MIND, BRAIN, AND DRUG

MIND, BRAIN, AND DRUG

An Introduction to Psychopharmacology

DAWSON HEDGES

Brigham Young University

COLIN BURCHFIELD

Columbus Air Force Base

Boston   New York   San Francisco

Mexico City   Montreal   Toronto   London   Madrid   Munich   Paris

Hong Kong   Singapore   Tokyo   Cape Town   Sydney

Executive Editor: *Karon Bowers*
Series Editorial Assistant: *Deb Hanlon*
Marketing Manager: *Pamela Laskey*
Production Editor: *Beth Houston*
Editorial Production Service: *Walsh & Associates, Inc.*
Composition Buyer: *Linda Cox*
Manufacturing Buyer: *JoAnne Sweeney*
Electronic Composition: *Publishers' Design and Production Services, Inc.*
Cover Administrator: *Joel Gendron*

For related titles and support materials, visit our online catalog at www.ablongman.com.

Between the time website information is gathered and then published, it is not unusual for some sites to have closed. Also, the transcription of URLs can result in typographical errors. The publisher would appreciate notification where these errors occur so that they can be corrected in subsequent editions.

Library of Congress Cataloging-in-Publication Data

Hedges, Dawson.
    Mind, brain, and body : an introduction to psychopharmacology / Dawson Hedges, Colin Burchfield
        p. cm.
    Includes bibliographical references and index.
    ISBN 0-205-35556-0
    1. Psychopharmacology. I. Burchfield, Colin. II. Title.

RM315.H44 2006
615'.78—dc22

                                                                                                2005048905

Printed in the United States of America

10 9 8 7 6 5 4 3 2 1   09 08 07 06 05

CONTENTS

CHAPTER SIX

The Psychostimulants, Amphetamines, Cocaine, Caffeine, and Nicotine   127

CHAPTER ELEVEN

First- and Second-Generation Antipsychotics and Anticholinergics   256

CHAPTER TWELVE

The Neurobiology and Treatment of Dementia   280

CHAPTER THIRTEEN

St. John's Wort, Gingko, Kava, and Valerian   299

PREFACE

In his 1958 paper, the Swiss psychiatrist Roland Kuhn (1958) wrote concerning his observations of the effects of imipramine on behavior that "An important field of research opens up here, rendered accessible for the first time by the recent development of psychopharmacology, and touching not only problems of psychiatry but also those of general psychology, religion, and philosophy." Although Kuhn was writing at the beginning of the current practice of therapeutic psychopharmacology that encompasses drugs used in the treatment of depression, bipolar disorder, anxiety disorders, and dementia, it is clear that humans have used drugs that affect the central nervous system for centuries. For example, the hallucinogen mescaline has been used for approximately 5,700 years (Bruhn et al., 2002).

The intent of this book is to provide a succinct but thorough and current introduction to the rapidly changing field of psychopharmacology, including not only drugs used therapeutically, such as antidepressants and antipsychotics, but also those used in many cases illegally, such as cocaine. Included also are alcohol, nicotine, and caffeine, readily available drugs that also affect the brain. This book is written for upper-division undergraduate students in psychology and the neurosciences, for nursing students, and for graduate students in clinical psychology. It is in no way meant to be an exhaustive review of the clinical practice of psychopharmacology but rather a means of making the basic ideas and vocabulary of psychopharmacology more broadly accessible. That is, this book is not meant as a prescribing guide, nor should it be used as such.

Containing the first four chapters, Section 1 introduces the physiology of the neuron to facilitate an understanding of drug action. An introduction to neuroanatomy is covered here also. Key to a grasp of psychopharmacology is a knowledge of neurotransmitters and their receptors, a task also taken up in this section. The time course of a drug as it passes through the body and brain and its interactions with the body are covered in the chapter on pharmacokinetics and pharmacodynamics. Finally, in the first section is a review of the neurobiology associated with several mental disorders, including depression, anxiety disorders, schizophrenia, and attention-deficit, hyperactivity disorder.

Section 2 includes the remainder of the chapters and comprises the core of the book. In this section, the main classes of psychotropic drugs—those drugs that primarily affect the brain and behavior—are covered. Section 2 discusses sedatives, hypnotics, anxiolytics, psychostimulants including cocaine and nicotine, opiates, marijuana, hallucinogens, inhalants, antidepressants, mood-stabilizing drugs, antipsychotics, and some herbal medications with psychoactive properties, such as St. John's wort and ginkgo. Because of the projected increase of people suffering from Alzheimer's disease (Samuels & Grossman, 2003), Chapter 12 contains a discussion of the neurobiology of not only Alzheimer's disease but also that of several other dementias. This chapter also covers some of the drugs used in the treatment of dementia.

Although not drugs, electroconvulsive therapy, transcranial magnetic stimulation, and vagal nerve stimulation affect the brain and behavior. These modalities in some cases have neurobiological effects similar to the effects of certain antidepressant drugs. As such, electroconvulsive therapy, transcranial magnetic stimulation, and vagal nerve stimulation are included in an appendix.

When drugs are presented in this book, the discussion usually is organized around their mechanisms of action, metabolism, interactions with other drugs, adverse effects, and clinical uses. As a general rule, when the uses of psychotropic drugs are discussed, the psychopharmacological literature is the source and not necessarily approval from the U.S. Food and Drug Administration, because it is the effects of the drugs on the brain, behavior, and emotion that are of primary interest in this book. Addiction, withdrawal, and treatment of dependency issues are discussed where relevant.

Learning the names of marketed psychotropic drugs can be daunting, since drugs are named both according to their generic name and to their brand name or names. To facilitate their memorization, when a drug is introduced, the generic name will be given with the brand name or names in parentheses. When the drug is subsequently mentioned, only the generic name will be given. However, drugs are listed alphabetically both by their generic and by their brand names in Appendices 2 and 3. The names of the pharmaceutical companies producing the drugs are listed in Appendix 2. A related issue is the comparison of brand-name drugs to their generic equivalents. Even though the active drug is the same, the two preparations are not necessarily equivalent as they can, with some drugs, differ in several important factors (Borgheini, 2003).

With its emphasis on neurobiology, this text derives its aims and purposes from a philosophy that has its roots in antiquity (e.g., the ancient physician Galen) wherein human suffering is explained and treated using biological theories and biological treatments. Like all subjects, psychopharmacology is in need of critical thought evaluating its underlying assumptions, evidence, and implications. In evaluating psychotropic drugs, for example, the distinction between efficacy and effectiveness is important. Efficacy considers how well a drug performs under controlled conditions. In contrast, effectiveness is a measure of drug performance in every day, clinical conditions that may be less than ideal (Jaffe & Levine, 2003).

There are a variety of methods of evaluating drugs. Case reports rely upon observations made concerning one particular case or possibly a series of cases. For example, a physician may note that a person has responded to a drug not previously known to have affected the disorder in question. New adverse effects may also be subjects of case reports. While provocative and useful in the generation of hypotheses, case reports are nevertheless limited by small numbers of people. Open-label studies are those in which both the subject and investigator know who is getting how much of what drug. Frequently reported in the psychopharmacology literature, open-label studies can be limited by bias but, like case reports, serve to generate hypotheses about drug efficacy and adverse effects. The gold standard of clinical psychotropic drug evaluation is the randomized, placebo-controlled, double-blind study. In this type of study, research participants are randomly assigned to one arm of a study. Typically, a randomized, placebo-controlled, double-blind study compares a chemically inert substance—the placebo (Latin: *placebo* = I shall please)—against one or more active drugs. To diminish bias, the study is double blind—neither the participants nor the investigators know who is on what drug.

Despite the primacy of the randomized, placebo-controlled, double-blind clinical trial in the evaluation of psychotropic drug efficacy, numerous factors suggest that even these studies have numerous pitfalls that confound interpretation of the results. Underreporting of negative trials—those trials that do not find a difference between active drug and placebo—may contaminate the interpretation of positive trials, as it is estimated that only 50 percent of negative trials are published (Thase, 1999). Just because a drug has been approved by the U.S. Food and Drug Administration does not mean that the drug is necessarily effective, as approximately a third of the published clinical trials on approved antidepressants are negative (Thase, 1999). Imprecision of diagnosis, unrepresentative participant samples, nonspecific response, and bias may limit the usefulness of controlled clinical trials (Parker et al., 2003), paradoxically placing some of the burden of evaluation in psychopharmacology on clinical lore and case studies. This is not to say that controlled clinical trials are meaningless, but rather that their findings require careful evaluation. "Use it quickly, while it's still safe," quipped an anonymous clinician (Settle, 1998), further underscoring the importance of vigilant monitoring even after a drug demonstrates clinical utility assessed by double-blind, placebo-controlled trials.

Related to drug evaluation is the issue of so-called off-label use of medication. Before gaining approval for marketing in the United States, the U.S. Food and Drug Administration must first approve a drug based upon its efficacy and safety for one or more specific indications. Even though approved only for certain indications, once a drug is available, it may be used for other, nonapproved uses or for nonapproved groups, such as children—that is, off-label use (O'Reilly & Dalal, 2003). In fact, in the United States drugs of all classes are frequently prescribed for off-label uses (O'Reilly & Dalal, 2003), and this off-label use is legal (Beck & Azari, 1998). Such off-label use, however, does carry liability to the prescriber (O'Reilly & Dalal, 2003). As this book approaches psychopharmacology from a neurobiological and pharmacological perspective and is not meant as a guide to prescription, the uses described for drugs generally are based upon actual practice and research support and not necessarily on approval from the Food and Drug Administration.

I thank the many patients whom I have treated and who taught me the often difficult and frustrating art of psychopharmacology. In addition, I thank the grad-

uate students in clinical psychology who have suffered through my psychopharmacology class with patience. Their insights and questions have greatly added to
this book.

—Dawson Hedges

We also thank the reviewers who persevered through the various versions of
the text. Their thoughtful comments and suggestions have greatly improved the
text:

A. Michael Anch, St. Louis University; Karen L. Ball, Alma College; Peter C.
Butera, Niagara University; Richard A. Deyo, Winona State University; Michael
Gadell, Del Mar College; Stephen Heinrichs, Boston College; Gloria J. Lawrence,
Wayne State College; Fred Leavitt, California State University Hayward; Edison
Perdoma, Minnesota State University, Mankato; Kim A. Roberts, California State
University Sacramento; Allen Salo, University of Maine at Presque Isle; Ines
Segert, University of Missouri; Stephen M. Siviy, Gettysburg College; Leland C.
Swenson, Loyola Marymount University; and George A. Wolford, Southwest Mis-
souri State University, Earthnet Institute, Canyon College.

REFERENCES

Beck JM, Azari ED (1998): FDA, off-label use, and informed consent: Debunking myths and mis-
conceptions. Food and Drug Law Journal 53:71–104.

Borgheini G (2003): The bioequivalence and therapeutic efficacy of generic versus brand-name
psychoactive drugs. Clinical Therapeutics 25:1578–1592.

Bruhn JG, De Smet PAGM, El-Seedi HR, Beck O (2002): Mescaline use for 5700 years. Lancet
359 (letter):1866.

Jaffe AB, Levine J (2003): Efficacy and effectiveness of first- and second-generation antipsychotics in schizophrenia. Journal of Clinical Psychiatry 64 (supplement 17): 3–6.

Kuhn R (1958): The treatment of depressive states with G-22355 (imipramine hydrochloride).
American Journal of Psychiatry 115:459–464.

O'Reilly J, Dalal A (2003): Off-label or out of bounds? Presciber and marketer liability for unap-
proved uses of FDA-approved drugs. Annals of Health Law 12:295–324.

Parker G, Anderson IM, Haddad P (2003): Clinical trials of antidepressants are producing meaningless results. British Journal of Psychiatry 183:102–104.

Samuels SC, Grossman H (2003): Emerging therapeutics for Alzheimer's disease: An avenue of
hope. CNS Spectrums 8:834–845.

Settle EC Jr (1998): Bupropion sustained release: Side effect profile. Journal of Clinical Psychiatry 59 (supplement 4):32–36.

Thase M (1999): How should efficacy be evaluated in randomized controlled trials of treatments
for depression? Journal of Clinical Psychiatry 60(supplement 1):23–31.

THE NEUROBIOLOGICAL BASIS OF PSYCHOTROPIC DRUG ACTION

CHAPTER ONE

NEURONS, SYNAPSES, AND THE BRAIN:
A Brief Introduction to Neuroscience

In order to facilitate an understanding of psychopharmacology, it is helpful to have a basic understanding of the organization of the nervous system. To begin with, the fundamental unit of the brain is the neuron. Although neurons have many features in common with other cells in the body, they are also highly specialized for their primary roles of transmitting and processing information. For example, neurons have dendrites—specialized regions that receive information for other neurons—and axons—cellular processes extending from the neurons that transmit information to other neurons. Information travels through a neuron as an electrochemical wave known as an action potential.

Bounded by the membranes of the incoming neuron and the outgoing neurons, the synapse is the area at which interneuronal communication occurs. Intraneuronal communication occurs by means of a wave of depolarization known as an action potential, which can cause a neuron to release chemical messengers called neurotransmitters into the synapse, where the neurotransmitter diffuses across the synaptic space to interact with the next neuron. This interaction may result in yet another action potential being generated in the downstream neuron.

The brain itself is organized into an incredible variety of regions, each having a role in overall brain function. The brainstem, located just above the spinal cord, contains areas involved in heart and respiratory function. Near the brainstem is the cerebellum, which is important in the coordination of movement, as well as for some types of memory and conditioned learning. The hypothalamus controls much of the response to stress, hormonal function, and regulation of temperature, blood volume, and appetite. Nearby is the thalamus, where information flowing from the brain to the rest of the body and from the body to the brain passes and to some extent is processed. The cerebral cortex is that part of the brain most visible when grossly inspected. Highly convoluted to increase surface area and mass, the cortex contains many areas of specialization. Parts of the cortex receive incoming information from all sensory modalities. Other regions of the cortex further integrate and process this information. Notable for its size in humans in relation to other areas of the brain is the frontal cortex, which is thought to be the neurobiological basis for planning, judgment, insight, and emotional control.

Neurons are the cells in the nervous system that process and transmit information. While this chapter focuses on neurons in the brain, neurons are also found in the spinal cord and peripheral nerves, including the vast networks of nerves in the gastrointestional system. In many ways, psychopharmacology is the study of neurotransmission—how information is transferred from one neuron to another, as well as the changes that neurotransmitter transmission induces in the neurons. As a prelude to the study of the mechanisms of drug action, adverse effects, abuse and dependency issues, and therapeutic uses in the ensuing chapters, this chapter introduces the basic features of the neuron, one of the fundamental units of the brain and a significant site for psychotropic drug action. Despite a bewildering variety of neurons located in complex patterns and circuits in the brain and varying from individual to individual like a person's unique fingerprint, certain fundamental features are common to all neurons. The first part of this chapter introduces these essential items. In the second part of this chapter, the basic features and organization of the brain are discussed. Although, as noted above, psychopharmacology in many ways is the study of how information is transferred from one neuron to another, the brain is where psychopharmacology happens. Even though all bodily organs are involved to some extent in psychopharmacology—such as the liver in drug breakdown and metabolism, the kidneys in drug excretion, and the other organs in unwanted side effects—it is in the brain that drugs produce both their therapeutic and unwanted behavioral effects. In this chapter, the basic features of brain anatomy, or neuroanatomy, are reviewed. While not meant to be a full course on neuroanatomy (a Ph.D. can be obtained in neuroanatomy), this chapter is a basic roadmap to the brain, with its major landmarks and pathways, or circuits, relevant for psychopharmacology outlined.

NEURONS

Like other organs of the body, the brain is composed of cells. Two main categories of brain cells are neurons and glial cells. Neurons are crucial for the proper functioning of the brain and are some of the basic elements of the brain. Brain functions—such as movement, sensation, cognition, and emotion—ultimately depend on neurons. Highly specialized, neurons receive, process, and transmit information in the nervous system of the body, including the brain (Brodal, 1992). While estimates of the number of neurons in the human brain vary, most range from approximately 20 billion (Spitzer, 1999) to 100 billion cells (Churchland, 1996). Adding to the complexity, each neuron on average makes contact with approximately 10,000 other neurons, tallying up to trillions of connections in each individual brain (Spitzer, 1999). These are big numbers to be sure and ironically lie outside most brains' ability to fully comprehend.

Neurons share many basic characteristics with other cells of the body. Like other cells, neurons have a cell body that houses the subcellular organelles that are necessary for cell replication, the synthesis of proteins, and the production of energy. Related to the processing and transmission of information, the neuron also possesses unique features and structures (see Figure 1.1), such as dendrites and axons that allow neurons to receive, process, and transmit information (Nicholls et al., 2001).

The Cell Body

Although neurons possess a variety of unique features, they are similar to other cells in the body in that they have a cell body (also called the soma or perikaryon) covered by a cellular membrane. In the cell body is a vast array of subcellular elements, or organelles, that contain the basic biochemical machinery for maintaining the neuron. The genetic code, deoxyribonucleic acid (DNA), resides in the nucleus, a key feature of the cell body. Proteins that are used throughout the neuron are synthesized in the cell body via complex cellular machinery and prepared for transport to other areas of the neuron. Energy is produced in the mitochondria, the powerhouse of the neuron and all other cells. A complex supporting framework, the cytoskeleton, is housed within the cell body and is composed of various neurofilaments and microtubules (Bear et al., 2001). In addition to providing structure and shape to the neuron, some of these cytoskeletal elements function to transport proteins and other molecules out of the cell body to more distant regions of the neuron (Swanson et al., 1999). The cell membrane is a complicated covering that surrounds the cell body, as well as other features of the neuron, such as the dendrites and axons. Far more than just housing the contents of

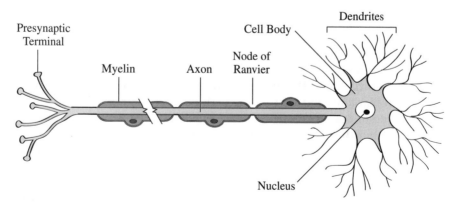

FIGURE 1.1 The Neuron

the neuron, the cell membrane is biologically active and home to myriads of bio-chemical processes and enzymes. Specialized channels allow substances, including ions and other biochemicals, to traverse the cellular membrane under tightly controlled circumstances (Swanson et al., 1999).

Receptors

Located within the cellular membrane in many cases, receptors are key regions for psychopharmacology. Receptors are intricate, three-dimensional protein structures that interact in a lock-and-key fit with other physiological elements—and most psychoactive drugs—to set off a chain of biochemical events that change in some way or maintain a cell's function (Wilcox et al., 1998). It is through their interactions with receptors that most psychoactive drugs initiate their behavioral effects, although complex post-receptor actions appear to be ultimately involved in drug effects. Many of the adverse effects of psychopharmacological drugs are also associated with the action of the drug on the receptors. Because of the importance of receptors and their physiology to an understanding of psychopharmacology, they are covered in additional detail in Chapter 2.

Dendrites

Neurons differ dramatically from other cells by the presence of dendrites. Although still a part of the neuron and covered by a cellular membrane, dendrites branch out from the cell body. Even though other parts of the neurons can and do receive input from other neurons, most input from other neurons is received via receptors on a neuron's dendrites (Ludwig & Pittman, 2003), from where the input is transmitted to the cell body. In contrast to the classical view that information flows only from dendrite to cell body, it appears that some dendrites may also transmit neuronal information from the cell body to the distal regions of the dendrite (Ludwig & Pittman, 2003).

As the Greek derivation of the word suggests, dendrites are tree-shaped structures extending in a three-dimensional configuration from the neuron (Greek: *dendron* = tree). Furthermore, the diameter of a dendrite decreases with increasing distance from the cell body. Most neurons have one or more dendrites. Dendrites significantly increase the surface area of the neuron, as well as the overall mass of the brain. Dendrite structure and shape are maintained by the neuron's neurofilaments and microtubules (Hof et al., 1999) and can differ markedly from neuron to neuron. Some neurons, for example, sport an extensive dendritic tree. Still others have dendrites that are much more modest.

The dendrites of some, though by no means all, neurons are covered with small protruding structures, known as dendritic spines, with some large neurons having up to 40,000 of these spines on their dendrites (Hof et al., 1999). The dendritic spines are specialized and biochemically complex areas of the dendrite that receive excitatory, but not inhibitory, input from other neurons (Thompson, 2003). Spines vary in morphology, and the strength of the synaptic transmission is related to the spine size. Spines also isolate their associated synapses from other synapses (Tashiro & Yuste, 2003). In part due to changes in dendritic spines that occur during learning, dendritic spines are hypothesized to be involved with the neurobiological basis of learning and memory (Stafstrom-Davis et al., 2001). In keeping with a role in learning, dendritic spines can change their shape within minutes, a finding that may underlie some of the plasticity found in the brain (Thompson, 2003).

Far from static appendages to a neuron, there is evidence that experience is associated, in many animal species, with changes in dendritic structure and arborization in certain areas of the brain, underscoring the importance of the dendrites in learning and memory (Kolb & Whishaw, 1998). This finding of neuronal changes and plasticity even in adult brains has challenged previously held notions that adult brains change little except to lose neurons.

Axons

Axons also distinguish neurons from the body's other cells. An integral part of the neuron and covered by the cellular membrane (although the axonal membrane is different from the rest of the neuronal membrane [Bear et al., 2001]), an axon is a cylindrical structure that transmits information from the neuron to another neuron or other cell of the body. Leaving the cell body from a small protrusion called the axon hillock, which forms the beginning of the axon, axons can extend to local areas or sites far removed from the cell body. As such, axons vary tremendously in size, from very short lengths in neurons that communicate only with other neurons in close proximity, to a meter or so in some axons in the peripheral nervous system (Bear et al., 2001). Axons often bifurcate, or split, into two or even many heads, increasing a neuron's ability to communicate with additional neurons. In fact, depending upon the type of neuron, axons may connect to several hundred neurons (Debanne, 2004). Axons contact other cells at specialized areas of the axonal membrane called the presynaptic terminals. Not only are these specialized areas of the axonal membrane found at the end of the axon, but an axon may have hundreds, or even thousands (Debanne, 2004) of these specialized areas known as *en passant* terminals located along its entire length (Bear et al., 2001). This feature allows an axon to communicate with many more additional neurons. Table 1.1 compares basic features of dendrites and axons.

The Action Potential

Action Potential Generation.   The action potential is the electrical impulse that transfers information within a neuron and ultimately causes a neuron to release neurotransmitter molecules, which communicate with other neurons. Initially forming in the axon hillock (Hof et al., 1999), the action potential is generated by the neuron's membrane changing in its permeability to different ions.

To understand the generation and propagation of the action potential, it is necessary to realize that ionic pumps, which require energy to maintain and are

TABLE 1.1   Dendrites and Axons

DENDRITE	AXON
Shape: Tree-shaped	*Shape:* Cylindrical
Function: Most input from other neurons is received via dendritic receptors (Ludwig & Pittman, 2003) from where the input is transmitted to the cell body.	*Function:* Transmits information from the neuron to another neuron or other cell of the body.
Components: Spines—Receive excitatory, but not inhibitory, input from other neurons (Thompson, 2003).	*Components:* Axon Hillock—Small protrusion from which the axon leaves the main cell body. Presynaptic Terminals—Specialized areas of axonal membrane that permit axons to contact other cells.

located in the neuronal membrane, keep the electrical charge of the neuron's interior negative relative to the outside of the cell by forcing a higher concentration of positively charged sodium ions outside of the neuron than inside. Furthermore, these pumps maintain a higher concentration of negatively charged chloride ions inside the cell than outside—positive sodium ions outside and negative chloride ions inside. Finally, positively charged potassium ions are kept in high concentrations in the interior of the cell, albeit not as high as the chloride ions inside the cell. The net result of all of this is that the interior of the resting cell is negatively charged relative to the outside at -70 millivolts (Carlson, 2001). However, if the neuron depolarizes to a certain threshold—that is, the negative charge inside the neuron lessens with respect to the outside—in response to a neurotransmitter binding to the cell's receptors or another action potential, ion channels within the neuron's membrane become more permeable to sodium ions. When these voltage-gated sodium channels become permeable to sodium, the electrochemical gradient—based on high sodium concentrations outside of the neuron compared to lower concentrations in the interior of the cell—drives sodium ions into the cell, reducing even more the negative charge within the neuron. Sodium channels then become less permeable to sodium—but not before potassium channels open up—allowing potassium ions to diffuse down their electrochemical gradient. Unlike sodium, potassium is maintained at relatively high intracellular levels, with positively charged potassium ions now traveling out of the cell, resulting in increased negative charge once again in the cell's interior (Bear et al., 2001). The rapid outflow of potassium with its accompanying positive charge initially hyperpolarizes (Carlson, 2001) and then restores the neuron to its original negative charge in relation to the outside of the cell. This situation readies the neuron to be capable of generating the next action potential after a small recovery or refractory period, during which the neuron is unable to generate an action potential.

Action Potential Propagation.   Depending upon activation of sodium channels (Debanne, 2004), an action potential in one part of the neuron induces depolarization in the adjacent area of the neuron, which in turn allows this region of the cell's membrane to generate an action potential. Thus, the action potential is a wave of depolarization that is the mechanism by which a neuron transmits information to those cells with which it synapses. Inhibitory input into a neuron from other neurons decreases the chances that the cell will generate an action potential. In contrast, excitatory input increases the chances that the neuron will mount an action potential (Bear et al., 2001).

Action potentials are either generated or not generated—there is no half of an action potential. If the threshold for an action potential is not reached, no action potential is formed; however, if the threshold is reached, an action potential is generated. That is, the formation of action potentials occurs as an all-or-none phenomenon (Carlson, 2001). The rate at which action potentials occur—the neuron's firing rate—adds important information over that supplied by the action potential itself (Carlson, 2001; Debanne, 2004).

Types of Neurons

While all neurons all have certain features in common with one another, such as the presence of a cell body, dendrites, and axons, there are a remarkable variety of neurons differing in shape, biochemistry, size, location, and function. In general, however, brain neurons can be classified into several main types, each with numerous subtypes (Hof et al., 1999). Inhibitory local interneurons contact only nearby neurons (Anderson, 2002). As implied in the name, these neurons are inhibitory; that is, they decrease the chances of the downstream neurons firing, or propagating a neuronal impulse. These local inhibitory neurons utilize the brain's primary inhibitory neurotransmitter, gamma amino benzoic acid (GABA) (Hof et al., 1999). Local spiny stellate cells are the next main type of neuron (Schubert et al., 2003). Unlike the inhibitory neurons, the spiny stellate cells are excitatory, increasing the chances of the downstream cell firing or propagating a neuronal impulse. The action of spiny stellate neurons is generally on neighboring neurons. A third type of brain neuron is the excitatory efferent cell, which transmits excitatory impulses to relatively distant parts of the nervous system and relys on the main excitatory neurotransmitter glutamate (Hof et al., 1999). Neurons are not just arranged in a haphazard fashion, like a sprawling suburban subdivision. Rather, they are organized with stereotactic precision into groups called nuclei and complex circuits.

THE SYNAPSE

Crucial for an understanding of neuronal function and psychopharmacology is the synapse, as it is here that many psychotropic drugs initiate their effects on the brain. Estimated to number in the trillions in a single human brain (Churchland, 1996), the synapse is the junction between two neurons. As such, the synapse is the region where communication between neurons occurs. In general, neuronal information flows from the presynaptic neuron—the one coming into the synapse—across the synapse to the postsynaptic neuron. In addition to this central tenet of synapse physiology, however, are findings that dendrites release certain neurotransmitters, such as dopamine, resulting in a potentially retrograde flow of neuronal information (Ludwig & Pittman, 2003). Although the neurons do not usually actually touch each other, the synapse itself is filled with extracellular fluid (composed of water, enzymes, and ions) and is bounded by the membrane of the incoming neuron (the presynaptic neuron) and the membrane of the outgoing neuron (the postsynaptic membrane). The classic synapse is between an incoming axon, transmitting information from the presynaptic neuron, and a dendrite from another neuron. However, many more arrangements are found. For example, there are synapses between axons and other axons, between axons and cell bodies, and even synapses in which an axon synapses with its own cell body, a so-called autosynapse.

Symmetric and Asymmetric Synapses

Although many different types of synapses exist, they can be roughly divided into two types by how they appear under an electron microscope (see Table 1.2). Asymmetric synapses are involved in the synaptic transmission of excitatory impulses, those that increase the chances of the postsynaptic cell generating an action potential. In contrast, symmetric synapses are associated with inhibitory transmission between neurons, transmissions that decrease the chances of the postsynaptic neuron forming an action potential (Hof et al., 1999). In the terminal region of the presynaptic neurons (that is, the region of the neuron that borders the synapse), neurotransmitter molecules are stored in specialized, membrane-bound sacs called vesicles.

Synaptic Neurotransmitter Release

When an action potential arrives at the presynaptic terminal, calcium ions flow into the region into the terminal region, initiating a sequence of biochemical reactions that fuse the vesicular membrane to the presynaptic membrane (Yoshihara & Littleton, 2002). After the membranes fuse, neurotransmitter molecules diffuse out of the vesicle and into the synapse, where neurotransmitter molecules diffuse

TABLE 1.2   Types of Synapses

ASYMMETRIC SYNAPSES	SYMMETRIC SYNAPSES
Involved in synaptic transmission of excitatory impulses (Hof et al., 1999).	Involved in synaptic transmission of inhibitory impulses (Hof et al., 1999).

through the extracellular fluid. Depending on the type of neurotransmitter and local conditions, several possible fates await the neurotransmitter.

1. Acting as a negative feedback loop, the neurotransmitter molecules can bind to receptors located on the presynaptic cell, the so-called autoreceptors, which in some cases signal the presynaptic neuron to stop releasing the neurotransmitter (White & Wang, 1984).

2. The neurotransmitter also may bind to reuptake receptors, which transport the neurotransmitter back into the presynaptic neuron (Amara, 1992), where it can be repackaged into another vesicle in preparation for the next action potential.

3. Some neurotransmitters are broken down, or metabolized, in and around the synapse by subtypes of the enzyme monoamine oxidase, a process that terminates the action of the neurotransmitter (Robinson, 2002).

4. Finally, the neurotransmitter may diffuse across the synapse and bind to postsynaptic receptors, initiating a number of responses in the postsynaptic neuron, depending on the kind of cell, its current state, and the type neurotransmitter.

The release of neurotransmitters into the synapse is an important and fundamental mechanism of neuronal communication. It is also the process through which most psychoactive drugs initiate their effects.

After the vesicle has released its neurotransmitter into the synaptic space, the vesicular membranes are taken back into the terminal region of the neuron. The vesicular membranes are then reformed into a new vesicle (Zucker et al., 1999) and filled again with neurotransmitter in preparation for the next action potential.

NEUROGLIAL CELLS

Outnumbering neurons approximately ten to one and totaling approximately one trillion in an individual human brain (Bear et al., 2001), the neuroglial cells in many ways function as the supporting cast of the neurons. Depending upon the type of neuroglial cell and its proximity to a neuron, the neuroglial cell can help determine a neuron's function (see Table 1.3). Some neuroglial cells secrete a variety of substances that provide supportive functions to neurons. Others are involved in phagocytosing (i.e., ingesting) neuronal debris, and still others are involved in immunological function in the brain.

Oligodendrocytes and Myelin

A specific type of neuroglial cell, an oligodendrocyte wraps its lipid-rich membranes around the axons of certain neurons to form a multilayered myelin sheath (cells in the peripheral nervous system that myelinate axons are schwann cells) (Quarles, 2002). A second role for the oligodendrocyte is to support the axon

TABLE 1.3 Types of Neuroglial Cells

OLIGODENDROCYTES AND MYELIN	ASTROCYTES	MICROGLIAL CELLS
Act to speed the action potential by insulating the axon, preventing the charge from leaking across the axonal membrane.	Provide a framework and guidance system for young neurons that are migrating to various brain regions. They also produce nerve growth factors.	Appear to function as immune cells; mediate the inflammatory response; scavenge cellular debris, dead cells, and other material; and secrete brain-derived neurotrophic factor.

(Edgar & Garbern, 2004). In fact, the relationship between the oligodendrocyte and the neuron appears complex and bidirectional, with each cell acting to support the other (Edgar & Garbern, 2004). For its part in addition to its supportive role, myelin acts to speed the action potential by insulating the axon, preventing the charge from leaking across the axonal membrane. Between myelinated segments on an axon are short [less than one micrometer in length (Rasband, 2004)] unmyelinated regions known as the nodes of Ranvier, which have high concentrations of sodium channels and which increase the speed of the action potential (Edgar & Garbern, 2004).

In an unmyelinated axon, the speed of the action potential down the axon is proportional to the diameter of the axon—the larger the cross-section of the neuron, the faster the action potential. However, size constraints limit the number of large-diameter axons. Myelin acts to speed the conduction of the action potential on relatively small-diameter axons. The change in membrane voltage generated by an action potential is passively conducted through myelinated regions of the axon until the action potential is regenerated at the next node of Ranvier (Carlson, 2001). In effect, the action potential jumps from node of Ranvier to node of Ranvier on myelinated axons, a process known as salutatory conduction (Carlson, 2001), resulting in faster transmission than if it had to regenerate at every point along the neuron (Hof et al., 1999). Furthermore, salutatory conduction requires less neuronal energy expenditure, as fewer action potentials are generated (Carlson, 2001).

Certain diseases result in a loss of myelin and illustrate the importance of myelin for the proper function of both the central and peripheral nervous systems. Multiple sclerosis, the most common demyelinating disease (Edgar & Garbern, 2004), for example, is associated with a loss of myelin in both the central and peripheral nervous systems. The symptoms and signs attendant to multiple sclerosis—loss of motor, bowel, and bladder control; interference with sensation, including vision (Adams & Victor, 1989); and cognitive deficits (Bobholz & Rao, 2003)—demonstrate the importance of myelin. Demonstrating the importance of the oligodendrocyte in supporting its neuron, the chronic changes associated with multiple sclerosis may be due to axonal degeneration thought secondary to the loss of myelin (Edgar & Garbern, 2004).

Astrocytes

A second type of neuroglial cell is the astrocyte. Ubiquitous in the brain and occupying one-quarter to one-half of the brain volume in many brain regions, astrocyte precursors provide a framework and guidance system for young neurons that are migrating to various brain regions (Parnavelas & Nadarajah, 2001). In humans and many other animals, the astrocytes form part of the blood-brain barrier (Abbott, 2002), which is a series of very close cellular junctions in the capillaries of the brain that prevent large molecules from exiting the blood vessels and entering the brain. The blood-brain barrier functions to maintain the environment of the brain within narrow metabolic limits by screening out compounds—like drugs and toxins—that might compromise brain function. In fact, a major requirement of psychotropic drugs is that they be able to pass the blood-brain barrier.

An additional function of astrocytes is the production of nerve growth factors (Koo & Choi, 2001). Nerve growth factors are proteins that are necessary for proper growth of neurons; they have an important role in the maintenance and even in some cases regeneration of damaged neurons. Certain astrocytes also take in toxic substances in many different brain diseases and trauma. In addition to their critical role in the blood-brain barrier, astrocytes also are involved in the regulation of blood flow through the cerebral microcirculation (Anderson & Nedergaard, 2003). Finally, astrocytes appear to have receptors for some neurotransmitters (Anderson & Nedergaard, 2003), although the effects of psychotropic drugs on these astrocyte receptors are largely unknown.

Microglial Cells

A third type of neuroglial cell is the microglial cell. These poorly understood cells appear to function as immune cells in the brain (Kim et al., 2002), mediating the inflammatory response in the brain (Polazzi & Contestabili, 2002). The microglial cells also behave much like a macrophage does in the rest of the body, scavenging cellular debris, dead cells, and other material (Polazzi & Contestabili, 2002). In addition, the microglial cells also secrete brain-derived neurotrophic factor (Nakajima et al., 2002), an important substance involved with neuron growth.

OVERVIEW OF NEUROANATOMY

The human brain weighs from 1250 to 1450 grams and occupies approximately 1400 cubic centimeters (Woolsey et al., 2003). Neuroanatomy can be a complicated affair because neurons are grouped into complex relationships with one another in the nervous system to form groups of neurons called nuclei. As a start, however, the nervous system can be classified into two main divisions: the central nervous system and the peripheral nervous system.

The central nervous system consists of the brain and the spinal cord, which are further subdivided into many specific regions. Within the brain, neurons are often organized into nuclei, simply a cluster of neurons and tracts, or pathways, that communicate between nuclei. Important regions of the brain covered here are the brainstem, the cerebellum, the midbrain, the basal ganglia, the hippocampus, the amygdala, and the temporal, parietal, and frontal lobes. The peripheral nervous system likewise can be grouped into several different systems, such as the somatic nervous system and the autonomic nervous system. The autonomic nervous system, in turn, is divided into the sympathetic nervous system and the parasympathetic nervous system, two generally opposing but otherwise similar systems that control glands and involuntary muscles.

The Peripheral Nervous System

The peripheral nervous system is the collection of nerves that is outside of the brain and spinal cord. It is composed of nerves and, in some cases, groups of neurons or nuclei. The peripheral nervous system either transmits information from the central nervous system to muscles and glands or sends information to the central nervous system. There are, of course, exceptions to this general setup. For example, some reflex arcs have no or only minimal involvement with the central nervous system, but the general pattern is true in most instances. Two important subdivisions of the peripheral nervous system exist: the somatic (or voluntary) nervous system and the autonomic (or involuntary) nervous system.

The Somatic Nervous System. The somatic division of the peripheral nervous system connects the central nervous system to voluntary muscles, that is, those muscles that are under our willful control, such as the muscles that control finger movement during writing. The somatic nervous system relies principally upon acetylcholine for its neurotransmitter, which carries information from the somatic nerve to the muscle of interest (Bear et al., 2001). This arrangement of nerve, synapse between nerve and muscle, and muscle is called the neuromuscular junction.

The Autonomic Nervous System. Alternatively, the autonomic nervous system functions in a somewhat different way from the somatic system. Unlike the somatic division, the autonomic nervous system is connected to involuntary muscles and, in some cases, various glands, such as salivary, tear, or sweat glands. Involuntary muscles are those that operate without conscious control, such as the iris in the eye, the heart, and muscles in the blood vessels. To take things a step further, the autonomic nervous system can be subdivided into sympathetic and parasympathetic portions. The sympathetic nervous system readies the body for what is often called the fight-or-flight response. Energy is readied for some type of action. If faced with an anxiety-inducing situation—a tiger bounding into the room or an upcoming examination—the sympathetic nervous system activates. Energy is mobilized and blood shunted to organs that are used for fighting or flee- ing. When the sympathetic nervous system is in operation, heart rate and breath- ing rate increase, blood flow diverts from the digestive system to the muscles to prepare for action, and pupils dilate to allow for maximum visual acuity. All of these responses happen quickly and without conscious input. The parasympa- thetic nervous system, in contrast, generally operates in a diametrical capacity to the sympathetic portion. That is, whereas the sympathetic nervous system mobi- lizes energy for consumption, the parasympathetic system tends to conserve en- ergy and works under nonstress conditions. In these situations, the sympathetic nervous system shuts down and the parasympathetic system takes the helm and diverts blood flow away from voluntary muscles to the digestive system. Heart and respiratory rates slow, and pupils constrict (Bear et al., 2001). Compare, for ex- ample, the amount of ambient light needed to read an interesting book to the amount needed when reading something a bit more boring. Because pupils dilate when we are interested in what we are reading—that is, when the sympathetic nervous system is activated—less background light is required.

While the peripheral nervous system is not of primary interest in psy- chopharmacology—after all, it is the brain and behavior that are the main con- cerns of psychopharmacology—it does play an important role mediating many of the adverse effects of psychoactive drugs that plague psychopharmacology. For in- stance, changes in heart rate, blood pressure, and salivation that commonly occur with some psychotropic drugs can be a result of that drug interacting with the pe- ripheral nervous system.

The Central Nervous System

It is in the central nervous system that the primary effects of the drugs used in psy- chopharmacology appear to happen. That is, it is the biochemical alterations in central nervous system neurons and synapses that are thought to lead to behav- ioral and emotional changes. The spinal cord, that aspect of the central nervous system that connects the peripheral nervous system to the brain, is of paramount importance to the proper function of the nervous system. However, the focus here will be on the brain, as that is where the drugs used in psychopharmacology operate.

Brainstem.   At the top of the spinal cord is the brainstem. This anatomical fea- ture of the brain, which does indeed look like a stem, connects the rest of the brain to the spinal cord. The brainstem contains several principal subdivisions, each with a unique anatomy and function.

Medulla Oblongata.   First, the medulla oblongata is that part of the brainstem that lies nearest the spinal cord. Central respiratory (Ramirez & Richter, 1996) and car- diac (Sapru, 2002) centers are located in the medulla and control some aspects of heart and lung function. Descending neuronal tracts transmitting information from the brain to the spinal cord and ascending tracts transmitting information from the periphery through the spinal cord to the brain all pass through the relatively narrow medulla. A small region of damage, therefore, in the medulla—from a stroke, for instance—can result in large neurological deficits.

Pons.   Rostral to the medulla is the pons, which is similar to the medulla in that it contains important respiratory centers (Nogues et al., 2002) and neurons transmitting information to and from the rest of the brain.

Cerebellum.   Tucked into the angle made by the brainstem and the rest of the brain is what looks like a much smaller brain. This "little brain," or cerebellum, is involved in coordinating rapidly alternating movements. Damage to the cerebellum, as often happens in alcoholism, results in dysmetria (jerky, poorly coordinated movements) (Hallett & Massaquoi, 1993). The cerebellum also is involved in gait (Earhart & Bastian, 2001). In addition to its motor function, the cerebellum is implicated in attention (Coull & Nobre, 1998). Furthermore, cerebellar abnormalities have been associated with autism, schizophrenia, and affective disorders (Allen & Courchesne, 2003). The cerebellum also is important in conditioned learning (Ohyama et al., 2003). In a study of twenty patients with neurological disease only identified in the cerebellum, Schmahmann and Sherman (1998) found evidence for deficit in in cognition and behavior, including planning, verbal fluency, and abstract reasoning, showing further the importance of the cerebellum in cognition.

Midbrain.   At the top of the brainstem and located in about the middle of the brain is the appropriately named midbrain. Importantly for psychopharmacology, the ventral tegmental region of the midbrain contains the cell bodies of neurons that are involved in addiction (PE Phillip et al., 2003) and behavior that is modulated by rewards (Schultz, 2001). Furthermore, the midbrain appears to be important in the etiology of psychosis (Nopoulos, 2001).

Hypothalamus.   The hypothalamus is a small region deep within the brain that has a myriad of functions, including roles in the regulation of appetite and mating behavior (Nicholls et al., 2001). The hypothalamus is also crucial in what is known as homeostasis, the exquisite regulation of the body's internal milieu (Nicholls et al., 2001): Blood pressure and volume, body temperature, and electrolyte concentration are all controlled to some degree by the hypothalamus. Furthermore, the hypothalamus regulates the autonomic nervous system, including both the sympathetic and parasympathetic divisions (Card et al., 1999). Another important role of the hypothalamus is its control of much of the endocrine system. The hypothalamus is connected by a small stalk to the body's master gland, the pituitary (Card et al., 1999). Hence, the hypothalamus synthesizes many hormones that travel through from the hypothalamus to the pituitary where they stimulate the release of pituitary hormones from the anterior pituitary lobe. Some of these hormones include thyroid-releasing hormone, growth hormone, prolactin, adrenocorticotropic-releasing hormone (ACTH), and the reproductive hormones follicle-stimulating hormone and luteinizing hormone. These hormones in turn are transported via the circulatory system to other glands and organs and are involved in the hormonal, or endocrine, regulation of many bodily functions. Pituitary axons also project from the hypothalamus to the posterior lobe of the pituitary gland where they release the hormones oxytocin and vasopressin (Amar & Weiss, 2003). Via its connections with the pituitary, the hypothalamus regulates the hypothalamic-pituitary-adrenal (HPA) axis, an important system in the processing of stress. In response to stress, the hypothalamus releases corticotropin-releasing hormone (CRH), which releases ACTH from the anterior lobe of the pituitary. ACTH, in turn, travels through the bloodstream to the adrenal glands, which are located on top of the kidneys. In response to ACTH, the adrenal glands release cortisol, a crucially important hormone involved in the stress response, which mobilizes energy and suppresses the immune system. Entering the brain via the bloodstream, cortisol interacts with the hypothalamus in a negative feedback loop to inhibit further release of CRH, maintaining the HPA axis under exquisite control.

The hypothalamus is also important in the control of some biological rhythms. The suprachiasmatic nuclei in the hypothalamus, for example, contain a region that appears responsible for many circadian rhythms in behavior and physiology (Hastings et al., 2003). Containing its own circadian rhythms (Kalat, 2004), the suprachiasmatic nucleus also appears to use input from the eye in order to regulate circadian rhythms (Lee et al., 2003).

Thalamus.   The thalamus is located above the hypothalamus, where it relays certain neuronal information going from higher brain regions to the peripheral nervous system. Furthermore, almost all of the information going from the peripheral nervous system to higher brain areas is transmitted through the thalamus (Behrens et al., 2003). Far from a homogenous entity, the thalamus is composed of several distinct nuclei (Behrens et al., 2003), each with a specific function. In addition to being a simple relay station for the brain, the thalamus also processes much of the information going through it. For example, cerebrovascular damage to the thalamus has been associated with a severe and disabling chronic pain syndrome (Awerbuch & Sandyk, 1990). Abnormalities in the thalamus have also been associated with schizophrenia (Torrey, 2002).

Limbic Structures: Amygdala and Hippocampus.   A poorly understood but seemingly increasingly important brain region is that referred to as the limbic system. Sometimes conceptualized as the emotional center of the brain, the whole concept of a limbic system has undergone extensive revision since it was first described. Despite this, it does appear that the limbic system is involved in memory, learning, and emotion. Two limbic system structures are reviewed here: the amygdala and the hippocampus.

Amygdala.   The amygdala is a small, and as its name implies, almond-shaped (Latin: *amygdala* = almond) structure located bilaterally in the brain. It appears to have a role in the perception of facial expression (LaBar et al., 2003), including fearful expressions (Whalen et al., 2001) and the perception of emotion (ML Phillips et al., 2003). Consistent with its role in the interpretation of facial affect, the amygdala processes stressful stimuli and is involved in the response to stress (McEwen, 2003).

Hippocampus.   Located near the amygdala, the seahorse-shaped hippocampus (Greek: *hippocampus* = seahorse) is another important structure of the limbic system. The hippocampus is, perhaps, best known for its role in explicit (Eichenbaum, 2001) and spatial (Knierim, 2003) memory. However, the hippocampus also seems to be involved in the stress response (McEwen, 2003) and regulation of the HPA axis. Hippocampal abnormalities have been reported in major depression (Frodl et al., 2002), posttraumatic stress disorder (Hull et al., 2002), schizophrenia (Jessen et al., 2003), and Alzheimer's disease (Jack et al., 2002), although the significance of these findings is not completely understood.

Basal Ganglia.   Deep within the brain are the basal ganglia, which include the caudate nucleus, the putamen, and the globus pallidus. This region of the brain is involved in the regulation of movement and is an important brain site for the generation of several pernicious adverse effects associated with some drugs used in psychopharmacology (Hardie & Lees, 1988). Typically associated with movement regulation, the basal ganglia also appear to have other functions, including a role in some aspects of behavior. For example, obsessive-compulsive disorder has been associated with abnormalities in the caudate nucleus (Micallef & Blin, 2001).

Parkinson's disease also illustrates the importance of the basal ganglia to overall brain function, including both behavioral and motor aspects. In Parkinson's disease, dopamine-containing neurons in the nigrostriatal pathway of the basal ganglia die (Shimohama et al., 2003), resulting in the well-known features of Parkinson's disease: a slow, pill-rolling tremor, difficulty initiating and stopping movement, slow movements (bradykinesia) (McDonald et al., 2003), depression in approximately half of the cases (McDonald et al., 2003), and eventually in approximately 40 percent of cases, dementia (Emre, 2003). By blocking dopamine receptors in the basal ganglia, some antipsychotic medications can cause drug-induced symptoms of Parkinson's disease (Hardie & Lees, 1988).

Cerebral Cortex.   The cerebral cortex is that part of the brain that is so clearly visible upon inspection. *Cortex*, in Latin, means bark. Indeed, the cortex covers the rest of the brain like bark on a tree. While only a few millimeters thick, the cortex is stunningly complex and, in most but not all regions, is composed of six different layers, each composed of its own distinctive cell types, organization, and function (Brodal, 1992). The cortex is highly convoluted, with many fissures, or sulci (singular, sulcus), and ridges, or gyri (singular, gyrus). The cerebral topography of furrows and ridges increases the surface area of the cortex, allowing for an increased cortical volume to be fit into a given cranium. The cerebral cortex also forms a large part of the so-called gray matter of the brain (Brodal, 1992), the place where neuronal cell bodies are located, as opposed to the axons—the white matter—many of which are white due to their covering of myelin. Furthermore, regional specializations are found in the cerebral cortex, with some areas having one function and others another. The central sulcus, a large fissure, divides the cerebral cortex into front and back halves. Immediately posterior to the central sulcus is the somatosensory cortex. This region of the cortex interprets incoming sensory information like touch from the rest of the body. Damage here results in a sensory deficit from the opposite side of the body. The cerebral cortex is also divided into two halves, a left and a right hemisphere, connected by the corpus collosum (Kalat, 2004). Several additional regions of the cerebral cortex require additional discussion (Figure 1.2 shows the lobes of the brain).

The Temporal Lobe.   Located laterally in each hemisphere are the temporal lobes, which provide the sensory cortex for auditory input (Kalat, 2004). In the medial regions of the temporal lobes are the hippocampus and other areas such as the parahippocampal and entorhinal cortices, which are integral to the function of declarative memory (Squire et al., 2004).

The Parietal Lobe.   Comprising approximately 20 percent of the cerebral cortex (Behrmann et al., 2004) and located posterior to the central sulcus but superior to the temporal lobe are the parietal lobes. The somatosensory cortex is in the anterior portions of the parietal lobes, with the posterior regions of the parietal cortex involved in several aspects of cognition including selective attention (Behrmann et al., 2004), arithmetic (Dehaene et al., 2004), and even some elements of determining the self from others (Decety & Chaminade, 2003).

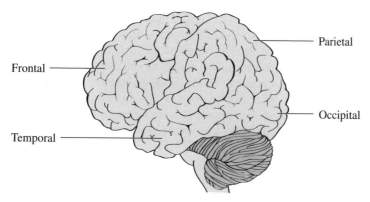

FIGURE 1.2   Lobes of the Brain

The Visual Cortex.   Moving still farther back towards the posterior pole of the cortex is the visual, or calcarine, cortex, the area of the cortex specialized for interpretation of visual input from the eye. Some types of damage to the visual cortex can produce cortical blindness, or blindsight, the inability to really see despite otherwise having an intact eye and visual system (Stoerig & Cowey, 1997). Other types of damage to the occipital cortex and other cortical regions (Cummings, 1985; Marciani et al., 1991) can produce prosopoagnosia, the inability to recognize faces, even those of loved ones, even though all other aspects of vision and cognition are intact (Cummings, 1985). A person with prosopoagnosia may recognize other features of a person, such as the hands or clothing, but cannot recognize a person by face alone.

The Frontal Cortex.   Anterior to the central sulcus is the frontal cortex. Bordering the central sulcus and forming the most posterior aspect of the frontal cortex is the motor cortex, where voluntary movements are controlled. Damage here results in paralysis in the corresponding part of the opposite side of the body. Control for the lower extremity is located near the top of the brain in the motor cortex, while that for the face is located toward the bottom. The frontal cortex also contains the motor speech center, or Broca's area (Brodal, 1992). Damage here, as fairly often occurs in strokes, results in a motor aphasia: People with this type of aphasia know what they want to say, but because the control for the motor aspect of speech is lost, articulation is poor or nonexistent and speech sounds garbled and inarticulate.

The area of the brain located anterior to the motor cortex is the frontal cortex. In humans, the frontal cortex is highly developed in comparison to other species, and it is here that so many of the functions that make humans unique are thought to be located. Emotional control and executive functions appear based in large part in the frontal cortex (Fuster, 2002). Perhaps the most famous case of frontal lobe damage is that of Phineas Gage. As the classic story goes, in 1848, Phineas Gage was foreman on a blasting team that was building a railroad through Vermont. Gage was reportedly conscientious, considerate, patient, and reliable. Although the details of exactly what happened are unclear, while tamping a blast, the charge exploded prematurely and Gage found his head in the path of a three-foot-long tamping rod. The entire rod went through Gage's frontal cortex to land in some nearby bushes. Remarkably, Gage survived the incident, but his frontal lobes were extensively damaged. Even though Gage's cognitive and intellectual abilities appeared intact, friends and doctors noted troubling changes in Gage after the accident. For example, his personality deteriorated to the point that he appeared to be a different man. No longer able to hold a job, Gage wandered from place to place, eventually dying penniless and unemployed in California about twelve years after the accident (Damasio, 1995). Although the relationship between Gage's accident and subsequent changes in behavior may not be as clear as is commonly reported due to limited information about Gage, including a lack of evidence about what Gage was like prior to the injury (Macmillan, 2000), the case of Phineas Gage remains of importance as it is an attempt to correlate frontal lobe function with personality (Macmillan, 2000).

Association Cortex.   The function of much of the cortex remains but poorly understood. Large regions are simply referred to as association cortex, where information from a variety of sensory modalities is thought to be integrated and further processed (Brodal, 1992).

SUMMARY

The brain is composed of approximately 100 billion neurons that make contact with sometimes thousands of other neurons, resulting in trillions of connections between neurons within the brain. Like other cells in the body, neurons are composed of a cell body, in which proteins are synthesized and energy produced. However, neurons are highly specialized for their primary function of processing and transmitting information. Unlike other cells, neurons have dendrites, which are regions of the neuron specialized for receiving information from other neurons. Far from static structures, dendrites are constantly in flux, remodeling response to the brain's needs and environment. Axons are also specialized regions of the neuron. Their main function, however, is to transmit information from the neuron to another. Generated by complex electrochemical processes, action potentials carry information through the neuron and interact with the presynaptic membrane of a neuron to release neurotransmitter into the synapse. This allows one neuron to communicate with another as well as to initiate negative feedback loops in the presynaptic cell to carefully regulate the amount of neurotransmitter released into the synapse. Neurotransmitters are then removed from the synapse by several processes including reuptake into the presynaptic neuron to be repackaged for later release into the synapse and degradation by enzymes into other biochemical products.

In addition to neurons, brains are composed of glial cells, which outnumber neurons approximately ten to one. Many types of glial cells exist and perform a variety of housekeeping functions in the brain. Oligodendrocytes, for instance, make myelin, a fatty substance that ensheaths some axons and greatly increases the speed of the action potential. Other glial cells form part of the blood-brain barrier, that structure of glial cells and capillaries that serves to limit the biochemicals and other substances that can gain entry to the brain. Still other glial cells appear to have a role in the immune system in the brain, while others ingest debris from cellular breakdown.

The nervous system itself can be divided into the peripheral and central nervous systems. The peripheral nervous system consists of the somatic and autonomic systems. The somatic nervous system controls voluntary muscles, while the autonomic system governs involuntary muscles and many glands. The autonomic nervous system can be further subdivided into the sympathetic and parasympathetic divisions. The sympathetic nervous system functions mainly to ready the body for the expenditure of energy—fight or flight. Alternatively, the parasympathetic division generally prepares the body for energy conservation, although the relationship between the sympathetic and parasympathetic nervous systems can be more complex than this. The central nervous system consists of the brain and spinal cord. Located at the top of the spinal cord and connecting the cord to the rest of the brain is the brainstem. The brainstem consists of several different structures, such as the medulla oblongata and the pons. Important centers for cardiac and respiratory control are located in the brainstem, as are all ascending and descending tracts conveying information to and from the brain. The cerebellum occupies the angle between the brainstem and the rest of the brain. Once thought to be primarily involved with the coordination of movement, the cerebellum may also have essential roles in cognition and memory. Moving further toward the front of the brain, the hypothalamus regulates the autonomic nervous system and hypothalamic-pituitary-adrenal axis. In addition, the hypothalamus maintains homeostasis in the body. Located nearby is the thalamus, where information traveling both from and toward the cortical areas of the brain passes and is to some extent processed.

Next, the limbic system is composed of a variety of brain structures, particularly the hippocampus, which is important for explicit and spatial memory and the stress response. The amygdala also regulates the stress response and is involved in the perception of facial expression. The basal ganglia, that region of the brain made up of the caudate, putamen, and globus pallidus, controls and regulates movements and also appears to have some sort of a role in obsessive-compulsive disorder. The basal ganglia mediate many of the side effects from antipsychotic medications.

Finally, massively developed in humans, the frontal cortex appears to be involved in the regulation of emotion and executive functioning. Injury to the frontal cortex can result in personality change.

STUDY QUESTIONS

1. Describe the basic cellular components of the nervous system and their functions.
2. List the main divisions and functions of the nervous system.
3. Describe how the action potential results in neurotransmitter release into the synapse.
4. What role do sodium channels have in the development of the action potential?
5. Name the principal structures and their functions of the brain.
6. Explain how a neuron is organized, including the dendrites and the axon.

REFERENCES

Abbott NJ (2002): Astrocyte-endothelial interactions and blood-brain barrier permeability. Journal of Anatomy 200:629–638.

Adams RD, Victor M (1989): *Principles of Neurology* (4th ed.) New York: McGraw-Hill.

Allen G, Courchesne E (2003): Differential effects of developmental cerebellar abnormalities on cognitive and motor functions in the cerebellum: An fMRI study of autism. American Journal of Psychiatry 160:262–273.

Amar AP, Weiss MH (2003): Pituitary anatomy and physiology. Neurosurgery Clinics of North America 14:11–23.

Amara SG (1992): A tale of two families. Nature 360:420–421.

Anderson CM, Nedergaard M (2003): Astrocyte-mediated control of cerebral microcirculation. Trends in Neuroscience 26:340–344.

Anderson SA (2002): Determination of cell fate within the telencephalon. Chemical Senses 27:573–575.

Awerbuch GI, Sandyk R (1990): Mexiletine for thalamic pain. International Journal of Neuroscience 55:129–133.

Bear MF, Connors BW, Paradiso MA (2001): *Neuroscience: Exploring the Brain.* Baltimore: Lippincott Williams & Wilkens.

Behrens TEJ, Johansen-Berg J, Woolrich MW, Smith SM, Wheeler-Kingshott CAM, Boulby PA, Barker GJ, Sillery EL, Sheehan K, Ciccarelli O, Thompson AJ, Brady JM, Matthews PM (2003): Non-invasive mapping of connections between human thalamus and cortex using diffusion imaging. Nature Neuroscience 6:750–757.

Behrmann M, Geng JJ, Shomstein S (2004): Parietal cortex and attention. Current Opinion in Neurobiology 14:212–217.

Bobholz JA, Rao SM (2003): Cognitive dysfunction in multiple sclerosis: Review of recent developments. Current Opinion in Neurology 16:283–288.

Brodal P (1992): *The Central Nervous System: Structure and Function.* New York: Oxford University Press.

Card JP, Swanson LW, Moore RY (1999): The hypothalamus: An overview of regulatory systems. In MJ Zigmond, FE Bloom, SC Landis, JL Roberts, LR Squire (eds.), *Fundamental Neuroscience.* San Diego, CA: Academic Press.

Carlson NR (2001): *Physiology of Behavior.* Boston: Allyn and Bacon.

Churchland PM (1996): *The Engine of Reason, the Seat of the Soul.* Cambridge, MA: MIT Press.

Coull JT, Nobre AC (1998): Where and when to pay attention: The neural systems for directing attention to spatial locations and to time intervals as revealed by both PET and fMRI. Journal of Neuroscience 18:7426–7435.

Cummings JL (1985): *Clinical Neuropsychiatry.* Orlando, FL: Grune & Stratton.

Damasio AR (1995): *Descartes' Error: Emotion, Reason, and the Human Brain.* New York: Avon Books.

Debanne D (2004): Information processing in the axon. Nature Reviews: Neuroscience 5:304–316.

Decety J, Chaminade T (2003): When the self represents the other: A new cognitive neuroscience view on psychological identification. Consciousness and Cognition 12:577–596.

Dehaene S, Molko N, Cohen L, Wilson AJ (2004): Arithmetic and the brain. Current Opinion in Neurobiology 14:218–224.

Earhart GM, Bastian AJ (2001): Selection and coordination of human locomotor forms following cerebellar damage. Journal of Neurophysiology 85:759–769.

Edgar JM, Garbern J (2004): The myelinated axon is dependent upon the myelinating cell for support and maintenance: Molecules involved. Journal of Neuroscience Research 76:593–598.

Eichenbaum H (2001): The hippocampus and declarative memory: Cognitive mechanisms and neural codes. Behavioural Brain Research 127:199–207.

Emre M (2003): Dementia associated with Parkinson's disease. Lancet Neurology 2:229–237.

Frodl T, Meisenzahl EM, Zetzsche T, Born C, Groll C, Jager M, Leinsinger G, Bottlender R, Hahn K, Moller HJ (2002): Hippocampal changes in patients with a first episode of major depression. American Journal of Psychiatry 159:1112–1118.

Fuster JM (2002): Frontal lobe and cognitive development. Journal of Neurocytology 31:373–385.

Hallett M, Massaquoi SG (1993): Physiologic studies of dysmetria in patients with cerebellar deficits. Canadian Journal of Neurological Sciences 20 (supplement 3):S83–92.

Hardie RJ, Lees AJ (1988): Neuroleptic-induced Parkinson's syndrome: Clinical features and results of treatment with levodopa. Journal of Neurology, Neurosurgery, and Psychiatry 51:850–854.

Hastings MH, Reddy AB, Maywood ES (2003): A clockwork web: Circadian timing in brain and periphery, in health and disease. Nature Reviews. Neuroscience: 4:649–661.

Hof PR, Trapp BD, de Vellis J, Claudio L, Colman DR (1999): The cellular components of nervous tissue. In MJ Zigmond, FE Bloom, SC Landis, JL Roberts, LR Squire (eds.), *Fundamental Neuroscience*. San Diego, CA: Academic Press.

Hull AM (2002): Neuroimaging findings in post-traumatic stress disorder. Systematic review. British Journal of Psychiatry 181:102–110.

Jack CR Jr., Dickson DW, Parisi JE, Xu YC, Cha RH, O'Brien PC, Edland SD, Smith GE, Boeve BF, Tangalos EG, Kokmen E, Petersen RC (2002): Antemortem MRI findings correlate with hippocampal neuropathology in typical aging and dementia. Neurology 58:750–757.

Jessen F, Scheef L, Germeshausen L, Tawo Y, Kockler M, Kuhn KU, Maier W, Schild HH, Heun R (2003): Reduced hippocampal activation during encoding and recognition of words in schizophrenia patients. American Journal of Psychiatry 160:1305–1312.

Kalat JW (2004): *Biological Psychology* (8th ed.). Toronto, Ontario: Thomson/Wadsworth.

Kim WK, Ganea D, Jonakait GM (2002): Inhibition of microglial CD40 expression by pituitary adenylate cyclase-activating polypeptide is mediated by interleukin-10. Journal of Neuroimmunology 126:16–24.

Knierim JJ (2003): Hippocampus and memory. Can we have our place and fear it too? Neuron 37:372–374.

Kolb B, Whishaw IQ (1998): Brain Plasticity and Behavior. Annual Review of Psychology 49: 43–64.

Koo H, Choi BH (2001): Expression of glial cell line-derived neurotrophic factor (GDNF) in the developing human fetal brain. International Journal of Developmental Neuroscience 19: 549–558.

LaBar KS, Crupain MJ, Voyvodic JT, McCarthy G (2003): Dynamic perception of facial affect and identity in the human brain. Cerebral Cortex 13:1023–1033.

Lee HS, Nelms JL, Nguyen M, Silver R, Lehman MN (2003): The eye is necessary for a circadian rhythm in the suprachiasmatic nucleus. Nature Neuroscience 6:111–112.

Ludwig M, Pittman Q (2003): Talking back: Dendritic neurotransmitter release. Trends in Neurosciences 26:255–261.

Macmillan M (2000): *An Odd Kind of Fame: Stories of Phineas Gage*. Cambridge MA: MIT Press.

Marciani MG, Carlesimo GA, Maschio MC, Sabbadini M, Stefani N, Caltagirone C (1991): Comparison of neuropsychological, MRI and computerized EEG findings in a case of prosopoagnosia. International Journal of Neuroscience 60:27–32.

McDonald WM, Richard IH, DeLong MR (2003): Prevalence, etiology, and treatment of depression in Parkinson's disease. Biological Psychiatry 54:363–375.

McEwen BS (2003): Mood disorders and allostatic load. Biological Psychiatry 54:200–207.

Micallef J, Blin O (2001): Neurobiology and clinical pharmacology of obsessive-compulsive disorder. Clinical Neuropharmacology 24:191–207.

Nakajima K, Tohyama Y, Kohsaka S, Kurihara T (2002): Ceramide activates microglial to enhance the production/secretion of brain-derived neurotrophic factor (BDNF) without induction of deleterious factors in vitro. Journal of Neurochemistry 80: 697–705.

Nicholls JG, Martin AR, Wallace BG, Fuchs PA (2001): *From Neuron to Brain*. Sunderland, MA: Sinauer Associates.

Nogues MA, Roncoroni AJ, Benarroch E (2002): Breathing control in neurological diseases. Clinical Autonomic Research 12:440–449.

Nopoulos PC, Ceilley JW, Gailis EA, Andreasen NC (2001): An MRI study of midbrain morphology in patients with schizophrenia: Relationship to psychosis, neuroleptics, and cerebellar neural circuitry. Biological Psychiatry 49:13–19.

Ohyama T, Nores WL, Murphy M, Mauk MD (2003): What the cerebellum computes. Trends in Neurosciences 26:222–227.

Parnavelas JG, Nadarajah B (2001): Radial glial cells. Are they really glia? Neuron 31:881–884.

Phillips ML, Drevets WC, Rauch SL, Lane R (2003): Neurobiology of emotion perception I: The neural basis of normal emotion perception. Biological Psychiatry 54:504–514.

Phillips PE, Stuber GD, Heien MI, Wightman RM, Carelli RM (2003): Subsecond dopamine release promotes cocaine seeking. Nature 422:614–618.

Polazzi E, Contestabili A (2002): Reciprocal interactions between microglial and neurons: From survival to pathology. Reviews in the Neurosciences 13:221–242.

Quarles RH (2002): Myelin sheaths: Glycoproteins involved in their formation, maintenance and degeneration. Cellular and Molecular Life Sciences 59:1851–1871.

Ramirez JM, Richter DW (1996): The neuronal mechanisms of respiratory rhythm generation. Current Opinion in Neurobiology 6:817–825.

Rasband MN (2004): It's "juxta" potassium channel! Journal of Neuroscience Research 76: 749–757.

Robinson DS (2002): Monoamine oxidase inhibitors: A new generation. Psychopharmacology Bulletin 36: 124–138.

Sapru HN (2002): Glutamate circuits in selected medullo-spinal areas regulating cardiovascular function. Clinical and Experimental Pharmacology & Physiology 29:491–496.

Schmahmann JD, Sherman JC (1998): The cerebellar cognitive affective syndrome. Brain 121: 561–579.

Schubert D, Kotter R, Zilles K, Luhmann HJ, Staiger JF (2003): Cell type-specific circuits of cortical layer IV spiny neurons. Journal of Neuroscience 23:2961–2970.

Schultz W (2001): Reward signaling by dopamine neurons. Neuroscientist 7:293–302.

Shimohama S, Sawada H, Kitamura Y, Taniguchi T (2003): Disease model: Parkinson's disease. Trends in Molecular Medicine 9:360–365.

Spitzer M (1999): *The Mind within the Net.* Cambridge, MA: MIT Press.

Squire LR, Stark CE, Clark RE (2004): The medial temporal lobe. Annual Review of Neuroscience 27:279–306.

Stafstrom-Davis CA, Ouimet CC, Feng J, Allen PB, Greengard P, Houpt TA (2001): Impaired conditioned taste aversion learning in spinophilin knockout mice. Learning & Memory 8:272–278.

Stoerig P, Cowey A (1997): Blindsight in man and monkey. Brain 120:535–559.

Swanson LW, Lufkin T, Colman DR (1999): Organization of nervous systems. In MJ Zigmond, FE Bloom, SC Landis, JL Roberts, LR Squire (eds.), *Fundamental Neuroscience.* San Diego, CA: Academic Press.

Tashiro A, Yuste R (2003): Structure and molecular organization of dendritic spines. Histology and Histopathology 18:617–634.

Thompson SM (2003): Ephrins keep dendritic spines in shape. Nature Neuroscience 6:103–104.

Torrey EF (2002): Studies of individuals with schizophrenia never treated with antipsychotic medications: A review. Schizophrenia Research 58:101–115.

Whalen PJ, Shin LM, McInerney SC Fischer H, Wright CI, Rauch SL (2001): A functional MRI study of human amygdala responses: Facial expressions of fear versus anger. Emotion 1:70–83.

White FJ, Wang RY (1984): Pharmacological characterization of dopamine autoreceptors in the rat ventral tegmental area: Microiontophoretic studies. Journal of Pharmacology and Experimental Therapeutics 231:275–280.

Wilcox RE, Gonzales RA, Miller JD (1998): Introduction to neurotransmitters, receptors, signal transduction, and second messengers. In AF Schatzberg, CB Nemeroff (eds.), *Textbook of Psychopharmacology* (2nd ed.). Washington, DC: American Psychiatric Press.

Woolsey TA, Hanaway J, Gado MH (2003): *The Brain Atlas: A Visual Guide to the Human Central Nervous System.* Hoboken, NJ: John Wiley & Sons.

Yoshihara M, Littleton JT (2002): Synaptotagmin I functions as a calcium sensor to synchronize neurotransmitter release. Neuron 36:897–908.

Zucker RS, Kullmann DM, Bennett M (1999): Release of neurotransmitters. In MJ Zigmond, FE Bloom, SC Landis, JL Roberts, LR Squire (eds.), *Fundamental Neuroscience.* San Diego, CA: Academic Press.

CHAPTER TWO

NEUROTRANSMITTERS AND RECEPTORS

Neurotransmitters are the biochemicals that carry information from one neuron to another. When an action potential arrives at the terminal axonal membrane, a neurotransmitter may be released into the synapse, where it can then diffuse through the synaptic fluids and interact with the receptors on either the presynaptic neuron or the postsynaptic neuron. Many different types of neurotransmitters exist, each with its own functions and neuroanatomical location. Dopamine, serotonin, and norepinephrine are common neurotransmitters that appear to have important roles in psychopharmacology because many psychotropic drugs appear to interact with these neurotransmitters.

Neurotransmitters interact with protein structures referred to as receptors. Receptors are often located in the neuronal membrane and interact in a lock-and-key fit with neurotransmitters. A given neurotransmitter may have many different types of receptors that interact with only that neurotransmitter. However, each of these receptors functions in a way unique from the other receptors. For example, while serotonin has several different kinds of receptors, each of these has its own physiological role.

Most psychotropic drugs appear to initiate their responses by interacting in some way with receptors, making psychopharmacology, in many ways, the study of receptor physiology. The interaction of a neurotransmitter or psychoactive drug is merely the beginning of a complicated biochemical chain of events that involves numerous other events. All of these events appear to be involved in generating the final behavioral responses. Furthermore, many of the adverse effects that so plague psychopharmacology also appear to be mediated through receptors. The binding of neurotransmitters to receptors, in some cases, results in the opening of ion channels in the neuronal membrane, which results in a fast cellular response to the neurotransmitter. In other cases, the binding of a neurotransmitter to its receptor results in a complex chain of biochemical reactions involving numerous other chemical entities called second messengers. Ultimately, these second messengers are thought to lead to physiological or behavioral responses.

This chapter discusses neurotransmitters and receptors. Psychopharmacology includes the study of neurotransmitters and receptors because this is where psychotropic drugs usually appear to initiate their effects. The general features and definitions of the neurotransmitters are covered here, as well as individual neurotransmitters relevant for an understanding of psychopharmacology, including acetylcholine, norepinephrine, serotonin, gamma aminobutyric acid, glutamate, and dopamine. The majority of psychotropic drugs appear to initiate their effects within the brain. Hence, psychotropic drugs may be associated with changes in behavior and emotion, possibly due, at least in part, to an interaction with the brain at a receptor level.

However, the binding of neurotransmitter to receptor is only the beginning of the story of psychopharmacology. Other and usually even more poorly understood events occur in the neuron that presumably lead to the behavioral and emotional changes occurring from the use of these drugs. For example, antidepressant-induced neurogenesis (that is, the growth of new neurons) in the hippocampus may be necessary for changes in mood associated with antidepressants (Santarelli et al., 2003). Complex reactions of biochemicals referred to as second messengers (the neurotransmitter is considered to be the first messenger) often carry out the actions initiated by the binding of the neurotransmitter to its receptor.

Neurotransmitters are the biochemicals that transmit neuronal information from one neuron to another. That is, neurotransmitters participate in interneuronal communication. As most psychotropic drugs interact with the receptors of various neurotransmitters, it is through modulation and alteration of neurotransmitter function that these drugs initiate their effects within the brain. In most cases, receptors are named after the neurotransmitter to which they bind. After synthesis in the neuron, neurotransmitters are stored in membrane-enclosed vesicles (Deutch & Roth, 1999) located where the presynaptic neuron is in close proximity to the postsynaptic neuron. Action potentials traveling through the presynaptic neuron in conjunction with calcium cause the neurotransmitter-containing vesicles to fuse with the presynaptic membrane (Matthews, 1996), which in turn releases the neurotransmitter into the synapse between the pre- and postsynaptic membranes.

Once in the synapse, several outcomes await the neurotransmitter, depending on both type of the neurotransmitter and local synaptic conditions (see also Chapter 1). First, some types of neurotransmitters, such as serotonin and norepinephrine, may diffuse through the extracellular fluid of the synapse to interact with presynaptic autoreceptors, which diminish further release of the neurotransmitter (Nutt, 2002) in a negative feedback system that regulates the amount of neurotransmitter in the synapse.

Alternatively, reuptake or transporter receptors may bind with certain neurotransmitters and transport the neurotransmitter back into the presynaptic neuron from which it came. Because these receptors are involved in the actual taking of neurotransmitters through the presynaptic membrane and back into the neuron, these uptake receptors can be referred to as transport mechanisms. They include specific receptors and the cellular ability to transport the neurotransmitter through the membrane. For example, serotonin reuptake receptors bind with synaptic serotonin to regulate the amount of serotonin in the synapse by transporting serotonin into the presynaptic neuron (Suhara et al., 2003). Once inside the presynaptic neuron, the neurotransmitter is repackaged into vesicles (Nagatsu, 2000), where is stored until another action potential releases additional neurotransmitter into the synapse. Many psychotropic drugs initiate their effects by blocking reuptake receptors, which in turn inhibits the uptake of neurotransmitter into the presynaptic neuron. This drug action, in effect, increases the availability of the neurotransmitter in the synapse and enhances its synaptic effects. For instance, a commonly prescribed antidepressant, fluoxetine (Prozac), blocks the uptake receptor for the neurotransmitter serotonin (Vaswani et al., 2003), increasing the actions of serotonin in the synapse in a process that is believed to initiate the antidepressant effects of fluoxetine.

Enzymes in the vicinity of the presynaptic membrane degrade certain neurotransmitters such as acetylcholine (Nagatsu, 2000). The enzyme monoamine oxidase binds with the neurotransmitters serotonin, norepinephrine, and dopamine to metabolize them into other biochemicals (Cesura & Pletscher, 1992), thus regulating the amount of neurotransmitter in the synapse.

Finally, the neurotransmitter may diffuse across the synapse and bind to receptors located on the postsynaptic membrane and, in effect, transmit information from one neuron to another. The response elicited in the postsynaptic neuron depends upon the type of neurotransmitter and the specific type of receptor involved.

Two main types of responses may occur. First, the binding of the neurotransmitter may result in ion channels opening in the postsynaptic neuron, in turn allowing either positively or negatively charged ions to enter into the cell. This fast transmission occurs in less than a millisecond (Greengard, 2001). The influx of positively or negatively charged ions can either depolarize or hyperpolarize respectively the postsynaptic neuron. If the cell is hyperpolarized from an influx of negatively charged ions, it becomes less likely to generate an action potential, and the neurotransmitter is said to have an inhibitory effect. For example, in adult neurons, the neurotransmitter gamma aminobutyric acid (GABA) binds to GABA$_A$ receptors to cause negatively charged chloride ions to flow into the neuron with resultant hyperpolarization (Simeone et al., 2003). If, on the other hand, the cell is depolarized from an inflow of positively charged ions, the effect from the neurotransmitter is excitatory, as the cell is more likely to mount an action potential. Some receptors for the excitatory neurotransmitter glutamate, for instance, result in ion channels opening and subsequently depolarizing (Madden, 2002) the postsynaptic membrane.

Second, the binding of the neurotransmitter to its receptor can activate other biochemical substances such as second messengers (Struder & Weicker, 2001) (the neurotransmitter is the first messenger), protein kinases, and protein phosphatases (Greengard, 2001) to alter neuronal function. This process is slower than fast, ion-channel-coupled transmission and is on the order of hundreds of milliseconds to minutes (Greengard, 2001).

G-proteins are important second messengers linked to many types of receptors that often serve to couple the receptor to other proteins in the chain. Some dopamine receptors are linked to g-proteins, and abnormal function of some g-proteins has been linked to some mental disorders (Manji, 1992). As can be seen, in many cases, the binding of a neurotransmitter to its receptors is only the beginning of a complex chain of chemical reactions that activate and modify a series of proteins, all of which result in a change in the function of the neuron.

Other molecules in addition to neurotransmitters can bind to receptors, often in a very specific manner. Many psychotropic drugs at least initiate their actions on the brain by binding to receptors normally utilized by naturally occurring neurotransmitters. When a drug is added to an already delicately balanced neurotransmitter-receptor system, the effect of the drug may take several forms.

First, the drug may cause the receptor to work like it would if it were bound by a naturally occurring neurotransmitter. In this case, for instance, the postsynaptic neuron could become either hyperpolarized or depolarized depending on what type of receptor is involved. But the important point is that the receptor, even though bound by a drug, is doing what it would do if it were bound by its naturally occurring neurotransmitter. In this situation, then, the drug is said to be a receptor agonist (Ross, 1990). See Table 2.1.

Second, the drug may prohibit the receptor from doing what it would do in the presence of its neurotransmitter, such that the receptor function is essentially blocked or antagonized. A drug that inhibits a receptor from doing what it would normally do is referred to as a receptor antagonist (Ross, 1990). Drug action, however, often involves combinations of both agonism and antagonism of different receptors. Fluoxetine (Prozac), for instance, is thought to initiate its actions by antagonizing the serotonin uptake receptors (Vaswani et al., 2003), blocking the presynaptic neuron from taking serotonin back into the cell and repackaging it into vesicles. This action results in serotonin being in the synapse for longer periods and increasing serotonin's agonism on its own receptors.

TABLE 2.1   Receptor Agonist, Antagonist, and Partial Agonist

TYPE	ACTION
Agonist	Causes the receptor to work like it would if it were bound by a naturally occurring neurotransmitter.
Antagonist	Prohibits the receptor from doing what it would do in the presence of its neurotransmitter.
Partial Agonist	Behave like weak agonists, weakly causing the receptor to do what it would normally do in the presence of its neurotransmitter, but only partially.

Finally, and perhaps slightly more complicated, is partial agonism. Partial agonists behave like weak agonists, weakly causing the receptor to do what it would normally do in the presence of its neurotransmitter (Pliska, 1999). If relatively high levels of naturally occurring neurotransmitter and a partial agonist are present, the partial agonist competes with the neurotransmitter for receptor occupancy. Those receptors occupied by the partial agonist, then, are actually agonized to a lesser extent than those agonized by the neurotransmitter. The net effect of the partial agonist, in this circumstance, is a relative antagonism compared to what would occur if just a neurotransmitter were present. On the other hand, in conditions of low neurotransmitter in which very little agonism from the neurotransmitter is occurring, a partial agonist actually *increases* receptor agonism and thus acts as a relative agonist. The anxiolytic drug buspirone (Buspar) is an example (for some of its mechanisms) of a partial agonist for serotonin. In conditions of high synaptic serotonin, buspirone partially agonizes serotonin receptors and prevents the naturally occurring serotonin from fully agonizing its receptors (Ninan et al., 1998). Conversely, by the same mechanism, buspirone operating against a backdrop of low naturally occurring serotonin increases the agonist activity on the serotonin receptors (Ninan et al., 1998).

The binding between neurotransmitters and the receptors is highly specific. While neurotransmitters usually have more than one receptor, only the neurotransmitter in question interacts with its own receptors—dopamine does not interact with serotonin's receptors, and serotonin does not bind with those of dopamine. In contrast, many drugs used in psychopharmacology lack this specificity. For example, tricyclic antidepressants antagonize serotonin and norepinephrine uptake transporter receptors while, at the same time, antagonizing acetylcholine and histamine receptors (Feighner, 1999).

Far from being static entities on the neuronal cell membrane, receptors are highly dynamic, frequently changing both numbers and density on the cell membrane as well as binding efficiency. Agonist drugs may increase the action on a receptor and, to compensate, a neuron may express fewer receptors on its membrane or decrease the efficiency with which the receptors bind to the neurotransmitter in a process known as down regulation. In conditions of a relative lack of neurotransmitter, as occur when receptors are antagonized by a psychotropic drug, up regulation, that is, an increase in overall receptor number or binding efficiency, may occur as the neuron attempts to counter the paucity of neurotransmitter. To illustrate the changes in receptors that can occur in response to drugs and neurotransmitter changes, the chronic administration of the antidepressant imipramine (Tofranil), which increases synaptic concentration of certain neurotransmitters, down regulates rat cortical alpha-adrenorecptors (Subhash et al., 2003).

Although neurotransmitter physiology is only beginning to be unraveled, a basic knowledge of certain neurotransmitters is crucial to understand the mechanisms of action of many psychotropic medications and drugs of abuse. While the complete actions of these drugs on neurotransmitter systems are unknown, many psychotropic drugs appear to have intimate ties with the following neurotransmitters, which are summarized in Table 2.2.

TABLE 2.2   Neurotransmitters and Their Functions

NEUROTRANSMITTER	FUNCTIONS IN THE BRAIN
Serotonin (5-hydroxytriptamine)	Regulation of emotion, anxiety, agitation, and gastrointestinal function
Norepinephrine (noradrenaline)	Regulation in emotion, attention, as well as a modulatory function in the brain
Dopamine	Regulation of movement and involved in the etiology of psychoses
Acetylcholine	Functions in memory, learning, and movement
Gamma aminobutric acid (GABA)	The brain's primary inhibitory neurotransmitter and increases the overall inhibitory tone of the brain
Glutamate	The brain's primary excitatory neurotransmitter and involved in affective, sensory, and motor function, as well as learning, memory, cognition, and synaptic plasticity

SEROTONIN

Serotonin, or 5-hydroxytriptamine, is a common neurotransmitter found in many different animals, including jellyfish (Vaswani et al., 2003) and humans. A monoamine located not only in the brain but also throughout the body, serotonin is involved in functions as diverse as platelet function in the blood's coagulation response to blood vessel diameter. Serotonin is synthesized in cells by tryptophan hydroxylase from an amino acid precursor tryptophan (Hamon et al., 1981), an amino acid that the body obtains from dietary sources.

Although serotonin is found throughout the brain, it is also involved in the function of other organ systems. For example, serotonin is found in heavy concentrations in the gastrointestinal tract, where it is involved in bowel motility. Any drug affecting serotonin function, therefore, has the potential to interfere with physiological processes throughout the body (Vaswani et al., 2003). Serotonin also has a role in cardiovascular and renal physiology (Doggrell, 2003).

Serotonin is synthesized in neurons whose cell bodies lie in the dorsal raphe nuclei in the brainstem (Tork, 1990). From here, the axons of these neurons project to virtually every major region of the brain (Vaswani et al., 2003). As might be anticipated from such a ubiquitous distribution, serotonin is involved in many different brain functions and appears to have a role in a variety of different types of behavior and emotions, making it a prime target for psychotropic drugs.

Further amplifying the neurobiological effects of serotonin on the functions of the brain and other organs are the numerous kinds of serotonin receptors. There are at least fourteen different types of serotonin receptors, each with its own physiology and function (Roth, 1994). These are different kinds of serotonin *receptors*, not different types of serotonin itself. These receptors are involved in widely varying functions and have different locations within the brain (Roth, 1994). Some of these serotonin receptors are of particular relevance to psychotropic drug action and require some discussion here (see Table 2.3).

For example, the serotonin type 1A receptor may be involved in the regulation of mood, and the binding of serotonin to this receptor has been hypothesized to result in an antidepressant response (Blier & Ward, 2003). This receptor may be a mechanism by which many of the available antidepressants initiate their antidepressant effects (Blier & Ward, 2003). By blocking the uptake of synaptic serotonin into the presynaptic neuron, many antidepressants elevate the concentration of serotonin in the synapse and increase the binding of serotonin to its receptors, including the 1A receptor. Unfortunately, this mechanism of antidepressant drug effect is relatively nonspecific, in that other serotonin receptors in addition to the 1A receptors are affected, a feature that can lead to some of the adverse effects associated with these drugs (Calabrese et al., 2003).

Serotonin 1B receptors may be involved in mood, aggression, and anxiety (Clark & Neumaier, 2001). Another serotonin receptor of importance for psychopharmacology is the type 2 receptor. Serotonin type 2 receptors may be associated with sexual function, and stimulation of these receptors by serotonin may be related to the sexual dysfunction found with some types of antidepressants (Berk et al., 2000). In addition to the role of serotonin 2 receptors in sexual function, serotonin type 2a receptors are implicated in psychosis (de Angelis, 2002).

Located in both the gastrointestional system and in the brain, serotonin type 3 receptors appear to be involved with gastrointestional function (Walton, 2000). Some limited evidence supports of role for serotonin type 3 receptors in anxiety (Olivier et al., 2000). Agonism of these receptors, as can occur from many antidepressants, can result in various forms of gastrointestional disturbance, including pain, nausea and vomiting, and diarrhea. Some serotonin 3 subtype antagonist medications are used to treat the nausea and vomiting associated with cancer

TABLE 2.3 Some Serotonin Receptors and Their Functions

TYPE	PUTATIVE FUNCTIONS
Serotonin type 1A receptors	Regulation of mood
Serotonin type 2 receptors	Sexual function, may be involved with psychosis
Serotonin type 3 receptors	Involved in gastrointestinal function and possibly anxiety

chemotherapy (Walton, 2000) and have been found possibly to be associated with anxiolysis (Olivier et al., 2000).

Serotonin dysfunction appears to be important in the neurobiology of suicide (van Heeringen, 2003). While this has an obvious relationship to the serotonin abnormalities posited to occur in depression, some researchers have speculated that serotonin may be involved in the regulation of impulsivity and aggression (Krakowski, 2003).

Serotonin also appears to have a role in other forms of psychopathology. For example, some anxiety disorders may also have serotonin underpinnings (Charney, 2003). Furthermore, as some drugs that increase the transmission of serotonin decrease the obsessions and compulsions of obsessive-compulsive disorder, serotonin has been speculated to have a role in obsessive-compulsive disorder (Zohar et al., 2000). The advent of serotonin-altering drugs that appear efficacious in schizophrenia has extended the hypothesized role of serotonin to psychotic disorders (Conley & Kelly, 2002). Consistent with this is the observation that some hallucinogenic drugs such as lysergic acid diethylamide (acid, LSD) affect certain serotonin receptors (Gresch et al., 2002). Serotonin components to eating (Monteleone et al., 2000) and sexual (Meston & Frohlich, 2000) behaviors also have been proposed.

After release into the synapse from the presynaptic neuron, serotonin is removed from the synapse by two main mechanisms. First, serotonin can be taken up by the serotonin transporter system after binding to specific receptors here into the presynaptic neuron (Suhara et al., 2003). Second, the enzyme monoamine oxidase metabolizes synaptic serotonin into other biochemical products (Cesura & Pletscher, 1992).

In summary, serotonin is a major neurotransmitter with a ubiquitous distribution in the many different organ systems of the body. Its association with many behaviors and emotions makes it a prime target for psychotropic drug action, and, indeed, many psychotropic drugs spanning several different classes of medications appear to interact at some level with the serotonin system.

NOREPINEPHRINE

Like serotonin, norepinephrine (noradrenaline) is another monoamine neurotransmitter found throughout the body and brain that is involved in a host of body functions, including a key role in the performance of the autonomic nervous system as well as emotion. Norepinephrine and two other monoamines, epinephrine (adrenaline) and dopamine, are frequently referred to as catecholemines and are important neurotransmitters. Like the other catecholemines, norepinephrine is synthesized from the amino acid tyrosine.

The cell bodies of the neurons that synthesize norepinephrine are located in the brainstem in the pons in an area called the locus coeruleus (Hardy et al., 2002). From here, axons from these neurons extend throughout much of the brain, including the hypothalamus, the frontal cortex, and the hippocampus (Gorman, 1999). Norepinephrine specifically interacts with alpha 1, alpha 2, beta 1, and beta 2 adrenergic receptors (Bloom, 1990).

Several antidepressants block the uptake of synaptic norepinephrine into the presynaptic neuron (Westenberg, 1999), increasing the action of norepinephrine on postsynaptic norepinephrine receptors. Similar to serotonin, norepinephrine is removed after release from the synapse by a reuptake mechanism into the presynaptic neuron (Brunello et al., 2002) or is metabolized by monoamine oxidase (Cesura & Pletscher, 1992).

Like serotonin, norepinephrine has been postulated to be involved in the regulation of emotion. If fact, there is evidence that the serotonin and norepinephrine system are closely related to and overlap each other in the regulation of mood and are not two independently operating neural systems (Gorman, 1999). Together, the place of norepinephrine and serotonin in the pathophysiology of depression is known as the monoamine hypothesis of depression. This hypothesis posits that aberrations in serotonin and norepinephrine play a crucial role in the etiology of depression (Bymaster et al., 2003). Bolstered in large part by the reputed antidepressant response of many drugs that inhibit reuptake of serotonin, norepinephrine, or both, the monoamine hypothesis has guided the development of both antidepressant drugs themselves and theories of affective regulation. Despite several limitations to the monoamine hypothesis of depression (Healy, 1997; Valenstein, 1998) suggesting that the monoamine hypothesis of depression requires substantial revision, drugs that interfere with brain monoamines remain important agents in the treatment of depression, and the monoamine hypothesis continues to be a factor in the development of new antidepressant drugs (Bymaster et al., 2003).

In addition to its effects on mood and affect, norepinephrine also appears to be involved in the regulation of attention and information processing (Berridge & Waterhouse, 2003). Indeed, some drugs that are used in the treatment of attention-deficit, hyperactivity disorder inhibit norepinephrine reuptake (Simpson & Perry, 2003)

Finally, it is thought that, in part due to its wide distribution throughout the brain, that norepinephrine may have a diffuse modulatory effect on brain function (Berridge & Waterhouse, 2003), setting the overall tone of the brain, much like a thermostat adjusting the overall temperature of a building. In summary, then, despite the limitations of a simplistic interpretation of the monoamine hypothesis of depression, norepinephrine is an important neurotransmitter in psychopharmacology (Berridge & Waterhouse, 2003) and is modulated by several psychoactive drugs. Its proposed brain functions include regulation of mood, attention, and a general regulation of brain function.

DOPAMINE

The most common catecholamine in the brain (Vallone et al., 2000), dopamine is a neurotransmitter that is intimately connected with the development of psychopharmacology. Synthesized from norepinephrine, dopamine functions in several different circuits of the brain. One dopamine pathway involves the nigrostriatal pathway, a group of neurons located in the basal ganglia. In Parkinson's disease, the dopamine-containing neurons of the substantia nigra die out, leading to the typical symptoms (Shimohama et al., 2003), with bradykinesia or slow movement, tremor, and rigidity becomingly increasingly prominent as the disease advances.

Another dopamine pathway in the brain is the tuberoinfundibular pathway, which functions to control the secretion of the hormone prolactin (Compton & Miller, 2002). Secreted by the pituitary gland, prolactin is involved in milk production (hence the name), and elevated prolactin can lead to menstrual disturbances, infertility, inappropriate lactation, and impotence (Tansey & Schlechte, 2001). Blockade of dopamine receptors in the tuberoinfundibular pathway by certain antipsychotic drugs can increase prolactin levels (Wieck & Haddad, 2003), leading to the clinical presentation of elevated prolactin.

Finally, the mesocorticolimbic pathway has dopamine as its neurotransmitter. This pathway originates and has its and dopamine-containing neurons in the midbrain and projects to cortical and limbic areas. The mesocorticolimbic pathway may mediate proposed dopamine reward centers, a function that could be part of a neurobiological basis of addictive behaviors (Noble, 1996). Like both serotonin and norepinephrine, the concentration of dopamine in the synapse is carefully regulated. After release into the synapse, transporter mechanisms in the presynaptic membrane bind with dopamine and take it back into the presynaptic neuron (Hitri et al., 1994).

Monoamine oxidase also breaks dopamine down to other metabolites (Cesura & Pletscher, 1992). Both the reuptake transporter and monoamine oxidase are important sites of drug action on dopamine, underlying the mechanisms of action of both therapeutic medications and drugs of abuse on dopamine.

The dopamine hypothesis of schizophrenia proposes that altered dopamine function is related to the etiology of schizophrenia (Willner, 1997). However, the dopamine hypothesis of schizophrenia is controversial, and several factors argue that additional brain regions and neurotransmitters are involved in schizophrenia. For instance, first-generation antipsychotic medications, which antagonize dopamine subtype 2 receptors, have important limitations in efficacy (Conley & Kelly, 2002) Second-generation antipsychotics that, in addition to dopamine subtype 2 receptor antagonism, also antagonize serotonin subtype 2 receptors may be more effective for some symptoms of schizophrenia than the first-generation antipsychotics (Conley & Kelly, 2002). Finally, increasing evidence supports abnormalities in the major excitatory neurotransmitter glutamate as having a part in the genesis of schizophrenia (Burbaeva et al., 2003). Not restricted to only schizophrenia, dopamine also appears to have a role in the etiology of Tourette's disorder and attention-deficit, hyperactive disorder (Vallone et al., 2000).

To summarize, dopamine is a major neurotransmitter in several brain pathways: the substantia nigra-basal ganglia, the tuberoinfundibular, and the mesocorticolimbic pathways. These circuits underlie a number of different brain functions, including the regulation of movement. Finally, dopamine appears to be an important component of the neurological basis of addiction and reinforcement.

ACETYLCHOLINE

One of the earliest and most thoroughly described neurotransmitters, acetylcholine has crucial functions in both the central and peripheral nervous systems. Acetylcholine is synthesized from choline and acetyl coenzyme A by the enzyme choline acetyltranferase (Lefkowitz et al., 1990). Like other neurotransmitters, the synaptic concentration of acetylcholine is carefully regulated to maintain proper function of acetylcholine-containing synapses. The enzyme acetylcholinesterase breaks down acetylcholine in the synapse and accounts for a major removal system for this neurotransmitter (Lefkowitz et al., 1990).

A variety of compounds exist that can bind to acetylcholinesterase, an action that prevents this enzyme from breaking down and terminating the action of acetylcholine. These agents can either bind irreversibly or reversibly to acetylcholine esterase. Several drugs exist that reversibly inhibit the action of this enzyme, the so-called acetylcholinesterase inhibitors—medications that are used in the treatment of Alzheimer's disease (Nordberg & Svennson, 1998). Irreversible inhibitors of acetylcholine esterase, however, tend to be toxins. For example, irreversible inhibitors of acetylcholine esterase include sarin (Abu-Qare & Abou-Donia, 2002) and soman (Raveh et al., 2003), potentially lethal nerve gases that strongly bind to acetylcholine esterase. In the periphery, acetylcholine is the neurotransmitter at the neuromuscular junction of both voluntary and involuntary muscles.

Acetylcholine binds to two broad types of receptors: nicotinic and muscarinic. Nicotinic receptors are found in the central and peripheral nervous systems and are the receptor of the neuromuscular junction (Astles et al., 2002). There are several subtypes of nicotinic receptors (Paterson & Nordberg, 2000), which appear to be involved with several mental disorders, including Alzheimer's disease and schizophrenia (Paterson & Nordberg, 2000).

There are five known types of muscarinic receptors (Anagnostaras et al., 2003). Muscarinic receptors appear to play fundamental roles in memory, learning, and movement. Blockade of muscarinic receptors, a common occurrence with many types of psychotropic medications, can result in memory and attentional impairment (Anagnostaras et al., 2003), particularly in populations already prone to such disturbances (e.g., such as people with brain damage and the elderly). Antagonism of muscarinic receptors can cause blurred vision and dry mouth (Richelson, 1987).

Several main acetylcholine pathways are found in the brain. The main acetylcholine system has its cell bodies in the nucleus basalis of Meynert. From here, acetylcholine-containing neurons project throughout the cortex and hippocampus. Loss of neurons in the nucleus basalis of Meynert is associated with Alzheimer's disease (Iraizoz et al., 1999).

In summary, acetylcholine is found both in the central and peripheral nervous systems, where it interacts with nicotinic and muscarinic receptors. Nicotinic receptors are located in the neuromuscular junction of voluntary muscles and are also found in the brain. Acetylcholinesterase breaks down acetylcholine in the synapse to carefully regulate to amount of synaptic acetylcholine. An important function of acetylcholine appears to be in memory and learning, and die-out of some acetylcholine-containing neurons is associated with Alzheimer's disease. Even antagonism of muscarinic receptors as is common from several different psychotropic medications can cause problems with memory and confusion.

GAMMA AMINOBUTYRIC ACID (GABA)

Gamma aminobutyric acid (GABA) is the brain's primary inhibitory neurotransmitter (Simeone et al., 2003) and decreases the chances of a postsynaptic neuron from firing. Like many other neurotransmitters, GABA is cleared from the synapse by transporter molecules in the presynaptic membrane that take GABA back up into the presynaptic neuron (Natsch et al., 1997). Certain anticonvulsant drugs, in fact, appear to inhibit the reuptake of GABA (Natsch et al., 1997).

There are two main types of GABA receptors, both widely distributed throughout the brain (Simeone et al., 2003): $GABA_A$ and $GABA_B$. When agonized by GABA, the $GABA_A$ receptor causes an influx of negatively charged chloride ions, which tends to hyperpolarize the neuron (Stein & Nicoll, 2003) by increasing its negative charge relative to the exterior of the cell. In some neurons, $GABA_A$ receptors may also lead to neuronal excitation (Stein & Nicoll, 2003). $GABA_B$ receptors are also inhibitory, although unlike $GABA_A$ receptors, they are linked G proteins (Stein & Nicoll, 2003). Some drugs, such as the benzodiazepine alprazolam (Xanax), bind to a site on the GABA receptor (Barbee, 1993). The GABA system may have a role in the etiology of anxiety (Lydiard, 2003) and depression (Tunnicliff & Malatynska, 2003).

In summary, GABA is a major inhibitor neurotransmitter that utilizes two main types of receptors: $GABA_A$ and $GABA_B$. When agonized by GABA, the $GABA_A$ receptor hyperpolarizes the neuron, diminishing the chances of that neuron mounting an action potential. Benzodiazepines bind to the $GABA_A$ receptor.

GLUTAMATE

The brain's primary excitatory neurotransmitter (Tamminga & Frost, 2001), glutamate, like GABA, is found throughout the brain. In fact, glutamate receptors are thought to be located on the majority of the brain's neurons and are involved in affective, sensory, and motor function (Tamminga & Frost, 2001). Glutamate also is involved in learning, memory, cognition (Fonnum, 1984), and synaptic plasticity (Banke & Traynelis, 2003). Similar to many other neurotransmitters, after release from the presynaptic neuron, glutamate is taken up by a glutamate transporter system into the presynaptic neuron (Palmada & Centelles, 1998). Glutamate has three main types of receptors, the proposed functions of which give an idea of the diverse brain processes that involve glutamate (see Table 2.4).

Agonization of kainate receptors by glutamate, for example, results in ion channels opening rapidly, allowing an influx of ions that depolarize the postsynaptic neuron (Huettner, 2003). The kainate receptor may be involved in the pathophysiology of epilepsy (Lerma, 1998). Metabotropic receptors are linked to G proteins (Pin & Acher, 2002). Increasingly studied in neuropsychiatric disorders, certain types of metabotropic receptors have been postulated to be involved with the genesis of anxiety (Gorman, 2003).

The third major type of glutamate receptor is the N-methyl-D-aspartate (NMDA) receptor, which is located throughout the brain, including the hippocampus. The street drug phencyclidine or ecstasy antagonizes the NMDA receptors, which can result in psychosis (Marino & Conn, 2002). In fact, the psychosis produced from phencyclidine closely resembles that of schizophrenia (Guochuan et al., 1998). In addition, NMDA antagonists have analgesic properties (Hewitt, 2003). In response to brain injury from a variety of causes such as stroke, trauma, and hypoxia (conditions of low oxygen), excess glutamate may be released into the synapse where it then agonizes NMDA receptors, a process that paradoxically can lead to further brain insult by what is known as excitotoxicity (Zipfel et al., 1996). NMDA antagonists are sometimes used immediately after the occurrence of a stroke in an attempt to prevent this additional brain damage. Dysfunction of the glutamate NMDA receptors is proposed to be integral in the development of schizophrenia, particularly as glutamate is thought to be involved in guiding the development of brain circuitry, processes believed to play a role in the etiology of schizophrenia (Tamminga & Frost, 2001). Furthermore, glutamate function has been reported to be abnormal in the thalamus of people with schizophrenia (Smith et al., 2001). These and other findings have contributed to the glutamate hypothesis of schizophrenia.

In addition to their roles in psychosis and excitotoxicity, NMDA receptors are important in learning and memory (Riedel et al., 2003). Far from operating in a vacuum, glutamate has clear interactions with other neurotransmitters, including dopamine and GABA systems (Tamminga & Frost, 2001). Furthermore, early

TABLE 2.4 Glutamate Receptors and Their Functions

TYPE	SOME POSSIBLE FUNCTIONS
Kainate receptors	Epilepsy (Lerma, 1998)
Metabotropic receptors	Anxiety (Gorman, 2003)
N-methyl-D-aspartate (NMDA) receptors	Role in development of schizophrenia (Marino & Conn, 2002), learning, and memory (Riedel et al., 2003)

evidence suggests that glutamate may have a crucial role in the regulation of the hypothalamic-pituitary-adrenal axis stress response (Mathew et al., 2001), and antagonism of NMDA may result in antidepressant and anxiolytic effects (Skolnick, 1999).

In summary, glutamate is an excitatory neurotransmitter with numerous functions. Glutamine's kainate receptors appear to be involved with epilepsy and its metabotropic receptors may have a role in anxiety. Important for their role in psychosis are NMDA receptors.

OPIOID NEUROPEPTIDES

Opiate narcotics such as heroin, morphine, opium, and a host of others do a brisk business in addiction, abuse, and legitimate medical uses such as pain control. These drugs operate through systems of receptors, like many other drugs. However, the receptors utilized by the opiates do not exist just so they can interact with heroin, but rather, naturally occurring opiate-like substances exist in the brain and interact with the opiate receptor family.

There are two main groups of endogenous opiate neuropeptides. The first group consists of enkephalins, endorphins, and dynorphins, and the second comprises the endomorphins (Okada et al., 2002). The exact functions of the opiate neuropeptides are elusive, although opiate neuropeptides appear to be involved in the processing of painful sensory input (Inturrisi, 2002) and mood regulation (Raynor et al., 1994).

There are three main types of opiate receptors, all of them coupled to G proteins: mu, kappa, and delta (Okada et al., 2002). Opiate antagonists such as naltrexone decrease the craving of some alcoholics for alcohol (Romach et al., 2002). Several different opiate receptors have been described.

MELATONIN

Although it is a neurohormone, rather than a neurotransmitter, melatonin is briefly considered here because of its effects on behavior. Produced in the pineal gland (Bergstom & Hakanson, 1998), melatonin appears to be important in the functioning of biological clocks (Stehle et al., 2003) and the induction of sleep (Bergstrom & Hakanson, 1998). In response to light conditions relayed from the retina, the suprachiasmatic nucleus of the hypothalamus, a crucial element of the brain's biological clock (Stehle et al., 2003), signals the pineal gland to increase the production of melatonin in response to dark conditions (Delagrange et al., 2003). Melatonin also seems to alter circadian rhythms (Rajaratnam et al., 2003) and is used for some sleep disorders as well as for the disrupted sleep cycles associated with jet lag (Cardinali et al., 2002). Other evidence suggests a role for melatonin in bowel motility and anxiolysis (Delagrange et al., 2003). A melatonin agonist and antagonist of serotonin 2C receptors, agomelatine may have antidepressant properties (Loo et al., 2002).

SUMMARY

Neurotransmitters and receptors, along with second messengers, form the basis of neuronal communication. It is at the level of neurotransmitter receptors that most psychotropic drugs interact with the neuronal transmission of information. The brain is home to many different kinds of neurotransmitters, and it is likely that additional ones will be discovered. Each neurotransmitter has its own specific functions that are mediated by receptors located in cell membranes. While the interaction between a neurotransmitter and its receptor is highly specific, each neurotransmitter may have more than one receptor with which it interacts. However, each receptor has its own effects on the neuron, a property that tends to amplify the action of the neurotransmitter. Serotonin-containing neurons originate in the dorsal raphe nuclei in the brainstem and project throughout the brain. Serotonin is involved in such diverse functions as emotion, mood, anxiety, appetite, sleep, and psychosis. Norepinephrine is produced in neurons whose cell bodies are in the locus coeruleus of the brainstem. Like serotonin-containing neurons, neurons that produce norepinephrine project widely throughout the brain and are involved in mood and attention.

Three major dopamine pathways exist in the brain, and each can be affected by certain psychotropic medications. The nigrostriatal pathway projects from the substantia nigra to other nuclei in the basal ganglia. Degeneration of these neurons, as occurs in Parkinson's disease, or antagonism of their postsynaptic dopamine-2 receptors by some types of antipsychotic drugs results in tremors, stiffness, and bradykinesia. Dopamine in the tuberoinfundibular pathway inhibits the release of prolactin. Blockade of this dopamine pathway, again from some antipsychotic drugs, releases prolactin, which may result in lactation and menstrual disturbances. The final dopamine pathway projects from the midbrain to the cortex and limbic system. This mesocorticolimbic pathway is thought to be involved in addiction and reward behavior.

Other pathways, including those whose degeneration is associated with Alzheimer's disease, utilize acetylcholine. Acetylcholine interacts with both nicotinic and muscarinic receptors, which are found in both the central and peripheral nervous system. In the periphery, acetylcholine and its nicotinic receptors act at the neuromuscular junction of voluntary muscles, while acetylcholine and its peripheral muscarinic receptors act at the neuromuscular junction of involuntary muscles. In the brain, muscarinic receptors appear to be involved in learning and memory. Antagonism of these receptors from certain drugs may result in confusion and memory deficits.

The brain's primary inhibitory neurotransmitter is GABA, which is distributed ubiquitously throughout the brain. GABA has two main types of receptors, both of which are inhibitory: GABA$_A$, coupled to chloride ion channels, which, when opened, hyperpolarize the neuron; and GABA$_B$, which is linked to G proteins.

With its receptors distributed throughout the brain, glutamate is the brain's primary excitatory neurotransmitter. Mediated by kainaic acid, metabotropic, and NMDA receptors, glutamate is associated with a variety of actions, including cognition and psychosis.

The binding of a neurotransmitter to its receptor is only the beginning of a complex process by which neurotransmitters affect neuronal function. In many cases, the receptors are coupled to ion channels in the cell's membrane, and the influx of ions alters the neuron's function. Other receptors are coupled with other biochemicals called second messengers that, in turn, are coupled to other molecules, and so on. Activation of these chains of chemical reactions also results in changes in neuronal and brain function, albeit not as quickly as that occurring with the opening or closing of membrane ion channels.

STUDY QUESTIONS

1. Describe the similarities and differences between agonists, antagonists, and partial agonists.
2. How does the traditional antipsychotic medication haloperidol (Haldol) result in lactation in non-nursing women or even in men?
3. Describe the process by which the antidepressant amitriptyline (Elavil), which antagonizes muscarinic receptors, could produce a dry mouth and confusion.
4. What are the differences between a receptor coupled to an ion channel and one coupled to a series of second messenger?
5. Based on events occurring in the synapse—including reuptake systems, presynaptic receptors, postsynaptic receptors, and enzymatic degradation—design a drug to prolong the time dopamine spends in the synapse.
6. List four possible outcomes of a neurotransmitter in the synapse.

REFERENCES

Abu-Qare AW, Abou-Donia MB (2002): Sarin: Health effects, metabolism, and methods of analysis. Food and Chemical Toxicology 40:1327–1333.

Anagnostaras SG, Murphy GG, Hamilton SE, Mitchell SL, Rahnama NP, Nathanson NM, Silva AJ (2003): Selective cognitive dysfunction in acetylcholine M$_1$ muscarinic receptor mutant mice. Nature Neuroscience 6:51–58.

Astles PC, Baker SR, Boot JR, Broad LM, Dell CP, Keenan M (2002): Recent progress in the development of subtype selective nicotinic acetylcholine receptor ligands. Current Drug Targets: CNS and Neurological Disorders 1:337–348.

Banke TG, Traynelis SF (2003): Activation of NR1/NR2B NMDA receptors. Nature Neuroscience 6:144–152.

Barbee JG (1993): Memory, benzodiazepines, and anxiety: Integration of theoretical and clinical perspectives. Journal of Clinical Psychiatry 54 (supplement):86–97.

Bergstrom WH, Hakanson DO (1998): Melatonin: The dark force. Advances in Pediatrics 45:91–106.

Berk M, Stein DJ, Potgieter A, Maud CM, Els C, Janet ML, Viljoen E (2000): Serotonin targets in the treatment of antidepressant induced sexual dysfunction: A pilot study of granisetron and sumitriptan. International Clinical Psychopharmacology 15:291–295.

Berridge CW, Waterhouse BD (2003): The locus coeruleus-noradrenergic system: Modulation of behavioral state and state-dependent cognitive processes. Brain Research. Brain Research Reviews 42:33–84.

Blier P, Ward NM (2003): Is there a role for 5-HT1A agonists in the treatment of depression? Biological Psychiatry 53:193–203.

Bloom FE (1990): Neurohumoral transmission and the central nervous system. In AF Gilman, TW Rall, AS Nies, P Taylor (eds.), *Goodman and Gilman's The Pharmacological Basis of Therapeutics*. Elmsford, NY: Pergamon Press.

Brunello N, Mendlewicz J, Kasper S, Leonard B, Montgomery S, Nelson J, Paykel E, Versiani M, Racagni G (2002): The role of noradrenaline and selective noradrenaline reuptake inhibition in depression. European Neuropsychopharmacology 12:461–475.

Burbaeva GS, Boksha IS, Turishcheva MS, Vorobyeva EA, Savushkina OK, Tereshkina EB (2003): Glutamine synthetase and glutamate dehydrogenase in the prefrontal cortex of patients with schizophrenia. Progress in Neuropsychopharmacology & Biological Psychiatry 27:675–680.

Bymaster FP, McNamara RK, Tran PV (2003): New approaches to developing antidepressants by enhancing monoaminergic neurotransmission. Expert Opinion on Investigational Drugs 12:531–543.

Calabrese JR, Londborg PD, Shelton MD, Thase ME (2003): Citalopram treatment of fluoxetine-intolerant depressed patients. Journal of Clinical Psychiatry 64:562–566.

Cardinali DP, Brusco LI, Lloret SP, Furio AM (2002): Melatonin in sleep disorders and jet lag. Neuroendocrinology Letters 23 (supplement 1):9–13.

Cesura AM, Pletscher A (1992): The new generation of monoamine oxidase inhibitors. Progress in Drug Research 38:171–297

Charney DS (2003): Neuroanatomical circuits modulating fear and anxiety behaviors. Acta Psychiatrica Scandinavica Supplementum 417:38–50.

Clark MS, Neumaier JF (2001): The 5-HT1B receptor: Behavioral implications. Psychopharmacology Bulletin 35:170–185.

Compton MT, Miller AH (2002): Psychopharmacology Bulletin 36:143–164.

Conley RR, Kelly DL (2002): Current status of antipsychotic treatment. Current Drug Targets. CNS and Neurological Disorders 1:123–128.

de Angelis L (2002): 5-HT2A antagonists in psychiatric disorders. Current Opinion in Investigational Drugs 3:106–112.

Delagrange P, Atkinson J, Boutin JA, Casteilla L, Lesieur D, Misslin R, Pellissier S, Penicaud L, Renard P (2003): Therapeutic perspectives for melatonin agonists and antagonists. Journal of Endocrinology 15:442–448.

Deutch AY, Roth RH (1999): Neurotransmitters. In MJ Zigmond, FE Bloom, SC Landis, JL Roberts, LR Squire (eds.), *Fundamental Neuroscience*. San Diego, CA: Academic Press.

Doggrell SA (2003): The role of 5-HT on the cardiovascular and renal systems and the clinical potential of 5-HT modulation. Expert Opinion on Investigational Drugs 12:805–823.

Feighner JP (1999): Mechanism of action of antidepressant medications. Journal of Clinical Psychiatry 60 (supplement 4):4–11.

Fonnum F (1984): Glutamate: A neurotransmitter in mammalian brain. Journal of Neurochemistry 42:1–11.

Gorman JM (1999): The role of norepinephrine in depression, pp. 625–626. In JM Gorman, CB Nemeroff, chairs. The role of norepinephrine in the treatment of depression (academic highlights). Journal of Clinical Psychiatry 60:623–631.

Gorman JM (2003): New molecular targets for antianxiety interventions. Journal of Clinical Psychiatry 64 (supplement 3): 28–35.

Greengard P (2001): The neurobiology of slow synaptic transmission. Science 294:1024–1030.

Gresch PJ, Strickland LV, Sanders-Bush E (2002): Lysergic acid diethylamide-induced Fos expression in rat brain: Role of serotonin-2A receptors. Neuroscience 114:707–713.

Guochuan T, van Kammen DP, Chen S, Kelley ME, Grier A, Coyle JT (1998): Glutamatergic neurotransmission involves structural and clinical deficits in schizophrenia. Biological Psychiatry 44:667–674.

Hamon M, Bourgoin S, Artaud F, El Mestikawy S (1981): The respective roles of tryptophan hydroxylase in the regulation of serotonin synthesis in the central nervous system. Journal of Physiology 77:269–279.

Hardy J, Argyropoulos S, Nutt DJ (2002): Venlafaxine: a new class of antidepressant. Hospital Medicine 63:549–552.

Healy DM (1997): *The Antidepressant Era.* Boston: Harvard University Press, pp. 157–15.

Hewitt J (2003): N-methyl-D-aspartate-enhanced analgesia. Current Pain and Headache Reports 7:43–47.

Hitri A, Hurd YL, Wyatt RJ, Deutsch SI (1994): Molecular, functional and biochemical characteristics of the dopamine transporter: Regional differences and clinical relevance. Clinical Neuropharmacology 17:1–22.

Huettner JE (2003): Kainate receptors and synaptic transmission. Progress in Neurobiology 70:387–407.

Inturrisi CE (2002): Clinical pharmacology of opioids for pain. Clinical Journal of Pain 18:4–13.

Iraizoz I, Guijarro JL, Gonzalo ML, deLacalle S (1999): Neuropathological changes in the nucleus basalis correlate with clinical measures of dementia. Acta Neuropathologica 98:186–196.

Krakowski M (2003): Violence and serotonin: Influence of impulse control, affect regulation, and social functioning. Journal of Neuropsychiatry and Clinical Neurosciences 15:294–305.

Lachowiez JE, Sibley DR (1997): Molecular characteristics of mammalian dopamine receptors. Pharmacology & Toxicology 81:105–113.

Lefkowitz RJ, Hoffman BB, Taylor P (1990): Neurohumoral transmission: The autonomic and somatic nervous systems. In AF Gilman, TW Rall, AS Nies, P Taylor (eds.), *Goodman and Gilman's The Pharmacological Basis of Therapeutics.* Elmsford, NY: Pergamon Press.

Lerma J (1998): Kainate receptors: An interplay between excitatory and inhibitory synapses. FEBS Letters 430:100–104.

Loo H, Hale A, D'haenen H (2002): Determination of the dose of agomelatine, a melatoninergic agonist and selective 5-HT(2C) antagonist in the treatment of major depressive disorder: A placebo-controlled dose range study. International Clinical Psychopharmacology 17:239–247.

Lydiard RB (2003): The role of GABA in anxiety disorders. Journal of Clinical Psychiatry 64 (supplement 3):21–27.

Madden DR (2002): The inner workings of the AMPA receptors. Current Opinion in Drug Discovery & Development 5:741–748.

Marino MJ, Conn PJ (2002): Direct and indirect modulation of the N-methyl-D-aspartate receptor. Current Drug Targets. CNS and Neurological Disorders 1:1–16.

Manji HK (1992): G proteins: Implications for psychiatry. American Journal of Psychiatry 149:746–760.

Mathew SJ, Coplan JD, Smith ELP, Schoepp DD, Rosenblum LA, Gorman JM (2001): Glutamate-hypothalamic-pituitary-adrenal axis interactions: Implications for mood and anxiety disorders. CNS Spectrums 6:555–564.

Matthews G (1996): Neurotransmitter release. Annual Review of Neuroscience 19:219–233.

Meston CM, Frohlich PF (2000): The neurobiology of sexual function. Archives of General Psychiatry 57:1012–1030.

Monteleone P, Brambilla F, Bortolotti F, Maj M (2000): Serotonergic dysfunction across eating disorders: Relationship to eating behaviour, purging behaviour, nutritional status, and general psychopathology. Psychological Medicine 30:1099–1110.

Nagatsu T (2000): [Molecular mechanisms of neurotransmission]: Rinsho Shinkeigaku 40:1185–1188.

Natsch S, Hekster YA, Keyser A, Deckers CL, Meinardi H, Renier WO (1997): Newer anticonvulsant drugs: Role of pharmacology, drug interactions and adverse reactions in drug choice. Drug Safety 17:228–240.

Ninan PT, Cole JO, Yonkers KA (1998): Nonbenzodiazepine anxiolytics. In AF Schatzberg, CB Nemeroff (eds.), *Textbook of Psychopharmacology*. Washington DC: American Psychiatric Press.

Noble E (1996): Alcoholism and the dopaminergic system: A review. Addiction Biology 1:333–348.

Nordberg A, Svennson AL (1998): Cholinesterase inhibitors in the treatment of Alzheimer's disease: A comparison of tolerability and pharmacology. Drug Safety 19:465–480.

Nutt DJ (2002): The neuropharmacology of serotonin and noradrenaline in depression. International Clinical Psychopharmacology 17 (supplement 1): S1–12.

Okada Y, Tsuda Y, Bryant SD, Lazarus LH (2002): Endomorphins and related opiate peptides. Vitamins and Hormones 65:257–279.

Olivier B, van Wijngaarden I, Soudijn W (2000): 5-HT(3) receptor antagonists and anxiety: A preclinical and clinical review. European Neuropsychopharmacology 10:77–95.

Palmada M, Centelles JJ (1998): Excitatory amino acid neurotransmission. Pathways for metabolism, storage and reuptake of glutamate in brain. Frontiers in Bioscience 3:D701–718.

Paterson D, Nordberg A (2000): Neuronal nicotinic receptors in the human brain. Progress in Neurobiology 61:75–111.

Pin JP, Acher F (2002): The metabotropic glutamate receptors: Structure, activation mechanism and pharmacology. Current Drug Targets. CNS and Neurological Disorders 1:297–317.

Pliska V (1999): Partial agonism: Mechanisms based on ligand-receptor interactions and on stimulus-response coupling. Journal of Receptor and Signal Transduction Research 19:597–629.

Rajaratnam SM, Dijk DJ, Middleton B, Stone BM, Arendt J (2003): Melatonin phase-shifts human circadian rhythms with no evidence of changes in the duration of endogenous melatonin secretion or the 24-hour production of reproductive hormones. The Journal of Clinical Endocrinology and Metabolism 88:4303–4309.

Raveh L, Brandeis R, Gilat E, Cohen G, Alkalay D, Rabinovitz I, Sonego H, Weissman BA (2003): Anticholinergic and antiglutamatergic agents protect against soman-induced brain damage and cognitive dysfunction. Toxicological Sciences 75:108–116.

Raynor K, Kong H, Chen Y, Yasuda K, Yu L, Bell GI, Reisine T (1994): Pharmacological characterization of the cloned kappa-, delta-, and mu-opioid receptors. Molecular Pharmacology 45:330–334.

Richelson E (1987): Pharmacology of antidepressants. Psychopathology 20 (supplement 1):1–12.

Riedel G, Platt B, Micheau J (2003): Glutamate receptor function in learning and memory. Behavioural Brain Research 140:1–47.

Romach KM, Sellers EM, Somer GR, Landry M, Cunningham GM, Jovey RD, McKay C, Boislard J, Mercier C, Pepin JM, Perreault J, Lemire E, Baker RP, Campbell W, Ryan D (2002): Naltrexone in the treatment of alcohol dependence: A Canadian trial. Canadian Journal of Clinical Pharmacology 9:130–136.

Ross EM (1990): Pharmacodynamics: Mechanisms of drug action and the relationship between drug concentration and effects. In AF Gilman, TW Rall, AS Nies, P Taylor (eds.), *Goodman and Gilman's The Pharmacological Basis of Therapeutics*. Elmsford, NY: Pergamon Press.

Roth BL (1994): Multiple serotonin receptors: Clinical and experimental aspects. Annals of Clinical Psychiatry 6:67–78.

Santarelli L, Saxe M, Gross C, Surget A, Battaglia F, Dulawa S, Weisstaub N, Lee J, Duman R, Arancio O, Belzung C, Hen R (2003): Requirement of hippocampal neurogenesis for the behavioral effects of antidepressants. Science 301:805–809.

Shimohama S, Sawada H, Kitamura Y, Taniguchi T (2003): Disease model: Parkinson's disease. Trends in Molecular Medicine 9:360–365.

Simeone TA, Donevan SD, Rho JM (2003): Molecular biology and ontogeny of gamma-aminobutyric acid (GABA) receptors in the mammalian central nervous system. Journal of Child Neurology 18:39–48.

Simpson D, Perry CM (2003): Atomoxetine. Paediatric Drugs 5:407–415.

Skolnick P (1999): Antidepressants for the new millennium. European Journal of Pharmacology 375:31–40.

Smith RE, Haroutunian V, Davis KL, Meador-Woodruff JH (2001): Vesicular glutamate transporter transcript expression in the thalamus in schizophrenia. Neuroreport 17:2885–2887.

Stehle JH, von Gall C, Korf HW (2003): Melatonin: A clock-output, a clock-input. Journal of Neuroendocrinology 15:383–389.

Stein V, Nicoll RA (2003): GABA generates excitement. Neuron 37:375–378.

Struder HK, Weicker H (2001): Physiology and pathophysiology of the serotonergic system and its implications on mental and physical performance. Part I. International Journal of Sports Medicine 22:467–481.

Subhash MN, Nagaraja MR, Sharada S, Vinod KY (2003): Cortical alpha-adrenoceptor down regulation by tricyclic antidepressants in the rat brain. Neurochemistry International 43:603–609.

Suhara T, Takano A, Sudo Y, Ichimiya T, Inoue M, Yasuno F, Ikoma Y, Okubo Y (2003): High levels of serotonin transporter occupancy with low-dose clomipramine in comparative occupancy study with fluvoxamine using positron emission tomography. Archives of General Psychiatry 60:386–391.

Tamminga CA, Frost DO (2001): Changing concepts in the neurochemistry of schizophrenia. American Journal of Psychiatry 158:1365–1366.

Tansey MJ, Schlechte JA (2001): Pituitary production of prolactin and prolactin-suppressing drugs. Lupus 10:660–664.

Tork I (1990): Anatomy of the serotonergic system. Annals of the New York Academy of Sciences 600:9–34.

Tunnicliff G, Malatynska E (2003): Central GABAergic systems and depressive illness. Neurochemical Research 28:965–976.

Valenstein, E. (1998). *Blaming the Brain: The Truth about Drugs and Mental Health.* New York: Free Press.

Vallone D, Picetti R, Borrelli E (2000): Structure and function of dopamine receptors. Neuroscience and Biobehavioral Reviews 24:125–132.

van Heeringen K (2003): The neurobiology of suicide and suicidality. Canadian Journal of Psychiatry 48:292–300.

Vaswani M, Linda FK, Ramesh S (2003): Role of selective serotonin reuptake inhibitors in psychiatric disorders: A comprehensive review. Progress in Neuro-Psychopharmacology & Biological Psychiatry 27:85–102.

Walton SM (2000): Advance in the uses of 5-HT3 receptor antagonists. Expert Opinion on Pharmacotherapy 1:207–223.

Westenberg HG (1999): Pharmacology of antidepressants: Selectivity or multiplicity? Journal of Clinical Psychiatry 60 (supplement 17):4–8.

Wieck A, Haddad PM (2003): Antipsychotic-induced hyperprolactinaemia in women: Pathophysiology, severity and consequences. Selective literature review. British Journal of Psychiatry 182:199–204.

Willner P (1997): The dopamine hypothesis of schizophrenia: Current status, future prospects. International Clinical Psychopharmacology 12:297–308.

Zipfel GJ, Babcock DJ, Lee JM, Choi DW (2000): Neuronal apoptosis after CNS injury: The roles of glutamate and calcium. Journal of Neurotrauma 17:857–869.

Zohar J, Chopra M, Sasson Y, Amiaz R, Amital D (2000): Obsessive compulsive disorder: Serotonin and beyond. World Journal of Biological Psychiatry 1:92–100.

CHAPTER THREE

PHARMACOKINETICS AND PHARMACODYNAMICS

This chapter describes how the body handles drugs and how drugs interact with the body to produce their desired and unwanted effects. Pharmacokinetics is about the passage of a drug through the body. For example, a drug must somehow get into the body, whether through the mouth, intravenously, or directly through the skin. Depending upon the route of entry of the drug into the body, the drug may have to run a biological gauntlet before getting to its destination. If absorbed from the gastrointestional tract, as many medications are, the drug must go through first-pass metabolism, a process that may reduce the concentration of a drug even before it gets to the blood circulation. Once in the bloodstream, a drug must navigate through the body to get to its target organ. Some drugs may be unable to pass through the blood-brain barrier either because they are insoluble in lipids or because they are simply too large. Similar factors determine whether a drug crosses the placental barrier.

In addtion to interacting with its target organ or organs to produce its desired and unwanted effects, a drug must be metabolized and eliminated from the body. One of the most common methods of metabolism is for the drug to pass through a system of enzymes, located primarily in the liver, that metabolize, or change, the drug into metabolites, which may be active drugs themselves. The cytochrome P450 system, as it is called, contains a host of enzymes that metabolize specific drugs and is a major source of the drug-drug interactions that can so complicate psychopharmacology and other branches of medicine.

The rate at which a drug is metabolized determines its half-life, which in turn affects how long it takes for the drug to achieve steady state, the point at which its blood concentration no longer fluctuates wildly with each additional dose of medication. Half-life also determines how long it takes the body to completely eliminate a drug.

Pharmacodynamics is the interaction of the drug with the body to elicit a clinical effect and includes such concepts as potency, efficacy, and dose-response curves. The effects a drug has on the body can be amplified by active metabolites, which are essentially new drugs the cytochrome P450 system has synthesized from the original drug.

Related to pharmacokinetics and pharmacodynamics, tolerance and dependence are driven in part by cellular changes that occur in response to drugs. Finally, this chapter discusses the importance of therapeutic drug monitoring, because determination of drug concentrations in the body utilizes pharmacokinetic and pharmacodynamic principles. For some drugs, such as the mood stabilizer lithium, monitoring of blood concentrations is crucial both for efficacy and safety. At the current state of knowledge, other drugs require little or no monitoring.

Pharmacokinetics and pharmacodynamics address, respectively, the passage of a drug through the body and the mechanisms by which the drug affects the body. Pharmacokinetics concerns the route of drug entry into the body (e.g., oral, intravenous, or nasal routes) and the absorption, distribution, metabolism, and elimination of the drug. Some drugs, when absorbed from the stomach or small intestine, are extensively metabolized in the lining of these organs. This first-pass metabolism can substantially reduce the availability of the drug in the rest of the body (Benet et al., 1990). Other drugs may be excluded from entry into the brain because they are not lipid (or fat) soluble and hence are unable to cross the blood-brain barrier, which contains substantial amounts of lipids. Pharmacokinetics also includes drug metabolism—that is, how the body eliminates or clears the drug. While the liver and kidney are the two main organs involved in drug metabolism, other organs such as the small intestine play a role in drug metabolism. In contrast, pharmacodynamics concerns the mechanisms by which drugs induce therapeutic and adverse effects.

PHARMACOKINETICS

Route of Administration

Pharmacokinetics refers to the movement of drugs through the body with time (Holford & Sheiner, 1981). A drug enters the body by some route, is distributed through various body tissues, is usually metabolized, and then is eliminated from the body. The route of administration of a drug is the first point at which a drug interacts with the body. Drugs may enter the body through numerous routes including the mouth, rectum, spinal fluid, skin, nasal cavity, and lungs.

The oral administration of psychotropic drugs, particularly those used clinically, is a common route of administration. For oral administration to work, the drug must get into and stay in the stomach. Vomiting and nausea can prohibit the oral administration of a drug, as anyone who has developed nausea while on antibiotics knows. For example, nausea from the antidepressant fluoxetine (Prozac) can lead to cessation of the drug treatment (Beasley et al., 2000). Drugs differ in how readily they are absorbed from the gastrointestinal tract. The antidepressant paroxetine (Paxil) is an example of one drug that is generally well absorbed when taken orally (Bourin et al., 2001).

Although less frequently used in psychopharmacology than oral drug administration, other routes of drug administration are possible. For example, vomiting or unconsciousness in some conditions may require rectal drug administration. Generally administered orally, the anticonvulsant topiramate (Topamax) is an example of a drug that may be given rectally (Conway et al., 2003). Some drugs can be administered intrathecally, or directly into the cerebral spinal fluid, which bathes the brain and spinal cord. Under certain circumstances, some opiates such as hydromorphone and morphine have been used intrathecally for chronic pain (Ackerman et al., 2003). Subcutaneous administration is another route by which drugs can enter the body. For example, to bypass stomach acidity, insulin is generally given subcutaneously (Belmin & Valensi, 2003).

Yet another way that a drug can be delivered to the body is by intramuscular injection, in which a bolus of drug is placed via a needle into muscle tissue. Intramuscular injection of some antipsychotic medications such as olanzapine (Zyprexa) can be administered for rapid behavioral control (Altamura et al., 2003), particularly in emergency settings. Another form of intramuscular injections of psychotropic drugs consists of depot preparations of antipsychotics that are released slowly from the muscle and thus provide a long-term supply of the medication. Haldol decanoate is one such depot preparation (Altamura et al., 2003). Depot antipsychotics can be used in some cases of noncompliance with oral antipsychotics (Barnes & Curson, 1994).

With intravenous administration, a drug is given directly into the bloodstream. Heroin (Bravo et al., 2003) and cocaine (Smith et al., 2001), for instance, can be administered intravenously. Some drugs are administered by inhalation. Tobacco smoking, for example, takes nicotine into the lungs where it is absorbed into the bloodstream. In addition to its intravenous route of administration (Nestor et al., 1989), the illegal drug methamphetamine also can be used by inhaling the smoked drug (Cook et al., 1993).

Drugs also can enter the body across mucus membranes or skin. Cocaine, for instance, can diffuse across the mucus membranes of the nose (i.e., "snorting") (Jeffcoat et al., 1989) to gain rapid access to the bloodstream and brain. Similarly, nicotine is available in a transdermal patch for use in smoking cessation (Haxby, 1995).

The route of administration is important also for drugs of abuse. Users of illicit drugs, for instance, employ routes of drug administration to ensure rapid penetration of the brain of adequate amounts of drug (Quinn et al., 1997). Smoking a drug results in fast access to the brain; intravenous administration increases the drug's availability (Quinn et al., 1997).

Absorption

After administration, a drug must be absorbed from the body region it entered into other body compartments in order to exert a therapeutic effect. If taken orally, a psychotropic drug must be absorbed from the stomach or small intestine into the bloodstream and pass into the brain. Drug absorption is dependent upon a variety of factors, such as drug solubility, gastrointestional motility, and pH (Burton et al., 2002). Drug absorption also can be affected by the presence of food in the stomach. For example, food in the stomach slows the rate of absorption of the antidepressant reboxetine (Edrolas, not available in the United States), yet the final degree of absorption of reboxetine is unchanged (Fleishaker, 2000). Absorption rates can vary from drug to drug. The antidepressant sertraline (Zoloft) is an example of a drug that is relatively slowly absorbed from the gastrointestional tract (DeVane et al., 2002).

Distribution

The distribution of a drug through the body is also an important aspect of pharmacokinetics and is dependent upon drug permeability and blood flow to different organs (Daniel, 2003). Lipid solubility is particularly important in determining which drugs can enter into the brain. Composed of tight capillary junctions and astrocytic processes, the blood-brain barrier restricts the passage of many substances from the blood to the brain (Benet et al., 1990), protecting the brain from potentially harmful substances (de Boer et al., 2003). Because of the blood-brain barrier, many potentially effective drugs are excluded from the brain because they are not lipophillic enough to pass the blood-brain barrier (Misra et al., 2003), an important notion in drug development. Lipid solubility is affected by whether a drug is ionized or nonionized, with the nonionized form generally being more lipophillic (Benet et al., 1990). The Henderson-Hasselbalch equation can be used to calculate the concentrations of the ionized and nonionized forms of the drug at a given pH (Benet et al., 1990), providing a measure of how lipid soluble a drug is.

In addition to lipid solubility, a variety of transporter mechanisms have been identified in the blood-brain barrier that allow brain entry of substances that otherwise could not gain access to the brain (de Boer et al., 2003). Transport mechanisms, for instance, may convey some drugs across the blood-brain barrier. For example, some evidence suggests that the antidepressant citalopram (Celexa) is taken through the blood-brain barrier by a transporter mechanism (Rochat et al., 1999). As with the blood-brain barrier, high-lipid solubility allows drugs to cross the placental barrier and enter into fetal circulation. Highly lipid soluble drugs also can enter into breast milk. In contrast, drugs low in lipid solubility have a more limited distribution, as they are unable to penetrate into highly lipid areas of the body.

An additional factor affecting how a drug is distributed throughout the body is protein binding. In the blood, drugs may bind to several different proteins (such as albumin), and many drugs in psychopharmacology may be highly protein bound, in some cases having 90 percent of the drug bound to blood proteins (DeVane, 2002). Because albumin has a large molecular weight (that is, it is a large molecule), a drug bound to albumin cannot fit through the gap junctions of the capillaries and remains in the bloodstream along with its bound drug. Even with highly protein-bound drugs, some of the drug exists in an unbound, or free, form that can result in pharmacological effects (DeVane, 2002).

Protein binding of drugs is a potential source of drug-drug interactions, as drugs can displace each other from protein-bound positions increasing the amount of unbound drug (DeVane, 2002). However, in actual practice, this type of drug-drug interaction may be of less concern than previously thought (DeVane, 2002).

Metabolism and Elimination

All drugs are eliminated from the body in some form, and different organ systems are involved in both the preparation of drugs for elimination from the body and in the discharge process itself. The liver is a major location for drug metabolism, including those drugs used in psychopharmacology (DeVane, 2002). In the liver is an extensive array of enzymes known as the cytochrome P450 system—enzymes that are responsible for a significant proportion of drug metabolism.

Cytochrome P450 enzymes convert drugs into more water-soluble compounds,, allowing them to be eliminated by the kidney. In addition, cytochrome P450 enzymes may convert drugs to other compounds, or metabolites, that may be pharmacologically active drugs themselves, having pharmacological properties similar to or different from their parent compounds. For example, the commonly prescribed antidepressant imipramine is converted by cytochrome P450 enzymes into an active metabolite desipramine (McLeod et al., 2000), a metabolite that has the potential to interfere with certain aspects of treatment (McLeod et al., 2000) (in fact, desipramine is marketed as a drug in its own right).

Many different cytochrome P450 enzymes exist, each having its own signature of drugs that it metabolizes. The cytochrome P450 3A3/4 metabolizes some frequently prescribed antidepressants, as well as steroids, certain benzodiazepines, and carbamazepine (used in epilepsy and bipolar disorder) (Ketter et al., 1995). Conversely, some drugs inhibit certain cytochrome P450 enzymes. Cytochrome P450 2D6 enzymes, for example, metabolize some tricyclic antidepressants and are inhibited by some of the specific serotonin reuptake inhibitor antidepressants (Ketter et al., 1995).

The inhibition of some cytochrome P450 enzymes by drugs can lead to drug-drug interactions. For example, specific serotonin reuptake inhibitor antidepressants disrupt the metabolism of tricyclic antidepressants, potentially increasing tricyclic levels into potentially toxic ranges (Ketter et al., 1995). The antidepressant paroxetine (Paxil) is both metabolized by and inhibits the cytochrome P450 2D6 enzyme (Bourin et al., 2001).

Many drugs have what are known as first-pass metabolism. In addition to the liver, cytochrome P450 enzymes are located in other body sites as well, including the walls of the small intestine (Shen et al., 1997). Because of the location of these enzymes in the small intestine, for many drugs metabolism begins as soon as they are absorbed from the gastrointestinal tract where they interact with these enzymes even before reaching the circulation. First-pass effects can also occur for some drugs because blood leaving the gastrointestinal tract passes through the liver before reaching the rest of the circulatory system, again subjecting these drugs to the possibility of extensive metabolism. Although it is well absorbed orally, paroxetine is highly subject to first-pass metabolism (Bourin et al., 2001). First-pass metabolism converts the antidepressant sertraline (Zoloft) to a weakly active metabolite desmethyl-sertraline, which is ultimately present in higher concentrations than the parent drug sertraline (DeVane et al., 2002).

Other organs in addition to the liver and gastrointestinal tract are involved in the metabolism and elimination of drugs. For instance, some cytochrome P450 enzymes are found in the brain, which may be involved in the metabolism of the anxiolytic drug alprazolam (Xanax) to an active metabolite (Pai et al., 2002). The lungs too metabolize some drugs (Boer, 2003) and are involved in the elimination of other drugs. For example, a percentage of a metabolite of alcohol, acetaldehyde, is eliminated through the lungs and can be measured in breath (Jones, 1995).

The kidney is involved in the excretion of the water-soluble metabolites of most drugs. While nearly all of the drugs used in psychopharmacology are metabolized through the liver, two important exceptions are excreted in unchanged forms by the kidney. The mood stabilizer lithium is not metabolized by the liver or any other enzymes but instead is excreted unchanged by the kidney (Wang & Ketter, 2002). Under condition of kidney disease or dehydration, lithium levels may rise to toxic concentrations. Under conditions of low blood volume, as occurs in dehydration from vomiting, exercise, and excessive sweating, the kidney's clearance of lithium decreases, with resulting increased serum concentrations of lithium, which may reach toxic levels (Thomsen & Schou, 1999). Kidney disease also affects the elimination of other drugs and their metabolites, and dosages often must be altered to compensate for cases of kidney failure. The second drug that is entirely cleared by the kidney is gabapentin (Neurontin) (Wang & Ketter, 2002), a medication used in the treatment of epilepsy (Btaiche & Woster, 1995), which may have efficacy for generalized anxiety disorder (Sramek et al., 2002).

Drug Half-Life and Steady State

Drug Half-Life.   Drugs have a half-life (t1/2), defined as the time taken for the body via metabolism to eliminate one-half of the drug (Benet et al., 1990). Thus, after one half-life of a drug, 50 percent of the original concentration of the drug remains, assuming that no additional drug has been taken. After two half-lives, 25 percent of the original concentration is present, and so on. After five half-lives, approximately 3 percent of the original amount of drug remains in the body. As a general rule, five or six half-lives of a drug are considered to be the time it takes for a drug to be cleared from the body. Half-life varies, often dramatically, from drug to drug. For instance, methylphenidate (Ritalin), a commonly prescribed drug for both child and adult attention-deficit disorder, has a half-life of approximately two to three hours (Kimko et al., 1999) (thus, methylphenidate is cleared from the body in anywhere from ten to fifteen hours, assuming it takes approximately five half-lives for the drug to be eliminated). Conversely, fluoxetine (Prozac) has a half-life of four to six days (Emmanuel et al., 1999), requiring twenty to thirty days to be cleared from the body. The half-life of fluoxetine's active metabolite, norfluoxetine, has an even longer half-life of about four to sixteen days (Emmanuel et al., 1999).

Not only does half-life vary from drug to drug, but also from person to person, depending on the types and amounts of cytochrome P450 enzymes. For instance, approximately 7 percent of Caucasians and 1 percent of Asians are considered poor metabolizers of drugs whose metabolism involves cytochrome P450 2D6, an enzyme that metabolizes numerous psychotropic drugs (Bertilsson et al., 2002). The poor metabolizers are at risk for higher than expected concentrations of those drugs that are metabolized by cytochrome P450 2D6. Serum concentrations of drugs can vary dramatically from person to person, even at the same dose. For example, concentrations of the antidepressant sertraline (Zoloft) can vary up to fifteen-fold from person to person (DeVane et al., 2002). Even though cytochrome P450 2D6 activity does not seem to change with age (Shulman & Ozdemir, 1997), the half-life of drugs metabolized by this enzyme may increase due to age- and disease-related changes in blood flow to the liver and in kidney function (Shulman & Ozdemir, 1997), making age a factor in half-life variability.

Steady State.   A second pharmacokinetic principle is related also to half-life and the rate of drug metabolism. Consistent dosing of a drug—be it once, twice, or three times daily—results in a steady inflow of drug into the body. However, the drug concentrations in the body under normal liver and kidney function do not increase indefinitely. Instead, after a period of approximately five half-lives, a condition of relative steady state is reached (Benet et al., 1990). Steady state occurs when the amount of drug entering the body over a given time period equals the amount of drug leaving the body, with the resulting blood concentrations of the drug remaining relatively constant. The blood concentrations of the drug are not entirely constant during steady state, because blood concentrations rise after a drug is absorbed and drop slightly before the next dose is absorbed into the circulation, resulting in a saw-tooth pattern of peak and trough drug concentration versus time but with no increasing slope to the overall pattern.

In a way, steady state can be thought of as the reverse of the time taken to eliminate a drug completely from the body after it is no longer being dosed— again, it is the time period of roughly five half-lives of the drug that guides how long these processes take. Because of the five half-life requirement for steady state conditions to occur, this amount of time is required to get the drug into a steady state not only after a drug has been initiated but also after a dose change has been made. Key pharmacokinetic features are summarized in Table 3.1.

PHARMACODYNAMICS

Pharmacodynamics concerns drug action (Holford & Sheiner, 1981), including interactions with receptors that elicit both therapeutic and adverse effects. Pharmacodynamic considerations include potency and efficacy, receptor occupancy, and therapeutic drug monitoring.

TABLE 3.1   Key Pharmacokinetic Features of Drugs

Administration	Oral: Through the mouth. Rectal: Through the rectum. Intrathecally: Directly into the cerebral spinal fluid. Subcutaneously: Into the skin. Intramuscular Injection: Into the muscles. Intravenously: Into the veins. Inhalation: Through the mouth. Across the mucus membranes or skin.
Absorption	If taken orally, a drug must be absorbed from the stomach or small intestine into the bloodstream and pass into the brain.
Distribution	Depends upon drug permeability and blood flow to different organs. The blood-brain barrier, for example, restricts the passage of many substances from the blood to the brain, protecting the brain from potentially harmful substances.
Metabolism and Elimination	Drugs are eliminated from the body in some form, and different organ systems are involved in both the preparation of drugs for elimination from the body and in the discharge process itself. The liver is a major location for drug metabolism, including those drugs used in psychopharmacology. The kidney is involved in the excretion of the water-soluble metabolites of most drugs.
Drug Half-Life	After one-half life of a drug, 50 percent of the original concentration of the drug remains, assuming that no additional drug has been taken. As a general rule, five or six half-lives of a drug are considered to be the time it takes for a drug to be cleared from the body.
Steady State	After a period of approximately five half-lives, a condition of relative steady state is reached. This occurs when the amount of drug entering the body over a given time period equals the amount of drug leaving the body, with the resulting blood concentrations of the drug remaining relatively constant.

Potency and Efficacy

Drugs can differ from one another in potency and efficacy. Potency is the amount of drug necessary to produce a certain effect. In psychopharmacology, this is often related to the efficiency with which a drug binds to its receptors. For example, benzodiazepines differ in potency (Ashton, 1994). While the end therapeutic effect is the same regardless of whether a high- or low-potency benzodiazepine is used, the amount of drug required to produce this effect is different between the low- and high-potency drugs. A high-potency drug is not necessarily superior to a low-potency drug if the dose of the latter can be increased to make up for the diminished potency (Nies, 1990). Potency becomes important for first-generation antipsychotic drugs, which can be classified according to their potency. While the overall type of side effects produced is usually the same for both high- and low-potency antipsychotics, the propensity to induce these adverse effects differs between high- and low-potency antipsychotics. For example, the high potency antipsychotics, such as haloperidol (Haldol), appear more likely to cause movement disorders than do the low-potency antipsychotics, such as thioridazine (Mellaril) (Schillevoort et al., 2001).

Distinct from potency, efficacy refers to a drug's maximum possible effects, not to the amount of drug required to produce a given effect (Nies, 1990). A drug that lowers depression by 50 percent would be considered to have greater efficacy than a drug that only produces a 30 percent reduction in depression. Additionally, no matter how high the dose of the latter drug was increased, the maximum efficacy of 30 percent would not increase further. That is, once a drug's maximum effect has been achieved, no additional increases in dose will result in greater efficacy—the response versus dose curve becomes flat (change in efficacy/change in dose = 0). Key pharmacodynamic features are summarized in Table 3.2.

Dose-Response Curves

Response versus drug dose can be illustrated by drug-response curves. If the concentration of a drug at a given site of interest (e.g., at a particular receptor), or the drug dose is plotted on the x-axis and the strength of the drug's therapeutic effect (response) is along the y-axis, the resulting graph is a dose-response curve, a relationship that can aid in evaluating dosing strategies (Mossman, 1997). In some cases, the resulting curve may have a sigmoid shape, although curves may be concave or linear (Nies, 1990). In those conditions that generate a sigmoid curve, at low drug concentrations or dose, the magnitude of the response is small, as the dose is subtherapeutic (Mossman, 1997). As concentrations of the drug or dose begin to rise, the curve may rise steeply, indicating an increasing therapeutic effect as the dose of drug is increased. At higher concentrations or doses, the curve flattens as increasing drug levels at the site of interest fail to result in increased therapeutic responses—that is, therapeutic responses do not increase indefinitely. Doses or concentrations at the initial portion of the curve are subtherapeutic, but increasing the dose in the final flat portion of the curve does not result in added clinical improvement (Mossman, 1997). The value of dose-response curves can be illustrated by a study done with first-generation antipsychotic drugs. The dose-response curves for first-generation antipsychotic drugs flattened at certain doses, above which little clinical improvement occurred, even though adverse effects continued to increase. That is, the risk-benefit ratio increased sharply above a particular dose (Mossman, 1997).

The shape and position of the dose-response curve vary from drug to drug; some drugs have a flatter curve, whereas others have a much steeper shape. Importantly, sigmoid curves for a given drug vary from person to person (Nies,

TABLE 3.2 Key Pharmacodynamic Features

Potency	The amount of drug necessary to produce a certain effect.
Efficacy	A drug's maximum possible effects, not the amount of drug required to produce a given effect.
Drug-Response Curves	The graph that occurs from plotting a measure of drug response against drug dose.

1990), depending upon individual differences in metabolism and receptor types and concentrations.

A closely related principle to the dose-response curve of therapeutic response is the dose-response curve of adverse effects, a curve that may well have a different location from the therapeutic sigmoid curve. In fact, the separation between the dose-response curve for therapeutic effects and that for toxic effects is a key factor in the likelihood of developing toxicity (DeVane, 1998). The greater the separation between curves, the less the chance of toxicity, as therapeutic levels are reached at concentrations much lower than those necessary for toxicity. Some drugs, however, have therapeutic and toxicity sigmoid curves that are closely positioned to one another. Lithium, for example, has a narrow therapeutic window (Dodds, 2000), as concentrations required for therapeutic effects are very close to those that can cause toxicity.

Most drugs used in psychopharmacology interact with more than one receptor. Tricyclic antidepressants illustrate this one-drug, multiple-receptor notion because they interact not only with serotonin and norepinephrine reuptake receptors but also with acetylcholine, alpha-adrenergic, and histamine receptors. The effects generated from each drug-receptor interaction—be they therapeutic or adverse—have their own dose-response curves (DeVane, 1998). In the case of a tricyclic antidepressant, therefore, dose-response curves exist for the therapeutic effects from serotonin and norepinephrine reuptake inhibition and for the adverse effects spawned from the interaction with acetylcholine, alpha-adrenergic, and histamine receptors.

Related to dose-response curves for both therapeutic and adverse effects are the LD_{50} and ED_{50}. LD_{50} stands for the drug dose that is lethal for 50 percent of the study population, and ED_{50} for the dose that is effective for 50 percent of the study population (Nies, 1990). The ratio of the LD_{50} to the ED_{50} is known as the therapeutic index (Nies, 1990), a number that provides important safety data about a drug. That is, the higher the therapeutic index, the greater the separation is between the LD_{50} and the ED_{50}. Lithium, or example, has a low therapeutic index (Wang & Ketter, 2002), and thus the dose that results in clinical response is close to the dose that causes lithium toxicity, whereas drugs with a high therapeutic index have a greater separation between their clinically effective doses and the doses that can cause toxicity.

DRUG CONCENTRATION MEASUREMENT

Related to both pharmacokinetics and pharmacodynamics is the measurement of plasma drug concentrations. For many drugs it is possible to measure the concentration of the drug in blood. Even though drug concentrations are not measured routinely for the many of the drugs used in psychopharmacology, several drugs do require regular measurements, such as lithium and in some cases tricyclic antidepressants (Preskorn et al., 1993). A clinician may measure blood concentrations of a drug for a number of reasons: to ascertain whether a drug is at a therapeutic concentration for those drugs that have these concentrations established, to diminish the chances of toxicity occurring, to anticipate and monitor drug-drug interactions, and, finally, to determine patient compliance with a drug regimen.

Some drugs appear to be associated with a therapeutic concentration level. That is, optimal clinical response is thought to occur for most people at drug concentrations above a minimum level, with concentrations of the drug below this level generally not leading to clinical improvement. An important example of this is lithium, as lithium appears to have approximate minimum effective plasma levels (McIntyre et al., 2001).

While therapeutic concentrations have not been established for most antidepressants—and indeed there may not be a correlation between clinical response and blood concentration for some psychotropic drugs including antidepressant specific serotonin reuptake inhibitors (Vaswani et al., 2003)—some of the tricyclic antidepressants have relatively well-established concentration levels that can serve as dosing guidelines. For example, the tricyclic antidepressant doxepin (Sinequan) may have a therapeutic plasma concentration range, even though the actual numbers in this range have been challenged (Leucht et al., 2001).

Drug-drug interactions can lead to one drug's increasing or decreasing a second drug's concentration, with the potential for increased side effects, toxicity, or loss of efficacy to occur. To anticipate or monitor the degree of an interaction, drug levels may be monitored (Mitchell, 2001). The antidepressant fluoxetine can interact with several other drugs, and its concentrations may be monitored to evaluate the potential drug-drug interaction (Lundmark et al., 2001), even though there is no clear relationship between fluoxetine concentrations and therapeutic response (Rasmussen & Brosen, 2000).

As many drugs, including many used in psychopharmacology, are toxic above certain concentrations, blood level monitoring is often used to minimize risks of toxicity (Mitchell, 2001). Because of its narrow therapeutic window and consequent risk of toxicity, lithium levels require monitoring not only to ensure effective plasma levels but also to avoid lithium-induced toxicity.

In addition to the above reasons for monitoring plasma drug concentrations, clinicians may determine plasma drug concentrations to evaluate whether a patient is compliant with treatment (Mitchell, 2001). For example, therapeutic drug monitoring may be used to evaluate a patient's compliance with the antidepressant fluoxetine (Lundmark et al., 2001), particularly as it is no easy task to remember to take a drug every day for months or even years, especially if side effects are present.

TOLERANCE AND DEPENDENCE

Two additional important factors in psychopharmacology related to pharmacokinetics and pharmacodynamics are tolerance and dependence. Tolerance generally refers to the need for higher doses to obtain the same effect (Holford & Sheiner, 1981) or loss of a drug effect at the same dose, be it a therapeutic effect or the induction of euphoria from illicit drugs. In psychopharmacology, tolerance can occur as a result of pharmacokinetics, in which the concentration of a drug drops with time. For example, the anticonvulsant and mood-stabilizing drug carbamazepine induces its own metabolism, which can result in a drop in carbamazepine concentration (Pippenger, 1987) with a potential for loss of therapeutic effects. To overcome this drop in concentration, the dose may be increased, restoring the original therapeutic effects.

Tolerance can also occur as a result of pharmacodynamic changes, in which something in the body is changing in response to the drug. Some antidepressant medications, for instance, appear to lose their effectiveness over time due to what may be pharmacodynamic changes (Fava, 2003). As an example of neurobiological changes that may be relevant to the development of pharmacodynamic tolerance, the benzodiazepine lorazepam (Ativan), when given chronically to rats, alters hippocampal glutamate (Bonavita et al., 2003). Etorphine, an opiate agonist, down regulates opiate mu receptors and results in subsequent changes in protein physiology (Patel et al., 2002), illustrating another mechanism by which drug tolerance may occur. That is, tolerance may develop through receptor down regulation (Holford & Sheiner, 1981). Drugs may also change gene expression, leading to tolerance. Long-term cannabis use, for example, alters certain genes that may be involved in the development of tolerance (Grigorenko et al., 2002).

Sensitization occurs when there is an increased effect from the drug with the passage of time but at a constant drug concentration (Holford & Sheiner, 1981), although some cases of sensitization may be due to the presence of active metabolites (Holford & Sheiner, 1981). Sensitization with time has been postulated to explain the delay between initiation of antidepressant treatment and clinical response (Antelman et al., 1997).

Closely related to tolerance is dependence, which is the physiological or psychological need to continue to take the drug. Physical dependence results in a withdrawal syndrome when the dose of the drug is decreased or the drug is withdrawn altogether. Withdrawal syndromes exist for many drugs relevant to psychopharmacology including alcohol, opiates (Kosten & O'Connor, 2003), and some antidepressants (Black et al., 2000). Withdrawal symptoms can vary from drug to drug and from person to person and may be relatively mild to severe and life threatening. The withdrawal associated with alcohol cessation is well known and can consist of agitation, sweating, tremor, nausea and vomiting, hallucinations (delirium tremens), and seizures (Kosten & O'Connor, 2003), whereas withdrawal from specific serotonin reuptake inhibitor antidepressants can produce lightheadedness, anxiety, headaches, insomnia, and diarrhea (Black et al., 2000). Psychological dependence, or addiction, encompasses drug craving, which is generally considered a fundamental aspect of drug addiction (Franken, 2003). Drug craving can be elicited by various classically conditioned, drug-related cues (Franken, 2003). The underlying neurobiology of drug craving is just beginning to be unraveled but may involve dopamine receptors (Volkow et al., 2002), as well as the amygdala and hippocampus (Volkow et al., 2002). Other neurotransmitters systems too have been implicated in craving, including serotonin, opiates, and glutamate (Franken, 2003).

SUMMARY

This chapter has discussed the basic principles of pharmacokinetics and pharmacodynamics. Although there are significant overlaps between these two concepts, pharmacokinetics is what the body does to the drug, while pharmacodynamics generally refers to what the drug does to the body (Holford & Sheiner, 1981).

Pharmacokinetics

Drugs can enter the body via oral, nasal, mucosal, epithelial, rectal, and pulmonary routes. In psychopharmacology, oral administration is by far the most common route, although some drugs are given intramuscularly, particularly some antipsychotics in depot, or long-lasting preparations. In order to pass the blood-brain barrier—that is, to get into the brain—a drug generally must be lipophillic, although transport mechanisms across the blood-brain barrier appear to exist for some drugs. Otherwise, a drug cannot enter into brain tissue. Drugs also are bound in differing degrees to proteins found in the blood, the most common of which is albumin. The drug-protein relationship exists in equilibrium, with some drug being unbound or free. It is the free drug that is capable of interacting with receptors, not the bound drug. Drug-drug interactions can occur if one drug displaces another drug from its binding sites on the protein, resulting in an increase in the amount of free drug.

Located primarily in the liver, the cytochrome P450 system is a large family of enzymes that metabolizes drugs into water-soluble products for excretion by the kidneys, or into pharmacologically active metabolites. Active metabolites may have similar or different mechanisms of action from their parent drug. Cytochrome P450 enzymes are also located to a lesser extent in the gastrointestional tract and the brain. Thus, drugs may undergo extensive metabolism even as they are absorbed for the gastrointestional tract, a process known as the first-pass effect. The rate of metabolism varies from drug to drug and from person to person. Half-life is defined as the amount of time required for a reduction in 50 percent of the original drug concentration. Half-life varies widely from drug to drug. Half-life also can vary considerably from person to person, with large differences in drug concentration occurring from similar doses. As a general rule, five or six half-lives are necessary for a drug to be cleared from the body. It also takes about five or six half-lives from initiation of the drug or from dose changes to reach a period of steady state.

Pharmacodynamics

Potency refers to the amount of drug required to produce a given clinical (or adverse) effect. This differs from efficacy, which is the maximal drug response that can occur; even if the dose is increased, no further increase in clinical effect occurs after maximal efficacy has been achieved. Both potency and efficacy vary from drug to drug and even with the same drug from person to person. When drug response on the y-axis is plotted against dose, or concentration of the drug at a receptor, on the x-axis, a dose-response curve results, for both therapeutic and toxic effects, with an initial slow rise in drug effect followed by a relatively rapidly increasing portion of the curve in which a change in dose is correlated with an increase in response or adverse effect. Finally, the dose-response curves flatten for therapeutic effects as maximal efficacy is reached.

Drug concentrations in the blood may be monitored for several reasons in psychopharmacology. Several drugs have defined therapeutic levels, and levels can serve as a guide to ensure adequate dosing strategies. Levels can be monitored also to help avoid toxicity and anticipate drug-drug interactions. Finally, levels are sometimes monitored to evaluate compliance.

Tolerance is the need for higher doses of a drug to achieve the same clinical effect. A related effect is dependence, which is the physiological or psychological need to continue taking the drug. Both tolerance and dependence are underpinned by neuronal changes.

STUDY QUESTIONS

1. List the advantages and disadvantages of the various routes of administration for drugs (oral, intramuscular, etc.)
2. How does a drug's solubility in fat tissue affect the volume in the body into which a drug may be distributed?
3. How does the blood-brain barrier limit drug from gaining access into the brain?
4. What is the first-pass effect?
5. What does the cytochrome P450 system of enzymes do? Where are these enzymes located?
6. List two ways by which drug-drug interactions can be generated.
7. What is an active metabolite?
8. What is half-life and how is it related to metabolism?
9. How is half-life related to steady state?
10. Discuss dose-response curves.
11. Under what circumstances may drug concentration in the blood be measured?
12. Describe the differences between tolerance and dependence.
13. What are some of the neurobiological bases of tolerance?

REFERENCES

Ackerman LL, Follett KA, Rosenquist RW (2003): Long-term outcomes during treatment of chronic pain intrathecal clonidine or clonidine/opioid combinations. Journals of Pain and Symptom Management 26:668–677.

Altamura AC, Sassella F, Santini A, Montresor C, Fumagalli S, Mundo E (2003): Intramuscular preparations of antipsychotics: Uses and relevance in clinical practice. Drugs 63:493–512.

Antelman SM, Soares JC, Gershon S (1997): Time-dependent sensitization—possible implications for clinical psychopharmacology. Behavioural Pharmacology 8:505–514.

Ashton H (1994): Guidelines for the rational use of benzodiazepines. When and what to use. Drugs 48:25–40.

Barnes TR, Curson DA (1994): Long-term depot antipsychotics. A risk-benefit assessment. Drug Safety 10:464–479.

Beasley CM Jr., Koke SC, Nilsson ME, Gonzales JS (2000): Adverse events and treatment discontinuations in clinical trials of fluoxetine in major depression: An updated meta-analysis. Clinical Therapeutics 22:1319–1330.

Belmin J, Valensi P (2003): Novel drug delivery systems for insulin: Clinical potential for use in the elderly. Drugs & Aging 20:303–312.

Benet LZ, Mitchell JR, Sheiner LB (1990): Pharmacokinetics: The dynamics of drug absorption, distribution, and elimination. In AF Gilman, TW Rall, AS Nies, P Taylor (eds.), *Goodman and Gilman's The Pharmacological Basis of Therapeutics*. Elmsford, NY: Pergamon Press.

Bertilsson L, Dahl ML, Dalen P, Al-Shurbaji A (2002): Molecular genetics of CYP2D6: Clinical relevance with focus on psychotropic drugs. British Journal of Clinical Pharmacology 53:111–122.

Black K, Shea C, Dursun S, Kutcher S (2000): Selective serotonin reuptake discontinuation syndrome: Proposed diagnostic criteria. Journal of Psychiatry & Neuroscience 25:255–261.

Boer F (2003): Drug handling by the lungs. British Journal of Anesthesia 91:50–60.

Bonavita C, Ferrero A, Cereseto M, Velardez M, Rubio M, Wikinski S (2003): Adaptive changes in the rat hippocampal glutamatergic neurotransmission are observed during long-term treatment with lorazepam. Psychopharmacology 166:163–167.

Bourin M, Chue P, Guillon Y (2001): Paroxetine: A review. CNS Drug Reviews 7:25–47.

Bravo MJ, Barrio G, de la Fuente L, Royuela L, Domingo L, Silva T (2003): Reasons for selecting an initial route of heroin administration and for subsequent transitions during a severe HIV epidemic. Addiction 98:749–760.

Btaiche IF, Woster PS (1995): Gabapentin and lamotrigine: Novel antiepileptic drugs. American Journal of Health-System Pharmacy 52:61–69.

Burton PS, Goodwin JT, Vidmar TJ, Amore BM (2002): Predicting drug absorption: How nature made it a difficult problem. Journal of Pharmacology and Experimental Therapeutics 303:889–895.

Conway JM, Birnbaum AK, Kriel RL, Cloyd JC (2003): Relative bioavailability of topiramate administered rectally. Epilepsy Research 54:91–96.

Cook CE, Jeffcoat AR, Hill JR, Pugh DE, Patetta PK, Sadler BM, White WR, Perez-Reyes M (1993); Pharmacokinetics of methamphetamine self-administered to human subjects by smoking S-(+)-methamphetamine hydrochloride. Drug Metabolism and Disposition 21: 717–723.

Daniel WA (2003): Mechanisms of cellular distribution of psychotropic drugs. Significance for drug action and interactions. Progress in Neuropsychopharmacology & Biological Psychiatry 27:65–73.

de Boer AG, van der Sandt IC, Gaillard PJ (2003): The role of drug transporters at the blood-brain barrier. Annual Review of Pharmacology and Toxicology 43:629–656.

Devane CL (1998): Principles of pharmacokinetics and pharmacodynamics. In AF Shatzberg, CB Nemeroff (eds.), *Textbook of Psychopharmacology*. Washington, DC: The American Psychiatric Press.

Devane CL (2002): Clinical significance of drug binding, protein binding, and binding displacement drug interactions. Psychopharmacology Bulletin 36:5–21.

Devane CL, Liston HL, Markowitz JS (2002): Clinical pharmacokinetics of sertraline. Clinical Pharmacokinetics 41:1247–1266.

Dodds G (2000): Lithium therapy. Scottish Medical Journal 45:171–173.

Emmanuel NP, Ware MR, Brawman-Mintzer O, Ballenger JC, Lydiard RB (1999): Once-weekly dosing of fluoxetine in the maintenance of remission in panic disorder. Journal of Clinical Psychiatry 60:299–301.

Fava GA (2003): Can long-term treatment with antidepressant drugs worsen the course of depression? Journal of Clinical Psychiatry 64:123–133.

Fleishaker JC (2000): Clinical pharmacokinetics of reboxetine, a selective norepinephrine reuptake inhibitor for the treatment of patients with depression. Clinical Pharmacokinetics 39:413–427.

Franken IHA (2003): Drug craving and addiction: Integrating psychological and neuropsychopharmacological approaches. Progress in Neuro-Psychopharmacology & Biological Psychiatry 27:563–579.

Grigorenko E, Kittler J, Clayton C, Wallace D, Zhuang S, Bridges D, Bundey S, Boon A, Pagget C, Hayashizaki S, Lowe G, Hampson R, Deadwyler S (2002): Assessment of cannabinoid induced gene changes: Tolerance and neuroprotection. Chemistry and Physics of Lipids 121: 257–266.

Haxby DG (1995): Treatment of nicotine dependence. American Journal of Health-System Pharmacy 52:265–281.

Holford NHG, Sheiner LB (1981): Pharmacokinetic and pharmacodynamic modeling in vivo. CRC Critical Reviews in Bioengineering 5:273–322.

Jeffcoat AR, Perez-Reyes M, Hill JM, Sadler BM, Cook CE (1989): Cocaine disposition in humans after intravenous injection, nasal insufflation (snorting), or smoking. Drug Metabolism and Disposition 17:153–159.

Jones AW (1995): Measuring and reporting the concentration of acetaldehyde in human breath. Alcohol and Alcoholism 30:271–285.

Ketter TA, Flockhart DA, Post RM, Denicoff K, Pazzaglia PJ, Marangell LB, George MS, Callahan AM (1995): The emerging role of cytochrome P450 3A in psychopharmacology. Journal of Clinical Psychopharmacology 15:387–398.

Kimko HC, Cross JT, Abernathy DR (1999): Pharmacokinetics and clinical effectiveness of methylphenidate. Clinical Pharmacokinetics 37:457–470.

Kosten TR, O'Connor PG (2003): Management of drug and alcohol withdrawal. New England Journal of Medicine 348:1786–1795.

Leucht S, Steimer W, Kreuz S, Abraham D, Orsulak PH, Kissling W (2001): Doxepin plasma concentrations: Is there really a therapeutic range? Journal of Clinical Psychopharmacology 21:432–439.

Lundmark J, Reis M, Bengtsson F (2001): Serum concentrations of fluoxetine in the clinical treatment setting. Therapeutic Drug Monitoring 23:139–147.

McIntyre RS, Mancini DA, Parikh S, Kennedy SH (2001): Lithium revisited. Canadian Journal of Psychiatry 46:322–327.

McLeod DR, Hoehn-Saric R, Porges SW, Kowalski PA, Clark CM (2000): Therapeutic effects of imipramine are counteracted by its metabolite, desipramine, in patients with generalized anxiety disorder. Journal of Clinical Psychopharmacology 20:615–621.

Misra A, Ganesh S, Shahiwala A, Shah SP (2003): Drug delivery to the central nervous system: A review. Journal of Pharmacy & Pharmaceutical Sciences 6:252–273.

Mitchell PB (2001): Therapeutic drug monitoring of psychotropic medications. British Journal of Clinical Pharmacology 52 (supplement 1): 45S–54S.

Mossman D (1997): A decision analysis approach to neuroleptic dosing: Insights from a mathematical model. Journal of Clinical Psychiatry 58:66–73.

Nestor TA, Tamamoto WI, Kam TH, Schultz T (1989): Crystal methamphetamine-induced acute pulmonary edema: A case report. Hawaii Medical Journal 48:457–458, 460.

Nies AS (1990): Principles of therapeutics. In AF Gilman, TW Rall, AS Nies, P Taylor (eds.), *Goodman and Gilman's The Pharmacological Basis of Therapeutics.* Elmsford, NY: Pergamon Press.

Pai HV, Upadhya SC, Chinta SJ, Hegde SN, Ravindranath V (2002): Differential metabolism of alprazolam by liver and brain cytochrome (P4503A) to pharmacologically active metabolites. The Pharmacogenomics Journal 2:243–258.

Patel MB, Patel CN, Rajashekara V, Yoburn BC (2002): Opioid agonists differentially regulate mu-opioid receptors and trafficking proteins in vivo. Molecular Pharmacology 62: 1464–1470.

Pippenger CE (1987): Clinically significant carbamazepine drug interactions: An overview. Epilepsia 28 (supplement 3): S71–76.

Preskorn SH, Burke MJ, Fast GA (1993): Therapeutic drug monitoring. Principles and practice. Psychiatric Clinics of North America 16:611–645.

Quinn DI, Wodak A, Day RO (1997): Pharmacokinetics and pharmacodynamic principles of illicit drug use and treatment of illicit drug users. Clinical Pharmacokinetics 33:344–400.

Rasmussen BB, Brosen K (2000): Is therapeutic drug monitoring a case for optimizing clinical outcome and avoiding interactions of the selective serotonin reuptake inhibitors? Therapeutic Drug Monitoring 22:143–154.

Rochat B, Baumann P, Audus KL (1999): Transport mechanisms for the antidepressant citalopram in brain microvessel epithelium. Brain Research 831:229–236.

Schillevoort I, de Boer A, Herings RM, Roos RA, Jansen PA, Leufkens HG (2001): Antipsychotic-induced extrapyramidal syndromes. Risperidone compared with low- and high-potency conventional antipsychotic drugs. European Journal of Pharmacology 57:327–331.

Shen DD, Kunze KL, Thummel KE (1997): Enzyme-catalyzed processes of first-pass hepatic and intestinal drug extraction. Advanced Drug Delivery Reviews 27:99–127.

Shulman RW, Ozdemir V (1997): Psychotropic medications and cytochrome P450 2D6: Pharmacokinetic considerations in the elderly. Canadian Journal of Psychiatry 42 (supplement 1):4S–9S.

Smith BJ, Jones HE, Griffiths RR (2001): Physiological, subjective and reinforcing effects of oral and intravenous cocaine in humans. Psychopharmacology 156:435–444.

Sramek JJ, Zarotsky V, Cutler NR (2002): Generalised anxiety disorder: Treatment options. Drugs 62:1635–1648.

Thomsen K, Schou M (1999): Avoidance of lithium intoxication: Advice based on knowledge of renal lithium clearance under various circumstances. Pharmacopsychiatry 32:83–86.

Vaswani M, Linda FK, Ramesh S (2003): Role of selective serotonin reuptake inhibitors in psychiatric disorders: A comprehensive review. Progress in Neuropsychopharmacology & Biological Psychiatry 27:85–102.

Volkow ND, Fowler JS, Wang GJ, Goldstein RZ (2002): Role of dopamine, the frontal cortex and memory circuits in drug addiction: Insight from imaging studies. Neurobiology of Learning and Memory 78:610–624.

Wang PW, Ketter TA (2002): Pharmacokinetics of mood stabilizers and new anticonvulsants. Psychopharmacology Bulletin 36:44–66.

CHAPTER FOUR

THE BIOLOGY OF MENTAL DISORDERS

The subject of this chapter is the underlying neurobiology associated with mental disorders. A remarkable variety of approaches have been marshaled in the attempt to understand the nature and causes of mental disorders. Some of these approaches deny altogether that the brain has anything to do with mental illness. Still others maintain that malfunction of the brain is the sole cause of mental illness. Consonant with this latter perspective, the ancient Greek physician Hippocrates believed that the brain possessed the primary etiological factors in mental disorder. Hidden as it is from scrutiny by not only difficulties of access but also by sheer complexity, the brain has kept its secrets well, releasing them only in small and often cryptic quanta. However, from Hippocrates' notions that mental illnesses is the result of imbalances in the four basic physiological fluids, or humors, a theory that is reminiscent of current views of neurotransmitter dysfunction, to early twenty-first century ideas of brain function and dysfunction, an early and necessarily tentative biology of mental disorders is emerging. This chapter contains a broad survey of the main neurobiological findings associated with mood disorders, anxiety, schizophrenia, and attentional disorders.

Although it is likely that depression may have a myriad of necessary factors, including social, adaptive, and biological sources, to name but a few, a body of literature exists indicating several neurobiological abnormalities that are associated with mood disorders. Whether these are the cause of, a reaction to, or incidental to the process of mood disorders remains a point of contention. Although no genes or chromosomes associated with major depression have been identified, it does appear that depression tends to run in families, and monozygotic twins have higher concordance rates of depression than do dizygotic twins, suggesting, but by no means proving, a genetic component to the transmission of depression. Like major depression, there is likely a genetic component to some cases of bipolar disorder, although specific genes and chromosomes have not been identified. Alternatively, the monoamine hypothesis of mood disorders postulates disturbances of norepinephrine and serotonin and their relevant receptors as etiological factors in the presentation of depression. Intriguing abnormalities in the hypothalamic-pituitary-adrenal axis function have also been found in people suffering from major depression. For example, the dexamethasone suppression test, a measure of the responsiveness of negative feedback systems on this axis, indicates relative nonsuppression in 50 percent of individuals with major depression. Tantalizing reports of brain dysfunction are also found for bipolar disorder.

Anxiety disorders, too, are associated with numerous biological factors. Brain-imaging studies, for example, have indicated abnormalities in the caudate nucleus associated with obsessive-compulsive disorder. The neurobiology of posttraumatic stress disorder is complex, vast, and only poorly integrated. Somewhat counterintuitively, cortisol levels in the bloodstream may be low in individuals with chronic posttraumatic stress disorder, although not all studies have been consistent in this area. Despite controversy, there is evidence of hippocampal volume reduction in posttraumatic stress disorder. However, whether this represents a condition antedating posttraumatic symptoms or is the result of posttraumatic stress disorder is unknown. Panic disorder also appears to have associated neurobiological abnormalities. In addition to having higher rates of concordance in monozygotic than in dizygotic twins, some patients with panic disorder are abnormally sensitive to infusions of lactate, a procedure that elicits panic attacks in people with panic disorder but not in those without panic disorder.

Numerous studies in a vast array of literature have identified many neurobiological disturbances associated with some cases of schizophrenia. Hampered by a postulated heterogeneity (e.g., there may be many kinds of schizophrenia, each with a different etiology), the actual biology of schizophrenia has proven elusive but intriguing. Prominent among biological explanations of schizophrenia are those of genetic predisposition. Based in part on antipsychotic drug action, the dopamine hypothesis of schizophrenia, which posits that many of the symptoms of schizophrenia are due to abnormalities of dopamine physiology, particularly in mesolimbic and mesocortical circuits, has also received a great deal of attention. It is likely that the dopamine hypothesis alone, however, is inadequate and increasing data suggest a role for abnormal serotonin and glutamate function.

Likewise, attention-deficit, hyperactivity disorder (ADHD) has been associated with many different factors. Among the biological factors associated with ADHD are genetics, neuroanatomical difficulties, and neurochemical factors. For example, ADHD has been demonstrated to have high concordance rates among familial relatives of probands. Furthermore, due to the prefrontal cortex's role in impulse control, planning, and executive functioning, this brain region has been implicated in the presentation of the symptoms associated with ADHD. Finally, neurotransmitter function, specifically impaired function of norepinephrine and dopamine, has been implicated in the presentation of ADHD. As with the role of biology in the other psychological phenomena already considered, these findings remain equivocal.

Much, though not all, psychopharmacological drug development has been serendipitous. In fact, it has often been the case that psychotropic drug development was a pharmacological accident, albeit with often surprising effects (Pletscher,

1991). In their nascent stages, for example, the monoamine oxidase–inhibiting antidepressants were used to treat tuberculosis (Pletscher, 1991), with the anti-depressant effects observed only later. An important difficulty with psycho-pharmacological drug development is that the basic pathophysiology of most mental disorders remains elusive and only poorly understood. Further contributing to the challenge of psychopharmacology is that at least some mental disorders may be het-erogeneous, with perhaps several or even many different neurobiological conditions contributing to the same behavioral phenotype. Depression is a prime example in that there may be a variety of conditions that lead to its clinical presentation.

Finally, inferential problems, such as post hoc inference and post hoc propter hoc inference (Williams, 2001), complicate the search for underlying pathophys-iology in mental disorders. Post hoc inference amounts to essentially circular and tautological arguments of the form that, for example, since a central feature of a disorder is X (a symptom), and Y (a biological component or factor) is known to regulate the function of X, then a problem with Y is the cause of X. This, in essence, is similar to stating that some problem with the stomach is responsible for concussions because concussions often include the symptom of vomiting. Post hoc propter hoc inferences include such arguments that suggest that certain dis-orders are caused by chemical processes based on the chemical effects of certain drugs or neurotransmitters. This is akin, as Williams (2001) notes, to saying that a flu is due to a lack of aspirin in the bloodstream, given the finding that adminis-tration of aspirin to a flu sufferer results in a lessening of flu symptoms and an in-crease in aspirin-rich blood. Similarly, brain-imaging studies, particularly those involving volume differences between people with the disorder in question com-pared to controls, can be difficult to interpret because these investigations are primarily correlative, making it difficult to determine whether the brain abnor-malities and their associated behaviors, if present, cause the disorder, whether the disorder causes the brain abnormality, or whether both the brain abnormalities and the disorder are the result of another factor or factors.

Despite the complexity of the brain, the false starts, the sometimes conflict-ing findings, possible etiologic heterogeneity, and inferential difficulties, several promising theories of the neurobiology of depressive disorders, anxiety disorders, schizophrenia, attention-deficit disorder, and the dementias are slowly emerging. With these limitations and caveats in mind, this chapter presents a review of the neurobiological stratum of major mental disorders.

THE BIOLOGY OF MOOD DISORDERS

Genetics of Mood Disorders

As part of the search for the origins of mood disorders, observation has long sug-gested that mood disturbances tend to run in families. These notions have been confirmed by family studies that as a rule have found higher rates of major de-pression in first-degree relatives of people who have major depression than in the general population (Weissman et al., 1982). Similarly, bipolar disorder is more commonly found in the first-degree relatives of people with bipolar disorder than in the population at large (Weissman et al., 1984). Clearly suggesting that mood disorders cluster in families, these findings themselves still beg the overriding question of the genetic causes of depression, as familial transmission could be the result of nongenetic factors as well.

Consistent with the findings that mood disorders run in families are hypotheses that depression may be learned in a family context or be the result of other experiential factors, such as abuse of all sorts, socioeconomic difficulties, malnutrition, or a host of other factors. To find additional insight into this conundrum, concordance rates of bipolar and depressive disorders have been investigated. Based on the notion that if genetic causes are present in some degree, concordant rates should be higher in monozygotic twins (who in principle share 100 percent of their genetic material) than in dizygotic twins (who are no more closely related to each other than nontwin siblings). In general, these studies have found that mood disorders do indeed have higher concordance rates in monozygotic than in dizygotic twins (Malhi et al., 2000). For example, an estimated concordance rate for bipolar disorder in monozygotic twins is 57 percent and 14 percent for dizygotic twins (Cadoret, 1978). However, even in monozygotic twins, the concordance of affective disorders is not 100 percent, leaving room for other etiologies for these conditions (Alda, 1997). Epidemiological research, for example, finds that anywhere from 40 to 50 percent of depression may have a genetic basis (Sanders et al., 1999).

There are, of course, some problems with such epidemiological findings being used as a clear indication of the genetic basis of depression (see Torgersen, 1997). The first problem, as noted above, is that it is difficult to rule out experiential similarities in the higher concordance rates between monozygotic twins. That is, monozygotic twins spend more time together, are closer, and more frequently have the same friends and the same activities than fraternal twins. Furthermore, twin deliveries involve physical risk events, and twins are more prone to head injuries, thus potentiating the role of trauma in the presentation of disorder. Finally, experiential factors may be more important for twins than for the average siblings. Twins, for example, grow up with a sibling of the same age with whom they have to compete for attention and share many possessions.

Adoption studies have been used in order to help control for such factors. For example, one such study indicated that the biological parents of adoptees hospitalized in Denmark had a higher incidence of severe depression (but not mild depression) than did biological parents of controls (Wender et al., 1986).

Further limiting the explanatory power of solely genetic causes of affective disorders is that no firm genetic linkages have been identified (Merikangas et al., 2002). Conversely, Huntington's chorea and its presentation of abnormal movements, psychiatric deficits, and cognitive problems (Squitieri et al., 2001) is clearly linked to chromosome number four (Tsuang et al., 2000). No such clearly identified relationship exists for any of the affective disorders. Current thinking regarding the etiology of bipolar disorder, for instance, involves an interaction between environmental and perhaps several susceptibility genes (Rush, 2003).

The Monoamine Hypothesis

Historically and clinically, one of the more important biological theories of affective disorders, the monoamine hypothesis of depressive and bipolar disorders, posits that such conditions arise from abnormalities in the physiology of the so-called biogenic or monoamines (Hindmarch, 2001). Functioning in the brain and other parts of the body as neurotransmitters, the monoamines norepinephrine and serotonin are implicated in the etiology of depression (Bymaster et al., 2003).

Perhaps the most compelling evidence supporting the monoamine hypothesis came from the antidepressants themselves. That is, the antidepressants appeared to at least initiate their affective responses by increasing synaptic concentrations of some combination of monoamines (Valenstein, 1998). These observations were further buoyed by findings that the antihypertensive drug reserpine depleted neurons of monoamines and could result in depression (Healy, 1997). Even though these observations concerning reserpine formed an important part of the evidence for the monoamine hypothesis of affective disorders, some work suggests that reserpine may not cause depression as argued by Baumeister et al. (2003), suggesting that the monoamine hypothesis requires revision. Nevertheless, the monoamine hypothesis of depression remains an important force in antidepressant drug development (Bymaster et al., 2003). Evidence supporting the notion of monoamine dysfunction in affective disorders, however, comes from other sources as well. There have, for example, been more direct investigations of monoamine function in the brain. Such investigations include the observation of abnormalities in serotonin and norepinephrine function (Leonard, 2000).

Further arguments against the monoamine hypothesis suggest that it is an oversimplification of brain function. Clinical findings, for example, demonstrate that, even when successful, antidepressants that initiate their effects by manipulation of the monoamine neurotransmitters can require two to eight weeks before a therapeutic response occurs. This is the case even though changes in monoamine function happen within hours of the first dose. While a bane to clinical psychopharmacology and representing a substantial clinical challenge, this finding suggests that other crucial mechanisms are occurring well after monoamine function is altered (Hindmarch, 2001). As pointed out by Valenstein (1998), the number of changes in neurochemistry that occur during the several weeks required before an antidepressant induces affective changes is enormous, increasing the difficulty in sorting what changes are relevant to an understanding of antidepressant action and limiting the explanatory power of the monoamine hypothesis of depression.

Gamma Aminobutyric Acid (GABA)

Both depression and mania are associated with lowered levels of the major inhibitory neurotransmitter, gamma aminobutyric acid (White, 2003), which may be a trait marker of major depression (Petty et al., 1995). The GABA hypothesis suggests that low GABA levels are an underlying vulnerability for affective disorders (Petty, 1995). The GABA hypothesis need not be in conflict with the monoamine hypothesis as disturbances in both the GABA and monoamine systems could be involved in the etiology of affective disorders (Brambilla et al., 2003).

The Hypothalamic-Pituitary-Adrenal Axis and Corticotropin-Releasing Factor

Numerous other theories posit biological etiologies for depression. An alternative theory to the monoamine and GABA hypotheses, for example, implicates abnormalities in the hypothalamic-pituitary-adrenal axis and in cortisol regulation in the genesis and expression of depression (Parker et al., 2003). For example, cortisol levels are elevated in some people who have major depression (Bissette, 2003). Ultimately controlling release of cortisol, cortisol-releasing factor (CRF) is elevated in the cerebral spinal fluid of people with depression (Bissette, 2003) and may be increased in the locus coeruleus of depressed people (Bissette, 2003), a finding that provides a potential link between norepinephrine and cortisol-releasing factor. Further implicating cortisol-releasing factor in depression is research in animals showing that stress exposure in early life predicts elevated CRF in adulthood (Heim & Nemeroff, 2001), as well as some of the neurotransmitter abnormalities seen in depressed humans (Kaufman & Charney, 2001). Stress-induced CRF abnormalities in children are also hypothesized to account for some of the risk of developing depression as adolescents and adults (Kaufman & Charney, 2001). Hippocampal volume reduction has been found that correlates with the length of time a person has been depressed (Sheline et al., 1999), a finding that has been proposed to be due to increased levels of cortisol, as cortisol can cause hippocampal volume loss (Hoschl & Hajek, 2001), although hippocampal volume reduction may occur in early episodes of depression in people who have not had long periods of exposure to elevated cortisol (Frodl et al., 2002). Following the findings of abnormal hypothalamic-pituitary-adrenal function in depression, drugs designed to antagonize CRF subtype 1 receptors are in development as potential antidepressants (Nemeroff, 2002).

Consistent with the hypothesized role of the hippocampus in depression, some have hypothesized that antidepressant treatment may increase neurogenesis or the growth of new neurons in the hippocampus in animals (Santarelli et al., 2003), as well as prevent the volume reduction associated with depression (Vaidya & Duman, 2001).

Related to these findings are the observations that children who are exposed to stress are at risk for the development of depression as children, adolescents, and adults (Kaufman & Charney, 2001). Further supporting the relationship between stress and the development of depression, research in animal models links stress in early life with increased activity of the corticotropin-releasing hormone system (Heim & Nemeroff, 2001). Finally, animal analogue studies indicate that stress early in development can alter the function of several neurotransmitters and brain regions in a fashion similar to the abnormalities observed in humans with depression (Kaufman & Charney, 2001). Far from being completely deterministic, however, the effects of stress in development may be modified by both natural and experiential factors (Kaufman & Charney, 2001).

Neurotrophic Factors

In addition to cortisol and corticotropin-releasing factor, brain-derived neurotrophic factors appear to be involved in the basic neurobiology of depression. Brain neurotrophic factors are biochemicals that not only regulate brain growth and form during development but also are responsible for plasticity in adult neurons and even glial cells (Nestler et al., 2002). For instance, Shimizu and colleagues (2003) found lower levels of brain-derived neurotrophic factors in untreated patients with major depression compared to antidepressant-treated patients and controls without major depression, suggesting not only that brain-derived neurotrophic factors are important in the etiology of depression but also that antidepressants may increase brain-derived neurotrophic factors.

In support of the brain-derived-neurotrophic-factor hypothesis of depression, it appears that many antidepressants may elevate levels of brain-derived neurotrophic factors in the hippocampus and cortex (Vaidya & Duman 2001), suggesting that antidepressant-induced increases in brain-derived neurotrophic factor may be a mechanism of action of antidepressants. Related to this action, antidepressants can increase cyclic adenosine monophosphate response to element-binding protein (CREB), a substance that increases brain-derived neurotrophic hormone (Vaidya & Duman, 2001).

Immunological and Inflammatory Factors

A growing body of evidence suggests a link between the immune system and depression. For example, important elements in the inflammatory response, proinflammatory cytokines, are elevated in men with mild to moderate depression compared to levels in nondepressed men (Suarez et al., 2003). In geriatric patients, elevated levels of inflammation were associated with depression (Penninx et al., 2003).

Brain-Reward Systems

Less well supported for their role in depressive disorders than are hypothalamic-pituitary-adrenal axis and neurotrophic factors, brain-reward systems also may underlie some of the neurobiology of depression. For example, abnormalities in brain-reward systems have been implicated in specific symptoms of depression such as anhedonia (Tremblay et al., 2002). The brain-reward system consists of those circuits in the brain that are hypothesized to mediate pleasure, reward, and motivation and includes the mesocortical-dopamine pathways, which have received substantial attention for their role in the behavior of addiction. Because the mesocortical pathway contains dopamine and is integral in addiction, the effects of dopamine-altering compounds are believed to be an indication of the functional integrity of this aspect of the brain-reward system. Heightened dopamine release to a dextroamphetamine challenge correlates with the presence of depression (Tremblay et al., 2002). One interpretation of this finding is that altered function of the brain-reward systems could cause the anhedonia found in depression (Naranjo et al., 2001).

Perinatal Complications

A history of perinatal complications may be more common in people with bipolar disorder than in their siblings without bipolar disorder, suggesting that perinatal brain insult may be a possible factor in the etiology of bipolar disorder (Kinney et al., 1998). In their review of eight studies investigating the association between bipolar disorder and prenatal and perinatal complications, Buka and Fan (1999) concluded that these complications are more common for people who have bipolar disorder than for those who do not. In three of four studies reviewed that contained a comparison group of normal controls, for example, Buka and Fan (1999) found that prenatal and perinatal complications were more common in the bipolar group, with odds ratios ranging between 1.0 and 12.0. Buka and Fan (1999) pointed out, however, that these studies do not show the specific significance of the prenatal and perinatal complications and did not demonstrate which complications seemed to be most common among patients with bipolar disorder.

Kindling in Bipolar Disorder

An important theoretical approach to bipolar disorder (as well as epilepsy), particularly in regards to proposed mechanisms of some mood-stabilizing drugs, is that of kindling. For bipolar disorder, the theory of kindling posits that stress in susceptible people can trigger bipolar symptoms and alter neurocircuitry (White, 2003). Critically, kindling theory suggests that subsequent episodes of bipolar disorder can be induced with lower levels of stress than those required for the initial episode, eventually leading to bipolar episodes occurring in the absence of psychosocial stressors (White, 2003). Table 4.1 gives a summary of neurobiological findings associated with depression and bipolar disorder.

The Neuroanatomy of Affective Disorders

Several regions of the brain appear to have crucial roles in the neurobiology of depression. Because of its putative volume reduction in depression (Frodl et al., 2002) and proposed role in antidepressant response (Santarelli et al., 2003), the hippocampus is but one of the important regions for the neurobiological understanding of depression (Beyer & Krishnan, 2002). The prefrontal cortex and anterior cingulate region also appear to be important for the neurobiological understanding of depression. Abnormal functioning of the prefrontal cortex, as assessed by impairment of frontal lobe tasks in executive function, has been observed in elderly depressed subjects (Lockwood et al., 2002). Bipolar disorder

TABLE 4.1   Neurobiological Findings Associated with Mood Disorders

DISORDER	FINDINGS ASSOCIATED WITH THE DISORDER
Depression	Increased in first-degree relatives of people who have major depression. Abnormal monoamine function. Associated with lower gamma aminobutyric acid concentrations. Elevated cortisol. Lower levels of brain-derived neurotrophic factors patients with untreated major depression. Abnormal brain-reward system function.
Bipolar Disorder	Increased in first-degree relatives of people who have bipolar disorder. Mania is associated with lower levels of gamma aminobutyric acid. History of prenatal and perinatal complications. Kindling.

too is associated with abnormalities in the prefrontal and anterior cingulate regions (Blumberg et al., 2003).

In addition to the hippocampus, prefrontal cortex, and anterior cingulate regions, the amygdala, nucleus accumbens, and some hypothalamic areas also are implicated in the neuroanatomy of depression (Nestler et al., 2002). In familial depression, imaging studies have found reduced volume in the subgenual area of the prefrontal cortex (Ongur et al., 1998). In contrast to brains of individuals diagnosed with schizophrenia, Ongur et al. (1998) reported a reduction in glial cell number in the subgenual region of the prefrontal cortex in brains of individuals with familial depression and bipolar disorder (Ongur et al., 1998).

Medical and Neurological Problems in Depression

Important but often overlooked correlates of clinical depression are various medical and neurological problems. In these cases, medical diseases or neurological disorders in the brain can present with typical symptoms and signs of depression. Some endocrine disorders such as thyroid disease can mimic depression (Talbot-Stern et al., 2000). Resulting from elevated cortisol levels from the adrenal gland, Cushing's syndrome is associated with symptoms of depression (Sonino & Fava, 2001). Parkinson's disease, too, often includes a depressive element, generally thought to be out of proportion to the degree of neurological dysfunction present (Okun & Watts, 2002). Furthermore, depression is the presenting complaint of some patients who later develop the choreoform movements, psychosis, and dementia of Huntington's chorea (Craufurd et al., 2001). Neuroanatomical abnormalities associated with mood disorders are summerized in Table 4.2.

TABLE 4.2   The Neuroanatomy Associated with Mood Disorders

NEUROANATOMY	DISORDER	FINDINGS
Hippocampus	Depression	Putative volume reduction in depression (Frodl et al., 2002) and proposed role in antidepressant response (Santarelli et al., 2003).
Prefrontal Cortex and Anterior Cingulate Region	Depression	Abnormal in elderly depressed subjects (Lockwood et al., 2002).
	Bipolar	Associated with abnormalities in the prefrontal and anterior cingulate regions (Blumberg et al., 2003).
Subgenual Area of the Prefrontal Cortex	Depression	In familial depression, imaging studies have found reduced volume (Ongur et al., 1998).
	Depression and Bipolar	Ongur et al. (1998) reported a reduction in glial cell number.

THE BIOLOGY OF ANXIETY DISORDERS

The cost of anxiety disorders in 1990 in the United States was approximately $42.3 billion (Greenberg et al., 1999). Such costs have provided a strong impetus to better understand the pathophysiology of these common disorders. The search to better understand the neurobiology of anxiety has led to the amygdala and connections with the prefrontal cortex (Ninan, 1999). The finding that the amygdala is involved in the presentation of anxiety is not surprising, given the amygdala's role in fear and the emotional content of memory (Stein et al., 2002).

Generalized Anxiety Disorder (GAD)

Despite the controversy surrounding it status as a distinct disorder (Jetty et al., 2001) and motivated in part by reported efficacy of some drugs for GAD (e.g., Sheehan, 1999), an early neurobiology of GAD is beginning to emerge. For instance, serotonin and GABA function appear to be abnormal in some cases of GAD (Jetty et al., 2001). Such findings correspond nicely with the responses of some patients to serotonin-modulating antidepressants and benzodiazepines, which operate through the GABA system (Haefely, 1985). Consistent with these observations, Tiihonen et al. (1997a) found decreased benzodiazepine binding in the left temporal lobe in GAD patients in comparison to controls. Other findings include increased cortical and decreased basal-ganglia activity in GAD (Jetty et al., 2001).

Similar to depression, some hypotheses about the neurobiology of GAD also are focused on corticotropin-releasing hormone. One such hypothesis is that emotional stress from a variety of sources, mediated by corticotropin-releasing hormone and a genetic predisposition, may result in GAD and the inability to tolerate later stress well

(Jetty et al., 2001). The glutamate system too is implicated in the neurobiology of GAD, particularly metabotropic and N-methyl-D-aspartate glutamate receptors (Jetty et al., 2001), and drugs that interact with metabotropic glutamate receptors have shown possible anxiolytic-like behavior in animal models (Schoepp et al., 1999).

Obsessive-Compulsive Disorder (OCD)

Obsessive-compulsive disorder is also associated with a variety of abnormal neuroanatomical findings. Clinically, a relationship between basal ganglia function and OCD is often observed. For example, neurological disorders involving the basal ganglia may present with symptoms of OCD (Huguelet & McQuillan, 1996). Furthermore, patients who have OCD frequently manifest what are known as neurological soft signs (Huguelet & McQuillan, 1996), subtle abnormalities in movement and other neurological functions.

Likewise, neuroimaging studies have found volume reduction in the caudate nucleus of the basal ganglia (Huguelet & McQuillan, 1996). Based upon functional brain imaging studies, increased metabolic activity in OCD in the orbital frontal cortex that normalizes after treatment with specific-serotonin reuptake inhibitors has also been observed (Insel & Winslow, 1992). Increased metabolism also appears to occur in the caudate nucleus and anterior cingulate cortex of individuals with OCD (Micallef & Blin, 2001). Suggesting global structural brain disorganization, there also seems to be an overall reduction in the amount of white matter in the brain, as well as an increased volume of gray matter (Jenike et al., 1996). Finally, visuospatial function is also often abnormal in individuals diagnosed with OCD (Micallef & Blin, 2001).

In addition to these areas of altered metabolism, certain neurotransmitter and neurohormone abnormalities are associated with OCD. For example, based in part on cerebrospinal fluid studies and the pharmacological response to selective serotonin reuptake inhibitors, abnormal serotonin transmission is consistently implicated in the neurobiology of OCD, although the exact nature of the serotonin dysfunction in OCD in unknown (Micallef & Blin, 2001). The posterior pituitary hormone oxytocin, which stimulates uterine contraction during labor and delivery, appears to be elevated in the cerebral spinal fluid in a subgroup of people with OCD. Furthermore, in this subgroup, OCD symptom severity is correlated with oxytocin levels (Leckman et al., 1994).

Posttraumatic Stress Disorder (PTSD)

With clear environmental antecedents and a rich neurobiology, posttraumatic stress disorder has added new insights into the interface of stress and biology, with evidence suggesting disturbances in several different brain systems. Several different neurotransmitter systems, for example, appear to function abnormally in patients with PTSD. The hyperarousal, sleep difficulties, and anxiety associated with posttraumatic stress disorder would appear to suggest the involvement of norepinephrine. Indeed, some but not all studies have reported increased excretion of norepinephrine in patients with PTSD (Hageman et al., 2001). The opioid system, too, is implicated in the pathogenesis of PTSD. Friedman and Southwick (1995), for example, demonstrated that individuals with lowered resting levels of beta-endorphins appear to be readily susceptible to PTSD.

Corticotropin-releasing factor and cortisol also appear to be intimately involved in the neurobiology of PTSD. Although such findings are mixed, some data suggest that, somewhat counterintuitively, cortisol levels in individuals with chronic PTSD are lower than those in normal individuals (e.g., Yehuda et al., 1995). Further developing this observation, Yehuda et al. (1998a) have demonstrated that presentation with abnormally low cortisol levels in the emergency room immediately following motor vehicle accidents appears to be predictive of which individuals will develop PTSD three months later.

In contrast to cortisol levels, concentrations of corticotropin-releasing factor appear to be elevated in PTSD (Heim et al., 2001a). Because corticotropin-releasing factor drives part of the stress response, chronic elevations of this hormone could produce symptoms of PTSD. It is proposed that drugs currently in development that antagonize corticotropin-releasing factor might be useful in the treatment of PTSD (Hageman et al., 2001).

Because of its central role in the response to stress, the hippocampus also has a strong theoretical basis in the pathogenesis of PTSD. Following the findings of Bremner (1995) that hippocampal volume is reduced in male Vietnam-combat veterans, many researchers have found reduced hippocampal volume in patients with a variety of precipitating stressors, such as rape and childhood sexual abuse (Hull, 2002). All studies, however, have not replicated these findings, underscoring the need for additional understanding of hippocampal anatomy in PTSD (Agartz et al., 1999).

The cause of the volume reduction in the hippocampus of patients with PTSD and its relation to the disorder is under investigation. Without the benefit of hippocampal volume studies in people later exposed to stress, two approaches to the question exist. First, it is postulated that the abnormal hippocampal volume may be a result of the disorder (Hageman et al., 2001). Abnormalities in the hypothalamic-pituitary-adrenal axis in PTSD could account for these findings, in particular cortisol. However, as noted previously, cortisol levels in chronic PTSD may be diminished (Yehuda et al., 1995), weakening the theory that chronically elevated cortisol levels themselves are resulting in hippocampal volume reduction in PTSD. Alternatively, the hippocampal damage could be the result of not absolute cortisol concentrations, but rather the result of abnormally high sensitivity of cortisol receptors on the hippocampus (Yehuda, 1998b). In this case, even low cortisol levels might produce toxicity to the hippocampus.

The second approach to explaining hippocampal abnormalities in PTSD is that, perhaps, a congenitally small hippocampus is a risk factor for the development of PTSD and precedes the onset of the disorder (Sapolsky, 2002). From the perspective of this hypothesis, the small hippocampus inadequately regulates the hypothalamic-pituitary-adrenal stress response and allows for continued expression of the stress response.

QUESTION OF DIAGNOSIS: THE CASE OF THE PSEUDOPATIENT

Rosenhan published a provocative study in the journal *Science* in 1973. In this study, eight "pseudopatients" (one graduate student, three psychologists, a pediatrician, a psychiatrist, a painter, and a housewife) were admitted to twelve different hospitals in five different states on the East and West coasts. Each of these pseudopatients was admitted after complaining about hearing voices saying relatively innocuous words such as, "empty," "hollow," and "thud." While the facts of these pseudopatients' names, vocations, and employment were altered, no further alterations in life histories and circumstances were made. All of these, debatably, "normal" individuals were admitted to the psychiatric ward. All but one was admitted with a diagnosis of schizophrenia.

Following admission to the psychiatric ward, these pseudopatients ceased presentation of any symptoms of abnormality and began tracking their interactions in notebooks. In the absence of "abnormal" symptoms, it was quite common for other patients on the ward to tell the pseudopatients that they did not belong there. The psychiatric staff, however, did not surmise this. In fact, the length of hospitalization for these pseudopatients lasted anywhere from seven to fifty-two days, with an average stay of about nineteen days. During this time, these eight pseudopatients were given approximately 2,100 pills, including antidepressants and antipsychotics (none of which they ingested). Rosenhan noted that even the pseudopatients' tracking of their experiences was taken as an indication of psychological disturbance. Rosenhan suggests that the reason for this misinterpretation is that the behaviors of these pseudopatients were interpreted with reference to symptoms of psychological disorder. In other words, because these individuals were disordered, and because the location of the disorder, in atomistic fashion, continues to remain within the individual, the behaviors must be indicative of the disorder. In the end, all of the pseudopatients were discharged with a diagnosis of schizophrenia "in remission," an indication that the schizophrenia may merely be in hiding but remains within the individual just as a remitting form of cancer remains within a treated cancer patient.

REFERENCES

Rosenhan DL (1973): On being sane in insane places. Science 179:250–258.

Panic Disorder

Characterized not only by panic attacks but also by anticipatory anxiety of having a panic attack and avoidance of certain situations (Pollack & Marzol, 2000), panic disorder is associated with several neurobiological abnormalities, the significance of which remain poorly delineated. Some patients with panic disorder, for instance, have elevations in the nocturnal release of cortisol (Abelson & Curtis, 1996). Furthermore, a well-described finding in panic disorder is the induction of panic symptoms from intravenous infusion of lactate in the majority of people who have panic disorder but not in those without this disorder (Goetz et al., 1996). The mechanism of lactate-induced panic is unknown, but some investigation has found that the generation of panic symptoms from lactate is associated with abnormal GABA function in the dorsomedial nucleus of the hypothalamus (Shekhar & Keim, 1997).

Similarly, changes in the concentrations of blood carbon dioxide (CO_2) are associated with anxiety symptoms in people with panic disorder (Gorman et al.,

1994). Unlike the specificity of the response to lactate, changing CO_2 levels are associated with anxiety symptoms in people with other anxiety disorders, such as generalized anxiety disorder and social phobia (Krystal et al., 2001). Detecting changes in CO_2, receptors in the carotid arteries are hypothesized to signal brainstem respiratory regions where, in panic disorder and other anxiety disorders, a false suffocation alarm is mounted that leads to symptoms of anxiety (Klein, 1993). A small study has reported volume reduction in both the right and left amygdala in people with panic disorder compared to controls (Massana et al., 2003), a finding consistent with the function of the amygdala in processing stressful stimuli (McEwen, 2003).

Social Phobia

Although social phobia is the most common anxiety and ranks third in prevalence among all psychiatric disorders after substance abuse and depression (Pollack, 2002), relatively little is known about its associated neurobiology. Based in part upon drug response, social phobia is postulated to involve several different neurotransmitter systems. Putative treatment response to serotonin reuptake inhibitors, for example, implicates the serotonin system in the neurobiology of social phobia (Mathew et al., 2001). Norepinephrine with its role in the mediation of anxiety may also be involved in social phobia (Mathew et al., 2001), as well as GABA (Li et al., 2001).

The dopamine system also may be involved in the etiology of social phobia. In a study of eleven people with social phobia, reuptake sites for dopamine in the striatum were lower in patients with social phobia as compared to normal controls (Tiihonen et al., 1997b). Further implicating the dopamine system in the neurobiology of social phobia is the finding of reduced binding potential in dopamine type 2 receptors in individuals with social phobia as compared to controls (Schneier et al., 2000).

Just as the role of neurotransmitters in the etiology of social phobia remains but poorly understood, so does the genetics of social phobia. There does, however, seem to be a familial contribution in social phobia. One study, for example, found that first-degree relatives of a person with social phobia have a 15 percent chance of also having social phobia (Fyer et al., 1995). However, a low rate of concordance in monozygotic twins (Kendler et al., 1992) suggests that a role for nongenetic factors in the etiology of social phobia is also likely.

Neuroimaging studies of social phobia, also, are in their infancy. Most studies to date suggest abnormalities in the basal ganglia, consistent with findings of altered dopamine function in individuals with social phobia. Neuroimaging abnormalities are also reported for the amygdala, and some regions of the cortex in social phobia (Mathew et al., 2001) further implicating the role of the amygdala in social phobia is analogue research in macaque monkeys, which suggests that abnormal amygdala function results in increased activity of the amygdala's social-context evaluation role (Amaral, 2002). Table 4.3 shows neurobiological findings associated with anxiety disorder.

TABLE 4.3   Neurobiological Findings Associated with Anxiety Disorders

DISORDER	ASSOCIATED BIOLOGICAL FINDINGS/THEORIES
Generalized Anxiety Disorder	Serotonin and GABA function appear to be abnormal in some cases.
	Emotional stress from a variety of sources, mediated by corticotropin-releasing hormone and a genetic predisposition.
	The glutamate system too is implicated, particularly metabotropic and N-methyl-D-aspartate glutamate receptors.
Obsessive Compulsive Disorder	Neurological disorders involving the basal ganglia may present with symptoms.
	Neuroimaging studies have found volume reduction in the caudate nucleus of the basal ganglia.
	Increased metabolic activity in the orbital frontal cortex.
	Increased metabolism appears to occur in the caudate nucleus and anterior cingulate cortex.
	An overall reduction in the amount of white matter in the brain, as well as an increased volume of gray matter.
	Visuospatial function is also often abnormal.
	Abnormal serotonin transmission is consistently implicated in the neurobiology.
	The posterior pituitary hormone oxytocin appears to be elevated in the cerebral spinal fluid in a subgroup. Symptom severity is correlated with oxytocin levels.
Posttraumatic Stress Disorder	Increased excretion of noradrenaline.
	Lowered resting levels of beta-endorphins appear to contributing factor in susceptibility.
	Somewhat counterintuitively, cortisol levels in chronic cases are lower than normals.
	Concentrations of corticotropin-releasing factor appear to be elevated.
	Hippocampal volume is reduced in male.
	Vietnam-combat veterans. Many researchers have also found reduced hippocampal volume in patients with a variety of precipitating stressors, such as rape and childhood sexual abuse.
Panic Disorder	Some have elevations in the nocturnal release of cortisol.
	Generation of symptoms from lactate is associated with abnormal GABA function in the dorsomedial nucleus of the hypothalamus.
	Changes in the concentrations of blood carbon dioxide (CO_2) are associated with anxiety symptoms.
	A small study has reported volume reduction in both the right and left amygdala.

Table 4.3 *Continued*

DISORDER	ASSOCIATED BIOLOGICAL FINDINGS/THEORIES
Social Phobia	Putative treatment response to serotonin reuptake inhibitors implicates the serotonin system.
	Norepinephrine, as well as GABA, with its role in the mediation of anxiety may be involved.
	Reuptake sites for dopamine in the striatum are lower.
	Reduced binding potential in dopamine type 2 receptors.
	Most studies to date suggest abnormalities in the basal ganglia.
	Neuroimaging abnormalities are also reported for the amygdala, and some regions of the cortex.

THE BIOLOGY OF SCHIZOPHRENIA

Occurring worldwide with a prevalence of approximately 1.4 to 4.6 per 1,000 (Jablensky, 2000), schizophrenia is characterized by psychosis and considerable impairment (Wong & Van Tol, 2003). The causes of schizophrenia appear to be complex, and despite intense efforts spanning decades, the neurobiology of schizophrenia is only beginning to be understood.

Genetics

Highly heritable (O'Donovan et al., 2003), schizophrenia clearly has important genetic contributions (Wong & Van Tol, 2003). Twin studies show higher rates of concordance for schizophrenia in monozygotic twins than in dizygotic twins (Kendler 1983), and linkage studies have shown several suggestive possibilities, including linkage to chromosomes 1, 6, and 13 (O'Donovan et al., 2003), although these studies do require additional replication (O'Donovan et al., 2003). Complicating an understanding of its genetics, schizophrenia may be a collection of several different diseases with differing genetic abnormalities (Wong & Van Tol, 2003).

Risk Factors for the Development of Schizophrenia

Numerous risk factors for the subsequent development of schizophrenia have been identified. Certainly not present in every case, and arguing for the possibility of different etiologies for schizophrenia, the risk factors for schizophrenia may interact with an underlying genetic diathesis (Wong & Van Tol, 2003). Not every person, or even a majority of people, with these risk factors goes on to have schizophrenia.

Among the risk factors for schizophrenia are obstetrical complications (Kotlicka-Antczak et al., 2001) that include hypoxia, a difficult and prolonged labor, and physical trauma, such as could occur from the use of forceps in a difficult birth. Some maternal infections, such as herpes simplex virus type 2 during critical portions of pregnancy and fetal brain development, are also postulated to be associated with an elevated risk of subsequent schizophrenia in the offspring (Buka et al., 2001). The maternal-infection hypothesis of schizophrenia is suggested by an overrepresentation of certain months of births in people with schizophrenia. Likewise, maternal malnutrition at critical periods may be a factor for the development of schizophrenia in the child (Brown et al., 1996). For example, offspring of women who underwent starvation in Holland during the Dutch Hunger Winter of World War II had a higher than expected incidence of schizophrenia, schizophrenia personality spectrum disorders, and congenital malformations of the central nervous system (Hoek et al., 1998).

An additional intriguing finding related to the parents of individuals with schizophrenia is that advanced paternal age at the time of conception may be a risk factor for the development of schizophrenia (Byrne et al., 2003; Dalman & Allebeck, 2002; Malaspina et al., 2001), particularly for females with schizophrenia (Byrne et al., 2003). However, most children of fathers of advanced age do not develop schizophrenia (Malaspina et al., 2001). The reason for the association of advanced paternal age and schizophrenia in the offspring is unknown, but accumulating *de novo* mutations in the germ-cell line with increasing age have been postulated (Brown et al., 2002; Malaspina et al., 2001). *De novo* germ-cell line mutations could account for some of the persistence of schizophrenia in the population, in spite of the decreased reproduction associated with schizophrenia compared to the general population (Byrne et al., 2003; McGrath et al., 1999). Advanced maternal age may confer an increased risk of schizophrenia in male offspring (Byrne et al., 2003).

Along these lines of risk factors for schizophrenia, and illustrating the difficulty of ascertaining the contributions of risk factors to schizophrenia and proposing an infectious etiology, it is postulated that domestic cats may transmit infectious diseases that are, in some cases, associated with schizophrenia. For example, toxoplasmosis, carried by cats and capable of infecting human brain tissue, can produce a clinical picture that is similar to schizophrenia. In fact, there is suggestive evidence that people with schizophrenia are statistically more likely to have been exposed to pet cats (Torrey & Yolken, 1995).

Gender differences suggest possible hormonal influences on the expression and course of schizophrenia. Males may have a higher risk of developing schizophrenia than do women, although this notion remains controversial (Aleman et al., 2003). Furthermore, men seem to develop schizophrenia earlier than do women, again suggesting that male gender is a risk factor for schizophrenia. To further complicate these issues, however, are early findings that the possible predominance of schizophrenia in men may be a relatively recent phenomenon, which would then implicate factors other than gender itself in the proposed excess of men with schizophrenia (Aleman et al., 2003).

Neuroanatomy of Schizophrenia

Along with genetic explanations, two general approaches to the neurobiology of schizophrenia exist. First, the neurodevelopment tact posits that schizophrenia is a disorder of development, analogous to mental retardation. According to this approach, there is an abnormality of brain development in early life that leads to the development of schizophrenia later in life (McGrath et al., 2003). Conversely, the neurodegeneration hypothesis argues for a deteriorating neural substrate from once higher functioning neural tissue, much like people suffering from Alzheimer's dementia presumably once enjoyed a normally functioning brain (Lieberman, 1999). In fact, some data suggest that elements of both the neurodevelopmental hypothesis and the neurodegenerative hypothesis are at play in the pathogenesis of schizophrenia. For example, abnormalities in the cortex and white matter of the frontotemporal region are present at the first presentation of schizophrenia (Bagary et al., 2003), yet brain volume appears to continue to decrease even after the onset of schizophrenia (McGrath et al., 2003). Furthermore, Ho and colleagues (1993) found that even in treated patients with schizophrenia, progressive volumetric deficits continued to occur, particularly in the frontal lobes, although the cause of these changes is unknown. Schizophrenia is also associated with gray matter volume loss in the left planum temporale and left Heschl gyrus (both located in the superior temporal gyrus) that appears progressive; that is, gray matter volume deficits in these structures increase with time (Kasai, 2003). Early neurodevelopmental abnormalities, therefore, may be progressive, not static, in schizophrenia (McGrath et al., 2003).

Based upon brain-imaging work and autopsy studies, numerous brain regions appear to have abnormal anatomy in patients suffering from schizophrenia. Among these are the hippocampus, temporal and frontal lobes, and the thalamus (Krystal et al., 2001). Abnormalities in gray matter and cerebral spinal fluid volume are also reported to occur in a variety of brain regions in individuals diagnosed with schizophrenia, including the mediodorsal area of the thalamus (Ananth et al., 2002). In an epidemiological study of hippocampal volume and schizophrenia, van Erp et al. (2002) found smaller hippocampal volumes in people suffering with schizophrenia when compared to normal controls. Furthermore, the hippocampal volumes of nonpsychotic siblings of the individuals with schizophrenia had hippocampal volumes in between those of their siblings who had been diagnosed with schizophrenia and normal controls (van Erp et al., 2002). Similarly, volume reductions in Heschl's gyrus, an important region for auditory processing located in the superior temporal lobe, are also reported to occur in episodic schizophrenia (Hirayasu et al., 2000). A related structure in the superior temporal lobe that appears to have a role in language processing, the left planum temporale, also shows volume reduction in schizophrenia (Kwon et al., 1999).

The Dopamine Hypothesis of Schizophrenia

Finally, despite significant limitations (Valenstein, 1998), the dopamine hypothesis of schizophrenia has been an important factor regarding the neurobiology of schizophrenia. Spawned in part by the action of early antipsychotic medications to block dopamine receptors, particularly dopamine type 2 receptors (Conley & Kelly, 2002), the dopamine hypothesis maintains that schizophrenia is associated with abnormal brain dopamine function (Conley & Kelly, 2002). At least some of the clinical features of schizophrenia have been hypothesized as due to abnormal dopamine function in the mesocortical pathway in people with schizophrenia compared to controls (Tuppurainen et al., 2003).

Consistent with this approach, the potency of these antipsychotic medications at blocking the dopamine type 2 receptor correlated with their ability to treat some of the symptoms of schizophrenia (Conley & Kelly, 2002). Conversely, drugs that increase the transmission of dopamine, such as amphetamines and cocaine, produce a psychosis in certain people that can closely resemble schizophrenia (Ellison, 1994). Furthermore, certain people with schizophrenia show a different dopamine-releasing response in the basal ganglia to an amphetamine challenge compared to normal controls (Breier et al., 1997).

In addition to dopamine, numerous other neurotransmitters are implicated in the etiology of schizophrenia, including serotonin and glutamate. Characterized by multiple mechanisms of action, the newer antipsychotic medications antagonize among other receptors the serotonin type 2 receptors, suggesting that serotonin function too may be abnormal in schizophrenia (Conley & Kelly, 2002). The neurotransmitter glutamate and its receptors also appear to be involved in the neurobiology of schizophrenia (Hashimoto et al., 2003). Of particular interest is the N-methyl-D-aspartate receptor (Hashimoto et al., 2003). Antagonism of this receptor, as occurs with phencyclidine (PCP, angel dust) and the anesthetic agent ketamine can produce a behavioral state closely resembling schizophrenia (Hashimoto et al., 2003). NMDA antagonism can also produce neurological findings associated with schizophrenia. In nonschizophrenic subjects, for example, ketamine produces abnormalities in ocular smooth-pursuit movements that are similar to those found first-degree relatives of people with schizophrenia (Avila et al., 2002).

In summary, schizophrenia is a complex phenomenon with an intricate and poorly elucidated neurobiology. Genetic factors are thought to be of major importance in the etiology of schizophrenia, although it appears that environmental risk factors are involved in the genesis of at least some cases of schizophrenia. Finally, it may be the interaction between genes, environmental, and experiential risk factors that leads to the expression of schizophrenia (Malaspina, 2002). Table 4.4 displays biological findings associated with schizophrenia.

TABLE 4.4 The Biology Associated with Schizophrenia

TYPE OF BIOLOGY	FINDINGS/THEORIES
Genetics	Higher rates of concordance for monozygotic twins than in dizygotic twins and linkage studies have shown several suggestive linkages, including linkage to chromosomes 1, 6, and 13.
Neuroanatomy	Abnormalities in the cortex and white matter of the frontotemporal region are present at the first presentation (Bagary et al., 2003) yet brain volume appears to continue to decrease even after the onset.
	Progressive volumetric deficits continue to occur, particularly in the frontal lobes.
	Associated with gray matter volume loss in the left planum temporale and left Heschl's gyrus (both located in the superior temporal gyrus) that appears progressive.
	Abnormal hippocampus, temporal and frontal lobes, and the thalamus.
	Abnormalities in gray matter and cerebral spinal fluid volume, including mediodorsal area of the thalamus.
	Volume reductions in Heschl's gyrus, an important region for auditory processing located in the superior temporal lobe. A related structure in the superior temporal lobe that appears to have a role in language processing, the left planum temporale, also shows volume reduction.
	The dopamine hypothesis maintains that it is associated with abnormal brain dopamine function; the potency of antipsychotic medications at blocking the dopamine type 2 receptor correlated with their ability to treat some of the symptoms of schizophrenia.
	Antagonism of the N-methyl-D-aspartate receptor, as occurs with phencyclidine (PCP, angel dust) and the anesthetic agent ketamine can produce a behavioral state closely resembling schizophrenia.

THE BIOLOGY OF ATTENTION-DEFICIT, HYPERACTIVITY DISORDER

Characterized by inattention and hyperactivity and occurring in children and adults (Pary et al., 2002), attention-deficit, hyperactivity disorder (ADHD) tends to run in families. A genetic component to ADHD has been assumed, and indeed ADHD appears highly heritable (see Jensen, 2000). Twin studies show higher rates of ADHD concordance in monozygotic compared to dizygotic twins (Goodman & Stevenson, 1989). Molecular genetics sheds additional light on potential causes for ADHD by implicating several possible genes that may affect the expression of ADHD: genes for the dopamine subtype 2 and 4 receptors and the dopamine transporter gene

(Faraone & Biederman, 1998). These genes are of particular interest because findings of abnormal dopamine transmission are consistent with the postulated ability of drugs affecting the reuptake of dopamine to treat ADHD (Pary et al., 2002).

Even given these findings of strong genetic contributions to the manifestations of ADHD, however, as Peter Jensen (2000) points out, as in any complex disorder, and particularly those involving behavior, complex and only poorly understood interactions between genetics and environment may well be highly relevant to an understanding of ADHD. In support of complex genetic-environmental interactions, several environmental risk factors for the development of ADHD appear relevant in some cases of ADHD. For example, prenatal and perinatal complications, marital stress, and low social class are all associated with ADHD (Faraone & Biederman, 1998).

The clinical presentation of attention-deficit, hyperactive disorder with its poorly sustained attention, impulsivity, and hyperactivity (Pary et al., 2002) also suggests deficiencies in executive function. Furthermore, many of the putative neuroanatomical findings in attention-deficit, hyperactive disorder are related to the brain's executive function—that is, the frontal lobe and its connections. In support of this observation, volumetric neuroimaging studies have found reduced volumes in the basal ganglia, particularly the caudate and globus pallidus, as well as the prefrontal cortex (a brain region well known for its role in planning, impulse control, and emotional regulation), in people with attention-deficit disorder (Narbona-Garcia & Sanchez-Carpintero, 1999). Similarly, functional brain-imaging studies have shown decreased metabolism in the basal ganglia and frontal cortex (Pary et al., 2002). In a 1998 review, Zametkin and Liotta (1998) summarized several brain imaging studies of ADHD and found reports of abnormalities in ADHD compared to controls in a variety of brain regions, including the cerebral cortex, corpus collosum, caudate nucleus, globus pallidus, and anterior frontal

IGNORING POTENTIAL AND IMPORTANT CONFOUNDS?

Gied, Blumenthal, Molloy, and Castellanos (2001) conducted a review of over thirty neuroimaging studies on children diagnosed with ADHD. This report, like most in the field, concluded that the evidence from neuroimaging studies indicates that there is involvement of the right frontal–striatal circuitry with cerebellar modulation in ADHD. That is, this meta-analysis concluded that ADHD is a result of abnormalities of brain functioning in specific portions of the brain.

However, as noted by Leo and Cohen (2003), Giedd et al. did not report on a con-founding variable of tremendous importance for this area of investigation—whether participants had been previously treated with stimulants or other psychotropic medication. When analyzed as to whether the studies included in the meta-analysis by Giedd et al. had reported prior use of stimulants or other psychotropic medication, it was discovered that the majority of participants in these studies had had prior medication use, often for several months or years (Leo & Cohen, 2003). As the authors of this subsequent analysis noted, the prior use of medication by these participants invalidates any suggestion of ADHD-specific neuropathology because investigators cannot rule out the possibility that the changes discovered by neuroimaging were a result of this prior medication use. Furthermore, Leo and Cohen (2003) noted that the few recent studies using unmedicated participants diagnosed with ADHD have inexplicably avoided making basic comparisons of these subjects with controls. Without such comparisons of unmedicated children diagnosed with ADHD versus controls not diagnosed with ADHD, there is no way to conclusively interpret the data from the neuroimaging studies thus far conducted on children diagnosed with ADHD.

As a specific example of the difficulty in conclusively interpreting neuroanatomical data as indicating biological causation in ADHD, it may be helpful to critically analyze the study most often cited as evidence of neuroanatomical factors in the brain being responsible for ADHD. This study was conducted in 1990 by Zametkin and his colleagues (Zametkin et al., 1990), who investigated the cerebral glucose metabolism of normal adults and adults with histories of hyperactivity in childhood who continued to have ADHD symptoms into adulthood. The study indicated that hyperactivity in adults was linked with reduced metabolism of glucose in the premotor cortex and the superior prefrontal cortex of the brain. These two areas of the brain that Zametkin and his colleagues reported as having reduced activity have been associated with the control of attention, planning, and motor activity. From these findings, the authors reported that their study indicated that these brain areas in people with ADHD are not as active as they are in controls. These findings were then interpreted as indicating that ADHD is a brain disorder related to problems with controlling attention, planning, and motor activity.

The interpretation of this study and studies similar to it—that ADHD is a brain disorder, as suggested by Leo and Cohen's (2003) meta-analysis above—cannot be considered definitive. A critique of the Zametkin et al. (1990)

study, for example, pointed out that the study had some major confounds (Reid, Maag, & Vasa, 1994). As just one example, the study did not indicate whether the lower glucose-metabolism rates found in the brains of individuals with ADHD were a cause, a result, or unrelated to attention problems. Without such factors investigated and analyzed, no definitive conclusions can be made from such studies in terms of definitively attributing causal sufficiency to neuroanatomical factors.

Perhaps even more significant is the fact that Zametkin and his colleagues (1993) attempted, unsuccessfully, to replicate their own findings three years later. This new study was conducted with adolescents, and no significant differences were found between the brains of normal adolescents and those diagnosed with ADHD. In their retrospective analysis, the results from the first study were not as clear, either.

REFERENCES

Giedd JN, Blumenthal J, Molloy E, Castellanos FX (2001): Brain imaging of attention deficit/hyperactivity disorder. In J Wasserstein, LE Wolf, & FF Lefever (eds.), *Adult Attention Deficit Disorder: Brain Mechanisms and Life Outcomes* (Vol. 931, pp. 33–49). New York: New York Academy of Sciences.

Leo J, Cohen D (2003): Broken brains or flawed studies? A critical review of ADHD neuroimaging research. The Journal of Mind and Behavior 24:29–56.

Reid R, Maag JW, Vasa SF(1994): Attention deficit hyperactivity disorder as a disability category: A critique. Exceptional Children 60:198–214.

Zametkin AJ, Liebenauer LL, Fitzgerald GA, King AC, Minkunas DV, Herscovitch P, Yamad EM, Cohen RM (1993): Brain metabolism in teenagers with attention-deficit hyperactivity disorder. Archives of General Psychiatry 50: 333–340.

Zametkin AJ, Nordahl TE, Gross M, King AC, Semple WE, Rumsey J, Hamburger S, Cohen RM (1990): Cerebral glucose metabolism in adults with hyperactivity of childhood onset. The New England Journal of Medicine 323: 1361–1366.

regions. These authors also noted studies showing decreased cerebral volume and decreased blood flow to the brain as a whole, as well as specifically to the prefrontal and premotor cortex. Not all of these studies were consistent with each other, and, in fact, Zametkin and Liotta concluded that no neuroanatomical findings were diagnostic of ADHD.

In a recent review of the research concerning the neurobiology of attention-deficit disorder, Himelstein et al. (2000) noted differing findings of the neurobiology of this disorder but describe a convergence of evidence implicating the dopamine and norepinephrine circuits in the frontal-striatal brain region. These findings of impaired transmission of dopamine and norepinephrine are consistent with the clinical observations and research that drugs that increase the synaptic concentrations of these neurotransmitters seem to be effective in the treatment of ADHD (Pary et al., 2002). Affecting both dopamine and norepinephrine, for example, the stimulant methylphenidate (Ritalin, Concerta, Metadate) and dextroamphetamine (Dexedrine) inhibit the reuptake of both these neurotransmitters (Keating et al., 2001), thus increasing their overall synaptic concentrations. Biological findings that have been associated with ADHD are listed in Table 4.5.

TABLE 4.5   The Biology Associated with Attention-Deficit, Hyperactivity Disorder

TYPE OF BIOLOGY	FINDINGS/THEORIES
Genetics	Tends to run in families.
	Several possible genes that may affect the expression: genes for the dopamine subtype 2 and 4 receptors and the dopamine transporter gene.
	Prenatal and perinatal complications, marital stress, and low social class.
Neuroanatomy	Volumetric neuroimaging studies have found reduced volumes in the basal ganglia, particularly the caudate and globus pallidus, as well as the prefrontal cortex.
	Abnormalities in a variety of brain regions, including the cerebral cortex, corpus collosum, caudate nucleus, globus pallidus, and anterior frontal regions.
	Decreased cerebral volume and decreased blood flow to the brain as a whole, as well as specifically to the prefrontal and premotor cortex.
	Impaired transmission of dopamine and norepinephrine.
	Zametkin and Liotta (1998) concluded that no neuroanatomical findings were diagnostic.

SUMMARY

In the last several decades, substantial progress has been made in understanding the neurobiology of many mental disorders. Despite this progress, though, much of the biological etiology of these conditions remains enigmatic. Central nervous system drug development is both a result of increased understanding of the biology of mental disorders and a driving force for increased understanding because these drugs can be viewed as pharmacological probes into the workings of the brain.

Affective disorders are well known to be familial and increased concordance rates in monozygotic as opposed to dizygotic twins suggest a genetic component to the affective disorders, although no definite chromosomes or genes have been identified. Based in part on antidepressant drug action, the monoamine hypothesis of depression has traditionally been one of the dominant theories of the biology of depression. A number of limitations, however, suggest that other mechanisms are likely in the etiology of depression. Abnormalities in the hypothalamic-pituitary-adrenal axis appear to be involved. Forming the basis of the dexamethasone suppression test, the physiology of the stress hormone cortisol appears abnormal in some people with depression. Furthermore, cortisol-releasing factor is elevated in major depression and antagonists for this neurohormone are in development as antidepressants. Several other intriguing leads into the neurobiology of depression exist. Neurotrophic factors could be abnormal, and currently available antidepressants may increase these agents in key brain regions as part of their mechanisms of action.

An early neurobiology is also forming for the anxiety disorders. Generalized anxiety disorder appears to involve abnormalities in GABA and serotonin, findings that are consistent with the putative efficacy of GABA-facilitating and serotonin-enhancing drugs for this disorder. Obsessive-compulsive disorder is associated with pathology in the basal ganglia. In particular, people with obsessive-compulsive disorder may have smaller than normal caudate nuclei. Diminished volumes of gray and white matter have also been reported in obsessive-compulsive disorder. Data suggest decreased hippocampal volume in posttraumatic stress disorder. The etiology of this hippocampal volume reduction is unclear. It may be due to toxic effects from cortisol, although recent evidence suggests that small hippocampi may be present before the trauma. Furthermore, concentrations of cortisol appear to be lower than normal in PTSD with cortisol-releasing factor being elevated. Panic disorder is biologically characterized in some cases by increased nocturnal cortisol levels. Lactate infusions and elevated carbon dioxide blood concentrations can precipitate panic attacks in panic-disorder patients. Comparatively poorly studied, social phobia shows some abnormalities in dopamine and amygdala function.

Schizophrenia is characterized by multiple brain abnormalities, although a comprehensive neurobiology of schizophrenia is yet to be assembled. Demonstrating a clear genetic component, twin studies in schizophrenia show increased concordance rates in monozygotic compared to dizygotic twins. However, the identification of specific genes and chromosomes remains elusive. Obstetrical complications, maternal malnutrition, advanced paternal age, and maternal infections confer an increased risk of schizophrenia in the offspring. Numerous neuroanatomical findings suggest that hippocampal, frontal lobe, and thalamic abnormalities may have a role in the pathogenesis of schizophrenia.

Positing abnormal dopamine function in mesocortical and mesolimbic pathways, the dopamine hypothesis of schizophrenia is giving way to increasingly sophisticated ideas involving not only abnormalities of dopamine but also of serotonin, glutamate, and other neurotransmitters.

Attention-deficit, hyperactive disorder appears to be highly heritable and several candidate genes have been tentatively identified: Genes for dopamine receptor subtypes 2 and 4, as well as for the dopamine transporter structure, may be abnormal in ADHD. Other research indicates that abnormal functioning of the caudate and globus pallidus nuclei may be associated with ADHD.

STUDY QUESTIONS

1. Describe the known neurobiology of the depressive disorders.
2. Given what is known about the etiology of schizophrenia, design a novel drug for this disorder. What pharmacological features would you include?
3. Why is it important to know whether the putative hippocampal abnormalities in posttraumatic stress disorder proceed or are a result of trauma?
4. Describe the differences in the neurobiology between depression and obsessive-compulsive disorder.
5. Design a study to further elucidate the neurobiology of social phobia.
6. List some proposed risk factors for the development of schizophrenia.
7. How might antidepressants affect brain structure?
8. What is kindling and how does it relate to bipolar disorder?

REFERENCES

Abelson JL, Curtis GC (1996): Hypothalamic-pituitary-adrenal axis in panic disorder: 24-hour secretion of corticotropin and cortisol. Archives of General Psychiatry 53:323–331.

Agartz I, Momenan R, Rawlings RR, Kerich MJ, Hommerow et al. (1999): Hippocampal volume in patients with alcohol dependence. Archives of General Psychiatry 56:356–363.

Alda M (1997): Bipolar disorder: From families to genes. Canadian Journal of Psychiatry 42:378–387.

Aleman A, Kahn RS, Selten JP (2003): Sex differences in the risk of schizophrenia. Archives of General Psychiatry 60:565–571.

Amaral DG (2002): The primate amygdala and the neurobiology of social behavior: Implications for understanding social anxiety. Biological Psychiatry 51:11–17.

Ananth H, Popescu I, Critchley HD, Good CD, Frackowiak RS, Dolan RJ (2002): Cortical and subcortical gray matter abnormalities in schizophrenia determined through structural magnetic resonance imaging with optimized volumetric voxel-based morphometry. American Journal of Psychiatry 159:1497–505.

Avila MT, Weiler MA, Lahti AC, Tamminga CA, Thaker GK (2002): Effects of ketamine on leading saccades during smooth-pursuit eye movements may implicate cerebellar dysfunction in schizophrenia. American Journal of Psychiatry 159:1490–1496

Bagary MS, Symms MR, Barger GJ, Mutsatsa SH, Joyce EM, Ron MA (2003): Gray and white matter brain abnormalities in first-episode schizophrenia inferred from magnetization transfer imaging. Archives of General Psychiatry 60:779–788.

Baumeister AA, Hawkins MF, Uzelac SM (2003): The myth of reserpine-induced depression: Role in the historical development of the monoamine hypothesis. Journal of the History of Neuroscience 12:207–220.

Beyer JL, Krishnan KR (2002): Volumetric brain imaging findings in mood disorders. Bipolar Disorders 4:89–104.

Bissette G, Klimek V, Pan J, Stockmeier C, Ordway G (2003): Elevated concentrations of CRF in the locus coeruleus of depressed subjects. Neuropsychopharmacology 28:1328–1335.

Blumberg HP, Leung HC, Skudlarski P, Lacadie CM, Fredericks CA, Harris BC, Charney DS, Gore JC, Krystal JH, Peterson BS (2003): A functional magnetic resonance imaging study of bipolar disorder. Archives of General Psychiatry 60:601–609.

Brambilla P, Perez J, Barale F, Schettini G, Soares JC (2003): GABAergic dysfunction in mood disorders. Molecular Psychiatry 8:721–737, 715.

Breier A, Su TP, Saunders R, Carsan RE, Kolachana BS, de Bortolomeis A, Weinberger DR, Weisenfold N, Malhotra AK, Eckelman WC, Pickar D et al. (1997): Schizophrenia is associated with elevated amphetamine-induced synaptic dopamine concentrations: Evidence from a novel positron emission tomography method. Proceedings of the National Academy of Science USA 94:2569–2574.

Bremner JD, Randall P, Scott TM, Bronen RA, Seibyl JP, Southwick SM, Delaney RC, McCarthy G, Charney DS, Innis RB (1995): MRI-based measurement of hippocampal volume in patients with combat-related posttraumatic stress disorder. American Journal of Psychiatry 152:973–981.

Brown AS, Schaefer CA, Wyatt RJ, Begg MD, Goetz R, Bresnahan MA, Harkavy-Friedman J, Gorman JM, Malaspina D, Susser ES (2002): Paternal age and risk of schizophrenia in adult offspring. American Journal of Psychiatry 159:1528–1533.

Brown AS, Susser ES, Butler PD, Richardson Andrews R, Kaufmann CA, Gorman JM (1996): Neurobiological plausibility of prenatal nutritional deprivation as a risk factor for schizophrenia. Journal of Nervous and Mental Disorders 184:71–85.

Byrne M, Agerbo E, Ewald H, Eaton WW, Mortensen PB (2003): Parental age and risk of schizophrenia. Archives of General Psychiatry 60:673–678.

Buka SL, Fan AP (1999): Association of prenatal and perinatal complications with subsequent bipolar disorder and schizophrenia. Schizophrenia Research 39:113–119.

Buka SL, Tsuang MT, Torrey EF, Klebanoff MA, Bernstein D, Yolken RH (2001): Maternal infections and subsequent psychosis among offspring. Archives of General Psychiatry 58:132–137.

Bymaster FP, McNamara RK, Tran PV (2003): New approaches to developing antidepressants by enhancing monoaminergic neurotransmission. Expert Opinion on Investigational Drugs 12:531–543.

Cadoret RJ (1978): Evidence for genetic inheritance of primary affective disorder on adoptees. American Journal of Psychiatry 135:463–466.

Conley RR, Kelly DL (2002): Current status of antipsychotic drug treatment. Current Drug Targets. CNS and Neurological Disorders 1:123–128.

Craufurd D, Thompson JC, Snowden JS (2001): Behavioral changes in Huntington's disease. Neuropsychiatry, Neuropsychology, and Behavioral Neurology 14:219–226.

Dalman C, Allebeck P (2002): Paternal age and schizophrenia: Further support for an association. American Journal of Psychiatry 159:1591–1592.

Ellison G (1994): Stimulant-induced psychosis, the dopamine theory of schizophrenia, and the habenula. Brain Research. Brain Research Reviews 19:223–239.

Faraone SV, Biederman J (1998): Neurobiology of attention-deficit hyperactivity disorder. Biological Psychiatry 44:951–958.

Friedman MJ, Southwick SM (1995): Towards pharmacotherapy for PTSD. In MJ Friedman (ed.), *Neurobiological and Clinical Consequences of Stress: From Normal Adaptation to PTSD.* Philadelphia: Lippincott-Raven, pp. 464–481.

Frodl T, Meisenzahl EM, Zetzsche T, Born C, Groll C, Jager M, Leinsinger G, Bottlender R, Hahn K, Moller HJ (2002): Hippocampal changes in patients with a first episode of major depression. American Journal of Psychiatry 159:1112–1118.

Fyer AJ, Mannuzza S, Chapman TF, Martin LY, Klein DF (1995): Specificity in familial aggregation of phobic disorders. Archives of General Psychiatry 52:564–573.

Goetz RR, Klein DF, Gorman JM (1996): Symptoms essential to the experience of sodium lactate-induced panic. Neuropsychopharmacology 14:355–366.

Goodman R, Stevenson J (1989): A twin study of hyperactivity, II: The aetiological role of genes, family relationships and perinatal adversity. Journal of Child Psychology and Psychiatry 34:1137–1152.

Gorman JM, Papp LA, Coplan JD, Martinez JM, Lennon S, Goetz RR, Ross D, Klein DF, et al. (1994): Anxiogenic effects of CO_2 and hyperventilation in patients with panic disorder. American Journal of Psychiatry 151:547–553.

Greenberg PE, Sisitsky T, Kessler RC, Finkelstein SN, Berndt ER, Davidson JRT, Ballenger JC, Fyer AJ (1999): The economic burden of anxiety disorders in the 1990s. Journal of Clinical Psychiatry 60:427–435.

Haefely W (1985): The biological basis of benzodiazepine actions. In DE Smith, DR Wesson, MA Hingham (eds.), *The Benzodiazepines: Current Standards for Medical Practice.* Hingham, MA: MTP Press.

Hageman I, Anderson HS, Jørgensen MB (2001): Post-traumatic stress disorder: A review of psychobiology and pharmacotherapy. Acta Psychiatrica Scandinavica 104:411–422.

Hashimoto K, Fukushiuma T, Shimizu E, Komatsu N, Watanabe H, Shinoda N, Nakazato M, Kumakiri C, Okada S, Hasegawa H, Imai K, Iyo M (2003): Decreased serum levels of D-serine in patients with schizophrenia. Archives of General Psychiatry 60:572–576.

Healy D (1997): *The Antidepressant Era.* Cambridge, MA: Harvard University Press.

Heim C, Nemeroff CB (2001): The role of childhood trauma in the neurobiology of mood and anxiety disorders: Preclinical and clinical studies. Biological Psychiatry 49:1023–1039.

Heim C, Newport J, Bonsall R, Miller AH, Nemeroff CB (2001a): Altered pituitary-adrenal axis responses to provocative challenge tests in adult survivors of childhood abuse. American Journal of Psychiatry 158:175–581.

Himelstein J, Newcorn JH, Halperin JM (2000): The neurobiology of attention-deficit disorder hyperactivity disorder. Frontiers in Bioscience 5:D461–478.

Hindmarch I (2001): Expanding the horizons of depression: Beyond the monoamine hypothesis. Human Psychopharmacology 16:203–218.

Hirayasu Y, McCarley RW, Salisbury DF, Tanaka S, Kwon JS, Frumin M, Snyderman D, Yurgelun-Todd D, Kikinis R, Jolesz FA, Shenton ME (2000): Planum temporale and Heschl gyrus volume reduction in schizophrenia: A magnetic resonance imaging study of first-episode patients. Archives of General Psychiatry 57:692–699.

Ho BC, Andreasen NC, Nopoulos P, Arndt S, Magnotta V, Flaum M (2003): Progressive structural brain abnormalities and their relationship to clinical outcome. Archives of General Psychiatry 60:585–594.

Hoek HW, Brown AS, Susser E (1998): The Dutch famine and schizophrenia spectrum disorders. Social Psychiatry and Psychiatric Epidemiology 33:373–379.

Hoschl C, Hajek T (2001): Hippocampal damage mediated by corticosteroids—a neuropsychiatric research challenge. European Archives of Psychiatry and Clinical Neuroscience 251 (supplement 2):II81–88.

Huguelet P, McQuillan A (1996): [Neuroimaging and neurobiology of obsessive compulsive disorder: A review of recent developments in research]. Encephale 22:41–45.

Hull AM (2002): Neuroimaging findings in post-traumatic stress disorder. British Journal of Psychiatry 181:102–110.

Insel TR, Winslow JT (1992): Neurobiology of obsessive-compulsive disorder. Psychiatric Clinics of North America 15:813–824.

Jablensky A (2000): Epidemiology of schizophrenia: The global burden of disease and disability. European Archives of Psychiatry and Clinical Neuroscience 250:274–285.

Jenike MA, Breiter HC, Baer I, Kennedy DN, Savage CR, Olivaros MS, O'Sullivan RL, Shera DM, Rauch SL, Keuthen N, Roson BR, Caviness VS, Filipek PA, et al. (1996): Cerebral structural abnormalities in obsessive-compulsive disorder: A quantitative morphometric magnetic resonance imaging study. Archives of General Psychiatry 53:625–632.

Jensen PS (2000): ADHD: Current concepts on etiology, pathophysiology, and neurobiology. Child and Adolescent Psychiatric Clinics of North America 9:557–572.

Jetty PV, Charney DS, Goddard AW (2001): Neurobiology of generalized anxiety disorder. Psychiatric Clinics of North America 24:75–97.

Kasai K, Shenton ME, Salisbury DF, Hirayasu Y, Onitsuka T, Spencer MH, Yergelun-Todd DA, Kikinis R, Jolesz FA, McCarley RW (2003): Progressive decrease of left Heschl gryrus and planum temporale gray matter volume in first-episode schizophrenia. Archives of General Psychiatry 60:766–775.

Kaufman J, Charney D (2001): Effects of early stress on brain structures and function: Implications for understanding the relationship between child maltreatment and depression. Developmental Psychopathology 13:451–471.

Keating GM, McClellan K, Jarvis B (2001): Methylphenidate (OROS formulation). CNS Drugs 15:495–500.

Kendler KS (1983): Overview: A current perspective on twin studies of schizophrenia. American Journal of Psychiatry 140:1413–1425.

Kendler KS, Neal MC, Kessler RC, Heath AC, Eaves LJ (1992): The genetic epidemiology of phobias in women: The interrelationship of agoraphobia, social phobia, situational phobia, and simple phobia. Archives of General Psychiatry 49:273–281.

Kinney DK, Yurgelun-Todd DA, Tohen M, Tramer S (1998): Pre- and perinatal complications and risk for bipolar disorder: A retrospective study. Journal of Affective Disorders 50:117–124.

Klein DF (1993): False suffocation alarms, spontaneous panics, and related conditions: An integrative hypothesis. Archives of General Psychiatry 50:306–317.

Kotlicka-Antczak M, Gmitrowicz A, Sobow TM, Rabe-Jablonska J (2001): Obstetric complications and Apgar scores in early-onset schizophrenic patients with prominent positive and prominent negative symptoms. Journal of Psychiatric Research 35:249–257.

Krystal JH, D'Souza DC, Sanacora G, Goddard AW, Charney DS (2001): Current perspectives in the pathophysiology of schizophrenia, depression, and anxiety disorders. Medical Clinics of North America 85:559–577.

Kwon JS, McCarley RW, Hirayasu Y, Anderson JE, Fischer IA, Kikinis R, Jolesz FA, Shenton ME (1999): Left planum temporale volume reduction in schizophrenia. Archives of General Psychiatry 56:142–148.

Leckman JF, Goodman WK, North WG, Chappell PB, Price LH, Pauls DL, Anderson GM, Riddle MA, McSwiggan-Hardin McDougle CJ, et al. (1994): Elevated cerebral spinal fluid levels of oxytocin in obsessive-compulsive disorder. Comparison with Tourette's syndrome and healthy controls. Archives of General Psychiatry 51:782–792.

Leonard BE (2000): Evidence for a biochemical lesion in depression. Journal of Clinical Psychiatry 61 (supplement 6): 12–17.

Li D, Chokka P, Tibbo P (2001): Toward an integrative understanding of social phobia. Journal of Psychiatry and Neuroscience 26:190–202.

Lieberman JA (1999): Is schizophrenia a neurodegenerative disorder? A clinical and neurobiological perspective. Biological Psychiatry 46:729–739.

Lockwood KA, Alexopoulos GS, van Gorp WG (2002): Executive function in geriatric depression. American Journal of Psychiatry 159:1119–1126.

Malaspina D (2002): Pathways to psychosis. CNS Spectrums 7:25.

Malaspina D, Harlap S, Fennig S, Heiman D, Nahon D, Feldman D, Susser EA (2001): Advancing paternal age and the risk of schizophrenia. Archives of General Psychiatry 58:361–367.

Malhi GS, Moore J, McGuffin P (2000): The genetics of major depressive disorder. Current Psychiatry Reports 2:165–169.

Massana G, Serra-Grabulosa JM, Salgado-Pineda P, Gasto C, Junque C, Massana J, Mercader JM, Gomez B, Tobena A, Salamero M (2003): Amygdalar atrophy in panic disorder patients detected by volumetric magnetic resonance imaging. NeuroImage 19:80–90.

Mathew SJ, Coplan JD, Gorman JM (2001): Neurobiological mechanisms of social anxiety disorder. American Journal of Psychiatry 158:1558–1567.

McEwen BS (2003): Mood disorders and allostatic load. Biological Psychiatry 54:200–207.

McGrath JJ, Feron FP, Burne TH, Mackay-Sim A, Eyles DW (2003): The neurodevelopmental hypothesis of schizophrenia: Review of recent developments. Annals of Medicine 35: 86–93.

McGrath JJ, Hearle J, Jenner L, Plant K, Drummond A, Barkla JM (1999): The fertility and fecundity of patients with psychoses. Acta Psychiatrica Scandinavica 99:441–446.

Merikangas KR, Chakravarti A, Moldin SO, Araj H, Blangero JC, Burmeister M, Crabbe J, Jr., Depaulo JR, Jr., Foulks E, Freimer NB, Koretz DS, Lichtenstein W, Mignot E, Reiss AL, Risch NJ, Takahashi JS (2002): Future of genetics of mood disorders research. Biological Psychiatry 52:457–477.

Micallef J, Blin O (2001): Neurobiology and clinical pharmacology of obsessive-compulsive disorder. Clinical Neuropharmacology 24:191–207.

Naranjo CA, Tremblay LK, Busto UE (2001): The role the brain reward system in depression. Progress in Neuropsychopharmacology & Biological Psychiatry 25:781–823.

Narbona-Garcia J, Sanchez-Carpintero R (1999): [Neurobiology of attention deficit-hyperactivity disorder]. Review of Neurology 28 (supplement 2):S160–164.

Nemeroff CB (2002): New directions in the development of antidepressants: The interface of neurobiology and psychiatry. Human Psychopharmacology 17 (supplement 1):S13–16.

Nestler EJ, Barrot M, Dileone RJ, Eisch AJ, Gold SJ, Monteggia LM (2002): Neurobiology of depression. Neuron 34:13–25.

Ninan PT (1999): The functional anatomy, neurochemistry, and pharmacology of anxiety. Journal of Clinical Psychiatry 60 (supplement 22):12–17.

O'Donovan MC, Williams NM, Owen MJ (2003): Recent advances in the genetics of schizophrenia. Human Molecular Genetics 12 (supplement 2):R125–133.

Okun MS, Watts RL (2002): Depression associated with Parkinson's disease: Clinical features and treatment. Neurology 58 (4 supplement 1):S63–70.

Ongur D, Drevets WC, Price JL (1998): Glial reduction in the subgenual prefrontal cortex in mood disorders. Proceedings of the National Academy of Science USA 95:13290–13295.

Parker KJ, Schatzberg AF, Lyons DM (2003): Neuroendocrine aspects of hypercortisolism in major depression. Hormones and Behavior 43:60–66.

Pary R, Lewis S, Matuschka PR, Lippmann S (2002): Attention-deficit/hyperactivity disorder: An update. Southern Medical Journal 95:743–749.

Penninx BW, Kritchevsky SB, Yaffe K, Newman AB, Simonsick EM, Rubin S, Ferrucci L, Harris T, Pahor M (2003): Inflammatory markers and depressed mood in older persons: Results from the Heath, Aging, and Body Composition study. Biological Psychiatry 54:566–572.

Petty F (1995): GABA and mood disorders: A brief review and hypothesis. Journal of Affective Disorders 34:275–281.

Petty F, Kramer GL, Fulton M, Davis L, Rush AJ (1995): Stability of plasma GABA at four-year follow-up in patients with primary unipolar depression. Biological Psychiatry 37:806–810.

Pletscher A (1991): The discovery of antidepressants: A winding path. Experientia 47:4–8.

Pollack MH (2002): Comorbidity, neurobiology, and pharmacotherapy of social anxiety disorder. Journal of Clinical Psychiatry 62 (supplement 12):24–29.

Pollack MH, Marzol PC (2000): Panic: Course, complications and treatment of panic disorder. Journal of Psychopharmacology 14 (2 supplement 1): S25–30.

Rush AJ (2003): Toward an understanding of bipolar disorder and its origin. Journal of Clinical Psychiatry 64 (supplement 6):4–8.

Sanders AR, Dolora-Wadleigh SD, Gershon ES (1999): Molecular genetics of mood disorders. In DS Charney, EJ Nestler, BS Bunney (eds.), *Neurobiology on Mental Illness*. New York: Oxford, pp. 299–316.

Santarelli L, Saxe M, Gross C, Surget A, Battaglia F, Dulawa S, Weisstaub N, Lee J, Duman R, Arancio O, Belzung C, Hen R (2003): Requirement of hippocampal neurogenesis for the behavioral effects of antidepressants. Science 301:805–809.

Sapolsky RM (2002): Chickens, eggs and hippocampal atrophy. Nature Neuroscience 5:1111–1113.

Schneier FR, Liebowitz MR, Abi-Darham A, Zea-Ponce Y, Lin SH, Larueile M (2000): Low dopamine D_2 receptor binding potential in social phobia. American Journal of Psychiatry 157:457–459.

Schoepp DD, Jane DE, Monn JA (1999): Pharmacological agents acting at subtypes of metabotropic glutamate receptors. Neuropharmacology 38:1431–1476.

Sheehan DV (1999): Venlafaxine extended release (XR) in the treatment of generalized anxiety disorder. Journal of Clinical Psychiatry 60 (supplement 22):23–28.

Shekhar A, Keim SR (1997): The circumventricular organs form a potential neural pathway for lactate sensitivity: Implications for panic disorder. Journal of Neuroscience 17:9726–9735.

Sheline YI, Sanghavi M, Mintun MA, Gado MH (1999): Depression duration but not age predicts hippocampal volume loss in medically healthy women with recurrent major depression. Journal of Neuroscience 19:5034–5043.

Shimizu E, Hashimoto K, Okamura N, Koike K, Komatsu N, Kumakiri C, Nakazato M, Watanabe H, Shinoda N, Okada S, Iyo M (2003): Alterations of serum levels of brain-derived neurotrophic factor (BDNF) in depressed patients with or without major depression. Biological Psychiatry 54:70–75.

Sonino N, Fava GA (2001): Psychiatric disorders associated with Cushing's syndrome. Epidemiology, pathophysiology and treatment. CNS Drugs 15:361–373.

Squitieri F, Cannella M, Giallonardo P, Maglione V, Mariotti C, Hayden MR (2001): Onset and pre-onset studies to define the Huntington's disease natural history. Brain Research Bulletin 56:233–238.

Stein DJ, Westenberg HG, Liebowitz MR (2002): Social anxiety disorder and generalized anxiety disorder: Serotonergic and dopaminergic neurocircuitry. Journal of Clinical Psychiatry 63 (supplement 6):12–19.

Suarez EC, Krishnan RR, Lewis JG (2003): The relation of severity of depressive symptoms to monocyte-associated proinflammatory cytokines and chemokines in apparently healthy men. Psychosomatic Medicine 65:362–368.

Talbot-Stern JK, Green T, Royle TJ (2000): Psychiatric manifestations of systemic illness. Emergency Medicine Clinics of North America 18:199–209, vii–viii.

Tiihonen J, Kuikka J, Rasanen P, Lepola U, Koponen H, Liuska A, Lehmusvaana A, Vainio P, Konanen M, Bergstrom K, Yu M, Kinnunen I, Akerman K, Karhu J (1997a): Cerebral benzodiazepine receptor binding and distribution in generalized anxiety disorder: A fractal analysis. Molecular Psychiatry 2:463–471.

Tiihonen J, Kuikka J, Bergstrom K, et al. (1997b): Dopamine reuptake site densities in patients with social phobia. American Journal of Psychiatry 154:239–242.

Torgersen S (1997): Genetic basis and psychopathology. In SM Turner and M Hersen (eds.), Adult Psychopathology and Diagnosis (3rd ed.). New York: John Wiley.

Torrey EF, Yolken RH (1995): Could schizophrenia be a viral zoonosis transmitted from house cats? Schizophrenia Research 21:167–171.

Tremblay LK, Naranjo CA, Cardenas L, Herrmann N, Busto UE (2002): Probing brain reward system function in major depression. Archives of General Psychiatry 59:409–416.

Tsuang D, Almqvist EW, Lipe H, Strgar F, DiGiacomo L, Hoff D, Eugenio C, Hayden MR, Bird TD (2000): Familial aggregation of psychotic symptoms in Huntington's disease. American Journal of Psychiatry 157:1955–1959.

Tuppurainen H, Kuikka J, Viinamaki H, Husso-Saastamoinen M, Bergstrom K, Tiihonen J (2003): Extrastriatal dopamine D(2/3) receptor densitiy and distribution in drug-naive schizophrenic patients. Molecular Psychiatry 8:453–455.

Vaidya VA, Duman RS (2001): Depression – emerging insights from neurobiology. British Medical Bulletin 57:61–79.

Valenstein ES (1998): *Blaming the Brain: The Truth about Drugs and Mental Health.* New York: The Free Press.

van Erp TGM, Saleh PA, Rosso IM, Huttunen M, Lönnqvist J, Pirkola T, Salonen O, Vallanne L, Poutanen V-P, Standertskjöld-Nordenstam C-G, Cannon TD (2002): Contributions of genetic risk and fetal hypoxia to hippocampal volume in patients with schizophrenia or schizoaffective disorder, their unaffected siblings, and healthy unrelated volunteers. American Journal of Psychiatry 159:1514–1520.

Weissman MM, Gershon ES, Kidd KK, Prusoff BA, Leckman JF, Bibble E, Hamovit J, Thompson WB, Pauls DL, Gurott JJ (1984): Psychiatric disorders in the relatives of probands with affective disorders: The Yale University-National Institute of Mental Health Collaborative Study. Archives of General Psychiatry 41:13–21.

Weissman MM, Kidd KK, Prusoff BA (1982): Variability in rates of affective disorders in relatives of depressed and normal probands. Archives of General Psychiatry 39:1397–1403.

Wender PH, Kety SS, Rosenthal D, Schulsinger F, Ortmann J, Lunde I (1986): Psychiatric disorders in the biological and adoptive families of adopted individuals with affective disorders. Archives of General Psychiatry 43:923–929.

White HS (2003): Mechanisms of action of newer anticonvulsants. Journal of Clinical Psychiatry 64 (supplement 8):5–8.

Williams RN (2001): The biologization of psychotherapy: Understanding the nature of influence. In BS Slife, R Williams, S Barlow (eds.), *Critical Issues in Psychotherapy: Translating New Ideas into Practice.* Thousand Oaks, CA: Sage Publications.

Wong AH, Van Tol HH (2003): Schizophrenia: From phenomenology to neurobiology. Neuroscience and Biobehavioral Reviews 27:269–306.

Yehuda R, Kahana B, Binder-Byrnes K, Southwick SM, Mason JW, Giller EL (1995): Low urinary cortisol excretion in Holocaust survivors with posttraumatic stress disorder. American Journal of Psychiatry 152:982–986.

Yehuda R, McFarlane AC, Shalev AY (1998a): Predicting the development of posttraumatic stress disorder from the acute response to a traumatic event. Biological Psychiatry 44:1305–1313.

Yehuda R (1998b): Neuroendocrinology of trauma and posttraumatic stress disorder. In Yehuda (ed.), *Psychological Trauma.* Washington DC: American Psychiatric Press, pp. 97–131.

Zametkin AJ, Liotta W (1998): The neurobiology of attention-deficit/hyperactivity disorder. Journal of Clinical Psychiatry 59 (supplement 7):17–23.

THE PSYCHOTROPIC DRUGS: THEIR PHARMACOLOGY, METABOLISM, INTERACTIONS, ADVERSE EFFECTS, AND THERAPEUTIC USES

CHAPTER FIVE

SEDATIVE HYPNOTICS, ANXIOLYTICS, AND ALCOHOL

The anxiolytics and sedative hypnotics form a diverse group of medications that have been widely used across a variety of diagnoses. Because of adverse effects, the barbiturates are much less frequently used than formerly, even though they continue to have a role in some conditions, such as the treatment of epilepsy. The benzodiazepines, drugs that have a wider safety margin than the barbiturates, have largely taken over the role of the older sedative hypnotic barbiturates and are used widely, primarily for different types of anxiety and for the induction of sleep. Controversy from several issues surrounding the clinical use of benzodiazepines has prompted the search for alternative approaches, and in fact many of the so-called antidepressants are being used in areas that traditionally were filled by the benzodiazepines.

Alcohol is widely used and abused and is associated with numerous adverse affects, including addiction. This chapter reviews these major categories of medications, including alcohol, discussing their mechanisms of action, pitfalls, and uses.

Drugs classified as anxiolytics and sedative hypnotics include the barbiturates and similar compounds, benzodiazepines, gamma-hydroxybutyrate (GHB), zolpidem (Ambien), and alcohol. Following the introduction of the first barbiturate, barbital, in 1903 (Nemeroff, 2003), the barbiturates were in widespread use during the middle of the twentieth century for all sorts of psychiatric conditions, especially anxiety and insomnia. However, because of a wider margin of safety, or higher therapeutic index, the benzodiazepines have largely replaced the more dangerous barbiturates (Byerley & Gillin, 1984). Despite extensive use of the benzodiazepines, concerns about their safety and long-term efficacy continue (Lader, 1999), and drugs from other classes have invaded areas once considered the exclusive domain of benzodiazepines. For example, the selective serotonin reuptake inhibitors, discussed in Chapter 9, are now considered first-line treatment for certain anxiety disorders once considered the domain of the benzodiazepines (Rickels & Rynn, 2002).

THE BARBITURATES AND RELATED COMPOUNDS

The barbiturates saw considerable clinical use in the middle decades of the twentieth century until approximately the 1960s, when benzodiazepines became more widely available (Nemeroff, 2003). The barbiturates and closely related compounds have now been almost entirely replaced by the safer benzodiazepine and other medications. Despite this relative demotion in importance, some barbiturates continue to see use in several select situations, such as epilepsy. Available barbiturates include amobarbitol (Amytal), butabarbital (Butisol), methohexital (Brevital), phenobarbital (Luminal), and secobarbital (Seconal).

Several other drugs that are closely related to the barbiturates continue to see occasional use. These barbiturate-like drugs include meprobamate (Miltown) and chloral hydrate (Noctec). Because of the availability of the safer benzodiazepines, these other barbiturate-like drugs are used clinically only infrequently.

Mechanism of Action, Pharmacology, and Metabolism

The barbiturates interact with sites on the $GABA_A$ receptor, a common and fairly ubiquitous receptor for the neurotransmitter gamma aminobutyric acid (GABA), the primary inhibitory neurotransmitter in the brain. When GABA binds to the $GABA_A$ receptor, ion channels are activated that allow for an influx of chloride ions, which in turn hyperpolarize the neuron, increasing its negative charge compared to the exterior of the cell and rendering it less likely to generate an action potential (Simeone et al., 2003). By binding to additional sites on the $GABA_A$ receptor, barbiturates modulate this receptor (Rabow et al., 1995). The change in configuration of the $GABA_A$ receptor facilitates and prolongs the action of GABA on the receptor (Chebib & Johnston, 1999) and diminishes the chances that the neuron will generate an action potential, presumably leading to the clinical effects, such as sedations and anxiolysis, observed with these drugs.

Certain barbiturates including secobarbital, amobarbital, and phenobarbital inhibit the response of N-methyl-D-aspartate subtype of glutamate receptors, the brain's main excitatory neurotransmitter (Daniell, 1994). An additional mechanism of certain barbiturates may consist of inhibiting the entry of sodium ions into the neuron (Wartenberg et al., 1999), a process that also makes it less likely that the neuron will generate an action potential.

Like many other psychopharmacological drugs, barbiturates are metabolized by enzymes in the cytochrome P450 system in the liver. Furthermore, the barbiturates can induce increased activity in the cytochrome P450 enzymes that metabolize them (Ninan et al. 1998), resulting in diminished blood levels of some barbiturates over time at a given dose.

Drug-Drug Interactions

The barbiturates have the potential to interact with many other types of drugs, including valproic acid (Kapetanovic, 1981), a commonly used mood stabilizer and anticonvulsant (see Chapter 10). As some barbiturates, such as phenobarbital, can induce cytochrome P450 enzymes (Hoen et al., 2001), another source of drug-drug interaction is an increase in metabolism of certain drugs, with resulting elevations in blood concentrations.

Adverse Effects

A low margin of safety is one of the main hazards of the barbiturates (Sellers et al., 1999): The dose required for a therapeutic response is often precariously close to the dose that results in unwanted and even dangerous effects, such as respiratory suppression. The narrow therapeutic window of barbiturates leaves little margin for error or individual differences in sensitivity to the barbiturates and is one of the reasons that the benzodiazepines with their increased safety have largely replaced the barbiturates.

Addiction is a significant risk as all of the barbiturates carry a clear potential for psychological dependence (Whitlock, 1970). Coupled with this is physical dependence, as the body develops a dependence on barbiturates that results in a potentially lethal withdrawal syndrome that can include delirium and seizures (Morgan, 1990) if the drug is discontinued abruptly. Untreated, barbiturate withdrawal may deteriorate to delirium (Morgan, 1990), hallucinations, seizures, and even death (Coupey, 1997; Morgan 1990). Infants born to mothers taking barbiturates can also experience barbiturate withdrawal (Coupey, 1997).

While the barbiturates do induce drowsiness and sleep (Morgan, 1990) and have been used extensively for insomnia, they tend to alter sleep architecture, resulting in disrupted and potentially less efficient sleep and making them less-than-ideal sedative agents. In particular, the barbiturates tend to suppress rapid-eye-movement sleep (Lancel, 1999).

Respiratory suppression from barbiturate effects on brain centers involved in the control of breathing can result in death when high doses are ingested in intentional or unintentional barbiturate overdose. Use of other classes of drug instead of the barbiturates is sometimes preferred to avoid respiratory suppression, such as in controlling agitation in critical-care settings (Levine, 1994).

Uses

Mainly of historical importance, the barbiturates and their close relatives do still see occasional use in select clinical settings despite much more circumscribed indications than seen formerly. Some of the uses of the barbiturates and related drugs, however, can still be considered primary, while other uses are secondary, although in general other drugs are now used for conditions that formerly were treated by barbiturates (Morgan, 1990).

Primary Uses.   *Anesthesia.*   Some barbiturates are still used for anesthesia. For example, methohexital (Brevital) is a short-acting anesthetic agent that is used to induce anesthesia in preparation for electroconvulsive therapy (Gaines & Rees, 1992).

Epilepsy.   All of the barbiturates diminish a person's chances of having a seizure. Phenobarbital has been used extensively as an anticonvulsant and despite the availability of newer anticonvulsants still sees clinical use (Pellock, 2002).

Determination of Language Lateralization.   Amobarbital (Amytal) is used in the evaluation of memory and language localization in patients preparing for surgery to remove a focus of seizure activity from their brain (Diaz-Arrastia, 2002). In the so-called Wada test, amobarbital is injected into one of the carotid arteries to anesthetize for a few minutes the cerebral hemisphere on the same side. If the speech centers are located in the hemisphere anesthetized by the amobarbital, speech arrest occurs, enabling a determination of which hemisphere houses the speech centers for an individual person (Kolb & Whishaw, 2003).

Secondary Uses.   *Amytal Interview.*   Amobarbital (Amytal) has been used for the so-called Amytal interview in which a person is given amobarbitol to induce a state of disinhibition to facilitate an interview, in theory allowing the interviewer to extract otherwise guarded information (Kavirajan, 1999). For example, sources of stress have been proposed to be identified in cases of conversion disorder by use of serial Amytal interviews (Fackler et al., 1997). Any superiority of amobarbital compared to placebo to facilitate interviews is, however, poorly supported by controlled trials (Kavirajan, 1999) and the Amytal interview is little used now.

Brain Trauma.   An additional use of barbiturates is in cases of brain damage, such as from trauma or stroke. After severe brain trauma, intracranial pressure can rise, which has the potential to cause additional brain damage (Roberts, 2000). By decreasing the rate of cerebral metabolism and thus blood requirement, barbiturates are thought to lower the intracranial pressure (Robert, 2000). Roberts (2000), however, after reviewing barbiturate use in severe brain injury concluded that barbiturate use does not improve outcome.

Use in Analgesics.   The barbiturate butalbital is used in combination with aspirin and acetaminophen analgesics for the treatment of tension and migraine headaches (Silberstein & McCrory, 2001). Because of the risks associated with barbiturates, including dependence and withdrawal, the use of butalbital for headache is not a first-line choice (Silberstein & McCrory, 2001), with some authors arguing that the use of butalbital for this indication should be discontinued altogether (Young & Siow, 2002).

Alcohol Withdrawal.   Paraldehyde is occasionally used in the treatment of alcohol withdrawal and delirium tremens. Its use for these conditions, however, has been largely supplanted by the benzodiazepines, largely due to safety concerns (Shaw, 1995).

BENZODIAZEPINES

The benzodiazepines comprise a large class of commonly prescribed medications. Since the introduction of the first benzodiazepine, chlordiazepoxide (Librium), in 1961 (Bailey et al., 1994) and in part due to an improved safety profile compared to the barbiturates, the benzodiazepines have nearly completely supplanted the barbiturates (Morgan, 1990). Not without significant problems in their own right, the benzodiazepines continue to be used in the treatment of several different disorders (Lader, 1999).

The several different benzodiazepines may be classified based upon half-life (Bailey et al., 1994). According to this scheme, some benzodiazepines with short half-lives are triazolam (Halcion) (t1/2 = 2–4 hours) and midazolam (Versed) (t1/2 = 1.8 hours) (Bailey et al., 1994). Benzodiazepines with longer half-lives include halazepam (Paxipam) (t1/2 = 14 hours), alprazolam (Xanax) (t1/2 = 12–15 hours), temazepam (Restoril) (t1/2 = 10–15 hours), chlordiazepoxide (Librium) (t1/2 = 10–30), diazepam (Valium) (t1/2 = 20–80 hours), and flurazepam (Dalmane) (t1/2 = more than 100 hours) (Bailey et al., 1994). However, in part because of active metabolites, half-lives of the parent benzodiazepines do not necessarily predict the duration of action of the benzodiazepines (Bailey et al., 1994).

Mechanism of Action, Pharmacology, and Metabolism

The benzodiazepines initiate their effects by binding to the gamma aminobutyric acid type A (GABA$_A$) receptor. By binding to this site, the benzodiazepines facilitate the effects of GABA, resulting in an increased influx of chloride ions into the neuron (Sigel, 2002), hyperpolarizing the neuron and making it less likely to generate an action potential (Bailey et al., 1994).

Due to their shared mechanisms of action, the benzodiazepines all have several common pharmacological effects. They all tend to be sedating, a feature that leads to their use in anxiety and insomnia (Rickels & Rynn, 2002). Furthermore, the benzodiazepines have muscle-relaxant properties (Koga et al., 1992), and anticonvulsant activity (Tietz et al., 1989).

The benzodiazepines are extensively metabolized by the cytochrome P450 system in the liver. For instance, flunitrazepam is metabolized, among other enzymes, by the cytochrome P450 2C19 enzyme to desmethylflunitrazepam and 3-hydroxyflunitrazepam (Gafni et al., 2003). The cytochrome P450 enzymes convert many of the benzodiazepines to active metabolites, making for complex parent drug and active metabolite relationships (Bailey et al., 1994). Not all of the benzodiazepines have active metabolites. Lorazepam (Ativan) and oxazepam (Serax) do not undergo transformation to active metabolites (Bailey et al., 1994), making these drugs a consideration for clinical conditions in which simple metabolic schemes are essential. For example, elderly people may be particularly sensitive to some of the side effects of the benzodiazepines (Bailey et al., 1994), providing a possible advantage to benzodiazepines that are not transformed to other active benzodiazepines.

Drug-Drug Interactions

Benzodiazepines can interact with other drugs, such as with other central nervous system suppressants, such as barbiturates and alcohol, which may increase sedation and psychomotor impairment (Bailey et al., 1994). There have been reports describing interactions between benzodiazepines and other commonly prescribed drugs that require consideration. Nefazodone (Serzone), an antidepressant, for instance, inhibits one of the cytochrome P450 enzymes that is involved in the metabolism of alprazolam and triazolam, resulting in increased benzodiazepine concentrations (Greene & Barbhaiya, 1997) and elevating the chances of adverse effects from the benzodiazepines. Conversely, the discontinuation of nefazodone when prescribed concurrently with alprazolam can cause alprazolam concentrations to decrease, potentially inducing benzodiazepine withdrawal (Ninan, 2001).

Adverse Effects

Although generally safer than the barbiturates, the benzodiazepines can cause side effects of their own (Bailey et al., 1994). Some groups of people such as the elderly may be at particularly high risk to develop adverse effects from benzodiazepines (Lader, 1999). Their propensity to result in sedation (Curran, 1991), while helpful with insomnia, can produce daytime drowsiness that can interfere with a myriad of activities, and may result in accidents (Lader, 1999). Slurred speech, difficulty with gait, vertigo, and psychomotor difficulties are other adverse effects from benzodiazepine use (Lader, 1999). The benzodiazepines can also produce problems with memory (Curran, 1991), both after a single dose and when taken chronically (Kilic et al., 1999), and attention (Buffett-Jerrott & Stewart, 2002).

Benzodiazepines can result in behavioral disinhibition and dyscontrol similar to that associated with alcohol. For example, one study found patients taking alprazolam were more likely than those on placebo to have aggression in response to provocation (Bond et al., 1995). An important adverse phenomenon associated with benzodiazepines is date rape. Although associated with the rapidly acting (Schwartz et al., 2000) benzodiazepine flunitrazepam, several other benzodiazepines including clonazepam (Dowd et al., 2002), diazepam, oxazepam, and temazepam (Negrusz & Gaensslen, 2003), have been used to impair the victims' cognition, judgment, and memory during the sexual assault. Gamma-hydroxybutyrate, an endogenous analogue of GABA, is also used in date rape.

These drugs are also used to facilitate sexual assault because their affects occur quickly, and they produce anterograde amnesia for the assault (Schwartz et al., 2000). Flunitrazepam easily dissolves in liquid where it is colorless, odorless, and tasteless (Anglin et al., 1997), making flunitrazepam difficult to detect when given to people without their knowledge.

The benzodiazepines also carry a risk for tolerance, abuse (Bailey et al., 1994), and dependence (Lader, 1999), a significantly limiting factor in their use. In addition, flunitrazepam is abused as a club drug (Smith et al., 2002). Resulting in a faster onset of action, intranasal or intravenous use of flunitrazepam appears to result in a greater rate of abuse (Gambi et al., 1999).

Like the barbiturates, the benzodiazepines can result in a medically dangerous withdrawal syndrome, particularly if high doses of short-acting benzodiazepines are discontinued abruptly (Peturrson, 1994). Benzodiazepine withdrawal is characterized by anxiety, agitation, difficulty with sleep, headaches, sweating, and in some cases seizures (Peturrson, 1994).

Uses

Commonly prescribed, the benzodiazepines are used in a wide variety of clinical situations (Lader, 1999). Similar to the situation with barbiturates, benzodiazepine use can be categorized into primary uses, in which the benzodiazepines are commonly used, and secondary uses, situations for which benzodiazepines are occasionally prescribed.

Primary Uses. *Generalized Anxiety Disorder.* The benzodiazepines reduce anxiety (Curran, 1991) have been and continue to be used for generalized anxiety disorder (Rickels & Rynn, 2002), despite their risks of dependence. Various antidepressants, among them the specific serotonin reuptake inhibitors (SSRIs), have essentially replaced the benzodiazepines as first-line treatments for generalized anxiety (Vaswani et al., 2003).

Panic Disorder. Most benzodiazepines appear to be quite effective in diminishing or eliminating altogether the occurrence of panic attacks (Bruce et al., 2003). Like generalized anxiety disorder, though, the SSRIs, not benzodiazepines, are recommended as first-line agents in the treatment of panic disorder (Vaswani et al., 2003), although according to one study the benzodiazepines are still the most commonly prescribed class of drug for panic disorder (Bruce et al., 2003) and most patients on an SSRI for panic disorder also take a benzodiazepine (Bruce et al., 2003).

Social Phobia (Social Anxiety Disorder). The benzodiazepines appear efficacious for the treatment of social phobia, although their use is complicated by side effects and dependence (Versiani, 2000). Because of the limitations associated with the benzodiazepines, other agents, including certain antidepressants, may be a first-line treatment option for social phobia (Davidson et al., 1998).

Simple Phobia.   In certain severe cases of simple phobia that have been unresponsive to behavioral interventions, a benzodiazepine may be used as part of the overall treatment approach to simple phobia (Hollister, 1986).

Insomnia.   A frequent use of the benzodiazepines is for insomnia (Lader, 1999). Some experts recommend that if a benzodiazepine is used for insomnia, the duration of use should be kept to a minimum (Lader, 1999). In selected cases of insomnia that have not responded to other interventions, long-term use of benzodiazepines can be considered, although a complete sleep evaluation is warranted before starting such a course (Schenck et al., 2003). For the treatment of insomnia associated with depression, a benzodiazepine may be added to certain antidepressants (Schenck et al., 2003).

Alcohol Withdrawal.   In part because of their sedative and anticonvulsant properties, the benzodiazepines are first-line drugs in the treatment of alcohol withdrawal (Holbrook et al., 1999) and are safe and effective in diminishing and preventing the complications associated with alcohol withdrawal (Saitz & O'Malley, 1997).

Anesthesia.   Midazolam (Versed) is a benzodiazepine that commonly is used to sedate patients prior to procedures such as gastrointestinal endoscopy, where it also may confer amnesia for the procedure (Lazzaroni & Bianchi Porro, 2003) and laceration repair (Nordt & Clark, 1997). Flunitrazepam is used as a preanesthetic agent (Gafni et al., 2003) in preparation for other types of anesthesia.

Adjunctive Use in the Treatment of Mania.   An important use of benzodiazepines is as adjunctive treatment in bipolar disorder (Post et al., 1996). Benzodiazepines are used for the treatment of mania because of their sedative properties (Möller & Nasrallah, 2003), which can both decrease the agitation of mania (Alderfer & Allen, 2003) and induce sleep (Post et al., 1996), important elements in treating bipolar disorder.

Adjunctive Use in the Treatment of Schizophrenia.   While certainly not the mainstay of treatment for schizophrenia, the benzodiazepines do play an important adjunct role, as they can help with the agitation that often accompanies schizophrenia, particularly during stages of acute psychosis. Benzodiazepines also may help with akithisia, a feeling of restlessness and inability to sit and stand still that frequently accompanies the use of the older, traditional antipsychotics agents that still have a place in the treatment of schizophrenia.

Catatonia.   Argued to be a psychological disorder in its own right, catatonia can respond to treatment with benzodiazepines (Taylor & Fink, 2003).

Secondary Uses.   *Night Terrors and Sleep Walking.*   Drug treatment is generally not necessary for night terrors or sleep walking, disorders of stage three and four sleep. In certain cases, however, the use of a benzodiazepine may be required (Smeyatsky et al., 1992).

Muscle Relaxation. In addition to their behavioral effects, the benzodiazepines also produce muscle relaxation. For example, midazolam (Versed) can be used for muscle relaxation as part of the overall treatment in tetanus (Ernst et al., 1997).

Epilepsy. The benzodiazepines have anticonvulsant properties and are effective for several different types of seizures (Isojarvi & Tokola, 1998), although sedative side effects and tolerance have prevented widespread use of the benzodiazepines for many seizure disorders (Isojarvi & Tokola, 1998). However, the benzodiazepines diazepam (Valium) and lorazepam (Ativan) are important agents in the treatment of status epilepticus (Sirven & Waterhouse, 2003), a condition of continued seizure activity. In addition to their use in status epilepticus, the benzodiazepines are indicated for control of acute seizure activity (Isojarvi & Tokola, 1998).

Trigeminal Neuralgia. Trigeminal neuralgia, or tic douloureux, is a painful condition affecting the fifth cranial nerve and results in pain in the face and head (Kaufman, 1990). Although the anticonvulsant drug carbamazepine (Tegretol) is a first-line treatment for trigeminal neuralgia, the benzodiazepine clonazepam (Klonopin) is sometimes used for this condition (Sindrup & Jensen, 2002).

SODIUM OXYBATE (XYREM, GAMMA-HYDROXYBUTYRATE)

Another sedative-hypnotic is sodium oxybate. An illegally made and used form of the drug is known as gamma-hydroxybutyrate (GHB) (Teeter & Guthrie, 2001). Like flunitrazepam, GHB is illicitly used to facilitate sexual assault (Smith, 1999) and is frequently used in club-drug settings (Teeter & Guthrie, 2001). Naturally synthesized by the body, GHB may be an analog of GABA (Mason & Kerns, 2002), and, therefore, related to barbiturates and benzodiazepines. It remains unclear exactly how GHB and sodium oxybate work, but they may agonize the $GABA_B$ receptor (Krahn, 2003). Metabolized by the liver, sodium oxybate has a half-life of approximately one hour (Krahn, 2003). Associated with numerous and sometimes serious side effects, GHB use can result in euphoria (Gobaille et al., 2002), confusion, amnesia, respiratory suppression, vomiting, coma (Teeter & Guthrie, 2001), headache, dizziness, and enuresis (GHB Study, 2002). When abused, GHB has been reported to cause loss of consciousness, seizures, and extensive sweating (Degenhardt et al., 2002). Sodium oxybate is associated with headache, nausea, and enuresis (Krahn, 2003; U.S. Xyrem Multicenter Study Group, 2002). Possibly due to its induction of slow-wave sleep, sodium oxybate can cause somnambulism (sleep walking) (Krahn, 2003). Furthermore, GHB is associated with a withdrawal syndrome similar that seen with benzodiazepine and alcohol (Mason & Kerns, 2002).

DRUGS AND DATE RAPE

Imagine that you are at a club. Someone has bought you a drink. Not thinking about it, you tip it back and continue chatting with your friends. A few minutes later, you find yourself feeling nauseated and head to the bathroom. This is the last thing you remember before your friends, half an hour later, find you passed out in the bathroom, lacking the ability to stand on your own . . .

This is a common scenario for victims of the use of various club drugs. However, the results are often much more damaging, especially as many of these club drugs lead to unwanted sexual contact—rape. For this reason, several of these drugs have been labeled as "date rape" drugs. However, as the scenario above indicates, those on dates are not the only ones at risk. And, *both* women and men are potential victims (Harned, 2001). The most common date rape drugs on the market today are ketamine hydrochloride (K, Ket, Special K, Vitamin K, Vit K, Kit Kat, Keller, Kelly's day, Green, Blind squid, Cat valium, Purple, Special la coke, Super acid, and Super C), gammahydroxybutyrate (GHB, liquid ecstasy, scoop, or any other use of the acronym "GHB" such as Georgia Home Boy, Grievous Bodily Harm, etc.), flunitrazepam (rohypnol, roofies, rophies, rope, the forget pill, roche, R2, trip-and-fall), and alcohol.

It has been estimated that approximately one-half of all sexual assaults involve alcohol use by the perpetrator, the victim, or both (Abbey et al., 2001). This estimate may, in fact, be low. Though such numbers do not demonstrate a linear connection of alcohol to sexual assault (e.g., that alcohol causes sexual assault), there is a clear indication that alcohol is related to sexual assault. This is likely due to the additional fact that, similar to all of the date rape drugs listed, heavy alcohol use is related to sedation, loss of consciousness, loss of memory, and, as such, inability to resist sexual advances or sexual violence. In the case of actual date rapes, alcohol is likely to be the main avenue

for the ingestion of substances, either as itself or as a carrier, which permits the sexual perpetrator the ability to commit his or her act of sexual violence.

Producing symptoms similar to alcohol intoxication, flunitrazepam is benzodiazepine that is used legally in about sixty countries as an adjunct to general anesthesia. When dissolved in a drink, it is odorless and tasteless. After ingestion, it rapidly absorbs and takes effect in 20 to 30 minutes. When it is used in conjunction with alcohol, flunitrazepam can dramatically inflate the effects of alcohol, leaving the unknowing victim in a very precarious and dangerous place—especially given the fact that, when mixed with alcohol, there is a potential for overdose. Thankfully, some manufacturers of this drug have made it so that, when it is placed in a light-colored beverage, it turns the drink bright blue. When in a dark-colored drink, look out for cloudiness!

Originally used as a supplement for body-building, the substance gamma-hydroxybutyrate is also very dangerous. Depending on the dose, the drug can be related to feelings that range from mild euphoria to death. Furthermore, the range or response to the drug is narrow. When mixed with alcohol, the dose response drastically increases. Because it is usually distributed as a solution of unknown concentration, the use of this drug either in a club setting or in a date rape activity is extremely dangerous. That is, a dangerous amount of GHB, whether intentional or not, can easily be ingested, especially when it is mixed with alcohol. Only a small dose is necessarily, in some cases, to render a person unconscious within 5 to 10 minutes. Sometimes, there is a salty aftertaste associated with ingestion of GHB.

Finally, originally designed as an anesthetic and still used as such in children and animals, ketamine hydrochloride has also been associated with date rapes. This drug is associated with states of consciousness characterized by profound analgesia and amnesia, without the usually accompanying loss of consciousness. As this drug has recently been packaged in tablet forms that make it look like "ecstasy," many users may be unwittingly ingesting ketamine and experience its debilitating effects thinking they are ingesting ecstasy. That being the case, many may unknowingly be victims of its use, making its potential for use in sexual assaults even more insidious.

REFERENCES

Abbey A, Zawacki T, Buck PO, Clinton AM, McAuslan P (2001): Alcohol and sexual assault. Alcohol Research & Health 25:43–51.

Harned MS (2001): Abused women or abused men? An examination of the context and outcomes of dating violence. Violence Victimization 16:269–285.

Despite its potential for serious side effects and abuse, clinical trial data suggest that sodium oxybate may improve symptoms of narcolepsy such as sleep attacks and nighttime awakenings (GHB Study, 2002) by improving nighttime sleep (Krahn, 2003). In addition, sodium oxybate received United States Food and Drug Administration approval in 2002 for the treatment of cataplexy (muscle weakness associated with strong emotion that can occur in narcolepsy) (Krahn, 2003).

ZOLPIDEM (AMBIEN) AND ZALEPLON (SONATA)

Zolpidem and zaleplon are relatively recently released non-benzodiazepine hypnotics. Similar to benzodiazepines, zolpidem and zaleplon are considered here because of their hypnotic properties and similarity to the benzodiazepines. Zaleplon appears to initiate its sedative effects by selectively agonizing the omega 1 receptor of the alpha 1 subunit of the main GABA$_A$ receptor (Patat et al., 2001). Zolpidem also appears to bind to the omega 1 receptor (Terzano et al., 2003) of the alpha 1 subunit (Doble, 1999). Binding to the omega 1 receptor appears associated with sedation without effects on cognition and memory (Terzano et al., 2003). In contrast, the binding of benzodiazepines to the GABA receptor is less specific than that of zolpidem and zaleplon (Doble, 1999). Short acting, zolpidem has a half-life of approximately 2.4 hours, and zaleplon one of approximately 1 hour (Terzano et al., 2003). Generally well tolerated and safe (Wagner & Wagner, 2000), zolpidem can be associated with nausea, sleepiness, dizziness, and some memory deficits shortly after the drug is taken (Holm & Goa, 2000), although with minimal effects on cognition the day following use (Holm & Goa, 2000). Similarly, zaleplon appears to have little effect on cognition when used at the recommended dose (Patat et al., 2001). Zolpidem and zaleplon appear to cause less interference with sleep architecture than do the benzodiazepines (Wagner & Wagner, 2000). In comparison to benzodiazepines, zolpidem and zaleplon may have a lower potential for abuse (Wagner & Wagner, 2000). With efficacies similar to the benzodiazepines for the promotion of sleep (Wagner & Wagner, 2000), zolpidem (Holm &

Goa, 2000) and zaleplon (Patat et al., 2001) are indicated for the treatment of in-somnia for limited periods (Terzano et al., 2003).

PREGABALIN

Related to the sedative-hypnotics, pregabalin is a GABA analogue (Lauria-Horner & Pohl, 2003). Originally developed as an anticonvulsant (Ashton & Young, 2003), pregabalin appears to have an inhibitory effect on the nervous system (Lauria-Horner & Pohl, 2003). Early reports suggest that adverse effects with pregabalin are usually mild to moderate (Feltner et al., 2003) and consist of dizziness, drowsiness (Feltner et al., 2003), ataxia (difficulty with gait), and headaches (Lauria-Horner & Pohl, 2003). Preliminary data suggest that pregabalin may be an effective treatment for generalized anxiety disorder (Feltner et al., 2003; Pande et al., 2003). Pregabalin may also be effective in panic disorder, social phobia, and some pain disorders (Lauria-Horner & Pohl, 2003).

BUSPIRONE (BUSPAR)

Approved for use in generalized anxiety disorder by the United States Food and Drug Administration in 1986 (Apter & Allen, 1999), buspirone is a nonsedating anxiolytic drug that offers an important alternative in the treatment of anxiety (Goa & Ward, 1986). Despite a relatively slow onset of action, buspirone is effective in generalized anxiety disorder (Gorman, 2003).

Mechanism of Action, Pharmacology, and Metabolism

Buspirone appears to have a fairly complex mechanism of action, combining full and partial agonism properties. It is an agonist at presynaptic serotonin 1A receptors in the area of the dorsal raphe nuclei, receptors that are thought to initially decrease the release of serotonin until desensitization occurs (Blier & Ward, 2003). In addition to this effect, however, buspirone acts as a partial agonist on postsynaptic serotonin 1A receptors (Blier & Ward, 2003).

Importantly, buspirone does not interact with the GABA receptor (Taylor, 1988) and does not appear to have potential for abuse (Goa & Ward, 1986). Unlike benzodiazepines, buspirone does not impair psychomotor and cognitive performance (Goa & Ward, 1986; Troisi et al., 1993) and does not interact with alcohol (Malec et al., 1996). Furthermore, buspirone has no hypnotic and anticonvulsant properties (Goa & Ward, 1986). These factors combine to make buspirone a very different drug from the barbiturates and benzodiazepines.

A short half-life of approximately 2.5 hours (Mahmood & Sahajwalla, 1999) requires that buspirone be taken two to three times daily, resulting in some dosing inconvenience and contributing to the potential for missing doses. Like its putative mechanism of action, the metabolism of buspirone is relatively complex (Chouinard et al., 1999). The liver's cytochrome P450 metabolic system converts buspirone to several metabolites. One of buspar's main metabolites is 1-pyrimidinylpiperazine, an active drug in its own right (Mahmood & Sahajwalla, 1999).

Drug-Drug Interactions

Because it is free of interaction with the $GABA_A$ receptor, buspirone has a very different drug-drug interaction profile from the barbiturates and benzodiazepines. Unlike the barbiturates and benzodiazepines, buspirone does not interact with the effects of alcohol. Buspirone appears to be relatively free of many of the drug-drug interactions that plague many psychotropic medications (Chouinard et al., 1999), although certain other drugs, such as the antibiotic erythromycin, can increase buspirone levels in plasma (Mahmood & Sahajwalla, 1999). Like other serotonin agonists, buspirone may have the potential to cause a serotonin syndrome when combined with other drugs that increase the synaptic transmission of serotonin (Manos, 2000).

Adverse Effects

Although buspirone is generally well tolerated and devoid of many of the troubling and limiting effects that haunt the barbiturates and benzodiazepines, such as abuse potential, buspirone does have some side effects, including nausea, dizziness, and headaches (Sramek et al., 1999). Somewhat counterintuitively, buspirone may cause agitation and anxiety in some people (Liegghio et al., 1988). Buspirone results in less sedation than do the benzodiazepines (Goa & Ward, 1986). Like other serotonin agonists, buspirone may have the potential to cause a serotonin syndrome when combined with other drugs that increase the synaptic transmission of serotonin (Manos, 2000).

Uses

Generalized Anxiety Disorder. Buspirone is effective in the treatment of generalized anxiety disorder (Gorman, 2003; Rickels & Rynn, 2002). Its onset of action is, however, much slower than that of the benzodiazepines, requiring one to two weeks before a decrease in anxiety occurs (Goa & Ward, 1986). In children with prominent anxiety, buspirone may be a second or third choice behind certain anxiolytic antidepressants (Varley & Smith, 2003). Its lack of abuse potential and psychomotor effects make buspirone an important consideration in those cases of generalized anxiety disorder in which the SSRIs have not provided adequate treatment.

Social Phobia.   Although buspirone is an anxiolytic and social phobia is an anxiety disorder, buspirone at best appears to have only limited efficacy in social phobia (Davidson, 2003).

Obsessive-Compulsive Disorder.   The primary use of buspirone in obsessive-compulsive disorder is to augment other drugs to further diminish the severity of the obsessive-compulsive features (Jenike, 1993).

Agitation Associated with Alzheimer's Disease.   While ineffective for the underlying cognitive deterioration that accompanies Alzheimer's dementia, buspirone can be helpful in certain cases of Alzheimer's disease in which agitation becomes problematic (Tariot et al., 1997).

Depression.   Buspirone is used to augment antidepressants when they have resulted in only a partial improvement in the depression. In such cases, the addition of buspirone sometimes results in an improvement in the depression (Marangell, 2000).

Alcoholism with Comorbid Anxiety.   Buspirone may a have a role in treating combined alcoholism and anxiety (Cornelius et al., 2003), a condition in which its lack of interaction with alcohol may be a particular advantage (Malec et al., 1996).

ALCOHOL

Alcohol is widely used and abused worldwide. With some restrictions, alcohol is legal and readily obtained—and exerts profound effects on the brain and behavior. Approximately two-thirds of Americans drink alcohol (Andreasen & Black, 1991) and an estimated 15 to 20 percent of those who drink become dependent upon alcohol (Anthony & Helzer, 1995). With ramifications extending far beyond an individual brain, alcohol use is associated with far-reaching costly and detrimental effects on society at large. In Scotland, for instance, alcohol misuse is estimated to cost 1,071 million pounds sterling per year, which is greater than costs from many other illnesses such as stroke and diabetes mellitus (Varney & Guest, 2002). Furthermore, men are more likely than women to become dependent upon alcohol, with the number of women who have alcoholism only one-third that of the number of men (Limosin, 2002).

It is unclear why humans and other primates, and even other animals, have acquired such a taste and passion for alcohol in light of the overall negative consequences associated with excessive alcohol intake. Along this line, Dudley (2002) notes that for 40 million years, it is possible that the anthropoid lineage has been exposed to low levels of alcohol due to consumption of fermenting fruit. Dudley (2002) also describes several potential survival advantages of alcohol intake:

- Alcohol could have helped via smell in the location of fruit, identifying important stores of caloric intake.
- Alcohol could have increased the appetite to facilitate the consumption of large amounts of calories from a perishable food supply.
- The alcohol itself could have served as a source of caloric intake.

Alcoholism, then, could be in part a result of being genetically primed to consume alcohol. Whereas the amounts of alcohol in fermenting fruit is relatively low, the large amounts of alcohol now available, coupled with this possible evolutionary background, could lead to a predilection for alcoholism.

Mechanism of Action and Pharmacology

Neurotransmitter Systems Involved in Alcoholism.   In general, little is known about how alcohol exerts its effects in the brain (Aguayo et al., 2002), although many studies have suggested involvement with different neurotransmitter systems and anatomical regions in the brain. Alcohol appears to have many different effects on the brain, as well as on other organs, that are important for its behavioral, toxic, and physiological effects. Sim-Selley et al. (2002) found that rats trained to self-administer alcohol had diminished activity compared to controls of second messenger G proteins that are mediated by the opioid system in the prefrontal cortex, with no changes found in other brain regions such as the cingulate cortex, hippocampus, and amygdala. These findings suggest that the effects of alcohol may be mediated, at least in part, by the prefrontal opiate system and also indicate a connection between alcohol and the endogenous opiate system in the brain.

In a similar manner to benzodiazepines and barbiturates, alcohol interacts with the GABA$_A$ receptor, which appears to be involved with some of the behavioral effects of alcohol (Chester & Cunningham, 2002). Moreover, in rats, GABA antagonists reverse some of the behavioral effects of alcohol (Hyytia & Koob, 1995), further implicating the GABA system as a mediator of some of the effects of alcohol.

The chronic consumption of alcohol results in compensatory changes in several neurotransmitter systems including GABA, serotonin, glutamate, and acetylcholine (Blaho et al., 1996). When the amount of alcohol intake is substantially reduced or discontinued altogether, the alcohol-induced neurotransmitter adaptations can become pathologic and result in the alcohol withdrawal syndrome (Blaho et al., 1996). Alcohol withdrawal can progress from elevation in blood pressure, increased pulse, and nausea to seizures, hallucinations, confusion, and even death (Andreasen & Black, 1991). Benzodiazepines safely (Blaho et al., 1996) and effectively (Gatch & Lal, 1998) treat alcohol withdrawal.

Dopamine is implicated in the pathophysiology of alcoholism (Singh et al., 1999), and activation of the dopamine system in the striatum may be involved in the addiction and craving that occurs with alcoholism. In a model linking environmental and social factors with neurobiology, Heinz (2002), for example, suggests that the addiction of alcohol may be maintained by the conditioning of otherwise unimportant stimuli, such as sights, smells, and sounds, associated with alcohol consumption. These conditioned stimuli then release dopamine, which in turn stimulates reward craving—in this case, alcohol intake.

Not only interacting with brain dopamine and GABA systems, alcohol also antagonizes N-methyl-D-aspartate receptors, one of the same receptors with which glutamate interacts (Krystal et al., 2003). The antagonism of N-methyl-D-aspartate receptors may lead to some of the mood alterations that occur with alcohol use (Krystal et al., 2003). Alcohol releases endogenous opiates, which also can contribute to the elevated mood associated with alcohol intake (Singh et al., 1999).

Factors Involved in the Development of Alcoholism.   Alcohol consumption often begins in adolescence, and it is well known that adolescents and college students may engage in binge drinking. During adolescence, the prefrontal cortex and frontal dopamine projections continue to undergo developmental changes (Spear, 2002), potentially critical changes for mature brain functioning. This continued period of brain maturation coupled with adolescent exposure to alcohol have raised concerns that alcohol could both interfere with normal brain development and lead to increased risk for alcohol abuse and dependence as an adult. Unfortunately, no hard answers are yet available, with a recent paper concluding that additional research into these questions is required (Spear, 2002). Nevertheless, given the staggering use of alcohol among adolescents, this issue is an important one with possibly huge implications for society at large.

A related issue is the question of who develops alcoholism as adults and whether there are biochemical or neurobiological risk factors present even before the development of alcoholism. Several studies have shown that disruptive and delinquent behavior, impulsive behavior and poor impulse control, and concentration problems in children and adolescents are associated with adult alcoholism (e.g., Robbins, 1998; Rydelius, 1983). McCord reported that a mother's inability to control her son's disruptive behavior was an important factor predicting the development of alcoholism in the son (McCord, 1988). However, these findings are correlative and fail to resolve the question of etiology of both the disruptive behavior of childhood and adolescence and the alcoholism. Based on the available data, parental, neurobiological, genetic, and social factors could all play a role in the genesis of alcoholism (Baer et al., 2003), placing alcoholism firmly within the spectrum of complex disorders.

Alcohol-Drug Interactions

Alcohol has the potential to interact with a large variety of drugs through both pharmacokinetic and pharmacodynamic mechanisms (Mayer, 1984). For example, the presence of alcohol can slow or increase the metabolism of some antidepressant and antipsychotic drugs (Tanaka, 2003), as well as certain other drugs

(Fraser, 1997), resulting in elevated or lowered drug concentrations. The effects of alcohol with other central nervous system depressants such as benzodiazepines can be additive (Fraser, 1997), with additional sedation and central nervous system suppression occurring. When used with nonsteroidal anti-inflammatory drugs, alcohol increases the chances of gastrointestional bleeding over that associated with either agent alone (Fraser, 1997).

Physiologic and Cognitive Effects of Alcohol

Far from affecting the brain alone, alcohol can disrupt the physiology of multiple organs. As is well known, alcohol damages liver cells, or hepatocytes, resulting in several different types of liver disease (Lieber, 2001). The pancreas too can be damaged from alcohol, although the mechanism by which alcohol causes damage to the pancreas in unknown (Saluja & Bhagat, 2003). In addition to its effects on the liver and pancreas, alcohol damages the lining of the stomach and can lead to gastrointestional bleeding (MacMath, 1990). Another gastrointestional complication associated with alcohol is esophageal bleeding from rupture of blood vessels from the Mallory-Weiss syndrome (MacMath, 1990).

A variety of malnutrition and metabolic disorders are found in alcoholism. Gastrointestional disorders with resulting malabsorption and poor diet can contribute to the malnutrition observed in some cases of alcoholism (Butterworth, 1995). Alcoholism-associated thiamine deficiencies, for example, are found in the Wernicke-Korsokoff syndrome, a condition characterized by mental-status deterioration and memory deficits (Andreasen & Black, 1991). Thiamine deficiencies, in fact, may underlie much of the cognitive and memory deficits found in alcoholism, stressing the importance of nutrition in the treatment of alcoholism (Joyce, 1994). Caused by nicotinamide deficiency, alcoholic pellagra is yet another example of deterioration in brain function caused by malnutrition in some cases of alcoholism (Cook et al., 1998). Thyroid hormone abnormalities too are associated with alcoholism, and alcohol may be toxic to the thyroid gland, resulting in abnormal function of the hypothalamic-pituitary-thyroid axis (Hermann et al., 2002). Even chronic social drinking may be associated with some cognitive deficits, although not all studies support this conclusion (Parsons & Nixon, 1998).

The effects of alcohol and alcoholic drinks on cardiovascular physiology are multifaceted and intriguing, urging caution when interpreting the often inconsistent research findings in this area. An association has been suggested between limited alcohol consumption and improved cardiovascular health in human (Goldberg et al., 1995) and animal models (e.g., Roig et al., 1999). Daily intake of one to two glasses of alcohol appears to be related to an overall decrease in myocardial infarction (Lee & Regan, 2002). Red wine in particular seems to be more closely associated with cardiovascular protection than are other alcoholic drinks, such as beer (Rimm et al., 1996). However, wine is chemically complex and contains many compounds in addition to alcohol. For instance, wine has certain phenols that may have antioxidant properties (Kanner et al., 1994), and it is possible that it is these phenols, or other compounds, and not alcohol *per se* that contributes to the putative cardiovascular protection. In contrast, protective effects on cardiovascular health are not necessarily limited to wine alone (Belleville, 2002). Far from being resolved by available research findings, the results of studies of red wine on human cardiovascular health are often conflicting and difficult to interpret (Auger et al., 2002). With a slightly different approach to cardiovascular disease, in a study of male and female obese, hypertensive patients, red wine with lunch was found to lower blood pressure for much of the remainder of the day (Foppa et al., 2002), suggesting another way that red wine, although not necessarily alcohol, may interact with the cardiovascular system.

In contrast to the proposed benefits of alcohol on cardiovascular disease (Spies et al., 2001), alcohol can be directly toxic to the heart, where it can cause a cardiomyopathy (Lee & Regan, 2002). Alcohol also interferes with left ventricular function (Lee & Regan, 2002). In addition, high levels of alcohol intake are associated with cardiac arrhythmias (Spies et al., 2001) and high blood pressure (Lee & Regan, 2002); alcohol consumption may increase mortality in patients with coronary artery disease (Spies et al., 2001).

In humans and rhesus macaques, there appears to be a relationship between excessive alcohol intake, aggression, and brain serotonin function, with an important predictor of increased alcohol intake being impulsivity in both humans and some other primates (Gerald & Higley, 2002). In a paper exploring some of the evolutionary facets of alcoholism, Gerald and Higley (2002), speculate that some of the benefits in particular contexts associated with aggressive and impulsive behaviors may be involved in the genesis of alcoholism.

An important relationship exists between alcohol and aggression: both aggression towards others (Graham et al., 1998) and aggression directed against one's self. Alcohol consumption is a factor in many cases of violence, extending the already heavy burden of alcohol on society. Moreover, suicide is clearly linked to the use of alcohol, and completed suicide victims have had a high rate of alcohol disorders (Inskip et al., 1998).

Alcohol use can result in hallucinations and dementia (Greenberg & Lee, 2001). Alcohol consumption is associated with the well-known hangover, a condition that has both physical and psychological components. In addition to nausea, headache, and certain cardiac effects, alcohol hangovers are associated with cognitive and visual-spatial deficits (Wiese et al., 2000). Hangovers appear to have a number of causes including dehydration and direct effects from the alcohol itself (Wiese et al., 2000).

Teratogenic Effects of Alcohol

Tragically, alcohol can disrupt fetal development and affect multiple organ systems, including the brain. Fetal alcohol syndrome illustrates some of effects of alcohol on the developing fetus. Occurring in some children who were exposed to alcohol prior to birth, fetal alcohol syndrome is characterized by retarded body growth, short palpebral fissures (the distance between the medial corner of the eye and the outer corner, i.e., the width of the eye), flattened cheekbones due to poorly developed maxillary bones, and a thin upper lip (Astley & Clarren, 2001). Mental retardation also complicates fetal alcohol syndrome (Chaudhuri, 2000). Additionally, fetal alcohol syndrome patients often show difficulty with attention, distractibility, and both visual and auditory memory (Streissguth et al., 1989). The maximum amount of alcohol that can safely be taken during pregnancy is unknown, and even social drinking may cause cognitive deficits in the offspring (Streissguth et al., 1989), leading to the recommendations that absolutely no alcohol should be consumed during pregnancy.

In addition to fetal alcohol syndrome, prenatal exposure to alcohol may affect adult behavior in other ways. Prenatal exposure to alcohol, for example, is associated with alcohol problems twenty-one years later, even when family history of alcoholism and environmental factors are taken into account (Baer et al., 2003).

Alcoholism and Its Pharmacological Treatment

Alcoholism is characterized by a lack of control over alcohol consumption that is associated with various psychosocial problems (Singh et al., 1999). An extensive neurobiology appears to underlie alcohol dependence with the rewarding aspects of alcoholism involving dopamine, glutamate, and endogenous opiates (Anton, 2001). Craving appears to encompass glutamate and GABA systems (Anton, 2001). Alcoholism has a genetic component and may be associated with several genes, with each individual gene having a relatively small effect on the expression of alcoholism (Crabbe, 2002).

In part because of the neurobiological and genetic associations of alcoholism, a variety of drugs have been considered for the treatment of alcoholism, with varying though generally incomplete degrees of success. Certainly, drugs are used as only part of a much broader treatment approach involving educational (Gatch & Lal, 1998), psychological, and social interventions (Singh et al., 1999), such as Alcoholics Anonymous (Hartmann, 1997). The appropriate use of medications, however, is an important adjunct in the overall treatment of alcoholism. Several general types of drug treatment have been used in alcoholism, including disulfiram (Antabuse), acamprosate, opiate antagonists such as naltrexone (ReVia), and drugs that increase the transmission of serotonin (Singh et al., 1999).

Disulfiram (Antabuse).   Disulfiram irreversibly inhibits the action of the enzyme aldehyde dehydrogenase, an enzyme involved in the metabolic breakdown of alcohol. In the presence of alcohol, disulfiram increases levels of acetaldehyde, which results in a noxious reaction (Peterson, 1992) that is thought to deter people from consuming alcohol. Outcome studies of disulfiram, however, have been mixed. In general, while disulfiram may reduce drinking frequency, little evidence suggests that long-term abstinence is improved (Garbutt et al., 1999). Apart from its effects when combined with alcohol, disulfiram itself is associated with fatigue and headache, less commonly confusion, and potentially fatal liver damage (Chick, 1999).

Opioid Antagonists.   Because the endogenous opioid system appears to be involved in alcoholism (Singh et al., 1999), opiate antagonists have been investigated in the treatment of alcoholism. In theory, opiate receptor antagonism diminishes the euphoria associated with alcohol intake (Hartmann, 1997). The opiate antagonist naltrexone (ReVia, Trexan) may reduce relapse rates (Singh et al., 1999) and decrease craving for alcohol (Hartmann, 1997), but long-term abstinence does not appear to be significantly affected (Garbutt et al., 1999). Because it antagonizes opiate receptors, naltrexone can cause opiate withdrawal in people taking opiates in addition to naltrexone (Hartmann, 1997), making concurrent use of opiates a contraindication to naltrexone. In high doses, naltrexone can cause liver toxicity (Hartmann, 1997).

TABLE 5.1   Adverse Effects of Barbiturates, Benzodiazepines, and Alcohol

TYPE OF PSYCHOTROPIC	ADVERSE EFFECTS
Barbiturates	The dose required for a therapeutic response is often precariously close to the dose that results in unwanted and even dangerous effects; addiction is a significant risk; agitation, sweating, elevated blood pressure and heart rate, and an increased body temperature characterize withdrawal; change the structure of architecture of sleep, resulting in disrupted and potentially less efficient sleep; tend to suppress rapid-eye movement sleep; respiratory suppression from effects on brain centers involved in the control of breathing can result in death, and poor muscle coordination, clouded thinking and judgment, behavioral disinhibition, affective changes, and memory impairment, especially in the elderly; tend to suppress rapid-eye movement sleep; respiratory suppression from effects on brain centers involved in the control of breathing can result in death; and poor muscle coordination, clouded thinking and judgment, behavioral disinhibition, affective changes, and memory impairment, especially in the elderly.
Benzodiazepines	Daytime drowsiness; slurred speech; gait impairment; poor coordination and slowed reaction time; problems with memory; confusion; behavioral disinhibition and dyscontrol; and addiction and a medically dangerous withdrawal syndrome.
Buspirone	Dizziness, headaches, agitation, and anxiety.

TABLE 5.2   Clinical Uses of Main Classes of Sedative Hypnotics, Anxiolytics, and Alcohol

TYPE OF PSYCHOTROPIC	CLINICAL USES
Barbiturates	Anesthesia; epilepsy; insomnia; amytal interview; brain trauma; and alcohol withdrawal.
Benzodiazepines	Generalized anxiety disorder; panic disorder; social phobia (social anxiety disorder); posttraumatic stress disorder; simple phobia; insomnia; depression; alcohol withdrawal; anesthesia; mania (adjunctive); schizophrenia (adjunctive); night terrors; muscle relaxation; epilepsy; and trigeminal neuralgia.
Buspirone	Generalized anxiety disorder; social phobia, obsessive-compulsive disorder; agitation associated with Alzheimer's disorder; and depression.
Alcohol	Moderate doses may improve cardiovascular health, but this must be balanced against risks of addiction and other problems.

Drugs Increasing the Transmission of Serotonin.   As serotonin may be involved in alcoholism (Singh et al., 1999), drugs that increase the transmission of serotonin have been investigated for the treatment of alcoholism. Garbutt et al. (1999), however, concluded that little evidence supports the use of serotonergic drugs in alcoholism but suggest that they may have a role in cases of alcoholism comorbid for certain other psychiatric disorders such as depression and anxiety. For example, paroxetine (Paxil), a specific serotonin reuptake inhibitor used for depressive and anxiety disorders, was found helpful in people who had both social phobia and alcoholism in reducing anxiety and possibly even drinking (Randall et al., 2001).

Acamprosate (Campral).   Approved by the United States Food and Drug Administration in 1994 and also available in numerous other countries including France (Mason, 2001), acamprosate (Campral), which is structurally related to the amino acid homotaurine (Mason, 2001), affects the glutamate and GABA systems (Singh et al., 1999), may decrease the frequency of binge drinking (Garbutt et al. 1999), and appears to improve abstinence (Mason, 2001).

In Table 5.1, some adverse effects of barbiturates, benzodiazepines, and alcohol are listed.

Table 5.2 summarizes some at the clinical uses of sedative hypnotics, anxiolytics, and alcohol.

SUMMARY

The anxiolytics and sedative hypnotics comprise a diverse group of drugs that cause varying degrees of anxiolysis and sedation. The barbiturates are the oldest group of the anxiolytics and sedative hypnotics. Side effects and a low safety margin have greatly limited the use these drugs, although a few select barbiturates continue to see use in anesthesia, epilepsy, and in the mitigation of damage from various types of brain injury such as from stroke and trauma.

By acting at a site on the GABA$_A$ receptor, the benzodiazepines are thought to facilitate the action of GABA, the major inhibitory neurotransmitter of the brain. For several reasons, including increased safety, the benzodiazepines have largely replaced the barbiturates and, though no longer first-line drugs for some disorders, continue to be widely prescribed for a host of conditions, such as generalized anxiety disorder, panic disorder, social phobia, insomnia, epilepsy, and alcohol withdrawal. The benzodiazepines also are often used in conjunction with certain antidepressants that tend to disrupt sleep, although generally this use is for a short time only.

Side effects do complicate the clinical use of benzodiazepines, as they may result in drowsiness, slowed reaction time, reduced psychomotor function, disinhibition, falls, and addiction. A potentially dangerous withdrawal can occur if benzodiazepines are discontinued too rapidly.

Zolpidem and zaleplon are nonbenzodiazepine hypnotics that appear to act more selectively at the GABA$_A$ receptor than do benzodiazepines. Well tolerated and characterized by relatively short half-lives, zolpidem and zaleplon may have less abuse potential than benzodiazepines.

The anxiolytic buspirone has a very different mechanism of action from the barbiturates, benzodiazepines, zolpidem, and zaleplon, acting instead through presynaptic and postsynaptic serotonin 1A receptors—and not the GABA$_A$ receptor, as do the barbiturates and benzodiazepines. Because it does not interact with the GABA$_A$ receptor, buspirone is generally devoid of some of the side effects that are so troubling with the barbiturates and benzodiazepines. For example, buspirone does not result in addiction and impaired psychomotor performance. Likewise, it is not associated with a dangerous withdrawal syndrome. Although not generally considered the treatment of choice for most of the conditions for which it is used, buspirone continues to be prescribed for generalized anxiety disorder. Although there are exceptions, panic disorder does not seem to respond well to buspirone. Buspirone also sees some use as an augmenting agent in cases of depression and obsessive-compulsive disorder that have only partially responded to the primary drugs used to treat these conditions.

Widely abused, alcohol appears to affect the brain, as well as other organs, in a variety of ways. Similar to barbiturates and benzodiazepines, alcohol affects the GABA$_A$ receptor. Alcohol also seems to interact with the opiate dopamine and N-methyl-D-aspartate brain systems. Cessation of alcohol, particularly if abrupt, can result in a withdrawal syndrome characterized by elevated heart rate, increased body temperature, agitation, delirium tremens, seizures, and if untreated, death in some cases. The benzodiazepines are a safe and effective treatment for alcohol withdrawal. Alcohol is initially metabolized by alcohol dehydrogenase to aldehyde. Alcohol is toxic to many organs, including the brain, the thyroid gland, and gastrointestional system. Behavioral effects from alcohol are varied and pervasive. Alcohol impairs cognition and memory and increases aggression both towards others and the person using alcohol.

Although a large part of the treatment of alcoholism is based upon group and individual treatment, several drugs appear to have a role in the overall treatment of alcoholism. Disulfiram (Antabuse), for example, inhibits aldehyde dehydrogenase, resulting in an unpleasant build up of aldehyde, which presumably deters people from consuming alcohol while taking disulfiram. The opiate antagonists naltrexone (ReVia, Trexan) are used to treat alcoholism by supposedly inhibiting the reinforcing properties alcohol.

STUDY QUESTIONS

1. Describe the mechanism of action of the barbiturates and benzodiazepines.
2. In what ways does the mechanism of action of buspirone differ from that of the benzodiazepines?
3. Why does buspirone not have a potentially severe withdrawal syndrome as do barbiturates and benzodiazepines?
4. Outline a pharmacological treatment approach for generalized anxiety disorder. What drugs would you consider and why? If your first choice did not work, what would you consider as a second option and why?
5. Compare and contrast the side effects of buspirone and the benzodiazepines.
6. Design a drug for anxiety. What mechanisms of action would you consider and why? How would you minimize adverse effects from your new drug?
7. Describe the effects of alcohol on the brain.
8. Compare the use of benzodiazepines and barbiturates in the treatment of alcohol withdrawal. What are the advantages and disadvantages of each?
9. What neurobiological factors are related to alcohol dependence?

REFERENCES

Aguayo LG, Peoples RW, Yeh HH, Yevenes GE (2002): GABA(A) receptors as molecular sites of ethanol action. Direct or indirect actions? Current Topics in Medicinal Chemistry 2:869–885.

Alderfer BS, Allen MH (2003): Treatment of agitation in bipolar disorder across the life cycle. Journal of Clinical Psychiatry 64 (supplement 4):3–9.

Andreasen NC, Black DW (1991): *Introductory Textbook of Psychiatry*. Washington, DC: American Psychiatric Press.

Anglin D, Spears KL, Hutson HR (1997): Flunitrazepam and its involvement in date or acquaintance rape. Academy of Emergency Medicine 4:323–326.

Anthony JC, Helzer JE (1995): Epidemiology of drug dependence. In MT Tsuang, M Tohen, GEP Zahner (eds.), *Textbook in Psychiatric Epidemiology*. New York: Wiley-Liss.

Anton RF (2001): Pharmacologic approaches to the management of alcoholism. Journal of Clinical Psychiatry 62 (supplement 20):11–17.

Apter JT, Allen LA (1999): Buspirone: Future directions. Journal of Clinical Psychopharmacology 19:86–93.

Ashton H, Young AH (2003): GABA-ergic drugs: Exit stage left, enter stage right. Journal of Psychopharmacology 17:174–178.

Astley SJ, Clarren SK (2001): Measuring the facial phenotype of individuals with prenatal alcohol exposure: Correlations with brain dysfunction. Alcohol and Alcoholism 36:147–159.

Auger C, Caporiccio B, Landrault N, Teissedre PL, Laurent C, Cros G, Besançon P, Rouanet JM (2002): Red wine phenolic compounds reduce plasma lipids and apolipoprotein B and prevent early aortic athersclerosis in hypercholesterolemic golden Syrian hamsters (*Mesocricetus auratus*). Journal of Nutrition 132:1207–1212.

Baer JS, Sampson PD, Barr HM, Connor PD, Streissguth AP (2003): A 21-year longitudinal analysis of the effects of prenatal alcohol exposure on young adult drinking. Archives of General Psychiatry 60:377–385.

Bailey L, Ward M, Musa MN (1994): Clinical pharmacokinetics of benzodiazepines. Journal of Clinical Pharmacology 34:804–811.

Belleville J (2002): The French paradox: Possible involvement of ethanol in the protective effects against cardiovascular diseases. Nutrition 18:173–177.

Blaho K, Merigian K, Winbery S (1996): The pharmacology of alcohol withdrawal syndrome treatment reviewed: Efficacy, cost, and safety. American Journal of Therapeutics 3:79–96.

Blier P, Ward NM (2003): Is there a role for 5-HT1A agonists in the treatment of depression? Biological Psychiatry 53:193–203.

Bond AJ, Curran HV, Bruce MS, O'Sullivan G, Shine P (1995): Behavioral aggression in panic disorder after 8 weeks' treatment with alprazolam. Journal of Affective Disorders 35:117–123.

Bruce SF, Vasile RG, Goisman RM, Salzman C, Spencer M, Machan JT, Keller MB (2003): Are benzodiazepines still the medication of choice for patients with panic disorder with or without agoraphobia? American Journal of Psychiatry 160:1432–1438.

Buffett-Jerrott SE, Stewart SH (2002): Cognitive and sedative effects of benzodiazepine use. Current Pharmaceutical Design 8:45–58.

Butterworth RF (1995): Pathophysiology of alcoholic brain damage: Synergistic effects of ethanol, thiamine deficiency and alcoholic liver disease. Metabolic Brain Disease 10:1–8.

Byerley B, Gillin JC (1984): Diagnosis and management of insomnia. Psychiatric Clinics of North America 7:773–789.

Chaudhuri JD (2000): Alcohol and the developing fetus—a review. Medical Science Monitor 6:1031–1041.

Chebib M, Johnston GA (1999): The "ABC" of GABA receptors: A brief review. Clinical and Experimental Pharmacology and Physiology 26:937–940.

Chester JA, Cunningham CL (2002): GABA(A) receptor modulation of the rewarding and aversive effects of ethanol. Alcohol 26:131–143.

Chick J (1999): Safety issues concerning the use of disulfiram in treating alcohol dependence. Drug Safety 20:427–435.

Chouinard G, Lefko-Singh K, Teboul E (1999): Metabolism of anxiolytics and hypnotics: Benzodiazepines, buspirone, zoplicone, and zolpidem. Cellular and Molecular Neurobiology 19:533–552.

Cook CC, Hallwood PM, Thomson AD (1998): B vitamin deficiency and neuropsychiatric syndromes in alcohol misuse. Alcohol and Alcoholism 33:317–336.

Cornelius JR, Bukstein O, Salloum I, Clark D (2003): Alcohol and psychiatric comorbidity. Recent Developments in Alcoholism 16:361–374.

Coupey SM (1997): Barbiturates. Pediatrics in Review 18:260–264.

Crabbe JC (2002): Alcohol and genetics: New models. American Journal of Medical Genetics 114:969–974.

Curran HV (1991): Benzodiazepines, memory and mood: A review. Psychopharmacology 105:1–8.

Daniell LC (1994): Effect of anesthetic and convulsant barbiturates on N-methyl-D-aspartate receptor-mediated calcium flux in brain membrane vesicles. Pharmacology 49:296–307.

Davidson JR (2003): Pharmacotherapy of social phobia. Acta Psychiatrica Scandinavicum. Supplementum (417):65–71.

Davidson JR, Connor KM, Sutherland SM (1998): Panic disorder and social phobia: Current treatments and new strategies. Cleveland Clinic Journal of Medicine 65 (supplement 1):SI39–44.

Degenhardt L, Darke S, Dillon P (2002): GHB use among Australians: Characteristics use patterns and associated harm. Drug and Alcohol Dependence 67:89–94.

Diaz-Arrastia R, Frol AB, Garcia MC, Agostini MA, Chason DP, Lacritz LH, Cullum CM, Van Ness PC (2002): Bilateral memory dysfunction in epilepsy surgery candidates detected by the intracarotid amobarbital procedure (Wada memory test). Epilepsy & Behavior 3:82–91.

Doble A (1999): New insights into the mechanism of action of hypnotics. Journal of Psychopharmacology 13 (4 supplement 1):S11–20.

Dowd SM, Strong MJ, Janicak PG, Negrusz A (2002): The behavioral and cognitive effects of two benzodiazepines associated with drug-facilitated sexual assault. Journal of Forensic Sciences 47:1101–1107.

Dudley R (2002): Fermenting fruit and the historical ecology of ethanol investigation: Is alcoholism in modern humans an evolutionary hangover? Addiction 97:381–388.

Ernst ME, Klepser ME, Fouts M, Marangos MN (1997): Tetanus: Pathophysiology and management. Annals of Pharmacotherapy 31:1507–1513.

Fackler SM, Anfinson TJ, Rand JA (1997): Serial sodium Amytal interviews in the clinical setting. Psychosomatics 38:558–564.

Feltner DE, Crockatt JG, Dubovsky SJ, Cohn CK, Shrivastava RK, Targum SD, Liu-Dumaw M, Carter CM, Pande AC (2003): A randomized, double-blind, placebo-controlled, fixed-dose, multicenter study of pregabalin in patients with generalized anxiety disorder. Journal of Clinical Psychopharmacology 23:240–249.

Foppa M, Fuchs FD, Preissler L, Andrighetto A, Rosito GA, Duncan BB (2002): Red wine with the noon meal lowers post-meal blood pressure: A randomized trial in centrally obese, hypertensive patients. Journal of Studies in Alcoholism 63:247–251.

Fraser AG (1997): Pharmacokinetic interactions between alcohol and other drugs. Clinical Pharmacokinetics 33:79–90.

Gafni I, Busto UE, Tyndale RF, Kaplan HL, Sellers EM (2003): The role of cytochrome P450 2C19 activity in flunitrazepam metabolism in vivo. Journal of Clinical Psychopharmacology 23:169–175.

Gaines GY III, Rees DI (1992): Anesthetic considerations for electroconvulsive therapy. Southern Medical Journal 85:469–482.

Gambi F, Conti CM, Grimaldi MR, Giampietro L, De Bernardis B, Ferro FM (1999): Flunitrazepam: A benzodiazepine most used among drug abusers. International Journal of Immunopathology and Pharmacology 12:157–159.

Garbutt JC, West SL, Carey TS, Lohr KN, Crews FT (1999): Pharmacological treatment of alcohol dependence: A review of the evidence. Journal of the American Medical Association 281:1318–1325.

Gatch MB, Lal H (1998): Pharmacological treatment of alcoholism. Progress in Neuropsychopharmacology & Biological Psychiatry 22:917–944.

Gerald MS, Higley JD (2002): Evolutionary underpinnings of excessive alcohol consumption. Addiction 97:415–425.

GHB Study (2002): A double-blind, placebo-controlled multicenter trial comparing the effects of three doses of orally administered sodium oxybate with placebo for the treatment of narcolepsy. Sleep 25:42–49.

Goa KL, Ward A (1986): Buspirone. A preliminary review of its pharmacological properties and therapeutic efficacy as an anxiolytic. Drugs 32:114–129.

Gobaille S, Schleef C, Hechler V, Viry S, Aunis D, Maitre M (2002): Gamma-hydroxybutyrate increases tryptophan availability and potentiates serotonin turnover in rat brain. Life Sciences 70:2101–2112.

Goldberg DM, Hahn SE, Parkes GJ (1995): Beyond alcohol: Beverage consumption and cardiovascular mortality. Clinica Chimica Acta 237:155–187.

Gorman JM (2003): Treating generalized anxiety disorder. Journal of Clinical Psychiatry 64 (supplement 2): 24–29.

Graham K, Leonard KE, Room R, Wild C, Pihl RO, Bois C, Single E (1998): Alcohol and aggression: Current directions in research on understanding and preventing intoxicated aggression. Addiction 93:659–676.

Greenberg DM, Lee JW (2001): Psychotic manifestations of alcoholism. Current Psychiatry Reports 3:314–318.

Greene DS, Barbhaiya (1997): Clinical pharmacokinetics of nefazodone. Clinical Pharmacokinetics 33:260–275.

Hartmann PM (1997): Naltrexone in alcohol dependence. American Family Physician 55:1877–1879, 1883–1884.

Heinz A (2002): Dopaminergic dysfunction in alcoholism and schizophrenia—psychopathological and behavioral correlates. European Psychiatry 17:9–16.

Hermann D, Heinz A, Mann K (2002): Dysregulation of the hypothalamic-pituitary-thyroid axis in alcoholism. Addiction 97:1369–1381.

Hoen PA, Bijsterbosch MK, van Berkel TJ, Vermeulen NP, Commandeur JN (2001): Midazolam is a phenobarbital-like cytochrome P450 inducer in rats. Journal of Pharmacology and Experimental Therapeutics 299:921–92.

Holbrook AM, Crowther R, Lotter A, Cheng C, King D (1999): Diagnosis and management of acute alcohol withdrawal. Canadian Medical Association Journal 160:675–680.

Hollister LE (1986): Pharmacotherapeutic considerations in anxiety disorders. Journal of Clinical Psychiatry 47 (supplement):33–36.

Holm KJ, Goa KL (2000): Zolpidem: An update of its pharmacology, therapeutic efficacy and tolerability in the treatment of insomnia. Drugs 59:865–889.

Inskip HM, Harris EC, Barraclough B (1998): Lifetime risk of suicide for affective disorder, alcoholism and schizophrenia. British Journal of Psychiatry 172:35–37.

Isojarvi JI, Tokola RA (1998): Benzodiazepines in the treatment of epilepsy in people with intellectual disability. Journal of Intellectual Disability Research 42 (supplement 1):80–92.

Jenike MA (1993): Augmentation strategies for treatment-resistant obsessive-compulsive disorder. Harvard Review of Psychiatry 1:17–26.

Joyce EM (1994): Aetiology of alcoholic brain damage: Alcoholic neurotoxicity or thiamine malnutrition? British Medical Bulletin 50:99–114.

Kanner J, Frankel E, Grant R, German B, Kinsella E (1994): Natural antioxidants in grapes and wines. Journal of Agricultural and Food Chemistry 42:64–69.

Kapetanovic IM, Kupferberg JH, Porter RJ, Theodore W, Schulman E, Penry JK (1981): Mechanism of valproate-phenobarbital interaction in epileptic patients. Clinical Pharmacology and Therapeutics 29:480–486.

Kaufman DM (1990): *Clinical Neurology for Psychiatrists* (3rd ed.). Philadelphia, PA: W.B. Saunders.

Kavirajan H (1999): The amobarbitol interview revisited: A review of the literature since 1966. Harvard Review of Psychiatry 7:153–165.

Kilic C, Curran HV, Noshirvani H, Marks IM, Basoglu M (1999): Long-term effects of alprazolam on memory: A 3.5 year follow-up of agoraphobia/panic patients. Psychological Medicine 29:225–231.

Koga Y, Sato S, Sodeyama N, Takahashi M, Kato M, Iwatsuki N, Hashimoto Y (1992): Comparison of the relaxant effects of diazepam, flunitrazepam and midazolam on airway smooth muscle. British Journal of Anesthesia 69:65–69.

Kolb B, Whishaw IQ (2003): *Fundamentals of Human Neuropsychology* (5th ed.). New York: Worth.

Krahn LE (2003): Sodium oxybate: A new way to treat narcolepsy. Current Psychiatry 2:65–69.

Krystal JH, Petrakis IL, Mason G, Trevisan L, D'Souza DC (2003): N-methyl-D-aspartate receptors and alcoholism: Dependence, treatment, and vulnerability. Pharmacology & Therapeutics 99:79–94.

Lader MH (1999): Limitations on the use of benzodiazepines in anxiety and insomnia: Are they justified? European Neuropsychopharmacology 9 (supplement 6):S399–405.

Lancel M (1999): Role of $GABA_A$ receptors in the regulation of sleep: Initial sleep responses to peripherally administered modulators and agonists. Sleep 22:33–42.

Lauria-Horner BA, Pohl RB (2003): Pregabalin: A new anxiolytic. Expert Opinion on Investigational Drugs 12:663–672.

Lazzaroni M, Bianchi Porro G (2003): Preparation, premedication, and surveillance. Endoscopy 35:103–111.

Lee WK, Regan TJ (2002): Alcoholic cardiomyopathy: Is it dose-dependent? Congestive Heart Failure 8:303–306.

Levine RI (1994): Pharmacology of intravenous sedatives and opioids in critically ill patients. Critical Care Clinics 10:709–731.

Lieber CS (2001): Alcoholic liver injury: Pathogenesis and therapy in 2001. Pathologie-Biologie 49:738–752.

Liegghio NE, Yeragani VK, Moore NC (1988): Buspirone-induced jitteriness in three patients with panic disorder and one with generalized anxiety disorder. Journal of Clinical Psychiatry 49:165–166.

Limosin F (2002): [Clinical and biological specificities of female alcoholism]: Encephale 28:503–509.

MacMath TL (1990): Alcohol and gastrointestional bleeding. Emergency Medicine Clinics of North America 8:859–872.

Mahmood I, Sahajwalla C (1999): Clinical pharmacokinetics and pharmacodynamics of buspirone, an anxiolytic drug. Clinical Pharmacokinetics 36:277–287.

Malec TS, Malec EA, Dongier M (1996): Efficacy of buspirone in alcohol dependence: A review. Alcoholism, Clinical and Experimental Research 20:853–858.

Manos GH (2000): Possible serotonin syndrome associated with buspirone added to fluoxetine. Annals of Pharmacotherapy 34:871–874.

Marangell LB (2000): Augmentation of standard depression therapy. Clinical Therapeutics 22 (supplement A):A25–38.

Mason BJ (2001): Treatment of alcohol-dependent patients with acamprosate: A clinical review. Journal of Clinical Psychiatry 62 (supplement 20):42–48.

Mason PE, Kerns WP II (2002): Gamma hydroxybutryric acid (GHB) intoxication. Academy Emergency Medicine 9:730–739.

Mayer, JM (1984): Mechanisms of drug interactions with alcohol. Advances in Alcohol & Substance Abuse 3:7–19.

McCord J (1988): Identifying developmental paradigms leading to alcoholism. Journal of Studies on Alcohol 49:357–362.

Möller HJ, Nasrallah HA (2003): Treatment of bipolar disorder. Journal of Clinical Psychiatry 64 (supplement 6): 9–17.

Morgan WW (1990): Abuse liability of barbiturates and other sedative-hypnotics. Advances in Alcohol & Substance Abuse 9:67–82.

Negrusz A, Gaensslen RE (2003): Analytical developments in toxicological investigations of drug-facilitated sexual assault. Analytical and Bioanalytical Chemistry 376: 1192–1197.

Nemeroff CB (2003): Anxiolytics: Past, present, and future agents. Journal of Clinical Psychiatry 64 (supplement 3):3–6.

Ninan PT (2001): Pharmacokinetically induced benzodiazepine withdrawal. Psychopharmacology Bulletin 35:94–100.

Ninan PT, Cole JO, Yonkers KA (1998): Nonbenzodiazepine anxiolytics. In AF Schatzberg, CB Nemeroff (eds.), *Textbook of Psychopharmacology*. Washington DC: American Psychiatric Press.

Nordt SP, Clark RG (1997): Midazolam: A review of therapeutic uses and toxicity. Journal of Emergency Medicine 15:357–365.

Pande AC, Crockatt JG, Feltner DE, Janney CA, Smith WT, Weisler R, Londborg PD, Bielski RJ, Zimbroff DL, Davidson JRT, Liu-Dimow M (2003): Pregabalin in generalized anxiety disorder: A placebo-controlled trial. American Journal of Psychiatry 160:533–540.

Parsons OA, Nixon SJ (1998): Cognitive functioning in sober social drinkers: A review of the research since 1986. Journal of Studies on Alcohol 59:180–190.

Patat A, Paty I, Hindmarch I (2001): Pharmacodynamic profile of Zaleplon, a new non-benzodiazepine hypnotic agent. Human Psychopharmacology 16:369–392.

Pellock JM (2002): Treatment considerations: Traditional antiepileptic drugs. Epilepsy and Behavior 3:18–23.

Peterson EN (1992): The pharmacology and toxicology of disulfiram and its metabolites. Acta Psychiatrica Scandinavica. Supplementum 369:7–13.

Peturrson H (1994): The benzodiazepine withdrawal syndrome. Addiction 89:1455–1459.

Post RM, Ketter TA, Pazzaglia PJ, Denicoff K, George MS, Callahan A, Leverich G, Frye M (1996): Rational polypharmacy in bipolar affective disorders. Epilepsy Research. Supplement 11:153–180.

Rabow LE, Russek SJ, Farb DH (1995): From ion currents to genomic analysis: Recent advances in $GABA_A$ receptor research. Synapse 21:189–274.

Randall CL, Johnson MR, Thevos AK, Sonne SC, Thomas SE, Willard SL, Brady KT, Davidson JR (2001): Paroxetine for social anxiety and alcohol use in dual-diagnosed patients. Depression and Anxiety 14:255–262.

Rickels K, Rynn M (2002): Pharmacotherapy of generalized anxiety disorder. Journal of Clinical Psychiatry 63(supplement 14):9–16.

Rimm EB, Klatsky A, Grobbee D, Stampfer MJ (1996): Review of moderate alcohol consumption and reduced risk of coronary heart disease: Is the effect due to wine, beer or spirits? British Medical Journal 312:713–736.

Robbins LN (1998): The intimate connection between antisocial personality and substance abuse. Social Psychiatry and Psychiatric Epidemiology 33:393–399.

Roberts I (2000): Barbiturates for acute traumatic brain injury. Cochrane Database of Systematic Reviews CD000033.

Roig R, Cascón E, Arola L, Bladé C, Salvadó P (1999): Moderate red wine consumption protects the rat against oxidation in vivo. Life Sciences 64:1517–1524.

Rydelius PA (1983): Alcohol-abusing teenage boys: Testing a hypothesis on the relationship between alcohol abuse and social background factors, criminality and personality in teenage boys. Acta Psychiatrica Scandinavica 68:368–380.

Saitz A, O'Malley SS (1997): Pharmacotherapies for alcohol abuse. Withdrawal and treatment. Medical Clinics of North America 81:881–907.

Saluja AK, Bhagat L (2003): Pathophysiology of alcohol-induced pancreatic injury. Pancreas 27:327–331.

Schenck CH, Mahowald MW, Sack RL (2003): Assessment and management of insomnia. Journal of the American Medical Association 289:2475–2479.

Schwartz RH, Milteer R, LeBeau MA (2000): Drug-facilitated sexual assault ("date rape"). Southern Medical Journal 93:558–561.

Sellers EM, Hoornweg K, Busto UE, Romach MK (1999): Risk of drug dependence and abuse posed by barbiturate-containing analgesics. Canadian Journal of Clinical Pharmacology 6:18–25.

Shaw GK (1995): Detoxification: The use of benzodiazepines. Alcohol and Alcoholism 30:765–770.

Sigel E (2002): Mapping of the benzodiazepine recognition site on GABA(A) receptors. Current Topics in Medicinal Chemistry 2:833–839.

Silberstein SD, McCrory DC (2001): Butalbital in the treatment of headache: History, pharmacology, and efficacy. Headache 41:953–967.

Simeone TA, Donevan SD, Rho JM (2003): Molecular biology and ontogeny of gamma-amminobutyric acid (GABA) receptors in the mammalian central nervous system. Journal of Child Neurology 18:39–48.

Sim-Selley LJ, Sharpe AL, Vogt LJ, Brunk LK, Selley DE, Samson HH (2002): Effect of ethanol self-administration on mu- and delta-opioid receptor-mediated G-protein activity. Alcoholism, Clinical and Experimental Research 26:688–694.

Sindrup SH, Jensen TS (2002): Pharmacotherapy of trigeminal neuralgia. Clinical Journal of Pain 18:22–27.

Singh AN, Srivastava S, Jainar AK (1999): Pharmacotherapy of chronic alcoholism: A review. Drugs of Today 35:27–33.

Sirven JI, Waterhouse E (2003): Management of status epilepticus. American Family Physician 68:469–476.

Smeyatsky N, Baldwin D, Botros W, Gura R, Kurian T, Lambert MT, Patel AG, Steinert J, Priest RG (1992): The treatment of sleep disorders. South African Medical Journal, May 2 (supplement):1–8.

Smith KM (1999): Drugs used in acquaintance rape. Journal of the American Pharmaceutical Association 39:519–525.

Smith KM, Larive LL, Romanelli F (2002): Club drugs: Methylenedioxymethamphetamine, flunitrazepam, ketamine hydrochloride, and gamma-hydroxybutyrate. American Journal of Health-System Pharmacy 59:1067–1076.

Spear LP (2002): The adolescent brain and the college drinker: Biologic basis of the propensity to use and misuse alcohol. Journal of Studies on Alcohol, March (supplement):71–81.

Spies CD, Sanders M, Stangl K, Fernandez-Sola J, Preedy VR, Rubin E, Andreasson S, Hanna EZ, Kox WJ (2001): Effects of alcohol on the heart. Current Opinion in Critical Care 7:337–343.

Sramek JJ, Hong WW, Hamid S, Nape B, Cutler NR (1999): Meta-analysis of the safety and tolerability of two dose regimens of buspirone in patients with persistent anxiety. Depression and Anxiety 9:131–134.

Streissguth AP, Bookstein FL, Sampson PD, Barr HM (1989): Neurobehavioral effects of prenatal alcohol. Part III. PLS analyses of neuropsychologic tests. Neurotoxicology and Teratology 11:493–507.

Tanaka E (2003): Toxicological interactions involving psychiatric drugs and alcohol: An update. Journal of Clinical Pharmacy and Therapeutics 28:81–95.

Taylor DP (1988): Buspirone, a new approach to the treatment of anxiety. FASEB Journal 2:2445–2452.

Taylor MA, Fink M (2003): Catatonia in psychiatric classification: A home of its own. American Journal of Psychiatry 160:1233–1241.

Teeter CJ, Guthrie SK (2001): A comprehensive review of MDMA and GHB: Two common club drugs. Pharmacotherapy 21:1486–1513.

Terzano MG, Rossi M, Palomba V, Smerieri A, Parrino L (2003): New drugs for insomnia: Comparative tolerability of zopiclone, zolpidem and zaleplon. Drug Safety 26:261–282.

Tietz EI, Rosenberg HC, Chiu TH (1989): A comparison of the anticonvulsant effects of 1,4- and 1,5-benzodiazepines in the amygdala-kindled rat and their effects on motor function. Epilepsy Research 3:31–40.

Troisi JR II, Critchfield TS, Griffiths RR (1993): Buspirone and lorazepam abuse liability in humans: Behavioral effects, subjective effects and choice. Behavioural Pharmacology 4:217–230.

U.S. Xyrem Multicenter Study Group (2002): A randomized, double blind, placebo-controlled multicenter trial comparing the effects of three doses of orally administered sodium oxybate with placebo for the treatment of narcolepsy. Sleep 25:42–49.

Varley CK, Smith CJ (2003): Anxiety disorders in the child and teen. Pediatric Clinics of North America 50:1107–1138.

Varney SJ, Guest JF (2002): The annual societal cost of alcohol misuses in Scotland. Pharmacoeconomics 20:891–907.

Vaswani M, Linda FK, Ramesh S (2003): Role of selective serotonin reuptake inhibitors in psychiatric disorders: A comprehensive review. Progress in Neuropsychopharmacology & Biological Psychiatry 27:85–102.

Versiani M (2000): A review of 19 double-blind placebo-controlled studies in social anxiety disorder (social phobia). World Journal of Biological Psychiatry 1:27–33.

Wagner J, Wagner ML (2000): Non-benzodiazepines for the treatment of insomnia. Sleep Medicine Reviews 4:551–581.

Wartenberg HC, Urban BW, Duch DS (1999): Distinct molecular sites of anesthetic action: Pentobarbital block of human brain sodium channels is alleviated by removal of fast inactivation. British Journal of Anesthesia 82:74–80.

Whitlock FA (1970): The syndrome of barbiturate dependence. Medical Journal of Australia 29:391–396.

Wiese JG, Shlipak MG, Browner WS (2000): The alcohol hangover. Annals of Internal Medicine 132:897–902.

Young WB, Siow HC (2002): Should butalbital-containing analgesics be banned? Yes. Current Pain and Headache Reports 6:151–155.

CHAPTER SIX

THE PSYCHOSTIMULANTS, AMPHETAMINES, COCAINE, CAFFEINE, AND NICOTINE

The psychostimulants, which include methylphenidate, the amphetamines, and cocaine, as well as several other drugs, have a long and at times infamous history. Cocaine has been used by some cultures for centuries and now represents a major public health problem due to its potent addictive properties. Cocaine's mechanism of action appears to involve a blocking of the reuptake of dopamine, resulting in an increased concentration of dopamine in the synapse. Cocaine has few legitimate medical uses but sees widespread illicit use due to its ability to cause euphoria and heightened attention.

First synthesized by chemists in the 1880s, the amphetamines rapidly found their way into a variety of uses. For example, amphetamines were given to soldiers in the nineteenth and twentieth centuries to increase stamina and reduce battle fatigue. Amphetamines appear to increase synaptic dopamine levels and in addition increase the concentration of norepinephrine in the synapse. Unlike cocaine, which has few legitimate uses, the amphetamines are more complicated: On the one hand, many amphetamines—methamphetamine, for instance—are illegal, highly addicting, and associated with many social problems; on the other hand, other amphetamines, such as dextroamphetamine, are routinely prescribed for certain disorders, including attention-deficit, hyperactive disorder in both children and adults.

The remaining stimulants include methylphenidate, pemoline, and modafinil. Generally regarded as being less addicting than cocaine and many of the amphetamines, these drugs are widely prescribed. Methylphenidate is the most commonly prescribed psychotropic drug in children and has been in use since the mid-twentieth century. Its mechanism of action involves inhibiting the reuptake of both dopamine and norepinephrine, resulting in increased synaptic concentration of these neurotransmitters. Methylphenidate is an important drug for the treatment of both child and adult attention-deficit, hyperactive disorder.

Pemoline is generally regarded as a weak stimulant that also may increase synaptic dopamine, although its mechanism of action remains essentially unknown. Used much less frequently than methylphenidate, in part because of rare but potentially lethal liver damage associated with its use, pemoline does have a longer half-life and more prolonged behavioral effects than methylphenidate. This, coupled with its low-level addiction potential, results in continued use of pemoline in certain patient groups.

A more recent addition is atomoxetine, whose mechanism of action involves reuptake inhibition of norepinephrine. Not a stimulant in the usual sense, atomoxetine is considered here because of its efficacy in both childhood and adult attention deficit disorder. An advantage over methylphenidate is atomoxetine's lack of abuse potential.

Another recent addition is modafinil, which was released in the late 1990s. Although its mechanism of action essentially is unknown, modafinil, which appears to have a comparatively low potential for addiction, is used as a wake-promoting drug in narcolepsy, and preliminary evidence suggests that modafinil may be effective in attention-deficit, hyperactivity disorder.

Nicotine is considered in this chapter due to its stimulatory effects. Carrying the potential for addiction, nicotine interacts not only with acetylcholine nicotine receptors but also with other neurotransmitter systems including dopamine, GABA, and opiates. Nicotine may be involved with Alzheimer's disease and cognition. Several pharmacologic approaches exist for nicotine addiction. Nicotine replacement therapy is simply supplying nicotine without tobacco smoking. For instance, nicotine can be given, and then tapered and discontinued via nicotine gum and nicotine patches. Bupropion (Wellbutrin, Wellbutrin SR, Zyban) is an antidepressant drug that may facilitate the discontinuation of nicotine dependence.

The final drug reviewed in this chapter is caffeine. Widely used, caffeine appears to exert its stimulatory effects through antagonism of adenosine receptors. In addition to its wake-promoting effects, caffeine also can precipitate anxiety in certain people.

The psychoactive properties of the stimulant drugs, which include methylphenidate (Ritalin and others), the amphetamines (e.g., Dexedrine), and cocaine, have been long recognized. Cocaine has been used for centuries in some cultures, such as certain groups in South America (Dackis & O'Brien, 2003). In the 1880s, Sigmund Freud wrote several papers about cocaine and made several recommendations for its use, including a proposed role for cocaine in the treatment of morphine addiction (Brain & Coward, 1989). Few legitimate medical uses exist for cocaine today, yet it continues to be widely abused and is a significant public health problem (Brain & Coward, 1989). Cocaine is also of theoretical interest in that it shares many similarities in its mechanism of action with other stimulants, such as methylphenidate (Volkow et al., 2001).

The amphetamines too have a long history. First synthesized in 1887 (Murray, 1998), the amphetamines have been used for many different psychological disorders over the ensuing decades. In World War II, for instance, amphetamines were given to soldiers to reduce fatigue (Murray, 1998). Certain amphetamines, such as dextroamphetamine, are now used in the treatment of childhood and adult attention-deficit, hyperactive disorder (ADHD), as is Adderall, a combination of several different amphetamines (Spencer et al., 2001). On the illicit side, a veritable tribe of designer amphetamines have been synthesized and are commonly abused. Methamphetamine use, for instance, is not only increasing but may be associated with long-lasting neuronal deficits (Nordahl et al., 2003).

In addition to cocaine and the amphetamines, nonamphetamine, noncocaine stimulants are available. These drugs include methylphenidate (Ritalin and others), for which approximately 2.8 million prescriptions were written in the United States in 1995 for children and adolescents (Gray & Kagan, 2000), pemoline (Cylert), and phentermine. Modafinil (ProVigil) is a stimulant-like drug used for narcolepsy (Mitler & Hayduk, 2002). Even though it is not technically a stimulant, atomoxetine (Strattera) is considered here because it is primarily indicated for the treatment of ADHD (Kratochvil et al., 2003). Possibly the most widely used drug in the world (Nawrot et al., 2003), caffeine is reviewed in this chapter, as is nicotine, which in addition to its addictive properties (Glover et al., 2003) appears to have important effects on cognition (Levin & Rezvani, 2002).

METHYLPHENIDATE (RITALIN AND OTHERS), PEMOLINE (CYLERT), AND PHENTERMINE

In part due to the increased recognition of attention-deficit, hyperactive disorder (ADHD), the use of methylphenidate for ADHD has increased sharply (Volkow et al., 2003). Although methylphenidate is the most frequently prescribed drug for ADHD (Pelham et al., 1995), other stimulants are also used to treat ADHD, such as pemoline (Pelham et al., 1995). Another stimulant, phentermine, is sometimes used to treat obesity (Stafford & Radley, 2003).

Mechanism of Action, Pharmacology, and Metabolism

Methylphenidate blocks the reuptake of dopamine and norepinephrine from the synapse into the presynaptic neuron, thus increasing synaptic concentrations of both dopamine and norepinephrine, although its reuptake inhibition of dopamine is greater than that of norepinephrine (Turner et al., 2003). This mechanism of action, particularly as regards dopamine, is consistent with the findings that an abnormal form of the dopamine transporter gene is associated with ADHD (DiMaio et al., 2003). Methylphenidate is metabolized to ritalinic acid, the major main metabolite of methylphenidate (DeVane et al., 2000). Peak concentrations occur approximately two hours after oral ingestion of methylphenidate (Kimko et al., 1999). Methylphenidate has a short half-life of approximately two to three hours (Kimko et al., 1999), which necessitates multiple daily doses. Because of methylphenidate's short half-life, new preparations of methylphenidate have been produced that slow its absorption, providing formulations of methylphenidate that can be given once daily (Markowitz et al., 2003) in an effort to improve patient compliance (Swanson et al., 2003).

A second stimulant is pemoline, which is also used to treat ADHD but less often than methylphenidate is (Pelham et al., 1995). The mechanism of action of pemoline is unknown, but like other stimulants, pemoline may affect dopamine, as it is hypothesized that it affects presynaptic release of dopamine as well as inhibits its reuptake (Markowitz & Patrick, 2001). One potential advantage of pemoline, however, is a longer half-life than the regular-release form of methylphenidate, resulting in an increased duration of clinical effect and diminishing the need for multiple daily dosings (Pelham et al., 1995). Whereas the therapeutic effects of methylphenidate in ADHD may be observed in a matter of hours after the medication is given, pemoline may require up to eight weeks before an improvement is noted (Pelham et al., 1995). Other studies, however, have noted beneficial effects within two days after beginning a course of pemoline, particularly if higher doses are used (Pelham et al., 1995).

Like methylphenidate, phentermine appears to increase the synaptic concentrations of dopamine and norepinephrine (Ulus et al., 2000). Phentermine also may block monoamine oxidase, inhibiting the metabolic breakdown of serotonin and other neurotransmitters in a fashion similar to some monoamine oxidase inhibitors, like meclobemide (Ulus et al., 2000) (see Chapter 9 for discussion of monoamine oxidase inhibiting drugs). Thus, phentermine in addition to being a stimulant is in many respects a monoamine oxidase inhibitor and necessitates many of the precautions that the other monoamine oxidase inhibitors require. Caution especially is required when using phentermine with other drugs, such as ones that increase synaptic concentrations of serotonin; in fact, it may have been this property of phentermine that led to the heart valve damage and pulmonary hypertension when phentermine was combined with fenfluramine and dexfenfluramine as fen-phen (Ulus et al., 2000).

Drug-Drug Interactions

Like most other medications, methylphenidate has the potential to interact with other drugs. For example, methylphenidate can be involved in pharmacokinetic interactions (Markowitz & Patrick, 2001), potentially resulting in altered concentrations of certain drugs. Significant tooth grinding (bruxism) and abnormal movements have been reported in children taking methylphenidate and the anticonvulsant valproic acid (Gara & Roberts, 2000). Relatively little is known about drug-drug interactions with pemoline, and there are few reports to provide guidance, although there is a report of low blood pressure occurring in a person taking pemoline who underwent general anesthesia (Bohringer et al., 2000). Because of its monoamine-oxidase–inhibiting properties, phentermine should not be combined with other drugs that increase the transmission of serotonin, such as fenfluramine (Ulus et al., 2000). Finally, stimulants should not be combined with monoamine-oxidase–inhibiting antidepressants (Markowitz & Patrick, 2001) (see Chapter 9).

Adverse Effects

Many potential side effects may complicate treatment with methylphenidate, pemoline, and phentermine. Some of these have proven to be quite controversial (Biederman, 2003) and have been an important impetus in the search for alternative medications that can be more safely used in the place of methylphenidate, pemoline, and phentermine. Commonly seen problems are an elevated blood pressure and heart rate (Elia et al., 1999). Of significant concern in many cases is a diminished appetite (Elia et al., 1999) that can result in weight loss. In some children, there has been evidence of stunted growth from stimulants (Elia et al., 1999; Klein et al., 1988a). Although it remains controversial whether stimulants actually do result in slowed growth and diminished adult height (Elia et al., 1999; Klein et al., 1988b; Stevenson & Wolraich, 1989), more recent data suggest that methylphenidate may indeed suppress growth (Lisska & Rivkees, 2003). Because of these concerns, it is important to monitor weight and height in children and adolescents who are taking these medications, as well as to encourage nutritional eating habits.

The stimulants may cause psychotic symptoms (Cherland & Fitzpatrick, 1999). Although an uncommon occurrence, motor tics and involuntary muscle contractions can be caused or induced by the stimulants (Stevenson & Wolraich, 1989). Despite the propensity of stimulants to cause motor tics, methylphenidate has been safely used in children with mild to moderate tic disorders (Gadow et al., 1999).

A major concern with the stimulants is that of addiction and abuse, and methylphenidate does carry a potential for abuse (Kollins, 2003). The relationship between methylphenidate and substance abuse is complicated, though, because ADHD itself appears to be a risk factor for substance abuse (Biederman, 2003). However, conclusive evidence demonstrating elevated rates of substance abuse in adolescence and adulthood related to stimulant exposure has not been found (Biederman, 2003). Similarly, concern exists that methylphenidate may increase the risk of later drug addiction, although some evidence suggest that, in fact, treatment of adolescents diagnosed with ADHD with stimulants was associated with less substance abuse than untreated adolescents with ADHD (Biederman, 2003).

There is concern that methylphenidate is abused by certain groups, such as college students who are not prescribed methylphenidate. Teeter et al. (2003), for example, reported that out of a randomly selected sample of 3,500 undergraduate students from a large public university, 3 percent of the 2,250 students who responded reported nonprescription use of methylphenidate within the past year, suggesting that stimulant abuse among college students may be a significant source of drug abuse. This same study also found that college students who illicitly used methylphenidate were more likely than prescribed methylphenidate users and non-methylphenidate users to have used alcohol and other drugs.

Finally, pemoline is associated with liver damage, ranging from mild toxicity to life-threatening or fatal liver damage (Abbiati et al., 2002). For people taking pemoline, it is recommended that liver enzyme tests be obtained during treatment to monitor for liver damage (Adcock et al., 1998). In one controlled, short-term (four weeks on active drug) study using a double-blind crossover design involving twenty-one adolescents with ADHD, no evidence of liver disease was found (Bostic et al., 2000), although the limited time of pemoline exposure makes extrapolation to more prolonged use of pemoline difficult.

MODAFINIL (PROVIGIL)

Chemically unrelated to other stimulants (Rugino & Copley, 2001) such as methylphenidate and the amphetamines, modafinil (ProVigil) is a wake-promoting drug (Jasinski & Kovacevic-Ristanovic, 2000) that appears to work very differently from other, more traditional, stimulants (Jasinski & Kovacevic-Ristanovic, 2000). Modafinil is approved by the United States Food and Drug Administration as a wakefulness-promoting agent for daytime somnolence associated with narcolepsy (Rugino & Copley, 2001).

Mechanism of Action, Pharmacology, and Metabolism

While the mechanism of action of modafinil remains only incompletely understood (Rugino & Copley, 2001), it does appear to be different from that of other stimulants (Jasinski & Kovacevic-Ristanovic, 2000). Modafinil may affect the primary inhibitory neurotransmitter GABA and the excitatory neurotransmitter glutamate (Rugino & Copley, 2001). Presumably by altering the balance between GABA and glutamate—inhibition and excitation—modafinil may alter the activity of several brain structures involved in the control of the autonomic nervous system and regulation of other parts of the brain. The regions affected by modafinil include the hypothalamus, parts of the thalamus, part of the amygdala, and the hippocampus (Rugino & Copley, 2001). It also has been proposed that modafinil may interact with the hypocretin-orexin system in the hypothalamus (Sigel, 2000). Modafinil appears to have less potential for dependence than the other stimulants (Jasinski & Kovacevic-Ristanovic, 2000). Metabolized by the liver to two inactive compounds, modafinil acid and modafinil sulfone (Rugino & Copley, 2001), modafinil has a half-life of approximately 12 to 15 hours (Robertson & Hellriegel, 2003), allowing for once-daily dosing (Rugino & Copley, 2001).

Drug-Drug Interactions

Modafinil may inhibit some cytochrome P450 enzymes and induce others (Robertson & Hellriegel, 2003). For example, modafinil may interact with the benzodiazepine triazolam (Halcion) by inducing gastrointestional cytochrome enzyme P450 3A4 (Robertson & Hellriegel, 2003).

Adverse Effects

In general, modafinil appears to be well tolerated (Rugino & Copley, 2001). As might be expected from a wake-promoting drug, excessive stimulation can be an effect of modafinil (Teitelman, 2001). In addition, gastrointestional upset (Teitelman, 2001), headaches, lightheadedness, and tremors have been reported to result in some cases from modafinil treatment (Rugino & Copley, 2001).

THE AMPHETAMINES

First synthesized in 1887 (Murray, 1998), the amphetamines have been used for a variety of indications. Canadian, German, and English soldiers, for example, took amphetamines in World War II to combat fatigue, and the drug was used by U.S. soldiers in the Vietnam and Korean wars (Murray, 1998). Today, amphetamines such as dextroamphetamine (Dexedrine) (Greenhill et al., 2001) are used in the treatment of ADHD and other disorders. Also used to treat ADHD is Adderall (Spencer et al., 2001). Composed of both the right and left isomers of different amphetamines (Spencer et al., 2001), Adderall contains *d*-amphetamine saccharate, *d, l*-amphetamine aspartate, *d*-amphetamine sulfate, and *d, l*-amphetamine sulfate (Ahmann et al., 2001). Other amphetamines have been developed that are highly abusable. For example, an amphetamine derivative first synthesized in 1914 (Liberg et al., 1998), methylenedioxymethamphetamine (MDMA, ecstasy) is a popular drug of abuse that may be toxic to human neurons (Green et al., 2003; Lyles & Cadet, 2003).

Mechanism of Action

Amphetamines inhibit the presynaptic reuptake of dopamine, norepinephrine, and serotonin to increase the synaptic concentration of these neurotransmitters (Vanderschuren et al., 2003). In addition, through a process known as reverse transport, amphetamines facilitate the neuronal release of dopamine, norepinephrine, and serotonin, thus increasing synaptic levels of these neurotransmitters (Vanderschuren et al., 2003). Amphetamines also release these neurotransmitters from storage vesicles into the intracellular fluid, making these neurotransmitters available for reverse transport (Vanderschuren, 2003). Various chemical modifications to the basic amphetamine structure result in other psychoactive compounds. For example, the so-called designer drugs (Christopherson, 2000) methylenedioxyamphetamine (MDA), originally synthesized in 1910 (Christopherson, 2000), and methylenedioxymethamphetamine (MDMA, ecstasy) are amphetamine derivatives (see Chapter 8) that can promote socialization

(Hegadoren et al., 1999). MDMA also shares some similarity with hallucinogens (Freese et al., 2002) and is more fully discussed in Chapter 8. In addition to the re-uptake inhibition of dopamine and norepinephrine, dextroamphetamine also inhibits monoamine oxidase (Ramsay & Hunter, 2002), a mechanism that may contribute to its effects. Methylenedioxymethamphetamine releases serotonin (Schmued, 2003) and dopamine (Green et al., 2003) from neurons.

Behavioral Effects

Amphetamine use produces euphoria and a short-lived elevation in mood (Murray, 1998), although amphetamines are ineffective as antidepressants and, in fact, can result in depression in some cases (Murray, 1998). In addition, amphetamines diminish appetite (Murray, 1998).

Drug-Drug Interactions

Because of their effects on dopamine and norepinephrine, amphetamines should not be combined with monoamine oxidase inhibitor antidepressants (see Chapter 9) (Markowitz & Patrick, 2001). In fact, the combination of amphetamine and monoamine oxidase inhibitors has resulted in fatalities (Markowitz & Patrick, 2001). Furthermore, drugs that inhibit the cytochrome P450 enzyme 2D6, such as fluoxetine (Prozac; see Chapter 9) may possibly increase blood levels of amphetamines, as amphetamines are metabolized by the 2D6 enzyme (Markowitz & Patrick, 2001). More data are needed before clear conclusions about the potential for pharmacokinetic interactions between amphetamines and 2D6 inhibitors.

Adverse Effects

The side effects of the amphetamines are similar to those of methylphenidate. The amphetamines can diminish appetite (Elia et al., 1999), resulting in loss of weight. In a placebo-controlled trial, reported adverse effects from Adderall were diminished appetite, insomnia, stomach pain, and headaches with higher doses (Ahmann et al., 2001). In addition to these effects, cardiovascular effects also can occur, such has an elevated heart rate and increased blood pressure in some people taking these drugs (Elia et al., 1999). The psychosis associated with amphetamine (Murray, 1998) and methamphetamine use (Yui et al., 2000) is similar to that observed with schizophrenia and characterized by paranoia and hallucinations. Methamphetamine use also is associated with violence (Buffenstein et al., 1999).

The psychosis may last even after the methylenedioxymethamphetamine is no longer present in the body and can reoccur in response to stress (Yui et al., 2000). Regarding people with schizophrenia who have abused amphetamines, the relationship between the amphetamine use and schizophrenia is unclear (Dalmau et al., 1999): The person could have been at risk for the development of psychosis and the drug catalyzed the psychosis, or, alternatively, the amphetamine could have produced a long-lasting psychosis.

Addiction is of course an important adverse effect of amphetamines (Srisurapanont et al., 2001a). Unfortunately, given the adverse effects of amphetamine abuse, limited pharmacological treatments are available (Srisurapanont et al., 2001a). Intensive psychosocial and behavioral outpatient therapies generally are recommended for methamphetamine dependence, although certain groups such as those with psychosis and agitation and pregnant women may require inpatient treatment at least initially (Rawson et al., 2002).

Although methylenedioxymethamphetamine is used to produce euphoria and increased energy (Liberg et al., 1998), it is also associated with psychosis and depression (Shannon, 2000).

Furthermore, methylenedioxymethamphetamine causes long-term neurotoxic effects in serotonin neurons in nonhuman primates (Green et al., 2003). The effects of methylenedioxymethamphetamine on humans remain unclear (Lyles & Cadet, 2003), but neuronal damage in heavy users has been suggested (Green et al., 2003). Even a single dose of methylenedioxymethamphetamine has been associated with neuronal degeneration in rats (Schmued, 2003). Methylenedioxymethamphetamine also can produce renal failure, liver damage (Liberg et al., 1998), low serum sodium (hyponatremia) (Shannon, 2000), and a dose-dependent and potentially fatal rise in body temperature (Green et al., 2003). The discontinuation of amphetamines can produce a withdrawal syndrome characterized be a strong craving for amphetamine that can lead to relapse (Srisurapanont et al., 2001b). Unfortunately, there is no available pharmacologic treatment to attenuate amphetamine withdrawal (Srisurapanont et al., 2001b).

COCAINE

Obtained from the leaves of the coca plant (Brain & Coward, 1989), cocaine has been used for centuries for many different types of conditions, including, as is well known, recreation. The earliest known use of cocaine dates to before the twelfth century among the pre-Incas of Peru (Brain & Coward, 1989). In the mid-1880s, Sigmund Freud wrote a series of papers on cocaine and suggested several possible therapeutic uses, including roles in digestive disorders and asthma (Brain & Coward, 1989). Used by an estimated 1.5 million Americans in 1995 (Bolla et al., 1998), cocaine remains widely abused with few legitimate uses (Brain & Coward, 1989). Despite this, cocaine remains of interest in understanding the behavioral pharmacology of the stimulants (Schenk, 2002), and cocaine's potent addictive properties make it an important pharmacological model for understanding some aspects of brain reward systems and the neurobiology of addiction, dependence, and abuse.

Mechanism of Action, Pharmacology, and Metabolism

Cocaine appears to block the reuptake of dopamine (Lima et al., 2003), norepinephrine, and serotonin (Vanderschuren et al., 2003), increasing the synaptic concentrations of these neurotransmitters. Methylphenidate may block the reuptake of dopamine more potently than cocaine does (Vastag, 2001). Factors affecting the differences between cocaine and methylphenidate could be the rate at which dopamine is increased in the synapse. Unlike orally given methylphenidate, which may take an hour or so to reach the brain and increase synaptic dopamine levels, smoked or inhaled cocaine makes its way to the brain and increases dopamine in the synapse within seconds (Vastag, 2001). In fact, there appears to be a direct relationship between cocaine-induced euphoria and the speed with which cocaine binds to dopamine reuptake receptors (Dackis & O'Brien, 2003). Another difference between the mechanisms of action of cocaine and methylphenidate is that in addition to inhibiting the reuptake of dopamine, cocaine also interferes with the reuptake of serotonin (Lima et al., 2003). Cocaine also acutely increases and chronically depletes glutamate (Dackis & O'Brien, 2003). Another effect of cocaine is antagonism of cellular sodium channels, which can lead to cardiac arrythmias (Kolecki & Curry, 1997).

Drug-Drug Interactions

Like other drugs, cocaine can result in drug-drug interactions. For example, cocaine used together with alcohol may increase the euphoria and possibly buffer the dysphoria when coming off cocaine (Pennings et al., 2002). However, the combination of cocaine and alcohol can produce cocaethylene, a substance that is toxic to the heart (Pennings et al., 2002). Behaviorally, the concomitant use of cocaine and alcohol may result in increased violent thoughts (Pennings et al., 2002).

Behavioral and Physiological Effects

Cocaine use produces a myriad of behavioral and physiological effects. Among these is addiction. Cocaine alters the firing rate of dopaminergic neurons in mesocortical and mesolimbic pathways, an action that may underlie some of the addictive behavior associated with cocaine use (Bonci et al., 2003). Neuronal projections utilizing glutamate as their neurotransmitter from the prefrontal cortex to the nucleus accumbens in the limbic system also appear to underlie cocaine craving in addicts (Baker et al., 2003). There is no satisfactory treatment for cocaine dependence (Bolla et al., 1998). Although preliminary evidence shows that some drugs, including, for example, ibogamine, an alkaloid, may attenuate craving for cocaine (Levi & Borne, 2003), there are no available drugs in the United

States that are approved for the treatment of cocaine addiction (Dackis & O'Brien, 2003; Levi & Borne, 2002). Neither dopamine agonists (Soares et al., 2003) nor antidepressants (Lima et al., 2003) appear helpful in treating cocaine dependence itself. However, other drugs that alter dopamine transmission are under investigation for use in treating cocaine abuse (Gorelick et al., 2004). Some work, for example, suggests that partial dopamine agonists may be helpful in the treatment of cocaine dependence (Platt et al., 2002). Similarly, vigabatrin (not marketed in the United States) may improve abstinence from cocaine by indirectly decreasing dopamine transmission via increasing GABA, which suppresses dopamine action (Gorelick et al., 2004). Depression, cocaine craving (Lima et al., 2003), irritability, and sleep difficulties (Soares et al., 2003) can occur when cocaine is discontinued. Cocaine use is associated with a period of euphoria (Brain & Coward, 1989), which may be at least partially dependent upon cocaine's effects on serotonin transmission (Muller et al., 2003). Cocaine's effects on serotonin also may lead to the increased activity in animal models (Muller et al., 2003). Increased concentration and motor activity also occur from cocaine use (Camí and Farré, 2003). Cocaine use also can result in hallucinations (Brain & Coward, 1989) and other forms of psychosis (Yui et al., 1999). Finally, decision-making ability and judgment can be impaired by cocaine use (Bolla et al., 1998), which may be related to cocaine-induced changes in the frontal cortex (Bolla et al., 1998).

In addition to its effects on brain function and behavior, cocaine can adversely affect many other organs of the body. Because of its effects on sodium and potassium channels in cardiac cells, cocaine can result in heart arrythmias (Bauman & DiDomenico, 2002). In addition, cocaine use is associated with myocardial infarction and sudden death (Frishman et al., 2003). Cocaine can elevate blood pressure as well as lead to cerebrovascular accidents (Mochizuki et al., 2003), vasoconstriction, and increased body temperature (Brain & Coward, 1989). Cocaine can result in placental abruption and premature rupture of membranes during pregnancy (Addis et al., 2001).

ATOMOXETINE (STRATTERA)

Although not a stimulant (Simpson & Perry, 2003), atomoxetine is discussed here because of its indication for the treatment of ADHD. Atomoxetine differs from the stimulants in that it is not associated with dependence (Simpson & Perry, 2003), in part due to its lack of direct involvement with dopamine (Michelson et al., 2003).

Mechanism of Action and Pharmacology

Atomoxetine is a selective inhibitor of norepinephrine reuptake (Michelson et al., 2003), a mechanism that may be related to its effects in ADHD because norepinephrine appears to be important for attention and its maintenance (Christman et al., 2004). Unlike the stimulants, therefore, atomoxetine appears to have no action at the dopamine reuptake receptor. The half-life of atomoxetine is approximately three hours (Witcher et al., 2003).

Adverse Effects

Atomoxetine, in general, appears to be relatively well tolerated (Simpson & Perry, 2003). It is, however, associated with a slightly increased heart rate and small increases in systolic blood pressure in adults and increases in diastolic blood pressure in children and adolescents (Wernicke et al., 2003). In adults, atomoxetine has been associated with heart palpitations (Wernicke et al., 2003). Atomoxetine can decrease appetite (Simpson & Perry, 2003).

USES OF METHYLPHENIDATE, PEMOLINE, PHENTERMINE, MODAFINIL, ATOMOXETINE, AND THE AMPHETAMINES

Attention-Deficit, Hyperactivity Disorder (ADHD)

Characterized by problems with attention and increased activity (Himelstein et al., 2000), attention-deficit, hyperactivity disorder (ADHD) is the most common childhood psychiatric disorder with estimates of its prevalence varying from 2 percent to 18 percent (Rowland et al., 2002). The neurobiology of ADHD is characterized by deficits in dopamine and norepinephrine in frontal-striatal pathways (Himelstein et al., 2000), findings that may relate to the therapeutic effects of the stimulants for ADHD. The stimulants are the most commonly used drugs for the treatment of ADHD (Pelham et al., 1999). All in all, approximately 70 to 80 percent of people with ADHD have a favorable response to the stimulants, although the degree of response varies from person to person (Pierce, 1999). Both children and adults with ADHD respond favorably to stimulants (Spencer et al., 1996).

Methylphenidate is the most commonly prescribed stimulant for ADHD (Pelham et al., 1999). Because of methylphenidate's short half-life, longer-acting, once daily (Sonuga-Barke et al., 2004) preparations of methylphenidate, such as Metadate CD and Concerta, are used to increase compliance (Pelham et al., 2001). Although methylphenidate remains the active ingredient in Concerta, a Concerta tablet consists of an outer covering of regularly released methylphenidate covering an insoluble core tablet of methylphenidate, which is released by an osmotic pump (Sonuga-Barke et al., 2004) to allow for less frequent dosing compared to immediate-release forms of methylphenidate. Also consisting of methylphenidate, Metadate CD consists of a soluble capsule containing immediate-release beads of methylphenidate and other methylphenidate beads covered with an extended-release coating that delays the release of methylphenidate, prolonging its duration (Sonuga-Barke et al., 2004). Possibly because of a proposed decrease in efficacy when compared to regular-release methylphenidate, an older extended-release form of methylphenidate, Ritalin-SR, has not ever been widely used (Pelham et al., 1999). As many as 30 to 40 percent of ADHD patients, however, do not respond adequately to methylphenidate but may respond to other stimulants (Pelham et al., 1999).

Pemoline is also used in the treatment of ADHD and may have similar efficacy to methylphenidate (Pelham et al., 1995), although it is not generally considered a first-choice medication for ADHD, due in part to its potential for liver toxicity (Stevenson & Wolraich, 1989) and the need, therefore, of laboratory monitoring of liver function tests. Generally thought to have slower onset of action and less efficacy than methylphenidate for ADHD, some evidence has suggested that when given at higher doses, pemoline's efficacy is similar to that of methylphenidate (Elia et al., 1999). Pemoline appears moderately effective for the treatment of adult ADHD (Wilens et al., 1999).

Similar to other stimulants, modafinil appears to increase attention and improve concentration (Rugino & Copley, 2001). Because of these factors, modafinil has been considered for use in ADHD, and early evidence indicates a positive effect on features of ADHD in children (Rugino & Copley, 2001) and adults (Taylor & Russo, 2000).

Double-blind, placebo-controlled trials have shown that atomoxetine is efficacious in childhood and adult ADHD (Kratochvil et al., 2003). The results of an open-label trial comparing atomoxetine to methylphenidate in the treatment of childhood suggested similar efficacy for the two drugs (Kratochvil et al., 2002). Furthermore, once-daily dosing of atomoxetine may be effective in children and adolescents (Michelson et al., 2002), conferring an important advantage over drugs that require multiple daily dosings. A particular advantage of atomoxetine over methylphenidate and the amphetamines is its lack of abuse potential (Michelson et al., 2003).

Used less frequently than is methylphenidate for ADHD, dextroamphetamine is nevertheless an important drug for ADHD (Elia et al., 1999) and appears to be of similar efficacy to methylphenidate (Elia et al., 1991, 1999). As mentioned above, perhaps one reason that dextroamphetamine is not as widely used as methylphenidate in the treatment of ADHD is its reputation of causing more side effects than does methylphenidate (Pelham et al., 1995), although this difference has been questioned (Elia et al., 1999).

Adderall, with its mixture of amphetamines, is also used for ADHD (Spencer et al., 2001). With possibly a longer half-life than that of regular-release methylphenidate (Pelham et al., 1999), Adderall may simplify dosing schedules. Adderall contains several different amphetamines, including different isomers, that may have different properties and could result in a therapeutic response in a wider range of people than any one of these drugs alone (Pelham et al., 1999).

WHAT LONG-TERM INVESTIGATIONS OF ADHD MEDICATIONS DON'T TELL US

The recent multimodal treatment (MTA) study of children with ADHD (MTA Cooperative Group, 1999), the first to study the *long-term* benefits of psychostimulants for the treatment of ADHD, has been interpreted by Carey (2000) as indicating that neither methylphenidate (MPH) nor any other medication is a specific remedy for children now receiving the diagnosis of ADHD due to many of the same shortcomings that the literature has demonstrated in terms of the short-term outcomes (e.g., idiosyncratic response, nonmaintained benefits, inconsistency of findings). That is, Carey (2000) suggests that the findings from the MTA appear to indicate that medication alone does not completely account for alleviation of the symptoms related to ADHD.

One of the primary investigators in the MTA study, William E. Pelham, Jr. (1999), noted several potential confounds in interpreting the data from the MTA studies as even indicating superiority for medicine in the treatment of ADHD symptoms. These confounds include the following:

1. *Timing of the assessments relative to treatment intensity.* The two main treatment modalities used in the MTA studies—behavioral (BT) and pharmacological (MM)—were assessed at different points in time relative to the intensive phase of treatment. Specifically, MM effects were assessed at post-treatment while participants were actively medicated, but BT effects were assessed after therapist involvement was faded. In other words, the results reported for the MTA treatment compared active MM treatment versus inactive/withdrawn BT. The results of the study, therefore, do not give a clear comparison of two active treatments.

2. *No withdrawal condition for the medication.* The MTA investigators argued that since it was well known that the effects of medication would disappear immediately upon withdrawing the medication treatment, it was neither important nor interesting for either clinical or research purposes to withdraw the medication condition. This limitation has two implications:

a. No conclusions can be made from the MTA studies in terms of the long-term effects of MPH. The best that the results can indicate, given this limitation, is that the effects of MPH given steadily for 14 months are the same at the end of that time as at the beginning. That is, without withdrawing the medication, no conclusion could be drawn about the possible cumulative effects of medication and no *direct* comparison of treatment modalities can be made.

b. No conclusion can be drawn about whether children in the BT or combined conditions would have an advantage over children in the MM group had medication been withdrawn. As the vast majority of individuals who take medication discontinue such use in less than one year, this is an important question for most parents of ADHD children. That is, it is important for parents, who may not want their children to be on medication for the remainder of their lives, to know whether medication will have lasting effects after its discontinuation.

3. *Even without fading, BT was effective.* BT was as effective as medication as provided in the community and almost as effective as active medication as administered in the study despite the fact that BT was faded.

4. *Sequencing of behavioral and pharmacological treatments.* MM and BT were started simultaneously for children in the combined group, so the initial medication-titration trial was conducted before behavioral interventions had been systematically implemented. This

sequencing difference involves two further confounds:

a. *Lower end doses.* The children in combined-treatment (MM and BT) ended the study on 20 percent lower doses at endpoint than did the MM group. That is, while the MM group had dose increases by 20 percent at endpoint, the combined group did not have dose increases over the 14 months of treatment. The MM group increases were all due to deterioration of functioning of participants at their monthly checks. Hence, a possible prediction that can be made from the MTA study results is that medication may increase by 20 percent yearly for children being treated with combined interventions. This estimate is the lowest likely increase, given that the medication dose could not be lowered for the combined-treatment group in the MTA study. The outcome of the combined-treatment group may have increased with increased medication as parent and teacher ratings appear to increase with medication increases.

b. *Reduction in motivation.* The decision not to lag medication behind BT for the combined-treatment group may have reduced motivation and, consequently, the effort that parents and teachers exert in BT when a child is medicated. One outcome of the MTA studies suggests that prior medication may reduce parental and perhaps clinician effort in BT. This result indicates that the probability of a child's crossing over to medication was 50 percent if he or she had been medicated prior to the study, while it was only 15 percent if he or she had not previously received medication.

5. *No "no-treatment" comparison.* Nearly 70 percent of the community-treatment group (used as a comparison) were treated with stimulant medication by their community physicians. One-third of the participants in the MTA study had been previously med-

icated. Presumably, all, or nearly all, of the participants immediately returned to their pre-study medications when they were assigned to the community group. Thus, likely one-half of the remaining children were medicated during the year following baseline assessment, such that nearly 70 percent of the community-treatment group, in total, was medicated with a stimulant. Assessments prior to treatment also revealed that parents and teachers used behavioral interventions, even in the absence of documented professional involvement, at quite a high rate (in some cases, 90 percent of parents and teachers used such interventions). Hence, children in the community comparison group were receiving BT even though they were not provided this by the study or by ongoing, systematic contacts with professionals.

6. *No true comparisons even between treatment groups.* The high rate of parental and teacher use of behavioral intervention along with the finding (from the Pittsburgh portion of the MTA study) that those in the medication group were also receiving BT indicates that the MM comparison to the BT treatment does not reflect a differential response to MM over BT.

REFERENCES

Carey WB (2000): What the multimodal treatment study of children with attention-deficit/hyperactivity disorder did and did not say about the use of methylphenidate for attention deficits. Pediatrics 105:863–866.

MTA Cooperative Group (1999): A 14-month randomized clinical trial of treatment strategies for attention deficit hyperactivity disorder. Archives of General Psychiatry 56:1073–1086.

Pelham WE Jr. (1999): The NIMH multimodal treatment study for Attention-Deficit Hyperactivity Disorder: Just say yes to drugs alone? Canadian Journal of Psychiatry 44:981–990.

Depression

Stimulants can be used to augment antidepressant medications in cases of depression that have not fully responded to the antidepressants alone (Masand et al., 1998). For example, in an open trial, elderly depressed patients showed improvement in depression after methylphenidate was added to the antidepressant citalopram (Celexa) (Lavretsky & Kumar, 2001). Methylphenidate also is used to treat depression in cases of cancer (Homsi et al., 2000).

Narcolepsy

Narcolepsy is a sleep disorder that is characterized by excessive drowsiness in inappropriate circumstances (Mitler & Hayduk, 2002). Other features that may accompany narcolepsy include cataplexy (Mitler & Hayduk, 2002), which is the loss of muscle tone with strong emotion, paralysis when drifting off to sleep or just coming out of sleep—so-called sleep paralysis, and hypnogognic and hypnopompic hallucinations (Mitler & Hayduk, 2002), which are abnormal sensory experiences that occur when a person is just entering or coming out of sleep (Mitler & Hayduk, 2002). Stimulants are used to treat the excessive sleepiness that occurs in narcolepsy (Jasinski & Kovacevic-Ristanovic, 2000). Modafinil is approved as a wake-promoting agent in narcolepsy to decrease daytime sleepiness (Mitler & Hayduk, 2002). Unlike other stimulants that are used in the treatment of narcolepsy, modafinil does not seem to carry a high risk of addiction (Jasinski & Kovacevic-Ristanovic, 2000), making modafinil a reasonable alternative to other stimulants in this condition.

Non-Narcolepsy–Associated Daytime Drowsiness

A few very preliminary reports have suggested that modafinil may have a role in ameliorating daytime drowsiness from other causes in some people. For example, the drowsiness that results from sedating psychotropic drugs in patients with a history of brain trauma (Teitelman, 2001) and from opiates (Webster et al., 2003) has been reported to respond favorably to modafinil (Teitelman, 2001). Modafinil may reduce the daytime drowsiness in patients with myotonic dystrophy (Talbot et al., 2003), a neurological illness associated with excessive daytime sleepiness. As with many of the potential uses of modafinil, additional studies are required to further establish the efficacy and safety of modafinil in these so-called off-label uses of this drug.

Appetite Suppression

Phentermine in combination with fenfluramine formed the phen-fen treatment for obesity (Stafford & Radley, 2003). Although fenfluramine is no longer available (Stafford & Radley, 2003) due to possible involvement in heart valve disease

(Ulus et al., 2000), phentermine is still used for weight loss in obesity (Stafford & Radley, 2003).

Anesthesia

Even though it has few legitimate medical uses, cocaine continues to be used as a topical anesthetic for several procedures, including rhinological surgery (De et al., 2003), nasal intubation (Cara et al., 2003), and bronchoscopy (Osula et al., 2003). The anesthetic effects of cocaine appear to result from cocaine's blockade of sodium channel in neurons, which, in turn, inhibits the formation of an action potential (Brain & Coward, 1989). Table 6.1 summarizes clinical uses and adverse effects of psychostimulant medications. The possible uses of some nonprescribed psychostimulants are listed in Table 6.2.

TABLE 6.1   The Uses and Adverse Effects of Psychostimulant Medications

TYPE OF STIMULANT	USES	ADVERSE EFFECTS
Methylphenidate, Pemoline, and Phentermine	Attention-Deficit/ Hyperactivity Disorder (ADHD), Depression, Narcolepsy, Appetite Suppression	Elevated blood pressure and heart rate, diminished appetite, stunted growth, stomache pain, headaches, insomnia, psychosis, motor tics, involuntary muscle contractions, addiction, and liver damage.
Modafinil	Narcolepsy, ADHD, Non-Narcolepsy Associated Daytime Drowsiness	Overstimulation, gastrointestinal upset, headaches, light-headedness, and tremors.
Atomoxetine (not, technically, a stimulant)	ADHD	Slightly increased heart rate, small increases in systolic and diastolic blood pressure, and some heart palpitations.
The Amphetamines (dextroamphetamine, Adderall, methamphetamine, methylenedioxymethamphetamine)	ADHD, Narcolepsy, Weight Loss	Diminished appetite, cardiovascular effects (e.g., elevated heart rate and increased blood pressure), agitation, confusion, decreased inhibition, psychosis, paranoia, hallucinations, addiction, depression, and neuronal damage.

TABLE 6.2   The Uses and Adverse Effects of Nonprescribed Psychostimulants

TYPE OF STIMULANT	POSSIBLE USES	ADVERSE EFFECTS
Cocaine	No legitimate medical uses	Addiction, craving, paranoia, hallucinations, perforations of nasal septum, increased heart rate and blood pressure, vasoconstriction, diminished blood flow to brain and heart, and myocardial infarctions and strokes.
Nicotine	Possibly helpful lessening fatigue, increased attention, Alzheimer's disease	Addiction, lung disease, low birth weight, irritability, poor sleep, diminished concentration, agitation, and cravings.
Caffeine	Migraine headaches, enhancing seizure duration and length during electroconvulsive therapy	Vasoconstriction, increased heart rate and blood pressure, reduced cerebral blood flow, and reduced birth weight.

CAFFEINE

Quite possibly the most widely used drug in the world (Paluska, 2003), the stimulant (Fisone et al., 2004) caffeine is readily available from caffeinated soft drinks, coffee, tea, and chocolate (Nawrot et al., 2003). Caffeine is used by all age groups (Nawrot et al., 2003), including large numbers of adolescents, many of whom meet criteria for caffeine dependence and continue to use caffeine despite being aware of the physiological and psychological problems associated with their caffeine use (Bernstein et al., 2002).

Mechanism of Action, Pharmacology, and Metabolism

Caffeine antagonizes adenosine receptors (Ribeiro et al., 2002), which are involved in neuromodulation, affecting sleep, cognition, and arousal (Ribeiro et al., 2002) and which appear to be the primary mechanism through which caffeine exerts its effects (Paluska, 2003). Adenosine inhibits neuronal activity (Fisone et al., 2004), and by antagonizing adenosine receptors, caffeine diminishes the inhibition produced by adenosine, resulting in its stimulant effects. There are four known types of adenosine receptors, of which caffeine is thought to antagonize the A_1 and A_{2A} subtypes (Fisone et al., 2004). Adenosine A_1 receptors are found presynaptically in many brain regions, including the cerebral cortex and hippocampus, where they inhibit the release of dopamine, glutamate, and acetylcholine (Fisone et al., 2004). The distribution of adenosine A_{2A} receptors is more limited but many are found in the striatum, where they may be involved in caffeine-induced increases in motor activity (Fisone et al., 2004). In addition to its effects on adenosine receptors, caffeine may antagonize benzodiazepine receptors (see Chapter 5), although caffeine's antagonism of benzodiazepine receptors may be weaker than its antagonism of adenosine receptors (Nehlig et al., 1992). The effects of caffeine on benzodiazepine receptors are not negligible, because caffeine can interfere with the effects of concurrently consumed benzodiazepines (Nehlig et al., 1992).

The half-life of caffeine in adults ranges from three and a half to six hours (Nehlig et al., 1992) but varies with age and pregnancy status (Eskenazi, 1993). For example, the half-life of caffeine increases to ten hours by the end of pregnancy (Eskenazi, 1993), exposing both the woman and her fetus to additional caffeine. Moreover, the half-life of caffeine in the fetus is prolonged because a fetus lacks the necessary enzymes to efficiently metabolize caffeine (Eskenazi, 1993).

Like many other psychotropic drugs, caffeine use can result in physical dependence. When the caffeine dose is abruptly stopped or lowered, a withdrawal syndrome characterized by irritability, drowsiness, lowered mood, anxiety, and nausea may ensue (Dews et al., 2002).

Drug-Drug Interactions

Caffeine does have some interactions with other drugs. In people taking both caffeine and lithium, for instance, an abrupt lowering or cessation of the caffeine intake can result in clinically significant increases in lithium levels (Mester et al., 1995).

Behavioral Effects of Caffeine

The stimulant-like effects of caffeine are well known. In a study of healthy young adults who remained awake for fifty-four and a half hours straight, caffeine was as effective as the wake-promoting agent modafinil in maintaining performance and alertness, and both drugs were better than placebo (Wesensten et al., 2002). Caffeine also increases motor activity (Fisone et al., 2004). With these stimulant effects comes the potential for caffeine to induce anxiety. Young adults treated with caffeine show significantly greater anxiety compared to those treated with placebo (Scott et al., 2002). At high doses, caffeine is associated with agitation and even aggression (Yudofsky et al., 1990). During strenuous exercise, caffeine can improve endurance and performance (Paluska, 2003).

Caffeine in adults over age 65 prevented the late-afternoon decrement in memory performance that often occurs in older adults. Not necessarily due to effects on memory *per se*, this response could be from nonspecific changes in arousal levels (Ryan et al., 2002). Another effect of caffeine on cognition is its enhancement of concentration (Paluska, 2003).

In rats that have undergone extinction of cocaine self-administration behavior, caffeine results in the reintroduction of cocaine self-administration. Although the mechanism for this is unknown, some evidence suggests that it is not through adenosine receptor antagonism but rather through dopamine mechanisms that this effect on cocaine seeking occurs (Green & Schenk, 2002). In humans, caffeine use can result in tolerance and dependence (Paluska, 2003).

Physiological Effects of Caffeine

Resulting in vasodilation in tissues outside of the brain (Nehlig et al., 1992), caffeine is a cerebral vasoconstrictor, and a dose of 250 milligrams of caffeine, roughly the amount found in a single cup of coffee, can reduce cerebral blood flow by 30 percent (Hoecker et al., 2002). Caffeine also crosses the placenta (Eskenazi, 1993), exposing the fetus to caffeine intake by the mother. Furthermore, many women use caffeine during pregnancy (Watkinson & Fried, 1985), and concern exists about a proposed linkage between maternal caffeine consumption during gestation and reduced birth weight (Eskenazi, 1993; Watkinson & Fried, 1985). However, a large-scale, prospective epidemiological study from Sweden found no association between caffeine consumption during pregnancy and birth weight, gestational age, and birth weight normalized for gestational age after other confounding founders such as cigarette smoking and socioeconomic status were corrected (Clausson et al., 2002). Nevertheless, the safety of caffeine consumption during pregnancy remains controversial because caffeine restricts placental blood flow, increases the work done by the fetal heart, and is associated with an increased risk of spontaneous abortion (Eskenazi, 1993). Caffeine is excreted in breast milk (Eskenazi, 1993), prompting concerns for its use during lactation.

Caffeine has numerous other physiological effects. For example, another possible role of adenosine receptors involves neuroprotection. Caffeine and other adenosine antagonists are associated with a reduced risk of developing Parkinson's disease, although inadequate evidence exists to recommend the clinical use of caffeine to minimize the chances of acquiring this disease. This putative neuroprotective effect of caffeine and related compounds may be utilized as new adenosine drugs are developed (Schwarzchild et al., 2002).

Caffeine is used during electroconvulsive therapy to enhance seizure duration and length, especially in those cases complicated by a high seizure threshold that makes seizure induction and maintenance difficult. Furthermore, in patients undergoing electroconvulsive therapy, caffeine treatment resulted in a quicker onset of response and fewer cognitive side effects compared to non-caffeine-treated subjects (Calev et al., 1993). Case reports, however, have suggested that caffeine given in conjunction with electroconvulsive therapy may be associated with heart dysrhythmias, particularly in elderly patients who have a history of cardiac disease (Jaffe et al., 1990).

NICOTINE

Together with alcohol and caffeine, nicotine is one of the most widely used and abused drugs—it is legal, addictive, and readily available. Furthermore, nicotine is often used—and abused—together with alcohol (Rezvani & Levin, 2002), making this form of polypharmacy a common event. Nearly all smokers are dependent upon, or addicted to, nicotine (Peters & Morgan, 2002), and nicotine appears to be the primary factor leading to tobacco addiction and withdrawal when tobacco use is discontinued (Catania et al., 2003). Somewhat surprisingly, the strong potential for addiction from cigarette smoking has only been realized since about 1980 (Sullivan & Covey, 2002). When viewed in the context of an addictive drug, the numbers of people who casually use nicotine, primarily through smoking, are staggering. Over 50 million people in the United States alone smoke tobacco, including 13 percent of people over age 65 (Murray & Abeles, 2002). In the United States, over 400,000 deaths occur yearly that are attributed to tobacco (U.S. Department of Health and Human Services, 1990), findings that attest to the addictive properties of nicotine. Affecting not only the person dependent upon nicotine, cigarette smoking is a major risk factor for low-birth-weight babies, regardless of the nicotine concentration of the cigarettes (Mitchell et al., 2002).

Mechanism of Action and Pharmacology

The neurotransmitter acetylcholine exerts its effects through two general types of receptors: nicotine and muscarinic (see Chapter 2). Widely distributed among many species of animals, nicotine receptors are important in the brain function of numerous other animals in addition to humans. For example, nicotine receptors are found in the cuttlefish, *Sepia officinalis*, where they may be involved in predatory behavior (Halm et al., 2002). Like other addictive drugs, nicotine, the main psychoactive ingredient of tobacco, is strongly reinforcing and leads to repeated self-administration (Sullivan & Covey, 2002). Nicotine interacts with the nicotine receptor, which spans the neuronal membrane and is composed of five different subunits (Suemaru et al., 2002) forming a channel through which ions can flow (Clementi et al., 2000a). Comprising multiple subtypes (Clementi et al., 2000b), nicotine receptors are found at the neuromuscular junction and in the central and peripheral nervous systems (Hogg et al., 2003), where they appear to be important for many aspects of brain functioning, including attention, learning, and memory consolidation (Clementi et al., 2000b). Abnormalities of the nicotinic receptor, for example, are postulated to be involved in the pathogenesis of schizophrenia, depression, and anxiety, as well as in the attentional abnormalities found in some people with schizophrenia (Suemaru et al., 2002). Abnormal functions of nicotine receptors also are associated with Alzheimer's disease, Parkinson's disease, and a form of epilepsy (Hogg et al., 2003).

Far from affecting the nicotinic receptors in isolation, nicotine interacts with several other neurotransmitter systems. For example, nicotine alters the function of the dopamine-containing neurons in the mesolimbic pathway, and antagonism of mesolimbic dopamine function by other compounds can inhibit repeated self-administration of nicotine (Corrigall et al., 1992), suggesting that the addictive features of nicotine are mediated at least in part by the mesolimbic dopamine system (Glover et al., 2003). Furthermore, nicotine increases the release of dopamine in dopaminergic systems (Picciotto & Corrigall, 2002), including the finding that nicotine increases extracellular dopamine in the nucleus accumbens (Sziraki et al., 2002). When smoked, nicotine penetrates the brain in approximately 10 to 20 seconds (Le Houezec, 2003). In addition to the effects of nicotine on the brain's dopamine systems, nicotine also interacts with GABA, noradrenaline, and serotonin systems, all of which could be involved in the addictive properties of nicotine (Picciotto & Corrigall, 2002). Nicotine administration also results in the actual release of several neurotransmitters, such as norepinephrine, serotonin, and endorphins (Sullivan & Covey, 2002).

It is possible that some or all of these neurotransmitters may mediate the behavioral effects of nicotine. The interaction with norepinephrine may underlie increased attention associated with nicotine, and effects on GABA and endorphins could result in the anxiolysis observed from nicotine (Sullivan & Covey, 2002). When presented with visual cues relating to smoking, cigarette smokers deprived of nicotine who were studied with functional MRI scanning showed activation of prefrontal and mesolimbic regions consistent with postulated dopamine-based reward systems of addiction. Smoking cues also activated brain areas associated with visual-spatial attention, such as the anterior cingulate cortex (Due et al., 2002).

Connections and interactions also exist between nicotine and the brain's opiate system. In rats, morphine increases nicotine potency and effects (Pomerleau, 1998). Nicotine is involved in the release of naturally occurring opioids in several different brain regions, an action that is related to opioid reinforcement (Pomerleau, 1998). Conversely, the opiates heroin and morphine increase cigarette smoking in humans (Pomerleau, 1998). These findings not only indicate the complex relationship between brain nicotine and opiate systems but also suggest that opioids may be a factor in nicotine addiction and that nicotine may be involved in opiate dependence. Further evidence indicating that nicotinic and opiate systems are closely related comes from work evaluating the effects of opiate antagonism in people dependent on nicotine. In these people, the opioid antagonist naloxone resulted in signs and symptoms of *opiate* withdrawal, suggesting that nicotine dependence is mediated at least in part by mechanisms involving the opiate system (Krishnan-Sarin et al., 1999). Consistent with this notion is that naloxone also increases nicotine craving in nicotine-dependent people (Krishnan-Sarin et al., 1999). Thus, some of the behavioral effects of nicotine may be mediated by the brain's opiate system working in conjunction with dopamine reward pathways (George et al., 2000).

Nicotine also may affect the hypothalamic-pituitary-adrenal axis, the neuroendocrine system that figures so prominently in the biology of depression, stress, and anxiety. Before challenge with naloxone, cigarette smokers had lower concentrations of the hypothalamic-pituitary-adrenal axis hormone cortisol and a smaller release of cortisol after naloxone challenge (Krishnan-Sarin et al., 1999). While this finding is preliminary and requires additional investigation, a connection between cigarette smoking and the hypothalamic-pituitary-adrenal axis is intriguing as this axis may be involved in the biology of many mental disorders, particularly those involving stress (Heim et al., 2000).

Nicotine also may have a role in attention. For example, transdermally administered nicotine appears to improve attention in ADHD and healthy non-smoking adults (Levin & Rezvani, 2002).

Nicotine also appears to be involved in cognition, and nicotine and nicotine receptors appear to play key roles in the neurobiology of Alzheimer's disease. For example, electrophysiologically, nicotine enhances the P300 component of event-related brain potentials. In a study involving Alzheimer-disease patients, acute administration of nicotine increased the amplitude of visual but not auditory P300s in both patients treated with the cholinesterase inhibitor tetrahy-droaminoacridine (Tacrine) (a drug used to arrest the progression of Alzheimer's disease; see Chapter 12) and those untreated. There were, however, no changes in visual-task ability from nicotine (Knott et al., 2002). Although requiring additional study, these findings suggest a role for nicotine in cognition. In people with Alzheimer's disease, nicotine improves attention (Levin & Rezvani, 2002). Furthermore and not unsurprisingly, given the loss of acetylcholine-containing neurons in Alzheimer's disease, the binding of nicotine is reduced in the brains of patients with dementia (Zanardi et al., 2002).

Pathologically, Alzheimer's disease is characterized by beta-amyloid plaques and neurofibrillary tangles, lesions that are thought to be involved in the patho-genesis of this disease (Clark & Karlawish, 2003). In genetically altered mice that develop excessive beta-amyloid deposits in brain, an animal model of Alzheimer's disease, nicotine reduces this buildup of beta-amyloid material and may be a novel therapeutic approach to Alzheimer's disease (Nordberg et al., 2002). Nicotine also appears to protect some brain regions, such as the hippocampus and cerebral cortex, from the toxicity associated with beta-amyloid deposits (Zanardi et al., 2002), and other studies point to the potential benefits of nicotine in preventing the cognitive decline associated with aging (Murray & Abeles, 2002). Furthermore, in a study of nonsmokers exposed to nicotine administered via a transdermal patch, nicotine improved alertness (Griesar et al., 2002). Some cognitive improvement was found from nicotine administration in healthy volunteers genetically at risk for Alzheimer's disease, prompting the consideration of the use of nicotine agonists in some elderly people who are at risk for Alzheimer's disease (Howe & Price, 2002).

Caution is required in extrapolating the findings of possible cognitive improvement to other populations, such as adolescents. For instance, in adolescent rats, nicotine administration resulted in different patterns of nicotine receptor changes from those observed in adult rats. Furthermore, in female adolescent rats exposed to nicotine, cell damage and reduced cell size were observed in hippocampal neurons. These findings suggest, with awareness that these studies involved rats and not humans, that adolescence may be a particularly vulnerable period for nicotine-induced neuronal dysfunction (Slotkin, 2002).

People with schizophrenia have high rates of cigarette smoking (Goff et al., 1992). One reason for the high rate of tobacco smoking in people with schizophrenia may lie in the neurobiological effects of nicotine in people with schizophrenia. Schizophrenia is associated with abnormal inhibitory processing of certain types of auditory stimuli that is improved by nicotine (Simosky et al., 2002). Furthermore, nicotine can improve attention in people with schizophrenia (Levin & Rezvani, 2002).

Nicotine and associated cigarette smoking may be relevant factors in mother–infant relationships. Women who smoke cigarettes are less likely to breastfeed their babies compared to women who do not smoke. A postulated cause of this relationship between maternal smoking and decreased breastfeeding is that nicotine reduces milk volume, possibly by inhibiting prolactin (Amir & Donath, 2003; Howard & Lawrence, 1998). However, in their comprehensive review of the relationship between maternal smoking and decreased breastfeeding, Amir and Donath (2003) concluded that it is predominantly psychosocial factors and not physiological ones that result in less breastfeeding in mothers who smoke.

As with other addictive substances, the cessation of nicotine is associated with signs and symptoms of withdrawal that include depressive-like symptoms, a slowed heart rate, and difficulty sleeping (Cryan et al., 2003). Nicotine withdrawal can lead to resumption of smoking (Catania et al., 2003).

Drug-Drug Interactions

Nicotine can interact with other drugs. For example, in a rat model of working memory investigating cognitive effects of combined alcohol and nicotine, alcohol blocked the improvement in memory observed with low-dose nicotine and resulted in actual memory impairment under conditions of high-dose nicotine (Rezvani & Levin, 2002).

Pharmacological Approaches to Nicotine Dependence

Because of the overwhelming numbers of people addicted to nicotine and the mortality and morbidity associated with smoking, several pharmacological strategies exist to treat smoking. Nicotine replacement and the antidepressant bupropion (Wellbutrin, Zyban) without nicotine are two general approaches used for smoking cessation (Cryan et al., 2003), although the drug clonidine (Catapres) has been used as well (Glassman et al., 1984). Nicotine replacement and bupropion appear similarly efficacious in smoking cessation (Haustein, 2003). In certain cases, combination treatment involving two drugs may be indicated, although this increases the likelihood of side effects from nicotine (Peters & Morgan, 2002). To maximize treatment response, nicotine replacement or bupropion treatment should be combined with counseling (Glover et al., 2003).

Nicotine-Replacement Therapy.   Nicotine-replacement therapy is available in several forms including gum, a transdermal patch, inhaler, nasal spray, and subdermal tablet (Le Houezec, 2003). Nicotine-replacement therapy provides nicotine to the brain but much more slowly than when nicotine is smoked, possibly decreasing the reinforcing effects of nicotine (Le Houezec, 2003). Nicotine-replacement therapy is by no means a complete way of treating nicotine dependence. For example, nicotine gum may not eliminate the cravings for smoking, but it does diminish the subjective and observable features of nicotine withdrawal (Gross & Stitzer, 1989). Nicotine gum does not require a prescription. Effective in reducing nicotine withdrawal, the transdermal nicotine patch, unlike nicotine gum, also may alleviate craving for nicotine (Tonnesen et al., 1991).

Clonidine (Catapres).   An alpha 2-adrenoreceptor agonist, clonidine has been investigated for the treatment of withdrawal syndromes from alcohol and opiates and has been found in most but not all studies to reduce both withdrawal symptoms and craving for nicotine (Glassman et al., 1984).

Bupropion (Wellbutrin, Zyban).   Bupropion is marketed for both depression and smoking cessation, although its mechanism of action in smoking cessation remains unknown but appears independent of its effects on depression (Cryan et al., 2003). It does appear that bupropion affects some of the same brain-reward that nicotine does (Cryan et al., 2003), suggesting that modulation of brain-reward circuitry mediates some of the effects of bupropion on smoking cessation. In rats trained to discriminate between nicotine and saline, bupropion produced a nicotine-like effect but via a different mechanism of action from nicotine. Part of the mechanism of action of bupropion in smoking cessation, therefore, may be that it produces effects that serve as a substitute for nicotine (Young & Glennon, 2002). Bupropion may inhibit nicotine receptors (Haustein, 2003), suggesting another potential mechanism of action of buspirone in smoking cessation. In Table 6.3, pharmacological agents for smoking cessation and possible mechanisms of action are summarized.

SUMMARY

Despite continued controversy regarding their use and role in medicine, the stimulants are widely prescribed for several psychiatric disorders. Methylphenidate and cocaine inhibit the reuptake of dopamine into the presynaptic neuron terminal, increasing the concentration of dopamine in the synapse. Methylphenidate also inhibits the reuptake of norepinephrine, a finding that has prompted the investigation of other compounds, such as certain antidepressants, for use in

TABLE 6.3   Pharmacological Agents for Smoking Cessation and Mechanisms of Action

PHARMACOLOGICAL AGENT	POSSIBLE MECHANISMS OF ACTION
Nicotine Polacrilex Gum (OTC)	Replace the nicotine that is physiologically craved without also producing the non-nicotine-related health risks from smoking tobacco. Does not reduce craving but is used to taper doses of nicotine.
Nicotine Transdermal Patch (OTC)	Reduces both nicotine withdrawal and cravings.
Clonidine	Works as an alpha 2 agonist and has been demonstrated in most, but not all, studies to reduce both withdrawal symptoms and craving for nicotine.
Buproprion	Increases both dopamine and norepinephrine transmission, which could be involved in brain reward circuits. Also, may produce effects that serve as a substitute for nicotine.

attention-deficit, hyperactive disorder. In addition to its reuptake inhibition of dopamine, cocaine blocks the reuptake of norepinephrine and serotonin.

The amphetamines share a similar mechanism of action, with reuptake inhibition of dopamine and norepinephrine and, in addition, facilitation of presynaptic neurotransmitter-storage vesicle release of dopamine and norepinephrine. The mechanism by which modafinil exerts its effects is less well known but may involve effects on the GABA and glutamate systems.

The abuse potential of the stimulants remains an important concern for both the clinical and illicit use of these drugs. While all these compounds can result in abuse and addiction, individual differences do exist, with modafinil having less potential for abuse than some other stimulants.

The stimulants are used in the treatment of several different clinical conditions. Methylphenidate is used primarily for attention-deficit, hyperactive disorder in both children and adults and is the most frequently prescribed psychoactive drug in children. In addition to its use in ADHD, methylphenidate is sometimes used in combination with an antidepressant in cases of depression that have not responded adequately to other measures. The amphetamines, including dextroamphetamine and Adderall, which is a mixture of several different amphetamines, are also used for ADHD.

Modafinil has FDA approval for use as a wake-promoting agent in narcolepsy. Early reports have suggested that modafinil also may have efficacy for ADHD.

Nicotine and caffeine are two generally legal, easily accessible, and widely used drugs that are associated with significant brain involvement with resulting changes in behavior and cognition. Both have the potential for dependence and are associated with withdrawal symptoms upon abrupt lowering of the dose or discontinuation of the drug altogether.

Nicotine

Over 50 million people in the United States alone smoke tobacco and the majority of these are addicted to nicotine. Associated with low birth weight in babies exposed *in utero* to nicotine, nicotine is an agonist of the nicotine subtype of acetylcholine receptor. In addition to acetylcholine, nicotine interacts with dopamine, GABA, noradrenaline, and serotonin systems. Important connections exist between nicotine and the opiate system that appear to be involved with the addiction of nicotine. Nicotine and its receptors also may be involved with the pathogenesis of Alzheimer's dementia.

Several drugs from different biological approaches have been utilized with some success to aid in the stopping of nicotine use. Nicotine-replacement therapy, whether via oral, transdermal, or intranasal routes, can aid in smoking cessation. Another approach consists of using the antidepressant bupropion (Wellbutrin, Zyban). Although the mechanism of action of bupropion's effect on smoking cessation is unknown, it may involve bupropion's actions on dopamine.

Caffeine

Widely consumed by all age groups with addiction common even in adolescents, caffeine initiates its stimulant effects by antagonism of the neuromodulatory adenosine receptors. Caffeine use can produce heightened performance and alertness. Anxiety and agitation may also follow antagonism of the adenosine receptor. In addition to these stimulant-like effects, caffeine also causes cerebral vasoconstriction.

STUDY QUESTIONS

1. List the proposed mechanisms of action of methylphenidate. How does this action differ from that of cocaine?
2. Name several common adverse effects of the stimulants.
3. A 13-year-old child with attention-deficit disorder presents for treatment. List several possible pharmacological approaches and the advantages and disadvantages of each.
4. Describe the proposed mechanisms of action of modafinil.
5. List the clinical conditions for which the stimulants are used.
6. List several proposed mechanisms of action of alcohol.
7. How could these actions of alcohol on the brain relate to the observed behavioral effects of alcohol?
8. What is the mechanism of action of nicotine?
9. In addition nicotine receptors, what other neurotransmitter systems are involved with nicotine?

10. Describe nicotine's involvement with Alzheimer's dementia.

11. How does caffeine exert its stimulant-like effects?

REFERENCES

Abbiati C, Vecchi M, Rossi G, Donata MF, de Franchis R (2002): Inappropriate pemoline therapy leading to acute liver failure and transplantation. Digestive and Liver Disease 34:447–451.

Adcock KG, MacElroy DE, Wolford ET, Farrington EA (1998): Pemoline therapy resulting in liver transplantation. Annals of Pharmacotherapy 32:422–425.

Addis A, Moretti ME, Ahmed Syed F, Einarson TR, Koren G (2001): Fetal effects of cocaine: An updated meta-analysis. Reproductive Toxicology 15:341–369.

Ahmann PA, Theye FW, Berg R, Linquist AJ, Van Erem AJ, Campbell LR (2001): Placebo-controlled evaluation of amphetamine mixture-dextroamphetamine salts and amphetamine salts (Adderall): Efficacy rate and side effects. Pediatrics 107:E10.

Amir LH, Donath SM (2003): Does maternal smoking have a negative physiological effect on breastfeeding? The epidemiological evidence. Breastfeeding Reviews: Publication of the Nursing Mothers' Association of Australia 11:19–29.

Baker DA, McFarland K, Lake RW, Shen H, Tang XC, Toda S, Kalivas PW (2003): Neuroadaptation in cytstine-glutamate exchange underlie cocaine relapse. Nature Neuroscience 6:743–749.

Bauman JL, DiDomenico RJ (2002): Cocaine-induced channelopathies: Emerging evidence the on the multiple mechanisms of sudden death. Journal of Cardiovascular Pharmacology and Therapeutics 7:195–202.

Bernstein GA, Carroll ME, Thuras PD, Cosgrove PD, Roth ME (2002): Caffeine dependence in teenagers. Drug and Alcohol Dependence 66:1–6.

Biederman J (2003): Pharmacotherapy for attention-deficit/hyperactive disorder (ADHD) decreases the risk of substance abuse: Findings from a longitudinal follow-up of youths with and without ADHD. Journal of Clinical Psychiatry 64 (supplement 11):3–8.

Bohringer CH, Jahr JS, Rowell S, Mayer K (2000): Severe hypotension in a patient receiving pemoline during general anesthesia. Anesthesia and Analgesia 91:1131–1133.

Bolla KI, Cadet JL, London ED (1998): The neuropsychiatry of chronic cocaine abuse. The Journal of Neuropsychiatry and Clinical Neurosciences 10:280–289.

Bonci A, Bernardi G, Grillner P, Mercuri NB (2003): The dopamine-containing neuron: Maestro or simple musician in the orchestra of addiction? Trends in Pharmacological Sciences 24:172–177.

Bostic JQ, Biederman J, Spencer TJ, Wilens TE, Prince JB, Monuteaux MC, Sienna M, Polisner DA, Hatch M (2000): Pemoline treatment of adolescents with attention deficit hyperactivity disorder: A short-term controlled trial. Journal of Child and Adolescent Psychopharmacology 10:205–216.

Brain PF, Coward GA (1989): A review of the history, actions, and legitimate uses of cocaine. Journal of Substance Abuse 1:431–451.

Calev A, Fink M, Petrides G, Francis A, Fochtmann L (1993): Caffeine pretreatment enhances clinical efficacy and reduces cognitive effects of electroconvulsive therapy. Convulsive Therapy 9:95–100.

Camí JC, Farré M (2003): Drug addiction. New England Journal of Medicine 349:975–986.

Cara DM, Norris AM, Neale LJ (2003): Pain during awake nasal intubation after topical cocaine or phenylephrine/lidocaine spray. Anaesthesia 58:777–780.

Catania MA, Firenzuoli F, Crupi A, Mannucci C, Caputi AP, Calapai G (2003): *Hypericum perforatum* attenuates nicotine withdrawal signs in mice. Psychopharmacology 169:186–189.

Cherland E, Fitzpatrick R (1999): Psychotic side effects of psychostimulants: A 5-year review. Canadian Journal of Psychiatry 44:811–813.

Christman AK, Fermo JD, Markowitz JS (2004): Atomoxetine, a novel treatment for attention-deficit-hyperactivity disorder. Pharmacotherapy 24:1020–1036.

Christopherson AS (2000): Amphetamine designer drugs: An overview and epidemiology. Toxicology Letters 112–113, 127–131.

Clark CM, Karlawish JH (2003): Alzheimer disease: Current concepts and emerging diagnostic and therapeutic strategies. Annals of Internal Medicine 138:400–410.

Clausson B, Granath F, Ekbom A, Nordmark A, Signorello LB, Cnattingius S (2002): Effect of caffeine exposure during pregnancy on birth weight and gestational age. American Journal of Epidemiology 155:429–436.

Clementi F, Fornasari D, Gotti C (2000a): Neuronal nicotinic acetylcholine receptors: From structure to therapeutics. Trends in Pharmacological Sciences 21:35–37.

Clementi F, Fornasari D, Gotti C (2000b): Neuronal nicotinic receptors, important new players in brain function. European Journal of Pharmacology 393:3–10.

Corrigall WA, Franklin KBJ, Coen KM, Clark PBS (1992): The mesolimbic dopaminergic system is implicated in the reinforcing effects of nicotine. Psychopharmacology 107:285–289.

Cryan JF, Bruijnzeel AW, Skjei KL, Markou A (2003): Bupropion enhances brain reward function and reverses the affective and somatic aspects of nicotine withdrawal in the rat. Psychopharmacology 168:347–358.

Dackis CA, O'Brien (2003): Neurobiology of cocaine dependence limits development of pharmacologic treatments. Psychiatric Annals 33:565–570.

Dalmau A, Bergman B, Brismar B (1999): Psychotic disorders among inpatients with abuse of cannabis, amphetamine and opiates. Do dopaminergic stimulants facilitate psychiatric illness? European Psychiatry 14:366–371.

De R, Uppal HS, Shehab ZP, Hilger AW, Wilson PS, Courteney-Harris R (2003): Current practices of cocaine administration by UK otorhinolaryngologists. Journal of Laryngology and Otology 117:109–112.

DeVane CL, Markowitz JS, Carson SW, Boulton DW, Gill HS, Nahas Z, Risch SC (2000): Single-dose pharmacokinetics of methylphenidate in CYP2D6 extensive and poor metabolizers. Journal of Clinical Psychopharmacology 20:347–349.

Dews PB, O'Brien CP, Bergman J (2002): Caffeine: Behavioral effects of withdrawal and related issues. Food and Chemical Toxicology 40:1257–1261.

DiMaio S, Grizenko N, Joober R (2003): Dopamine genes and attention-deficit hyperactivity disorder: A review. Journal of Psychiatry & Neuroscience 28:27–38.

Due DL, Huettel SA, Hall WG, Rubin DC (2002): Activation of mesolimbic and visuospatial neural circuits elicited by smoking cues: Evidence from functional magnetic resonance imaging. American Journal of Psychiatry 159:954–960.

Elia J, Ambrosini PJ, Rapaport JL (1999): Treatment of attention-deficit-hyperactivity disorder. The New England Journal of Medicine 340:780–788.

Elia J, Borcherding BG, Rapaport JL, Keysor CS (1991): Methylphenidate and dextroamphetamine treatments of hyperactivity: Are there true nonresponders? Psychiatry Research 36:141–155.

Eskenazi B (1993): Caffeine during pregnancy: Grounds for concern? Journal of the American Medical Association 270:2973–2974.

Fisone G, Borgkvist A, Usiello A (2004): Caffeine as a psychomotor stimulant: Mechanism of action. Cellular and Molecular Life Sciences 61:857–872.

Freese TE, Miotto K, Reback CJ (2002): The effects and consequences of selected club drugs. Journal of Substance Abuse Treatment 23:151–156.

Frishman WH, Del Vecchio A, Sanal S, Ismail A (2003): Cardiovascular manifestations of substance abuse part 1: Cocaine. Heart Disease 5:187–201.

Gadow KD, Sverd J, Sprafkin J, Nolan EE, Grossman S (1999): Long-term methylphenidate therapy in children with comorbid attention-deficit hyperactivity disorder and chronic multiple tic disorder. Archives of General Psychiatry 56:330–336.

Gara L, Roberts W (2000): Adverse response to methylphenidate in combination with valproic acid. Journal of Child and Adolescent Psychopharmacology 10:39–43.

George TP, Verrico CD, Xu L, Roth RH (2000): Effects of repeated nicotine administration and footshock stress on rat mesoprefrontal dopamine systems: Evidence for opioid mechanisms. Neuropsychopharmacology 23:79–88.

Glassman AH, Jackson WK, Walsh BT, Roose SP, Rosenfeld B (1984): Cigarette craving, smoking withdrawal, and clonidine. Science 226:864–866.

Glover ED, Glover PN, Payne TJ (2003): Treating nicotine dependence. American Journal of the Medical Sciences 326:183–186.

Goff DC, Henderson DC, Amico E (1992): Cigarette smoking in schizophrenia: Relationship to psychopathology and medication side effects. American Journal of Psychiatry 149: 1189–1194.

Gorelick DA, Gardner EL, Xi Z-X (2004): Agents in development for the management of cocaine abuse. Drugs 64:1547–1573.

Gray JR, Kagan J (2000): The challenge of predicting which children with attention deficit-hyperactivity disorder will respond positively to methylphenidate. Journal of Applied Developmental Psychology 21:471–489.

Green AR, Mechan AO, Elliott JM, O'Shea E, Colado MI (2003): The pharmacology and clinical pharmacology of 3,4-methylenedioxymethamphatomine (MDMA, "ecstasy") Pharmacological Reviews 55:463–508.

Green TA, Schenk S (2002): Dopaminergic mechanism for caffeine-produced cocaine seeking in rats. Neuropsychopharmacology 26:422–430.

Greenhill LL, Pliszka S, Dulcan MK, Bernet W, Arnold V, Beitchman J, Bensons RS, Bukstein O, Kinlan J, McClellan J, Rue D, Shaw JA, Stock S, Kroeger K (2001): Summary of the practice parameters for the use of stimulant medications in the treatment of children, adolescents, and adults. Journal of the American Academy of Child and Adolescent Psychiatry 40:1352–1355.

Griesar WS, Zajdel DP, Oken BS (2002): Nicotine effects on alertness and spatial attention in non-smokers. Nicotine & Tobacco Research 4:185–194.

Gross J, Stitzer ML (1989): Nicotine replacement: Ten-week effects on tobacco withdrawal symptoms. Psychopharmacology 93:334–341.

Halm MP, Chichery MP, Chichery R (2002): The role of cholinergic networks of the anterior basal and inferior frontal lobes in the predatory behavior of Sepia officinalis. Comparative Biochemistry and Physiology. Part A, Molecular & Integrative Physiology 132:267–274.

Haustein KO (2003): Bupropion: Pharmacological and clinical profile in smoking cessation. International Journal of Clinical Pharmacology and Therapeutics 41:56–63.

Hegadoren KM, Bake GB, Bourin M (1999): 3,4-methylenedioxy analogues of amphetamine: Defining the risks to humans. Neuroscience and Biobehavioral Reviews 23:539–553.

Heim C, Newport DJ, Heit S, Graham YP, Wilcox M, Bonsall R, Miller AH, Nemeroff CB (2000): Pituitary-adrenal and autonomic responses to stress in women after physical and sexual abuse in childhood. Journal of the American Medical Association 284:592–597.

Himelstein J, Newcorn JH, Halperin JM (2000): The neurobiology of attention-deficit hyperactivity disorders. Frontiers in Bioscience 5:D461–478.

Hoecker C, Nelle M, Poeschl J, Beedgen B, Linderkamp O (2002): Caffeine impairs cerebral and intestinal blood flow velocity in preterm infants. Pediatrics 109:784–787.

Hogg RC, Raggenbass M, Bertrand D (2003): Nicotinic acetylcholine receptors: From structure to brain function. Reviews of Physiology, Biochemistry and Pharmacology 147:1–46.

Homsi J, Walsh D, Nelson KA, LeGrand S, Davis M (2000): Methylphenidate for depression in hospice practice: A case series. American Journal of Hospice & Palliative Care 17:393–398.

Howard CR, Lawrence RA (1998): Breast-feeding and drug exposure. Obstetrics and Gynecology Clinics of North America 25:195–217.

Howe MN, Price IR (2001): Effects of transdermal nicotine on learning, memory, verbal fluency, concentration, and general health in a healthy sample at risk for dementia. International Psychogeriatrics 13:465–475.

Jaffe R, Brubaker G, Dubin WR, Roemer R (1990): Caffeine-associated cardiac dysrhythmias during ECT: Report of three cases. Convulsive Therapy 6:308–313.

Jasinski DR, Kovacevic-Ristanovic R (2000): Evaluation of the abuse liability of modafinil and other drugs used for excessive daytime sleepiness associated with narcolepsy. Clinical Neuropharmacology 23:149–156.

Kimko HC, Cross JT, Abernathy DR (1999): Pharmacokinetics and clinical effectiveness of methylphenidate. Clinical Pharmacokinetics 37:457–470.

Klein RG, Landa B, Mattes JA, Klein DF (1988a): Methylphenidate and growth in hyperactive children: A controlled withdrawal study. Archives of General Psychiatry 45:1127–1130.

Klein RG, Mannuzza S (1988b): Hyperactive boys almost grown up. III. Methylphenidate effects on ultimate height. Archives of General Psychiatry 45:1131–1134.

Kolecki PF, Curry SC (1997): Poisoning by sodium channel blocking agents. Critical Care Clinics 13:829–848.

Kollins SH (2003): Comparing the abuse potential of methylphenidate versus other stimulants: A review of available evidence and relevance to the ADHD patient. Journal of Clinical Psychiatry (supplement 11):14–18.

Knott V, Mohr E, Mahoney C, Engeland C, Ilivitsky V (2002): Effects of acute nicotine administration on cognitive event-related potentials in Tacrine-treated and non-treated patients with Alzheimer's disease. Neuropsychobiology 45:156–160.

Kratochvil CJ, Heiligenstein JH, Dittman R, Spencer TJ, Biederman J, Wernicke J, Newcorn JH, Casat C, Milton D, Michelson D (2002): Atomoxetine and methylphenidate treatment in children with ADHD: A prospective, randomized, open-label trial. Journal of the American Academy of Child and Adolescent Psychiatry 41:776–784.

Kratochvil CJ, Vaughan BA, Harrington MJ, Burke WJ (2003): Atomoxetine: A selective noradrenaline reuptake inhibitor for the treatment of attention-deficit/hyperactivity disorder. Expert Opinion on Pharmacotherapy 4:1165–1174.

Krishnan-Sarin S, Rosen MI, O'Malley SS (1999): Naloxone challenge in smokers. Preliminary evidence of an opioid component in nicotine dependence. Archives of General Psychiatry 56:663–668.

Lavretsky H, Kumar A (2001): Methylphenidate augmentation of citalopram in elderly depressed patients. American Journal of Geriatric Psychiatry 9:298–303.

Le Houezec J (2003): Role of nicotine pharmacokinetics in nicotine addiction and nicotine replacement therapy: A review. International Journal of Tuberculosis and Lung Disease 7:811–819.

Levi MS, Borne RF (2002): A review of chemical agents in the pharmacology of addiction. Current Medicinal Chemistry 9:1807–1818.

Levin ED, Rezvani AH (2002): Nicotinic treatment of cognitive dysfunction. Current Drug Targets. CNS and Neurological Disorders 1:423–431.

Liberg JP, Hovda KE, Nordby G, Jacobsen D (1998): [Ecstasy – cool dope with long-lasting effects?]. Tidsskrift for den Norske Laegeforening 118:4384–4387.

Lima MS, Reisser AA, Soares BG, Farrell M (2003): Antidepressants for cocaine dependence. Cochrane Database of Systematic Reviews, CD002950.

Lisska MC, Rivkees SA (2003): Daily methylphenidate use slows the growth of children: a community based study. Journal of Pediatric Endocrinology & Metabolism 16:711–718.

Lyles J, Cadet JL (2003): Methylenedioxymethamphetamine (MDMA, Ecstasy) neurotoxicity: Cellular and molecular mechanisms. Brain Research. Brain Research Reviews 42:155–168.

Markowitz JS, Patrick KS (2001): Pharmacokinetic and pharmacodynamic drug interactions in the treatment of attention-deficit hyperactivity disorder. Clinical Pharmacokinetics 40:753–772.

Markowitz JS, Straughn AB, Patrick KS (2003): Advances in the pharmacotherapy of attention-deficit-disorder: Focus on methylphenidate formulations. Pharmacotherapy 23:1281–1299.

Masand PS, Anand VS, Tanquary JF (1998): Psychostimulant augmentation of second generation antidepressants: A case series. Depression and Anxiety 7:89–91.

Mester R, Toren P, Mizrachi I, Wolmer L, Karni N, Weizman A (1995): Caffeine withdrawal increases lithium blood levels. Biological Psychiatry 37:348–350.

Michelson D, Adler L, Spencer T, Reimherr FW, West SA, Allen AJ, Kelsey D, Wernicke J, Dietrich A, Milton D (2003): Atomoxetine in adults with ADHD: Two randomized, placebo-controlled studies. Biological Psychiatry 53:112–120.

Michelson D, Allen AJ, Busner J, Casat C, Dunn D, Kratochvil CJ, Newcorn J, Sallee FR, Sangal RB, Saylor K, West S, Kelsey D, Wernicke J, Trapp NJ, Harder D (2002): Once-daily atomoxetine treatment for children and adolescents with attention deficit hyperactivity disorder: A randomized, placebo-controlled study. American Journal of Psychiatry 159:1896–1901.

Mitchell EA, Thompson JM, Robinson E, Wild CJ, Becroft DM, Clark PM, Glavish N, Pattison NS, Pryor JE (2002): Smoking, nicotine and tar and risk of small for gestational age babies. Acta Paediatrica 91:323–328.

Mitler MM, Hayduk R (2002): Benefits and risks of pharmacotherapy for narcolepsy. Drug Safety 25:791–809.

Mochizuki Y, Zhang M, Golestaneh L, Thananart S, Coco M (2003): Acute aortic thrombosis and renal infarction in acute cocaine intoxication: A case report and review of literature. Clinical Nephrology 60:130–133.

Muller CP, Carey RJ, Huston JP (2003): Serotonin as an important mediator of cocaine's behavioral effects. Drugs of Today 39:497–511.

Murray JB (1998): Psychophysiological aspects of amphetamine-methamphetamine abuse. Journal of Psychology 132:227–237.

Murray KN, Abeles N (2002): Nicotine's effect on neural and cognitive functioning in an aging population. Aging & Mental Health 6:129–138.

Nawrot P, Jordan S, Eastwood J, Rotstein J, Hugenholtz A, Feeley M (2003): Effects of caffeine on human health. Food Additives and Contaminants 20:1–30.

Nehlig A, Daval J-L, Debry G (1992): Caffeine and the central nervous system: Mechanisms of action, biochemical, metabolic, and psychostimulant effects. Brain Research Reviews 17:139–170.

Nordahl TE, Salo R, Leamon M (2003): Neuropsychological effects of chronic methamphetamine on neurotransmitters and cognition: A review. Journal of Neuropsychiatry and Clinical Neurosciences 15:317–325.

Nordberg A, Hellstrom-Lindahl E, Lee M, Johnson M, Mousavi M, Hall R, Perry E, Bednar I, Court J (2002): Chronic nicotine treatment reduces beta-amyloidosis in the brain of a mouse model of Alzheimer's disease (APPsw). Journal of Neurochemistry 81:655–658.

Osula S, Stockton P, Abdelaziz MM, Walshaw MJ (2003): Intratracheal cocaine induced myocardial infarction: An unusual complication of fibreoptic bronchoscopy. Thorax 58:733–734.

Paluska SA (2003): Caffeine and exercise. Current Sports Medicine Reports 2:213–219.

Pelham WE Jr., Swanson JM, Furman MB, Schwindt H (1995): Pemoline effects on children with ADHD: A time-response by dose-response analysis on classroom measures. Journal of the American Academy of Child and Adolescent Psychiatry 34:1504–1513.

Pennings EJ, Leccese AP, Wolff FA (2002): Effects of concurrent use of alcohol and cocaine. Addiction 97:773–783.

Peters MJ, Morgan LC (2002): The pharmacotherapy of smoking cessation. Medical Journal of Australia 176:486–490.

Picciotto MR, Corrigall WA (2002): Neuronal systems underlying behaviors related to nicotine addiction: Neural circuits and molecular genetics. Journal of Neuroscience 22:3303–3305.

Pierce K (1999): Which stimulant to choose in ADHD? Child & Adolescent Psychopharmacology News 4:1–4.

Platt DM, Rowlett JK, Spealman RD (2002): Behavioral effects of cocaine and dopaminergic strategies for preclinical medication development. Psychopharmacology 163:265–282.

Pomerleau OF (1998): Endogenous opioids and smoking: A review of progress and problems. Psychoneuroendocrinology 23:115–130.

Ramsay RR, Hunter DJ (2002): Inhibitors alter the spectrum and redox properties of monoamine oxidase A. Biochimica et Biophysica Acta 1601:178–184.

Rawson RA, Gonzales R, Brethen P (2002): Treatment of methamphetamine use disorders: An update. Journal of Substance Abuse Treatment 23: 145–150.

Rezvani AH, Levin ED (2002): Nicotine-alcohol interactions and cognitive function in rats. Pharmacology, Biochemistry, and Behavior 72:865–872.

Ribeiro JA, Sebastiao AM, de Mendonca A (2002): Adenosine receptors in the nervous system: Pathophysiological implications. Progress in Neurobiology 68:377–392.

Robertson P Jr., Hellriegel ET (2003): Clinical pharmacokinetic profile of modafinil. Clinical Pharmacokinetics 42:123–137.

Rowland AS, Lesesne CA, Abramowitz AJ (2002): The epidemiology of attention-deficit/hyperactivity disorder (ADHD): A public health view. Mental Retardation and Developmental Disabilities Research Reviews 8:162–170.

Rugino TA, Copley TC (2001): Effects of modafinil in children with attention-deficit/hyperactivity disorder: An open-label study. Journal of the American Academy of Child and Adolescent Psychiatry 40:230–235.

Ryan L, Hatfield C, Hofstetter M (2002): Caffeine reduces time-of-day effects on memory performance in older adults. Psychological Science 13:68–71.

Schenk JO (2002): The functioning neuronal transporter for dopamine: Kinetic mechanisms and effects of amphetamines, cocaine and methylphenidate. Progress in Drug Research 59:111–131.

Schmued LC (2003): Demonstration and localization of neuronal degeneration in the rat forebrain following a single exposure to MDMA. Brain Research 974:127–133.

Schwarzchild MA, Chen JF, Ascherio A (2002): Caffeinated clues and the promise of adenosine A (2A) antagonists in PD. Neurology 58:1154–1160.

Scott WH Jr., Coyne KM, Johnson MM, Lausted CG, Sahota M, Johnson AT (2002): Effects of caffeine on performance of low intensity tasks. Perceptual and Motor Skills 94:521–532.

Shannon M (2000): Methylenedioxymethamphetamine (MDMA, "Ecstasy"). Pediatric Emergency Care 16:377–380.

Sigel J (2000): Narcolepsy. Scientific American 282:77–81.

Simosky JK, Stevens KE, Freedman R (2002): Current drug targets. CNS and Neurological Disorders 1:149–162.

Simpson D, Perry CM (2003): Atomoxetine. Paediatric Drugs 5:407–415.

Slotkin TA (2002): Nicotine and the adolescent brain. Insights from and animal model. Neurotoxicology and Teratology 24:369–384.

Soares BG, Lima MS, Reisser AA, Farrell M (2003): Dopamine agonists for cocaine dependence. Cochrane Database of Systematic Reviews, CD003352.

Sonuga-Barke EJS, Swanson JM, Coghill D, DeCory H, Hatch SJ (2004): Efficacy of two once-daily methylphenidate formulations compared across dose levels at different times of the day: Preliminary indications from a secondary analysis of the COMACS study data. BMC Psychiatry 4:28.

Spencer T, Biederman J, Wilens T, Faraone S, Prince J, Gerard K, Doyle R, Parekh A, Kagan J, Bearman SK (2001): Efficacy of a mixed amphetamine salts compound in adults with attention-deficit/hyperactivity disorder. Archives of General Psychiatry 58:775–782.

Srisurapanont M, Jarururaisin N, Kittirattanapaiboon P (2001a): Treatment for amphetamine dependence and abuse. Cochrane Database of Systematic Reviews, CD003022.

Srisurapanont M, Jarusuraisin N, Kittirattanapaiboon P (2001b): Treatment for amphetamine withdrawal. Cochrane Database of Systematic Reviews, CD003021.

Stafford RS, Radley DC (2003): National trends in antiobesity medication use. Archives of Internal Medicine 163:1046–1050.

Stevenson RD, Wolraich ML (1989): Stimulant medication therapy in the treatment of children with attention deficit hyperactivity disorder. Pediatric Clinics of North America 36:1183–1197.

Suemaru K, Araki H, Gomita Y (2002): [Involvement of neuronal nicotinic receptor in psychiatric disorders]. Nippon Yakurigaku Zasshi 119:295–300.

Sullivan MA, Covey LS (2002): Nicotine dependence: The role for antidepressants and anxiolytics. Current Opinion in Investigational Drugs 3:262–271.

Swanson J, Gupta S, Lam A, Shoulson I, Lerner M, Modi N, Lindemulder E, Wigal S (2003): Development of a new once-a-day formulation of methylphenidate for the treatment of attention-deficit/hyperactivity disorder. Archives of General Psychiatry 60:204–211.

Sziraki I, Sershen H, Hashim A, Lajtha A (2002): Receptors in the ventral tegmental area mediating nicotine-induced dopamine release in the nucleus accumbens. Neurochemical Research 27:253–261.

Talbot K, Stradling J, Crosby J, Hilton-Jones D (2003): Reduction in excess daytime sleepiness by modafinil in patients with myotonic dystrophy. Neuromuscular Disorders 13:357–364.

Taylor FB, Russo J (2000): Efficacy of modafinil compared to dextroamphetamine for the treatment of attention deficit hyperactivity disorder in adults. Journal of Child and Adolescent Psychopharmacology 10:311–320.

Teeter CJ, McCabe SE, Boyd CJ, Guthrie SK (2003): Illicit methylphenidate use in an undergraduate student sample: Prevalence and risk factors. Pharmacotherapy 23:609–617.

Teitelman E (2001): Modafinil for Narcolepsy. American Journal of Psychiatry 158 (letter): 970–971.

Tonnesen P, Norrezaard J, Simonsen K, Sawe U (1991): A double-blind trial of a 16-hour transdermal nicotine patch in smoking cessation. New England Journal of Medicine 325:311–315.

Turner, DC, Robbins TW, Clark L, Aron AR, Dowson J, Sahakian BJ (2003): Relative lack of cognitive effects of methylphenidate in elderly male volunteers. Psychopharmacology 168: 455–464.

Ulus IH, Maher TJ, Wurtman RJ (2000): Characterization of phentermine and related compounds as monoamine oxidase (MAO) inhibitors. Biochemical Pharmacology 59: 1611–1621.

U.S. Department of Health and Human Services (1990): The health benefits of smoking cessation: a report of the Surgeon General. Washington, DC: U.S. Government Printing Office.

Vanderschuren LJMJ, Beemster P, Schoffellmeer ANM (2003): On the role of noradrenaline in psychostimulant-induced psychomotor activity and sensitization. Psychopharmacology 169:176–185.

Vastag B (2001): Pay attention: Ritalin acts much like cocaine. Journal of the American Medical Association 286:905–906.

Volkow NS, Wang G-J, Fowler JS, Logan J, Gerasimov M, Maynard L, Ding Y-S, Gatley SJ, Gifford A, Franceschi D (2001): Therapeutic doses of oral methylphenidate significantly increase extracellular dopamine in the human brain. Journal of Neuroscience 21:RC121.

Watkinson B, Fried PA (1985): Maternal caffeine use before, during and after pregnancy and effects upon offspring. Neurobehavioral Toxicology and Teratology 7:9–17.

Webster L, Andrews M, Stoddard G (2003): Modafinil treatment of opioid-induced sedation. Pain Medicine 4:135–140.

Wernicke J, Faries D, Girod D, Brown J, Gao H, Kelsey D, Quintana H, Lipetz R, Michelson D, Heiligenstein J (2003): Cardiovascular effects of atomoxetine in children, adolescents, and adults. Drug Safety 26:729–740.

Wesensten NJ, Belenky G, Kautz MA, Thorne DR, Reichardt RM, Balkin TJ (2002): Maintaining alertness and performance during sleep deprivation: Modafinil versus caffeine. Psychopharmacology 159:238–247.

Witcher JW, Long A, Smith B, Sauer JM, Heilgenstein J, Wilens T, Spencer T, Biederman J (2003): Atomoxetine pharmacokinetics in children and adolescents with attention deficit hyperactivity disorder. Journal of Child and Adolescent Psychopharmacology 13:53–63.

Young R, Glennon RA (2002): Nicotine and bupropion share a similar discriminative stimulus effect. European Journal of Psychopharmacology 443:113–118.

Yudofsky SC, Silver JM, Hales RE (1990): Pharmacologic management of aggression in the elderly. Journal of Clinical Psychiatry 51 (10 supplement):22–28.

Yui K, Goto K, Ikemoto S, Ishiguro T, Angrist B, Duncan GE, Sheitman BB, Lieberman JA, Bracha SH, Ali SF (1999): Neurobiological basis of relapse prediction in stimulant-induced psychosis and schizophrenia: The role of sensitization. Molecular Psychiatry 4:512–523.

Yui K, Ikemoto S, Ishiguro T, Goto K (2000): Studies of amphetamine or methamphetamine psychosis in Japan: Relation of methamphetamine psychosis to schizophrenia. Annals of the New York Academy of Sciences 914:1–12.

Zanardi A, Leo G, Biagini G, Zoli M (2002): Nicotine and neurodegeneration in ageing. Toxicology Letters 127:207–215.

CHAPTER SEVEN

THE OPIATES

This chapter reviews the opiates, opiate neuropeptides, and opiate receptors. Derived from poppies, opium is the prototypical opiate drug, from which many other compounds are derived. In addition, many other opiates have been synthesized. Opiate pharmacology involves several naturally occurring opiate receptors that are located throughout the brain and spinal cord. Mu, kappa, and delta receptors all interact with opiates. For example, morphine, a commonly used opiate for analgesia, initiates its relief of pain by binding to mu receptors.

Composed of short chains of amino acids, endorphins, enkephalins, dynorphins, and endomorphins are neuropeptides that physiologically function much like neurotransmitters and are known as endogenous opiates. Through their interactions with mu, kappa, and delta receptors, the endogenous opiates affect a wide range of brain functions. For example, the endogenous opiates modulate pain transmission, memory, mood, and eating behavior.

Medical uses of exogenous opiates include pain management, particularly in cancer patients. Not without controversy, opiate medications are also used in select circumstances in other types of pain syndromes such as headache, although generally as an adjunct to other treatment approaches.

Use of exogenous opiates frequently leads to both psychological and physiological dependence. The psychological dependence is characterized by craving for opiates and compulsive drug seeking. In contrast, physiological dependence is characterized by a withdrawal syndrome that occurs when the dose is rapidly lowered or discontinued. Withdrawal from opiates is characterized by nasal congestion, sweating, restlessness, chilling, flushing, joint pain, and an increased craving for the drug. Because of the intense discomfort, associated medical concerns, and return to opiate use associated with the opiate withdrawal syndrome, medical intervention is often necessary. An important treatment approach to opiate withdrawal includes the use of long-acting opiates, such as methadone, whose dose can be gradually tapered in an effort to avoid precipitating withdrawal signs and symptoms.

Opiate dependence is a major public health problem whose treatment is often chronic and involves a variety of therapeutic approaches. In addition to psychosocial counseling, many opiate treatment programs utilize what is known as methadone maintenance. In methadone maintenance, methadone, or other long-acting opiate such as buprenorphine, is prescribed in an effort to supply the opiate in a relatively controlled setting in an attempt to avoid the use of heroin, contaminated needles, and crime. Not without controversy, methadone maintenance is associated with less heroin use, less infection with human immunodeficiency virus, and increased employment than therapy that does not use methadone maintenance.

The opiates are those drugs that come from opium, its derivatives, or are synthetic or semisynthetic analogues of opium-like drugs (Cherny, 1996). In addition to opium, which is found in poppies (*Papaver somniferum*) (Morimoto et al., 2001), numerous other opiates are available both by prescription and illegally. Widely used in pain control (O'Callaghan, 2001), morphine was isolated from opium in the early 1800s (O'Callaghan, 2001). Opiate dependence constitutes a major personal and public health concern (Fiellin & O'Connor, 2002). Long-acting methadone, another opiate, is a pharmacological mainstay in the treatment of opiate addiction (Cone & Preston, 2002). Other opiate drugs are hydromorphone (Dilaudid), oxycodone, and meperidine (Demerol) (Inturrisi, 2002). Table 7.1 shows some typical opiates and categorizes them as to whether they are naturally occurring, semisynthetic, or synthetic.

Opiates are thought to have been used since prehistoric times (Brune, 2002). Named after the Greek god of sleep Morpheus because of its powerful sedative, hypnotic, and analgesic properties, morphine was first synthesized in 1804 by the German chemist Frederick Serturner (Comer, 2001).

Although potent analgesics, morphine and other opium derivatives unfortunately also have strong abuse and addiction potential. It is estimated that in the United States there are approximately 800,000 people who are dependent on opiates (Fiellin & O'Connor, 2002). Hailed as a significant medical advance by its discoverer Heinrich Dreser (Boehm, 1968), heroin is widely abused (Cone & Preston, 2002).

TABLE 7.1   Classification of Opiates

Natural Opiates	■ Morphine (Boonstra et al., 2001) ■ Codeine (Boonstra et al., 2001)
Semisynthetic Opiates	■ Hydrocodone (Boonstra et al., 2001). ■ Hydromorphone (Dilaudid) (Boonstra et al., 2001). ■ Oxycodone (Cairns, 2001)
Synthetic Opiates	■ Meperidine (Demerol) (Clark et al., 1995) ■ Fentanyl (Duragesic) (Jeal & Benfield, 1992) ■ Alfentanil (Scholz et al., 1996) ■ Sufentanil (Scholz et al., 1996) ■ Methadone (Dolophine) (Davis & Walsh, 2001)

Though used for centuries (Brune, 2002), little was known of the opiates' mechanism of action. Finally, after considerable investigation, Pert and Snyder (1973) identified receptors in the brain that bind specifically to the opiates and that these receptors could be localized to certain regions of the brain, findings that spawned research investigating opiate pharmacology and the neurobiological underpinnings of opiate abuse and dependency.

MECHANISM OF ACTION, PHARMACOLOGY, AND METABOLISM

Endogenous Opiates and Their Receptors

Exogenous opiates initiate their behavioral and physiological actions by binding to opiate receptors located in the membranes of neurons (Singh et al., 1997). The brain does not come equipped with opiate receptors simply to allow for exogenous opiates to exert their effects. Rather, an intricate brain opiate system exists that involves several distinct types of opiate receptors and their naturally occurring ligands, the endogenous opiates.

The endogenous opiates are naturally occurring peptides—short chains of amino acids—that function essentially as neurotransmitters and are referred to as neuropeptides. Like exogenous opiates, endogenous opiates interact with opiate receptors (Singh et al., 1997). The endogenous opiate neuropeptides form an important class of substances involved in the neuronal transmission of information and are particularly prominent in the processing of pain stimuli (Inturrisi, 2002). Based in part upon their amino-acid sequences, the endogenous opiate peptides can be classified into two general groups: The endorphins, enkephalins, and dynorphins form one group, and the endomorphins 1 and 2 form the second (Okada et al., 2002). Among the best studied endogenous opiate neuropeptides are endorphins and enkephalins. Neuropeptides are produced from proneuropeptide precursors. For example, prodynorphin is the precursor of dynorphin (Vogt, 2002). The endogenous opiate system is involved extensively in the processing of pain, which is the reason for the analgesic effects of the *exogenous* opiates like morphine. Among other brain areas, the anterior cingulate cortex appears to be critical for opiate-induced analgesia and is activated by opiates (Petrovic et al., 2002).

An important element in the central nervous system processing of pain, dynorphin is released by spinal cord neurons and modulates incoming neuronal pain impulses at the spinal level and in the brain (Vogt, 2002). Dynorphin is also involved in chronic pain syndromes and can be elevated in chronic pain. Despite its role in blocking the transmission of some pain impulses, dynorphin may enhance pain impulses in some cases (Vogt, 2002), illustrating the complexity of pain processing.

Connected to opiate-mediated pain processing is substance P (McLean et al., 1985), a neuropeptide involved in pain (DeVane, 2001) and inflammation (O'-Connor et al., 2004) and found in some brain regions together with certain opiate receptors, (McLean et al., 1985). Because of the localization of substance P with opiate receptors, it is thought that the pain-producing effects of substance P are inhibited by opiates.

The endogenous and exogenous opiates initiate their effects by interacting with mu, kappa, and delta opiate receptors that are located in both the nervous system and peripheral body tissues (Okada et al., 2002). Mu opiate receptors, for instance, are located throughout the nervous system including sites in the peripheral nervous system, the spinal cord, brainstem, thalamus, and cortex (Inturrisi, 2002), as well as in the gastrointestional system (Miller & Lyon, 2003). Kappa opiate receptors are located throughout the nervous system, including sites in the nigro-striatal and mesocorticolimbic dopamine pathways (Kreek et al., 2002) and are involved in analgesia and respiratory depression (Sporer, 1999). Delta opiate receptors appear to have a role in spinal-cord level analgesia (Sporer, 1999).

Delta, kappa, and mu opiate receptors are coupled to G-proteins (Okada et al., 2002) and can diminish the release of presynaptic neurotransmitters, hyperpolarize the postsynaptic neuron (making it less likely to generate an action potential), alter the transmission of some GABA circuits (Inturrisi, 2002), and alter gene expression (Miller & Lyon, 2003). Furthermore, there are several subtypes of mu receptors (Pasternak, 2001). Mu_1 receptors appear to be involved in analgesia, whereas mu_2 receptors appear to mediate the respiratory depression associated with opiates, slowed bowel motility, miosis (small pupillary diameter), and dependence (Sporer, 1999). Opiate receptors can be antagonized pharmacologically by naloxone, an opiate receptor antagonist (Cherny, 1996).

In addition to their roles in analgesia and respiratory depression, the delta, mu, and kappa opiate receptors are involved in a diverse range of brain and other organ function:

- In addition to their role in pain processing and modulation, the opiate receptors are implicated in memory function (Okada et al., 2002).
- Heroin and morphine can produce a sense of tranquility (Camí & Farré, 2003).
- Agonism of mu receptors results in analgesia and euphoria (Miller & Lyon, 2003).
- Drugs that specifically agonize opiate delta receptors diminish pain but appear to have convulsive properties (Broom et al., 2002).
- Opiate peptides when given exogenously may have antidepressant properties, and drugs that inhibit enkephalinase, the enzyme that degrades enkephalins (thereby increasing available enkephalins), are associated with delta-receptor-mediated antidepressant properties in animal models (Broom et al., 2002).
- Specific delta agonists have antidepressant properties in the forced-swim test in animal studies (Broom et al., 2002), a behavioral test used to screen compounds for antidepressant potential.

- The antidepressants venlafaxine (Effexor) and mirtazapine (Remeron) affect opiate receptors, a mechanism of action that may relate to their putative efficacy in severe depression (Schreiber et al., 2002).
- Opiate receptors in rats regulate serotonin release in parts of the midbrain and forebrain (Tao & Auerbach, 2002).
- The endogenous opiate system may have an inhibitory and anxiolytic effect to emotionally laden stimuli in brain limbic regions (Liberzon et al., 2002).
- Mu receptor agonists increase the consumption of food (Smith et al., 2002).
- Transmission in the spinal projections of the locus coeruleus that diminish pain via norepinephrine mechanisms is increased by presynaptic delta opioid receptor activation by lessening GABA inhibition in this system (Pan et al., 2002), suggesting an additional mechanism by which opiate receptors are involved in pain processing.
- Peripheral effects of opiate receptors include a role in gastrointestinal motility, vascular function (Okada et al., 2002), respiration (mediated through brainstem opiate receptors), and, through mu receptors, regulation of pupillary diameter (Miller & Lyon, 2003). Furthermore, opiate receptors appear to be involved in several cardiovascular diseases, including hypertension and heart failure (Pugsley, 2002).

Sigma opiate receptors are also an important part of the endogenous opiate system, although much less is known about them than about delta, kappa, and mu receptors. In mice, sigma antagonists block some of the effects of cocaine, suggesting that one mechanism of cocaine may involve opiate sigma receptors (Matsumoto et al., 2002). Moreover, cocaine affects additional opiate receptors. Chronic administration of cocaine, for instance, increases mu and kappa receptor density. Cocaine also increases gene expression for prodynorphin (Collins et al., 2002). Sigma receptors also affect heart contractility and rhythm (Monassier & Bousquet, 2002).

Evidence suggests that the opiate system may vary significantly from one person to another. For example, the binding potential between opiate receptors and opiates differs between individuals (Zubieta et al., 2001). Furthermore, men and women may activate mu-opioid receptors differently in response to pain, with men displaying more mu receptor activation than women in certain brain regions (Zubieta et al., 2002).

EXOGENOUS OPIATES

In addition to heroin and other illicit opiates, several opiates are used clinically, primarily for the treatment of pain and opiate addiction. The exogenous opiates, including morphine, hydromorphone, meperidine, oxymorphone, levorphanol, and methadone (Inturrisi, 2002), mediate their effects through agonism of endogenous opiate receptors. Morphine, for instance, agonizes mu receptors, which blocks transmission of pain impulses into the spinal cord and alters cortical processing of pain stimuli (Vogt, 2002). For example, by decreasing calcium ion flow into neurons mediating pain transmission in the spinal cord, opiates diminish the release of substance P (Inturrisi, 2002), decreasing the perception of pain. Other exogenous opiates can act as agonists or antagonists of the opiate receptors, depending on the state of the opiate system of a given person (Inturrisi, 2002).

Via G-proteins linked to opiate receptors, exogenous opiates increase cyclic AMP, which appears to relate to cellular changes that may underlie the development of tolerance and physical dependence to exogenous opiates (Inturrisi, 2002).

The brain reward system located in the mesocorticolimbic dopamine pathway is a potential locus and mechanism of the reinforcing properties of exogenous opiates. Activating this pathway by releasing endogenous opiates, exogenous opiate drugs are related to feelings of euphoria and elevated energy, as well as reinforcement for consuming more opiate (Koob & Le Moal, 1997). Other brain regions, too, appear involved in opiate use. For example, when presented with opiate-related cues, increased blood flow evaluated by positron emission tomography occurred in the left medial frontal and left anterior cingulate cortex in people with a history of opiate dependence who had been abstinent anywhere from ten days to three years (Daglish et al., 2001).

Half-life varies among the exogenous opiates. Morphine has a half-life of approximately two to three and a half hours in the plasma, but its analgesic effects can persist for four to six hours (Inturrisi, 2002). Longer-acting preparations of morphine, such as MS-Contin, with analgesia effects lasting approximately eight to twelve hours, and Roxanol-SR, with effects lasting twenty-four hours, are available (Inturrisi, 2002). Methadone (Dolophine) has a plasma half-life of approximately twenty-four hours (Inturrisi, 2002).

Heroin is more lipophillic than other opiates and penetrates the brain within 15 to 20 seconds after intravenous administration, accounting not only for the so-called rush associated with heroin use but also for some of its toxicity (Sporer, 1999). Some metabolism of heroin occurs within the brain, where heroin is converted into morphine in approximately one-half hour after reaching the brain (Sporer, 1999). Other differences between exogenous opiates exist. For instance, according to a government report, OxyContin, a controlled release form of the exogenous opiate oxycodone, is twice a potent as morphine (U. S. Government Accounting Office, 2004).

The metabolism of exogenous opiates is important in understanding their clinical effects and some of their potential for toxicity. For example, codeine depends upon metabolic conversion to codeine-6-glucuronide and morphine for its analgesic effects (Vree et al., 2000). Via primarily the non-cytochrome P450 enzymes uridine diphosphate glucuronosyl transferases (Armstrong & Cozza, 2003), morphine is metabolized to 3-conjugate and a 6-conjugate metabolites. The 3-conjugate form (morphine-3-glucuronide; Inturrisi, 2002) does not appear to have analgesic properties and may, in fact, lower the analgesia from the parent drug morphine (Armstrong & Cozza, 2003). The morphine 6-conjugate form (morphine-6-glucuronide; Inturrisi, 2002), however, may be up to fifty times more potent as an analgesic than morphine itself (Armstrong & Cozza, 2003). Meperidine is metabolized to normeperidine (Clark et al., 1995), which is excitotoxic and can cause anxiety, tremors, and sometimes seizures (Inturrisi, 2002). Behavioral and physiological changes in optical intoxication are listed in Table 7.2.

ADVERSE EFFECTS

Dependence and tolerance issues are important to opiate use. Most people who are addicted to opiates are also physiologically dependent upon them (Inturrisi, 2002). Furthermore, tolerance—the requirement of ever higher amounts of drug to obtain the desired effects—occurs with opiate use (Harrison et al., 1998). In addition to abuse of heroin, exogenous opiates used in pain management are often abused. In their study of the medical use and abuse of the opiates fentanyl, hydromorphone, meperidine, morphine, and oxycodone, Gilson and colleagues (2004) found that abuse of all these opiates with the exception of meperidine increased between 1997 and 2002. Corresponding with this reported increase in opiate abuse, the diversion of OxyContin (controlled-release oxycodone) from legitimate uses to illegal use more than doubled between 2000 and 2002 (Gilson et al., 2004). Sometimes referred to as "poor man's heroin," or "oxy", or "killer" (Hays, 2004; Katz & Hays, 2004), OxyContin abuse does indeed appear to be increasingly abused (U.S. Government Accounting Office, 2004). In fact, the rise in abuse and dependence on controlled-release oxycodone has been referred to as an epidemic in some regions of the United States (Hays, 2004; Katz & Hays, 2004). And no wonder—the number of people reporting at least one nonmedical use of OxyContin increased from 221,000 in 1999 to 1,900,000 in 2002 (www.deadiversion.usdoj.gov/drugs_concern/oxycodone/oxycodone.htm). In their report of three adolescent cases that developed dependence upon controlled-release oxycodone, Katz and Hays (2004) note that controlled-release oxycodone can be

---

TABLE 7.2   Behavioral and Physiological Changes in Opioid Intoxication

- Maladaptive behavior or psychological changes (e.g., initial euphoria followed by apathy, dysphoria, or retardation, impaired judgment, or impaired social or occupational functioning) that developed during, or shortly after, opioid use (APA, 1994; Miller & Lyon, 2003).

- Pupillary constriction (or pupillary dilation due to anoxia from severe overdose) and one (or more) of the following signs, developing during, or shortly after, opioid use:

  1. drowsiness or coma

  2. slurred speech

  3. hypotension

  4. respiratory depression

  5. impairment in attention or memory (APA, 1994; Miller & Lyon, 2003).

used orally, snorted, or used intravenously and can result in a high similar to that obtained from heroin.

Opiate addiction may have an underlying genetic susceptibility. The gene coding for the mu opiate receptor, for example, has several polymorphisms, some of which alter the function of the receptor. Some of these polymorphisms are associated with an increased risk of opiate dependence (Lee & Smith, 2002). The A118G polymorphism, for example, of the mu opiate receptor may be associated with heroin abuse in Han Chinese living in Hong Kong (Szeto et al., 2001). Similar to other drugs of addiction, dependence upon opiates appears to involve the mesocorticolimbic dopamine pathway (Inturrisi, 2002). The rewarding properties of opiates may also be mediated through cannabinoid receptors (Mas-Nieto et al., 2001)

Because of the physiological dependence that occurs from opiate use, withdrawal signs and symptoms are associated with the cessation of opiate use, or even a reduction in dose. Mediated in part by the sympathetic nervous system and activation of the hypothalamic-pituitary-adrenal axis (Kreek et al., 2002), opiate withdrawal is characterized by myalgia (muscle pain), arthralgia (joint pain), nausea, insomnia, irritability, rhinorrhea (nasal congestion and discharge), diaphoresis (sweating), tachycardia (increased heart rate), dilated pupils, and piloerection (goose flesh) (Fiellin & O'Connor, 2002). Table 7.3 lists behavioral and physiological changes associated with opiate withdrawal.

The use of methadone, a long-acting opiate, during pregnancy is associated with a withdrawal syndrome in the neonate that correlates with the maternal dose of methadone. Up to 90 percent of newborns experience opiate withdrawal when higher doses of methadone were used by the pregnant mothers (Dashe et al., 2002).

TABLE 7.3   Behavioral and Physiological Changes in Opioid Withdrawal

- Three (or more) of the following, developing within minutes to several days after either the cessation of (or reduction in) opioid use that has been heavy and prolonged or administration of an opioid antagonist after a period of opioid use:

1. dysphoric mood

2. nausea or vomiting

3. muscle aches

4. lacrimation or rhinorrhea

5. pupillary dilation, piloerection, or sweating

6. diarrhea

7. yawning

8. fever

9. insomnia (APA, 1994; Miller & Lyon, 2003)

Opiate overdose is a serious and potentially lethal complication of opiate abuse. In Australia, deaths from heroin overdose increased from 1.3 per million in 1964 to 71.5 per million 1997—a fifty-five-fold increase (Hall et al., 1999). One-half of the mortality rate among regular users of heroin may be attributable to overdose (Sporer, 1999), most of which is associated with intravenous heroin use, although deaths from intranasal, intramuscular, subcutaneous, and oral routes do occur (Sporer, 1999). Overdose involving opiates often occurs in the context of other drug use (Sporer, 1999), such as alcohol and benzodiazepines (Sporer, 2003). One factor in deaths associated with heroin and other drugs that suppress respiration may be the increased respiratory suppression occurring from the combination of several drugs suppressing respiration (Sporer, 1999). Showing the enhanced lethality of oxycodone when combined with other drugs, a study of 1,014 deaths involving oxycodone found lower mean oxycodone levels in those cases in which other drugs had been ingested than in those in which oxycodone was the sole drug (Cone et al., 2004). Most of the fatalities associated with heroin overdose occur in a social context; that is, other people are present, although medical help is often not sought until too late (Sporer, 1999). The people who die from heroin overdose tend to be those who have heroin dependence, as opposed to new users, although, to be sure, even new users of heroin can die from overdose (Sporer, 1999).

Mediated by opiate effects on brainstem respiratory centers and augmented by concomitant use of alcohol and benzodiazepines (Inturrisi, 2002), respiratory suppression also can be a serious and lethal complication of exogenous opiate use (Camí & Farré, 2003). The most common cause of death in opiate overdose, in fact, is cessation of breathing (Inturrisi, 2002). Nausea and vomiting can complicate treatment with opiates and is thought to occur as a result of opiate interaction with the chemoreceptor regions in the brain (Inturrisi, 2002). Another gastrointestinal effect from exogenous opiates is constipation, which results from activation of receptors in the gastrointestinal tract that diminish bowel motility and secretions (Inturrisi, 2002). Because opiates increase smooth muscle tone, including the sphincter muscles in the bladder, exogenous opiates can result in urinary retention (Inturrisi, 2002). Finally, sedation is also a common adverse effect from opiate treatment, an effect that is exacerbated by the concurrent use of alcohol or benzodiazepines (Inturrisi, 2002). Drug interactions can occur with opiates. For example, meperidine should not be used in conjunction with monoamine-oxidase-inhibiting antidepressants (Clark et al., 1995) (see Chapter 9).

USES

Analgesia

Opiates can be quite effective in reducing the pain associated with headaches and other pain syndromes. Meperidine, for example, is prescribed in emergency rooms for migraine headaches (Clark et al., 1995). Because of their potential for addiction, however, the use of opiates is reserved for those cases in which other pain-relief techniques have proven ineffective and are often used only in conjunction with nonopiate medications, such as anti-inflammatory medication. Furthermore, experts recommend against using opiates as first-line treatment for migraine headaches (Snow et al., 2002), even though opiates can be quite effective in treating the pain of acute migraines. Opiates such as morphine and oxycodone (Cairns, 2001) are used in the management of pain that occurs in patients who have cancer (Cherny, 1996). The abuse potential in this population appears relatively low in people who do not have a history of substance abuse (Inturrisi, 2002). When opiates are used for the management of pain, opiate rotation can be used. This technique involves rotating through different opiates during treatment instead of continuously using the same opiate. Although the pharmacological basis for this practice is unknown, opiate rotation can improve analgesia while reducing adverse effects (Inturrisi, 2002).

Pain is a complex physiological phenomenon with a large psychological component. Illustrating this is the finding that some types of placebo analgesia, at least in part, depend upon the endogenous opiate system. In fact, a placebo analgesic response can be blocked by the opiate antagonist naloxone (Petrovic et al., 2002). Opiates are generally only part of the overall treatment of pain (Bannwarth, 1999).

Cough

The opiates are effective in alleviating coughing (Chung & Chang, 2002). However, the usefulness of the opiates in controlling cough is limited by opiate side effects and the risk of opiate dependence (Chung & Chang, 2002).

Management of Opiate Detoxification and Withdrawal

Opiate withdrawal poses a considerable clinical challenge for which a variety of approaches are in use. The mental and physical misery of opiate withdrawal can diminish a patient's motivation for abstinence and may lead to continued opiate use (Fiellin & O'Connor 2002). One way of treating the physiological cravings associated with withdrawal was pioneered by a research team at the Rockefeller University in New York. Their means of treatment involved the use of the psychopharmacological agent methadone, a long-acting opiate, concomitantly with a rehabilitation program directed at the "total resocialization" of the addicted person (Dole & Nyswander, 1967). After admission to a treatment facility, or even in an outpatient setting, the person addicted to opiates is often treated with a long-acting synthetic opiate, such as methadone. A full agonist at opiate mu receptors (Kreek et al., 2002), methadone has been used extensively for this purpose (Kreek et al., 2002) to control withdrawal signs and symptoms.

Buprenorphine, a long-acting, mu-opiate receptor partial agonist (Kreek et al., 2002) was approved in 2002 by the United States Food and Drug Administration for the treatment of opiate withdrawal. Its long half-life allows for a gradual decrement in blood and brain buprenorphine concentrations and minimizes or even prevents symptoms of opiate withdrawal. Buprenorphine has been demonstrated to be as equally effective as methadone and has fewer side effects (Blaine, 1992). In a study of opiate withdrawal complicated by concurrent abuse of other drugs, a combination of buprenorphine and carbamazepine (an anticonvulsant that is also used to treat bipolar disorder) was more effective than methadone and carbamazepine (Seifert et al., 2002). Furthermore, buprenorphine has fewer physical dependency characteristics than other opiates (Grant & Sonti, 1994) and can be discontinued without severe withdrawal symptoms. A partial agonist, buprenorphine produces the feelings of contentment associated with opiate use (Mendelson & Mello, 1992) but its partial agonist properties make unintentional overdose less likely (Kreek et al., 2002).

Methadone and buprenorphine are both opiates and carry their own risks of addiction, a concern that has motivated the search other alternatives to treat opiate withdrawal. One such nonopiate drug is clonidine (Catapres). Clonidine is an alpha 2-adrenoreceptor agonist and decreases norepinephrine release (Hoffman & Lefkowitz, 1990). Another approach to managing the acute withdrawal from opiates done in some centers is rapid opiate detoxification. In rapid opiate detoxification, opiate-addicted patients are placed under general anesthesia while the opiate antagonist naloxone (see page 164) is given (Wilson et al., 1999), with the intense withdrawal symptoms precipitated by the opiate antagonist occurring while the patient is under general anesthesia. In effect, rapid opiate detoxification rapidly substitutes an opiate antagonist for an opiate agonist as a means of beginning long-term opiate antagonist treatment (Streel & Verbanck, 2003).

Opiates suppress the locus coeruleus, which contains the nerve cell bodies of the brain's norepinephrine system, and opiate withdrawal results in increased activity of the locus coeruleus, which results in some of the symptoms of opiate withdrawal (Miller & Lyon, 2003). Clonidine via its alpha 2 agonism can suppress some of these withdrawal symptoms and can be used in the management of opiate withdrawal (Miller & Lyon, 2003). A trial comparing buprenorphine to clonidine in the treatment of heroin withdrawal found that more patients were retained and had fewer withdrawal symptoms with buprenorphine than with clonidine and other drugs used to symptomatically treat the withdrawal (Lintzeris et al., 2002). In addition, judicious use of benzodiazepines can relieve some of the agitation and insomnia of opiate withdrawal (Miller & Lyon, 2003).

Treatment of Opiate Addiction

Of the approximately 800,000 people in the United States who are dependent upon opiates, it is estimated that only 180,000 receive appropriate treatment (Fiellin & O'Connor, 2002). The costs of opiate addiction and its associated problems are immense. For example, in the United States in 1996, it was estimated that costs associated with heroin use totaled approximately $21 billion (Mark et al.,

2001). Many of the available treatment programs in the United States are federally regulated and performed in specially designated clinics. Because of new regulations, however, physicians with the proper qualifications can now treat some opiate dependency in an office-based setting, which offers several advantages over traditional opiate-treatment clinics, such as increased availability of treatment and less contact with other opiate-abusing patients (Fiellin & O'Connor, 2002).

The treatment of opiate dependency has both pharmacological and nonpharmacological components. The nonpharmacological aspect of the treatment of opiate addiction is based upon frequent psychosocial counseling in both group and individual settings. Specific focuses of therapy include relapse prevention, motivation, teaching coping skills and interpersonal skills, and compliance with treatment (Fiellin & O'Connor, 2002). Twelve-step programs like Narcotics Anonymous also can be helpful (Miller & Lyon, 2003). Another example of similar programs, Methadone Anonymous is a 12-step program for heroin-dependent people maintained on methadone that may have benefits not found in other treatment approaches, such as less concomitant use of cocaine and marijuana (Gilman et al., 2001).

Other psychotherapeutic approaches also have been investigated. One such intervention added a cognitive-behavioral component to routine counseling for people with opiate dependency. This technique was associated with less illegal drug use in women but not men (Pollack et al., 2002). Urine drug screens also are obtained in an effort to monitor abstinence and enhance motivation. Other mental and medical disorders, such as comorbid depression or psychosis, should be diagnosed and appropriately treated, as opiate dependency is frequently comorbid with other mental disorders (Fiellin & O'Connor, 2002).

In addition to psychosocial approaches, several drugs are available as adjuncts in the treatment of opiate addiction. Methadone maintenance, developed in 1964 for heroin addiction (Kreek, 1996), was the first effective drug treatment. Spawned in part from an increasing understanding of the neurobiology of addiction, as of 2002, over sixty drugs were under investigation for use in drug addiction, including opiate dependence and abuse (Tankosic, 2002). Other drugs used to treat opiate addiction are levomethadyl acetate hydrochloride oral solution (LAAM), buprenorphine (Subutex), and the opiate-receptor antagonist naltrexone (Kreek et al., 2002).

Methadone (Dolophine). Used in the maintenance treatment of opiate addiction since the 1960s (Dole & Nyswander, 1965), methadone is used in many countries for the treatment of opiate dependence (Mattick et al., 2002). Methadone is the most frequently used drug in the long-term treatment of opiate addiction, with approximately 350,000 people in the United States and Europe in methadone-maintenance treatment programs (Kreek et al., 2002). In addition to methadone's full agonism at the mu receptor (Kreek et al., 2002), methadone also antagonizes to some extent N-methyl-D-aspartate (NMDA) glutamate receptors (Kreek et al., 2002). Antagonism of NMDA receptors may prevent or inhibit the development of tolerance to opiates, which may account for the lack of tolerance seen with the long-term use of methadone (Kreek et al., 2002). Combined with behavioral interventions (Kreek et al., 2002), methadone is given in once-daily doses (Fiellin & O'Connor, 2002) and diminishes drug craving (Kreek et al., 2002). Controversial and associated with low rates of complete opiate abstinence at five years after discharge from the methadone program (Maddux & Desmond, 1992), the efficacy of methadone maintenance has been questioned (Mattick et al., 2002). A review study, however, comparing methadone-maintenance treatment to treatment that did not utilize methadone replacement found that methadone maintenance kept people in treatment and diminished heroin use more than did the treatment that did not use methadone, though it did not significantly diminish criminal activity (Mattick et al., 2002). Methadone treatment is associated with decreased infection with human immunodeficiency virus (Fiellin & O'Connor, 2002) and increased employment. Methadone maintenance also reduces fatal and nonfatal heroin overdose (Sporer, 2003).

Levomethadyl Acetate Hydrochloride Oral Solution (LAAM).   Approved by the United States Food and Drug Administration for maintenance treatment of opiate addiction and sharing a similar chemical structure with methadone (Kreek et al., 2002), LAAM's half-life allows it to be given only three times a week (Fiellin & O'Connor, 2002), diminishing the frequency that a person in treatment must report to the opiate clinic to receive medication but also weakening the supervision that the clinic can provide. A concern with LAAM is the possibility that it may prolong cardiac conduction times, resulting in an increased QT interval (Kreek et al., 2002), a condition that can lead to heart arrhythmias. For this reason, LAAM therapy of opiate dependency is generally used only when other drugs, such as methadone, have failed (Fiellin & O'Connor, 2002).

Buprenorphine (Subutex).   Acting as an opiate antagonist in conditions of high opiate concentrations and as an agonist under low or nonexistent opiate concentrations, buprenorphine is a partial agonist of opiate receptors (Fiellin & O'Connor, 2002). In addition to its actions at the mu receptor, buprenorphine also shows high affinity for kappa and delta opiate receptors, although its effects on the delta receptor appear relatively weak (Negus et al., 2002). Buprenorphine is the first drug approved for physician-office prescribing for opiate dependency (Kleber, 2002). An advantage of buprenorphine over methadone is that, because buprenorphine is a partial opiate agonist, it is safer than methadone in overdose, although fatalities can occur, particularly if the buprenorphine is taken with other drugs (Kleber, 2002). Because it is a partial opiate agonist, large doses of buprenorphine may precipitate withdrawal when heroin is used concomitantly (Clark et al., 2002). With a longer half-life than methadone, buprenorphine can be taken every other day and diminishes craving for opiates (Kleber, 2002).

Naltrexone.   By antagonizing opiate receptors (Kreek et al., 2002), naltrexone reduces the reinforcing properties of opiates by blocking their access to opiate receptors. This approach requires high compliance and motivation on the part of the opiate-addicted person, as the naltrexone must be regularly taken. If the naltrexone is discontinued, opiate receptors are again available for opiates. Furthermore,

TABLE 7.4   Treatment of Opiate Addiction

1. Frequent psychosocial counseling in both group and individual settings, focusing on relapse prevention, motivation, teaching coping skills and interpersonal skills, and compliance with treatment.

2. Urine drug screens to monitor abstinence and enhance motivation.

3. Diagnosis and treatment of comorbid disorders.

4. Adjunct opiate-maintenance treatment designed to diminish use of opiates obtained on the street and provide some supervision to the person taking the drug and to gradually decrease the dose:
   a. Methadone
   b. Levomethadyl Acetate Hydrochloride Oral Solution (LAAM)
   c. Buprenorphine (Subutex)
   d. Naltrexone

while naltrexone blocks the effects of opiates, it does little to block the craving for opiates (Kleber, 2002). Due to these and possibly other factors, naltrexone alone is relatively ineffective in the treatment of opiate addiction (Kreek et al., 2002). Nalmefene (Revex) is another opiate antagonist that has been used for opiate addiction (Kreek et al., 2002). Table 7.4 summarizes the treatment of opiate addiction.

SUMMARY

The endogenous opiates consist of several naturally occurring neurotransmitter-like substances that occur throughout the central nervous system. Endorphins, enkephalins, dynorphins, and endomorphins agonize mu, delta, and kappa opiate receptors to modulate and regulate a host of brain functions. The endogenous opiates are a crucial component in pain processing and modulation systems. In addition to their role in pain physiology, endogenous opiates are involved with certain aspects of memory, food consumption, gastrointestinal motility, cardiovascular function, anxiolysis, and mood regulation.

The exogenous opiates are a large class of opiates that also act through mu, kappa, and delta opiate receptors. Heroin, morphine, hydrocodone, oxycodone, and methadone are but a few of the many available exogenous opiates. Although often abused, many of the exogenous opiates have legitimate medical uses, centering mainly on the management of pain syndromes. Even though they are highly effective analgesics, the use of opiates in pain management remains controversial and the risk of addiction and other complications require a search for other options and judicious use of opiates.

Opiate dependency is a major worldwide health problem whose treatment consists of two basic stages. Detoxification is a particularly vulnerable time that often results in resumption of the opiate. To manage the withdrawal syndrome that can occur when the opiate dose is stopped or even lowered, methadone, buprenorphine, or LAAM can be used to control the withdrawal symptoms and allow for tapered dose reduction. Because buprenorphine is a partial opiate agonist, it may cause less dependence than other opiates, making it a reasonable choice to manage opiate withdrawal. Clonidine can also be used to manage the opiate withdrawal syndrome, although the side effects of clonidine often limit its use.

Requiring different treatment approaches, the long-term management of opiate addiction poses a considerable clinical challenge. Psychosocial interventions consisting of both individual and group counseling are often combined with long-term methadone maintenance. Substituting the relatively controlled use of methadone for illicit opiate use, methadone maintenance can decrease intravenous drug use and increase employment. In addition to methadone, other long-acting opiates can be used for long-term maintenance therapy in opiate clinics. The partial agonist buprenorphine can be prescribed in physicians' offices and may have less abuse potential than methadone.

STUDY QUESTIONS

1. Describe the known functions of the endogenous opiate system.
2. Before treating a patient with chronic pain with an opiate, what factors should be considered?
3. Describe the known relevant neurobiology of opiate addiction.
4. What is the mechanism of the opiate withdrawal syndrome and what are its clinical characteristics?
5. What options are available to treat the opiate withdrawal syndrome?
6. Compare and contrast methadone, buprenorphine, and LAAM. Which would you use in a long-term, opiate-substitution program and why?

REFERENCES

American Psychiatric Association. (1994). *Diagnostic and Statistical Manual of Mental Disorders* (4th ed.). Washington, DC: Author.

Armstrong SC, Cozza KL (2003): Pharmacokinetic drug interactions of morphine, codeine, and their derivatives: Theory and clinical reality, part I. Psychosomatics 44:167–171.

Bannwarth B (1999): Risk-benefit assessment of opioids in chronic noncancer pain. Drug Safety 21:283–296.

Boehm G (1968): At last—a nonaddicting substitute for morphine? Today's Health, 46:69–72.

Blaine JD (1992): Introduction. In JD Blaine (ed.), *Buprenorphine: An Alternative Treatment for Opioid Dependence* (pp. 1–4). Washington, DC: U.S. Department of Health and Human Services.

Boonstra B, Rathbone DA, Bruce NC (2001): Engineering novel biocatalytic routes for production of semisynthetic opiate drugs. Biomolecular Engineering 18:41–47.

Broom DC, Jutkiewicz EM, Rice KC, Traynor JR, Woods JH (2002): Behavioral effects of delta-opioid receptor agonists: Potential antidepressants. Japanese Journal of Pharmacology 90:1–6.

Brune K (2002): Next generation of everyday analgesics. American Journal of Therapeutics 9:215–223.

Cairns R (2001): The use of oxycodone in cancer-related pain: A literature review. International Journal of Palliative Nursing 7:522–527.

Camí H, Farré M (2003): Drug addiction. New England Journal of Medicine 349:975–986.

Cherny NI (1996): Opioid analgesics: Comparative features and prescribing guidelines. Drugs 51:713–737.

Chung KF, Chang AB (2002): Therapy for cough: Active agents. Pulmonary Pharmacology & Therapeutics 15:335–338.

Clark NC, Lintzeris N, Muhleisen PJ (2002): Severe opiate withdrawal in a heroin user precipitated by a massive buprenorphine dose. Medical Journal of Australia 176:166–167.

Clark RF, Wei EM, Anderson PO (1995): Meperidine: Therapeutic use and toxicity. Journal of Emergency Medicine 13:797–802.

Collins SL, Kunko PM, Ladenheim B, Cadet JL, Carroll FI, Izenwasser S (2002): Chronic cocaine increases kappa-opioid receptor density: Lack of effect by selective dopamine uptake inhibitors. Synapse 45:153–158.

Comer RJ (2001): *Abnormal Psychology* (4th ed.). New York: Worth Publishers.

Cone EJ, Fant RV, Rohay JM, Caplan YH, Ballina M, Reder RF, Haddox JD (2004): Oxycodone involvement in drug abuse deaths. II. Evidence for toxic multiple drug-drug interactions. Journal of Analytical Toxicology 28:217–225.

Cone EJ, Preston KL (2002): Toxicologic aspects of heroin substitution treatment. Therapeutic Drug Monitoring 24:193–198.

Daglish MR, Weinstein A, Malizia AL, Wilson S, Melichar JK, Britten S, Brewer C, Lingford-Hughes A, Myles JS, Grasby P, Nutt DJ (2001): Changes in regional cerebral blood flow elicited by craving memories in abstinent opiate-dependent subjects. American Journal of Psychiatry 158:1680–1686.

Dashe JS, Sheffield JS, Olscher DA, Todd SJ, Jackson GL, Wendel GD (2002): Relationship between maternal methadone dosage and neonatal withdrawal. Obstetrics and Gynecology 100:1244–1249.

Davis MP, Walsh D (2001): Methadone for relief of cancer pain: A review of pharmacokinetics, pharmacodynamics, drug interactions and protocols of administration. Supportive Care in Cancer 9:73–83.

DeVane CL (2001): Substance P: A new era, a new role. Pharmacotherapy 21:1061–1069.

Dole, VP, & Nyswander, M (1965). A medical treatment for diacetylmorphine (heroin) addiction: A clinical trial with methadone hydrochloride. Journal of the American Medical Association 193:646–650.

Dole VP, Nyswander M (1967). The miracle of methadone in the narcotics jungle. Roche Report 4:1–2, 8, 11.

Fiellin D, O'Connor P (2002): Office-based treatment of opioid-dependent patients. New England Journal of Medicine 347:817–823.

Gilman SM, Galanter M, Dermatis H (2001): Methadone Anonymous: A 12-step program for methadone maintained heroin addicts. Substance Abuse 22:247–256.

Gilson AM, Ryan KM, Joranson DE, Dahl JL (2004): A reassessment of trends in the medical use and abuse of opioid analgesics and implications for diversion control: 1997–2002. Journal of Pain and Symptom Management 28:176–188.

Grant SJ, Sonti G (1994). Buprenorphine and morphine produce equivalent increases in extracellular single unit activity of dopamine neurons in the ventral tegmental area in vivo. Synapse 16:181–187.

Hall WD, Degenhardt LJ, Lynskey MT (1999): Opioid overdose mortality in Australia, 1964–1997: Birth-cohort trends. Medical Journal of Australia 171:34–37.

Harrison LM, Kastin AJ, Zadina JA (1998): Opiate tolerance and dependence: receptors, G-proteins, and antiopiates. Peptides 19:1603–1630.

Hays LR (2004): A profile of OxyContin addiction. Journal of Addictive Diseases 23:1–9.

Hoffman BB, Lefkowitz RL (1990): Catecholamines and sympathomimetic drugs. In Gilman AF, Rall TW, Nies AS, Taylor P (eds.), *Goodman and Gilman's The Pharmacological Basis of Therapeutics*. Elmsford, NY: Pergamon Press.

Inturrisi CE (2002): Clinical pharmacology of opioids for pain. Clinical Journal of Pain 18:S3–13.

Jeal W, Benfield P (1997): Transdermal fentanyl. A review of its pharmacological properties and therapeutic efficacy in pain control. Drugs 53:109–138.

Katz DA, Hays LR (2004): Adolescent OxyContin abuse. Journal of the American Academy of Child and Adolescent Psychiatry 43:231–234.

Kleber HD (2002): Treating addicts is now easier. Clinical Psychiatry News 30:21.

Koob GF, Le Moal M (1997): Drug abuse: Hedonic homeostatic dysregulation. Science 278:52–58.

Kreek MJ (1996): Opiates, opioids, and addiction. Molecular Psychiatry 1:232–254.

Kreek MJ, LaForge KS, Butelman E (2002): Pharmacotherapy of addictions. Nature Reviews. Drug Discovery 1:710–726.

Lee NM, Smith AP (2002): Opioid receptor polymorphisms and opioid abuse. Pharmacogenomics 3:219–227.

Liberzon I, Zubieta JK, Fig LM, Phan KL, Keoppe RA, Taylor SF (2002): mu-Opioid receptors and limbic responses to aversive emotional stimuli. Proceedings of the National Academy of Sciences of the United States of America 99:7084–7089.

Lintzeris N, Bell J, Bammer J, Jolley DJ, Rushworth L (2002): A randomized controlled trial of buprenorphine in the management of short-term ambulatory heroin withdrawal. Addiction 97:1394–1404.

Maddux JF, Desmond DP (1992): Methadone maintenance and recovery from opioid dependence. American Journal of Drug and Alcohol Abuse 18:63–74.

Mark TL, Woody GE, Juday T, Kleber HD (2001): The economic costs of heroin addiction in the United States. Drug and Alcohol Dependence 61:195–206.

Mas-Nieto M, Pommier B, Tzavara ET, Caneparo A, Da Nascimento S, Le Fur G, Rogues BP, Noble F (2001): Reduction of opioid dependence by the CB1 antagonist SR141716A in mice: Evaluation of the interest in pharmacotherapy of opioid addiction. British Journal of Pharmacology 132:1809–1816.

Matsumoto RR, McCracken KA, Pouw B, Zhang Y, Bowen WD (2002): Involvement of sigma receptors in the behavioral effects of cocaine: Evidence from novel ligands and antisense oligodeoxynucleotides. Neuropharmacology 42:1043–1055.

Mattick RP, Breen C, Kimber J, Davoli M (2002): Methadone maintenance therapy versus no opioid replacement therapy for opioid dependence. Cochrane Database Syst Rev:CD002209.

McLean S, Skirboll LR, Pert CB (1985): Comparison of substance P and enkephalin distribution in rat brain: An overview using radioimmunocytochemistry. Neuroscience 14:837–852.

Mendelson JH, Mello N (1992): Human laboratory studies of buprenorphine. In JD Blaine (ed.), *Buprenorphine: An Alternative Treatment for Opiate Dependence* (pp. 38–60). Washington, DC: U.S. Department of Health and Human Services.

Miller NS, Lyon D (2003): Biology of opiates affects prevalence of addiction, options for treatment. Psychiatric Annals 33:559–564.

Monassier L, Bousquet P (2002): Sigma receptors: from discovery to highlights of their implications in the cardiovascular system. Fundamental & Clinical Pharmacology 16:1–8.

Morimoto S, Suemori K, Moriwaki J, Taura F, Tanaka H, Asao M, Tanaka M, Suemune H, Shimohigashi Y, Shoyama Y (2001): Morphine metabolism in the opium poppy and its possible physiological function. Biochemical characterization of the morphine metabolite, bismorphine. Journal of Biological Chemistry 276:38179–38184.

Negus SS, Bidlack JM, Mello NK, Furness MS, Rice KC, Brandt MR (2002): Delta opioid antagonist effects of buprenorphine in rhesus monkeys. Behavioural Pharmacology 13:557–570.

O'Callaghan JP (2001): Evolution of a rational use of opioids in chronic pain. European Journal of Pain 5 (supplement A):21–26.

O'Connor TM, O'Connell J, O'Brien DI, Goode T, Bredin CP, Shanahan F (2004): The role of substance P in inflammatory disease. Journal of Cellular Physiology 201:167–180.

Okada Y, Tsuda Y, Bryant SD, Lazarus LH (2002): Endomorphins and related opioid peptides. Vitamins and Hormones 65:257–279.

Pan YZ, Li DP, Chen SR, Pan HL (2002): Activation of delta-opioid receptors excites spinally projecting locus coeruleus neurons through inhibition of GABAergic inputs. Journal of Neurophysiology 88:2675–2683.

Pasternak GW (2001): Insights into mu opioid pharmacology the role of mu opioid receptor subtypes. Life Sciences 68:2213–2219.

Pert, C.B., & Snyder, S.H. (1973). Opiate receptor: Demonstration in nervous tissue. Science 179:1011–1014.

Petrovic P, Kalso E, Petersson KM, Ingvar M (2002): Placebo and opioid analgesia—imaging a shared neuronal network. Science 295:1737–1740.

Pollack MH, Penava SA, Bolton E, Worthington JJ, Allen GL, Farach FJ, Otto MW (2002): A novel cognitive-behavioral approach for treatment-resistant drug dependence. Journal of Substance Abuse and Treatment 23:335–342.

Pugsley MK (2002): The diverse molecular mechanisms responsible for the actions of opioids on the cardiovascular system. Pharmacology & Therapeutics 93:51–75.

Scholz J, Steinfath M, Schulz M (1996): Clinical pharmacokinetics of alfentanil, fentanyl and sufentanil. An update. Clinical Pharmacokinetics 31:275–292.

Schreiber S, Bleich A, Pick CG (2002): Venlafaxine and mirtazapine: Different mechanisms of antidepressant action, common opioid-mediated antinociceptive effects—a possible opioid involvement in severe depression? Journal of Molecular Neuroscience 18:143–149.

Seifert J, Metzner C, Paetzold W, Borsutzky M, Passie T, Rollnik J, Wiese B, Emrich HM, Schneider U (2002): Detoxification of opiate addicts with multiple drug abuse: A comparison of buprenorphine vs. methadone. Pharmacopsychiatry 35:159–164.

Singh VK, Bajpai K, Biswas S, Haq W, Khan MY, Mathur KB (1997): Molecular biology of opioid receptors: Recent advances. Neuroimmunomodulation 4:285–297.

Smith SL, Harrold JA, Williams G (2002): Diet induced obesity increases mu opioid receptor binding in specific regions in rat brain. Brain Research 953:215–222.

Snow V, Weiss K, Wall EM, Mottur-Pilson C (2002): Pharmacologic management of acute attacks of migraine and prevention of migraine headache. Annals of Internal Medicine 137:840–849.

Sporer KA (1999): Acute heroin overdose. Annals of Internal Medicine 130:584–590.

Sporer KA (2003): Strategies for preventing heroin overdose. British Medical Journal 326:442–444.

Streel E, Verbanck P (2003): Ultra-rapid opiate detoxification: From clinical applications to basic science. Addiction Biology 8: 141–146.

Szeto CY, Tang NL, Lee DT, Stadlin A (2001): Association between mu-opioid receptor gene polymorphisms and Chinese heroin addicts. Neuroreport 12:1103–1106.

Tankosic, T (2002). Potential pharmacotherapy of drug and alcohol addiction. CNS News 4:21–22.

Tao R, Auerbach SB (2002): Opioid receptor subtypes differentially modulate serotonin efflux in the rat central nervous system. Journal of Pharmacology and Experimental Therapeutics 303:549–556.

Use of opioids to treat acute headaches remains controversial. CNS News, 4, 8.

U.S. Government Accounting Office. (2004): OxyContin abuse and diversion and efforts to address the problem: Highlights of a government report. Journal of Pain & Palliative Care Pharmacotherapy 18:109–113.

Vogt, BA (2002). Knocking out the DREAM to study pain. New England Journal of Medicine 347:362–364.

Vree TB, van Dongen RT, Koopman-Kimenai PM (2000): Codeine analgesia is due to codeine-6-glucuronide, not morphine. International Journal of Clinical Practice 54:395–398.

Wilson LB, DeMaria PA Jr., Kane HL, Reining KM (1999): Anesthesia-assisted rapid opiate detoxification: A new procedure in the postanesthesia care unit. Journal of Perianesthesia Nursing 14:207–212.

Zubieta JK, Smith YR, Beuller JA, Xu Y, Kilbourn MR, Jewett DM, Meyer CR, Koeppe RA, Stohler CS (2001): Regional mu opioid receptor regulation of sensory and affective dimensions of pain. Science 293:311–315.

CHAPTER EIGHT

MARIJUANA, HALLUCINOGENS, PHENCYCLIDINE, AND INHALANTS

Marijuana, the hallucinogens, phencyclidine (PCP), and the inhalants are widely used and associated with substantial morbidity, including addiction. This chapter discusses the history, postulated mechanisms of action and pharmacology, intoxication states, and withdrawal syndromes of these substances.

The most commonly used illicit drug in the United States, marijuana is obtained from *cannabis sativa*, which can be grown in most temperate regions of the world. Although marijuana contains numerous cannabinoids, one of its principal psychoactive ingredients is delta 9-tetrahydrocannabinol. This compound appears to initiate its effects through agonism of endogenous cannabinoid receptors that have numerous physiological functions. Behavioral effects of marijuana include euphoria as well as psychosis in some cases. Cognitive and memory dysfunction also occur. The abrupt discontinuation of marijuana is associated with a withdrawal syndrome characterized by irritability and diminished appetite.

Although many hallucinogens are clandestinely available, this chapter focuses on lysergic acid diethylamide (LSD), psilocybin, bufotenine, mescaline, and 3, 4-methylenedioxymethamphetamine (MDMA). Demonstrating the variation in sources that characterize the hallucinogens, LSD is chemically synthesized, psilocybin is found in psilocybe mushrooms, bufotenine is obtained from a species of toad, and mescaline is found in a certain type of cactus. These drugs appear to initiate their effects by agonizing serotonin type 2 receptors. MDMA seems to increase the release of serotonin and dopamine. The hallucinogens alter emotions and produce hallucinations. Unlike many other psychoactive drugs, the hallucinogens are not associated with a withdrawal syndrome.

Originally developed as an anesthetic, PCP antagonizes N-methyl-D-aspartate receptors. A similar drug, ketamine, is still used in some situations as an anesthetic. In addition to euphoria, PCP can produce a psychotic state that closely resembles acute schizophrenia.

The inhalants are readily available in many common household and industrial products. Requiring no special equipment to use, the inhalants are widely abused among children and adolescents, ranking fourth in this population behind alcohol, nicotine, and marijuana. Inhalants come from many sources such as glue, gasoline, and paint. Toluene, acetone, and benzene are found in many of the inhalants and appear to underlie the toxic and addictive properties of many inhalants. Increasing the activity of dopamine neurons in the mesocorticolimbic like many drugs of abuse, toluene also modulates the activity of GABA, N-methyl-D-aspartate, and glycine receptors. Associated not only with euphoria, inhalants can also cause neurological disturbances, seizures, and death.

In 2000, approximately 14 million Americans were users of illegal drugs (Khalsa et al., 2002). Many of these people abused marijuana (Khalsa et al., 2002), the hallucinogens (Borowiak et al., 1998), and inhalants (Riegel & French, 2002). Associated not only with acute intoxication states (Brust, 1993), these drugs may in certain cases produce long-term neurobehavioral changes. For example, marijuana use can worsen the course of psychosis in some people with psychosis (Degenhardt & Hall, 2002). Furthermore, abuse and addiction (Borowiak et al., 1998; Khalsa et al., 2002; Riegel & French, 2002) can accompany use of these substances. Many of these substances occur naturally in certain plants and fungi. Marijuana, for instance, is found in the hemp plant (Brust, 1993), and psilocybe mushrooms contain the hallucinogens psilocybin and psilocin (Gross, 2002). In addition to the naturally occurring substances, other psychoactive drugs, such as lysergic acid diethylamide (LSD) and phencyclidine (Vetulani, 2001) are synthesized, often illegally, in laboratories. Many highly abusable psychoactive compounds, however, are not generally even considered to be drugs. For instance, aromatic hydrocarbons and the solvent toluene are inhalants, not generally regarded as drugs, yet they are used by children and adolescents for their euphoria-inducing qualities (Vetulani, 2001). Although differing in mechanism of action and behavioral effects, marijuana, the hallucinogens, phencyclidine, and inhalants are discussed in this chapter because of their significant effects on behavior and widespread use. Other drugs of abuse are reviewed in Chapters 5 (sedative hypnotics and alcohol), 6 (amphetamines, stimulants, cocaine, caffeine, and nicotine), and 7 (the opiates).

MARIJUANA

Obtained from the hemp plant (*Cannabis sativa*) (Brust, 1993) and used for centuries in India and China (Brust, 1993), the earliest known references to marijuana date to 2700 B.C. (Julien, 1995). In China, marijuana was (Blum, 1969; Culliton, 1970) listed in the herbal compendiums of the Chinese emperor Shen Nung, written in about 2737 B.C. Approximately seven million people use marijuana at least weekly in the United States (Bolla et al., 2002). In fact, marijuana is the most commonly used illicit drug in the United States (Khalsa et al., 2002). In

1993, over 23 percent of adults in the 19- to 32-year range had used marijuana in the last year (Johnston et al., 1994), with 12.9 percent of this population reporting use in the previous month. More recently, it has been reported that one-third of the individuals studied in the National Household Survey on Drug Abuse had used marijuana in the past (Bobashev & Anthony, 1998).

Mechanism of Action and Pharmacology

Ordinarily smoked, marijuana also can be ingested (Brust, 1993). When smoked, behavioral effects can occur within seconds to minutes (Grotenhermen, 2003); taken orally, the behavioral effects of marijuana do not occur for approximately 30 to 90 minutes (Grotenhermen, 2003). *Cannabis sativa* contains at least sixty cannabinoids (Hart et al., 2002); the primary active ingredient of marijuana, however, appears to be delta 9-tetrahydrocannabinol (Wilson & Nicoll, 2002), the chemical that appears to be responsible for most of the central nervous system effects of marijuana.

Marijuana mediates its behavioral effects by agonizing cannabinoid receptors. At least two types of cannabinoid receptors exist: those in the central nervous system, the cannabinoid receptors type 1, which appear to be coupled to G-proteins (Basavarajappa & Hungund, 2002), and those outside the central nervous system, cannabinoid receptors type 2 (Khalsa et al., 2002). Via cannabinoid receptors, the cannabinoids found in marijuana appear to act as neuromodulators and may have neuroprotective and glial-cell-modulatory properties (Carter & Weydt, 2002). Furthermore, it is the cannabinoid 1 receptors that appear responsible for the behavioral and rewarding effects of cannabis (Tanda & Goldberg, 2003). Although found widely throughout the brain and located in almost every brain area, cannabinoid 1 receptors are nevertheless distributed unevenly, with relatively high densities in limbic and association regions (Howlett et al., 2004). Cannabinoid 2 may be involved in immune function, and cannabinoid 2 messenger RNA has been found in tonsils, spleen, and thymus (Howlett et al., 2004), tissues involved in the immune response.

Similar to the opiate receptors, which interact with naturally occurring opiates found in the brain (see Chapter 7), endogenous substances known as endocannabinoids agonize presynaptic cannabinoid receptors and decrease the release of other neurotransmitters (Camí & Farré, 2003). Resulting in similar effects as the active ingredient of marijuana (Maccarrone & Finazzi-Agro, 2002), primary endocannabinoids are anandamide (arachidonylethanolamide), 2-arachidonoylglyercol (Howlett et al., 2004; Maccarrone & Finazzi-Agro, 2002), and noladin ether (2-arachidonylglycerylether) (Camí & Farré, 2003; Howlett et al., 2004).

Although little is known about the synthesis and release of anandamide and 2-arachidonoylglycerol, activation of muscarinic acetylcholine and metabotropic glutamate receptors in rats results in release of endocannabinoids in the hippocampus, suggesting a relationship between endocannabinoids and the brain muscarinic acetylcholine and glutamate systems (Kim et al., 2002). While in the synapse, endocannabinoids interact with a transporter molecule that regulates their synaptic concentrations by taking them back into the presynaptic neuron where they are degraded into other compounds (Maccarrone & Finazzi-Agro, 2002). Endogenous cannabinoids may function in a retrograde fashion; that is, they can be released from the postsynaptic neuron and diffuse backwards across the synapse to interact with cannabinoid 1 receptors on the presynaptic neuron (Wilson & Nicoll, 2002).

The physiological effects of endocannabinoids via the cannabinoid receptors are only but poorly understood. Despite this paucity of information, however, evidence suggests multiple functions for endocannabinoids, ranging from cognitive to cardiovascular responses. For example, the endocannabinoids appear to be involved with pain control, the promotion of appetite, suckling, blockade of working memory, cardiovascular modulation, embryonic development (Khalsa et al., 2002), and cognition (Wilson & Nicoll, 2002). Anandamide is also important for the function of sperm cells in humans. Other proposals for the function of endocannabinoids include immune regulation and even psychomotor control (Khalsa et al., 2002). Furthermore, chronic alcohol intake in rodents increases the synthesis of anandamide and 2-arachidonylglycerol, which in turn down regulates the cannabinoid 1 receptor (Basavarajappa & Hungund, 2002), suggesting an important mechanism of action of alcohol. Further strengthening the putative link between alcohol and the endocannabinoid system in rodents, antagonism of cannabinoid 1 receptors inhibits the voluntary consumption of alcohol (Basavarajappa & Hungund, 2002).

In addition to its effects on cannabinoid receptors, delta 9-tetrahydrocannabinol increases the release of dopamine in the mesolimbic pathway (Tanda et al., 1997), similar to some other drugs of addiction (Camí & Farré, 2003). The actions of delta 9-tetrahydrocannabinol on mesolimbic dopamine suggest that at least some of the effects of marijuana are mediated by the same brain reward system through which other recreational and abuse-prone psychopharmacological agents operate (Gardner & Lowinson, 1991). The brain cannabinoid system also affects the opiate system, another mechanism by which cannabis dependence is thought to occur (Tanda & Goldberg, 2003).

In a study evaluating the effects of delta 9-tetrahydrocannabinol with positron emission tomography, Mathew and colleagues (2002) found increased regional cerebral blood flow, a measure of brain activation, after intravenous infusion of delta 9-tetrahydrocannabinol in frontal, insular, and cingulate brain regions, with increased regional cerebral blood flow in the right brain hemisphere. Behavioral intoxication peaked at 30 minutes after infusion and remained present 120 minutes after infusion. These functional imaging studies thus suggest that marijuana can affect a relatively wide range of brain regions.

The acute use of marijuana can cause relaxation, euphoria, a sense that time is slowed (Brust, 1993), and a feeling of well-being (Grotenhermen, 2003). Paranoia can also occur (Brust, 1993). The effects of marijuana involve a dose-dependent impairment of memory and cognitive functions, such as attending, speaking, problem solving, and concept formation (Azorlosa et al., 1992; Dewey, 1986; Ferraro, 1976).

The effects of the cannabinoid 1 receptor antagonist rimonabant may help clarify the roles of the endocannabinoid system. Rimonabant may have role in obesity and tobacco addiction (Howlett et al., 2004).

Although marijuana is generally smoked, a process that allows marijuana to penetrate the lungs where it is rapidly absorbed (Grotenhermen, 2003), the subjective effects of smoked marijuana and orally ingested delta 9-tetrahydrocannabinol are similar, although some effects of the smoked marijuana are more pronounced. Orally ingested delta 9-tetrahydrocannabininol was less likely than smoked marijuana to be associated with irritability in the days following use. Both routes of administration resulted in an increase in appetite for about three days (Hart et al., 2002).

Marijuana is metabolized into an active biologically metabolite, 11-hydroxy-delta 9-tetrahydrocannabinol, and into an inactive metabolite, 11-nor-9-carboxy-delta 9-tetrahydrocannabinol (Huestis et al., 1992).

Drug-Drug Interactions

Marijuana inhibits the cytochrome P450 3A4 isoenzyme (McLeod et al., 2002). Because this enzyme is involved in the metabolism of many drugs, marijuana has the potential for numerous drug-drug interactions. For example, sildenafil (Viagra), used to treat erectile dysfunction, is metabolized by the cytochrome P450 3A4 enzyme (McLeod et al., 2002). McLeod and colleagues (2002) report a case of myocardial infarction occurring in a young man who had used both sildenafil and marijuana, raising the possibility that marijuana, by blocking the 3A4 isoenzyme, inhibited the metabolism of sildenafil, with subsequent toxic levels possibly leading to the myocardial infarction. Smoked marijuana may also decrease levels of some antipsychotic medications, such as clozapine (Clozaril) and olanzapine (Zyprexa) by inducing cytochrome P450 enzymes that metabolize them. If the marijuana is abruptly stopped, the cytochrome enzymes metabolizing clozapine and olanzapine may decrease, resulting in increased drug levels and possible negative side effects (Zullino et al., 2002). In part because marijuana is illegal, its drug-drug interaction profile is incompletely described.

Adverse Effects

A hallmark of marijuana use is its production of psychological dependence, similar to other addicting drugs. Several risk factors have been identified for marijuana abuse and dependence: marijuana availability, pressure from peer groups, poor self-esteem, parental mental disorders, and experience with legal drugs (von Sydow et al., 2002). Marijuana abuse is also associated with such personality factors as low extraversion and high openness to experience (Flory et al., 2002).

Because of the high prevalence of marijuana abuse and dependence, drugs are being investigated for their use in minimizing marijuana dependence. For example, mice treated concurrently with delta 9-tetrahydrocannabinol and the benzoflavone moiety from *Passiflora incarnata* (Passion Flower) showed less tolerance and dependence than those given delta 9-tetrahydrocannabinol alone (Dhawan et al., 2002). Coupled with marijuana dependence is a withdrawal syndrome initiated by the abrupt cessation of marijuana use and characterized by irritability, diminished appetite, anxiety (Khalsa et al., 2002), depression, muscle pain, poor sleep (Haney et al., 2002), and anger (Budney et al., 2003). The onset of the marijuana withdrawal syndrome occurs between one and three days after marijuana cessation and lasts for approximately four to fourteen days (Budney et al. 2003). The antidepressant nefazodone (Serzone) may diminish the anxiety and muscle pain that occur during marijuana withdrawal (Haney et al., 2002), although further research is required. In mice undergoing withdrawal from delta 9-tetrahydrocannabinol, the benzoflavone moiety from *Passiflora incarnata* also attenuated withdrawal features (Dhawan et al., 2002). In part because cannabis is highly lipid soluble, it is readily stored in fat and slowly released. This slow release of marijuana attenuates marijuana withdrawal (Tanda & Goldberg, 2003). Finally, psychosocial interventions, such as relapse prevention and support groups, appear effective in the treatment of marijuana abuse and dependency (Steinberg et al., 2002; Stephens, Roffman, & Simpson, 1994).

Marijuana use has been associated with the initiation of other drugs (Morral, 2002), such as amphetamines and opiates—the so-called gateway effect. In their review, reassessment, and analysis of the marijuana gateway effect, Morral and colleagues (2002) note that evidence for the gateway effect consists of three broad findings: (1) the increased risk of marijuana users compared to nonusers to later use other drugs, (2) the robust tendency for adolescents to use marijuana before initiating the use of other drugs, and (3) the relationship between the frequency of marijuana use and likelihood of initiating other drugs. Alternatively, Morral and colleagues (2002) argue based on analysis of their model that although a gateway effect may indeed exist, the correlation between marijuana use and the propensity to use other drugs could be due to an underlying common factor that leads to both marijuana and other drug use.

Also associated with marijuana use are serious neurobehavioral consequences. Anxiety and panic attacks can occur from high doses of marijuana (Grotenhermen, 2003). Marijuana used acutely also can cause a psychosis that generally resolves with cessation of marijuana (Zammit et al., 2002). Marijuana-induced psychosis can vary in its presentation, ranging from depersonalization to paranoia and hallucinations (Johns, 2001). Alternatively, marijuana use in adolescence also is associated with the development of chronic schizophrenia, even after marijuana is no longer being consumed (Andreasson et al., 1987). People who have schizophrenia and who use marijuana tend to have had an earlier age of schizophrenia onset and have more severe positive symptoms such as hallucinations and delusions (Bersani et al., 2002). Illustrating the complexity of the relationship between schizophrenia and drug use, several factors are considered relevant in explaining the association between marijuana and schizophrenia: other drugs, such as amphetamines that are often used in addition to marijuana, premorbid personality traits, and the use of marijuana as a form of self-treatment (Zammit et al., 2002).

However, Zammit and colleagues (2002) in an epidemiological study found evidence of a causal relationship between marijuana use and the later development of schizophrenia independent of other risk factors. However, this study is limited in that it is retrospective and did not sample the entire population of marijuana users, potentially leading to a biased sample. Although the neurobiology of this proposed relationship is not known, delta 9-tetrahydrocannabinol releases dopamine in the mesolimbic pathway (Tanda et al., 1997).

As also noted above, marijuana worsens cognitive function (Solowij et al., 2002), a finding with major public and individual heath implications, given the widespread use of marijuana. Solowij and colleagues (2002) found that heavy, long-term marijuana use worsens attention and memory, effects that persisted beyond the period of acute intoxication. Furthermore, these cognitive impairments worsened with increased years of marijuana use. As measured by a radial-arm maze, a test of spatial memory function in rats, delta 9-tetrahydrocannabinol impairs rat spatial memory through the acetylcholine system (Mishima et al., 2002). Furthermore, delta 9-tertrahydrocannabinol reduces the release of acetylcholine in the rat hippocampus. Acetylcholinesterase inhibitors (such as tetrahydroaminoacridine) both reduce the diminished release of hippocampal acetylcholine and lessen the impairments in spatial memory from delta 9-tetrahydrocannabinol in rats (Mishima et al., 2002). Delta 9-tetrahydrocannabinol also appears to worsen episodic memory in a dose-dependent fashion (Curran et al., 2002).

Marijuana use also impairs cardiac function and increases heart rate and affects blood pressure (Grotenhermen, 2003). Overall, marijuana increases cardiac work (Khalsa et al., 2002). Orthostatic hypotension (lightheadedness upon standing) may also occur from marijuana use (Sidney, 2002). Marijuana appears to cause its cardiovascular effects via the autonomic nervous system (Sidney, 2002).

By suppressing the secretion of gonadotropins from the pituitary gland and by possible direct effects on the ovaries and testes, marijuana lowers levels of leutinizing hormone and follicle-stimulating hormone (Brust, 1993). Although the effects of marijuana on pregnancy and reproductive function are controversial (Grotenhermen, 2003), one study found that use of marijuana during the second trimester of pregnant teenagers is related to reduced height among the offspring when evaluated at age 6 compared to controls who were not exposed to intrauterine marijuana (Cornelius et al., 2002).

The smoke inhaled from marijuana use is similar to tobacco smoke, with the exception that tobacco smoke contains nicotine, whereas marijuana smoke has cannabinoids (Tashkin et al., 2002). As such, marijuana smoke itself is a source of adverse effects from marijuana. In general, the long-term use of marijuana is associated with numerous adverse effects on respiratory function, such as chronic bronchitis, wheezing, chronic cough, and shortness of breath with exertion (Tashkin et al., 2002). Microscopic damage from long-term marijuana smoking occurs in the airways (Tashkin et al., 2002). Marijuana smoke also contains known carcinogens (Tashkin et al., 2002), making marijuana smoking a risk factor for the development of cancer.

Uses (Controversial)

The legitimate medical uses of marijuana remain controversial; however, marijuana does have several potentially therapeutic effects (Grotenhermen, 2003). Furthermore, marijuana's agonism of the endogenous endocannabinoid receptor and structural similarity to endocannabinoids suggest that positive effects may occur from marijuana use. These potential uses must be balanced against the risks associated with a drug that is addictive and causes many adverse effects including negative neurobehavioral outcomes. The clinical use of marijuana is further hampered by only limited pharmacokinetic and pharmacodynamics information. Furthermore, the overall safety and efficacy data of marijuana are weak (Roth, 2002). Inhalation of marijuana via smoking is associated with risk of cancer and other adverse effects as mentioned above, a problem that may be mitigated by oral, rectal, or parenteral (i.e., administered at a site outside of the gastrointestinal tract, such as intramuscularly or intravenously) delivery of marijuana (Kalant, 2001). Synthetic cannabinoid analogues could produce cannabinoid-like compounds that separate therapeutic effects from harmful ones.

Nausea.   Marijuana diminishes nausea and vomiting (Kalant, 2001) and dronabinol (Marinol), synthetic delta 9-tetrahydrocannabinol, l is approved as a treatment for the severe nausea and vomiting that often occur from cancer chemotherapy (Howlett et al., 2004).

Appetite Stimulation.   Marijuana increases appetite and can lead to weight gain. Although generally considered a negative effect of marijuana, the appetite stimulation from marijuana may be a benefit in people suffering from wasting syndrome (Kalant, 2001), a condition of health-threatening weight loss associated with severe disease, such as cancer. As previously mentioned, dronabinol is approved for use in AIDS wasting syndromes (Howlett et al., 2004).

Analgesia.   Marijuana has potentially clinically useful analgesia effects (Kalant, 2001). In particular, cannabinoids diminish inflammatory and neuropathic pain and appear to interact with sites in the brain, spinal cord, and peripheral nervous system (Beaulieu & Rice, 2002).

Intraocular Pressure Reduction.   Marijuana can diminish the increased intraocular pressure that occurs in glaucoma, although this effect is not generally robust or long-lasting enough to justify the therapeutic use of marijuana in glaucoma (Kalant, 2001). However, the discovery of ocular cannabinoid receptors may allow for a topical application of marijuana that circumvents some of the problems associated with smoking marijuana to alleviate intraocular pressure (Jarvinen et al., 2002).

Bronchodilation. Marijuana dilates the bronchi of the lungs, a potentially therapeutic effect in asthma, a disease characterized by bronchial restriction. However, this effect is often weak and short lived, suggesting that marijuana may be an inappropriate clinical intervention for asthma (Kalant, 2001).

Epilepsy. Marijuana reduces seizure threshold and may have a role in epilepsy (Kalant, 2001).

Tourette's Syndrome. In a placebo-controlled trial, delta 9-tetrahydrocannabinol significantly improved tics and obsessive-compulsive behavior. The authors of this study speculated that the clinical effects in Tourette's syndrome were from the 11-delta 9-tetrahydrocannabinol metabolite of marijuana (Muller-Vahl et al., 2002). Table 8.1 lists the proposed mechanism of action, adverse effects, and some proposed but controversial uses of marijuana.

THE HALLUCINOGENS

The hallucinogens are a diverse group of drugs loosely classified together on the basis of their ability to cause hallucinations in one or more sensory modalities at doses that are not necessarily otherwise toxic (Leikin et al., 1989). Cognition and alertness are thus preserved even in the presence of hallucinations. Although a variety of drugs could arguably be included under such a rubric, this section focuses on lysergic acid diethylamide (LSD), psilocybin, bufotenine, mescaline, and 3, 4-methylenedioxymethamphetamine (MDMA, ecstasy). In his fascinating review of the hallucinogens, Nichols (2004) argues that MDMA should not be classified with the hallucinogens because of its unique pharmacology. With this point in mind, however, MDMA is considered here primarily because of its consciousness-altering effects, even though its mechanism of action differs from that of the more traditionally defined hallucinogens. The name *hallucinogen* itself may not be en-

TABLE 8.1 Marijuana: Mechanism of Action, Adverse Effects, and Uses

Mechanism of Action	Agonizes cannabinoid receptors
Adverse Effects	Psychological and physiological dependence, psychosis, worsened cognitive functioning, including deficits in attention and memory; increased heart rate and blood pressure, orthostatic hypotension; lowered levels of leutinizing hormone, follicle-stimulating hormone, estrogens, and testosterone
Some Proposed but Controversioal Uses	Nausea, appetite stimulation, analgesia, intraocular pressure reduction, bronchodilation, epilepsy, and Tourette's syndrome

tirely accurate because at doses normally used, the so-called hallucinogens may not necessarily induce hallucinations, although other effects on consciousness are produced (Nichols, 2004). Other terms for the hallucinogens are used particularly in the nonscientific literature. Designating these substances as psychedelic and psychomimetic drugs is common (Nichols, 2004), but in this review, the term hallucinogen will be used.

Many types of hallucinogens occur naturally in some plants and fungi. Psilocybin and related substance psilocin are found in psilocybe mushrooms (*Psilocybe semilanceata*) (Gross, 2002). Bufotenine is found in the venom of *Bufo alvarius*, a toad found in the Sonoran desert (Weil & Davis, 1994). In addition to these naturally occurring hallucinogens, numerous types of hallucinogens have been artificially synthesized, such as lysergic acid diethylamide (LSD).

Many naturally occurring hallucinogens have been used for millennia. Some of the hallucinogens have been (and are currently) used as sacraments in religious rites and have been ascribed with mystical and magical properties. Groups of Native Americans, for example, have used extracts from peyote cactus and psilocybin-containing mushrooms in religious rites (Brust, 1993). Furthermore, mescaline has been used for centuries (Bruhn et al., 2002).

Mechanism of Action and Pharmacology

LSD. LSD affects serotonin function (Backstrom et al., 1999), including interacting with the serotonin 2C receptor (Backstrom et al., 1999). LSD also decreases the firing rate of serotonin-producing neurons in the raphe nuclei (Aghajanian, 1970). However, research suggests that LSD agonism or partial agonism on cortical serotonin 2A receptors is an important aspect of the behavioral effects of LSD (Nichols, 2004). Glutamate transmission also may be affected by LSD and other hallucinogens (Nichols, 2004). Possibly unique to LSD compared to other hallucinogens is the suggestion that LSD may increase dopamine transmission (Nichols, 2004).

Physiologically, LSD causes headache, nausea, and blurred vision (Brust, 1993). Euphoria, alterations in hearing and vision, hallucinations, and a subjective sense time prolongation also follow the use of LSD (Brust, 1993). An often-frightening feeling of time reversal can sometimes occur (Brust, 1993). The blending of perceptions from different sensory modalities—synesthesia—occurs with LSD use. For example, in the synesthesia associated with LSD use, people may hear sights, feel colors, and see sounds. Visual hallucinations of bright colors may be followed by increasingly complex hallucinations that can be beautiful or hideous (Brust, 1993). In addition, the behavioral changes accompanying LSD use can include dysphoria, anxiety, and frank paranoia, the so-called bad trip, which can be associated with suicide and homicide (Frosh et al., 1965). Even after the acute behavioral effects of LSD have stopped, a person may reexperience, generally only for a short period, the behavioral changes and hallucinations associated with the use of LSD, although in this case, no additional LSD was used. These "flashbacks" may occur for months (Brust, 1993). The mental effects of LSD can be viewed as primarily altering consciousness (Nichols, 2004). The effects on consciousness from LSD appear to depend in part on the expectations of the user, as well as the environment in which the drug is taken (Nichols, 2004). Finally, the effects of LSD can persist for 10 to 12 hours (Nichols, 2004).

Psilocybin.   Obtained from psilocybe mushrooms (Gross, 2002), psilocybin use may result in mood changes, visual hallucinations, illusions, and changes in thinking patterns (Vollenweider et al., 1999). Psilocybin can also produce a behavioral state similar to that seen in early-onset schizophrenia, an effect that is blocked by the serotonin subtype 2A antagonist ketanserin (Vollenweider et al., 1998). Consistent with the finding of serotonin subtype 2 receptor down regulation that occurs in rats treated with LSD (Buckholtz et al., 1990), psilocybin is an agonist of serotonin subtype 1A (Vollenweider et al., 1999) and 2A receptors (Umbricht et al., 2003). In addition to and possibly a result of its agonism of serotonin subtype 1A and 2A receptors, psilocybin appears to modulate dopamine release in the basal ganglia (Vollenweider et al., 1999) and increases glucose metabolism in several brain regions including the prefrontal and anterior cingulate cortices (Vollenweider et al., 1997). This psilocybin-induced increase in metabolism is similar to that seen in acute schizophrenia, in contrast to the decreased metabolism found in chronic schizophrenia (Vollenweider et al., 1997). Psilocybin is actually an inactive prodrug for the active compound psilocin, which is metabolized from psilocybin (Nichols, 2004). The behavioral effects of psilocybin do not appear to last longer than approximately five hours (Nichols, 2004).

Mescaline.   The psychoactive component of peyote (Nichols, 2004), and with psychological effects similar to LSD (Brust, 1993), mescaline, or 3, 4, 5-trimethoxyphenylethylamine (Ghansah et al., 1993), is derived from the buttons of the peyote cactus, *Lophophora williamsii* (Bruhn et al., 2002). Archeological evidence suggests that mescaline has been in use for approximately 5,700 years, originally having been used in North America (Bruhn et al., 2002). In addition to inhibiting acetylcholine transmission at the neuromuscular junction (Ghansah et al., 1993), mescaline may act as a partial agonist at serotonin subtype 2A receptors (Aghajanian & Marek, 1999). Like LSD, the effects of mescaline can be present for approximately 10 to 12 hours (Nichols, 2004).

MDMA.   MDMA has features in common with both methamphetamine (see Chapter 6) and the hallucinogens (Freese et al., 2002). Although it has been suggested that MDMA possesses both amphetamine-like and hallucinogen-like effects, its psychopharmacological effects are relatively free of the hallucinations produced by LSD and related compounds (Greer & Tolbert, 1986; Nichols, 1986). It appears to release serotonin from neurons and may increase synaptic concentrations of dopamine also (Schmidt, 1987). As is the case with amphetamine, MDMA also has some dopamine-releasing action. Analogue studies of MDMA have shown that, following the serotonin-releasing action, there is an acute depletion of cortical serotonin between three and six hours after administration, with recovery of normal serotonin levels within 24 hours. However, a second phase of depletion may occur several days later, which is suggestive of a neurotoxic reaction (Schmidt, 1987). The serotonin attenuation from even one-time use of MDMA appears to result in depressed moods, to which women may be more susceptible than men (Verheyden et al., 2002). Even limited use of MDMA may cause permanent neuronal damage to serotonin-producing neurons (Ricuarte et al., 1985; Schmidt, 1987). Psychologically, MDMA produces a sense of bliss and emotional intimacy to others (Westreich, 2002). The most common positive psychological effects of MDMA are enhanced communication, empathy, understanding, cognitive insight, or mental association changes, euphoria, perceptual distortions, and transcendental experiences. Common negative effects are physiological and include elevation of blood pressure and pulse, muscle tension and jaw clenching, fatigue, insomnia, sweating, blurred vision, loss of motor coordination, and anxiety (Siegel, 1986). It appears that, with continued use of MDMA, the positive psychological effects often decrease, while the negative physiological effects often increase (Barnes, 1988).

Adverse Effects

LSD.   In addition to its behavioral effects, lysergic acid diethylamide can cause an elevated heart rate, increased blood pressure, fever, seizures, and coma (Brust, 1993). The extreme agitation that can occur from lysergic acid diethylamide can often be controlled by talking down, but some cases require pharmacological intervention. In these situations, benzodiazepines are generally preferred over antipsychotic medications, as antipsychotics may exacerbate the agitation (Brust, 1993). Unlike many drugs of abuse, animals do not self-administer LSD, mescaline, and psilocybin (Carroll, 1990), and dependence does not occur from these drugs (Nichols, 2004). There is also no withdrawal syndrome associated with these hallucinogens (Brust, 1993). The lack of dependence and a withdrawal syndrome should not be construed that these drugs are safe, as accidents and the so-called bad trips can occur (Nichols, 2004).

Psilocybin.   Intoxication with psilocybe mushrooms can produce unintended effects in other organs. For example, a case report has described the induction a cardiac arrhythmia and myocardial infarction in an 18-year-old who had ingested psilocybe mushrooms (Borowiak et al., 1998).

MDMA.   When used in so-called rave parties in which participants, usually teenagers, intensely dance for long periods, MDMA is associated with dehydration and increased body temperatures that can lead to muscle cell damage and kidney failure (Westreich, 2002). MDMA use also can lead to psychosis (Westreich, 2002). Possible mechanisms of action and adverse effects of several hallucinogens are shown in Table 8.2.

TABLE 8.2   The Hallucinogens: Mechanism of Action and Adverse Effects

TYPE	MECHANISM OF ACTION	ADVERSE EFFECTS
LSD	Affects serotonin subtype 2 receptors and serotonin transmission.	Tachycardia, nausea, dilated pupils, altered emotions, bizarre ideas, hallucinations, dysphoria, anxiety, paranoia, fever, and coma.
Psilocybin	Agonize serotonin subtype 1A and 2A receptors.	Mood changes, visual hallucinations, illusions, and changes in thinking patterns, behavioral state similar to that seen in early-onset schizophrenia, cardiac arrhythmia.
MDMA	Potently releases serotonin from neurons and increases synaptic concentrations of dopamine.	Neuronal damage, fatigue, insomnia, sweating, blurred vision, loss of motor coordination, and anxiety, dehydration, increased body temperatures that can lead to muscle cell damage and kidney failure, and psychosis.

PHENCYCLIDINE

The development of phencyclidine (PCP) was quite serendipitous. While searching for psychoactive drugs with psychotherapeutic properties, chemists synthesized PCP, which psychopharmacologists recognized as having several unique effects on animals (Domino, 1980). Phencyclidine (PCP) was developed as an anesthetic in the 1950s (Brust, 1993) but was discontinued because of its toxic effects on behavior such as delirium, agitation, and psychosis, including during the postoperative period (Mendyk & Fields, 2002). Partly due to the ease of its synthesis (Brust, 1993), PCP has become a widely used illicit drug that goes by several names, including "angel dust" (Brust, 1993). Sometimes sprinkled on marijuana or parsley in order to be smoked, PCP can also be swallowed, sniffed, or injected (Brust, 1993).

Other drugs similar to PCP have been synthesized. One such psychopharmacological agent is ketamine (Ketalar), which has a similar mechanism of action and effects to PCP (Umbricht et al., 2003). This compound was found to have the most therapeutic value as an anesthetic of any of the synthesized compounds. While possessing the more positive features of PCP (e.g., high therapeutic index, minimal effect on respiration, and elevation of blood pressure and cardiac output), ketamine does not induce convulsions and is shorter acting than PCP (Domino, 1980). Possessing essentially the same pharmacodynamic properties as PCP, ketamine also possesses essentially the same psychotic symptoms and perceptual distortions in vision, audition, body image, and sense of time associated with PCP, but to a lesser degree (Hansen et al., 1988).

Mechanism of Action and Pharmacology

PCP and ketamine are antagonists of N-methyl-D-aspartate (NMDA) receptors (Umbricht et al., 2003; Wang et al., 2001), one of the primary receptors of the excitatory neurotransmitter glutamate (see Chapter 2). Subchronic treatment with PCP in rodents increases dopamine activity in the striatum (Balla et al., 2003), similar to the dopamine hyperactivity noted in schizophrenia (Balla et al., 2003). Furthermore, PCP enhances the increased dopamine from amphetamines in rodents (Balla et al., 2003). In addition to antagonizing NMDA receptors and affecting dopamine transmission, PCP also appears to have affinity for serotonin 2 and dopamine 2 receptors (Kapur & Seeman, 2002).

In humans, PCP causes a behavioral state that closely resembles schizophrenia (Javitt & Zukin, 1991). Whereas amphetamine intoxication produces clinical findings that are similar to the positive symptoms of schizophrenia, such as paranoia, PCP use can cause both the positive (such as paranoia) and negative symptoms (e.g., withdrawal, lack of motivation) of schizophrenia (Javitt & Zukin, 1991). Because of its NMDA antagonism and induction of features found in schizophrenia, PCP has been instrumental in furthering the understanding of the etiology of schizophrenia (Javitt & Zukin, 1991). One possibility is that schizophrenia may be associated with abnormal structure or function of the NMDA receptor (Javitt & Zukin, 1991). However, the effects of PCP on dopamine and serotonin function, in addition to its effects on NMDA receptors, confound the interpretation of studies investigating the relationship between NMDA receptors and psychosis (Kapur & Seeman, 2002).

The behavioral effects associated with PCP vary and include euphoria, relaxation, dysphoria, paranoia, and a sense of time being slowed (Brust, 1993). Distortions of sensation can also occur (Brust, 1993).

Drug-Drug Interactions

PCP inhibits the cytochrome P450 2B6 isoenzyme (Jushchyshyn et al., 2003). The metabolism of drugs that rely upon this isoenzyme, therefore, could be inhibited with subsequent increases in drug levels.

Adverse Effects

PCP causes a myriad of behavioral and physical changes that can be difficult to manage in clinical and other settings and may be life threatening (Brust, 1993). Behavioral changes, including psychosis, agitation, disinhibition, and aggression, predominate in the early stages of phencyclidine intoxication. As the degree of PCP intoxication increases, stupor occurs, although deep-pain responses remain intact. Coma can develop along with loss of all pain responses in later stages on intoxication (Milhorn, 1991). Cognitive impairments are also associated with PCP use. In chronic users of PCP, impairments in acquisition, recall, and delayed recall as assessed by the Randt Memory Test improved after use of PCP was discontinued or reduced (Cosgrove & Newell, 1991). PCP use is reinforcing, and nonhuman primates and rats self-administer PCP (Marquis & Moreton, 1987).

These reinforcing properties of PCP give it a high addiction and abuse potential that can cause some major difficulties in treatment. A quiet environment free from disruptive stimuli is important in the management of acute phencyclidine intoxication (Brust, 1993). Benzodiazepines are used in some cases of phencyclidine intoxication (Brust, 1993). In extreme cases of psychosis associated with phencyclidine, electroconvulsive therapy is reported to be helpful (Dinwiddie et al., 1988). Withdrawal from PCP is characterized by craving, anxiety, sweating, and tremors (Brust, 1993).

Unfortunately, PCP appears to interfere with fetal development, leading to both physical and behavioral abnormalities. When matched for demographical variables, infants who had prenatal exposure to PCP had more physical abnormalities, poorer attention, hypertonia, and diminished reflexes (Golden et al., 1987). Like cocaine, prenatal exposure to PCP causes intrauterine growth retardation and signs of withdrawal in the neonate (Tabor et al., 1990). Long-term behavioral changes occur in rats that had prenatal exposure to PCP (Wang et al., 2001).

INHALANTS

Widely abused by children and adolescents, the inhalation of organic solvents and other inhalants presents a significant public health problem (Brouette & Anton, 2001; Riegel & French, 2002). In adolescents, inhalants are the fourth most frequently abused class of drug, after nicotine, alcohol, and marijuana (Riegel & French, 2002). Many inhalants are available in most households, providing easy access to these substances. Furthermore, special equipment is not required to use the inhalants, and they are readily abused. Although glue is the most frequently abused (Zabedah et al., 2001), numerous common, easily obtainable, and inexpensive organic solvents can be used as inhalants such as various cleaning agents, gasoline, aerosols, marker pens, paints, paint remover, and fingernail polish (Brust, 1993). Furthermore, inhalants are not illegal and can thus be easily obtained even by children. Because many inhalants have legitimate, nonmedical uses, they are all the more difficult to regulate. Volatile solvents are a commonly abused but diverse group of inhalants (Brouette & Anton, 2001). Used as an anesthetic agent, nitrous oxide (laughing gas) also can be considered an abusable inhalant and is found in whipping cream containers (Balster, 1998). Other inhalants include volatile alkyl nitrites, such as amyl nitrite, and chlorofluorocarbons, such as Freon (Balster, 1998).

As the name inhalant implies, the inhalants are generally taken into the body via the respiratory system by smelling, snorting, inhalation from a bag containing the substance ("bagging"), spraying the material into the mouth, or putting a rag containing the substance into the mouth ("huffing") (Brouette & Anton, 2001).

Mechanism of Action and Pharmacology

Given the widespread abuse of inhalants and their ready availability, there is surprisingly little known about the neurobiological effects of these substances, although some clues do exist. For instance, a component shared by many inhalants is toluene, an industrial organic solvent, which can produce euphoria and hallucinations (Riegel & French, 2001). Other commonly abused organic inhalants are acetone and benzene (Kucuk et al., 2000). Although its mechanism of action in the brain is not entirely understood (Balster, 1998), toluene may modulate the activity of NMDA glutamate receptors, gamma-aminobutyric acid receptors, and glycine receptors (Bale et al., 2002). Toluene may also alter the function of certain types of acetylcholine nicotinic receptors (Bale et al., 2002). In rats, toluene, like many drugs of abuse, increases the firing rates of mesolimbic dopamine-containing neurons (Riegel & French, 2002), a property that appears to be important for addiction to occur (Camí & Farré, 2003). Toluene in rats also increases extracellular dopamine in the prefrontal cortex (Gerasimov et al., 2002).

Grossly observable brain structure changes from inhaled toluene shown by brain magnetic resonance imaging have also been reported. For instance, chronic toluene inhalation in humans appears to cause white matter (myelinated axons) changes and abnormalities in the thalamus (Aydin et al., 2002). The white matter abnormalities associated with toluene inhalation appear to begin in paraventricular regions and extend into other white matter areas with continued abuse of toluene (Aydin et al., 2002). When measured by single photon emission computed tomography (SPECT), late adolescent inhalant abusers, who had not abused substances for an average of approximately five-and-a-half months prior to the study, had significant abnormalities in brain blood flow with areas of both increased and decreased blood perfusion (Kucuk et al., 2000).

The mechanism of nitrous oxide in abuse is unclear. Some evidence suggests that the anesthetic effects of nitrous oxide may be mediated at least in part by release of endogenous opiates (Balster, 1998) (see Chapter 7), endogenous-opiate release does not appear to account for the intoxication and reinforcement observed with nitrous oxide (Balster, 1998). One study reported evidence that nitrous oxide diminishes excitatory neurotransmission by antagonizing N-methyl-D-aspartate glutamate receptors (Jevtović-Todorović et al., 1998). Similarly, the mechanism of action of the volatile alkyl nitrites is poorly described, although they may produce vasodilation (Balster, 1998).

Intoxication from many inhalants produces euphoria, gait disturbances, double vision, and slurred speech (Brust, 1993). Seizures, psychosis, and coma can also occur (Brust 1993). Intoxication from nitrous oxide can result in a dissociative-like state (Brouette & Anton, 2001). Nitrites are used to augment sexual behavior (Brouette & Anton, 2002). Fatalities are associated with the use of inhalants and can result from trauma and cardiac damage (Bowen et al., 1999). CNS atrophy and renal damage has also been associated with chronic use of some of these substances—for example, toluene (Jaffe, 1990).

Adverse Effects

Numerous adverse neurological sequelae are reported in people who chronically abuse inhalants (Rosenberg et al., 2002). Compared to controls who abused other drugs, primarily alcohol and cocaine, inhalant abusers had more impairment in working memory and executive function (Rosenberg et al., 2002). A case report found an association between chronic toluene abuse and visual abnormalities, tremor, sensory problems, and spinal cord lesions (Sakai et al., 2000). Many organic solvents including toluene can also cause liver toxicity (Brautbar & Williams, 2002).

Toluene use by pregnant women may significantly impair fetal development and can produce findings in the offspring known as the fetal solvent syndrome. The abnormalities found in children who had *in utero* exposure to toluene are similar to those observed in fetal alcohol syndrome (Costa et al., 2002). Although the mechanism underlying the effects of toluene on the fetus are unknown, preliminary *in vitro* evidence suggests that toluene may interfere with astrocyte function in the developing brain (Costa et al., 2002).

Treatment

Little information is available regarding treatment for inhalant use. Because of the potential for the inhalants to damage other body organs, a physical workup should be done, as well as testing for cognitive deficits (Brouette & Anton, 2001). A withdrawal syndrome from volatile solvents consisting of nausea, tremor, difficulty with sleep, and irritability may occur and last approximately two to five days (Brouette & Anton, 2001). Benzodiazepines have been considered for use in managing the withdrawal from inhalants (Brouette & Anton, 2001). Twelve-step programs and cognitive-behavioral approaches are used by some clinicians for the treatment of inhalant abuse but are in need of additional research (Brouette & Anton, 2001).

SUMMARY

Used in some cases for several thousand years, marijuana and the hallucinogens continue to flourish illicitly in conjunction with relatively recently synthesized and now illegal drugs such as PCP. Marijuana, the hallucinogens, PCP, and the inhalants each possess unique mechanisms of action, and their use results in different behavioral, cognitive, and perceptual abnormalities.

Smoked by millions of people in the United States alone, marijuana is obtained from *Cannabis sativa*, which possesses numerous cannabinoids. One key psychoactive cannabinoid compound in marijuana is delta 9-tetrahydrocannabinol, which seems to be responsible for many of the psychoactive effects from marijuana. Marijuana appears to initiate its effects by interacting with cannabinoid type 1 receptors, which are located in the brain, and cannabinoid type 2 receptors, which are located outside of the central nervous system. Endogenous cannabinoids, or endocannabinoids, agonize both types of cannabinoid receptors and are involved in a wide range of functions both within and without the central nervous system. Two principal endocannabinoids are anandamide and 2-arachidonoylglycerol. Endocannabinoids may be closely associated with brain acetylcholine and glutamate systems. Furthermore, the endocannabinoids appear to have a role in pain control, appetite regulation, cardiovascular function, and embryonic development.

The acute use of marijuana produces a relaxed euphoric, dream-like state with a sense that time is slowed. Psychosis can also occur from marijuana use and can present as paranoia or auditory hallucinations. Impairment of cognition and memory is dose dependent. Marijuana dependence may be medicated by mesocorticolimbic dopamine pathways, and the cessation of marijuana use is associated with a withdrawal syndrome consisting of irritability, diminished appetite, depression, poor sleep, and muscle pain.

The legitimate uses of marijuana remain a point of sharp disagreement. Proposed but by no means generally accepted uses of marijuana are in the amelioration of nausea, particularly that occuring from chemotherapy, the promotion of appetite in wasting syndromes, the relief of some types of pain, and the treatment of epilopsy.

The hallucinogens consist of many drugs, some of which occur naturally in plants and fungi, and some of which are synthesized. A hallmark of the hallucinogens is their ability to cause hallucinations in one or more sensory modalities at doses that are not otherwise considered toxic. LSD agonizes serotonin type 2 receptors and alters emotions and causes hallucinations. Reactions from LSD can be frightening and may reoccur as flashbacks. Related to LSD, psilocybin is found in psilocybe mushrooms and causes mood changes and hallucinations and alters thinking patterns. Psilocybin agonizes serotonin 1A and 2A receptors. Mescaline also acts as a partial agonist at serotonin subtype 2A receptors. Sharing features with both hallucinogens and amphetamines, MDMA produces a sense of emotional intimacy, increased communication, empathy, and euphoria, although even limited use of MDMA is associated with permanent brain changes.

Originally developed as an anesthetic, the clinical use of PCP was so severely limited by agitation, delirium, and psychosis that it is no longer used medically. Both PCP and ketamine antagonize NMDA glutamate receptors. PCP use is associated with euphoria, perceptual distortions, dysphoria, and sense that time is slowed. Of importance to schizophrenia research, PCP can produce a psychotic state characterized by paranoia, withdrawal, and diminished motivation.

Inhalants are found in many common household and industrial substances, such as glue, paint, cleaning agents, gasoline, and aerosols. Easily obtained by children and adolescents, the inhalants are widely abused by this population. Many inhalants contain toluene, an industrial organic solvent that can produce euphoria and hallucinations. In addition to altering firing patterns in mesocorticolimbic dopamine neurons like many other drugs of addiction, toluene modulates GABA and NMDA receptors, appears to cause white matter abnormalities, and results in changes in cerebral blood-flow patterns. Impairments in working memory and executive function are associated with inhalant use, in addition to other medical problems such as liver toxicity.

STUDY QUESTIONS

1. Discuss the neurobiological mechanism that appears to underlie addiction in many drugs of abuse.
2. Outline the endocannabinoid system, including its receptors and functions.
3. Discuss the clinical effects of acute marijuana intoxication.
4. Describe the neurobiological effects of the hallucinogens.
5. What are features of LSD intoxication?
6. Which neurotransmitter receptors appear to be affected by LSD?
7. What is the mechanism of action of PCP and ketamine?
8. List several neurobiological effects of toluene.

REFERENCES

Aghajanian GK, Foote WE, Sheard MH (1970): Action of psychotogenic drugs on midbrain raphe neurons. Journal of Pharmacology and Experimental Therapeutics 171:178–187.

Andreasson S, Allebeck P, Engstrom A, Rydberg U (1987): Cannabis and schizophrenia. A longitudinal study of Swedish conscripts. Lancet 2:1483–1486.

Aydin K, Spencer S, Demir T, Ogel K Tunaci A, Minareci O (2002): Cranial MR findings in chronic toluene abuse by inhalation. American Journal of Neuroradiology 23:1173–1179.

Azorlosa JL, Heishman SJ, Stitzer ML, Mahaffey JM (1992): Marijuana smoking: Effect of varying delta-9-tetrahydrocannabinol content and number of puffs. Journal of Pharmacology and Experimental Therapeutics 261:114–122.

Backstrom JR, Chang MS, Chu H, Niswender CM, Sanders-Bush E (1999): Agonist-directed signaling of serotonin 5-HT2C receptors: Differences between serotonin and lysergic acid diethylamide (LSD). Neuropsychopharmacology 21 (supplement):77S–81S.

Bale AS, Smothers CT, Woodward JJ (2002): Inhibition of neuronal nicotinic acetylcholine receptors by the abused solvent, toluene. British Journal of Pharmacology 137:375–383.

Balla A, Sershen H, Serra M, Koneru R, Javitt DV (2003): Subchronic continuous phencyclidine administration potentiates amphetamine-induced frontal cortex dopamine release. Neuropsychopharmacology 28:34–44.

Balster RL (1998): Neural basis of inhalant abuse. Drug and Alcohol Dependence 51:207–214.

Barnes DM (1988): New data intensify the agony over ecstasy. Science 240:864–866.

Basavarajappa BA, Hungund BL (2002): Neuromodulatory role of the endocannabinoid signaling system in alcoholism: A review of prostaglandins, leukotrienes, and essential fatty acids 66:287–299.

Beaulieu P, Rice AS (2002): [The pharmacology of cannabinoid derivatives: Are there applications to treatment of pain?]. Annales Francaises d'Anesthesie et de Reanimation 21:493–508.

Bersani G, Orlandi V, Kotzalidis GD, Pancheri P (2002): Cannabis and schizophrenia: Impact on onset, course, psychopathology, and outcomes. European Archives of Psychiatry and Clinical Neuroscience 252:86–92.

Blum R (1969): *Society and drugs* (Vol. 1). San Francisco: Jossey-Boss.

Bobashev GV, Anthony JC (1998): Clusters of marijuana use in the United States. American Journal of Public Health 148:1168–1173.

Bolla KI, Brown K, Eldreth D, Tate K, Cadet JL (2002): Dose-related neurocognitive effects of marijuana. Neurology 59:1337–1343.

Borowiak KS, Ciechanowski K, Waloszczk P (1998): Psilocybin mushroom (Psilocybe semilanceata) intoxication with myocardial infarction. Journal of Toxicology. Clinical Toxicology 36:47–49.

Bowen SE, Daniel J, Balster RL (1999): Deaths associated with inhalant abuse in Virginia from 1987 to 1996. Drug and Alcohol Dependence 53:239–245.

Brautbar N, Williams J (2002): Industrial solvents and liver toxicity: Risk assessment, risk factors and mechanisms. International Journal of Hygiene and Environmental Health 205: 479–491.

Brouette T, Anton R (2001): Clinical review of inhalants. The American Journal on Addictions 10:79–94.

Bruhn JG, De Smet PAGM, El-Seedi HR, Beck O (2002): Mescaline use for 5700 years. Lancet 359 (letter):1866.

Brust JC (1993): Other agents. Phencyclidine, marijuana, hallucinogens, inhalants, and anticholinergics. Neurology Clinics 11:555–561.

Buckholtz NS, Zhou DF, Freedman DX, Potter WZ (1990): Lysergic acid diethylamide (LSD) administration selectively downregulates serotonin 2 receptors in rat brain. Neuropsychopharmacology 3:137–148.

Budney AJ, Moore BA, Vandrey RG, Hughes JR (2003): The time course and significance of cannabis withdrawal. Journal of Abnormal Psychology 112:393–402.

Camí J, Farré M (2003): Drug addiction. New England Journal of Medicine 349:975–986.

Carroll ME (1990): PCP and hallucinogens. Advances in Alcohol and Substance Abuse 9:167.

Carter GT, Weydt P (2002): Cannabis: Old medicine with new promise for neurological disorders. Current Opinion in Investigational Drugs 3:437–440.

Cornelius MD, Goldschmidt L, Day NL, Larkby C (2002): Alcohol, tobacco, and marijuana use among pregnant teenagers: 6-year follow-up of offspring growth effects. Neurotoxicology and Teratology 24:703–710.

Cosgrove J, Newell TG (1991): Recovery of neuropsychological functions during reduction in use of phencyclidine. Journal of Clinical Psychology 47:159–169.

Costa LG, Guizzetti M, Burry B, Oberdoerster J (2002): Developmental neurotoxicity: Do similar phenotypes indicate a common mode of action? A comparison of fetal alcohol syndrome, toluene embryopathy and maternal phenylketonuria. Toxicology Letters 127:197–205.

Culliton BJ (1970): Pot facing stringent scientific examination. Scientific News 97:102–105.

Curran HV, Brignell C, Fletcher S, Middleton P, Henry J (2002): Cognitive and subjective dose-response effects of acute oral Delta 9-tetrahydrocannabinol (THC) in infrequent cannabis users. Psychopharmacology: 164:61–70.

Degenhardt L, Hall W (2002): Cannabis and psychosis. Current Psychiatry Reports 4:191–196.

Dewey WL (1986): Cannabinoid pharmacology. Pharmacological Reviews 38:151–178.

Dhawan K, Kumar S, Sharma A (2002): Reversal of cannabinoids (delta9-THC) by the benzoflavone moiety from methanol extract of Passiflora incarnata Linneaus in mice: A possible therapy for cannabinoid addiction. Journal of Pharmacy and Pharmacology 54:875–881.

Dinwiddie SH, Drevets WC, Smith DR (1988): Treatment of phencyclidine-associated psychosis with ECT. Convulsive Therapy 4:230–235.

Domino EF (1980): History and pharmacology of PCP and PCP-related analogs. Journal of Psychedelic Drugs 12:223–227.

Ferraro DP (1976): A behavioral model of marihuana tolerance. In MC Braude & S Szara (eds.), *The Pharmacology of Marihuana* (pp. 475–486). New York: Raven Press.

Flory K, Lynam D, Milich R, Leukefeld C, Clayton R (2002): The relations among personality, symptoms of alcohol and marijuana abuse, and symptoms of comorbid psychopathology: Results from a community sample. Experimental and Clinical Psychopharmacology 10:425–434.

Freese TE, Miotto K, Reback CJ (2002): The effects and consequences of selected club drugs. Journal of Substance Abuse Treatment 23:151–156.

Frosh W, Robbins E, Stern M (1965): Untoward reactions to lysergic acid diethylamide (LSD) resulting in hospitalization. New England Journal of Medicine 273:1235.

Gardner EL, Lowinson JH (1991): Marijuana's interaction with brain reward systems: Update 1991. Pharmacology, Biochemistry, and Behavior 40:571–580.

Gerasimov MR, Schiffer WK, Marstellar D, Ferrieri R, Alexoff D, Dewey SL (2002): Toluene inhalation produces regionally specific changes in extracellular dopamine. Drug and Alcohol Dependence 65:243–251.

Ghansah E, Kopsombut P, Malleque MA, Brossi A (1993): Effects of mescaline and some of its analogs on cholinergic neuromuscular transmission. Neuropharmacology 32:169–174.

Golden NL, Kuhnert BR, Sokol RJ, Martier S, William T (1987): Neonatal manifestations of maternal phencyclidine exposure. Journal of Perinatal Medicine 15:185–191.

Greer G, Tolbert R (1986): Subjective reports of the effects of MDMA in a clinical setting. Journal of Psychoactive Drugs 18:319–327.

Gross ST (2002): Psychotropic drugs in developmental mushrooms: A case study review. Journal of Forensic Science 47:1298–1302.

Grotenhermen F (2003): Pharmacokinetics and pharmacodynamics of cannabinoids (2003): Clinical Pharmacokinetics 42:327–360.

Haney M, Hart CL, Ward AS, Foltin RW (2003): Nefazodone decreases anxiety during marijuana withdrawal in humans. Psychopharmacology 165:57–165.

Hansen G, Jensen SB, Chandresh L, Hilden T (1988): The psychotropic effect of ketamine. Canadian Journal of Psychology 36:527–531.

Hart CL, Ward AS, Haney M, Comer SD, Foltin RW, Fischman MW (2002): Comparison of smoked marijuana and oral Delta (9)-tetrahydrocannabinol in humans. Psychopharmacology 164:407–415.

Howlett AC, Breivogel CS, Childers SR, Deadwyler SA, Hampson RE, Porrino LJ (2004): Cannabinoid physiology and pharmacology: 30 years of progress. Neuropharmacology 47:345–358.

Huestis MA, Henningfield JE, Cone EJ (1992): Blood cannabinoids. I. Absorption of THC and formation of 11-OH-THC and THCCOOH during and after smoking marijuana. Journal of Analytical Toxicology 16:276–282.

Jaffe JH (1990): Drug addiction and drug abuse. In AG Gilman, TW Rall, AS Nies, P Taylor (eds.), *The Pharmacological Basis of Therapeutics* (pp. 522–573). Elmsford, NY: Pergamon Press.

Jarvinen T, Pate DW, Laine K (2002): Cannabinoids in the treatment of glaucoma. Pharmacology & Therapeutics 95:203–220.

Javitt DC, Zukin SR (1991): Recent advances in the phencyclidine model of schizophrenia. American Journal of Psychiatry 148:1301–1308.

Jevtović-Todorović V, Todorović SM, Mennerick S, Powell S, Dikranian K, Benshoff N, Zorumski CF, Olney JW (1998): Nitrous oxide (laughing gas) is an NMDA antagonist, neuroprotectant and neurotoxin. Nature Medicine 4:460–463.

Johns A (2001): Psychiatric effects of cannabis. British Journal of Psychiatry 178:116–122.

Johnston LD, O'Malley RM, Bachman JG (1994): *National Survey Results on Drug Use from the Monitoring the Future Study, 1975–1993.* Rockville, MD: National Institute on Drug Abuse.

Julien RM (1995): *A Primer of Drug Action: A Concise, Nontechnical Guide to the Actions, Use and Side Effects of Psychoactive Drugs* (7th ed.). New York: W.H. Freeman and Company.

Jushchyshyn MI, Kent UM, Hollenberg PF (2003): The mechanism-based inactivation of human cytochrome P450 2B6 by phencyclidine. Drug Metabolism and Disposition: The Biological Fate of Chemicals 31:46–52.

Kalant H (2001): Medicinal use of cannabis: History and current status. Pain Research & Management 6:80–91.

Kapur S, Seeman P (2002): NMDA receptor antagonists ketamine and PCP have direct effects on the dopamine D (2) and serotonin 5-HT (2) receptors—implications for models of schizophrenia. Molecular Psychiatry 7:837–844.

Khalsa JH, Genser S, Francis H, Martin B (2002): Clinical consequences of marijuana. Journal of Clinical Pharmacology 42:7S–10S.

Kim J, Isokawa M, Ledent C, Alger BE (2002): Activation of muscarinic acetylcholine receptors enhances the release of endogenous cannabinoid in the hippocampus. Journal of Neuroscience 22:10182–10191.

Kucuk NO, Kilic EO, Ibis E, Aysev A, Gencoglu EA, Aras G, Soylu A, Erbay G (2000): Brain SPECT findings in long-term inhalant abuse. Nuclear Medicine Communications 21:769–773.

Leikin JB, Krantz AJ, Zell-Kanter M, Barkin RL, Hyrhorczuk DO (1989): Clinical features and management of intoxication due to hallucinogenic drugs. Medical Toxicology and Adverse Drug Experience 4:324–350.

Maccarrone M, Finazzi-Agro A (2002): Endocannabinoids and their actions. Vitamins and Hormones 65:225–255.

Mathew RJ, Wilson WH, Turkington TG, Hawk TC, Coleman RE, DeGrado TR, Provenzale J (2002): Time course of tetrahydrocannabinol-induced changes in regional cerebral blood flow measured with positron emission tomography. Psychiatry Research 116:173–185.

McLeod AL, McKenna CJ, Northridge DB (2002): Myocardial infarction following the combined recreational use of Viagra and cannabis. Clinical Cardiology 25:133–134.

Mendyk SL, Fields DW (2002): Acute psychotic reactions: Consider "Dip Dope" intoxication. Journal of Emergency Nursing 28:432–435.

Milhorn HT Jr (1991) Diagnosis and management of phencyclidine intoxication. American Family Physician 43:1293–1302.

Mishima K, Egashira N, Matsumoto Y, Iwasaki K, Fujiwara M (2002): Involvement of reduced acetylcholine release in delta (9)-tetrahydrocannabinol-induced impairment of spatial memory in the 8-arm radial maze. Life Sciences 72:397–407.

Morral AR, McCaffrey DF, Paddock SM (2002): Reassessing the marijuana gateway effect. Addiction 97:1493–1504.

Muller-Vahl KR, Schneider U, Koblenz A, Jobges M, Kolbe H, Daldrup T, Emrich HM (2002): Treatment of Tourette's syndrome with Delta 9-tetrahydrocannabinol (THC): A randomized crossover trial. Pharmacopsychiatry 35:57–61.

Nichols DE (1986): Differences between the mechanism of action of MDMA, MBDB, and the classic hallucinogens. Identification of a new therapeutic class: Entactogens. Journal of Psychoactive Drugs 18:305–313.

Nichols DE (2004): Hallucinogens. Pharmacology & Therapeutics 101:131–181.

Ricuarte G, Bryan G, Strauss L, Seiden L, Schuster C (1985): Hallucinogenic amphetamine selectively destroys serotonin nerve terminals. Science 229:986–987.

Riegel AC, French ED (2002): Abused inhalants and central reward pathways: Electrophysiological and behavioral studies in the rat. Annals of the New York Academy of Science 965:281–291.

Rosenberg NL, Grigsby J, Dreisbach J, Busenbark D, Grigsby P (2002): Neuropsychologic impairment and MRI abnormalities associated with chronic solvent abuse. Journal of Toxicology. Clinical Toxicology 40:21–34.

Roth VE (2002): Should physicians support the medical use of marijuana? No: Evidence of its safety and efficacy is weak. Counterpoint. Western Journal of Medicine 176:77.

Sakai T, Honda S, Kuzuhara S (2000): [Encephalomyopathy demonstrated on MRI in a case of chronic toluene intoxication]. Rinsho Shinkeigaku 40:571–575.

Schmidt CJ (1987): Neurotoxicity of the psychedelic amphetamine, methylenedioxymethamphetamine. Journal of Pharmacology and Experimental Therapeutics 240:1–7.

Sidney S (2002): Cardiovascular consequences of marijuana use. Journal of Clinical Pharmacology 42 (supplement 11):64S–74S.

Siegel RK (1986): MDMA: Nonmedical use and intoxication. Journal of Psychoactive Drugs 18:349–354.

Solowij N, Stephens RS, Roffman RA, Babor T, Kadden R, Miller M, Christiansen K, McRee B, Vendetti J (2002): Cognitive functioning of long-term heavy cannabis users seeking treatment. Journal of the American Medical Association 287:1123–1131.

Steinberg KL, Roffman RA, Carroll KM, Kabela E, Kadden R, Miller M, Duresky D (2002). Tailoring cannabis dependence treatment for a diverse population. Addiction 97 (supplement 1):135–142.

Stephens RS, Roffman RA, Simpson EE (1994): Treating adult marijuana dependence: A test of the relapse prevention model. Journal of Counseling & Clinical Psychology 62:92–99.

Tabor BL, Smith-Wallace T, Yonekura ML (1990): Perinatal outcome associated with PCP versus cocaine use. American Journal of Drug and Alcohol Abuse 16:337–348.

Tanda G, Goldberg SR (2003): Cannabinoids: Reward, dependence, and underlying neurochemical mechanisms—a review of recent preclinical data. Psychopharmacology 169:115–134.

Tanda G, Pontieri FE, Di Chiara G (1997): Cannabinoid and heroin activation of mesolimbic dopamine transmission by a common mu1 opioid receptor mechanism. Science 276:2048–2050.

Tashkin DP, Baldwin GC, Sarafian T, Dubinett S, Roth MD (2002): Journal of Clinical Pharmacology 42 (supplement 11): 71S–81S.

Umbricht D, Vollenweider FX, Scmid L, Grubel C, Skrabo A, Huber T, Koller R (2003): Effects of the 5-HT(2A) agonist psilocybin on mismatch negativity generation and AX-continuous performance task: Implications for the neuropharmacology of cognitive deficits in schizophrenia. Neuropsychopharmacology 28:170–181.

Verheyden SL, Hadfield J, Calin T, Curran HV (2002): Sub-acute effects of MDMA (+/−3,4-methylenedioxymethamphetamine, "ecstasy") on mood: Evidence of gender differences. Psychopharmacology 161:23–31.

Vetulani J (2001): Drug addiction. Part I. Psychoactive substances in the past and present. Polish Journal of Pharmacology 53:201–214.

Vollenweider FX, Leenders KL, Scharfetter C, Magui P, Stadelmann O, Angst J (1997): Positron emission tomography and fluorodeoxyglucose studies of metabolic hyperfrontality and psychopathology in the psilocybin model of psychosis. Neuropsychopharmacology 16:357–372.

Vollenweider FX, Vontobel P, Hell D, Leenders KL (1999): 5-HT modulation of dopamine release in basal ganglia in psilocybin-induced psychosis in man—PET study with [11C]raclopride. Neuropsychopharmacology 20:424–433.

Vollenweider J, Vollenweider-Scherpenhuyzen MF, Babler A, Vogel H, Hell D (1998): Psilocybin induces a schizophrenia-like psychosis in humans via a serotonin-2 agonist action. Neuroreport 9:3897–3902.

von Sydow K, Lieb R, Pfister H, Hofler M, Wittchen HU (2002): What predicts incident use of cannabis and progression to abuse and dependence? A 4-year prospective examination of risk factors in a community sample of adolescents and young adults. Drug and Alcohol Dependence 68:49–64.

Wang C, McInnis J, Ross-Sanchez M, Shinnick-Gallagher P, Wiley JL, Johnson KM (2001): Long-term behavioral and neurodegenerative effects of perinatal phencyclidine administration: Implications for schizophrenia. Neuroscience 107:535–550.

Weil AT, Davis W (1994): Bufo alvarius: A potent hallucinogen of animal origin. Journal of Ethnopharmacology 41:1–8.

Westreich LM (2002): Teachable moments: Turning alcohol and drug emergencies into catalysts for change. Current Psychiatry 1:50–57.

Wilson RI, Nicoll RA (2002): Endocannabinoid signaling in the brain. Science 296:678–682.

Zabedah MY, Razak M, Zakiah I, Zuraidah AB (2001): Profile of solvent abusers (glue sniffers) in East Malaysia. Malaysian Journal of Pathology 23:105–109.

Zammit S, Allebeck P, Andreasson S, Lundberg I, Lewis G (2002): Self reported cannabis use as a risk factor for schizophrenia in Swedish conscripts of 1969: Historical cohort study. British Medical Journal 325:1199.

Zullino DF, Delessert D, Eap CB, Preisig M, Baumann P (2002): Tobacco and cannabis smoking cessation can lead to intoxication with clozapine or olanzapine. International Clinical Psychopharmacology 17:141–143.

CHAPTER NINE

THE ANTIDEPRESSANTS

The antidepressants are among the most commonly prescribed of all medications. While there are several different classes of antidepressants and several dozen individual drugs, many have similar mechanisms of action, with all primarily resulting in increased concentrations of serotonin or norepinephrine or both in the synapse, although other changes also occur. In addition to depression, the antidepressants are used in a variety of other conditions, including anxiety disorders, eating disorders, and chronic pain. Despite widespread use of the antidepressants, questions remain regarding their overall clinical effectiveness, particularly for long-term use.

The antidepressants are a diverse group of drugs united by their ability to alleviate depression. In addition to this effect, certain antidepressants also are used for a wide range of mental disorders, including anxiety, obsessive-compulsive disorder, social anxiety, posttraumatic stress disorder (Vaswani et al., 2003), and chronic pain control (Barkin & Fawcett, 2000). There are several different types of antidepressants that are currently available in the United States and other countries, which include some of the older groups such as the tricyclic antidepressant and monoamine oxidase inhibitors as well as newer ones like the specific serotonin reuptake inhibitors and a variety of other agents. In fact, more than twenty antidepressants are available in the United States as of 2003 (Richelson, 2003). Despite their differences, most of the antidepressants are thought to initiate their antidepressant actions by manipulation at the synapse of various neurotransmitters, such as serotonin, norepinephrine, and dopamine (Richelson, 2003). In addition to their therapeutic effects, the antidepressants may affect many other organs in the body, often producing adverse effects that can result in discontinuation of the drug, lack of compliance, physical illness, and even in rare cases death. Adverse effects can be highly variable, both from drug to drug and from one person to the next. One person may tolerate well a particular antidepressant while another may suffer from severe side effects from the same medication. Furthermore, a particular effect may be problematic for one person but therapeutic for another. For example, the antidepressant mirtazapine (Remeron) tends to cause sedation

(Burrows & Kremer, 1997). Some people do not experience sedation at all from mirtazapine, while others are unable to take the medication because of its sedative effects. Still others find that the sedation from mirtazapine is helpful in that it improves sleep.

Another major problem with antidepressants is that there seems to be a delay of anywhere from approximately two to three weeks (Elena Castro et al., 2003), or longer, from the time a person begins a course of treatment with an antidepressant until a significant clinical response occurs. However, this treatment-response delay hypothesis has been questioned, as some data suggest that a response to antidepressants may occur within two weeks after starting treatment (Szegedi et al., 2003). For someone who is severely depressed and possibly even suicidal, even a short delay between the initiation of treatment and response can be stressful and potentially lethal. The reasons for the putative delay in treatment response are not known, but it may be related to inhibitory serotonin 1A receptors. That is, on serotonin-producing neurons in the raphe nuclei in the brainstem, serotonin interacts with 1A receptors located on the cell bodies and dendrites to decrease neuronal firing (Elena Castro et al., 2003), a mechanism that may delay the response to antidepressants.

Despite widespread availability, the efficacy of antidepressants in treating depression has been questioned. For example, a meta-analysis by Kirsch and Sapirstein (1998) concluded that 75 percent of the response to an antidepressant is actually due to placebo, with only about 25 percent of the response as a result of the antidepressant. Kirsch and Sapirstein also suggested that when an antidepressant is compared against a nonantidepressant with side effects similar to those of the antidepressant being evaluated (a so-called active placebo), the difference between placebo response and antidepressant response diminishes even further. In a second study of the efficacy data supporting the United States Food and Drug Administration's approval of the six most prescribed antidepressants approved between 1987 and 1999, Kirsch and colleagues (2002) concluded that the effects of the antidepressants are minimal. These and other similarly provocative findings (Khan et al., 2000) call for additional careful study about the uses of these drugs.

The effectiveness of antidepressants in naturalistic, long-term studies (studies that more closely resemble actual clinical conditions instead of the simplified clinical-drug-trial environment), however, are mixed, with some showing continued features of depression (Reimherr et al., 2001). These findings underscore the need for close monitoring of people who are being treated with antidepressants and emphasize the need for additional research into the long-term effectiveness of these medications and the treatment of depression in general.

Several classes of antidepressants are available, including the tricyclic antidepressants, monoamine oxidase inhibitors, specific serotonin reuptake inhibitors, dual-action antidepressants, and atypical antidepressants. Although all of these classes are used for the treatment of depression, they vary in their uses for other disorders, adverse effects, and drug-drug interactions.

THE TRICYCLIC ANTIDEPRESSANTS

Originally thought to have antipsychotic properties (Kuhn, 1958), the tricyclic antidepressants (TCAs) were the mainstay of the pharmacological treatment of depression from the 1960s until the early 1990s (Fava, 2003). Scourged by many adverse effects, some of which can be serious (Feighner, 1999), the TCAs are no longer first-line choices for the treatment of depression, having been replaced by specific-serotonin reuptake inhibitors (Thase & Kupfer, 1996), although they remain important agents in some types of depression (Parker, 2001).

In the late 1950s, Roland Kuhn, a professor of clinical psychiatry at the University of Zurich, obtained a supply of imipramine, one of the first TCAs. Knowing little if anything about the clinical use of this drug, Kuhn treated more than 500 people with imipramine over a period of three years. The group of people Kuhn treated with imipramine was comprised of people diagnosed with schizophrenia, depression, organic mental disorders, and other conditions (Kuhn, 1958). Kuhn's prescient observations described much of what is currently known about the clinical effects of TCAs today. Kuhn had noticed that imipramine was generally ineffective for schizophrenia but very helpful for people who had certain types of depression. He further noted that bipolar depression tended to respond less favorably than did depression with no history of mania (Kuhn, 1958).

There are nine TCAs on the market in the United States: imipramine (Tofranil and others), desipramine (Norpramin), amitriptyline (Elavil and others), nortriptyline (Pamelor and others), protriptyline (Vivactyl), trimipramine (Surmontil), doxepin (Sinequan and others), clomipramine (Anafranil), amoxapine (Asendin), and one closely related compound, a tetracyclic, maprotoline (Ludiomil).

Mechanism of Action, Pharmacology, and Metabolism

Despite intense study and interest, exactly how the TCAs—or any class of antidepressant for that matter—exert their antidepressant effects remains undiscovered (Donati & Rasenick, 2003). It is known, however, that all of the TCAs inhibit the reuptake of both serotonin and norepinephrine (Westenberg, 1999) to varying degrees into the presynaptic neuron. The reuptake inhibition of these neurotransmitters increases the amount of serotonin and norepinephrine in the synapse, prolonging the action of serotonin and norepinephrine in the synapse.

Despite the many similarities that the TCAs share with each other, they also differ from one another in their relative abilities to block the reuptake of serotonin and norepinephrine into the presynaptic neuron. For example, desipramine and nortriptyline primarily inhibit the reuptake of norepinephrine (Brunello et al., 2002), while clomipramine mainly inhibits the uptake of serotonin (Schatzberg, 2002). Amoxapine is unique in that it also blocks dopamine receptors (Tao et al., 1985), a feature that may confer antipsychotic properties to this drug (Anton & Burch, 1990).

The tricyclic antidepressants as a class undergo significant first-pass metabolism and are highly protein bound (Rudorfer & Potter, 1999). In addition, the tricyclic antidepressants are primarily metabolized through the cytochrome P450 system, which can produce active metabolites that may have not only antidepressant properties but also adverse effects (Rudorfer & Potter, 1999). For example, imipramine is converted to desipramine, amitriptyline to nortriptyline, and clomipramine to desmethylclomipramine (Rudorfer & Potter, 1999). Furthermore, desmethylclomipramine levels may be twice as high as those of clomipramine (Rudorfer & Potter, 1999). There is large interindividual variation in rates of TCA metabolism: The same dose of a TCA given to different people may result in vastly different plasma concentrations. A person who metabolizes a TCA slowly will be at greater risk of adverse effects from the drug. Conversely, a fast metabolizer may not achieve therapeutic drug concentrations and have an inadequate response to treatment (Bertilsson et al., 1997). Also, certain races may more slowly metabolize these drugs. Asians on average, for instance, have lower activity of the cytochrome P450 2D6 isoenzyme than do Caucasians (Bertilsson et al., 1997). As a general rule, though, most TCAs have a half-life in the blood of approximately twenty-four hours (Rudorfer & Potter, 1999), although protriptyline has a half-life of approximately three days (Rudorfer & Potter, 1999).

Drug-Drug Interactions

The TCAs can interact with other drugs, including other antidepressants. For example, the specific serotonin-reuptake inhibiting antidepressants fluoxetine (Prozac) and paroxetine (Paxil) inhibit some of the cytochrome P450 enzymes that are involved in the metabolism of several TCAs (Sproule et al., 1997), which can then elevate TCA levels. Despite this potential for interactions, the TCAs can still be used in some conditions with specific serotonin reuptake inhibitors (Nelson, 1998). Conversely, some anticonvulsant medications such as carbamazepine (Tegretol) can increase the metabolic rates of TCAs (Monaco & Cicolin, 1999) and lower concentrations of the TCAs.

Adverse Effects

Like many other types of drugs, the TCAs have the potential to cause unwanted, unpleasant, and sometimes dangerous side effects, many of which can be grouped into three main categories: anticholinergic, cardiovascular, and antihistaminic effects.

Anticholinergic side effects occur from a TCAs propensity to block acetylcholine muscarinic receptors, which are important for numerous body and brain functions. By interfering with these crucial receptors, for example, the TCAs may cause deficits in memory (Spring et al., 1992). Constipation (Feighner, 1999) can occur from diminished bowel motility. Diminished salivation not only results in an unpleasantly dry mouth but is associated with dental cavities as well (Peeters et al., 1998). The anticholinergic effects from TCAs can prevent the lens of the eye focusing appropriately with subsequent blurred vision. Blockade of cardiac acetyl-choline receptors may also account for some of the increased heart rate seen from TCAs (Harrigan & Brady, 1999). Although some of this elevation in heart rate may be from antagonism of cardiac acetylcholine receptors, it also probably occurs from norepinephrine reuptake inhibition (Ross et al., 1983). TCAs also can affect the electrical activity of the heart, with resulting electrocardiogram (EKG) changes. For example, TCAs can prolong cardiac conduction intervals, the time it takes for an electrical impulse to travel through the conduction system of the heart. By blocking channels that allow sodium ions to flow into the heart muscle cell, the TCAs can slow the electrical impulse that allows the chambers of the heart to beat with proper timing (Harrigan & Brady, 1999).

The TCAs are associated with sudden death, possibly due to cardiac arrythmias resulting from slowed conduction of the electrical impulse through the heart (Witchel et al., 2003). Furthermore, death rates are elevated in people who have had a myocardial infarction (heart attack) and are then treated with a TCA (Roose, 2001).

By blocking alpha-adrenergic receptors on blood vessels, the TCAs also can impair a person's ability to maintain blood pressure, particularly when going from a sitting or lying position to standing. This orthostatic hyotension is a frequent cause of lightheadedness in people taking TCAs. Particularly in the elderly, ortho-static hypotension can be a cause of falls (Joo et al., 2002).

Cardiovascular effects often complicate TCA overdose. By slowing cardiac conduction intervals, TCAs can result in cardiac arrythmias (Goldberg et al., 1985) and heart block (Feighner, 1999), particularly in TCA overdose. Prolongation of cardiac conduction intervals can lead to the potentially lethal arrhythmia Tor-sades de Pointes (Davison, 1985)

The tricyclic antidepressants affect sleep quality and architecture. The TCAs suppress rapid-eye movement (REM) (Sharpley & Cowen, 1995), and de-sipramine interferes with sleep continuity (Shipley et al., 1985). The TCAs can block histamine receptors resulting in drowsiness and weight gain (Fernstrom & Kupfer, 1988).

Uses

Depression.   For a period of approximately thirty years only ending in the 1990s, the TCAs were the mainstay of the pharmacological treatment of depres-sion (Fava, 2003). However, newer so-called dual-action antidepressants, such as venlafaxine (Effexor) and mirtazapine (Remeron) may be more effective in the treatment of depression than many of the tricyclic antidepressants with fewer ad-verse effects (Gupta et al., 2003). Although generally regarded as third- or fourth-line treatments for depression (Nierenberg et al., 2003), the TCAs do have a role in cases that have not responded to other antidepressants (Nierenberg et al., 2003) and may be particularly effective in cases of severe depression (Parker, 2001; An-derson, 2000), although this assertion remains tentative and in need of additional supporting data. For bipolar depression, there is some suggestion that the TCAs may worsen the overall course of the disorder by increasing the rate of affective cycling (Altshuler et al., 1995). Like most if not all antidepressants, the TCAs have the propensity to precipitate an affective switch in bipolar disorder, potentially driving a person from depression to mania (Altshuler et al., 1995).

Obsessive-Compulsive Disorder.   While most TCAs are thought to be ineffective for obsessive-compulsive disorder (OCD), clomipramine (Anafranil), by virtue of its potent reuptake inhibition of serotonin, can provide relief from the often debilitating obsessions and compulsions that characterize this disorder (Hollander et al., 2000).

Panic Disorder.   Although not considered first-line treatment for panic disorder, the TCAs do appear to be effective anti-panic agents (Sheehan, 1999; Jefferson, 1997).

Generalized Anxiety Disorder.   While not generally considered a first-line treatment for generalized anxiety disorder (GAD) because of their propensity for side effects, the TCAs can be used to treat this disorder (Rickels & Rynn, 2002), particularly when other medications, such as the SSRIs for instance, have not been helpful. Compared to benzodiazepines, TCAs have a slower onset of anxiolysis (Rickels & Rynn, 2002).

Attention-Deficit, Hyperactivity Disorder.   Although stimulant medications such as methylphenidate (Ritalin) comprise the mainstay of treatment for attention-deficit, hyperactivity disorder (ADHD) (Elia et al., 1999), concerns about addiction potential have led to the consideration of other medications for the treatment of this often chronic disorder of both children and adults. Among other medications, the TCAs are used for this condition and have been shown to be effective for at least some people with ADHD (Pliszka, 2003). The efficacy of TCAs for ADHD may wane, however, further limiting their use in this population (Elia et al, 1999).

Chronic Pain.   In addition to their use in depression, the TCAs are used in the treatment of chronic pain conditions (Barkin & Fawcett, 2000), such as fibromyalgia (Lawson, 2002) and chronic low-back pain (Staiger et al., 2003). Although the mechanism by which tricyclic antidepressants cause analgesia is unknown (Carter & Sullivan, 2002), it may involve serotonin and norepinephrine systems, N-methyl-D-aspartate receptor antagonism, or changes in membrane potassium channels (Lawson, 2002). The effects of TCAs on chronic low-back pain do not appear to be related to whether the patient also suffers from depression (Staiger et al., 2003).

Nocturnal Enuresis.   Nocturnal enuresis or bedwetting is a common problem among children (Harari & Moulden, 2000). Although behavioral interventions, such as a bedwetting alarm, are generally preferred (Harari & Moulden, 2000),

TABLE 9.1   Tricyclic Antidepressants

MECHANISM OF ACTION	ADVERSE EFFECTS	USES
Block the reuptake of both serotonin and norepinephrine to varying degrees into the presynaptic neuron.	Confusion, forgetfulness, constipation, diminished salivation, blurred vision, increased heart rate, lightheadedness, cardiac arrythmias, sedation, weight gain, excessive sweating, swelling in the ankles and feet, and disruption of certain stages of sleep, and, potentially, overdose.	Depression, Obsessive-Compulsive Disorder (clomipramine), Panic Disorder, Generalized Anxiety Disorder, Attention-Deficit/Hyperactivity Disorder, Chronic Pain, Nocturnal Enuresis, and Narcolepsy.

TCAs may diminish nocturnal enuresis through several potential mechanisms: via their inhibition of the detrusor muscle of the bladder (Sullivan & Abrams, 1999), anticholinergic effects (Sullivan & Abrams, 1999) that also inhibit bladder contraction, and possible elevation of the low nocturnal levels of antidiuretic hormone associated with nocturnal enuresis (Tomasi et al., 2001). Limiting the use of the TCAs in nocturnal enuresis are high relapse rates (Harari & Moulden, 2000).

Narcolepsy.   In addition to daytime sleepiness, some cases of narcolepsy are characterized by cataplexy, the loss of muscle tone, which is often precipitated by emotion (Thorpy, 2001). While the stimulant medications methylphenidate (Ritalin) and modafinil (ProVigil) are used to treat narcolepsy (Thorpy, 2001), the TCAs can be used to treat cataplexy (Thorpy, 2001). Table 9.1 summarizes the proposed mechanisms of action, adverse effects, uses of the TCAs.

THE MONOAMINE OXIDASE INHIBITORS

Like the TCAs, the monoamine oxidase inhibitors (MAOIs) were first developed in the late 1950s (Crane, 1957), after it was observed that MAOIs used to treat tuberculosis appeared to have antidepressant effects (Hardy et al., 2002). Introduced in 1957 (Ban, 2001), the MAOI iproniazid proved toxic to the liver and was withdrawn (Nelson et al., 1978). Although the MAOIs are effective in the treatment of depression, a number of factors, including mandatory dietary restrictions (Ban, 2001), have limited the use of these medications (Ban, 2001). Despite the limitations associated with their use, four MAOIs are currently available in the United States: phenelzine (Nardil), tranylcypromine (Parnate), isocarboxazide (Marplan), and selegiline (Eldepryl).

Mechanism of Action, Pharmacology, and Metabolism

The MAOIs are thought to initiate their antidepressant effects by inhibiting monoamine oxidase, an enzyme that is involved in the metabolic breakdown of some neurotransmitters. Two types of monoamine oxidase exist: monoamine oxidase A and monoamine oxidase B. The genes that code for both types are on the X chromosome (Cesura & Pletscher, 1992). Monoamine oxidase A appears to metabolize primarily serotonin and norepinephrine, thus regulating the amounts of these neurotransmitters in the synapse, while monoamine oxidase B seems to metabolize dopamine (Cesura & Pletscher, 1992). When these enzymes are blocked by the MAOIs, the actions of dopamine, serotonin, and norepinephrine in the synapse are prolonged, an effect that is thought to initiate the antidepressant effects from these medications.

Phenelzine, tranylcypromine, and isocarboxazide are nonspecific inhibitors of monoamine oxidase, inhibiting both monoamine oxidase A and B. Importantly, they also bind irreversibly to monoamine oxidase (Schatzberg, 2002), permanently inhibiting this enzyme.

L-deprenyl (Selegiline), in contrast, selectively inhibits mainly monoamine oxidase B (Cesura & Pletscher, 1992) and generally acts only in the brain, although it also binds irreversibly. A transdermal patch preparation of selegiline may target selectively brain monoamine oxidase A and B, while sparing intestinal monoamine oxidase A (Amsterdam, 2003). An additional MAOI moclobemide (Aurorix), not available in the United States although used in other parts of the world, binds both specifically and *reversibly* to monoamine oxidase B (Bonnet, 2003). Moclobemide is metabolized through the cytochrome P450 2C19 enzyme (Bonnet, 2003). Selegiline is metabolized to amphetamine (Akhondzadeh et al., 2003).

Drug-Drug Interactions

The MAOIs can interact with many other drugs, including other MAOIs, SSRIs, TCAs (Feighner, 1999), certain over-the-counter medications (Livingston & Livingston, 1996), and a variety of foods, requiring dietary restrictions (Gardner et al., 1996). Many of these interactions can be dangerous (Livingston & Livingston, 1996). One of the most well-described interactions is what is known as the cheese reaction, which involves the amino acid tyramine that is found in many foods. While the mechanism of the interaction is not known with certainty, one factor that may account for tyramine-MAOI interaction is the blockade of tyramine metabolism by MAOIs, as tyramine in the gastrointestinal tract is metabolized by monoamine oxidase A (Cesura & Pletscher, 1992). By blocking this metabolic pathway, MAOIs increase tyramine concentrations (DiMartini, 1995), which may lead to the clinical effects of the interaction due to the effects of increased tyramine. The combination of tyramine-containing foods and a MAOI can cause a dramatic rise in blood pressure, or hypertensive crisis (Feighner, 1999). The reaction between tyramine and MAOIs also is characterized by flushing, sweating, elevated heart rate, and tremor (DiMartini, 1995). While the list of foods and drinks that must be avoided if someone is taking a MAOI is long, examples of foods to be avoided include but are not limited to aged cheeses and meats, potentially spoiled meat, yeast extract, and sauerkraut (Gardner et al., 1996). Soybean products should not be used by people taking MAOIs (Shulman & Walker, 1999). Moclobemide does not seem to require as severe dietary restrictions as do the irreversible MAOIs (Bonnet, 2003), although caution when consuming foods rich in tyramine is advised (Livingston & Livingston, 1996). A double-blind, placebo-controlled trial of transdermally delivered selegiline without dietary restrictions found no clinical symptoms of elevated blood pressure due to a selegiline-tyramine interaction, a finding presumably due to sparing of intestinal monoamine oxidase A by transdermally delivered selegiline (Amsterdam, 2003).

Consisting of confusion, agitation, excessive sweating, elevated heart rate, and increased reflexes (Mason et al., 2000), a serotonin syndrome can occur when monoamine oxidase inhibitors are combined with drugs that increase the transmission of serotonin (Gillman, 1998), such as tricyclic antidepressants and specific serotonin reuptake inhibitors (Chan et al., 1998).

Adverse Effects

In addition to their interactions with certain foods and other drugs, the MAOIs can cause a variety of side effects. With the exception of moclobemide, the MAOIs decrease REM sleep (Sharpley & Cowen, 1995). Weight gain with all of its attendant health risks may also occur (Feighner, 1999). Like the TCAs, the MAOIs also can cause orthostatic hypotension (Feighner, 1999), the drop in blood pressure upon standing. MAOIs can also cause sexual dysfunction (Feighner, 1999). Moclobemide is associated with insomnia, nausea, and dizziness (Bonnet, 2003). In a double-blind, placebo-controlled study of major depression comparing transdermal selegiline to placebo, typical MAOI-induced adverse effects were not observed (Bodkin & Amsterdam, 2002).

Uses

Depression.   Although effective in the treatment of depression, the dietary restrictions and side effects associated with the MAOIs have significantly limited their use (Pletscher, 1991), even though the MAOIs appear particularly effective in the treatment of atypical depression (Posternak, 2003). In addition to being well tolerated, transdermally delivered selegiline may be an effective treatment for major depression (Bodkin & Amsterdam, 2002), with one double-blind, placebo-controlled trial showing modest but statistically significant improvement in transdermally delivered selegiline compared to placebo (Amsterdam, 2003).

TABLE 9.2   Monoamine Oxidase Inhibitors

MECHANISM OF ACTION	ADVERSE EFFECTS	USES
Block monoamine oxidase, which is involved in the metabolic breakdown of some neurotransmitters.	Adverse interactions with foods containing tyramine, decreased REM sleep, weight gain, orthostatic hypotension, dry mouth, constipation, swelling, headaches, and sexual dysfunction.	Depression, Social Phobia, Panic Disorder, Parkinson's Disease, and Migraine Headaches.

Social Phobia.   The MAOIs can be very effective in diminishing the anxiety occurring with social phobia (Scott & Heimberg, 2000). However, the availability of other treatments, such as the specific serotonin reuptake inhibitors, and the adverse effects associated with the MAOIs have limited the use of the MAOIs in the treatment of social phobia (Scott & Heimberg, 2000).

Panic Disorder.   Although effective for panic disorder, safety and tolerability issues again restrict the use of MAOIs to those cases in which other modalities have not produced a sufficient response (Simon & Pollack, 2000).

Parkinson's Disease.   Selegiline improves symptoms of Parkinson's disease (Romrell et al., 2003).

Migraine Headache.   Although monoamine oxidase inhibitors appear effective in preventing migraine headaches (Silberstein, 1997), safety concerns limit their use to cases that have not responded to other treatments (Noble & Moore, 1997).

Attention-Deficit, Hyperactivity Disorder (ADHD).   Preliminary data suggest that selegiline may be helpful in the treatment of ADHD (Akhondzadeh et al., 2003). Because selegiline is metabolized to amphetamine (Akhondzadeh et al., 2003), it may be that its putative effects in ADHD result not from monoamine oxidase inhibition alone, but also from the amphetamine metabolite. Proposed mechanisms of action, effects, and uses of monoamine oxidase inhibitors are listed in Table 9.2.

THE SPECIFIC SEROTONIN REUPTAKE INHIBITORS

Since the introduction of fluoxetine (Prozac) in the late 1980s (Nemeroff, 2003), the specific serotonin reuptake inhibitors (SSRIs) have rapidly increased in popularity (Nemeroff, 2003). Their ease of dosing, comparatively few side effects, and efficacy have led to the SSRIs becoming the treatment of choice for most depression (Nemeroff, 2003). By 1998, there were five SSRIs available in the United States: fluoxetine (Prozac), sertraline (Zoloft), paroxetine (Paxil), fluvoxamine (Luvox), and citalopram (Celexa). A more recent introduction is escitalopram (Lexapro).

Mechanism of Action, Pharmacology, and Metabolism

The SSRIs are thought to initiate their antidepressant effects by blocking the reuptake of serotonin into the presynaptic neuron, increasing the overall amount of serotonin in the synapse (Vaswani et al., 2003). Unlike most TCAs, which block the reuptake of both serotonin and norepinephrine, the SSRIs are more specific in that they generally block the reuptake of primarily only serotonin (Vaswani et al., 2003)—hence the term *specific serotonin reuptake inhibitors*. While the SSRIs are fairly specific for serotonin reuptake blockade, some of the SSRIs show weak reuptake inhibition of norepinephrine (Bourin et al., 2001). Paroxetine is the most potent of the SSRIs for the reuptake inhibition of norepinephrine (Bourin et al., 2001). In addition, the SSRIs do not interact with histamine and adrenergic receptors (Vaswani et al., 2003). It is important to realize that while the SSRIs are relatively specific for serotonin, the serotonin itself acts nonspecifically, interacting with all serotonin receptors, not just those involved in affective regulation (Vaswani et al., 2003). The SSRIs differ from one another in how strongly they inhibit the reuptake of serotonin, with paroxetine (Bourin et al., 2001) being the most potent in this regard. However, the strength of reuptake inhibition of serotonin does not appear to correlate with the antidepressant response, as all of the SSRIs appear equally efficacious in large groups of people (Vaswani et al., 2003). Citalopram is the most selective of the SSRIs for reuptake inhibition of serotonin (Baumann, 1996).

The synaptic serotonin reuptake from the SSRIs is only a small part of an extensive cascade of biochemical changes that occur from SSRI use. For example, fluoxetine (and possibly other SSRIs as well) may change both presynaptic and postsynaptic serotonin 1A receptor properties. This alteration may occur via SSRI-induced modification of G proteins that are coupled to the serotonin 1A receptor (Elena Castro et al., 2003). In rats, presynaptic autoreceptors appear to be desensitized at the G-protein level by fluoxetine treatment, while postsynaptic hippocampal serotonin 1A receptors become hypersensitive (Elena Castro et al., 2003). These findings may be relevant in understanding the mechanism of action of SSRIs in that the serotonin 1A receptor has been implicated as having a role in depressive disorders (Hensler, 2003) and presynaptic serotonin 1A autoreceptor desensitization is postulated to underlie the therapeutic efficacy of SSRIs and other antidepressants that desensitize this receptor (Hensler, 2003).

Certain antidepressants may increase hippocampal neurogenesis (Santarelli et al., 2003). In a series of experiments linking serotonin and hippocampal neurogenesis, Santarelli and colleagues (2003), found that mice genetically lacking serotonin 1a receptors did not respond behaviorally or with hippocampal neurogenesis to fluoxetine treatment. This finding suggests that serotonin-mediated hippocampal neurogenesis may be a mechanism of SSRIs' antidepressant action.

The SSRIs are all extensively metabolized by the liver by cytochrome P450 enzymes. The half-life of sertraline, paroxetine, and fluvoxamine is approximately one day. Citalopram has a similar half-life of around 35 hours. However, fluoxetine has a considerably longer half-life of one to four days (Vaswani et al., 2003). This means that it can take nearly a month for fluoxetine to reach a steady state in the blood and a month for fluoxetine to leave the body after its dosing has been discontinued. To further complicate things, fluoxetine is metabolized in the liver by cytochrome P450 enzymes to an active metabolite called norfluoxetine, which has a half-life of seven to fifteen days (Vaswani et al., 2003), enabling norfluoxetine potentially to remain in the body for six weeks or longer after the fluoxetine has been discontinued.

Drug-Drug Interactions

The SSRIs can inhibit the enzymes in the cytochrome P450 system of the liver that metabolizes many different kinds of drugs, enabling the SSRIs to have the potential to interact with a wide variety of drugs (Sproule et al., 1997). Furthermore, each of the individual SSRIs inhibits different cytochrome P450 enzymes to varying degrees. Therefore, despite the similarity in the mechanism of action of the SSRIs, the drug-drug interactions can vary widely from SSRI to SSRI (Vaswani et al., 2003). Compared to other SSRIs, citalopram may have fewer drug-drug interactions via the cytochrome P450 system (Parker & Brown, 2000). As a class, drug-drug reactions between SSRIs and many other drugs have been reported. For example, the SSRIs can interact with some antipsychotics and with TCAs (Vaswani et al., 2003). Fluoxetine can increase levels of the benzodiazepines alprazolam (Xanax) and diazepam (Valium) (Sproule et al., 1997).

Adverse Effects

Due in part to their lack of binding to histamine and dopamine receptors (Vaswani et al., 2003), the SSRIs may have fewer side effects than the TCAs and are less lethal in overdose than the TCAs (Peretti et al., 2000). However, they do have significant adverse effects, some of which can be quite serious. Furthermore, even though the SSRIs are quite similar to one another, there do appear to be some differences in side effects between one SSRI and another. For example, some people who cannot tolerate fluoxetine can be treated with citalopram (Calabrese et al., 2003). When serotonin type 2 receptors are stimulated by these drugs, gastrointestinal upset and pain, as well as nausea (Calabrese et al., 2003), may result, although this side effect may be short lived. Stimulation of serotonin type 3 receptors from SSRI-induced reuptake inhibition also may result in gastrointestinal upset and nausea, as serotonin type 3 receptor antagonists are used to treat nausea (Walton, 2000). Headaches are also fairly common in the initial stages of SSRI treatment (Calabrese et al., 2003), usually resolving within the first few weeks of treatment. Unlike the other SSRIs and similar to the TCAs, paroxetine can block acetylcholine receptors (Vaswani et al., 2003).

A common problem with the use of these drugs in both men and women is the induction of a variety of sexual dysfunctions (Calabrese et al., 2003), including ejaculatory delay (Rosen et al., 1999), that often continue while someone is on the drug. SSRI-induced ejaculatory delay and other sexual dysfunction may be related to activation of serotonin subtype 2 receptors from SSRIs and may respond to high-dose sildenafil (Viagra) (Seidman et al., 2003). In fact, SSRIs are used to treat premature ejaculation (Seidman et al., 2003). Other sexual dysfunction may involve SSRI-induced stimulation of serotonin subtype 2 receptors (Berk et al., 2000).

The SSRIs also diminish REM sleep (Sharpley & Cowen, 1995) and are associated with both weight loss and gain in different patients (Vaswani et al., 2003), and long-term use of the SSRIs may cause weight gain (Sussman et al., 2001). The mechanism of the gain in weight remains unknown (Van Ameringen et al., 2002).

Like many antidepressants, the SSRIs appear to have a withdrawal syndrome (Black et al., 2000), especially the ones with shorter half-lives like paroxetine (Black et al., 2000). These symptoms of withdrawal can occur with abrupt discontinuation of the drug and are characterized by dizziness, insomnia, headache, nausea, irritability, and anxiety (Black et al., 2000)

Several studies have suggested a link between the use of SSRIs and suicide, particularly in children and adolescents (Gunnell & Ashby, 2004). The evidence is less clear in adults, although the possibility of SSRI-induced suicide does exist even in adults (Gunnell et al., 2005). Even though much of the research is investigating the relationship between SSRIs and suicide, it is possible that other classes of antidepressants may also increase suicide (Gunnell et al., 2005). Due to a reported declining rate of suicide in the United States (Grunebaum et al., 2004), in the face of putative SSRI-induced suicide, additional research is needed to further assess the risk-benefit ratio of SSRIs and possibly other classes of antidepressants in depression.

Uses

Depression.   Because they appear to be as effective as other antidepressants, have possibly fewer side effects (Hardy et al., 2002), and have convenient, once-a-day dosing, the SSRIs generally have become the first-line treatment for most types of depression (Thase & Kupfer, 1996). Their role in very severe depression is less clear, with some evidence favoring TCAs for this condition (Anderson, 2000; Parker, 2001). Furthermore, some of the dual-action antidepressants (see below) may be more effective in the treatment of major depression than are the SSRIs (Richelson, 2003). Like other antidepressants, the SSRIs can force a switch from depression to mania in susceptible people, although they may be somewhat safer in this regard than the TCAs (Thase & Sachs, 2000). All of the SSRIs appear equally efficacious for depression overall, although one report found that 42 to 71 percent of people whose depression has not responded to one SSRI will respond to a second SSRI (Sussman & Stahl, 1996), suggesting some differences in individual SSRIs. Some findings have suggested that SSRIs may lose efficacy over time in the treatment of depression (Feighner, 1999). Fluoxetine also is available in an enteric-coated, delayed-release preparation that can be given once weekly (Wagstaff & Goa, 2001), with a possible improvement in compliance (Wagstaff & Goa, 2001). Of the SSRIs, citalopram is the least expensive (Parker & Brown, 2000), providing an advantage in terms of cost.

Anorexia Nervosa.   The SSRIs are frequently used as part of the overall treatment of anorexia nervosa (Vaswani et al., 2003), particularly if another disorder such as depression or obsessive-compulsive disorder is present, although the positive effects from the SSRI may be short lived, unless coupled with therapy (Vaswani et al., 2003)

Bulimia Nervosa and Binge-Eating Disorder.   The SSRIs are often used in conjunction with psychotherapy in the treatment of bulimia (Vaswani et al, 2003), although their positive effects tend to be short lived. Fluoxetine (Arnold et al., 2002), fluvoxamine (Hudson et al., 1998), and sertraline (McElroy et al., 2000) are associated with improvement in placebo-controlled trials in binge-eating disorder patients.

Obsessive-Compulsive Disorder.   Along with the TCA clomipramine, the SSRIs have become an important part of the pharmacological treatment of obsessive-compulsive disorder (OCD) (Vaswani et al., 2003), either alone or in combination with forms of behavioral interventions. No one SSRI has been shown to be more effective for OCD than any other, and fluoxetine, fluvoxamine, paroxetine, and sertraline all have U.S. Food and Drug Administration approval for the treatment of obsessive-compulsive disorder (Hollander et al., 2003a). Trichotillomania, a disorder whose hallmark involves obsessively and impulsively plucking body and scalp hair, may respond to an SSRI, although the results from placebo-controlled studies have shown mixed results, with some studies showing positive responses to SSRIs and others noting no improvement (van Minnen et al., 2003).

Body Dysmorphic Disorder (Dysmorphophobia).   Body dysmorphic disorder may respond favorably to specific serotonin reuptake inhibitors (including the TCA clomipramine) (Phillips & Najjar, 2003).

Posttraumatic Stress Disorder.   While many classes of psychotropic medications have been used to treat posttraumatic stress disorder (PTSD), the SSRIs can provide some relief in this condition (Vaswani et al., 2003), although psychotherapy too appears to play a key role in this disorder. SSRIs also can be used to treat posttraumatic stress disorder in children and adolescents (Donnelly, 2003).

Generalized Anxiety Disorder and Social Anxiety Disorder.   The SSRIs appear beneficial for both generalized anxiety disorder and panic disorder to the point where they now are considered first-line treatment for generalized and social anx-

TABLE 9.3   Selective Serotonin Reuptake Inhibitors

MECHANISM OF ACTION	ADVERSE EFFECTS	USES
Block the reuptake of serotonin into the presynaptic neuron, increasing the overall amount of serotonin in the synapse.	Gastrointestinal upset and pain, nausea, agitation, anxiety, headaches, dry mouth, constipation, confusion, sexual dysfunction, diminishment of REM sleep, weight loss and gain, and a withdrawal syndrome (characterized by dizziness, insomnia, headache, nausea, irritability, and anxiety).	Depression, Anorexia Nervosa, Bulimia Nervosa, Binge-Eating Disorder, Obsessive-Compulsive Disorder, Body Dysmorphic Disorder, Posttraumatic Stress Disorder, Generalized Anxiety Disorder, Social Anxiety Disorder, and Panic Disorder.

iety disorders (van der Linden et al., 2000; Vaswani et al., 2003). An advantage of the SSRIs over benzodiazepines is their lack of abuse potential (Rickels & Rynn, 2002).

Panic Disorder.   Although many drugs appear to be effective in the treatment of panic disorder, the SSRIs are often the first-line treatment for panic disorder (Vaswani et al., 2003). A disadvantage of the SSRIs in panic disorder is the longer delay compared to benzodiazepines before therapeutic effects appear (Sheehan, 2002). In fact, however, in actual practice, benzodiazepines still appear to be used more frequently for the treatment of panic disorder than do the SSRIs (Bruce et al., 2003).

Narcolepsy.   Similar to the TCAs, the SSRIs can be used to treat the cataplexy associated with narcolepsy (Thorpy, 2001). Table 9.3 summarizes the proposed mechanism of action, adverse effects, and uses for the SSRIs.

ATYPICAL AND DUAL-ACTION ANTIDEPRESSANTS

In addition to the TCAs, MAOIs, and SSRIs, several other antidepressants are available, including bupropion (Wellbutrin, Wellbutrin SR, Zyban), mirtazapine (Remeron), trazodone (Desyrel), nefazodone (Serzone), and venlafaxine (Effexor). Some of these, such as bupropion, have a relatively unique mechanism of action. Others combine reuptake inhibition of serotonin and norepinephrine, the so-called dual-action antidepressants, some of which may have greater antidepressant efficacy than other antidepressants (Richelson, 2003).

Bupropion

First marketed in the United States in 1988 (Settle, 1998), bupropion (Wellbutrin, Wellbutrin SR, Wellbutrin XL, and Zyban) is an antidepressant whose mechanism of action is different from other available antidepressants (Richelson, 2003). Increasing the duration of action, sustained-release forms [bupropion SR (Davidson & Connor, 1998) and bupropion XL (Stahl et al., 2004)] have been introduced to allow bupropion to be given once a day, instead of two or three times daily as was the original, immediate-release preparation. Zyban is simply bupropion SR marketed to help in smoking cessation.

Mechanism of Action, Pharmacology, and Metabolism. Unlike many antidepressants, bupropion does not appear to directly affect the serotonin system, blocking instead the reuptake of dopamine (Feighner, 1999) and norepinephrine (Richmond & Zwar, 2003) into the presynaptic neuron to initiate its antidepressant effects (Feighner, 1999). Bupropion also appears to suppress the firing of the locus coeruleus, a finding thought to be relevant for the antidepressant effects of bupropion (Davidson & Connor, 1998). Bupropion also inhibits nicotinic acetylcholine receptors (Haustein, 2003), although the clinical implications of this action are unknown. Unlike the TCA, bupropion does not interact with histamine and acetylcholine receptors (Feighner, 1999). Bupropion is metabolized to hydroxybupropion, threobupropion, erythrohydrobupropion (Stahl et al., 2004). Hydroxybupropion appears to inhibit the reuptake of norepinephrine and dopamine and may antagonize the nicotinic acetylcholine receptor (Damaj et al., 2004). As such, hydroxybupropion is an active metabolite that may contribute to the antidepressant effects of bupropion (Sanchez & Hyttel, 1999). Concentrations of hydroxybupropion and erythrohydrobupropion in cerebral spinal fluid are approximately six times higher than those of bupropion. Even more striking, threobupropion cerebral spinal fluid concentrations are forty times greater the concentration of bupropion (Davidson & Connor, 1998).

Drug-Drug Interactions. Bupropion can interact with several drugs. For example, bupropion inhibits the metabolism of tricyclic antidepressants (Haustein, 2003). In a study evaluating the effects of bupropion on fluoxetine, paroxetine, or venlafaxine (Effexor), bupropion did not significantly alter plasma levels of fluoxetine or paroxetine, but did increase venlafaxine concentrations (Kennedy et al., 2002), suggesting a bupropion-venlafaxine interaction.

Adverse Effects. Common side effects from bupropion include dry mouth, insomnia (Tracey, 2002), and nausea (Stahl et al., 2004). Bupropion appears to cause less sexual dysfunction than other antidepressants (Labbate et al., 2003). When added to fluoxetine, paroxetine, or venlafaxine in people who had antidepressant-induced sexual dysfunction, bupropion diminished the amount of sexual dysfunction (Kennedy et al., 2002). Seizures have been a concern with the immediate-release formulation of bupropion (Settle, 1998); however, the sustained-release formulation of bupropion appears to be associated with seizures in approximately one in 1,000 cases (Tracey, 2002). In fact, in patients without additional risk factors for seizures, the seizure rate for sustained-release bupropion may be similar to other antidepressants (Dunner et al., 1998). Seizures can complicate the course of bupropion overdose (Balit et al., 2003; Tracey, 2002). The sustained-release form of bupropion may cause fewer adverse effects overall compared to the immediate-release form (Settle, 1998).

Uses.   *Depression.*   Bupropion is effective for the treatment of depression (Settle, 1998) and can be a treatment option for patients whose depression has not responded adequately to a trial of an SSRI (Fava et al., 2003). A small, open trial of bupropion sustained-release in depressed adolescents showed a favorable response to bupropion (Glod et al., 2003). Some evidence suggests that bupropion is less likely than many other antidepressants to induce switching in bipolar depression, making bupropion a consideration for bipolar depression (Thase & Sachs, 2000).

Smoking Cessation.   Bupropion appears effective for the cessation of smoking (Tracey, 2002) in people with and without a history of depression (Richmond & Zwar, 2003). A randomized, double-blind, placebo-controlled trial found the slow-release form of bupropion in combination with counseling to be more effective than placebo for smoking cessation (Tonnesen et al., 2003). Bupropion and nicotine-replacement therapy appear similar in efficacy (Haustein, 2003). Bupropion inhibits acetylcholine nicotinic receptors (Haustein, 2003), which may be part of its mechanism in smoking cessation.

Attention-Deficit, Hyperactive Disorder.   Although stimulants such as methylphenidate (Ritalin) are the most commonly used drug for the treatment of attention-deficit disorder (ADHD) (Pelham et al., 1999), other drugs have been found at least somewhat helpful in this disorder, among them bupropion (Pliszka, 2003). Bupropion may be an alternative in case in which the use of a stimulant is inappropriate. Table 9.4 lists the proposed mechanism of action, adverse effects, and uses of bupropion.

Mirtazapine (Remeron)

Mirtazapine is an effective antidepressant (Benkert et al., 2002) with a unique mechanism of action (Nutt, 2002).

Mechanism of Action, Pharmacology, and Metabolism.   Mirtazapine is thought to initiate its antidepressant effects by blocking what are known as α_2-receptors on the *presynaptic* neuron (Anttila & Leinonen, 2001). These receptors serve as a negative feedback system: Norepinephrine from the synapse binds to these receptors, signaling to the presynaptic neuron to stop releasing additional norepinephrine and into the synapse. By blocking these receptors, mirtazapine

TABLE 9.4   Bupropion

MECHANISM OF ACTION	ADVERSE EFFECTS	USES
Block the reuptake of dopamine and norepinephrine into the presynaptic neuron.	Dry mouth, insomnia, seizures, and death from overdose.	Depression, Smoking Cessation, and Attention-Deficit, Hyperactivity Disorder.

disrupts the negative feedback loop, allowing for more norepinephrine to be released into the synapse. Norepinephrine then interacts with α_1 receptors on serotonin-containing neurons to increase the firing rate of these cells (Nicholas et al., 2003). In addition to the blockade of alpha-receptors, mirtazapine also blocks postsynaptic serotonin 2 receptors (Anttila & Leinonen, 2001). So while the overall transmission of serotonin is increased, it is diminished at this subtype of serotonin receptor. Because stimulation of the serotonin type 2 receptor may be involved in anxiety and sexual dysfunction, mirtazapine actually may result in fewer of these untoward effects than some other antidepressants, as the SSRIs (Nutt, 2002). In addition, mirtazapine antagonizes postsynaptic serotonin type 3 receptors (Nicholas et al., 2003). As stimulation of these receptors is thought to result in nausea and vomiting, mirtazapine may produce fewer of these gastrointestinal problems than other antidepressants that stimulate serotonin type 3 receptors (Nutt, 2002). Finally, mirtazapine blocks histamine type 1 receptor (Nicholas et al., 2003), an action that is important in the generation of some of the adverse effects associated with mirtazapine.

Metabolized by cytochrome P450 enzymes, including the 2D6 isoenzyme (Kirchheiner et al., 2004), mirtazapine is converted into a variety of metabolites, including one active metabolite, desmethylmirtazapine, which is significantly less potent than mirtazapine itself (Störmer et al., 2000). A half-life of approximately twenty to forty hours (Feighner, 1999) allows for once-daily dosing of mirtazapine.

Drug-Drug Interactions. Drug interactions can occur when mirtazapine is combined with other drugs. For example, when given concurrently to healthy people, mirtazapine and amitriptyline alter the pharmacokinetics slightly of each other, although tolerability does not seem to be affected (Sennef et al., 2003). The anticonvulsant phenytoin (Dilantin) can decrease concentrations of mirtazapine, possibly through induction of cytochrome P450 enzymes that metabolize mirtazapine (Spaans et al., 2002).

Adverse Effects. Generally well tolerated (Nutt, 2002), mirtazapine does cause some side effects. Drowsiness can be a particular problem with this medication (Nicholas et al., 2003). Unlike TCAs, SSRIs, and MAOIs (Sharpley & Cowen, 1995), mirtazapine does not interfere with REM sleep and actually increases sleep continuity and decreases sleep latency without additionally affecting sleep architecture (Winokur et al., 2000). Tolerance to the sedating effects of mirtazapine may occur with time (Winokur et al., 2000). Although the mechanism of mirtazapine's effects on sleep are unknown, histamine antagonism, effects on alpha-adrenergic receptors, and serotonin 2 receptor antagonism have been suggested as possibilities (Winokur et al., 2000). Another effect from mirtazapine is increased appetite (Nicholas et al., 2003) and weight gain (Burrows & Kremer, 1997), necessitating close monitoring of weight during treatment with mirtazapine (Vanina et al., 2002). Mirtazapine may be associated with less sexual dysfunction than some other antidepressants (Labbate et al., 2003). Mirtazapine is also associated with increased total cholesterol but not LDL levels (Nicholas et al., 2003).

Uses.   *Depression.*   Mirtazapine is an effective antidepressant (Wade et al., 2003) and appears to be as effective as the TCAs (Benkert et al., 2002). Of both clinical and theoretical significance, mirtazapine may result in an antidepressant response faster than do the SSRIs (Benkert et al., 2002; Blier, 2003). An open-label study reported improvement from mirtazapine in treatment-resistant depression (Wan et al., 2003).

Anxiety Disorders.   Early evidence suggests that mirtazapine may be effective for at least some anxiety disorders. For instance, open-label studies have found improvement in mirtazapine-treated subjects in social phobia (Van Veen et al., 2002) and panic disorder (Sarchiapone et al., 2003). In addition, a placebo-controlled, double-blind study found that mirtazapine resulted in some improvement in post-traumatic stress disorder (Davidson et al., 2003). Table 9.5 shows the proposed mechanism of action, adverse effects, and use of mirtazapine.

Trazodone (Desyrel) and Nefazodone (Serzone)

Trazodone (Marek et al., 1992) and nefazodone (Schatzberg, 2000) are antidepressants with relatively unique mechanisms of action (Haria et al., 1994).

Mechanism of Action, Pharmacology, and Metabolism.   Both trazodone and nefazodone appear to initiate their antidepressant effects by weakly blocking the reuptake of serotonin into the presynaptic neuron and by blocking serotonin 2 receptors (Schatzberg, 2000). In addition, nefazodone possesses norepinephrine reuptake blocking properties (Pallanti et al., 2002). Similar to mirtazapine, these drugs increase the overall transmission of serotonin while at the same time blocking some serotonin receptors. Trazodone, and more weakly nefazodone, also bind to α_1-adrenergic receptors (Feighner, 1999). Further complicating their mechanism of action, both trazodone (Rothman & Baumann, 2002) and nefazodone are metabolized to a compound called metachlorophenylpiperazine (M-CPP), an active metabolite that may block reuptake of serotonin and act to directly stimulate serotonin 2 and to a lesser extent serotonin 1A receptors (Pallanti et al., 2002). Nefazodone does not interrupt sleep architecture as many other antidepressants do (Sharpley et al., 1996). Finally, trazodone and nefazodone do not antagonize his-

TABLE 9.5   Mirtazapine

MECHANISM OF ACTION	ADVERSE EFFECTS	USE
Block α_2-receptors on the presynaptic neuron; reuptake inhibition of serotonin and norepinephrine.	Drowsiness, increased appetite, weight gain, increased cholesterol, but not LDL levels, and rarely, effects on white blood cell production.	Depression.

tamine and acetylcholine receptors (Feighner, 1999), making them relatively devoid of antihistaminic and anticholinergic adverse effects. Nefazodone has significant first-pass metabolism effects (Green & Barbhaiya, 1997). In addition to its conversion to M-CPP, nefazodone is converted to two other pharmacologically active metabolites, hydroxyl-nefazodone and triazoledione (Green & Barbhaiya, 1997). Furthermore, nefazodone inhibits the cytochrome P450 enzyme 2D6 (Green & Barbhaiya, 1997) and 3A4 (Dresser et al., 2000).

Drug-Drug Interactions.   Because of its interactions with cytochrome P450 enzymes, nefazodone can interact with several drugs, including the benzodiazepines triazolam (halcion) and alprazolam (Xanax), as well as with carbamazepine (Tegretol) (Green & Barbhaiya, 1997). Trazodone appears to have clinically significant interactions with the anticoagulant warfarin (Coumadin) (Small & Giamonna, 2000).

Adverse Effects.   Common side effects from trazodone include drowsiness (Feighner, 1999), orthostatic hypotension, lowered blood pressure, and dizziness (Hayes & Kristoff, 1986). Less common but dramatic is priaprism (Hayes & Kristoff, 1986), a painful, sustained erection that can result in tissue damage and may be related to trazodone's effects on the α_1-adrenergic receptor (Feighner, 1999). Trazodone also has been associated with cardiac arrythmias (Haria et al., 1994). Generally reasonably well tolerated, nefazodone can result in nausea, drowsiness, headache, dry mouth (Augustin et al., 1997), lightheadedness, and blurred vision (Ellingrod & Perry, 1995). Possibly due to its antagonism of serotonin 2c receptors, nefazodone induces less sexual dysfunction than do the SSRIs (Pallanti et al., 2002). Unlike TCAs, most MAOIs, and SSRIs, nefazodone tends to increase slow-wave sleep, possibly through its antagonism of serotonin 2a and 2c (Sharpley & Cowen, 1995). In contrast to trazodone, nefazodone does not seem to cause priaprism (Andrews & Nemeroff, 1994). Finally, nefazodone is associated with liver toxicity (Lucena, 2003).

Uses.   *Depression.*   Trazodone is more effective than placebo for the treatment of depression (Workman & Short, 1993) and appears to be effective in geriatric depression (Haria et al., 1994). Nefazodone also appears to be effective in the treatment of depression (Ellingrod & Perry, 1995). Possibly because of its antagonism of serotonin 2 receptors, nefazodone may improve sleep architecture and is a possible option for people with depression complicated by insomnia (Thase, 1999).

Insomnia.   Because of its sedating and nonaddictive properties, trazodone is used in the short-term treatment of insomnia and provides and alternative to the use of benzodiazepines (Lenhart & Buysse, 2001). Trazodone also is used to treat the insomnia associated with the SSRIs (Dording et al., 2002). A possible reason for trazodone's ability to improve sleep is that it appears to increase slow-wave sleep but does not affect other aspects of sleep architecture (Ware & Pittard, 1990), effects that have been hypothesized to occur from trazodone's alpha-adrenergic blocking properties combined with its diminished norepinephrine reuptake inhibition and anticholinergic action (Ware & Pittard, 1990).

Generalized Anxiety Disorder. Both trazodone (Gale, 2002) and nefazodone (Hedges et al., 1996) may be effective for the treatment of generalized anxiety disorder, although additional evidence is required to better understand the role of these drugs in the treatment of generalized anxiety disorder.

Panic Disorder. Early evidence also supports the use of nefazodone for panic disorder (Papp et al., 2000).

Erectile Dysfunction. Trazodone may have some use as a treatment for erectile dysfunction (Vitezic & Pelcic, 2002). Table 9.6 summarizes the mechanism of action, adverse effects, and uses of nefazodone and trazodone.

Venlafaxine (Effexor)

One of the newer antidepressants, venlafaxine (Effexor) may result in higher remission rates in the treatment of depression than SSRIs and possibly have a faster onset of antidepressant action (Hardy et al., 2002).

Mechanism of Action, Pharmacology, and Metabolism. Venlafaxine is considered to be a dual-action antidepressant, selectively inhibiting the reuptake of both serotonin and norepinephrine (Hardy et al., 2002). At its lower doses, venlafaxine primarily inhibits the reuptake of serotonin (Hardy et al., 2002), with both serotonin and norepinephrine reuptake inhibition occurring at higher doses (Roseboom & Kalin, 2000), conferring a dual-action mechanism to venlafaxine. Additionally, venlafaxine may block to some extent the reuptake of dopamine at high doses (Feighner, 1999).

Venlafaxine is metabolized in the liver to 0-desmethylvenlafaxine, which also inhibits the reuptake of serotonin and norepinephrine (Marazziti, 2003). Ven-

TABLE 9.6   Nefazodone/Trazodone

MECHANISM OF ACTION	ADVERSE EFFECTS	USES
Weakly block the reuptake of serotonin into the presynaptic neuron and by blocking serotonin 2a and 2c receptors.	Drowsiness, orthostatic hypotension (trazodone), priaprism (trazodone), lightheadedness, gastrointestinal complaints, nausea, and an increase in slow-wave sleep.	Depression, Insomnia, Generalized Anxiety Disorder, and Panic Disorder.

lafaxine's relatively short half-life of about five hours (Hardy et al., 2002) requires multiple daily dosing of venlafaxine, although the sustained-release form of venlafaxine has an effective half-life of approximately 15 hours (Hardy et al., 2002). Venlafaxine is approximately 27 percent protein bound (Augustin et al., 1997).

Drug-Drug Interactions.   Venlafaxine appears to have relatively few effects on the enzymes of the cytochrome P450 system, and although it does inhibit some of these enzymes, its propensity to interact with other drugs is relatively low (Hardy et al., 2002). Venlafaxine carries the potential to result in a serotonin syndrome if combined with other medications that affect serotonin, such as monoamine oxidase inhibitors (Hardy et al., 2002).

Adverse Effects.   Venlafaxine may result in nausea, insomnia, lightheadedness, drowsiness, sexual dysfunction, headaches, and agitation (Hardy et al., 2002). Particularly at higher doses (Feighner, 1999), venlafaxine can cause elevations in blood pressure (Thase, 1998), necessitating blood pressure monitoring in people taking venlafaxine (Feighner, 1999). When the venlafaxine dose is abruptly lowered or discontinued, a withdrawal syndrome characterized by worsening mood, anxiety, flu-like symptoms, and sleep disturbance can occur (Hardy et al., 2002). In pediatric populations, venlafaxine may be associated with hostility, suicidal ideation, and self-harm (Wyeth, 2003).

Uses.   *Depression.*   Venlafaxine is an important drug for the treatment of depression. An important advantage of venlafaxine over the TCAs is greater safety in overdose (Hardy et al., 2002). Venlafaxine may have a faster onset of action than other antidepressants (Blier, 2003; Feighner, 1999), which may be related to the observation that venlafaxine may down regulate the beta-adrenergic receptor faster than other antidepressants (Feighner, 1999).

Generalized Anxiety Disorder and Panic Disorder.   Preliminary evidence supports the use of venlafaxine for the treatment of generalized anxiety disorder (Hardy et al., 2002) and panic disorder (Ninan, 2000). Venlafaxine has been suggested also for use in cases of treatment-resistant panic disorder (Mathew et al., 2001). Venlafaxine's lack of abuse and addiction potential provides an advantage over some other drugs used to treat anxiety, such as the benzodiazepines.

Obsessive-Compulsive Disorder.   Preliminary data suggest that venlafaxine may be helpful in the treatment of obsessive-compulsive disorder, even in some cases that have not previously responded to specific serotonin reuptake inhibitors (Hollander et al., 2003b; Marazziti, 2003). Albert and colleagues (2002) reported that according to their study venlafaxine might have efficacy similar to clomipramine in the treatment of obsessive-compulsive disorder, with fewer adverse effects.

Chronic Pain Syndrome.   Emerging evidence suggests that venlafaxine may have a role in the management of chronic pain, as it appears to be at least effective as the

TCAs for pain control but with potentially fewer adverse effects (Barkin & Fawcett, 2000).

Attention-Deficit, Hyperactivity Disorder. Venlafaxine has had some use in the treatment of attention-deficit, hyperactivity disorder (ADHD), particularly in adults (Hedges et al., 1995) and may be an option for some cases of ADHD (Ninan, 2000). The putative mechanism of action, adverse effects, and uses of venlafaxine are shown in Table 9.7.

Duloxetine (Cymbalta)

Approved by the United States Food and Drug Administration in 2004 (Franklin, 2004), duloxetine potently inhibits the reuptake of serotonin and norepinephrine, making it a dual-action antidepressant (Schatzberg, 2003). Duloxetine may also inhibit the reuptake of dopamine (Schatzberg, 2003). Effective for major depression, duloxetine may have a faster onset of action than other antidepressants (Schatzberg, 2003). Well tolerated, duloxetine is associated with some sedation, dry mouth, and nausea (Schatzberg, 2003).

Reboxetine (Edronax)

Reboxetine is a newly developed drug that, although available in many countries, has not yet received approval from the U.S. Food and Drug Administration for release in the United States. Nevertheless, its mechanism of action makes it a potentially important antidepressant.

Mechanism of Action, Pharmacology, and Metabolism. Reboxetine is a relatively selective reuptake inhibitor of norepinephrine (Montgomery &

TABLE 9.7   Venlafaxine

MECHANISM OF ACTION	ADVERSE EFFECTS	USES
Selectively inhibit the reuptake of both serotonin and norepinephrine.	Nausea, insomnia, lightheadedness, drowsiness, sexual dysfunction, headaches, and agitation, elevations in blood pressure, hostility, suicidal ideation, self-harm, and a withdrawal syndrome (characterized by worsening mood, anxiety, flu-like symptoms, and sleep disturbance).	Depression, Generalized Anxiety Disorder, Panic Disorder, Obsessive-Compulsive Disorder, Chronic Pain Syndrome, and Attention-Deficit, Hyperactivity Disorder.

Schatzberg, 1998). Early data suggest that reboxetine has relatively little interaction with cytochrome P450 enzymes (Montgomery, 1998).

Adverse Effects.   Reboxetine appears to be fairly well tolerated in general. Side effects from reboxetine include dry mouth, constipation, and excessive sweating (Kasper et al., 2000). Reboxetine is also associated with insomnia early in the course of therapy (Stahl et al., 2002). Notably, reboxetine appears to have relatively few adverse effects on sexual function (Clayton et al., 2003).

Uses.   *Depression.*   Reboxetine appears to be effective for the treatment of major depression (Kasper et al., 2000), including severe depression (Montgomery et al., 2003).

Panic Disorder.   Reboxetine has been reported to reduce the number of panic attacks (Versiani et al., 2002). Dannon and colleagues (2002) reported that reboxetine was effective for panic attacks in patients who had not responded to SSRIs.

OTHER PUTATIVE MECHANISMS OF ANTIDEPRESSANT ACTION

The antidepressants discussed in this chapter affect reuptake primarily of serotonin or norepinephrine, or both. A myriad of post-receptor effects, however, has been postulated to further develop an understanding of antidepressant action. One such effect may involve modifications in receptor function. For example, treatment with antidepressants that increase synaptic serotonin results in a nearly immediate increase in synaptic serotonin, even though it generally takes two to four weeks for an antidepressant response to occur. A possible mechanism for this delay in treatment response may be that the rate of neuronal firing in the serotonin-containing cells of the brainstem's raphe nuclei is decreased by antidepressants that increase synaptic concentrations of serotonin via interaction with somatodendritic serotonin 1A autoreceptors (Schatzberg, 2002). Stimulation of presynaptic serotonin 1A autoreceptors results in diminished release of serotonin into the synapse. Chronic antidepressant treatment, however, results in down regulation of serotonin 1A receptors, allowing for an increase in synaptic serotonin (Schatzberg, 2002), a process that corresponds with the delay in antidepressant response.

Many antidepressants and electroconvulsive therapy as well (see Appendix 1) down regulate, or result in less efficient binding with norepinephrine, beta-adrenergic receptors (Sulser, 1984). Beta receptor down regulation occurs from both antidepressants that inhibit the reuptake of norepinephrine and those that inhibit serotonin reuptake (Donati & Rasenick, 2003).

Antidepressants may have potent effects on neuronal structure itself. For example, antidepressant treatment may alter the expression of neuronal genes (Hyman & Nestler, 1996). In fact, chronic antidepressant treatment appears to stimulate the formation of new neurons in the adult rat hippocampus (Donati &

■ ■ ■ ■ ■ ▬▬▬▬▬▬▬▬▬▬▬

HOW BLIND IS THE DOUBLE-BLIND?

Double-blind, randomized clinical trials are considered the "gold standard" of antidepressant research. Through the use of placebos, such studies attempt to "blind" both the participant and investigator as to a subject's true medication status. Unfortunately, studies concerning the maintenance of this "double-blind" indicate that this standard is hardly ever reached (Moncrieff, 2001). In fact, Slife, Burchfield, and Hedges (2002) summarize how several limitations affect the simple interpretation of findings from randomized, double-blind clinical trials. Some of the methodological limitations of these trials include the following:

- *Unblinding*: The potential for active drugs to produce unintended physiological and psychological experiences (e.g., side effects) can unmask the blinding because the side effects may reveal to both participants and investigators which participants received which medication (Moncrieff, 2001; Moncrief et al., 1998).
- *Wash out*: The finding that a placebo whose side effects resemble those of the active drug may not significantly separate from the active drug (Antonnucio et al., 1999; Greenberg et al., 1992; Kirsch & Sapirstein, 1998).
- *Early subject withdrawal*: May include the exclusion from analysis of individuals who withdraw early from treatment and results in higher effects sizes for antidepressants (Bollini et al., 1999; Colditz et al., 1989; O'Sullivan et al., 1991; Schultz et al., 1996).
- *Withdrawal symptoms*: Discontinuing antidepressant treatment may result in a set of withdrawal symptoms that can be mistaken for relapse, thus depressing the outcome of the placebo group (Moncrieff, 2001).
- *The nonspecificity of antidepressant response*: The finding that some *non-*

antidepressant medications can be used to effectively treat depression, including some antipsychotics, barbiturates, benzodiazepines, and buspirone (Moncrieff, 2001; Thase & Kupfer, 1996).
- *Sponsorship effects*: The finding that the study sponsor is the strongest predictor of drug efficacy in clinical trials (Freemantle, 2000; Friedberg et al., 1999).

These methodological limitations appear to indicate that the double-blind, randomized clinical trials of antidepressants may be less than ideal and, as suggested by Moncrieff (2001), "that depression is susceptible to a variety of non-disease-specific pharmacological actions, such as sedation or psychostimulation, as well as the effects of suggestion" (p. 292).

REFERENCES

Antonuccio DO, Danton WG, DeNelsky GY, Greenberg RP, Gordon JS (1999): Raising questions about antidepressants. Psychotherapy and Psychosomatics 68:3–14.

Bollini P, Pampallona S, Tibaldi G, Kupelnick B, Munniza C (1999): Effectiveness of antidepressants: Meta-analysis of dose-effect relationships in randomized clinical trials. British Journal of Psychiatry 174:297–303.

Colditz GA, Miller JN, Mosteller F (1989): How study design affects outcomes in comparisons of therapy, I: Medical. Statistical Medicine 8:441–454.

Freemantle N, Anderson IM, Young P (2000): Predictive value of pharmacological activity for the relative efficacy of antidepressant drugs: Meta-regression analysis. British Journal of Psychiatry 177:292–302.

Friedberg M, Saffran B, Stinson TJ, Nelson W, Bennett CL (1999): Evaluation of conflict of interest in economic analyses of new drugs used in oncology. Journal of the American Medical Association 282:1453–1457.

Greenberg RP, Bornstein RF, Greenberg MD, Fisher S (1992): A meta-analysis of antidepressant outcome under "blinder" conditions. Journal of Consulting & Clinical Psychology 60:664–669.

Kirsch I, Sapirstein G (1998): Listening to prozac but hearing placebo: A meta-analysis of antidepressant medication. Prevention & Treatment, 1, Article 0002a.

Moncrieff J (2001): Are antidepressants overrated? A review of methodological problems in antidepressant trials. The Journal of Nervous and Mental Disease 189:288–295.

Moncrieff J, Wessely S, Hardy R (1998): Meta-analysis of trials comparing antidepressants with active placebos. British Journal of Psychiatry 172:227–231.

O'Sullivan G, Noshivani H, Marks I, Monteiro W, Leiliot P (1991): Six year follow up after exposure and clomipramine therapy for ob-

sessive-compulsive disorder. Journal of Clinical Psychiatry 52:150–155.

Schultz KF, Grimes DA, Altman DG, Hayes RH (1996): Blinding and exclusions after allocation in randomized clinical trials: Survey of published parallel group trials in obstetrics and gynaecology. British Medical Journal 312:742–744.

Slife BD, Burchfield CM, Hedges DW (2002): *Hook Line and Sinker: Psychology's Uncritical Acceptance of Biological Explanation*. Paper presented at the Rocky Mountain Psychological Association Meeting, Park City, Utah, 5 April 2002.

Thase ME, Kupfer DJ (1996): Recent developments in the pharmacotherapy of mood disorders. Journal of Consulting & Clinical Psychology 64:646–659.

Rasenick, 2003). Antidepressants also may alter the function of neurotrophic factors, chemicals that regulate the survival on neurons (Nestler et al., 2002). For example, the expression one of the most prevalent types of neurotrophic factors in the adult brain, brain-derived neurotrophic factor, is increased by chronic antidepressant treatment (Nibuya et al., 1995). In support of these ideas, it appears that many antidepressants may elevate levels of brain-derived neurotrophic factors in the hippocampus and cortex (Vaidya & Duman, 2001). This finding suggests that antidepressant-induced increases in these biochemicals may be a mechanism of action of antidepressants. Related to this action, antidepressants can increase cyclic adenosine monophosphate response to element binding protein (CREB), a substance that increases brain-derived neurotrophic hormone (Vaidya & Duman, 2001).

Antidepressants may change the function of G proteins, which in many cases are coupled to receptors. Because they conduct and amplify intraneuronal communication, G proteins can have a profound effect on neuronal function. Due to the complexity of the G-protein system, antidepressants could alter G proteins at several different points. For example, antidepressants may affect the coupling between a receptor and G protein, or the antidepressant could affect the properties of the G protein itself (Donati & Rasenick, 2003).

SUMMARY

In addition to their key role in the treatment of depression, antidepressant medications are used in many other disorders, including anxiety, obsessive-compulsive disorders, and pain control. Despite several different mechanisms of action, all available antidepressants appear to manipulate serotonin, norepinephrine, or both at the synapse, an effect thought to initiate the antidepressant response. It is necessary to assume that other changes occur, as the synaptic serotonin and norepinephrine alterations happen immediately, whereas the antidepressant effects may not be observed for two to eight weeks.

While antidepressants are a widely used and accepted part of standard medical practice, several studies have suggested that the effectiveness of antidepressants for treatment of depression may be overrated. Concerns such as these reinforce the need for continued research with these drugs and underscore the importance of careful and judicious clinical use of these medications. Tricyclic antidepressants appear to initiate their effects by blocking the reuptake of serotonin or norepinephrine, or both, although the relative amounts amount of reuptake inhibition varies among the different tricyclic antidepressants. Effective for depression and other disorders, the tricyclic antidepressants are associated with significant adverse effects and high lethality in overdose. Although curtailed in their use by adverse effects and dietary restrictions, monoamine oxidase inhibitors inhibit monoamine oxidase, with subsequent elevations in synaptic serotonin and norepinephrine. The specific serotonin reuptake inhibitors selectively inhibit the reuptake of serotonin and appear effective for several disorders in addition to depression, such as generalized anxiety disorder, panic disorder, social phobia, and obsessive-compulsive disorder. Bupropion is an atypical antidepressant that appears to inhibit the reuptake of dopamine and norepinephrine, but not serotonin. It is also used as an aid in smoking cessation and may be effective for attention-deficit disorder. Nefazodone and trazodone also are atypical antidepressants that inhibit the reuptake of serotonin and, in the case of nefazodone, norepinephrine. In addition, nefazodone and trazodone antagonize post-synaptic serotonin 2 receptors, a factor that may account for a different adverse effect profile from antidepressants that indiscriminately agonize multiple serotonin receptors. For example, trazodone and nefazodone are not associated with as many sexual adverse effects as are the specific serotonin reuptake inhibitors. Dual-action antidepressants such as mirtazapine, venlafaxine, and duloxetine inhibit the reuptake of both serotonin and norepinephrine and may be associated with a faster onset of action than other antidepressants.

Although much of the research involving antidepressant action has focused on the effects of antidepressants at the level of neurotransmitters, the antidepressants appear to initiate multiple post-receptor changes in neuronal function and even structure.

STUDY QUESTIONS

1. For each main class of antidepressant, describe the putative mechanism of the antidepressant effect.
2. Why are reversible monoamine oxidase inhibitors safer than nonreversible monoamine oxidase inhibitors?

3. List two possible reasons for the delay in antidepressant response after antidepressant treatment is initiated.

4. Why might dual-action antidepressants be more effective than more traditional antidepressants?

5. If you were to design a novel antidepressant, what features would you include in its mechanism of action and metabolism and why?

6. List one antidepressant from each of the main classes of antidepressants and tell why that particular antidepressant is so classified.

7. Which classes of antidepressants have drugs suitable for the treatment of obsessive-compulsive disorder?

8. Describe the limitations associated with antidepressants and their use.

REFERENCES

Akhondzadeh S, Tavakolian R, Davari-Ashtiani R, Arabgol F, Amini H (2003): Selegiline in the treatment of attention deficit hyperactivity disorder in children: A double-blind and randomized trial. Progress in Neuropsychopharmacology & Biological Psychiatry 27:841–845.

Albert U, Aguglia E, Maina G, Bogetto F (2002): Venlafaxine versus clomipramine in the treatment of obsessive-compulsive disorder: A preliminary single-blind, 12-week, controlled study. Journal of Clinical Psychiatry 63:1004–1009.

Altshuler LL, Post RM, Leverich GS, Mikalauskas K, Rosoff A, Ackerman L (1995): Antidepressant-induced mania and cycle acceleration: A controversy revisited. American Journal of Psychiatry 152:1130–1138.

Amsterdam JD (2003): A double-blind, placebo-controlled trial of the safety and efficacy of selegiline transdermal system without dietary restrictions in patients with major depressive disorder. Journal of Clinical Psychiatry 64:208–214.

Anderson IM (2000): Selective serotonin reuptake inhibitors versus tricyclic antidepressants: A meta-analysis of efficacy and tolerability. Journal of Affective Disorders 58:19–36.

Andrews JM, Nemeroff CB (1994): Contemporary management of depression. American Journal of Medicine 97 (6A):24S–32S.

Anton RF Jr., Burch EA Jr. (1990): Amoxapine versus amitriptyline combined with perphenazine in the treatment of psychotic depression. American Journal of Psychiatry 147:1203–1208.

Anttila SA, Leinonen EV (2001): A review of the pharmacological and clinical profile of mirtazapine. CNS Drug Reviews 7:249–264.

Anttila SA, Leinonen EV (2001): A review of the pharmacological and clinical profile of mirtazapine. CNS Drug Review 8:249–264.

Arnold LM, McElroy SL, Hudson JI, Welge JA, Bennett AJ, Keck PE Jr. (2002): A placebo-controlled, randomized trial of fluoxetine in the treatment of binge-eating disorder. Journal of Clinical Psychiatry 63:1028–1033.

Augustin BG, Cold JA, Jann MW (1997): Venlafaxine and nefazodone, two pharmacologically distinct antidepressants. Pharmacotherapy 17:511–530.

Balit CR, Lynch CN, Isbister GK (2003): Bupropion poisoning: A case series. Medical Journal of Australia 178:61–63.

Ban TA (2001): Pharmacotherapy of depression: A historical analysis. Journal of Neural Transmission 108:707–716.

Barkin RL, Fawcett J (2000): The management challenges of chronic pain: The role of antidepressants. American Journal of Therapeutics 7:31–47.

Baumann P (1996): Pharmacology and pharmacokinetics of citalopram and other SSRIs. International Clinical Psychopharmacology 11 (supplement 1):5–11.

Benkert O, Muller M, Szegedi A (2002): An overview of the clinical efficacy of mirtazapine. Human Psychopharmacology 17 (supplement 1): S23–S26.

Bertilsson L, Dahl ML, Tybring G (1997): Pharmacogenetics of antidepressants: Clinical aspects. Acta Psychiatrica Scandinavica 391 (supplement):14–21.

Black K, Shea C, Dursun S, Kutcher S (2000): Selective serotonin reuptake inhibitor discontinuation syndrome: Proposed diagnostic criteria. Journal of Psychiatry & Neuroscience 25:255–261.

Blier P (2003): The pharmacology of putative early-onset antidepressant strategies. European Neuropsychopharmacology 13:57–66.

Bodkin JA, Amsterdam JD (2002): Transdermal selegiline in major depression: A double-blind, placebo-controlled, parallel-group study in outpatients. American Journal of Psychiatry 159:1869–1875.

Bonnet U (2003): Moclobemide: Therapeutic use and clinical studies. CNS Drug Reviews 9:97–140.

Bourin M, Chue P, Guillon Y (2001): Paroxetine: A review. CNS Drug Reviews 7:25–47.

Bruce SF, Vasile RG, Goisman RM, Salzman C, Spencer M, Machan JT, Keller MB (2003): Are benzodiazepines still the medication of choice for patients with panic disorder with or without agoraphobia? American Journal of Psychiatry 160:1432–1438.

Brunello N, Mendlewicz J, Kasper S, Leonard B, Montgomery S, Nelson J, Paykel E, Versiani M, Racagni G (2002): The role of noradrenaline and selective noradrenaline reuptake inhibition in depression. European Neuropsychopharmacology 12:461–475.

Burrows GD, Kremer CM (1997): Mirtazapine: Clinical advantages in the treatment of depression. Journal of Clinical Psychiatry 17 (supplement 1):34S–39S.

Calabrese JR, Londborg PD, Shelton MD, Thase ME (2003): Citalopram treatment of fluoxetine-intolerant depressed patients. Journal of Clinical Psychiatry 64:562–566.

Carter GT, Sullivan MD (2002): Antidepressants in pain management. Current Opinion in Investigational Drugs 3:454–458.

Cesura AM, Pletscher A (1992): The new generation of monoamine oxidase inhibitors. Progress in Drug Research 38:171–297.

Chan BS, Graudins A, Whyte IM, Dawson AH, Braitberg G, Duggins GG (1998): Serotonin syndrome resulting from drug interactions. Medical Journal of Australia 169:523–525.

Clayton AH, Zajecka J, Ferguson JM, Filipiak-Reisner JK, Brown MT, Schwartz GE (2003): Lack of sexual dysfunction with the selective noradrenaline reuptake inhibitor reboxetine during treatment for major depressive disorder. International Clinical Psychopharmacology 18:151–156.

Crane GE (1957): Iproniazid (marsilid) phosphate: A therapeutic agent for mental disorders and debilitating disease. Psychiatry Research, Report 8:142–152.

Damaj MI, Carroll FI, Eaton JB, Navarro HA, Blough BE, Mirza S, Lukas RJ, Martin BR (2004): Enantioselective effects of hydroxy metabolites of bupropion on behavior and on function of monoamine transporters and nicotinic receptors. Molecular Pharmacology 66:675–682.

Dannon PN, Iancu I, Grunhaus L (2002): The efficacy of reboxetine in the treatment-refractory patients with panic disorder: An open label study. Human Psychopharmacology 17:329–333.

Davidson JR, Connor KM (1998): Bupropion sustained release: A therapeutic overview. Journal of Clinical Psychiatry 59 (supplement 4): 25–31.

Davidson JR, Weisler RH, Butterfield MI, Casat CD, Connor KM, Barnett S, van Meter S (2003): Mirtazapine vs. placebo in posttraumatic stress disorder: A pilot trial. Biological Psychiatry 53:188–191.

Davison ET (1985): Amitriptyline-induced Torsades de Pointes. Successful therapy with atrial pacing. Journal of Electrocardiology 18:299–301.

DiMartini A (1995): Isoniazid, tricyclics and the "cheese reaction." International Clinical Psychopharmacology 10:197–198.

Donati RJ, Rasenick MM (2003): G protein signaling and the molecular basis of antidepressant action. Life Sciences 73:1–17.

Donnelly CL (2003): Pharmacologic treatment approaches for children and adolescents with posttraumatic stress disorder. Child and Adolescent Clinics of North America 12:251–269.

Dording CM, Mischoulon D, Petersen TJ, Kornbluh R, Gordon J, Nierenberg AA, Rosenbaum JE, Fava M (2002): The pharmacologic management of SSRI-induced side effects: A survey of psychiatrists. Annals of Clinical Psychiatry 14:143–147.

Dresser GK, Spence JD, Bailey DG (2000): Pharmacokinetic-pharmacodynamic consequences and clinical relevance of cytochrome P450 3A4 inhibition. Clinical Pharmacokinetics 38: 41–57.

Dunner DL, Zisook S, Billow AA, Batey SR, Johnston JA, Ascher JA (1998): A prospective safety surveillance study for bupropion sustained-release in the treatment of depression. Journal of Clinical Psychiatry 59:366–373.

Elena Castro M, Diaz A, del Olmo E, Pazos A (2003): Chronic fluoxetine induces opposite changes in G protein coupling in pre and postsynaptic 5-HT1A receptors in rat brain. Neuropharmacology 44:93–101.

Elia J, Ambrosini PJ, Rapaport JL (1999): Treatment of attention-deficit hyperactivity disorder. The New England Journal of Medicine 340:780–788.

Ellingrod VL, Perry PJ (1995): Nefazodone: A new antidepressant. American Journal of Health-System Pharmacy 52:2799–2812.

Fava M (2003): Depression with physical symptoms: Treating to remission. Journal of Clinical Psychiatry 64 (supplement 7):24–28.

Feighner JP (1999): Mechanism of action of antidepressant medications. Journal of Clinical Psychiatry 60 (supplement 4):4–11.

Fernstorm MH, Kupfer DJ (1988): Antidepressant-induced weight gain: A comparison of four medications. Psychiatry Research 26:265–271.

Franklin D (2004): Duloxetine gains FDA approval for major depression. Clinical Psychiatry News 32:1, 8.

Gale CK (2002): The treatment of generalised anxiety disorder. A systematic review. Panminerva Medica 44:283–286.

Gardner DM, Shulman KI, Walker SE, Tailor SA (1996): The making of a user friendly MAOI diet. Journal of Clinical Psychiatry 57:99–104.

Gillman PK (1998): Serotonin syndrome: History and risk. Fundamental & Clinical Pharmacology 12:482–491.

Glod CA, Lynch A, Flynn E, Berkowitz C, Baldessarini RJ (2003): Open trial of bupropion SR in adolescent major depression. Journal of Child and Adolescent Psychiatric Nursing 16:123–130.

Goldberg RJ, Capone RJ, Hunt JD (1985): Cardiac complications following tricyclic antidepressant overdose. Issues for monitoring policy. Journal of the American Medical Association 254:1772–1775.

Green DS, Barbhaiya RH (1997): Clinical pharmacokinetics of nefazodone. Clinical Pharmacokinetics 33:260–275.

Grunebaum MF, Ellis SP, Li S, Oguendo MA, Mann W (2005): Antidepressants and suicide risk in the United States, 1985–1999. Journal of Clinical Psychiatry 65:1456–1462.

Gunnell D, Ashby D (2004): Antidepressants and suicide: What is the balance of benefit and harm? British Medical Journal 329:34–38.

Gunnell D, Saperia J, Ashby D (2005): Selective serotonin reuptake inhibitors (SSRIs) and suicide in adults; meta-analysis of drug comparison data from placebo controlled randomised controlled trials submitted to the MHRA's safety review. British Medical Journal 330:385.

Gupta RK, Tiller JW, Burrows GD (2003): Dual action antidepressants and some important considerations. Australian and New Zealand Journal of Psychiatry 37:190–195.

Harari MD, Moulden A (2000): Nocturnal enuresis: What is happening? Journal of Paediatrics and Child Health 36:78–81.

Hardy J, Argyropoulos S, Nutt DJ (2002): Venlafaxine: A new class of antidepressant. Hospital Medicine 63:549–552.

Haria M, Fitton A, McTavish D (1994): Trazodone. A review of its pharmacology, therapeutic use in depression and therapeutic potential in other disorders. Drugs & Aging 4:331–355.

Harrigan RA, Brady WJ (1999): ECG abnormalities in tricyclic antidepressant ingestion. American Journal of Emergency Medicine 17:387–393.

Haustein KO (2003): Bupropion: Pharmacological and clinical profile in smoking cessation. International Journal of Clinical Pharmacology and Therapeutics 41:56–66.

Hayes PE, Kristoff CA (1986): Adverse reactions to five new antidepressants. Clinical Pharmacy 5:471–480.

Hedges DW, Reimherr FW, Rogers A, Strong RE, Wender PH (1995): An open trial of venlafaxine in adult patients with attention deficit hyperactivity disorder. Psychopharmacology Bulletin 31:779–783.

Hedges DW, Reimherr FW, Strong RE, Halls CH, Rust C (1996): An open trial of nefazodone in adult patients with generalized anxiety disorder. Psychopharmacology Bulletin 32:671–676.

Hensler JG (2003): Regulation of 5-HT1A receptor function following agonist or antidepressant administration. Life Sciences 72:1665–1682.

Hollander E, Friedberg J, Wasserman S, Allen A, Birnbaum M, Koran L (2003b): Venlafaxine in treatment-resistant obsessive-compulsive disorder. Journal of Clinical Psychiatry 64:546–550.

Hollander E, Kaplan A, Allen A, Cartwright C (2000): Pharmacotherapy for obsessive-compulsive disorder. Psychiatric Clinics of North America 23:643–656.

Hollander E, Koran LM, Goodman WK, Greist JH, Ninan PT, Yang H, Li D, Barbato LM (2003a): A double-blind, placebo-controlled study of the efficacy and safety of controlled-release fluvoxamine in patients with obsessive-compulsive disorder. Journal of Clinical Psychiatry 64:640–647.

Hudson JI, McElroy SL, Raymond NC, Crow S, Keck PE Jr., Carter WP, Mitchell JE, Strakowski SM, Pope HG Jr., Coleman BS, Jonas JM (1998): Fluvoxamine in the treatment of binge-eating disorder: A multicenter, placebo-controlled, double-blind trial. American Journal of Psychiatry 155:1756–1762.

Hyman SE, Nestler EJ (1996): Initiation and adaptation—a paradigm for understanding psychotropic drug action. American Journal of Psychiatry 153:151–162.

Jefferson JW (1997): Antidepressants in panic disorder. Journal of Clinical Psychiatry 58 (supplement 2):20–24.

Joo JH, Lenze EJ, Mulsant BH, Begley AE, Weber EM, Stack JA, Mazumdar S, Reynolds CF III, Pollock BG (2002): Risk factors for falls during treatment of late-life depression. Journal of Clinical Psychiatry 63:936–941.

Kasper S, el Giamal N, Hilger E (2000): Reboxetine: The first selective noradrenaline reuptake inhibitor. Expert Opinion on Pharmacotherapy 1:771–782.

Kennedy SH, McCann SM, Masellis McIntyre RS, Raskin J, McKay G, Baker GB (2002): Combining bupropion SR with venlafaxine, paroxetine, or fluoxetine: A preliminary report on pharmacokinetic, therapeutic, and sexual dysfunction effects. Journal of Clinical Psychiatry 63:181–186.

Khan A, Warner HA, Brown WA (2000): Symptom reduction and suicide risk in patients treated with placebo in antidepressant clinical trials: An analysis of the Food and Drug Administration database. Archives of General Psychiatry 57:311–317.

Kirchheiner J, Henckel HB, Meineke I, Roots I, Brockmoller J (2004): Impact of the CYP2D6 ultrarapid metabolizer genotype on mirtazapine pharmacokinetics and adverse events in healthy volunteers. Journal of Clinical Psychopharmacology 24:647–652.

Kirsch I, Moore TJ, Scoboria A, Nicholls SS (2002): The emperor's new drugs: An analysis of antidepressant medication data submitted to the U.S. Food and Drug Administration. Prevention & Treatment 5, article 23.

Kirsch I, Sapirstein G (1998): Listening to Prozac but hearing placebo: A meta-analysis of antidepressant medication. Prevention & Treatment 1, article 0002a.

Kuhn R (1958): The treatment of depressive states with G-22355 (imipramine hydrochloride). American Journal of Psychiatry 115:459–464.

Labbate LA, Croft HA, Oleshansky MA (2003): Antidepressant-related erectile dysfunction: Management via avoidance, switching antidepressants, antidotes, and adaptation. Journal of Clinical Psychiatry 64 (supplement 10):11–19.

Lawson K (2002): Tricyclic antidepressants and fibromyalgia: What is the mechanism of action? Expert Opinion on Investigational Drugs 11:1437–1445.

Lenhart SE, Buysse DJ (2001): Treatment of insomnia in hospitalized patients. Annals of Pharmacotherapy 35:1449–1457.

Livingston MG, Livingston HM (1996): Monoamine oxidase inhibitors: An update on drug interactions. Drug Safety 14:219–227.

Lucena, MI, Carvagal A, Andrade RJ, Velasco A (2003); Antidepressant-induced hepatotoxicity. Expert Opinion Drug Safety 2:249–252.

Marazziti D (2003): Venlafaxine treatment of obsessive-compulsive disorder: Case reports. CNS Spectrums 8:421–422.

Marek GJ, McDougle CJ, Price LH, Seiden LS (1992): A comparison of trazodone and fluoxetine: Implications for a serotonergic mechanism of antidepressant action. Psychopharmacology 109:2–11.

Mason PJ, Morris VA, Balcezak TJ (2000): Serotonin syndrome. Presentation of 2 cases and review of the literature. Medicine 79:201–209.

Mathew SJ, Coplan JD, Gorman JM (2001): Management of treatment-refractory panic disorder. Psychopharmacology Bulletin 35:97–110.

McElroy SL, Casuto LS, Nelson EB, Lake KA, Soutullo CA, Keck PE Jr., Hudson JI (2000): Placebo-controlled trial of sertraline in the treatment of binge eating disorder. American Journal of Psychiatry 157:1004–1006.

Monaco F, Cicolin A (1999): Interactions between anticonvulsant and psychoactive drugs. Epilepsia 40 (supplement 10):S71–76.

Montgomery SA (1998): Chairman's overview: The place of reboxetine in antidepressant therapy. Journal of Clinical Psychiatry 59 (supplement 14): 26–29.

Montgomery SA, Ferguson JM, Schwartz GE (2003): The antidepressant efficacy of reboxetine in patients with severe depression. Journal of Clinical Psychopharmacology 23:45–50.

Montgomery SA, Schatzberg AF (1998): Reboxetine: A new selective antidepressant for the treatment of depression. Journal of Clinical Psychiatry 59 (supplement 14):3.

Nelson JC (1998): Augmentation strategies with serotonergic-noradrenergic combinations. Journal of Clinical Psychiatry 59 (supplement 5):65–68.

Nelson SD, Mitchell JR, Snodgrass WR, Timbrell JA (1978): Hepatotoxicity and metabolism of iproniazid and isopropylhydrazine. Journal of Pharmacology and Experimental Therapeutics 206:574–585.

Nemeroff CB (2003): Advancing the treatment of mood and anxiety disorders: The first 10 years' experience with paroxetine. Psychopharmacology Bulletin 37 (supplement 1):6–7.

Nestler EJ, Barrot M, DiLeone RJ, Eisch AJ, Gold SJ, Monteggia LM (2002): Neurobiology of depression. Neuron 34:13–25.

Nibuya M, Morinobu S, Durman RS (1995): Regulation of BDNF and trkB mRNA in rat brain by chronic electroconvulsive seizure and antidepressant drug treatments. Journal of Neuroscience 15:7639–7547.

Nicholas LM, Ford AL, Eposito SM, Ekstrom D, Golden RN (2003): The effects of mirtazapine on plasma lipid profiles in health subjects. Journal of Clinical Psychiatry 64:883–889.

Nierenberg AA, Papakostas GI, Petersen T, Kelly KE, Iacoviello BM, Worthington JJ, Tedlow J, Alpert JE, Fava M (2003): Nortriptyline for treatment-resistant depression. Journal of Clinical Psychiatry 64:35–39.

Ninan PT (2000): Use of venlafaxine in other psychiatric disorder. Depression and Anxiety 12 (supplement 1):90–94.

Noble SL, Moore KL (1997): Drug treatment of migraine: Part II. Preventive therapy. American Family Physician 56:2279–2286.

Nutt DJ (2002): Tolerability and safety aspects of mirtazapine. Human Psychopharmacology 17 (supplement 1):S37–41.

Pallanti S, Baldini Rossi N, Sood E, Hollander E (2002): Nefazodone treatment of pathological gambling: A prospective open-label controlled trial. Journal of Clinical Psychiatry 63:1034–1039.

Papp LA, Coplan JD, Martinez JM, de Jesus M, Gorman JM (2000): Efficacy of open-label nefazodone treatment in patients with panic disorder. Journal of Clinical Psychopharmacology 20:544–546.

Parker G (2001): "New" and "old" antidepressants: All equal in the eyes of the lore? British Journal of Psychiatry 179:95–96.

Parker NG, Brown CS (2000): Citalopram in the treatment of depression. Annals of Pharmacotherapy 34:761–771.

Peeters FP, deVries MW, Vissink A (1998): Risks for oral health with the use of antidepressents. General Hospital Psychiatry 20:150–154.

Pelham WE, Aronoff HR, Midlam JK, Shapiro CJ, Gnagy EM, Chronis AM, Onyango AN, Forehand G, Nguyen A, Waxmonsky J (1999): A comparison of Ritalin and Adderall: Efficacy and time-course in children with attention-deficit/hyperactivity disorder. Pediatrics 103:e43.

Peretti S, Judge R, Hindmarch I (2000): Safety and tolerability considerations: Tricyclic antidepressants vs. selective serotonin reuptake inhibitors. Acta Psychiatrica Scandinavica. Supplementum 403:17–25.

Phillips KA, Najjar F (2003): An open-label study of citalopram in body dysmorphic disorder. Journal of Clinical Psychiatry 64:715–720.

Pletscher A (1991): The discovery of antidepressants: A winding path. Experientia 47:4–8.

Pliszka SR (2003): Non-stimulant treatment of attention-deficit/hyperactive disorder. CNS Spectrum 8:253–258.

Posternak MA (2003): Biological markers of atypical depression. Harvard Review of Psychiatry 11:1–7.

Reimherr FW, Strong RE, Marchant BK, Hedges DW, Wender PH (2001): Factors affecting return of symptoms 1 year after treatment in a 62-week controlled study of fluoxetine in major depression. Journal of Clinical Psychiatry 62 (supplement 22):16–23.

Richelson E (2003): Interactions of antidepressants with neurotransmitter transporters and receptors and their clinical relevance. Journal of Clinical Psychiatry 64 (supplement 13):5–12.

Richmond R, Zwar N (2003): Review of bupropion for smoking cessation. Drug and Alcohol Review 22:203–220.

Rickels K, Rynn M (2002): Pharmacotherapy of generalized anxiety disorder. Journal of Clinical Psychiatry 63 (supplement 14):9–16.

Romrell J, Fernandez HH, Okun MS (2003): Rationale for current therapies in Parkinson's disease. Expert Opinion on Pharmacotherapy 4:1747–1761.

Roose SP (2001): Depression, anxiety, and the cardiovascular system: The psychiatrist's perspective. Journal of Clinical Psychiatry 62(supplement 8):19–22.

Roseboom PH, Kalin NH (2000): Neuropharmacology of Venlafaxine. Depression and Anxiety 12 (supplement 1):20–29.

Rosen RC, Lane RM, Menza M (1999): Effects of SSRIs on sexual function: A critical review. Journal of Clinical Psychopharmacology 19:67–85.

Ross RI, Zavadil AP III, Calil NM, Linnoila M, Kitanaka I, Blombery P, Kopin IJ, Potter WZ (1983): Effects of desmethylimipramine on plasma norepinephrine, pulse, and blood pressure. Clinical Pharmacology and Therapeutics 33:429–437.

Rothman RB, Baumann MH (2002): Serotonin releasing agents. Neurochemical, therapeutic and adverse effects. Pharmacology, Biochemistry, and Behavior 71:825–836.

Rudorfer MV, Potter WZ (1999): Metabolism of tricyclic antidepressants. Cellular and Molecular Neurobiology 19:373–409.

Sanchez C, Hyttel J (1999): Comparison of the effects of antidepressants and their metabolites on reuptake of biogenic amines and on receptor binding. Cellular and Molecular Neurobiology 19:467–489.

Santarelli L, Saxe M, Gross C, Surget A, Battaglia F, Dulawa S, Weisstaub N, Lee J, Duman R, Arancio O, Belzung C, Hen R (2003): Requirement of hippocampal neurogenesis for the behavioral effects of antidepressants. Science 301:805–809.

Sarchiapone M, Amore M, De Risio S, Carli V, Faia V, Poterzio F, Balista C, Camardese G, Ferrari G (2003): Mirtazapine in the treatment of panic disorder: An open-label trial. International Clinical Psychopharmacology 18:35–38.

Schatzberg AF (2000): New indications for antidepressants. Journal of Clinical Psychiatry 61 (supplement 11):9–17.

Schatzberg AF (2002): Pharmacological principles of antidepressant efficacy. Human Psychopharmacology 17 (supplement 1):S17–S22.

Schatzberg AF (2003): Efficacy and tolerability of duloxetine, a novel dual uptake inhibitor, in the treatment of major depression. Journal of Clinical Psychiatry 64 (supplement 13):30–37.

Scott EL, Heimberg RG (2000): Social phobia: An update on treatment. Psychiatric Annals 30:678–686.

Seidman SN, Pesce VC, Roose SP (2003): High-dose sildenafil citrate for selective serotonin reuptake inhibitor-associated ejaculatory delay: Open clinical trial. Journal of Clinical Psychiatry 64:721–725.

Sennef C, Timmer CJ, Sitsen JM (2003): Mirtazapine in combination with amitriptyline: A drug-drug interaction study in healthy subjects. Human Psychopharmacology 18:91–101.

Settle EC Jr. (1998): Bupropion sustained release: Side effect profile. Journal of Clinical Psychiatry 59 (supplement 4):32–36.

Sharpley AL, Cowen PJ (1995): Effect of pharmacologic treatments on the sleep of depressed patients. Biological Psychiatry 37:85–98.

Sharpley AL, Williamson DJ, Attenburrow ME, Pearson G, Sargent P, Cowen PJ (1996): The effects of paroxetine and nefazodone on sleep: A placebo-controlled trial. Psychopharmacology 126:50–54.

Sheehan DV (1999): Current concepts in the treatment of panic disorder. Journal of Clinical Psychiatry 60 (supplement 18):16–21.

Sheehan DV (2002): The management of panic disorder. Journal of Clinical Psychiatry 63 (supplement 14):17–21.

Shipley JE, Kupfer DJ, Griffin SJ, Dealy RS, Coble PA, McEachran AB, Grochocinski VJ, Ulrich R, Perel JM (1985): Comparison of effects of desipramine and amitriptyline on EEG sleep of depressed patients. Psychopharmacology 85:14–22.

Shulman KI, Walker SE (1999): Refining the MAOI diet: Tyramine content of pizzas and soy products. Journal of Clinical Psychiatry 60:191–193.

Silberstein SD (1997): Preventive treatment of migraine: An overview. Cephalalgia 17:67–72.

Simon NM, Pollack MH (2000): The current status of the treatment of panic disorder: Pharmacotherapy and cognitive-behavioral therapy. Psychiatric Annals 30:689–696.

Small NL, Giamonna KA (2000): Interaction between warfarin and trazodone. Annals of Pharmacotherapy 34:734–736.

Spaans E, van den Heuvel MW, Schnabel PG, Peeters PA, Chin-Kon-Sung UG, Colbers EP, Sitsen JM (2002): Concommitant use of mirtazapine and phenytoin: A drug-drug interaction study in healthy male subjects. European Journal of Clinical Pharmacology 58:423–429.

Spring B, Gelenberg AJ, Garvin R, Thompson S (1992): Amitriptyline, clovoxamine and cognitive function: A placebo-controlled comparison in depressed outpatients. Psychopharmacology 108:327–332.

Sproule BA, Naranjo CA, Brenmer KE, Hassan PC (1997): Selective serotonin reuptake inhibitors and CNS drug interactions. A critical review of the evidence. Clinical Pharmacokinetics 33:454–471.

Stahl SM, Mendels J, Schwartz GE (2002): Effects of reboxetine on anxiety, agitation, and insomnia: Results of a pooled evaluation of randomized clinical trials. Journal of Clinical Psychopharmacology 22:388–392.

Stahl SM, Pradko JF, Haight BR, Modell JG, Rockett CB, Learned-Coughlin S (2004): A review of the neuropharmacology of bupropion, a dual norepinephrine and dopamine reuptake inhibitor. Journal of Clinical Psychiatry 6:159–166.

Staiger TO, Gaster B, Sullivan MD, A Deyo R (2003): Systematic review of antidepressants in the treatment of chronic low back pain. Spine 28:2540–2545.

Störmer E, von Moltke LL, Shader RI, Greenblatt DJ (2000): Metabolism of the antidepressant mirtazapine in vitro: Contributions of cytochromes P-450 1A2, 2D6, and 3A4. Drug Metabolism and Disposition 28:1168–1175.

Sullivan J, Abrams P (1999): Pharmacological management of incontinence. European Urology 36 (supplement 1):89–95.

Sulser F (1984): Antidepressant treatments and regulation of norepinephrine-receptor-coupled adenylate cyclase systems in brain. Advances in Biochemical Psychopharmacology 39:249–261.

Sussman N, Ginsberg DL, Bikoff J (2001): Effects of nefazodone on body weight: A pooled analysis of selective serotonin reuptake inhibitor- and imipramine-controlled trials. Journal of Clinical Psychiatry 62:256–260.

Szegedi A, Müller MJ, Anghelescu I, Klawe C, Kohnen R, Benkert O (2003): Early improvement under mirtazapine and paroxetine predicts later stable response and remission with high sensitivity in patients with major depression. Journal of Clinical Psychiatry 64:413–420.

Tao GK, Harada DT, Kootsikas ME, Gordon MN, Brinkman JH (1985): Amoxapine-induced tardive dyskinesia. Drug Intelligence & Clinical Pharmacy 19:548–549.

Thase ME (1998): Effects of venlafaxine on blood pressure: A meta-analysis of original data from 3744 depressed patients. Journal of Clinical Psychiatry 59:502–508.

Thase ME (1999): Antidepressant treatment of the depressed patient with insomnia. Journal of Clinical Psychiatry 60 (supplement 17):28–31.

Thase ME, Kupfer DJ (1996): Recent developments in the pharmacotherapy of mood disorders. Journal of Consulting and Clinical Psychology 64:646–659.

Thase ME, Sachs GS (2000): Bipolar depression: Pharmacotherapy and related therapeutic strategies. Biological Psychiatry 48:558–572.

Thorpy M (2001): Current concepts in the etiology, diagnosis and treatment of narcolepsy. Sleep Medicine 2:5–17.

Tomasi PA, Siracusano S, Monni AM, Mela G, Delitala G (2001): Decreased nocturnal urinary antidiuretic hormone excretion in enuresis is increased by imipramine. BJU International 88:932–937.

Tonnesen P, Tonstad S, Hjalmarson A, Lebargy F, Van Spiegel PI, Hide A, Sweet R, Townsend J (2003): A multicentre, randomized, double-blind, placebo-controlled, 1-year study of bupropion SR for smoking cessation. Journal of Internal Medicine 254:184–192.

Tracey JA (2002): Zyban—is there a cause for concern? Expert Opinion on Drug Safety 1:303–305.

Vaidya VA, Duman RS (2001): Depression—emerging insights from neurobiology. British Medical Bulletin 57:61–79.

Van Ameringen M, Mancini C, Pipe B, Campbell M, Oakman J (2002): Topiramate treatment of SSRI-induced weight gain in anxiety disorders. Journal of Clinical Psychiatry 63:981–984.

Vanina Y, Podolskaya A, Sedky K, Shahab H, Siddiqui A, Munshi F, Lippmann S (2002): Body weight changes associated with psychopharmacology. Psychiatric Services 53:842–847.

van Minnen A, Hoogduin KAL, Keijsers GPJ, Hellenbrand I, Hendriks GJ (2003): Treatment of trichotillomania with behavioral therapy or fluoxetine. Archives of General Psychiatry 60:517–522.

Van Veen JF, Van Vliet IM, Westenberg HG (2002): Mirtazapine in social anxiety disorder: A pilot study. International Clinical Psychopharmacology 17:315–317.

Vaswani M, Linda FK, Ramesh S (2003): Role of selective serotonin reuptake inhibitors in psychiatric disorders: A comprehensive review. Progress in Neuropsychopharmacology & Biological Psychiatry 27:85–102.

Versiani M, Cassano G, Perugi G, Benedetti A, Mastalli L, Nardi A, Savino M (2002): Reboxetine, a selective norepinephrine reuptake inhibitor, is an effective and well-tolerated treatment for panic disorder. Journal of Clinical Psychiatry 63:31–37.

Vitezic D, Pelcic JM (2002): Erectile dysfunction: Oral pharmacotherapy options. International Journal of Clinical Pharmacology and Therapeutics 40:393–403.

Wade A, Crawford GM, Angus M, Wilson R, Hamilton L (2003): A randomized, double-blind, 24-week study comparing the efficacy and tolerability of mirtazapine and paroxetine in depressed patients in primary care. International Clinical Psychopharmacology 18:133–141.

Wagstaff AJ, Goa KL (2001): Once-weekly fluoxetine. Drugs 61:2221–2228.

Walton SM (2000): Advances in the use of 5-HT3 receptor antagonists. Expert Opinion on Pharmacotherapy 1:207–223.

Wan DD, Kundhur D, Solomons K, Yatham LN, Lam RW (2003): Mirtazapine for treatment-resistant depression: A preliminary report. Journal of Psychiatry & Neuroscience 28:55–59.

Ware JC, Pittard JT (1990): Increased deep sleep after trazodone use: A double-blind placebo-controlled study in health young adults. Journal of Clinical Psychiatry 51 (supplement):18–22.

Westenberg HG (1999): Pharmacology of antidepressants: Selectivity or multiplicity? Journal of Clinical Psychiatry 60 (supplement 17):4–8.

Winokur A, Sateia MJ, Hayes JB, Bayles-Dazet W, MacDonald MM, Gary KA (2000): Acute effects of mirtazapine on sleep continuity and sleep architecture in depressed patients: A pilot study. Biological Psychiatry 48:75–78.

Witchel HJ, Hancox JC, Nutt DJ (2003): Psychotropic drugs, cardiac arrhythmias, and sudden death. Journal of Clinical Psychopharmacology 23:58–77.

Workman EA, Short DD (1993): Atypical antidepressants versus imipramine in the treatment of major depression: A meta-analysis. Journal of Clinical Psychiatry 54:5–12.

Wyeth (2003): Letter to health care professionals, 22 August 2003.

CHAPTER TEN

THE MOOD STABILIZERS

Lithium has long been an integral part of the pharmacological treatment of bipolar disorder, despite its association with numerous adverse effects. Although it appears to affect many different brain functions, it remains unclear which of these if any accounts for lithium's therapeutic effects, even though progress in understanding lithium's effects on intraneural signal transmission is being made. Increasingly, the anticonvulsants—drugs like carbamazepine, valproic acid, and lamotrigine—are being used in the treatment of bipolar disorder. The mechanism of action of the anticonvulsants in bipolar disorder remains uncertain, although these drugs too appear to affect many different systems in the brain, some of them showing similarities to lithium's effects on intraneural signal transmission. In addition to their uses in bipolar disorder, lithium and the anticonvulsants are used for other conditions, such as aggression.

The mood stabilizers are a group of drugs that share as a common property the ability to treat mania. An additional characterization of a mood stabilizer is that it treats of one or both phases of bipolar disorder (i.e., mania or depression) (Dunner, 2003). While lithium has been used for several decades and remains an important drug in the treatment of bipolar disorder (Dunner, 2003), a variety of other medications now are available (Kahn & Chaplan, 2002). Most of these newer drugs were originally marketed as anticonvulsants, although there are several exceptions (Kahn & Chaplan, 2002). Like the antidepressants, the mood stabilizers can be effective in a variety of clinical conditions in addition to their mood-stabilizing effects. For example, lithium can be used for certain types of aggression (Fava, 1997). The mood stabilizers are far from adequate for the treatment of bipolar disorder, however, and, unfortunately, many people with bipolar disorder require trials with several different mood stabilizers at one time or another (Kahn & Chaplan, 2002). An additional complicating factor in the treatment of mania is that in practice one mood stabilizer alone may not result in adequate and prolonged mood stabilization. Polypharmacy then becomes a necessity for some cases of bipolar disorder (Grof, 2003; Kahn & Chaplan, 2002). Additionally, some of the newer, second-generation antipsychotics are seeing increasing use in bipolar disorder (Kahn & Chaplan, 2002); these drugs are discussed in Chapter 11. There is some evidence that, even though in many ways diverse, the molecular mechanisms for mood stabilization may be similar for both lithium and at least some of the mood-stabilizing anticonvulsants (Kahn & Chaplan, 2002).

LITHIUM

An element discovered in 1817 (Gray et al., 2003), lithium's therapeutic properties have long been recognized (Gray et al., 2003). In 1949, John Cade, an Australian psychiatrist, reported that lithium calmed people who suffered from mania (Cade, 1949). Further reports on lithium's antimanic properties followed (Schou, 1997a) and lithium saw increasing use as an agent to treat mania. Lithium was the dominant drug for bipolar disorder until the 1990s (Jefferson, 2002), when other agents began to vie for that position. Lithium, however, remains a first-line medication for mania (Möller & Nasrallah, 2003), and has several other uses.

Mechanism of Action, Pharmacology, and Metabolism

Although it is unknown by exactly what mechanism lithium exerts its mood-stabilizing properties (Manji & Lenox, 1998), it is clear that it causes a myriad of changes in the brain that could play a role in its effects on mood regulation. It is not known, however, which, if any, of these actions contributes to lithium's mood-stabilizing properties (Agam & Shaltiel, 2003). Even though its exact mechanisms of action are unknown, considerable progress has elucidated several candidate mechanisms of lithium's mood-stabilizing properties. Foremost are lithium's effects on second-messenger systems (a series of biochemical reactions that change neuronal function) and signal transduction (Brunello & Tascedda, 2003), mechanisms that can alter neuronal responses to many neurotransmitters (Bebchuk et al., 2000).

Lithium, for instance, inhibits the enzyme that converts inositol monophosphates to myoinositol, leading to increased neuronal levels of inositol monophosphates and reduced levels of myoinositol (O'Donnell et al., 2003), a substance that affects communication between neurons. Lithium also decreases the transport of myoinositol into neurons (Coyle & Duman, 2003). The myoinositol-depletion hypothesis proposes that lithium's reduction of myoinositol leads to the affective stabilization associated with lithium treatment, although this theory is not universally accepted because the relationship is between lithium and inositol is complex (Manji & Lenox, 1998). By inhibiting inositol monophosphatase (Coyle & Duman, 2003), lithium also inhibits the enzyme protein kinase C (Brunello & Tascedda, 2003), another important substance in signal transduction (Bebchuk et al., 2000).

Lithium inhibits other enzymes that could be involved in its therapeutic effects. For example, lithium strongly inhibits 3' (2')-phosphoadenosine-5'-phosphate phosphatase, an enzyme that may be present in abnormal levels in the frontal cortex of people with bipolar disorder (Agam & Shaltiel, 2003). Another second messenger affected by lithium is cyclic adenosine monophosphate (cAMP) (Manji & Lenox, 1998).

In addition to effects on second-messenger systems and similar to post-synaptic events proposed for antidepressants (see Chapter 9), lithium may have neuroprotective or neurotrophic actions as suggested by findings of lithium-induced increases in N-acetyl-aspartate (Moore et al., 2000), which is thought to be a function of neuronal integrity, and in bcl-2, a putative neuroprotective protein (Manji et al., 2000). Consistent with these findings of lithium's possible neuroprotective or neurotrophic effects, lithium increases hippocampal neurogenesis in adult mice (Chen et al., 2000) and gray matter in the human hippocampus and caudate nucleus of patients with bipolar disorder (Gray et al., 2003). Lithium affects gene expression and subsequent protein synthesis for a variety of neuronal substances (Brunello & Tascedda, 2003). Intriguingly, lithium has been suggested to alter circadian rhythms (Coyle & Duman, 2003).

Unlike most other psychotropic medications, lithium it not metabolized through the liver and has no metabolites, being cleared from the body instead almost entirely by the kidneys (Jefferson, 2002). Lithium levels per dose can be lower during the time that a person with bipolar disorder has mania than when the person is does not have mania (Dunner, 2003). The reason for this is not clear, but may be related to the higher urine output during mania than during euthymia (Dunner, 2003).

Drug-Drug Interactions

Despite its lack of metabolism in the liver and metabolites (Jefferson, 2002), lithium still interacts with a variety of other drugs, demanding proper education of people taking this drug. For example, several common over-the-counter anti-inflammatory drugs can increase the lithium concentrations (Jefferson, 2002), potentially resulting in lithium toxicity. Thiazide diuretics, drugs used for treatment of various cardiovascular disorders, elevate lithium levels (Jefferson, 2002).

Adverse Effects

Lithium has a narrow therapeutic window: Doses and blood levels that are high enough to produce therapeutic responses can be precariously close to the doses and blood levels that can cause adverse effects and toxicity (Möller & Nasrallah, 2003). This narrow therapeutic window requires that lithium levels be kept within a tight range to achieve clinical efficacy but to avoid toxicity. Lithium toxicity is characterized by difficulty walking, tremors, slurred speech, and nausea and vomiting (Jefferson, 2002). Severe lithium intoxication can lead to coma and death (Dunner, 2003). Dehydration increases the risk of elevated lithium levels and toxicity (Jefferson, 2002).

Cognitive dysfunction—difficulties with memory, thinking, motivation, and concentration—also can complicate lithium treatment (Möller & Nasrallah, 2003). Affecting the endocrine system, lithium interferes with thyroid function, most commonly resulting in diminished production of thyroid hormone (Möller & Nasrallah, 2003), low levels of which can affect mood (Jefferson, 2002). Conversely, lithium can also produce hyperthyroidism (Jefferson, 2002). By effecting the kidney, lithium can cause polyuria, when an increased volume of urine is produced, which can lead to dehydration and subsequent lithium toxicity (Jefferson, 2002). Lithium also has been implicated in actual kidney damage resulting in renal insufficiency, but this effect of lithium may occur less frequently than previously thought (Manji & Lenox, 1998), although, if possible, other drugs should be considered in lieu of lithium in people with a history of renal disease (Jefferson, 2002). In addition, lithium is associated with weight gain (Nemeroff, 2003) and skin irritations, such as acne and psoriasis (Jefferson, 2002). Lithium also can result in gastrointestional and cardiac abnormalities (Möller & Nasrallah, 2003), as well as tremor (Jefferson, 2002). Unfortunately, since many women with bipolar disorder have child-bearing potential, lithium also can interfere with prenatal development. Although lithium exposure in the first trimester of pregnancy may not be associated with the rare but severe congenital heart malformation Ebstein's Anomaly as much as previously thought (Llewellyn et al., 1998), it is associated with other cardiac abnormities (Llewellyn et al., 1998), prompting caution when lithium is used in women of child-bearing potential.

Uses

Bipolar Disorder.   Despite its adverse effects and the availability of other drugs, lithium remains an important drug in the treatment of bipolar disorder (Möller & Nasrallah, 2003), although approximately 50 percent of bipolar patients treated with lithium fail to have a satisfactory response (Nemeroff, 2003). In addition, response rates appear lower with lithium in cases that are complicated by depressive features in contrast to mania alone (Kahn & Chaplan, 2002). While many studies have suggested that lithium is effective for acute mania (Kahn & Chaplan, 2002), the long-term efficacy of lithium has been questioned, because many bipolar patients continue to have significant symptoms while on lithium (Harrow et al., 1990). At least a component of the difficulty controlling affective symptoms on long-term lithium maintenance is medication noncompliance (Silverstone et al., 1998), which may occur in over 60 percent of bipolar patients for whom lithium is prescribed (Colom et al., 2000). In fact, noncompliance with lithium may be the most common cause of poor treatment response in people with bipolar disorder (Schou, 1997b). Factors associated with treatment noncompliance in bipolar patients are comorbid personality disorders (Colom et al., 2000) and substance abuse (Keck et al., 1997). Because a substance abuse history has been reported in one study to occur in almost 60 percent of people with bipolar disorder (Cassidy et al., 2001), and comorbid substance abuse is associated with a more difficult course of the illness (Cassidy et al., 2001), substance abuse among bipolar patients is a significant factor in medication noncompliance. Not unique to lithium, noncompliance with medication occurs with other mood stabilizers as well (Kleindienst & Greil, 2003). Despite its limitations, lithium treatment may decrease the mortality rate associated with untreated bipolar disorder (Manji & Lenox, 1998).

Several subtypes of mania do not appear to respond as well to lithium as to other mood stabilizers. For example, lithium treatment may be associated with a relatively poor response when used for rapid-cycling bipolar disorder, mixed mania (mania with concurrent depressive symptoms), and mania from medical conditions (Möller & Nasrallah, 2003).

Augmentation of Antidepressants.   Although usually not as effective for major depression as most other antidepressants, lithium can be added to an anti-depressant to obtain a more complete resolution of partially treated depression (Heit & Nemeroff, 1998). Lithium appears to have some but still less than ideal effects on bipolar depression (Kahn & Chaplan, 2002).

Schizoaffective Disorder.   Although inadequately studied, schizoaffective disorder, particularly those cases with predominant affective features, may respond to lithium (Baethge, 2003).

Aggression.   Lithium may be helpful in reducing aggression in prison inmates and in people with mental retardation (Fava, 1997). Furthermore, lithium can be effective in reducing the aggression associated with conduct disorder in children and adolescents (Silva et al., 1993).

Cluster Headaches.   Cluster headaches typically occur in cycles and are characterized by severe but short-lived, one-sided pain that occurs in a distribution around the eye (van Liet et al., 2003). Circadian rhythm abnormalities may be involved with cluster headaches (May & Leone, 2003). Even though other drugs are used in the management of cluster headaches, lithium can be used prophylactically to prevent reoccurrence of cluster headaches (Ekbom & Hardebo, 2002). Table 10.1 summarizes the adverse effects and uses of lithium.

TABLE 10.1   Lithium

ADVERSE EFFECTS	USES
Narrow therapeutic window may lead to lithium toxicity characterized by difficulty walking, slurred speech, confusion, coma, and even death; cognitive dysfunction (e.g., memory, thinking, motivation, and concentration); interferes with thyroid function (most commonly resulting in low thyroid hormone); can impair kidney's ability to concentrate urine; weight gain; tremors; drowsiness; diarrhea; skin irritations; gastrointestinal and cardiac abnormalities; and interference with prenatal development.	Bipolar Disorder, Depression, Schizoaffective Disorder, Aggression, and Cluster Headaches.

CARBAMAZEPINE

Carbamazepine (Tegretol), one of the now several drugs that were originally developed as anticonvulsants, along with lithium and valproic acid is an important agent for the treatment of bipolar disorder (Evins, 2003).

Mechanism of Action, Pharmacology, and Metabolism

While carbamazepine's mechanism of mood stabilization is not fully known, it is thought to have a variety of effects in the brain (Manji & Lenox, 2000). Carbamazepine, for instance, inhibits neuronal sodium channels (Bonifacio et al., 2001), interfering with action potential generation. Perhaps of more relevance to carbamazepine's mechanism of action in mood stabilization and similar to lithium and valproic acid is carbamazepine's regulation of certain intraneuronal signaling pathways and effects on gene expression (Li et al., 2002). For example, carbamazepine appears to diminish the formation of the neuronal signaling agent cyclic adenosine monophosphate via direct or indirect inhibition of adenylyl cyclase (Manji & Lenox, 2000).

Carbamazepine is cleared from the body via metabolism (Eadie, 1991). One product of carbamazepine metabolism is carbamazepine-10, 11-epoxide, a compound that has anticonvulsant properties similar to carbamazepine (Eadie, 1991).

Drug-Drug Interactions

Carbamazepine is an inducer of the enzymes that metabolize certain drugs and can thus decrease the concentrations of some drugs, including tricyclic antidepressants, and some antipsychotic medications (Spina & Perucca, 2002). As such, carbamazepine has the potential to lower these drug concentrations to below therapeutic levels. In addition, the metabolism of carbamazepine can be inhibited by valproic acid and fluoxetine (Prozac) (Dunner, 2003). Conversely, carbamazepine can increase the metabolism of valproic acid (Dunner, 2003). Therapeutic drug monitoring can be useful to evaluate potential drug-drug interactions between carbamazepine and other drugs (Spina & Perucca, 2002). Finally, carbamazepine induces the enzymes that metabolize itself, sometimes requiring dose increases to maintain therapeutic levels (Nemeroff, 2000).

Adverse Effects

Carbamazepine use is associated with several adverse effects. Drowsiness, double vision, and dizziness can complicate carbamazepine therapy (Nemeroff, 2000). Although relatively rare, carbamazepine can suppress the bone marrow's production of both white and red blood cells (Nemeroff, 2003), as well as the thrombocytes (Dunner, 2003), blood elements essential for coagulation of blood, requiring laboratory surveillance in people taking this drug (Dunner, 2003). Like many anticonvulsants, carbamazepine can damage liver cells (Nemeroff, 2003), necessitating monitoring of liver function during carbamazepine therapy. Rashes also complicate the use of carbamazepine (Dunner, 2003) including the potentially lethal rash of the Stevens-Johnson syndrome (Nemeroff, 2000), which is characterized by fever and an extensive rash that can involve mucus membranes (Herbert & Ralston, 2001). Carbamazepine can also cause cardiac abnormalities (Dunner, 2003). Although the mechanism is poorly elucidated, carbamazepine is associated with weight gain (Biton, 2003).

Uses

Epilepsy.   One of carbamazepine's primary indications is in the treatment of epilepsy (Pugh & Garnett, 1991).

Bipolar Disorder.   Carbamazepine appears to be as effective as lithium in the control of acute mania (Nemeroff, 2003). While carbamazepine's short-term efficacy appears similar to that of lithium, there have been some indications that carbamazepine's effects may wane with time, and it may not be an effective drug for the long-term treatment of bipolar disorder (Sachs & Thase, 2000).

Schizoaffective Disorder.   Similar to lithium, carbamazepine may have a role in the treatment of schizoaffective disorder, particularly when affective symptoms predominate (Baethge, 2003).

Depression.   Although not generally considered an antidepressant, carbamazepine may diminish the reoccurrence of major depressive episodes (Blacker, 1996).

Aggression.   An additional role for carbamazepine is in the treatment of aggression, such as that associated with dementia, brain damage, and personality disorders (Fava, 1997).

Trigeminal Neuralgia and Diabetic Neuropathy.   Trigeminal neuralgia is a painful condition involving the trigeminal or fifth cranial nerve, resulting in pain in the face (Kaufman, 1990). Carbamazepine can provide some relief from this condition (Jensen, 2002). In addition, carbamazepine is used to reduce the pain associated with diabetic neuropathy (Jensen, 2002). Table 10.2 lists the adverse effects and uses of carbamazepine.

TABLE 10.2   Carbamazepine

ADVERSE EFFECTS	USES
Too high a dose is associated with behaviors much like alcohol intoxication (e.g., slurred speech and difficulty walking); double vision, vertigo; suppression of the bone marrow's production of both white, red blood cells, and thrombocytes; and can damage liver cells.	Epilepsy, Bipolar Disorder, Depression, Aggression, and Trigeminal Neuralgia.

VALPROIC ACID

The most frequently prescribed anticonvulsant in the world (Perucca, 2002), valproic acid (valproate, sodium divalproex, Depakote, and Depakene) is an anticonvulsant that like carbamazepine is used as a mood stabilizer (Calabrese et al., 2002).

Mechanism of Action, Pharmacology, and Metabolism

Valproic acid has a myriad of effects on the brain, although it is unknown which of these actions account for its mood-stabilizing properties. For example, valproic acid facilitates the transmission of the brain's major inhibitory neurotransmitter, GABA (Perucca, 2002), a mechanism with implications for both the treatment of epilepsy and bipolar disorder. Valproic acid also diminishes to flow of sodium ions into the neuron (Perucca, 2002), resulting in changes in the action potential, and possibly leading to an increased neuronal stability. Valproic acid also may affect substance P, a substance that appears to be involved in the etiology of mood disorders (Lieb et al., 2003). For instance, in addition to inhibiting substance P's effects on interleukin-6 (which is increased during depression), valproic acid down regulated substance P receptors, actions not shared with lithium and carbamazepine (Lieb et al., 2003). Other evidence suggests that valproic acid may, like lithium, increase inositol monophosphates and decrease myoinositol (O'Donnell et al., 2003), as well as decrease the transport of myoinositol into neurons (Coyle & Duman, 2003). Also similar to lithium, valproic acid inhibits protein kinase C and affects gene expression of neuronal proteins (Brunello & Tascedda, 2003). Valproic acid also dampens the effects of excitatory amino acids (Perucca, 2002). Finally, valproic modulates dopamine and serotonin (Perucca, 2002).

Valproic acid is metabolized by the liver and has a half-life of approximately 9 to 18 hours (Perucca, 2002). Several metabolites are formed from valproic acid, including 2-en valproic acid, a compound that may have anticonvulsant action (Eadie, 1991).

Drug-Drug Interactions

Because of its tendency to inhibit the metabolism of certain drugs, among them the anticonvulsant and mood stabilizer lamotrigine (Lamictal) and the barbiturate phenobarbital, valproic acid can increase the concentrations of certain drugs in the body (Perucca, 2002).

Adverse Effects

Valproic acid affects a variety of organ systems in the body. It can cause nausea, vomiting (Nemeroff, 2003), and other gastrointestional problems. Liver failure, for instance, is rare but can happen, particularly in young children (Nemeroff, 2003). Likewise, severe and possibly fatal pancreatitis in children and adults taking valproic acid has been reported (Dunner, 2003). Central nervous system side effects include sedation and tremor (Perucca, 2002). Weight gain is a frequent complication of valproic acid treatment (Bowden, 2003) and can lead to noncompliance with treatment. Incomplete evidence has indicated that valproic acid use may be associated with polycystic ovaries (Perucca, 2002), although the putative relationship between valproic acid and polycystic ovaries has been questioned (Swann, 2001). Valproic acid is associated with elevated levels of ammonia that may result in an encephalopathy (Perucca, 2002). Finally, valproic acid is associated with a 1 to 3 percent risk (Perucca, 2002) of neural tube defects in the offspring if taken during the first trimester of pregnancy (Bowden, 2003).

Uses

Epilepsy.   Valproic acid is useful in the treatment of all types of seizures (Perucca, 2002).

Bipolar Disorder.   For the treatment of acute mania, valproic acid appears to be as effective as lithium (Bowden et al., 1994). One possible advantage for valproic acid over other mood stabilizers in the treatment of acute mania is that its dose can be "loaded" or titrated rapidly to effective levels, even perhaps intravenously (Grunze, 1999a). Its efficacy for the long-term treatment of bipolar disorder is less well established (Kahn & Chaplan, 2002). However, valproic acid may be more effective than lithium for mixed mania (Möller & Nasrallah, 1993) but is usually considered to be a fairly weak antidepressant, although it may have some efficacy in bipolar depression (Bowden, 2003). Certain types of bipolar disorder may respond better to valproic acid than to lithium. For example, some evidence favors valproic acid over lithium in rapid-cycling bipolar disorder [defined as at least four mood episodes, of either mania or depression, or both, or two full bipolar cycles, per year (APA, 1994)] and dysphoric mania (a mood state consisting of mixed depression and mania) (Calabrese & Delucchi, 1990).

Anxiety.   Some evidence suggests that valproic acid may have a role in the treatment of anxiety (Davis et al., 2000). For example, in an open-label study, valproic acid was effective in social anxiety disorder (Kinrys et al., 2003).

TABLE 10.3   Valproic Acid

ADVERSE EFFECTS	USES
Nausea; vomiting; other gastrointestinal problems; liver failure; severe and potentially fatal pancreatitis in children; sedation; tumor; cognitive dulling; weight gain; polycystic ovaries; elevated levels of ammonia that may result in an encephalopathy; and neural tube defects.	Epilepsy, Bipolar Disorder, Anxiety, and Aggression and Impulsivity.

Aggression.   Valproic acid may have some use in the treatment of aggression associated with dementia, brain damage, and personality disorders (Fava, 1997). Adverse effects and uses of valproic acid are shown in Table 10.3.

LAMOTRIGINE

Lamotrigine (Lamictal) is one of the newer anticonvulsant and mood-stabilizing drugs that increasingly is used for bipolar disorder (Xie & Hagan, 1998). In addition to its putative mood-stabilizing properties, lamotrigine may have antidepressant properties (Barbosa et al., 2003).

Mechanism of Action, Pharmacology, and Metabolism

The mechanism by which lamotrigine exerts its putative mood-stabilizing effects is unknown, although its mechanism of action may include the inhibition of voltage-dependent sodium channels (Xie & Hagan, 1998) and of the excitatory amino-acid neurotransmitters glutamate and aspartate (Barbosa et al., 2003). Also relevant to lomotrigine's putative efficacy in mood stabilization is its possible antagonism of serotonin subtype 3 receptors and purported ability to increase dopamine transmission (Barbosa et al., 2003). Lamotrigine undergoes little first-pass metabolism and is eventually metabolized to an inactive compound (Keck & McElroy, 2002).

Drug-Drug Interactions

The combination of lamotrigine and valproic acid increases the occurrence of the so-called Stevens-Johnson syndrome, a severe, potentially life-threatening rash (Calabrese, Sullivan, et al., 2002) thought to involve an allergic response to lamotrigine (Calabrese, Sullivan, et al., 2002). Valproic acid inhibits the metabolism of lamotrigine, requiring a reduction in lamotrigine dose (Calabrese, Sullivan, et al., 2002). By inducing its metabolism, carbamazepine lowers levels of lamotrigine (Calabrese, Sullivan, et al., 2002).

Adverse Effects

Lamotrigine in general appears to be fairly well tolerated by most people (Kahn & Chaplan, 2002). It does rarely cause the aforementioned Stevens-Johnson syndrome (Kahn & Chaplan, 2002), characterized by a severe, potentially lethal rash that can occur not only on the skin but also on mucus membranes (Herbert & Ralston, 2001). In addition to concurrent use with valproic acid, other risk factors for the occurrence of this rash are use in children (Messenheimer, 1998) and rapid increase of the dose (Calabrese, Sullivan, et al., 2002). Complicating this is lamotrigine's propensity to cause other rashes that are not themselves harmful but can

TABLE 10.4   Lamotrigine

ADVERSE EFFECTS	USES
Stevens-Johnson syndrome; headaches; insomnia; excessive sleeping; dizziness; double vision; ataxia; and nausea.	Epilepsy and Bipolar Disorder.

be difficult to distinguish from the early stages of Stevens-Johnson syndrome (Calabrese, Sullivan, et al., 2002). Other adverse effects from lamotrigine are headaches, insomnia, excessive sleeping, dizziness, double vision, ataxia (difficulty with gait), and nausea (Calabrese, Sullivan, et al., 2002).

Uses

Epilepsy.   Lamotrigine is an anticonvulsant (Btaiche & Woster, 1995).

Bipolar Disorder.   Although generally not recommended for the treatment of acute mania, lamotrigine is recommended for rapid-cycling mania and bipolar depression (Möller & Nasrallah, 2003). A potential drawback is the requirement that the dose of lamotrigine be increased slowly to avoid precipitating the Stevens-Johnson syndrome (Dunner, 2003). Accumulating evidence also suggests that lamotrigine may have antidepressant properties in both major depression and bipolar depression (Barbosa et al., 2003), although additional controlled-trial data are required to fully evaluate the use of lamotrigine in depression. Table 10.4 summarizes the adverse effects and uses of lamotrigine.

GABAPENTIN

Gabapentin (Neurontin) is another anticonvulsant (Maneuf et al., 2003) that has been evaluated for bipolar disorder. While its efficacy for seizure control is well established (Maneuf et al., 2003), additional research is required to define its role in bipolar and other psychological disorders. A placebo-controlled trial of gabapentin as an adjunctive medication in combination with other mood stabilizers in outpatients with bipolar disorder showed no benefits from gabapentin in mood stabilization (Pande et al., 2000), although it may effective in reducing bipolar features when added to other mood stabilizers (Kahn & Chaplan, 2002).

Mechanism of Action, Pharmacology, and Metabolism

Gabapentin's mechanism of action remains unknown. As its chemical structure is derived from GABA (Wheeler, 2002), gabapentin was originally thought to be a GABA mimetic, although this mechanism has been significantly questioned (Maneuf et al., 2003). Gabapentin does affect some neuronal calcium channels

TABLE 10.5   Gabapentin

ADVERSE EFFECTS	USES
Drowsiness and ataxia.	Seizures, Bipolar Disorder, Anxiety, and Insomnia.

and neurotransmitter release (Maneuf et al., 2003; Wheeler, 2002). Similar to lithium, gabapentin is eliminated by the kidneys (Wang & Ketter, 2002).

Drug-Drug Interactions

Gabapentin has few or no pharmacokinetic interactions (Dunner, 2003; Wang & Ketter, 2002).

Adverse Effects

Generally well tolerated (Dunner, 2003), gabapentin nevertheless may cause unwanted effects. One of the most common is its tendency to cause drowsiness (Swann, 2001). Gabapentin also may cause weight gain (DeToledo et al., 1997; Swann, 2001) and dizziness (Dunner, 2003).

Uses

Seizures.   Gabapentin is an anticonvulsant (Nemeroff, 2000) that can be added to other anticonvulsant drugs for the treatment of epilepsy (Maneuf et al., 2003).

Bipolar Disorder.   Although used for the treatment of bipolar disorder (Evins, 2003), little evidence supports this use (Evins, 2003; Kahn & Chaplan, 2002). It may be useful, however, for bipolar disorder comorbid for anxiety (Kahn & Chaplan, 2002) and as an added drug to preexisting mood stabilizers (Kahn & Chaplan, 2002).

Anxiety.   There is some evidence suggesting that gabapentin may be effective in the treatment of social anxiety disorder (Blanco et al., 2002).

Neuropathic Pain.   In addition to its uses in epilepsy and bipolar disorder, gabapentin is used in the treatment of neuropathic pain (Wheeler, 2002). Table 10.5 lists the adverse effects and uses of gabapentin.

OTHER ANTICONVULSANT MOOD STABILIZERS

Several other anticonvulsants are beginning to be used in bipolar disorder. Although certainly not as well established as lithium, carbamazepine, and valproic acid for the treatment of bipolar disorder (Kahn & Chaplan, 2002), these newer agents do have some preliminary promise. For example, topiramate (Topamax) is a recently introduced anticonvulsant that is increasingly used in psychiatry in part because it too appears to have at least some mood-stabilizing properties (Calabrese, Shelton, et al., 2002), although the putative efficacy of topiramate in bipolar disorder is based upon small, open-label (Calabrese et al., 2001) testing.

Topiramate seems to have a wide range of pharmacological effects. Similar to valproic acid, it inhibits sodium channels (Keck & McElroy, 2002) and increases GABA effects, possibly by enhancing GABA$_A$ receptors (Van Ameringen et al., 2002). Topiramate also may antagonize glutamate action at alpha-amino-3-hydroxy-5-methyl-4-isoxazolepropionic acid/kainite receptors (Van Ameringen et al., 2002).

Generally well tolerated, topiramate can cause cognitive deficits (Nemeroff, 2003). Topiramate also can result in paresthesias (Calabrese et al., 2001), uncomfortable sensations in various parts of the body. Topiramate also is associated with diminished sweating (oligohydrosis) and elevated body temperature, particularly in children (Ortho-McNeil, 2003).

In addition to its role in bipolar disorder and epilepsy, topiramate has been used with some initial success in binge-eating disorder (McElroy et al., 2003) and bulimia (Hoopes et al., 2003), in part possibly because unlike many other mood-stabilizing drugs, such as lithium and valproic acid, topiramate often results in weight loss (Nemeroff, 2003). Topiramate also may have efficacy in the prevention of migraine headaches (Edwards et al., 2003).

Tiagabine (Gabitril) is another newer anticonvulsant (Bazil, 2002) that is starting to see use as a psychotropic agent, especially in bipolar disorder (Kaufman, 1998). Tiagabine appears to inhibit GABA reuptake (Kaufman, 1998). However, results from an open trial of tiagabine in acute mania found no antimanic effects from tiagabine (Grunze et al., 1999b), and a review concluded that tiagabine does not appear to be an effective option for acute mania (Carta et al., 2002). Generally causing few adverse affects (Bauer et al., 2002), severe nausea and vomiting have been reported from tiagabine (Grunze et al., 1999b), and slow titration of the tiagabine dose is required to avoid severe side effects (Carta et al., 2002).

OTHER NONANTICONVULSANT MOOD STABILIZERS

In addition to lithium and the anticonvulsant mood stabilizers, other drugs have been considered and investigated for use in bipolar disorder, particularly in those cases that do not respond adequately to lithium and anticonvulsants. Included in this category are drugs known as calcium-channel antagonists (Malhi & Berk, 2002), such as verapamil (Calan, Isoptin). Most frequently used in cardiology, these drugs block neuronal calcium channels, inhibiting inflow of calcium into the cell and disrupting firing patterns, and appear to have at least some therapeutic effect in bipolar disorder (Wisner et al., 2002), although additional research is needed to fully understand the role of the calcium-channel antagonists in the treatment of bipolar disorder (Wisner et al., 2002). These drugs may have a role in the treatment of bipolar disorder in people who cannot tolerate lithium. Omega-3 fatty acids also may have mood-stabilizing properties (Malhi & Berk, 2002). Limited data suggest that the cholinesterase inhibitor (by blocking cholinesterase, acetylcholine levels in the brain are increased) donepezil (Aricept) may have efficacy in bipolar disorder, although additional studies are needed (Burt et al., 1999).

The newer antipsychotic drugs, medications such as olanzapine (Zyprexa) and risperidone (Risperdal) also are used for the treatment of bipolar disorder (Malhi & Berk, 2003). In addition to their antipsychotic properties, which are often required for in acute mania, these newer antipsychotics may have mood-stabilizing properties, attributes that have made this class of medication a potential alternative to more traditional mood stabilizers in certain cases (Nemeroff, 2003).

SUMMARY

The mood stabilizers are composed of several different types of medications, including lithium, some anticonvulsants, and atypical antipsychotic medications. Like the antidepressants, the mood stabilizers are used for other conditions in addition to bipolar disorder, such as aggression. As a general rule, the mood stabilizers are better at controlling acute mania than depression, although early evidence has suggested that lamotrigine may be somewhat better for depression than some of the other mood stabilizers.

The mood stabilizers have numerous actions. Lithium, carbamazepine, and valproic acid have important effects on neuronal signal transduction that may modulate neuronal function. Carbamazepine, valproic acid, lamotrigine, and topiramate affect neuronal sodium channels. Valproic acid and topiramate appear to increase GABA function, and gabapentin may affect the function of neuronal calcium channels and neurotransmitter release. In addition, lamotrigine and topiramate may affect excitatory neurotransmitters. In many cases of bipolar disorder, more than one mood stabilizer is used in the same person. Increasingly, the newer antipsychotics are being used in bipolar disorder, although additional information and clinical experience needs to be obtained before the relative roles of the mood stabilizers and the new antipsychotics can be clarified.

STUDY QUESTIONS

1. Describe some of the main effects that lithium causes in the brain.
2. How might lithium's putative effects on circadian rhythms relate to its effects in bipolar disorder?
3. Summarize the putative mechanisms of action of the mood stabilizers.
4. What is the theoretical importance of the anticonvulsants' effects on GABA?

5. What clinical factors should considered in the decision to initiate treatment for bipolar disorder with valproic acid as opposed to lithium?

6. Adverse effects frequently limit treatment and often result in inability to tolerate the drug. Discuss the common side effects associated with lithium, carbamazepine, valproic acid, lamotrigine, gabapentin, and topiramate.

7. How serious is lithium noncompliance?

8. If you were to design a new mood stabilizer, what features would you include in its mechanism of action and why?

REFERENCES

Agam G, Shaltiel G (2003): Possible role of 3' (2')-phosphoadenosine-5' phosphate phosphatase in the etiology and therapy of bipolar disorder. Progress in Neuropsychopharmacology & Biological Psychiatry 27:723–727.

American Psychiatric Association (1994): *Diagnostic and Statistical Manual* (4th ed.). Washington, DC: APA Press.

Baethge C (2003): Long-term treatment of schizoaffective disorder: Review and recommendations. Pharmacopsychiatry 36:45–56.

Barbosa L, Berk M, Vorster M (2003): A double-blind, randomized, placebo-controlled trial of augmentation with lamotrigine or placebo in patients concomitantly treated with fluoxetine for resistant major depressive episodes. Journal of Clinical Psychiatry 64:403–407.

Bauer J, Bergmann A, Reuber M, Stodieck SR, Genton P (2002): Tolerability of tiagabine: A prospective open-label study. Epileptic Disorders 4:257–260.

Bazil CW (2002): New antiepileptic drugs. Neurology 8:71–81.

Bebchuk JM, Arfken CL, Dolan-Manji S, Murphy J, Hasanat K, Manji HK (2000): A preliminary investigation of a protein kinase C inhibitor in the treatment of acute mania. Archives of General Psychiatry 57 (letter):95–97.

Biton V (2003): Effect of antiepileptic drugs on bodyweight: Overview and clinical implications for the treatment of epilepsy. CNS Drugs 17:781–791.

Blacker D (1996): Maintenance treatment of major depression: A review of the literature. Harvard Review of Psychiatry 4:1–9.

Blanco C, Antia SX, Liebowitz MR (2002): Pharmacotherapy of social anxiety disorder. Biological Psychiatry 51:109–120.

Bowden CL (2003): Valproate. Bipolar Disorders 5:189–202.

Bowden CL, Brugger AM, Swann AC, Calabrese JR, Janicak PG, Petty F, Dilsaver SC, Davis JM, Rush AJ (1994): Efficacy of divalproex vs. lithium and placebo in the treatment of mania. Journal of the American Medical Association 27:918–924.

Brunello N, Tascedda F (2003): Cellular mechanisms and second messengers: Relevance to the psychopharmacology of bipolar disorders. International Journal of Neuropsychopharmacology 6:181–189.

Btaiche IF, Woster PS (1995): Gabapentin and lamotrigine: Novel antiepileptic drugs. American Journal of Health-System Pharmacy.

Burt T, Sachs GS, Demopulos C (1999): Donepezil in treatment-resistant bipolar disorder. Biological Psychiatry 45:959–964.

Cade J (1949): Lithium salts in the treatment of psychotic excitement. Medical Journal of Australia 2:349–352.

Calabrese JR, Delucchi GA (1990): Spectrum of efficacy of valproate in 55 patients with rapid-cycling bipolar disorder. American Journal of Psychiatry 147:431–434.

Calabrese JR, Keck PE Jr., McElroy SL, Shelton MD (2001): A pilot study of topiramate as monotherapy in the treatment of acute mania. Journal of Clinical Psychopharmacology 21:340–342.

Calabrese JR, Shelton MD, Rapport DJ, Kimmel SE (2002): Bipolar disorders and the effectiveness of novel anticonvulsants. Journal of Clinical Psychiatry 63 (supplement 3):5–9.

Calabrese JR, Sullivan JR, Bowden CL, Suppes T, Goldberg JF, Sachs GS, Shelton MD, Goodwin FK, Frye MA, Kusumakar V (2002): Rash in multicenter trials of lamotrigine in mood disorders: Clinical relevance and management. Journal of Clinical Psychiatry 63:1012–1019.

Carta MG, Hardoy MC, Grunze H, Carpiniello B (2002): The use of tiagabine in affective disorders. Pharmacopsychiatry 35:33–34.

Cassidy F, Ahearn EP, Carroll BJ (2001): Substance abuse in bipolar disorders. Bipolar Disorders 3:181–188.

Chen G, Rajkowska G, Du F, Seraji-Bozorgzad N, Manji HK (2000): Enhancement of hippocampal neurogenesis by lithium. Journal of Neurochemistry 75:1729–1734.

Colom F, Vieta E, Martinez-Aran A, Reinares M, Benabarre A, Gasto C (2000): Clinical factors associated with treatment noncompliance in euthymic bipolar patients. Journal of Clinical Psychiatry 61:549–555.

Coyle JT, Duman RS (2003): Finding the intracellular signaling pathways affected by mood disorder treatments. Neuron 38:157–160.

Davis LL, Ryan W, Adinoff B, Petty F (2000): Comprehensive review of the psychiatric uses of valproate. Journal of Clinical Psychopharmacology 20:(supplement 1):1S–17S.

DeToledo JC, Toledo C, DeCerce J, Ramsay RE (1997): Changes in body weight with chronic, high-dose gabapentin therapy. Therapeutic Drug Monitoring 19:394–396.

Dunner DL (2003): Drug interactions of lithium and other antimanic/mood-stabilizing medications. Journal of Clinical Psychiatry 64 (supplement 5):38–43.

Eadie MJ (1991): Formation of active metabolites of anticonvulsant drugs. A review of their pharmacological and therapeutic significances. Clinical Pharmacokinetics 21:27–41.

Edwards KR, Potter DL, Wu SC, Kamin M, Hulihan J (2003): Topiramate in the preventive treatment of episodic migraine: A combined analysis from pilot, double-blind, placebo-controlled trials. CNS Spectrum 8:428–432.

Ekbom K, Hardebo JE (2002): Cluster headache: Aetiology, diagnosis, and management. Drugs 62:61–69.

Evins AE (2003): Efficacy of newer anticonvulsant medication in bipolar spectrum mood disorders. Journal of Clinical Psychiatry 64 (supplement 8):9–14.

Fava M (1997): Psychopharmacologic treatment of pathologic aggression. Psychiatric Clinics of North America 20:427–451.

Gray NA, Zhou R, Du J, Moore GJ, Manji HK (2003): The use of mood stabilizers as plasticity enhancers in the treatment of neuropsychiatric disorders. Journal of Clinical Psychiatry 64 (supplement 5):3–17.

Grof P (2003): Selecting effective long-term treatment for bipolar patients: Monotherapy and combinations. Journal of Clinical Psychiatry 64 (supplement 5):53–61.

Grunze H, Erfurth A, Amann B, Giupponi G, Kammerer C, Walden J (1999a): Intravenous valproate loading in acutely manic and depressed bipolar I patients. Journal of Clinical Psychopharmacology 19:303–309.

Grunze H, Erfurth A, Marcuse A, Amann B, Normann C, Walden J (1999b): Tiagabine appears not to be efficacious in the treatment of acute mania. Journal of Clinical Psychiatry 60:759–762.

Harrow M, Goldberg JF, Grossman LS, Meltzer HY (1990): Outcome in manic disorders. A naturalistic follow-up study. Archives of General Psychiatry 47:665–671.

Heit S, Nemeroff CB (1998): Lithium augmentation of antidepressants in treatment-refractory depression. Journal of Clinical Psychiatry 59 (supplement 6):28–33.

Herbert AA, Ralston JP (2001): Cutaneous reactions to anticonvulsant medications. Journal of Clinical Psychiatry 62 (supplement 14):22–26.

Hoopes SP, Reimherr FW, Hedges DW, Rosenthal NR, Kamin M, Karim R, Capece JA, Karvois D (2003): Treatment of bulimia nervosa with topiramate in a randomized, double-blind, placebo-controlled trial, part 1: Improvement in binge and purge measures. Journal of Clinical Psychiatry 64:1335–1341.

Jefferson JW (2002): Rediscovering the art of lithium therapy. Current Psychiatry 1:18–24.

Jensen TS (2002): Anticonvulsants in neuropathic pain: Rationale and clinical evidence. European Journal of Pain 6 (supplement A):61–68.

Kahn D, Chaplan R (2002): The "good enough" mood stabilizer: A review of the clinical evidence. CNS Spectrum 7:227–237.

Kaufman DM (1990): *Clinical Neurology for Psychiatrists*. Philadelphia: W. B. Saunders.

Kaufman KR (1998): Adjunctive tiagabine treatment of psychiatric disorders: Three cases. Annals of Clinical Psychiatry 10:181–184.

Keck PE, McElroy SL (2002): Clinical pharmacodynamics and pharmacokinetics of antimanic and mood-stabilizing medications. Journal of Clinical Psychiatry 63 (supplement 40):3–11.

Keck PE Jr., McElroy SL, Strakowski SM, Bourne ML, West SA (1997): Compliance with maintenance treatment in bipolar disorder. Psychopharmacology Bulletin 33:87–91.

Kinrys G, Pollack MH, Simon NM, Worthington JJ, Nardi AF, Versiani M (2003): Valproic acid for the treatment of social anxiety disorder. International Clinical Psychopharmacology 18:169–172.

Kleindienst N, Greil W (2003): Lithium in the long-term treatment of bipolar disorders. European Archives of Psychiatry and Clinical Neuroscience 253:120–125.

Li X, Ketter TA, Frye MA (2002): Synaptic, intracellular, and neuroprotective mechanisms of anticonvulsants: Are they relevant for the treatment and course of bipolar disorders? Journal of Affective Disorders 69:1–14.

Lieb K, Treffurth Y, Hamke M, Akundi RS, von Kleinsorgen M, Fiebich BL (2003): Valproic acid inhibits substance P-induced activation of protein kinase C epsilon and expression of the substance P receptor. Journal of Neurochemistry 86:69–76.

Llewellyn A, Stowe ZN, Strader JR Jr. (1998): The use of lithium and management of women with bipolar disorder during pregnancy and lactation. Journal of Clinical Psychiatry 59 (supplement 6):57–64.

Malhi GS, Berk M (2002): Pharmacotherapy of bipolar disorder: The role of atypical antipsychotics and experimental strategies. Human Psychopharmacology 17:407–412.

Maneuf YP, Gonzalez MI, Sutton KS, Chung FZ, Pinnock RD (2003): Cellular and molecular action of the putative GABA-mimetic, gabapentin. Cellular and Molecular Life Sciences 60:742–750.

Manji HK, Lenox RH (1998): Lithium: A molecular transducer of mood-stabilization in the treatment of bipolar disorder. Neuropsychopharmacology 19:161–166.

Manji HK, Lenox RH (2000): The nature of bipolar disorder. Journal of Clinical Psychiatry 61 (supplement 13):42–57.

Manji HK, Moore GJ, Chen G (2000): Lithium up-regulates the cytoprotective protein Bcl-2 in the CNS in vivo: A role for neurotrophic and neuroprotective effects in manic depressive illness. Journal of Clinical Psychiatry 61 (supplement 9):82–96.

May A, Leone M (2003): Update on cluster headache. Current Opinion in Neurology 16:333–340.

McElroy SL, Arnold LM, Shapira NA, Keck PE Jr., Rosenthal NR, Karim MR, Kamin M, Hudson JI (2003): Topiramate in the treatment of binge-eating disorder associated with obesity: A randomized, placebo-controlled trial. American Journal of Psychiatry 160:612.

Messenheimer JA (1998): Rash in adult and pediatric patients treated with lamotrigine. The Canadian Journal of Neurological Sciences 25:S14–S18.

Möller HJ, Nasrallah HA (2003): Treatment of bipolar disorder. The Journal of Clinical Psychiatry 64 (supplement 6):9–17.

Moore G, Bebchuck JM, Hasanat K, Chen G, Seraji-Bozorgzad N, Wild IB, Faulk MW, Koch S, Glitz DA, Jolkovsky L, Manji HK (2000): Lithium increases N-acetyl-aspartate in the human brain: In vivo evidence in support of bcl-2's neurotrophic effects? Biological Psychiatry 48:1–8.

Nemeroff CB (2000): An ever-increasing pharmacopoeia for the management of patients with bipolar disorder. Journal of Clinical Psychiatry 61 (supplement 13):19–25.

Nemeroff CB (2003): Safety of available agents used to treat bipolar disorder: Focus on weight gain. Journal of Clinical Psychiatry 64:532–539.

O'Donnell T, Rotzinger S, Nakashima TT, Hanstock CC, Ulrich M, Silverstone PH (2003): Chronic lithium and sodium valproate both decrease the concentration of myoinositol and increase the concentration of inositol monophosphates in rat brain. European Neuropsychopharmacology 13:199–207.

Ortho-McNeil (2003): Letter to Healthcare Professionals.

Pande AC, Crockatt JG, Janney CA, Werth JL, Tsaroucha G (2000): Gabapentin in bipolar disorder: A placebo-controlled trial of adjunctive therapy. Gabapentin Bipolar Disorder Study Group. Bipolar Disorders 2:249–255.

Perucca E (2002): Pharmacological and therapeutic properties of valproate: A summary after 35 years of clinical experience. CNS Drugs 16:695–714.

Pugh CB, Garnett WR (1991): Current issues in the treatment of epilepsy. Clinical Pharmacy 10:335–358.

Sachs GA, Thase ME (2000): Bipolar disorder therapeutics: Maintenance treatment. Biological Psychiatry 48:573–581.

Schou M (1997a): Forty years of lithium treatment. Archives of General Psychiatry 54:9–13.

Schou M (1997b): The combat of non-compliance during prophylactic lithium treatment. Acta Pyschiatrica Scandinavica 95:361–363.

Silva RR, Ernst M, Campbell M (1993): Lithium and conduct disorder. Encephale 19:585–590.

Silverstone T, McPherson H, Hunt N, Romans S (1998): How effective is lithium in the prevention of relapse in bipolar disorder? A prospective naturalistic follow-up study. Australian and New Zealand Journal of Psychiatry 32:61–66.

Spina E, Perucca E (2002): Clinical significance of pharmacokinetic interactions between antiepileptic and psychotropic drugs. Epilepsia 43 (supplement 2):37–44.

Swann AC (2001): Major system toxicities and side effects of anticonvulsants. Journal of Clinical Psychiatry 62 (supplement 14):16–21.

Van Ameringen M, Mancini C, Pipe B, Campbell M, Oakman J (2002): Topiramate treatment for SSRI-induced weight gain in anxiety disorders. Journal of Clinical Psychiatry 63:981–984.

van Liet JA, Vein AA, Le Cessie S, Ferrari MD, van Dijk JG (2003): Impairment of trigeminal sensory pathways in cluster headache. Cephalalgia 23:414–419.

Wang PW, Ketter TA (2002): Pharmacokinetics of mood stabilizers and new anticonvulsants. Psychopharmacology Bulletin 36:44–66.

Wheeler G (2002): Gabapentin. Current Opinion in Investigational Drugs 3:470–477.

Wisner KL, Peindl KS, Perel JM, Hanusa BH, Piontek CM, Baab S (2002): Verapamil treatment for women with bipolar disorder. Biological Psychiatry 51:745–752.

Xie X, Hagan RM (1998): Cellular and molecular actions of lamotrigine: Possible mechanisms of efficacy in bipolar disorder. Neuropsychobiology 38:119–130.

CHAPTER ELEVEN

FIRST- AND SECOND-GENERATION ANTIPSYCHOTICS AND ANTICHOLINERGICS

The typical, or first-generation, antipsychotics dominated the treatment of schizophrenia for much of the last half of the twentieth century. Generally thought relatively effective for the positive symptoms of schizophrenia, the typical antipsychotics are generally thought to have had little beneficial effect on the negative symptoms of schizophrenia and in addition caused many debilitating adverse affects. In the early 1990s, the atypical, or second, antipsychotics began to be widely introduced. In addition to treating the positive symptoms of schizophrenia, such as delusions and hallucinations, the newer atypical antipsychotics also appear to have some effect on the often recalcitrant negative symptoms of schizophrenia, such as lack of motivation and apathy. Furthermore, the atypical antipsychotics cause far fewer neurological adverse effects than do the typical antipsychotics. Due in part to these factors, the atypical antipsychotics have dramatically altered the way schizophrenia and other psychotic disorders are treated, although these drugs do cause serious side effects of their own.

Because of the propensity of particularly the typical antipsychotics to cause various and often debilitating neurological adverse effects, other drugs, primarily the anticholinergic agents, are used in conjunction with the antipsychotics, although less so with the newer atypical agents.

The first typical antipsychotic, chlorpromazine (Thorazine), was introduced in 1952 (Bennett, 1998). By the 1960s, it was suggested that the typical antipsychotics, or neuroleptics as they were sometimes called (Bennett, 1998), worked via the brain's dopamine system, a hypothesis strengthened by the findings in the 1970s that typical antipsychotics antagonized dopamine receptors (Bennett, 1998). The introduction of chlorpromazine was followed by the synthesis and release of additional typical antipsychotics. For example, the first clinical report of haloperidol (Haldol) appeared in 1958 (Granger, 1999).

These drugs, now referred to as typical antipsychotics, neuroleptics [meaning to control the neuron (Casey, 1997)], major tranquilizers (Itil & Wadud, 1975), and first-generation antipsychotics not only diminished the agitation of psychosis but also improved the associated thought disorder (Casey, 1997). Unfortunately, soon after the typical antipsychotics began to be used, significant adverse effects were noted (Casey, 1997). For example, the typical antipsychotics induced muscle movement disorders (Casey, 1997). In addition, the therapeutic response to the typical antipsychotics was all too often incomplete (Lieberman & Perkins, 2002). Specifically, the so-called positive symptoms of schizophrenia—delusions, hallucinations, and overtly disorganized behavior (Andreasen & Black, 1991)—did somewhat respond to the typical antipsychotics, but the perhaps even more pernicious negative symptoms—such as lack of motivation, apathy, and affective difficulties (Andreasen & Black, 1991)—did not (Lieberman & Perkins, 2002).

Despite the significant limitations of the typical antipsychotics, no significant breakthroughs in the treatment of schizophrenia occurred until 1991 when clozapine (Clozaril) was released in the United States (Casey, 1991). Developed in the 1960s but withdrawn due to agranulocytosis [decreased production of white blood cells (Nemeroff et al., 2002)], clozapine is effective for some people who are unresponsive to the earlier antipsychotics (Sernyak et al., 2003). Since the introduction of clozapine, several other atypical antipsychotics, or second-generation antipsychotics, have been released in the United States and other parts of the world. Unlike first-generation antipsychotics, atypical or second-generation antipsychotics cause substantially fewer of the neurological adverse effects (Love, 1996) that have so plagued the use of first-generation antipsychotics, as well as less elevation of the hormone prolactin (Kapur & Seeman, 2001), increased concentrations of which can cause menstrual dysfunction, lactation, breast development in men, and disturbances in sexual function (Haddad & Wieck, 2004).

THE TYPICAL OR FIRST-GENERATION ANTIPSYCHOTICS

The typical antipsychotics were essentially the only drugs available for the treatment for schizophrenia from the introduction of chlorpromazine (Thorazine) to 1991 when the first atypical antipsychotic, clozapine, became available (Casey, 1991). Despite the difficulties surrounding their use and the availability of the often more expensive atypical antipsychotics, the typical antipsychotics continue to see clinical use in some situations (Tempier & Pawliuk, 2003). Several typical antipsychotics are marketed in the United States, including chlorpromazine (Thorazine), thioridazine (Mellaril), trifluoperazine (Stelazine), fluphenazine (Prolixin), thiothixene (Navane), haloperidol (Haldol), droperidol (Inapsine), loxapine (Loxitane), pimozide (Orap), and molindone (Moban).

258   CHAPTER ELEVEN

Mechanism of Action, Pharmacology, and Metabolism

The typical antipsychotics can be organized into six different chemical classes as shown in Table 11.1.

All of the typical antipsychotics block dopamine type 2 receptors in the brain. In fact, a typical antipsychotic's ability to bind to the dopamine type 2 receptor is inversely related to its clinically effective dose (Seeman et al., 1976). That is, the more readily the drug binds to the dopamine type 2 receptor, the lower its effective dose. Antagonism of the dopamine type 2 receptor appears necessary for an antipsychotic effect (Kapur & Mamo, 2003), although others are involved (Sundram et al., 2003). Specifically, it is thought that dopamine antagonism in the mesolimbic system is related to the antipsychotic properties of the atypical antipsychotics (Maguire, 2002). Even though all of the typical antipsychotics block dopamine type 2 receptors, these drugs differ in the potency, or strength, of their binding to these receptors (Meltzer et al., 1998). Low-potency typical antipsychotics, for example (Schwartz & Brotman, 1992), such as chlorpromazine and thioridazine, bind with less affinity to dopamine type 2 receptors than do high-potency typical antipsychotics (Schwartz & Brotman, 1992), such as haloperidol and fluphenazine.

In addition to their effects on dopamine type 2 receptors, the typical antipsychotics interact with other neurotransmitter receptors. For example, haloperidol binds to dopamine type 1, alpha 1 adrenergic, and serotonin type 2 receptors (Casey, 1997). Furthermore, the low-potency typical antipsychotics have greater antagonistic effects on acetylcholine receptors than do the high-potency antipsychotics (Casey, 1997).

The typical antipsychotics tend to have fairly substantial first-pass metabolism effects (Balant-Gorgia & Balant, 1987). As a general rule, the half-lives of most of the typical antipsychotics are generally about twenty-four hours (Balant-Gorgia & Balant, 1987), allowing for once-a-day dosing in most cases. Like most

TABLE 11.1   Classification of Typical Antipsychotic Drugs

CHEMICAL CLASS	EXAMPLE
Phenothiazines	Chlorpromazine, Thioridazine, Fluphenazine (Czekalla et al., 2001)
Thioxanthenes	Thiothixene (Shehata et al., 2000)
Butyrophenones	Haloperidol, Droperidol (Czekalla et al., 2001)
Dibenzoxazepines	Loxapine (Heel et al., 1978)
Diphenylbutylpiperadines	Pimozide (Czekalla et al., 2001)
Dihydroindolones	Molindone (Owen & Cole, 1989)

other psychotropic medications, these drugs are metabolized by the liver (Balant-Gorgia & Balant, 1987), primarily by cytochrome P450 enzymes 1A2 and 2D6 (Meyer et al., 1996).

Drug-Drug Interactions

The typical antipsychotics can interact with several other drugs, requiring caution in clinical practice as many of these reactions have the potential to be quite serious (Meyer et al., 1996). For example, the SSRIs can inhibit the liver's cytochrome P450 enzymes involved with the metabolism of the typical antipsychotics, resulting in increased blood and brain levels of typical antipsychotics and possibly leading to toxicity (Meyer et al., 1996). The beta blocker propranolol (Inderal) can increase typical antipsychotic levels (Meyer et al.,1996).

Adverse Effects

The potential for frequent, often severe, and sometimes permanent adverse effects of the typical antipsychotics have severely limited their use overall and have led to the search for other better tolerated agents. The adverse effects from typical antipsychotic medications can be organized into several broad classes based on how they are generated: acetylcholine inhibition (Meltzer, 1998), dopamine blockade in the tuberoinfundibular and nigrostriatal pathways (Maguire, 2002), and side effects from other mechanisms (Meltzer et al., 1998).

The typical antipsychotics block acetylcholine receptors, producing what are commonly referred to as anticholinergic effects (Meltzer et al., 1998), which include a dry mouth, constipation, urinary hesitation, and blurred vision. In some cases, anticholinergic effects from particularly typical antipsychotics can deteriorate to memory deficits, confusion, and delirium (Meltzer et al., 1998).

By antagonizing dopamine receptors in the nigrostriatal system (Maguire, 2002) leading to an excess of acetylcholine transmission (Glazer, 2000), the typical antipsychotics are notorious for causing what are known as extrapyramidal effects, which occur in approximately 50 percent to 75 percent of people taking them (Casey, 1997). Several types of extrapyramidal effects can occur. For example, akathisia, literally the inability to sit or stand still, is a form of EPS characterized by an inner feeling of restlessness (Friedman & Wagner, 1987; Kulkarni & Naidu, 2003) that can lead to medication noncompliance (Gerlach, 2002). Propranolol can be used to diminish akathisia (Fischel et al., 2001). Other drugs too have been investigated to control akathisia. For example, in a double-blind study, the serotonin antagonist cyproheptadine appeared to be as effective as propranolol in diminishing akathisia (Fischel et al., 2001).

Muscles spasms called dystonia (Kulkarni & Naidu, 2003) that affect most muscles in the neck (torticollis) (Skorin et al., 1987) and muscles that control eye movements (oculogyric crisis) (Skorin et al., 1987) can occur during treatment with atypical antipsychotics (Skorin et al., 1987). The typical antipsychotics can produce a drug-induced Parkinson's disease (Hassin-Baer et al., 2001) that is characterized by slowed movements, resting and action tremor, and muscle rigidity (Hassin-Baer et al., 2001).

Tardive dyskinesia, abnormal and involuntary movements of the face, tongue, limbs, and trunk, may complicate typical antipsychotic therapy (Kulkarni & Naidu, 2003). These disfiguring movements can take a variety of forms but tend to be slow, writhing, and purposeless (Najib, 1999). The exact prevalence of tardive dyskinesia in people taking typical antipsychotic medication is unknown, but an average of estimated prevalence rates has been reported at 24 percent (Kulkarni & Naidu, 2003). The prevalence of tardive dyskinesia after just one year of treatment is approximately 5 to 10 percent (Kane et al., 1998). Occurring not only during drug treatment, tardive dyskinesia can develop when typical antipsychotics are withdrawn (Najib, 1999). Often permanent, tardive dyskinesia improves or resolves completely in only approximately 10 percent to 30 percent of cases (Bai et al., 2003), even after the typical antipsychotic is discontinued (Kulkarni & Naidu, 2001). Although clearly associated with typical antipsychotic medication, the mechanism by which these medications induce tardive dyskinesia is not known. A variety of mechanisms are proposed, however, including hypersensitivity in the dopamine system, an altered balance between dopamine and acetylcholine systems, free radicals produced from atypical neuroleptics (Kulkarni & Naidu, 2003), and altered glutamate function (Kulkarni & Naidu, 2001). Abnormalities in serotonin, gamma amino benzoic acid (GABA), and norepinephrine may be involved in the pathogenesis of tardive dyskinesia as well (Kulkarni & Naidu, 2001). The elderly, women, and people with affective disorders (Casey, 1988), such as major depression and bipolar disorder, have an increased chance of developing tardive dyskinesia as a result of treatment with typical antipsychotics. Because of the seriousness and high prevalence of tardive dyskinesia, numerous treatments have been considered. Baclofen (a muscle relaxant), diazepam, valproic acid, and vitamin E are among the medications that may reduce symptoms of tardive dyskinesia (Soares & McGrath, 1999). Tardive dyskinesia has been major area of concern to psychopharmacologists and patients alike and has significantly hampered the pharmacological treatment of psychosis, especially in the era before the atypical antipsychotic medications were available.

An additional serious problem with the typical antipsychotics is neuroleptic malignant syndrome. This potentially lethal condition can occur after exposure to a typical antipsychotic, often in the context of treatment initiation or increase in dose (Chandran et al., 2003), and is characterized by muscle rigidity, high fever, elevated heart rate and blood pressure, and profuse sweating (Lappa et al., 2002). Alterations in consciousness such as confusion also result and death can occur, particularly if untreated. The death rate of untreated neuroleptic malignant syndrome was reported to be 21 percent in one study (Sakkas et al., 1991). Treatment consists primarily of stopping the offending neuroleptics and providing supportive treatment (Chandran et al., 2003): fever reduction measures and hydration (Chandran et al., 2003). Because neuroleptic malignant syndrome may be the caused by antagonism of brain dopamine receptors (Chandran et al., 2003), dopamine agonists—for example, bromocriptine—can help in reducing the symptoms of neuroleptic malignant syndrome (Chandran et al., 2003). The muscle relaxant dantrolene also may be beneficial in neuroleptic malignant syndrome (Chandran et al., 2003).

In addition to antagonizing dopamine receptors in mesolimbic and nigrostriatal pathways (Maguire, 2002), typical neuroleptics also antagonize dopamine receptors in the tuberoinfundibular pathway, which leads to an increase in the hormone prolactin (Maguire, 2002) in both men and women, although women may have typical antipsychotic-induced elevations in prolactin somewhat more frequently than men (Haddad & Wieck, 2004). Elevated prolactin can cause menstrual abnormalities, including irregular menstrual periods, a cessation of menstruation, and even early menopause (Maguire, 2002). Milk production or galactorrhea can occur (Maguire, 2002). Sexual dysfunction too is associated with prolactin elevation and includes diminished libido and delay in orgasm (Maguire, 2002). Increased prolactin levels can result in decreased concentrations of estrogen and testosterone, alterations that are associated with diminished bone density (Maguire, 2002). Finally, increased prolactin levels are associated with depression (Maguire, 2002).

Other adverse effects from the typical antipsychotic medications are orthostatic hypotension [lowered blood pressure upon standing (Meltzer et al., 1998)] from antagonism of alpha 1 adrenergic receptors (Meltzer et al., 1998). These drugs also can slow down the electrical impulses that course through the heart coordinating the heart's contractions (Meltzer et al., 1998). Serious heart arrhythmias can result from this prolongation of cardiac conduction intervals (Meltzer et al., 1998), particularly with thioridazine (Czekalla et al., 2001). Droperidol (Inapsine) is also implicated as being associated with prolonged cardiac conduction intervals (Shale et al., 2003). Typical antipsychotics are also associated with sedation and cognitive deficits (Meltzer et al., 1998). Weight gain is associated with the use of typical antipsychotics (Meltzer et al., 1998), although molindone may not be associated with weight gain (Owen & Cole, 1989).

In general, the high-potency typical antipsychotics, such as haloperidol, tend to cause more extrapyramidal symptoms but less sedation and fewer anticholinergic effects than do the low-potency antipsychotics such as Thorazine (Meltzer et al., 1998). Table 11.2 categorizes and lists adverse effects from typical (first-generation) antipsychotics.

Uses

The typical antipsychotics all appear to be equally efficacious in the treatment of psychosis but differ in their adverse side effects (Remington, 2003). However, in many of the following indications, the newer and presumably safer atypical antipsychotics (Conley & Kelly, 2002) are being used with increasing frequency, in many instances supplanting the use of the older typical antipsychotics.

Schizophrenia.   The typical antipsychotics appear to have some benefit in the treatment of the positive symptoms of schizophrenia (Maguire, 2002). Not only

TABLE 11.2   The Typical Antipsychotics: Types of Adverse Effects

TYPES	ADVERSE EFFECTS
Acetylcholine inhibition	Dry mouth; decreased bowel motility resulting in constipation; dry eyes; blurred vision; and problems with memory and confusion.
Dopamine blockade in the tuberoinfundibular and nigrostriatal pathways	Extrapyramidal effects including akathisia, characterized by a feeling of restlessness, and dystonia; tremor, rigidity or muscle stiffness; tardive dyskinesia (abnormal and involuntary movements of the face, tongue, limbs, and trunk); neuroleptic malignant syndrome (characterized by extreme muscle rigidity, high fever, and profuse sweating); increase in the amount of prolactin in the body, resulting in lactation, menstrual abnormalities, ovulation problems, lowered estrogen and testosterone concentrations, and impotence.
Other mechanisms	Orthostatic hypotension; severe and even fatal heart arrhythmias; prolonged cardiac conduction intervals.

limited by their propensity for adverse effects (Worrel et al., 2000), the typical antipsychotics do not treat the negative symptoms associated with schizophrenia (Worrel et al., 2000). So saying, some evidence suggests that low-dose first-generation antipsychotic medications may be as effective overall as the newer second-generation antipsychotic medications (Geddes et al., 2000).

Despite the limitations of the typical antipsychotics for the treatment of schizophrenia, the decanoate forms—the long-lasting injectable preparations—of haloperidol and fluphenazine still are used, particularly in patients who have been noncompliant with the oral forms of antipsychotic medications (Barnes & Curson, 1994). An additional feature of the decanoate forms is that the clinicians administering these drugs know immediately if someone does not show up for a scheduled injection, allowing appropriate action to be taken (Barnes & Curson, 1994). If relapse should occur, the clinician knows that the relapse is not the result of noncompliance on the part of the patient (Kane et al., 2003). A potential disadvantage is that if the need arises—for example, severe adverse effects develop—the decanoate medication cannot be immediately discontinued (Kane et al., 2003). However, decanoate medications do not appear to be associated with increased risks of adverse effects compared to oral typical antipsychotic medications (Glazer & Kane, 1992; Kane et al., 2003).

Although the practice is poorly studied (Tempier & Pawliuk, 2003), typical and atypical antipsychotics are sometimes combined. In one study, for example, 19 percent of outpatients with chronic psychiatric disorders were taking both typical and atypical antipsychotics (Tempier & Pawliuk, 2003). This combined use may have been due to true polypharmacy in an attempt to increase the clinical response by using more than one drug type or to both typical and atypical being used while one drug was being slowly withdrawn and another added (Tempier & Pawliuk, 2003).

Mania.   In the acute forms of mania, the typical antipsychotics were frequently used, particularly before the availability of the atypical antipsychotics (Yatham, 2002) and appear to have mood-stabilizing properties (Möller & Nasrallah, 2003). However, the potential for adverse effects such as tardive dyskinesia from the typical antipsychotic limits the use of the typical antipsychotics in mania (Yatham, 2002).

Acute Agitation.   The typical antipsychotics have for years been used to treat extreme agitation and aggression. Several of these drugs can be given intramuscularly, resulting in less agitation in a few minutes. For example, haloperidol is often used in emergency situations when rapid sedation is indicated. Despite its lack of approval from the U.S. Food and Drug Administration for this use and its potential to prolong cardiac-conduction intervals, droperidol is also used to rapidly sedate highly agitated patients (Shale et al., 2003).

Tourette's Disorder.   Typical antipsychotics, particularly haloperidol (Jimenez-Jimenez & Garcia-Ruiz, 2001) and pimozide, are effective in the treatment of Tourette's syndrome to suppress tics (Muller-Vahl, 2002), although they are not necessarily considered first-line agents for Tourette's disorder (Kossof & Singer, 2001).

Depression with Psychotic Features.   Many if not most cases of psychotic depression do not respond to an antidepressant alone. Because of this, an antipsychotic is often prescribed in conjunction with an antidepressant, at least temporarily, in cases of major depression with psychotic features (Wheeler Vega et al., 2000).

Mental Retardation.   The typical antipsychotics, including chlorpromazine, haloperidol, and thioridazine (Buck & Sprague, 1989), have been used in people with mental retardation for behavioral and psychiatric problems (Advokat et al., 2000), although the typical antipsychotics are associated with more adverse effects in the mentally retarded population than are the atypical antipsychotics (Advokat et al., 2000).

Stuttering.   Although stuttering generally resolves by adulthood and rarely requires drug intervention, haloperidol may be beneficial in reducing stuttering in some cases (Lawrence & Barclay, 1998). Table 11.3 summarizes the potential uses of typical (first-generation) antipsychotics.

TABLE 11.3   Uses of Typical Antipsychotics

Schizophrenia

Mania

Acute Agitation

Tourette's Disorder

Depression with Psychotic Features

Behavioral and Psychiatric Disturbances Associated with Mental Retardation

Stuttering

ATYPICAL OR SECOND-GENERATION ANTIPSYCHOTICS

Because of the many problems associated with the typical antipsychotics and questions concerning their efficacy (Worrel et al., 2000), new compounds have been developed to try to circumvent these difficulties. The first of these atypical or second-generation antipsychotics, clozapine (Clozaril) became available in the United States in 1990 (Iqbal et al., 2003). Causing fewer extrapyramidal symptoms than do the typical antipsychotics, the side-effect profile of clozapine suggests that a drug can possess antipsychotic properties without having to cause extrapyramidal symptoms, findings that counter the previously held notion that a drug had to cause extrapyramidal effects in order to be an effective antipsychotic (Hippius, 1999). While certainly not without significant problems of their own (Newcomer, 2001), the atypical antipsychotics are replacing the older, typical antipsychotics in many instances due to their efficacy not only for the psychosis of schizophrenia but also for the cognitive, mood, and negative symptoms of schizophrenia, as well as a lower incidence of extrapyramidal symptoms and tardive dyskinesia (Tandon & Jibson, 2003). Several atypical antipsychotics are now available in the United States: clozapine (Clozaril), risperidone (Risperdal), olanzapine (Zyprexa), quetiapine (Seroquel), and ziprasidone (Geodon). Another atypical antipsychotic, amisulpride, is as yet unavailable in the United States but is used in other countries including France (Leucht et al., 2002). Aripiprazole (Abilify) was introduced in late 2002 and is an atypical antipsychotic whose pharmacology differs from the other atypical antipsychotics in that it appears to be a partial dopamine 2 agonist (Burris et al., 2002). In general, the atypical antipsychotics differ from the typical antipsychotics in a variety of ways including having markedly less propensity to cause extrapyramidal effects (Love, 1996) and elevations in prolactin concentration (Kapur & Seeman, 2001).

Mechanism of Action, Pharmacology, and Metabolism

The exact mechanism of action of the atypical antipsychotics remains unknown. Furthermore, each atypical antipsychotic varies considerably from the other atypical antipsychotics (Breier, 2001). Despite this added complexity, several theories exist that attempt to account for what is known about the pharmacology of the atypical antipsychotics. Like their close relatives the typical antipsychotics, the atypical antipsychotics also antagonize dopamine type 2 receptors (Breier, 2001). Risperidone may have the greatest degree of dopamine type 2 receptor binding compared to the other atypical antipsychotics (Breier, 2001). Preliminary findings raise the possibility that the dopamine type 2 receptor need only be occupied transiently as opposed to continuously by quetiapine, and possibly other atypical antipsychotics, in order to achieve improvement in first-episodes schizophrenia (Tauscher-Wisniewski et al., 2002). In addition to its blockade of dopamine type 2 receptors, clozapine also antagonizes prefrontal dopamine type 1 receptors, which may be important in the genesis of schizophrenia's negative symptoms (Remington, 2003). Furthermore, clozapine and olanzapine block dopamine type 4 receptors but so does haloperidol (Kapur & Seeman, 2001). Clozapine and olanzapine also antagonize muscarinic, alpha-adrenergic, and histamine receptors (Casey, 1997). Amisulpride antagonizes presynaptic dopamine 2 and 3 receptors in the frontal cortex, which increases dopamine transmission in this region and is hypothesized to improve the negative symptoms of schizophrenia (Pani, 2002). Improvement in positive symptoms from amisulpride may be in part due to its decrease in dopamine transmission subcortical regions via dopamine 2 receptor and dopamine 3 receptor antagonism in the nucleus accumbens (Pani, 2002). In contrast to other atypical antipsychotics, amisulpride does not antagonize serotonin receptors (Leucht et al., 2002).

Aripiprazole appears to act as a partial agonist of dopamine 2 receptors (Burris et al., 2002). That is, when dopamine activity is high, aripiprazole acts as an antagonist at dopamine 2 receptors and when dopamine activity is low, aripiprazole behaves as an agonist at dopamine 2 receptors (Weiden, 2003).

In addition to effects on dopamine receptors, however, the second-generation antipsychotics block a wide variety of other receptors, including serotonin, subtype 2A receptors (Ichikawa et al., 2001), which may relate to their therapeutic effects. Yet, the typical or first-generation antipsychotics loxapine (Kapur et al., 1997) and chlorpromazine also antagonize the serotonin, subtype 2A receptors, suggesting that other factors are involved in the mechanisms of action of second-generation antipsychotics. For example, the *ratio* of the dopamine to serotonin antagonism differs among the atypical antipsychotics. This dopamine/serotonin blockade ratio has been postulated to be important for the therapeutic effects exerted by the atypical antipsychotics (Deutch et al., 1991). In addition to its action at dopamine 2 receptors, aripiprazole acts as a partial agonist at serotonin 1A receptors (Buckley, 2003) and antagonizes serotonin 2A receptors (Bowles & Levin, 2003).

Some data suggest that too much dopamine in the mesolimbic pathway results in the positive symptoms of schizophrenia, while the negative symptoms of schizophrenia are associated with too little dopamine in the frontal cortex. It had been proposed that the atypical antipsychotics may block mesolimbic dopamine type 2 receptors, presumably decreasing positive symptoms. Because serotonin may act as an inhibitor of dopamine, antagonism of serotonin type 2 receptors in the frontal cortex may increase dopamine function in this area, a possible mechanism of negative symptom reduction and improved cognitive function in schizophrenia (Ichikawa et al., 2003).

Additional evidence suggests that it is the rapid dissociation of the atypical antipsychotic from the dopamine type 2 receptor itself that accounts for the atypical features of these drugs (Remington, 2003). In effect, the dopamine receptor is occupied enough by the atypical antipsychotic to decrease psychosis but not enough to produce extrapyramidal effects and increases in prolactin (Kapur & Seeman, 2001).

Other neurotransmitters and their receptors, in addition to serotonin and dopamine, are affected by second-generation antipsychotic medications. At least some second-generation antipsychotics appear to affect glutamate function (Heresco-Levy, 2003), a mechanism that may result in some of olanzapine's effects on negative symptoms (Goff et al., 2002). Work in animals has suggested that olanzapine and risperidone may affect glutamate's N-methyl-D-aspartate (NMDA) receptors in the hippocampus as part of their therapeutic mechanism of action (Tarazi et al., 2003). Down-regulation of NMDA receptors in the caudate and putamen may underlie the lowered likelihood of extrapyramidal effects from second-generation antipsychotics (Tarazi et al., 2003). The glutamate and dopamine models are not necessarily exclusive, as dopamine inhibits glutamine release (Remington, 2003), indicating an interaction between the two neurotransmitter systems.

Several cytochrome P450 enzymes metabolize the atypical antipsychotics. For example, cytochrome P450 2D6 metabolizes to some extent risperidone, olanzapine, and clozapine, while cytochrome P450 3A4 is involved in the metabolism of clozapine and quetiapine. Cytochrome P450 2C19 and 1A2 also contribute to the metabolism of some of the atypical antipsychotics (Prior et al., 1999).

Half-lives vary somewhat among the atypical antipsychotics, with clozapine having a half-life of approximately 12 hours at steady state (Keck & McElroy, 2002); quetiapine, 5 hours (Gefvert et al., 1998); ziprasidone, 6 to 7 hours (Caley & Cooper, 2002); risperidone, approximately 10 hours (after single dose) (Tauscher et al., 2002); and olanzapine, approximately 24 hours (after single dose) (Tauscher et al., 2002). The metabolism of the atypical antipsychotics is through cytochrome P450 enzymes (Keck & McElroy, 2002; Meltzer et al., 1998), where some atypical antipsychotics are converted to active metabolites. Quetiapine, for instance, has at least eleven metabolites, of which two may be pharmacologically active but present in relatively low concentrations (Nemeroff et al., 2002). Clozapine is metabolized to an active metabolite, norclozapine (Keck & McElroy, 1991). An active metabolite of risperidone is 9-OH-risperidone (Keck & McElroy, 1991).

Drug-Drug Interactions

Because they are metabolized by cytochrome P450 enzymes (Meltzer et al., 1998), the atypical antipsychotics have the potential to interact with several other drugs. Inhibitors of relevant cytochrome P450 enzymes can increase atypical antipsychotic concentrations. For example, by interfering with cytochrome P450 1A2, the specific serotonin reuptake inhibiting antidepressant fluvoxamine (Luvox) can increase concentrations of olanzapine and clozapine (Meltzer et al., 1998). Because as clozapine can inhibit the production of blood cells in the bone marrow, it should not be used with other bone-marrow-suppressing drugs, such as carbamazepine (Meltzer et al., 1998).

Adverse Effects

One major advantage of the atypical antipsychotics over the typical ones is the greatly diminished chances of causing extrapyramidal side effects, especially tardive dyskinesia (Geddes et al., 2000; Möller & Nasrallah, 2003). In contrast to the 5 to 10 percent prevalence of tardive dyskinesia after one year of treatment with typical antipsychotic medications, the atypical antipsychotics appear to have a 0.5 to 1 percent incidence of tardive dyskinesia per year (Tandon & Jibson, 2003)—a reduced but nevertheless real problem from use of these drugs. The frequency of extrapyramidal symptoms from clozapine treatment, in fact, may equal that of placebo (Iqbal et al., 2003), suggesting that clozapine has little or no propensity to precipitate extrapyramidal symptoms. Although the atypical neuroleptics are thought to induce neuroleptic malignant syndrome less frequently than typical neuroleptics, cases of atypical neuroleptics associated with neuroleptic malignant syndrome have been reported (Reeves et al., 2002). In contrast to clozapine, risperidone does seem to cause a dose-dependent increase in extrapyramidal effects (Breier, 2001).

As a class, the atypical antipsychotics have minimal effects on prolactin elevation, with clozapine and quetiapine not appearing to elevate prolactin levels, even at high doses (Haddad & Wieck, 2004). Olanzapine can elevate prolactin at higher doses (Haddad & Wieck, 2004). However, amisulpride (Haddad & Wieck, 2004) and risperidone are associated with prolactin increases (Maguire, 2002; Remington, 2003) similar in magnitude to those produced by typical antipsychotics (Haddad & Wieck, 2004).

Clozapine can cause agranulocytosis (Alphs & Campbell, 2002), a condition in which the bone marrow stops producing granulocytes, important infection-fighting white blood cells. Although the incidence of agranulocytosis with clozapine is only about 1 to 2 percent (Alphs & Campbell, 2002), the seriousness and potential lethality of this requires that people taking clozapine have their blood monitored weekly for the first six months of treatment and every other week afterwards for the duration of clozapine treatment (Meltzer et al., 1998). In most cases, this intensive surveillance system is able to detect impending agranulocytosis before the point of no return is reached, allowing for appropriate interventions to be taken—such as stopping the clozapine and providing supportive treatment (Meltzer et al., 1998).

Seizures too may complicate treatment with some atypical antipsychotics. While it is likely that several of the atypical antipsychotics can increase slightly the chances of a seizure occurring (Meltzer et al., 1998), clozapine is associated with a well-documented, dose-dependent increase in seizures (Devinsky et al., 1991; Meltzer et al., 1998). That is, the seizure risk from clozapine seems to be dose related, with higher doses causing more seizures (Miller, 2000), at an incidence of approximately 4 percent at the higher dose ranges (Meltzer et al., 1998). For example, in one study, doses less than 300 mg/day were associated with a seizure incidence of 1 percent, whereas doses between 300 mg/day and 599 mg/day had a seizure incidence of 2.7 percent, and doses over 599 mg/day had a seizure incidence of 4.4 percent (Devinsky et al., 1991). Risk factors for an increased risk of clozapine-induced seizures include a history of seizures (Wilson & Claussen, 1994) and concurrent use of other drugs that lower the seizure threshold (Devinsky et al., 1991; Toth & Frankenburg, 1994).

Clozapine also causes excessive salivation (Miller, 2000). Clozapine can also result in prolonged drowsiness and elevated heart rate (Alphs & Campbell, 2002). Clozapine and olanzapine are associated with anticholinergic effects (Meltzer et al., 1998), which can produce constipation with clozapine (Meltzer et al., 1998). Although generally benign (Levin et al., 2002), clozapine-induced constipation has resulted in death (Levin et al., 2002). Effective management of constipation from clozapine includes good hydration, a high-fiber diet, and bulk laxatives (Miller, 2000).

Weight gain is a major problem associated with the atypical antipsychotics (Osser et al., 1999), with olanzapine possibly the worst culprit for this (Möller & Nasrallah, 2003), although weight gain does occur with the other atypical antipsychotics, particularly clozapine (Meltzer et al., 1998). Quetiapine may result in less weight gain than other atypical antipsychotics (Möller & Nasrallah, 2003), as does aripiprazole (Buckley, 2003) and possibly amisulpride (Sechter et al., 2002). The atypical antipsychotics, especially clozapine and olanzapine (Atmaca et al., 2003), and possible quetiapine (Casey et al., 2004) also have been linked to elevations in triglycerides (Atmaca et al., 2003), mandating periodic monitoring of triglycerides in patients on atypical antipsychotics. Ziprasidone, risperidone, and aripiprazole may affect triglycerides less than clozapine and olanzapine (Casey et al., 2004). Olanzapine (Koller & Doraiswamy, 2002) and clozapine (Sernyak et al., 2003) are associated with diabetes mellitus. Some of the atypical antipsychotics, such as olanzapine, can cause sedation (Meltzer et al., 1998). All of the atypical antipsychotics can cause orthostatic hypotension via antagonism of alpha 1 adrenergic receptors (Meltzer et al., 1998). Finally, quetiapine, ziprasidone, and other atypical antipsychotics may cause some prolongation of cardiac conduction intervals, increasing the risk of cardiac arrhythmias (Breier, 2001; Czekalla et al., 2001; Gupta et al., 2003). Table 11.4 summarizes the adverse effect associated with a typical (second-generation) antipsychotics.

TABLE 11.4 Adverse Effects Associated with Atypical Antipsychotics

Fewer extrapyramidal effects, including tardive dyskinesia, compared to typical antipsychotics

Less elevation of prolactin—risperidone, however, can elevate prolactin

Clozapine causes agranulocytosis

Seizures, particularly clozapine

Excessive salivation, particularly clozapine

Elevated heart rate

Anticholinergic effects, particularly clozapine and olanzapine

Weight gain, particularly with olanzapine and clozapine; may be less with quetiapine and aripiprazole

Elevated triglycerides

Possible induction of diabetes

Orthostatic hypotension

Prolongation of cardiac conduction intervals, especially ziprasidone

Uses

Because of their efficacy in controlling the symptoms of schizophrenia and their propensity to cause many fewer extrapyramidal adverse effects, such as tardive dyskinesia, the atypical antipsychotics have to a great extent supplanted the older typical antipsychotics, becoming the treatment of first choice in many clinical situations that were once dominated by the typical antipsychotics (Kinon et al., 2001). These ideas have not been unchallenged, however. In a published meta-analysis, it was suggested that the typical antipsychotics haloperidol and chlorpromazine in low doses were approximately equally effective as the newer atypical antipsychotics, although they did have a tendency to cause somewhat more extrapyramidal effects than did the newer atypical antipsychotics (Geddes et al., 2000). So while the atypical antipsychotics have been hailed as a major step in the treatment of schizophrenia (Breier, 2001), the full import and limitations of their use remains to be fully elucidated.

Schizophrenia. In many cases of schizophrenia, the atypical antipsychotics are now often considered first-line treatment, both acutely and chronically, although not all authors agree (Davis et al., 2003). Because of its potential to induce agranulocytosis, clozapine is reserved for treatment-refractory schizophrenia (Kane et al., 2003), in which cases it can be effective. In fact, approximately 30 to 60 percent of people whose schizophrenia is unresponsive to typical antipsychotics show some positive response to clozapine (Buchanan, 1995; Iqbal et al., 2003). Clozapine may also have an advantage in cases of schizophrenia complicated by suicide ideation (Kane et al., 2003). On the other hand, only limited evidence suggests that the atypical antipsychotics are better for the positive symptoms of schizophrenia than the typical antipsychotics. A meta-analysis comparing atypical antipsychotics with typical antipsychotics, for example, found no convincing evidence that atypical antipsychotics are more effective or better tolerated in the treatment of schizophrenia than are typical antipsychotics (Geddes et al., 2000). A more recent meta-analysis, however, found some superiority for risperidone and olanzapine over typical antipsychotics, particularly for the negative symptoms of schizophrenia but also for positive symptoms (Davis et al., 2003). Moreover, compared to typical antipsychotics, the atypical antipsychotics risperidone and olanzapine are associated with fewer rehospitalizations among people hospitalized for schizophrenia (Rabinowitz, 2001). Overall, with the exception of clozapine, the atypical antipsychotics appear equally efficacious among themselves for the treatment of schizophrenia (Tandon & Jibson, 2003).

Unlike the typical antipsychotics, which are helpful for primarily the positive symptoms of schizophrenia, the atypical agents may have a therapeutic effect on negative symptoms (Csernansky, 2003; Möller, 2003). Affective and cognitive symptoms also complicate the course of schizophrenia, and some preliminary evidence suggests that the atypical antipsychotics may have an advantage of the typical antipsychotics in the treatment of these often highly debilitating disturbances of mood and cognition (Tandon & Jibson, 2003), although this assertion does require additional research. Risperidone is available in a long-acting injectable form (Marder et al., 2003) that can be given every two weeks (Marder et al., 2003).

Other Psychoses.   The atypical antipsychotics are used to treat psychosis for related to conditions other than schizophrenia. For example, they can be used in the treatment of the delusions and hallucinations that can occur during the course of Alzheimer's disease (Bassiony & Lyketsos, 2003).

Bipolar Disorder.   Increasingly, the atypical antipsychotics are being used to treat bipolar disorder (Möller & Nasrallah, 2003). It is unclear which of the atypical antipsychotic medications is most effective in bipolar disorder, but available evidence suggests that all may have similar efficacy (Möller & Nasrallah, 2003). In a placebo-controlled trial, olanzapine was found to be superior to placebo in the treatment of bipolar depression (Tohen et al., 2003).

Schizoaffective Disorder.   While mood stabilizers are sometimes used for the treatment of schizoaffective disorder, clozapine may be effective in the treatment of schizoaffective disorder, for both cases characterized by affective symptoms and those characterized by psychotic features (Baethge, 2003).

Major Depression with Psychotic Features.   In cases of major depression with psychotic features that are treated with antipsychotics and antidepressants,

TABLE 11.5   Uses of Atypical Antipsychotics

Schizophrenia

Bipolar disorder

Schizoaffective disorder

Major depression with psychotic features

Schizotypal personality disorder

Behavioral disturbances associated with dementia

Aggression

Tourette's syndrome

an atypical antipsychotic may be an appropriate measure in conjunction with an antidepressant (Wheeler Vega et al., 2003).

Schizotypal Personality Disorder.   According to one randomized, placebo-controlled study, low-dose risperidone resulted in statistically significant improvement in schizotypal personality disorder (Koenigsberg et al., 2003).

Behavioral Disturbances Associated with Dementia.   Atypical antipsychotics are frequently used to treat the numerous behavioral disturbances, such as agitation and aggression, psychosis (Street et al., 2000), and anxiety (Mintzer et al., 2001), that may accompany dementia.

Aggression.   The atypical antipsychotics also are used for the treatment of aggression associated with mental retardation and brain trauma (Fava, 1997). In people with psychosis, clozapine may have specific anti-aggressive properties (Adityanjee & Schulz, 2002). Quetiapine was associated with reduced aggression and irritability in an open trial of people with antisocial personality disorder in a forensic setting (Adityanjee & Schulz, 2002).

Tourette's Syndrome.   Like haloperidol and pimozide, atypical antipsychotics suppress tics in Tourette's syndrome (Muller-Vahl, 2002). For example, a placebo-controlled, eight-week trial found risperidone effective in reducing tics in Tourette's disorder (Scahill et al., 2003). Table 11.5 shows potential uses of the atypical (second-generation) antipsychotic.

DRUGS USED IN THE TREATMENT OF EXTRAPYRAMIDAL EFFECTS

Extrapyramidal symptoms all too often complicate the use of particularly the typical antipsychotic medications (Casey, 1997). Even some atypical antipsychotics can produce extrapyramidal effects, particularly in high doses (Marder & Meibach, 1994). Because extrapyramidal effects can lead to suffering and treatment non-compliance (Gerlach, 2002), several different types of medications have been recruited to combat these adverse effects.

The control of movement in the extrapyramidal system appears to involve several neurotransmitters, including dopamine, acetylcholine, and GABA. Dopamine and acetylcholine seem to work in a kind of balance, with blockade of dopamine, by a typical antipsychotic, for instance, resulting in a relative overdrive of acetylcholine (Glazer, 2000). This imbalance theoretically may be corrected in one of two ways: (1) addition of a dopamine agonist to restore dopamine transmission or (2) an acetylcholine antagonist or anticholinergic medication to lessen the acetylcholine overdrive. Both approaches have been used in the treatment of antipsychotic-induced extrapyramidal effects.

Anticholinergic Drugs

This group of drugs includes benztropine (Cogentin), trihexiphenidyl (Artane), procyclidine (Kemadrine), and biperidin (Akineton). All work by blocking the muscarinic subtype of acetylcholine receptors (Larson et al., 1991). Muscarinic subtype 1 receptors are found more in the brain than muscarinic subtype 2 receptors, which are in the heart. Biperidin may be more selective for muscarinic subtype 1 receptors and thus more likely to avoid anticholinergic adverse cardiac effects (Larson et al., 1994), such as an elevated heart rate. Other adverse effects from these drugs are what would be expected from the blockade of acetylcholine receptors and include dry mouth, decreased sweating (Goff et al., 1991), and constipation (Marder et al., 2003). In some cases, confusion and memory deficits can occur (Adler et al., 1993). All anticholinergic drugs can produce euphoria and may be abused, with trihexiphenidyl possibly carrying more abuse potential than other anticholinergic drugs (Buhrich et al., 2000). A withdrawal syndrome characterized by sweating, nausea, and vomiting (Marder et al., 2003) can occur when anticholinergic drugs are discontinued abruptly (Marder et al., 2003).

Used in some cases to treat Parkinson's disease (Brocks, 1999), the anticholinergics are used to alleviate extrapyramidal effects from typical and in some cases atypical antipsychotics (Holloman & Marder, 1997). Akathisia may respond only partially to anticholinergic agents (Tonda & Guthrie, 1994). Based on the available evidence, it is unclear whether the anticholinergic agents are effective in the treatment of tardive dyskinesia (Soares & McGrath, 2000).

In addition its use in some insomnia (Kudo & Kurihara, 1990) and Parkinson's disease (Carlson et al., 2000), the antihistamine diphenhydramine (Benadryl) is also used to treat extrapyramidal side effects and may have some efficacy in akathisia (Friedman & Wagner, 1987). Its mechanism of action in relieving extrapyramidal symptoms may be related to its antagonism of histamine receptors (van't Groenewout et al., 1995), as well as mechanisms that appear independent of histamine (Carlson et al., 2000).

TABLE 11.6   Drugs Used in the Treatment of Extrapyramidal Effects

1. Anticholinergic Drugs
    a. benztropine (Cogentin)
    b. trihexiphenidyl (Artane)
    c. procyclidine (Kemadrine)
    d. biperidin (Akineton)
2. Amantadine (Symmetrel)

Amantadine (Symmetrel)

Amantadine is an antiviral drug that is also used in the treatment of Parkinson's diseases, both alone and in combination with other drugs (Deleu et al., 2002). In addition to its use in Parkinson's disease, amantadine can alleviate extrapyramidal symptoms caused by antipsychotics (Holloman & Marder, 1997). Its mechanism of action not entirely understood, amantadine may increase dopamine transmission and cause weak inhibition of acetylcholine muscarinic receptors (Deleu et al., 2002), both of which effects may diminish extrapyramidal effects from antipsychotic-induced dopamine 2 antagonism. Amantadine undergoes comparatively little metabolism and most of it is eliminated via the kidneys (Deleu et al., 2002). In general amantadine is well tolerated, although its use can be associated with confusion, nightmares, and ankle swelling (Deleu et al., 2002). Table 11.6 lists the drugs that may be used in the treatment of extrapyramidal effects.

SUMMARY

The antipsychotic drugs are composed of two main subtypes: the older, typical, first-generation antipsychotics and the newer, atypical, second-generation antipsychotics. While effective for positive symptoms of schizophrenia, the typical antipsychotics are associated with extrapyramidal effects, including tardive dyskinesia, factors that have limited the use of these drugs. Some of the atypical antipsychotics appear to offer some improved treatment of schizophrenia's negative symptoms compared to the typical antipsychotics. Additionally, the atypical antipsychotics seem to result in much fewer extrapyramidal symptoms and tardive dyskinesia. While this does represent a significant improvement over the older typical antipsychotics, the atypical antipsychotics have serious adverse effects of their own, such as weight gain, elevated triglycerides, and increased risk of developing diabetes. The anticholinergics and other drugs used to treat the extrapyramidal adverse effects induced by antipsychotics continue to be used, particularly in conjunction with typical antipsychotics.

STUDY QUESTIONS

1. List several conditions in addition to schizophrenia for which both typical and atypical antipsychotics may be useful.
2. What are the primary differences between the typical and atypical antipsychotics?
3. Describe the putative mechanisms of action of the atypical antipsychotics.
4. Discuss several forms of extrapyramidal symptoms and how they are thought to be generated by the typical antipsychotic medications.
5. What is the presumed mechanism of action of the anticholinergic drugs?
6. For which patients would ziprasidone be contraindicated? Why?
7. How does the mechanism of action of aripiprazole differ from that of olanzapine?
8. What are potential adverse effects from atypical antipsychotics?
9. Why is clozapine reserved for cases of schizophrenia that have not responded to other antipsychotics?

REFERENCES

Adityanjee, Schulz SC (2002): Clinical use of quetiapine in disease states other than schizophrenia. Journal of Schizophrenia 63 (supplement 13):32–38.

Adler LA, Peselow E, Rosenthal M, Angrist B (1993): A controlled comparison of the effects of propranolol, benztropine, and placebo on akithisia: An interim analysis. Psychopharmacology Bulletin 29:283–286.

Advokat CD, Mayville EA, Matson JL (2000): Side effect profiles of typical antipsychotics, typical antipsychotics, or no psychotropic medications in persons with mental retardation. Research in Developmental Disabilities 21:75–84.

Alphs LD, Campbell BJ (2002): Clozapine: Treatment of mood symptoms. Psychiatric Annals 32:722–729.

Andreasen NC, Black DW (1991): *Introductory Textbook of Psychiatry*. Washington, DC: American Psychiatric Press.

Atmaca M, Kuloglu M, Tezcan E, Ustundag B (2003): Serum leptin and triglyceride levels in patients on treatment with atypical antipsychotics. Journal of Clinical Psychiatry 64:598–604.

Baethge C (2003): Long-term treatment of schizoaffective disorder: Review and recommendations. Pharmacopsychiatry 36:45–56.

Bai YM, Yu SC, Lin CC (2003): Risperidone for severe tardive dyskinesia: A 12-week randomized, double-blind, placebo-controlled study. Journal of Clinical Psychiatry 64:1342–1348.

Balant-Gorgia AE, Balant L (1987): Antipsychotic drugs. Clinical pharmacokinetics of potential candidates for plasma concentration monitoring. Clinical Pharmacokinetics 13:65–90.

Barnes TR, Curson DA (1994): Long-term depot antipsychotics. A risk-benefit assessment. Drug Safety 10:464–479.

Bassiony MM, Lyketsos CG (2003): Delusions and hallucinations in Alzheimer's disease: Review of the brain decade. Psychosomatics 44:388–401.

Bennett MR (1998): Monoaminergic synapses and schizophrenia: 45 years of neuroleptics. Journal of Psychopharmacology 12:289–304.

Bowles TM, Levin GM (2003): Aripiprazole: A new atypical antipsychotic drug. Annals of Pharmacotherapy 37:687–694.

Breier A (2001): A new era in the pharmacotherapy of psychotic disorders. Journal of Clinical Psychiatry 62 (supplement 2):3–5.

Brocks DR (1999): Anticholinergic drugs used in Parkinson's disease: An overlooked class of drugs from a pharmacokinetic perspective. Journal of Pharmacy & Pharmaceutical Sciences 2:39–46.

Buchanan RW (1995): Clozapine: Efficacy and safety. Schizophrenia Bulletin 21:579–591.

Buck JA, Sprague RL (1989): Psychotropic medication of mentally retarded residents in community long-term care facilities. American Journal of Mental Retardation 93:618–623.

Buckley PF (2003): Aripiprazole: Efficacy and tolerability profile of a novel-acting atypical antipsychotic. Drugs Today (Barcelona) 39:145–151.

Buhrich N, Weller A, Kevans P (2000): Misuse of anticholinergic drugs by people with serious mental illness. Psychiatric Services 51:928–929.

Burris KD, Molski TF, Xu C, Ryan E, Torrori K, Kikuchi T, Yocca FD, Molinoff PB (2002): Aripiprazole, a novel antipsychotic, is a high-affinity partial agonist at human dopamine D_2 receptors. The Journal of Pharmacology and Experimental Therapeutics 302:381–389.

Caley CF, Cooper CK (2002): Ziprasidone: The fifth atypical antipsychotic. Annals of Pharmacotherapy 36:839–851.

Carlson BB, Trevitt JT, Salamone JD (2000): Effects of H1 antagonism on cholinomimetic-induced tremulous jaw movements: Studies of diphenhydramine, doxepin, and mepyramine. Pharmacology, Biochemistry, and Behavior 65:683–689.

Casey DE (1988): Affective disorders and tardive dyskinesia. Encephale 14:221–226.

Casey DE (1997): The relationship of pharmacology to side effects. Journal of Clinical Psychiatry 58 (supplement 10):55–62.

Casey DE, Haupt DW, Newcomer JW, Henderson DC, Sernyak MJ, Davidson M, Lindenmayer J-P, Manoukian SV, Banerji MA, Lebovitz HE, Hennekens CH (2004): Antipsychotic-induced weight gain and metabolic syndrome abnormalities: Implications for increased mortality in patients with schizophrenia. Journal of Clinical Psychiatry 65 (supplement 7):4–18.

Chandran GJ, Mikler JR, Keegan DL (2003): Neuroleptic malignant syndrome: Case report and discussion. Canadian Medical Association Journal 169:439–442.

Conley RR, Kelly DL (2002): Current status of antipsychotic drug treatment. Current Drug Targets. CNS and Neurological Disorders 1:123–128.

Csernansky JG (2003): Treatment of schizophrenia: Preventing the progression of disease. Psychiatric Clinics of North America 26:367–379.

Czekalla J, Kollack-Walker S, Beasley CM Jr. (2001): Cardiac safety parameters of olanzapine: Comparison with other atypical and typical antipsychotics. Journal of Clinical Psychiatry 62 (supplement 2):35–40.

Davis JM, Chen N, Glick ID (2003): A meta-analysis of the efficacy of second-generation antipsychotics. Archives of General Psychiatry 60:553–564.

Deleu D, Northway MG, Hanssens Y (2002): Clinical pharmacokinetic and pharmacodynamic properties of drugs used in the treatment of Parkinson's disease. Clinical Pharmacokinetics 41:261–309.

Deutch AY, Moghaddam B, Innis RB, Krystal JH, Aghajanian GK, Bunney BS, Charney DS (1991): Mechanisms of action of atypical antipsychotic drugs. Implications for novel therapeutic strategies for schizophrenia. Schizophrenia Research 4:121–156.

Devinsky O, Honigfeld G, Patin J (1991): Clozapine-related seizures. Neurology 41:369–371.

Fava M (1997): Psychopharmacologic treatment of pathologic aggression. Psychiatric Clinics of North America 20:427–451.

Fischel T, Hermesh H, Aizenberg D, Zemishlany Z, Munitz H, Benjamini Y, Weizman A (2001): Cyproheptadine versus propranolol for the treatment of acute neuroleptic-induced akathisia: A comparative double-blind study. Journal of Clinical Psychopharmacology 21:612–615.

Friedman JH, Wagner RL (1987): Akathisia: The syndrome of motor restlessness. American Family Physician 35:145–149.

Geddes J, Freemantle N, Harrison P, Bebbington P (2000): Atypical antipsychotics in the treatment of schizophrenia. British Medical Journal 321:1371–1376.

Gefvert O, Bergstrom M, Langstrom B, Lundberg T, Lindstrom L, Yates R (1998): Time course of central nervous dopamine-D2 and 5-HT2 receptor blockade and plasma drug concentrations after discontinuation of quetiapine (Seroquel) in patients with schizophrenia. Psychopharmacology 135:119–126.

Gerlach J (2002): Improving outcome in schizophrenia: The potential importance of EPS and neuroleptic dysphoria. Annals of Clinical Psychiatry 14:47–57.

Glazer WM (2000): Extrapyramidal side effects, tardive dyskinesia, and the concept of atypicality. Journal of Clinical Psychiatry 61 (supplement 3):16–21.

Glazer WM, Kane JM (1992): Depot neuroleptic therapy: An underutilized treatment option. Journal of Clinical Psychiatry 53:426–433.

Goff DC, Arana GW, Greenblatt DJ, Dupont R, Ornsteen M, Harmatz JS, Shader RI (1991): The effect of benztropine on haloperidol-induced dystonia, clinical efficacy and pharmacokinetics: a prospective, double-blind trial. Journal of Clinical Psychopharmacology 11: 106–112.

Goff DC, Hennen J, Lyoo IK, Tsai G, Wald LL, Evins AE, Yurgelun-Todd DA, Renshaw PF (2002): Modulation of brain and serum glutamatergic concentrations following a switch from conventional neuroleptics to olanzapine. Biological Psychiatry 51:493–497.

Granger B (1999): [The discovery of haloperidol]. Encephale 25:59–66.

Gupta S, Nienhaus K, Shah SA (2003): Quetiapine and QTc issues: A case report. Journal of Clinical Psychiatry 64 (letter):612–613.

Haddad PM, Wieck A (2004): Antipsychotic-induced hyperprolactinaemia: Mechanisms, clinical features and management. Drugs 64:2291–2314.

Hassin-Baer S, Sirota P, Korczyn AD, Treves TA, Epstein B, Shabtai H, Martin T, Litvinjuk Y, Giladi N (2001): Clinical characteristics of neuroleptic-induced parkinsonism. Journal of Neural Transmission 108:1299–1308.

Heel RC, Brogden RN, Speight TM, Avery GS (1978): Loxapine: A review of its pharmacological properties and therapeutic efficacy as an antipsychotic agent. Drugs 15:198–217.

Heresco-Levy U (2003): Glutamatergic neurotransmission modulation and the mechanism of antipsychotic atypicality. Progress in Neuropsychopharmacology & Biological Psychiatry 27:1113–1123.

Hippius H (1999): A historical perspective of clozapine. Journal of Clinical Psychiatry 60 (supplement 12):22–23.

Holloman LC, Marder SR (1997): Management of acute extrapyramidal effects induced by antipsychotic drugs. American Journal of Health-System Pharmacy 54:2461–2477.

Ichikawa J, Ishii H, Bonaccorso S, Fowler WL, O'Laughlin IA, Meltzer HY (2001): 5-HT(2A) and D(2) receptor blockade increases cortical DA release via 5-HT(1A) receptor activation: A possible mechanism of atypical antipsychotic-induced cortical dopamine release. Journal of Neurochemistry 76:1521–1531.

Iqbal MM, Rahman A, Husain Z, Mahmud SZ, Ryan WG, Feldman JM (2003): Clozapine: A clinical review of adverse effects and management. Annals of Clinical Psychiatry 15:33–48.

Itil TM, Wadud A (1975): Treatment of human aggression with major tranquilizers, antidepressants, and newer psychotropic drugs. Journal of Nervous and Mental Disease 160:83–99.

Jimenez-Jimenez FJ, Garcia-Ruiz PJ (2001): Pharmacological options for the treatment of Tourette's disorder. Drugs 61:2207–2220.

Kane JM, Leucht S, Carpenter D, Docherty JP (2003): Introduction: Methods, commentary, and summary. Journal of Clinical Psychiatry 64 (supplement 12):1–100.

Kane JM, Woerner M, Lieberman J (1998): Tardive dyskinesia: Prevalence, incidence, and risk factors. Journal of Clinical Psychopharmacology 8 (supplement 4):52S–56S.

Kapur S, Mamo D (2003): Half a century of antipsychotics and still a central role for dopamine D (2) receptors. Progress in Neuropsychopharmacology & Biological Psychiatry 27:1081–1090.

Kapur S, Seeman (2001): Does fast dissociation from the dopamine D_2 receptor explain the action of atypical antipsychotics? A new hypothesis. American Journal of Psychiatry 158:360–369.

Kapur S, Zipursky R, Remington G, Jones C, McKay G, Houles S (1997): PET evidence that loxapine is an equipotent blocker of $5-HT_2$ and D_2 receptors: Implications for the treatment of schizophrenia. American Journal of Psychiatry 154:1525–1529.

Keck PE, McElroy SL (2002): Clinical pharmacodynamics and pharmacokinetics of antimanic and mood-stabilizing medications. Journal of Clinical Psychiatry 63 (supplement 4):3–11.

Kinon BJ, Roychowdhury SM, Milton DR, Hill AL (2001): Effective resolution with olanzapine of acute presentation of behavioral agitation and positive psychotic symptoms in schizophrenia. Journal of Clinical Psychiatry 62 (supplement 2):17–21.

Koenigsberg HW, Reynolds D, Goodman M, New AS, Mitropoulou V, Trestman RL, Silverman J, Siever LJ (2003): Risperidone in the treatment of schizotypal personality disorder. Journal of Clinical Psychiatry 64:628–634.

Koller EA, Doraiswamy PM (2002): Olanzapine-associated diabetes mellitus. Pharmacotherapy 22:841–852.

Kossof EH, Singer HS (2001): Tourette syndrome: Clinical characteristics and current management strategies. Paediatric Drugs 3:355–363.

Kudo Y, Kurihara M (1990): Clinical evaluation of diphenhydramine hydrochloride for the treatment of insomnia in psychiatric patients: Double-blind study. Journal of Clinical Pharmacology 30:1041–1048.

Kulkarni SK, Naidu PS (2001): Tardive dyskinesia: An update. Drugs of Today 37:97–119.

Kulkarni SK, Naidu PS (2003): Pathophysiology and drug therapy of tardive dyskinesia: Current concepts and future perspectives. Drugs of Today 39:19–49.

Lappa A, Podesta M, Capelli O, Castagna A, Di Placido G, Alampi D, Semerara F (2002): Successful treatment of a complicated case of neuroleptic malignant syndrome. Intensive Care Medicine 28:976–977.

Larson EW, Pfenning MA, Richelson E (1991): Selectivity of antimuscarinic compounds for muscarinic receptors of human brain and heart. Psychopharmacology 103:162–165.

Lawrence M, Barclay DM III (1998): Stuttering: A brief review. American Family Physician 57:2175–2178.

Leucht S, Pitschel-Walz G, Engel RR, Kissling W (2002): Amisulpride, an unusual "atypical" antipsychotic: A meta-analysis of randomized controlled trials. American Journal of Psychiatry 159:180–190.

Lieberman JA, Perkins DO (2002): Quetiapine fumarate: A 5-year update. Journal of Clinical Psychiatry 63 (supplement 13):3–4.

Love RC (1996): Novel versus conventional antipsychotic drugs. Pharmacotherapy 16:6S–10S.

Maguire GA (2002): Prolactin elevation with antipsychotic medications: Mechanisms of action and clinical consequences. Journal of Clinical Psychiatry 63 (supplement 4):56–62.

Marder SR, Conley R, Ereshefsky L, Kane JM, Turner MS (2003): Dosing and switching strategies for long-acting risperidone. Journal of Clinical Psychiatry 64 (supplement 16):41–46.

Marder SR, Meibach RC (1994): Risperidone in the treatment of schizophrenia. American Journal of Psychiatry 151:825–835.

Meltzer HY, Casey DE, Garver DL, Lasagna L, Marder SR, Masand PS, Miller D, Pickar D, Tandon R (Collaborative Working Group on Clinical Trial Evaluations) (1998): Adverse effects of the atypical antipsychotics. Journal of Clinical Psychiatry 59 (supplement 12):17–22.

Meyer MC, Baldessarini RJ, Goff DC, Centorrino F (1996): Clinically significant interactions of psychotropic agents with antipsychotic drugs. Drug Safety 15:333–346.

Miller DD (2000): Review and management of clozapine side effects. Journal of Clinical Psychiatry 61 (supplement 8):14–17.

Mintzer J, Faison W, Street JS, Sutton VK, Breier A (2001): Olanzapine in the treatment of anxiety symptoms due to Alzheimer's disease: A post hoc analysis. International Journal of Geriatric Psychiatry 16 (supplement 1):S71–S77.

Möller HJ (2003): Management of the negative symptoms of schizophrenia: New treatment options. CNS Drugs 17:793–823.

Möller HJ, Nasrallah HA (2003): Treatment of bipolar disorder. Journal of Clinical Psychiatry 64 (supplement 6):9–17.

Muller-Vahl KR (2002): The treatment of Tourette's syndrome: Current opinions. Expert Opinion on Pharmacotherapy 3:899–914.

Najib J (1999): Tardive dyskinesia: A review and current treatment options. American Journal of Therapeutics 6:51–60.

Nemeroff CB, Kinkead B, Goldstein J (2002): Quetiapine: Preclinical studies, pharmacokinetics, drug interactions, and dosing. Journal of Clinical Psychiatry 63 (supplement 13):5–11.

Newcomer JW (2001): Metabolic disturbances associated with antipsychotic use. Journal of Clinical Psychiatry 62 (supplement 27):3–4.

Osser DN, Najarian DM, Dufresne RL (1999): Olanzapine increases weight and serum triglyceride levels. Journal of Clinical Psychiatry 60:767–770.

Owen RR Jr., Cole JO (1989): Molindone hydrochloride: A review of laboratory and clinical findings. Journal of Clinical Psychopharmacology 9:268–276.

Pani L (2002): Clinical implications of dopamine research in schizophrenia. Current Medical Research and Opinion 18 (supplement 3):s3–7.

Prior TI, Chue PS, Tibbo P, Baker GB (1999): Drug metabolism and atypical antipsychotics. European Neuropsychopharmacology 9:301–309.

Rabinowitz J, Lichtenberg P, Kaplan Z, Mark M, Nahon D, Davidson M (2001): Rehospitalization rates of chronically ill schizophrenic patients discharged on a regimen of risperidone, olanzapine, or conventional antipsychotics. American Journal of Psychiatry 158:266–269.

Reeves RR, Torres RA, Liberto V, Hart RH (2002): Atypical neuroleptic malignant syndrome associated with olanzapine. Pharmacotherapy 22:641–644.

Remington G (2003): Understanding antipsychotic "atypicality": A clinical and pharmacological moving target. Journal of Psychiatry & Neuroscience 28:275–284.

Sakkas P, Davis JM, Janicak PG, Wang ZY (1991): Drug treatment of neuroleptic malignant syndrome. Psychopharmacology Bulletin 27:381–384.

Scahill L, Leckman JF, Schultz RT, Katsovich L, Peterson BS (2003): A placebo-controlled trial of risperidone in Tourette syndrome. Neurology 60:1130–1135.

Schwartz JT, Brotman AW (1992): A clinical guide to antipsychotic drugs. Drugs 44:981–992.

Sechter D, Peuskens J, Fleurot O, Rein W, Lecrubier Y (2002): Amisulpride vs. risperidone in chronic schizophrenia: Results of a 6-month double-blind study. Neuropsychopharmacology 27:1071–1081.

Seeman P, Lee T, Chau-Wong M, Wong K (1976): Antipsychotic drug doses and neuroleptic/dopamine receptors. Nature 261:717–719.

Sernyak MJ, Gulanski B, Leslie DL, Rosenheck R (2003): Undiagnosed hyperglycemia in clozapine-treated patients with schizophrenia. Journal of Clinical Psychiatry 64:605–608.

Shale JH, Shale CM, Mastin WD (2003): A review of the safety and efficacy of droperidol for the rapid sedation of severely agitated and violent patients. Journal of Clinical Psychiatry 64:500–505.

Shehata IA, El-Ashry SM, El-Sherbeny MA, El-Sherbeny DT, Belal F (2000): Fluorimetric determination of some thioxanthene derivatives in dosage forms and biological fluids. Journal of Pharmaceutical and Biomedical Analysis 22:729–737.

Skorin L Jr., Onofrey BE, DeWitt JD (1987): Phenothiazine-induced oculogyric crisis. Journal of the American Optometric Association 58:316–318.

Soares KV, McGrath JJ (1999): The treatment of tardive dyskinesia—a systematic review and meta-analysis. Schizophrenia Research 39:1–16.

Soares KV, McGrath JJ (2000): Anticholinergic medication for neuroleptic-induced tardive dyskinesia. Cochrane Database of Systematic Reviews CD000204.

Street JS, Clark WS, Gannon KS, Cummings JL, Bymaster FP, Tamura RN, Mitan SJ, Kadam DL, Sanger TM, Feldman PD, Tollefson GD, Breier A (2000): Olanzapine treatment of psychotic and behavioral symptoms in patients with Alzheimer disease in nursing care facilities: A double-blind, randomized, placebo-controlled trial. Archives of General Psychiatry 57:968–976.

Sundram S, Joyce PR, Kennedy MA (2003): Schizophrenia and bipolar affective disorder: Perspectives for the development of therapeutics. Current Molecular Medicine 3:393–407.

Tandon R, Jibson MD (2003): Efficacy of newer generation antipsychotics in the treatment of schizophrenia. Psychoneuroendocrinology 28 (supplement 1):9–26.

Tarazi FI, Baldessarini RJ, Kula NS, Zhang K (2003): Long-term effects of olanzapine, risperidone, and quetiapine on ionotropic glutamate receptor types: Implications for antipsychotic drug treatment. Journal of Pharmacology and Experimental Therapeutics 306:1145–1151.

Tauscher J, Jones C, Remington G, Zipursky RB, Kapur S (2002): Significant dissociation of brain and plasma kinetics with antipsychotics. Molecular Psychiatry 7:317–321.

Tauscher-Wisniewski S, Kapur S, Tauscher J, Jones C, Daskalakis ZJ, Papatheodorou G, Epstein I, Christensen BK, Zipursky RB (2002): Quetiapine: An effective antipsychotic in first-episode schizophrenia despite only transiently high dopamine-2 receptor blockade. Journal of Clinical Psychiatry 63:992–997.

Tempier RP, Pawliuk NH (2003): Conventional, atypical, and combination antipsychotic prescriptions: A 2-year comparison. Journal of Clinical Psychiatry 64:673–679.

Tohen M, Vieta E, Calabrese J, Ketter TA, Sachs G, Bowden C, Mitchell PB, Centorrino F, Risser R, Baker RW, Evans AR, Beymer K, Dubé S, Tollefson GD, Breier A (2003): Efficacy of olanzapine and olanzapine-fluoxetine combination in the treatment of bipolar I depression. Archives of General Psychiatry 60:1079–1088.

Tonda ME, Guthrie SK (1994): Treatment of acute neuroleptic-induced movement disorders. Pharmacotherapy 14:543–560.

Toth P, Frankenberg FR (1994): Clozapine and seizures: A review. Canadian Journal of Psychiatry 39:236–238.

van't Groenewout JL, Stone MR, Vo VN, Truong DD, Matsumoto RR (1995): Evidence for the involvement of histamine in the antidystonic effects of diphenhydramine. Experimental Neurology 134:253–260.

Weiden PJ (2003): Acute treatment of schizophrenia, pp. 1381–1382. In PJ Weiden, chair. New Developments in Antipsychotic Therapy [Academic Highlights]. Journal of Clinical Psychiatry 64:1379–1390.

Wheeler Vega JA, Mortimer AM, Tyson PJ (2000): Somatic treatment of psychotic depression: Review and recommendations for practice. Journal of Clinical Psychopharmacology 20:504–519.

Wilson WH, Claussen AM (1994): Seizures associated with clozapine treatment in a state hospital. Journal of Clinical Psychiatry 55:184–188.

Worrel JA, Marken PA, Beckman SE, Ruehter VL (2000): Atypical antipsychotic agents: A critical review. American Journal of Health-System Pharmacy 57:238–255.

Yatham LN (2002): The role of novel antipsychotics in bipolar disorders. Journal of Clinical Psychiatry 63 (supplement 3):10–14.

CHAPTER TWELVE

THE NEUROBIOLOGY AND TREATMENT OF DEMENTIA

Many different diseases are included in the dementia syndromes, each with its own neurobiological explanation and treatment approach. The most common type of dementia is Alzheimer's disease, which accounts for approximately 50 to 75 percent of all dementia and is characterized, pathologically, by beta-amyloid deposits and neurofibrillary tangles.

Vascular dementia accounts for approximately 10 to 15 percent of dementia cases. The diagnosis of vascular dementia depends upon the occurrence of both cognitive deficits and vascular disease, which may take the form of strokes or other cerebrovascular disease. Perhaps even more common than vascular dementia alone is the combination of vascular dementia with another type of dementia, particularly Alzheimer's dementia.

Dementia with Lewy bodies also accounts for approximately 10 to 15 percent of all dementia. Lewy bodies are inclusions seen in the cytoplasm of certain neurons in patients who have Parkinson-like diseases. Lewy-body dementia is characterized by fluctuating levels of consciousness, with patients alternating between periods of confusion and relative lucidity. Other features of this dementia are visual hallucinations and motor disorders, such as gait disturbances and rigidity.

Frontal-temporal dementia comprises approximately 5 percent of dementia and may present somewhat earlier in life than does Alzheimer's dementia. Findings of frontal-lobe dysfunction, such as difficulties with motivation, planning, and socially appropriate behavior, are predominant early in the illness, with memory deficits becoming more pronounced later in the course of the disease.

Numerous other causes of dementia exist and, although they are rare, must be considered in the evaluation of cognitive and behavioral changes. Medical conditions like thyroid disease and medications, both prescription and non-prescription, can worsen mental status, particularly in elderly patients. Normal-pressure hydrocephalus is another rare and sometimes partially reversible cause of dementia. Creutzfeldt-Jacob disease is still another rare type of dementia that presents as an aggressive and rapidly fatal disease, often resulting in death in as little as a few months after its initial presentation.

Most cases of dementia are irreversible, and existing treatment can do little more than ameliorate the cognitive and behavioral symptoms associated with the dementia. The first step in the treatment of dementia is the identification of any reversible factors that are causing or contributing to the dementia. Antipsychotics, antidepressants, anxiolytics, and mood stabilizers, for example, are used to treat the delusions, hallucinations, agitations, and aggression that accompany dementia. Yet, they do not affect the core cognitive deterioration. In an attempt to improve or stabilize the cognitive deficits of dementia, drugs have been developed that increase the amount of synaptic acetylcholine. These so-called cognitive enhancers have shown some efficacy in slowing the course of Alzheimer's dementia, especially if treatment is initiated early in the course of dementia. Other drugs, with different mechanisms of action, are also being investigated as to their ability to prevent, inhibit, or halt dementia, including memantine, an N-methyl-D-aspartate antagonist.

As the population of the United States and other developed countries ages, the incidence of age-related diseases is expected to rise considerably (Sleegers & van Duijn, 2001). Furthermore, because they primarily affect the elderly, the dementias are anticipated to become more widely prevalent in the next fifty years (Friedman, 2002). This scenario is of concern because currently approximately 10 percent of the population between ages 70 and 80, and 30 percent of those over age 80, already have some form of dementia (Morgan et al., 1993). While Alzheimer's disease is the most common dementia (Kasckow, 2002) and accounts for approximately 50 to 75 percent of all cases of dementia (Ott et al., 1995), many other diseases also contribute to the total burden of dementia. This burden, unlike the burden of many other diseases, often involves an impact on its victims' very personality, transforming intelligent and active people into empty shells of their former selves.

The diagnosis of dementia is primarily clinical (Wells & Whitehouse, 1996). There are no laboratory tests or brain imaging scans that definitively rule in or rule out the diagnosis. Although laboratory evaluations, including brain-imaging scanning, are utilized extensively in the evaluation and diagnosis of dementia (Kantarci & Jack, 2003), the diagnosis of dementia rests primarily on the evaluation of presenting signs and symptoms, particularly those related to cognitive and memory deficits. As separate diseases, each type of dementia is accompanied by its own neurobiology and course. Due to the anticipated increase in the prevalence of dementia and its devastating effects, the neurobiology of dementia is receiving increased attention in the hope of a better understanding of how to prevent these diseases from occurring and to aid in the development of more effective treatments.

Prevention and treatment issues concerning dementia are of paramount importance. Unfortunately, little is known about the prevention of most types of dementia, although intriguing clues do exist. Even less is understood about how to arrest or reverse dementia once it starts. Treatment, therefore, revolves around first attempting to discover whether any reversible factors, such as infection or drug use, may be causing or contributing to the patient's decline in cognitive ability. Behavioral disturbances associated with dementia, such as hallucinations, delusions, agitation, and aggression (Wragg & Jeste, 1989), are often managed— but not cured—not only by behavioral approaches but also by judicious use of antipsychotics, antidepressants, anxiolytics, and mood stabilizers (Cummings et al., 2002). Even more importantly, drugs are available that can slow the rate of cognitive deterioration in some cases of dementia. Although medications from several different classes are used to slow cognitive deterioration during the course of dementia, those most frequently used inhibit the enzyme acetylcholinesterase (Scarpini et al., 2003), which increases synaptic acetylcholine, a neurotransmitter long associated with cognitive function.

THE NEUROBIOLOGY OF DEMENTIA

Alzheimer's Dementia

Alzheimer's disease (AD) is the most common of the dementing diseases, affecting approximately 4.5 million people in the United States alone in the year 2000 (Herbert et al., 2003). With its increasing incidence, AD is predicted to afflict between over 8 million (by 2047) (Grossberg, 2003) and 13.2 million people by 2050 (Herbert et al., 2003). Named after the German psychiatrist Alois Alzheimer, who first described it in 1911 (Graeber et al., 1997), the characteristic brain changes found on autopsy in patients who had demonstrated cognitive impairment in life, AD generally occurs after age 60 and only rarely before age 50 (Small et al., 1997).

Concomitant with the primary cognitive and memory dysfunction in most AD patients are other behavioral symptoms not necessarily related to cognition (Lee & Lyketsos, 2003), including depression, agitation, psychosis (Cummings et al., 2002), irritability, and inappropriate behavior (Grossberg, 2003). Such conditions contribute substantially to overall morbidity. Other behavioral problems associated with AD are aggression and wandering. The time course of AD can vary widely, but on average the time between onset of symptoms and death is approximately ten years (Small et al., 1997).

Although its etiology is complex and includes environmental factors (Rocchi et al., 2003), a prominent genetic component appears to exist for AD, although there appear to be different genetic abnormalities and patterns of inheritance (Rogan & Lippa, 2002). Despite the complex genetics associated with AD (Clark & Karlawish, 2003), amyloid precursor protein, presenilin 1, and presenilin 2 are the three genes known to be linked to familial early-onset AD, even though they are found in fewer than 5 percent of all AD cases (Rocchi et al., 2003) and not all cases of familial Alzheimer's disease are associated with these genes (Ermak & Davies, 2002). Adding to the complexity, more than twenty mutations in the amyloid precursor gene could be related to early-onset AD (Kowalska, 2003). Apolipoprotein E is the fourth gene associated with AD (Ermak & Davies, 2002) and is found in some nonfamilial or sporadic, late-onset cases (Rocchi et al., 2003). Some families with familial AD can trace their ancestry to villages on the west bank of the Volga River that were founded by German settlers in the 1760s (Bird et al., 1988)

In addition the tantalizing genetics of AD, abnormalities in the neurotransmitter acetylcholine are implicated in the pathogenesis of AD. Acetylcholine-producing neurons in the basal forebrain, particularly in the nucleus basalis of Meynert, appear to degenerate in AD, resulting in less available acetylcholine (Whitehouse et al., 1982). Furthermore, in conjunction with the decrease in acetylcholine-producing neurons is a deficit in the enzymes necessary for the synthesis of acetylcholine (Perry et al., 1978), factors that combine to produce lower concentrations of acetylcholine. These findings are consistent with observations that acetylcholine-blocking agents often cause disturbances in cognition and memory and suggest a connection between AD, memory deficits, and drugs that antagonize acetylcholine receptors. However, severe loss of acetylcholine-producing neurons occurs only relatively late in the course of AD, possibly explaining why the severe memory loss associated with AD also comes late in its course (Tiraboschi et al., 2000a).

The finding that acetylcholine levels appear to relate to the presentation of AD has important treatment implications. For example, because acetylcholine levels can be manipulated pharmacologically, drugs that enhance this neurotransmitter serve as treatment options for AD. For this reason, such psychopharmacological agents are receiving a great deal of research attention (e.g., Nordberg & Svensson, 1998).

AD is also accompanied by several other characteristic pathological and biochemical findings. Mutations, for example, in the genes for amyloid precursor protein, presenilin 1, and presenilin 2 are associated with an increased synthesis of beta amyloid. Beta amyloid is found in the extracellular neuritic plaques that are pathologically associated with AD (Clark & Karlawish, 2003). Also highly characteristic of the pathology of AD are neurofibrillary tangles formed from abnormal tau proteins (Clark & Karlawish, 2003) [tau proteins are found in normal brain tissue (Trojanowski & Lee, 2002), where they are involved in intracellular transport and cell morphology (Brady et al., 1999)]. Neurofibrillary tangles are located in brain regions affected by AD (Sinha, 2002), and, in contrast to the extracellular beta amyloid plaques, neurofibrillary tangles are inside neurons and composed of wound filaments (Sinha, 2002).

A correlated finding in individuals with Down's syndrome suggests an interesting genetic link not mentioned above. That is, patients with Down's syndrome (Trisomy 21) can develop an Alzheimer-like dementia in mid life that is characterized by the same pathology (e.g., neurofibrillary tangle and beta-amyloid plaques) observed in Alzheimer's disease (Harman, 2002) and thus provides important clues to the etiology of Alzheimer's disease. In fact, some data suggest that all people with Down's syndrome who die after the age of 40 have brain changes similar to those seen in AD (Cairns, 1999).

Dementia with Lewy Bodies

Occurring in approximately 20 percent of cases of dementia (McKeith et al., 1996), dementia with Lewy bodies may represent a very different pathological process from that of AD. Long associated with Parkinson's disease and a hallmark of dementia with Lewy bodies, Lewy bodies are intracellular inclusions of alpha-synuclein and ubiquitin proteins found in the cytoplasm of the neuronal cell bodies in the striatal brain regions in patients suffering from Lewy-body disorders, such as Parkinson's disease and dementia with Lewy bodies (Duda et al., 2002; McKeith, 2002). In addition to the abnormal deposition of alpha-synuclein and ubiquitin, dementia with Lewy bodies, like AD, is associated with a reduction in acetylcholine (Tiraboschi et al., 2000b), possibly due to the formation of Lewy bodies in the nucleus basalis of Meynert (Rogan & Lippa, 2002).

In addition to their differing pathologies, several clinical features distinguish Lewy-body dementia from AD. Although patients with Lewy-body dementia do not manifest the full spectrum of Parkinson's disease, they do have features of this disorder in addition to their dementia, in contrast to AD, which generally does not manifest symptoms of Parkinson's disease. The characteristic slow, shuffling gait of Parkinson's disease, for example, may be present dementia with Lewy bodies in addition to motor rigidity (Ransmayr, 2002). A fluctuating mental status also often occurs with Lewy-body dementia, varying from lack of responsiveness to seeming coherence over the course of a day (McKeith, 2002). Furthermore, hallucinations, both visual and auditory, are more prevalent in Lewy-body dementia, as are well-formed delusions, in contrast to the less organized delusions present in individuals with AD (Ransmayr, 2002). Patients with Lewy-body dementia are also extremely sensitive to the adverse effects induced by antipsychotic medications, most probably because in Parkinson's disease, and presumably to some extent in Lewy-body dementia, dopamine-producing neurons die out, leaving a dopamine deficit that is exacerbated by dopamine-blocking antipsychotic medications; this degeneration of dopamine-producing neurons and sensitivity to dopamine antagonists makes the use of antipsychotics contraindicated in the treatment of dementia with Lewy bodies (McKeith, 2002). Related to this difference with AD, the enzyme responsible for the synthesis of acetylcholine, choline acteyltranferase, occurs in low levels early on in the course of Lewy-body dementia, whereas in AD the loss occurs relatively late in the disease course (Tiraboschi et al., 2002). Finally, also in contrast to AD, there does not appear to be a major genetic abnormality associated with Lewy-body dementia (Rogan & Lippa, 2002).

Vascular Dementia

The next form of dementia, vascular dementia, accounts for approximately the same amount of dementia as does Lewy-body dementia (American Psychiatric Association, 1997), although some authors suggest that it is the second most common type of dementia (Roman, 2003). Caused by disease in the vascular system supplying the brain, vascular dementia not only produces cognitive and memory deficits but may also result in a variety of neurological impairments as damage accumulates in regions of the brain involved in movement, gait, bladder control, motor reflexes, and regulation of affect. Such diseases in the vascular system supplying the brain, which can result in vascular dementia, include cerebrovascular accidents (Roman, 2002). Even disease in the brain's microcirculation may result in cognitive impairment and dementia (Kril et al., 2002). The relationship between vascular dementia and AD is complex but poorly understood. Early evidence, however, suggests that vascular dementia and AD may occur simultaneously in the same person (Kalaria, 2002). In fact, some investigators have postulated that vascular disease may be a risk factor for AD. It is also suggested that pure AD and pure vascular dementia may represent the extremes of a continuum, with the middle composed of mixed AD and vascular dementia (Kalaria, 2002).

Frontotemporal Dementia

Frontotemporal dementia is associated with neuronal degeneration that starts in the more frontal regions of the brain, in particular the frontal and temporal lobes (Kertesz & Munoz, 2002). Initial signs and symptoms of the dementia, therefore, are comprised of those typically found in cases of frontal lobe damage, such as impaired foresight, planning, executive function, and emotional regulation. These frontal lobe deficits tend to be more prominent early on than are difficulties with memory. As the disease progresses, however, memory problems become more pronounced.

A range of individual conditions are classified as frontotemporal dementias (Kowalska et al., 2002). Pick's disease, for instance, is an important, though rare, type of frontotemporal dementia, accounting for 2 percent or less of dementia (Coleman et al., 2002). Generally occurring in middle age, Pick's disease may present much earlier; a recent case report described a Pick's disease presenting at age 25 (Coleman et al., 2002). A pathological hallmark of Pick's disease is the finding of neuronal inclusions of tau proteins called Pick bodies in the cytoplasm of surviving neurons (Tolnay & Probst, 2001) Other frontotemporal dementias also are associated with abnormalities of tau proteins (Kowalska et al., 2002).

Other Dementias

The list of other conditions that are associated with dementia is long and complex, ranging from common medical disorders that may affect brain functioning to rare and poorly described conditions that are only just beginning to receive attention. For example, hypothyroidism is associated in some cases with dementia (Green, 2002). Mitochondrial encephalopathies too are associated with degeneration of brain tissue and muscle (Isozumi et al., 1994). Arising from abnormalities in the genes that code for the neuron's energy-producing apparatus, the mitochondria, mitochondrial encephalopathies are associated with brain degeneration (Isozumi et al., 1994) and dementia (Naviaux, 2000). Also associated with dementia, normal-pressure hydrocephalus, a form of hydrocephalus found in some adults

TABLE 12.1   The Dementias and Neurobiological Correlates

TYPES OF DEMENTIA	NEUROBIOLOGICAL CORRELATES
Alzheimer's Disease	■ Abnormal transmission of acetylcholine.
	■ Abnormalities in amyloid precursor protein.
	■ Neurofibrillary tangles and beta-amyloid plaques.
Dementia with Lewy Bodies	■ Lewy bodies—intracellular inclusions of alpha-synuclein and ubiquitin proteins found in the cytoplasm of the neuronal cell bodies in the striatal brain regions.
	■ Reduction in acetylcholine.
Vascular Dementia	■ Cerebrovascular disease.
Frontotemporal Dementia	■ Neuronal degeneration, beginning in the frontal regions of the brain (particularly the frontal and temporal regions).

and possibly in children (Bret et al., 2002), is characterized radiographically by enlarged brain ventricles (Goodman & Meyer, 2001). Clinically, patients with normal-pressure hydrocephalus tend to demonstrate gait abnormalities, urinary incontinence, and dementia. Neurosurgical shunting may result in improved cognitive function in this potentially reversible dementia syndrome (Hurley et al., 1999), although shunting in normal-pressure hydrocephaly is associated with complications (Bret et al., 2002). Spongiform encephalopathies are a cause of fatal neural degeneration (Lasmezas, 2003) that includes Creutzfeldt-Jakob disease, which leads to severe dementia and death (Rentz, 2003). Table 12.1 lists several types of dementia and their associated neurobiological findings.

THE COGNITIVE ENHANCERS

The neurotransmitter acetylcholine, with its relationship to cognition and memory, has received a great deal of attention, especially as it relates to potential treatments for dementias. Clinicians, for example, have long observed that drugs blocking brain acetylcholine receptors, such as tricyclic antidepressants and antipsychotics, can result in cognitive and memory disturbances, particularly in elderly and brain-damaged populations (Sunderland et al., 1987). Furthermore, as noted above, abnormalities in acetylcholine function, particularly lowered acetylcholine transmission, are described in AD (Nordberg & Svensson, 1998). Because of these factors, drugs that increase the amount of acetylcholine transmission have been developed. Two ways exist pharmacologically to increase acetylcholine transmission: First, the metabolism of acetylcholine can be slowed by pharmacologically inhibiting the enzymes that breakdown acetylcholine, and, second, the actions of acetylcholine can be mimicked by acetylcholine agonists acting directly on mus-carinic and nicotinic receptors (Messer, 2002).

Acetylcholinesterase Inhibitors

A key enzyme in the metabolism of acetylcholine is acetylcholinesterase. Acetyl-cholinesterase metabolizes acetylcholine into pharmacologically inactive metabo-lites. By inhibiting this enzyme, synaptic concentrations of acetylcholine are increased (Nordberg & Svensson, 1998). This action improves, at least temporar-ily, cognitive abilities in patients who have AD (Nordberg & Svensson, 1998) by increasing the interaction of acetylcholine with its muscarinic receptors, whose function is crucial for cognition and memory.

Butyrylcholinesterase is another enzyme that metabolizes acetylcholine (Nordberg & Svensson, 1998), although butyrylcholinesterase seems to break down acetylcholine in the gastrointestinal tract more so than in the brain. As AD progresses, however, brain butyrylcholinesterase increases (Giacobini, 2003), sug-gesting that butyrylcholinesterase inhibition may be beneficial in more advanced stages of AD (Stahl, 2000).

Acetylcholinesterase and butyrylcholinesterase exist in globular monomer, dimer, and tetramer forms, of which the tetramer form is the most common (Nordberg & Svensson, 1998). Based on these considerations, several drugs have been developed and are in clinical uses that inhibit acetylcholinesterase, some of which also inhibit butyrylcholinesterase. Many but not all of the therapeutic and adverse effects are thought to be a direct consequence of increased levels of acetyl-choline (e.g., Kasckow, 2002). Resulting in direct interaction with acetylcholine receptors, cholinergic agonists have been evaluated in AD. Unlike the acetyl-choline inhibitors, however, the available muscarinic agonists have had only a minimal clinical response (Messer, 2002). However, selective muscarinic subtype 1 agonists are in development that may have greater efficacy over available com-pounds (Messer, 2002).

Acetylcholine also interacts with nicotinic receptors. At the neuromuscular junction in the body, acetylcholine binds with nicotinic receptors to cause muscle cell contraction. In the brain, nicotinic receptors appear to be important in cogni-tion and attention. In addition, agonism of nicotinic receptors increases release of acetylcholine from acetylcholine-containing neurons, resulting in increased con-centrations of acetylcholine (Wevers & Schroder, 1999). Galantamine (Reminyl) is an acetylcholinesterase inhibitor that also modulates brain nicotinic receptors.

Despite their inability to reverse the course of or cure dementia (Nordberg & Svensson, 1998), the acetylcholinesterase inhibitors are generally considered to be the most effective intervention in AD and certain other dementias with positive ef-fects on cognition, activities of daily living, and behavior (Bonner & Peskind, 2002). The acetylcholinesterase inhibitors as a class appear to modestly delay by approximately six to twelve months (Ihl, 2002) the further development of cognitive and behavioral deficits in AD (Kasckow, 2002), increasing the time to nursing-home placement (Knopman & Morris, 1997). Possibly because of its associated deficits in acetylcholine, dementia with Lewy bodies also responds to acetylcholinesterase inhibitors (McKeith, 2002). In fact, the early and severe loss of cholinergic function in dementia with Lewy bodies may make this disease particularly amenable to acetylcholinesterase inhibition (Tiraboschi et al., 2002). However, although acetylcholinesterase inhibitors are used in some cases of frontotemporal dementia, they may also make certain of these dementias worse (Rogan & Lippa, 2002). Such findings, then, make the distinction among dementia of the Alzheimer's type, dementia with Lewy bodies, and frontotemporal dementia more than just an academic exercise.

Related to acetylcholine's stimulation of the gastrointestinal tract, the most common adverse effects associated with the cholinesterase inhibitors are primarily related to gastrointestinal function: nausea, vomiting diarrhea, and weight loss (Stahl, 2000). Because of increased acetylcholine transmission from acetylcholinesterase inhibitors, these drugs should be used with caution in people who have medical conditions sensitive to acetylcholine such as slow heart arrhythmias, asthma, and chronic obstructive pulmonary disease (Irizarry & Hyman, 2001). Cholinergic effects from acetylcholinesterase inhibitors at the neuromuscular junction can result in muscle cramping.

Tacrine (Cognex). Released in 1993, tacrine was the first available acetylcholinesterase inhibitor. In addition to its acetylcholinesterase inhibition, tacrine may increase the actual release of acetylcholine and binds to acetylcholine receptors (Wagstaff & McTavish, 1994). It is unknown, however, what these additional mechanisms mean clinically. Tacrine's main metabolite, 1-hydroxy-tacrine, which is found in higher concentrations than tacrine, is also an inhibitor of acetylcholine (Nordberg & Svensson, 1998). A short half-life, which necessitates multiple daily dosings, and the possibility of significant liver damage that requires monitoring of liver function tests, which are abnormal in approximately 30 percent of patients, limit use of tacrine to a relatively few patients who have AD (Kasckow, 2002).

Donepezil (Aricept). Approved in 1997, donepezil was the second acetylcholinesterase inhibitor to see clinical use. Although its mechanism of action is similar to that of tacrine, donepezil offers the advantages of a longer half-life (approximately 70 to 80 hours) (Bryson & Benfield, 1997). This longer half-life results in fewer daily dosings of donepezil than tacrine (an important factor in a cognitively impaired patient). Although by no means a cure for dementia, donepezil appears to maintain cognitive function in dementia for approximately a year before deterioration again sets in (Shigeta & Homma, 2001). In addition to its proposed role in improving or slowing the deterioration of the cognitive deficits of AD, donepezil may help with some of the accompanying behavioral disturbances, such as apathy and agitation (Cummings & Kaufer, 1996). Donepezil is also highly selective for acetylcholinesterase inhibition in contrast to other acetylcholinesterase inhibitors (Jann et al., 2002), a property that may result in relatively fewer side affects than observed with other acetylcholinesterase inhibitors.

Furthermore, unlike tacrine, donepezil is not associated with severe liver toxicity and, thus, does not require monitoring of liver function tests (Rogers & Friedhoff, 1998).

There are, however, some potential risks of using donepezil due to its specificity in inhibiting acetylcholinesterase. Demonstrating the potential for increased synaptic acetylcholine to cause mental status changes, a case study reported a delirium associated with donepezil (Kawashima & Yamada, 2002). This case report described a man treated with donepezil for AD who developed severe delirium that subsided upon discontinuation of the donepezil. For this reason, caution is recommended in the prescription of acetylcholinesterase inhibitors for the treatment of dementia.

Rivastigmine (Exelon). Like tacrine and donepezil, rivastigmine inhibits acetylcholinesterase. In addition, rivastigmine appears to inhibit the metabolism of butyrylcholinesterase (Cutler et al., 1998). The latter, as noted above, is also increased in individuals with AD (Nordberg & Svensson, 1998), possibly adding a therapeutic advantage for rivastigmine over tacrine and donepezil. Because of this unique mechanism of action, rivastigmine is sometimes referred to as a dual acetylcholinesterase inhibitor. Some evidence, though, suggests that the other acetylcholinesterase inhibitors also inhibit butyrylcholinesterase (Darvesh et al., 2003). An additional feature of rivastigmine is its preferential inhibition of the G1 form of acetylcholinesterase (Kasckow, 2002), which is the predominate form in AD (Atack et al., 1983). This is in contrast to G4, which is decreased in AD. It remains unknown, however, whether these additional pharmacological features translate into clinically meaningful differences compared to other acetylcholinesterase inhibitors (Jones, 2003). Lessening the potential for drug-drug interactions, rivastigmine is not metabolized through the liver's cytochrome P450 enzyme system (Geula, 2002). Beneficial not only for cognitive deficits, rivastigmine may also improve some of the behavioral problems associated with AD such as wandering, hallucinations, delusions, and irritability (Cummings et al., 2000). This feature potentially lessens the need for adjunctive medications including antipsychotic agents.

Approximately one-third of patients with Parkinson's disease develop dementia that is pathologically similar to AD (Korczyn, 2002). Because of this similarity between the two dementias, rivastigmine has been investigated in dementia of Parkinson's disease and found in early work to result in some cognitive improvement (Korczyn, 2002). Rivastigmine also has been shown to result in improvement in the hallucinations, delusions, and anxiety that is associated with Lewy-body dementia (McKeith et al., 2000).

There are, however, some potential difficulties associated with the prescription of rivastigmine. For example, due at least in part to its inhibition of butyrylcholinesterase, rivastigmine is associated with more negative gastrointestinal effects than are tacrine and donepezil (Rosler et al., 1999). Such adverse effects, however, may be diminished by administering the drug with food.

Galantamine (Reminyl).   Isolated from the European daffodil (*Galanthus nivalis*) (Howes et al., 2003) and the most recently introduced acetylcholinesterase inhibitor, galantamine has been available since 2000. In addition to acetylcholinesterase inhibition, galantamine modulates brain nicotinic receptors, which may increase the release of acetylcholine (Doggrell & Evans, 2003). However, the actual clinical significance of nicotinic receptors modulation in not yet known (Geula, 2002). Unfortunately, a relatively short half-life of approximately five hours (Kewitz, 1997) makes for multiple daily dosings. Table 12.2 summarizes the acetylcholinesterase inhibitors.

TABLE 12.2   The Acetylcholinesterase Inhibitors

Tacrine (Cognex)	■ Increases the release of acetylcholine and binds to acetylcholine receptors (Wagstaff & McTavish, 1994). ■ Short half-life necessitates multiple daily dosing. ■ Risk of liver damage (Kasckow, 2002). ■ Beneficial for cognitive deficits associated with Alzheimer's disease.
Donepezil (Aricept)	■ Similar chemical action to tacrine. ■ Half-life of approximately 70 to 80 hours necessitates fewer daily doses than tacrine (Bryson & Benfield, 1997). ■ May help with the accompanying behavioral disturbances (Cummings & Kaufer, 1996) as well as the cognitive deficits associated with Alzheimer's. ■ Highly selective for acetylcholinesterase inhibition (Jann et al., 2002), which means fewer side effects than other acetylcholinesterase inhibitors. ■ Not associated with liver toxicity (Rogers & Friedhoff, 1998). ■ Possibility of delirium associated with its use (Kawashima & Yamada, 2002).
Rivastigmine (Exelon)	■ Blocks the metabolism of butyrylcholinesterase as well as acetylcholinesterase (Cutler et al., 1998). ■ Lower potential for drug-drug interaction (Geula, 2002). ■ May help with the accompanying behavioral disturbances associated with dementia (Cummings et al., 2000).
Galantamine (Reminyl)	■ Modulates brain nicotinic receptors in addition to acetylcholinesterase inhibition (Doggrell & Evans, 2003). ■ Relatively short half-life (approximately five hours) means multiple daily dosings (Kewitz, 1997).

Memantine (Namenda). With a different mechanism of action from the acetylcholinesterase inhibitors and approved by the U.S. Food and Drug Administration for the treatment of AD in 2003 (Farlow, 2004), memantine antagonizes N-methyl-D-aspartate receptors, a mechanism that may be neuroprotective (Molinuevo et al., 2004) as excessive activity of N-methyl-D-aspartate receptors can result in neuronal toxicity due to damaging levels of calcium ions (Farlow, 2004). By antagonizing N-methyl-D-aspartate receptors excitotoxicity, memantine may prevent some of the neuronal damage occurring from excessive N-methyl-D-aspartate receptor activity. Some N-methyl-D-aspartate antagonists such as phencyclidine can result in considerable adverse effects (see Chapter 8), but the relatively low affinity of memantine for these receptors appears to result in comparatively few adverse effects. Memantine also may interact with nicotinic and serotonin subtype 3 receptors (Rogawski, 2004), although the significance for AD of this action is unknown (Rogawski, 2004). To date, memantine appears safe and well tolerated (van Dyck, 2004).

OTHER APPROACHES TO THE TREATMENT OF DEMENTIA

Because of the limitations of currently available treatments, new drugs and therapeutic ideas are under investigation as possible treatments for AD and other dementias. Many of these treatments are highly speculative and are unsupported by rigorous clinical trials. One such alternative approach to decreasing brain amyloid deposits involves the use of a vaccine to increase the immune clearance of amyloid (Friedman, 2002), although neurological side effects and autoimmune reactions have hampered the development of vaccines to prevent AD (McGeer & McGeer, 2003).

Irreversibly inhibiting monoamine oxidase B, selegiline (Eldepryl), in addition to its more accepted role in depression and Parkinson's disease, has also been evaluated in treatment of AD. Possibly because of its interference with the elevated levels of monoamine oxidase B observed in AD, the use of selegiline in AD has been predicted to result in cognitive improvement (Friedman, 2002). Alternatively, selegiline's mechanism of action could involve its antioxidant properties (Sano et al., 1997). The irreversible and nonspecific monoamine oxidase inhibitor tranylcypromine (Parnate) resulted in considerable toxicity in AD subjects, which made comparison to the much better tolerated selegiline difficult (Tariot et al., 1988). Even with selegiline, however, a meta-analysis found that, while there were short-term indications of cognitive improvements from selegiline, these did not differ significantly from those of placebo (Wilcock et al., 2002). Furthermore, in this meta-analysis, there was no indication of long-term positive effects on cognition from this drug.

Posited to prevent neural loss due to its antioxidant properties and free-radical scavenging, alpha-tocopherol (vitamin E) has also been investigated in AD (Tabet et al., 2000). Although the clinical effects of alpha-tocopherol in AD remain unclear (Tabet et al., 2000), alpha-tocopherol is routinely used as an adjunctive agent in the treatment of AD because of its good safety profile and few side effects (Bonner & Peskind, 2002).

Last, some potentially prophylactic treatments are under investigation. One such possible prophylactic treatment is statins. Used extensively as lipid-lowering drugs, statins may decrease the risk of developing AD (Jick et al., 2000). In contrast, non-statin, lipid-reducing drugs do not appear to reduce the risk of developing AD, arguing that mechanisms other than the effects of statins on lipids are relevant in the protection from AD. With an as yet unknown mechanism of action for cognitive protection, the antioxidant and anti-inflammatory properties of statins have been suggested as the mechanism by which these drugs appear to protect against Alzheimer's disease (Friedman, 2002). Similarly, anti-inflammatory medication may diminish the risk of developing AD (Knopman & Morris, 1997). There is some suggestion that nonsteroidal anti-inflammatory medications that interfere with the production of amyloid-beta (1-42) (a protein found in AD brains) (Imbimbo, 2004), such as ibuprofen, indomethacin, and sulindac, may be more effective in reducing the risk of developing AD than nonsteroidal anti-inflammatory drugs, like naproxen and aspirin, that may not inhibit the production of amyloid-beta (1-42) (Imbimbo, 2004).

Drugs Used to Treat Noncognitive Disturbances Associated with Dementia

While drugs that have specific actions on the cognitive and memory impairments of dementia are important for their treatment, there are associated behavioral features of dementia that also require treatment. In addition to the memory and cognitive deficits that are the *sine qua non* of dementia many people with dementia suffer from hallucinations, delusions, depression, agitation, and aggression (Wragg & Jeste, 1989). These features substantially complicate the care of these people and are a major reason for the institutionalization of individuals with dementia (O'Donnell et al., 1992). Although anticholinesterase inhibitors can improve some of these problems (Cummings & Kaufer, 1996), drugs from other classes are often used as well. Once widely used to treat the hallucinations, delusions, and other behavioral disturbances of AD, first-generation antipsychotics are limited by their extrapyramidal side effects and are contraindicated in dementia with Lewy bodies (McKeith et al., 1992). Moreover, antagonism of acetylcholine receptors from first-generation antipsychotics can exacerbate the already present cognitive deficits (Riva et al., 1998).

Other psychopharmacological agents, however, have been demonstrated to aid in the treatment of the associated behavioral disturbances of dementia and have fewer side effects than the first-generation antipsychotics. With generally fewer extrapyramidal effects than earlier antipsychotic drugs, for example, the second-generation antipsychotic risperidone (Risperdal), in low doses, has been shown to reduce the severity and amount of dementia-associated behavioral disturbances without worsening cognition (Rainer et al., 2001). Because of fewer extrapyramidal symptoms, the second-generation antipsychotics may offer an advantage over the older agents. Benzodiazepines are also sometimes used to treat the associated behavioral disturbances of dementia (Devanand, 1997). However, benzodiazepines can worsen cognitive and memory deficits and contribute to falls, particularly in elderly people (Chaimowicz et al., 2000; Moore & O'Keeffe, 1999). Finally, Buspirone (Buspar) in low doses can diminish agitation and aggression associated with dementia (Salzman, 2001).

SUMMARY

Many neurological and medical diseases can produce dementia, either from a process directly affecting brain tissue or from organ failure impinging upon brain function. Accounting for the majority of dementia, dementia of the Alzheimer's type (AD) generally affects people over the age of 65. Among the many observed neurobiological abnormalities in Alzheimer's disease is a degeneration of acetylcholine-producing neurons, particularly in the nucleus basalis of Meynert.

Numerous medications have been investigated for the treatment of AD. Based upon putative deficits in acetylcholine and upon clinical trial data, the mainstay of pharmacological treatment for AD are the acetylcholinesterase inhibitors donepezil, rivastigmine, and galantamine. Due to a short half-life and potential for liver toxicity in these pharmacological treatments, a fourth acetylcholinesterase inhibitor, tacrine, is little used clinically. Having in common acetylcholinesterase inhibition, which increases synaptic acetylcholine concentrations, the acetylcholinesterase inhibitors have potentially clinically significant differences. Rivastigmine, for instance, also inhibits butyrylcholinesterase, an enzyme that appears to be increased in AD. Alternatively, galantamine modulates nicotinic receptors, thusly increasing the release of acetylcholine into the synapse. At this time, the main therapeutic benefits of the acetylcholinesterase inhibitors appear to be an arrest of disease prevention, prolonging the time to nursing-home placement. Despite limited data supporting its use, alpha-tocopherol (vitamin E) is often prescribed as an adjunctive medication in the treatment of AD.

Several additional medications are being evaluated for use in AD, with varying degrees of support. Some of these drugs are designed with the intent to alter, fundamentally, the underlying disease process of AD, such as a vaccine that interferes with abnormal deposition of amyloid protein. Furthermore, lipid-lowering statins may lower the risk of developing AD, possibly through antioxidant or anti-inflammatory effects.

Characterized by a rapidly fluctuating mental status and hallucinations, dementia with Lewy bodies is pathologically distinct from AD. In addition to the Lewy-body cellular inclusions, an early degeneration of acetylcholine-producing neurons occurs in dementia with Lewy bodies, a loss that happens much earlier in the course of dementia than in AD. This early loss of acetylcholine suggests that acetylcholinesterase inhibitors may be helpful in slowing the progression of Lewy-body dementia, including diminishing the hallucinations and delusions that are prominent in this disease.

Finally, another form of cognitive deficits, vascular dementia occurs from strokes and disease in the cerebral vasculature. The treatment of vascular dementia includes intervention into the medical problems producing the disease, such as control of high blood pressure and elevated lipid levels. Because vascular dementia can occur in conjunction with and may serve as a risk factor for the occurrence of AD, acetylcholinesterase inhibitors may have a role in certain cases of vascular dementia.

STUDY QUESTIONS

1. Design a drug for Alzheimer's disease. What mechanism would you include and why?
2. For treatment purposes, why is it important to distinguish between Alzheimer's disease and frontotemporal dementia?
3. Describe the similarities and differences of tacrine, donepezil, rivastigmine, and galantamine.
4. What, if any, theoretical advantages does rivastigmine offer over donepezil?
5. In evaluating the proposed treatments for Alzheimer's disease, which drugs do you find most promising? Why?
6. An 80-year-old male presents with severe memory and cognitive deficits accompanied by severe agitation, hallucinations, and wandering. Outline a treatment program for this man, including differential diagnosis and drug approaches.

REFERENCES

American Psychiatric Association (1997): Practice guidelines for the treatment of patients with Alzheimer's disease and other dementias of late life. American Journal of Psychiatry 154:1–39.

Atack JR, Perry ED, Bronham JR, et al. (1983): Molecular forms of acetylcholinesterase in senile dementia Alzheimer's type: Selective loss of the intermediate (10S) form. Neuroscience Letters 40:199–204.

Bird TD, Lampe TH, Nemens EJ, Miner GW, Sumi SM, Schellenberg GD, Wijsman EM (1988): Familial Alzheimer's disease in American descendents of the Volga Germans: Probable genetic founder effect. Annals of Neurology 23:25–31.

Bonner LT, Peskind ER (2002): Pharmacologic treatments of dementia. Medical Clinics of North American 86:657–674.

Brady S, Colman DR, Brophy P (1999): Subcellular organization of the nervous system: Organelles and their functions. In MJ Zigmond, FE Bloom, SC Landis, JL Roberts, LR Squire (eds.), *Fundamental Neuroscience*. London UK: Academic Press.

Bret P, Guyotat J, Chazal J (2002): Is normal pressure hydrocephalus a valid concept in 2002? A reappraisal in five questions and a proposal for a new designation of the syndrome as "chronic hydrocephalus." Journal of Neurology, Neurosurgery and Psychiatry 73:9–12.

Bryson HM, Benfield P (1997): Donepezil. Drugs and Aging 10:234–239.

Cairns NJ (1999): Neuropathology. Journal of Neural Transmission. Supplementum 57:61–74.

Chaimowicz F, Ferreira Tde J, Miguel DF (2000): Use of psychoactive drugs and related falls among older people living in a community in Brazil. Rev Stade Saude Publica 34:631–635.

Clark CM, Karlawish JH (2003): Alzheimer disease: Current concepts and emerging diagnostic and therapeutic strategies. Annals of Internal Medicine 138:400–410.

Coleman LW, Digre KB, Stephenson GM, Townsend JJ (2002): Autopsy-proven, sporadic pick disease with onset at age 25 years. Archives of Neurology 59:856–859.

Cummings J, Anand R, Koumaras B, et al. (2000): Rivastigmine provides behavioral benefits to Alzheimer's disease patients residing in a nursing home: Findings from a 26-week trial. Neurology 54 (supplement 3):A468.

Cummings JL, Frank JC, Cherry D, Kohatsu ND, Kemp B, Hewett L, Mittman B (2002): Guidelines for managing Alzheimer's disease: Part II. Treatment. American Family Physician 65:2525–2534.

Cummings JL, Kaufer D (1996): Neuropsychiatric aspects of Alzheimer's disease: The cholinergic hypothesis revisited. Neurology 47:876–883.

Cutler NR, Polinsky RJ, Sramek JJ, et al. (1998): Dose-dependent CSF acetylcholine inhibition by SDZ ENA 713 in Alzheimer's disease. Acta Neurologica Scandinavia 97:244–250.

Darvesh S, Walsh R, Kumar R, Caines A, Roberts S, Magee D, Rockwood K, Martin E (2003): Inhibition of human cholinesterases by drugs used to treat Alzheimer disease. Alzheimer Disease and Associated Disorders 17:117–126.

Devanand DP (1997): Behavioral complications and their treatment in Alzheimer's disease. Geriatrics 52 (supplement 2):S37–39.

Doggrell SA, Evans S (2003): Treatment of dementia with neurotransmission modulation. Expert Opinion on Investigational Drugs 12:1633–1654.

Duda JE, Giasson BI, Mabon ME, Lee VM, Trojanowski JQ (2002): Novel antibodies to synuclein show show abundant striatal pathology in Lewy body diseases. Annals of Neurology 52:205–210.

Ermak G, Davies KJ (2002): Gene expression in Alzheimer's disease. Drugs of Today 38:509–516.

Farlow MR (2004): NMDA receptor antagonists: A new therapeutic approach for Alzheimer's disease. Geriatrics 59:22–27.

Friedman L (2002): New drugs, mechanisms are coming for Alzheimer's disease. Current Psychiatry 1:63–69.

Geula C (2002): Differential pharmacology of cholinesterase inhibitors, pp. 265–266. In Understanding changes in cholinergic function: Implications for treating dementia [Academic Highlights]. Journal of Clinical Psychiatry 63:259–269.

Giacobini E (2003): Cholinergic function and Alzheimer's disease. International Journal of Geriatric Psychiatry 18 (supplement 1):S1–5.

Goodman M, Meyer WJ (2001): Dementia reversal in post-shunt normal pressure hydrocephalus predicted by neuropsychological assessment. Journal of the American Geriatric Society 49:685–686.

Graeber MB, Kosel S, Egensperger R, Banati RB, Muller U, Bise K, Hoff P, Moller HJ, Fujisawa K, Mehraein P (1997): Rediscovery of the case described by Alois Alzheimer in 1911: Historical, histological and molecular genetic analysis. Neurogenetics 1:73–80.

Green A (2002): Biochemical investigations in patients with dementia. Annals of Clinical Biochemistry 39:211–220.

Grossberg GT (2003): Diagnosis and treatment of Alzheimer's disease. Journal of Clinical Psychiatry 64 (supplement 9):3–6.

Harman D (2002): Alzheimer's disease: Role of aging in pathogenesis. Annals of the New York Academy of Sciences 959:384–395.

Herbert LE, Scherr PA, Bienias JL, Bennett DA, Evans DA (2003): Alzheimer disease in the US population: Prevalence estimates using the 2000 census. Archives of Neurology 60:1119–1122.

Howes MJ, Perry NS, Houghton PJ (2003): Plants with traditional uses and activities, relevant to the management of Alzheimer's disease and other cognitive disorders. Phytotherapy Research 17:1–18.

Hurley RA, Bradley WG Jr., Latifi HT, Taber KH (1999): Normal pressure hydrocephalus: Significance of MRI in a potentially treatable dementia. Journal of Neuropsychiatry and Clinical Neuroscience 11:297–300.

Ihl R (2002): [Dementing disorders. What benefits do the new antidementia drugs have?] MMW Fortschritte der Medizin May 6, supplement 2:24–26, 26–29.

Imbimbo BP (2004): The potential role of non-steroidal anti-inflammatory drugs in treating Alzheimer's disease. Expert Opinion on Investigational Drugs 13:1469–1481.

Irizarry MC, Hyman BT (2001): Alzheimer's disease therapeutics. Journal of Neuropathology and Experimental Neurology 60:923–928.

Isozumi K, Fukuuchi Y, Tanaka K, Nogawa S, Ishihara T, Sakuta R (1994): A MELAS (mitochondrial myopathy, encephalopathy, lactic acidosis, and stroke-like episodes) mtDNA mutation that induces subacute dementia which mimics Creutzfelt-Jacob disease. Internal Medicine 33:543–546.

Jann MW, Shirley KL, Small GW (2002): Clinical pharmacokinetics and pharmacodynamics of cholinesterase inhibitors. Clinical Pharmacokinetics 41:719–739.

Jick H, Zornberg ZL, Jick SS, Seshadri S, Drachman DA (2000): Statins and the risk of dementia. Lancet 356:1627–1631.

Jones RW (2003): Have cholinergic therapies reached their clinical boundary in Alzheimer's disease? International Journal of Geriatric Psychiatry 18 (supplement 1):S7–S13.

Kalaria R (2002): Similarities between Alzheimer's disease and vascular dementia. Journal of the Neurological Sciences 15:203–204, 29–34.

Kantarci K, Jack CR Jr. (2003): Neuroimaging in Alzheimer disease: An evidence-based review. Neuroimaging Clinics of North America 13:197–209.

Kasckow J (2002): Cognitive enhancers for dementia: Do they work? Current Psychiatry 1:22–28.

Kawashima T, Yamada S (2002): Delirium caused by donepezil: A case study. Journal of Clinical Psychiatry 63 (letter):250–251.

Kertesz A, Munoz DG (2002): Frontotemporal dementia. Medical Clinics of North America 86: 501–518.

Kewitz H (1997): Pharmacokinetics and metabolism of galanthamine. Drugs of Today 33:265–272.

Knopman DS, Morris JC (1997): An update on primary drug therapies for Alzheimer's disease. Archives of Neurology 54:1406–1409.

Korczyn A (2002): Treatment of dementia in Parkinson's disease: Results with rivastigmine, pp. 262–263. In Understanding changes in cholinergic function: Implications for treating dementia [Academic Highlights]. Journal of Clinical Psychiatry 63:259–269.

Kowalska A (2003): Amyloid precursor protein gene mutations responsible for early-onset autosomal dominant Alzheimer's disease. Folia Neuropathologica 41:35–40.

Kowalska A, Takahashi K, Kozubsky W, Tabira T (2002): Microtubule associated protein (tau) gene variability in patients with frontotemporal dementia. Folia Neuropathol 40:1–5.

Kril JJ, Patel S, Harding AJ, Halliday JM (2002): Patients with vascular dementia due to microvascular pathology have significant hippocampal neuronal loss. Journal of Neurology, Neurosurgery, and Psychiatry 72:747–751.

Lasmezas CI (2003): The transmissible spongiform encephalopathies. Revue Scientifique et Technique 22:23–36.

Lee HB, Lyketsos CG (2003): Depression in Alzheimer's disease: Heterogeneity and related issues. Biological Psychiatry 54:353–362.

McGeer PL, McGeer E (2003): Is there a future for vaccination as a treatment for Alzheimer's disease? Neurobiology of Aging 24:391–395.

McKeith I (2002): Treating dementia with Lewy bodies, pp. 263–264. In Understanding changes in cholinergic function: Implications for treating dementia [Academic Highlights]. Journal of Clinical Psychiatry 63:259–269.

McKeith I, Del Ser T, Spano P, Emre M, et al. (2000): Efficacy of rivastigmine on dementia with Lewy bodies: A randomised, double-blind, placebo-controlled international study. Lancet 356:2031–2036.

McKeith I, Fairbairn A, Perry R, Thompson P, Perry E (1992): Neuroleptic sensitivity in patients with senile dementia of Lewy body type. British Medical Journal 305:673–678.

Messer WS Jr. (2002): The utility of muscarinic agonists in the treatment of Alzheimer's disease. Journal of Molecular Neuroscience 19:187–193.

Molinuevo JL, Garacia-Gil V, Villar A (2004): Memantive: An antiglutamatergic option for dementia. American Journal of Alzheimer's Disease and Other Dementias 19:10–18.

Moore AR, O'Keeffe ST (1999): Drug-induced cognitive impairment in the elderly. Drugs and Aging 15:15–28.

Morgan K, Lilley JM, Arie T, Byrne EJ, Jones R, Waite J (1993): Incidence of dementia in a representative sample. British Journal of Psychiatry 163:467–470.

Naviaux RK (2000): Mitochondrial DNA disorders. European Journal of Pediatrics 159 (supplement 3):S219–226.

Nordberg A, Svensson AL (1998): Cholinesterase inhibitors in the treatment of Alzheimer's disease: A comparison of tolerability and pharmacology. Drug Safety 19:465–480.

O'Donnell BF, Drachman, DA, Barnes HJ, Peterson KE, Swearer JM, Lew RA (1992): Incontinence and troublesome behaviors predict institutionalization in dementia. Journal of Geriatric Psychiatry and Neurology 5:45–52.

Ott A, Breteler MM, van Harskamp F, Claus JJ, van der Commen TJ, Grobbee DE, Hofman A (1995): Prevalence of Alzheimer's disease and vascular dementia: Association with education: The Rotterdam study. British Medical Journal 310:970–973.

Perry E, Perry R, Blessed G, et al. (1978): Changes in brain cholinesterases in senile dementia of Alzheimer's type. Neuropathological Applications of Neurobiology 4:273–277.

Rainer MK, Masching AJ, Ertl MG, Kraxberger E, Haushofer M (2001): Effect of Risperidone on behavioral and psychological symptoms and cognitive function in dementia. Journal of Clinical Psychiatry 62:894–900.

Ransmayr G (2002): [Dementia with Lewy bodies]. Wiener Medizinische Wochenschrift 152:81–84.

Rentz CA (2003): Creutzfeldt-Jakob disease: Two case studies. American Journal of Alzheimer's Disease and Other Dementias 18:171–180.

Riva E, Nobili A, Trecate F (1998): ["Judicious" use of neuroleptic drugs in the treatment of behavioral symptoms in the course of Alzheimer's disease]. Recenti Progression Medicina 89:598–603.

Rocchi A, Pellegrini S, Siciliano G, Murri L (2003): Causative and susceptibility genes for Alzheimer's disease: A review. Brain Research Bulletin 61:1–24.

Rogan S, Lippa CF (2002): Alzheimer's disease and other dementias: A review. American Journal of Alzheimer's Disease and Other Dementias 17:11–17.

Rogawski MA (2004): What is the rationale for new treatment strategies in Alzheimer's disease? CNS Spectrums 9 (supplement 5):6–12.

Rogers SL, Friedhoff LT (1998): Long-term efficacy and safety of donepezil in the treatment of Alzheimer's disease: An interim analysis of the results of a U.S. multicentre open label extension study. European Neuropharmacology 8:67–75.

Roman GC (2002): Vascular dementia revisited: Diagnosis, pathogenesis, treatment and prevention. Medical Clinics of North America 86:477–499.

Roman GC (2003): Vascular dementia: Distinguishing characteristics, treatment, and prevention. Journal of the American Geriatrics Society 51 (supplement Dementia):S296–304.

Rosler M, Anand R, Cicin-Sain A, Gauthier S, Agid Y, Dal-Blanco P, Stahelin HB, Hartman R, Gharabawim (1999): Efficacy and safety of rivastigmine in patients with Alzheimer's disease: International randomized controlled trial. British Medical Journal 318:633–638.

Salzman C (2001): Treatment of the agitation of late-life psychosis and Alzheimer's disease. European Psychiatry 16 (supplement 1):25s–28s.

Sano M, Ernesto C, Thomas RG, Klauber MR, Schafer K, Grundman M, Woodbury P, Growdon J, Cotman CW, Pfeiffer E, Schneider LS, Thal LJ (1997): A controlled trial of selegiline, alpha-tocopherol, or both as treatment for Alzheimer's disease: The Alzheimer's Disease Cooperative Study. New England Journal of Medicine 336:1216–1222.

Scarpini E, Scheltens P, Feldman H (2003): Treatment of Alzheimer's disease: Current status and new perspectives. Lancet Neurology 2:539–547.

Shigeta M, Homma A (2001): Donepezil for Alzheimer's disease: Pharmacodynamic, pharmaco-kinetic, and clinical profiles. CNS Drug Reviews 7:353–368.

Sinha S (2002): The role of beta-amyloid in Alzheimer's disease. Medical Clinics of North America 86:629–639.

Sleegers K, van Duijn CM (2001): Alzheimer's disease: Genes, pathogenesis, and risk prediction. Community Genetics 4:197–203.

Small GW, Rabins PV, Barry PP, et al. (1997): Diagnosis and treatment of Alzheimer's disease and related disorders: Consensus statement of the American Association for geriatric psychiatry, the Alzheimer's Association, and the American Geriatrics Society. Journal of the American Medical Association 278:1363–1371.

Stahl SM (2000): The new cholinesterase inhibitors for Alzheimer's disease, part 1: Their simi-larities are different. Journal of Clinical Psychiatry 61:710–711.

Sunderland T, Tariot PN, Cohen RM, et al. (1987): Anticholinergic sensitivity in patients with de-mentia of the Alzheimer's type and age-matched controls: A dose-response study. Archives of General Psychiatry 44:418–426.

Tabet N, Birks J, Grimley Evans J (2000): Vitamin E for Alzheimer's disease. Cochrane Database of Systematic Reviews CD002854.

Tariot PN, Sunderland T, Cohen RM, Newhouse PA, Muellar EA, Murphy DL (1988): Tranyl-cypromine compared with L-deprenyl in Alzheimer's disease. Journal of Clinical Psy-chopharmacology 8:23–27.

Tiraboschi P, Hansen LA, Alford M, Masliah E, Thal LJ, Corey-Bloom J (2000a): The decline in synapses and cholinergic activity is asynchronous in Alzheimer's disease. Neurology 55:1278–1283.

Tiraboschi P, Hansen LA, Alford M, et al. (2000b): Cholinergic dysfunction in diseases with Lewy bodies. Neurology 54:407–411.

Tiraboschi P, Hansen LA, Alford M, Merdes A, Masliah E, Thal LJ, Corey-Bloom J (2002): Early and widespread cholinergic losses differentiate dementia with Lewy bodies from Alzheimer disease. Archives of Clinical Psychiatry 59:946–951.

Tolnay M, Probst A (2001): Frontotemporal lobar degeneration. An update on clinical, patho-logical and genetic findings. Gerontology 47:1–8.

Trojanowski JQ, Lee VM-L (2002): The role of tau in Alzheimer's disease. Medical Clinics of North America 86:615–627.

van Dyck CH (2004): Understanding the latest advancers in pharmacologic interventions for Alzheimer's disease. CNS Spectrums 9 (supplement 5): 24–29.

Wagstaff A, McTavish D (1994): Tacrine: A review of its pharmacological and pharmacokinetic properties and their therapeutic potential in Alzheimer's disease. Drugs & Aging 4:1–31.

Wells CE, Whitehouse PJ (1996): Cortical dementia. In BS Fogel, RB Schiffer (eds.), SM Rao (as-sociate ed.), *Neuropsychiatry*. Baltimore, MD: Williams & Wilkins.

Wevers A, Schroder H (1999): Nicotinic acetylcholine receptors in Alzheimer's disease. Journal of Alzheimer's Disease 1:207–219.

Whitehouse PJ, Price DL, Struble RG, Clark AW, Coyle GT, DeLong MR (1982): Alzheimer's dis-ease and senile dementia: Loss of neurons in the basal forebrain. Science 215:1237–1239.

Wilcock GK, Birks J, Whitehead A, Evans SJ (2002): The effect of selegiline in the treatment of people with Alzheimer's disease: A meta-analysis of published trials. International Journal of Geriatric Psychiatry 17:175–183.

Wragg RE, Jeste DV (1989): Overview of depression and psychosis in Alzheimer's disease. Amer-ican Journal of Psychiatry 146:577–587.

■ ■ ■ ■ ■

CHAPTER THIRTEEN

ST. JOHN'S WORT, GINKGO, KAVA, AND VALERIAN

Used in many cases for millennia, herbal medications have been extensively used for the treatment of a wide range of conditions, including depression and anxiety. Furthermore, in recent years, sharp increases in the use of herbal medications have occurred around the world, including in the United States. This increase in the use of herbal medications can be attributed to a number of factors, not the least of which is patient autonomy and control. This chapter focuses on four herbal medications used widely for mental ailments such as depression, anxiety, and insomnia: St. John's wort, ginkgo, kava, and valerian. These preparations alter brain biochemistry in a number of ways and have been associated with adverse effects. An important consideration in the evaluation of herbal medications is the relative lack of well controlled trials establishing their use and safety.

St. John's wort, *Hypericum perforatum*, for example, contains numerous biologically active components, some of which may inhibit the reuptake of serotonin, norepinephrine, dopamine, and glutamate. In addition, St. John's wort may interact with GABA receptors. Furthermore, this herbal medication carries with it the potential to interact with other medications, particularly those drugs that increase the synaptic concentration of serotonin. Such an interaction has the potential of creating a serotonin syndrome. While St. John's wort is generally tolerated well, adverse effects can occur, including skin sensitivity to sunlight. The primary use of St. John's wort is for mild-to-moderate depression and, with less supporting evidence, anxiety, and possibly obsessive-compulsive disorder.

Next, ginkgo is prepared from *Ginkgo biloba* and has been used for thousands of years. Although its mechanism of action is poorly understood, gingko appears to act in a complex fashion that may involve the scavenging of membrane-damaging free radicals. Other mechanisms are likely such as increased peripheral and brain blood perfusion and enhanced acetylcholine function. Like St. John's wort, ginkgo is well tolerated but does produce some usually mild adverse effects like headache and heartburn. Its interaction with other drugs may be associated with easy bruising and bleeding. Ginkgo has been investigated as a treatment option for dementia and may stabilize the course of mild to moderate dementia.

Because of its ability to increase blood flow, ginkgo also has been used in some disorders of diminished peripheral blood flow.

Made from extracts of the kava kava plant (*Piper methysticum*), kava has traditionally been used in Polynesia but is seeing increased application in other parts of the world. With muscle-relaxing and anticonvulsant properties, kava may enhance GABA function and reduce anxiety. Although adverse effects from kava are usually mild and include gastrointestional upset, headaches, and skin reactions, kava has been banned in the United Kingdom because of rare but potentially fatal liver toxicity. Kava generally is used for anxiety and insomnia.

Valerian is produced from Valeriana officinalis and seems to interact with the GABA receptor. Additionally, it may inhibit the metabolism of GABA, thus increasing synaptic GABA. While it generally appears relatively safe, valerian has been associated with liver and kidney toxicity as well as with tremors. Primary uses of valerian are for insomnia, anxiety, and possibly depression.

Herbal medications have been used by various cultures for centuries as treatments and tonics for mental and physical complaints of different types. Medicinal plant pollens, for example, have been found in Neandertal burial sites in Iraq dating back 60,000 years (Krystal & Ressler, 2001; Secki & Shanidar, 1975). While it is, of course, unknown exactly what the Neandertals did with these plants, this finding is intriguing and suggests that the use of plants for treating disease may have been done for a very long time. Consonant with this suggestion, medicinal plants have been described in many ancient cultures, including Chinese, Assyrian, and Greek writings (Barrett et al., 1999; Krystal & Ressler, 2001).

Generally viewed as alternative medicine compared more traditional drugs, herbal remedies have seen staggering increases in use in recent years, not only in the United States but worldwide (Boniel & Dannon, 2001). In the United States alone, an estimated $27 billion is spent yearly on alternative medicine (Eisenberg et al., 1998), much of which includes herbal medications. Because of the Dietary Supplement Health and Education Act, the dietary supplements can bypass approval from the United States Food and Drug Administration (Pies, 2000) and enter the market with little available data concerning their efficacy (Sommer & Schatzberg, 2002), even if touted as effective for depression (Gorman, 2001). In addition, there is an overall paucity of safety studies for herbal medications (Gorman, 2001; Pies, 2000). As a case in point, little information exists about adverse drug-drug interactions between herbal medications and other psychotropic drugs (Gorman, 2001). Safety data too can be elusive for alternative medications that bypass the U.S. Food and Drug Administration—the removal in 2004 of the popular drug ephedrine from marketing as a dietary supplement because of safety concerns (Lipman, 2004) illustrates the need for caution and research concerning these alternative psychotropic agents. Even though good, rigorous data can be hard to find for herbal medicines, kava, St. John's wort, gingko, and valerian were among the top fifteen herbals sold in 1998 (Eisenberg et al., 1998).

Complementary and alternative therapies, which include not only herbal medications but also approaches such as exercise and relaxation, are used more frequently than are conventional medications (i.e., those approved by the Food and Drug Administration) by people with self-defined panic attacks and severe depression (Kessler et al., 2001). Furthermore, the majority of people who attend more conventional mental health clinics also use complementary and alternative treatments (Kessler et al., 2001). A study from the Netherlands (van Rijswijk et al., 2000) found that the prevalence of psychological problems was higher in the users of what the authors referred to as "over-the-counter psychotropics" than in non-users.

People may prefer herbal medications in part because they believe that this treatment approach offers safer and more holistic alternatives than do conventional medications (Yager et al., 1999). Also, it has been suggested that people want control in selecting and administering their own medications (see, for example, Healy, 1997), and the ready availability of herbal medications may provide people a degree of autonomy in treating mental distress. Moreover, many people believe that herbal medications are bereft of adverse effects (Wagner et al., 1999) and are therefore somehow natural and thus safer than conventional medications. An additional factor is that relatively few people tell their physicians that they are taking alternative medications (Druss & Rosenheck, 1999). Such a stance can increase the possibility of adverse drug-drug interactions.

Despite the overall lack of data regarding herbal medications, a number of studies have been done evaluating some of the herbal medications. After the initial public interest for these compounds, good clinical trials have in some cases dampened the enthusiasm noted above, leading to a more cautious appraisal of these medications (Davidson & Connor, 2001a). While there is evidence for the rational use of some herbal medications, it is often difficult to evaluate these compounds due to their often complex pharmacology, the lack of standardized dosing and concentrations, and the overall paucity of well-controlled studies (Beaubrun & Gray, 2000). Further complicating matters is that, in many cases, the known pharmacology of these preparations cannot account for the proposed clinical effects. Additive interactions among the various active components of a particular herbal medication may interact with each other and contribute to the drug's overall clinical effects (Spinella, 2002). Herbal medications can be obtained in health-food stores and pharmacies, often without any medical advice, and yet they are capable of altering mood and cognition, causing adverse effects, and interacting with other drugs (Boniel & Dannon, 2001).

ST. JOHN'S WORT

St. John's wort is the common name for the flowering herb *Hypericum perforatum* (Lee et al., 2003), whose yellow flowers (Meltzer-Brody, 2001) were used in the feast of St. John the Baptist (Gaster & Holroyd, 2000). Used for centuries in Europe as a tonic-like agent for depression and anxiety, St. John's wort also has been used for such diverse conditions as insomnia, ulcers, tumors, inflammation, nerve pain, cancer, hemorrhoids, burns, kidney disease, and scabies, among others (Fetrow & Avila, 1999; Meltzer-Brody, 2001; Upton, 1999). As St. John's wort is considered a dietary supplement in the United States, it has been able to bypass much of the rigorous testing required of antidepressants and anxiolytics (Gaster & Holroyd, 2000). Despite this, approximately thirty controlled clinical trials with varying methodologies have evaluated St. John's wort in the treatment of depression (Kessler et al., 2001), providing some reasonable information guiding comparisons with other antidepressants.

Despite the lack of careful evaluation, the sales of St. John's wort in the United States increased from $20 million in 1995 to $400 million in 1998 (Meltzer-Brody, 2001) (Blumenthal, 1999, puts the 1998 sales at $140 million), and in Germany, St. John's wort accounts for more than a quarter of all antidepressant prescriptions (Müller & Kasper, 1997), signaling that regardless of its marketing status and herbal origins, St. John's wort requires careful psychopharmacological consideration in regards to its efficacy, safety, and role in psychopharmacology.

Mechanism of Action, Pharmacology, and Metabolism

For a pretty, yellow, flowering herb, St. John's wort is surprisingly complex pharmacologically, containing at least ten biologically active constituents that include hypericin, hyperforin, pseudohypericin, xanthones, essential oils, tannic acid, and some amino acids, such as the neurotransmitter glutamate (Gaster & Holroyd, 2000), although it is unclear which if any of these is responsible for the antidepressant properties of St. John's wort. The concentrations of these compounds can vary depending upon the variety of St. John's wort and the conditions under which it was grown and processed (Wagner & Bladt, 1994).

Hypericin and hyperforin are the two components of St. John's wort that have been the most thoroughly evaluated (Beaubrun & Gray, 2000). Whereas some evidence has suggested that hypericin has monoamine-oxidase-inhibiting properties, this effect, if present at all, appears small and may not account for the antidepressant properties of St. John's wort (Müller et al., 1997). Furthermore, no cases of hypertensive crises of the type associated with typical monoamine oxidase inhibitors have been reported from St. John's wort (Cott, 1997).

On the other hand, hyperforin appears to inhibit the reuptake of serotonin, dopamine, norepinephrine, and glutamate (Meltzer-Brody, 2001), suggesting that some of the antidepressant effect from St. John's wort results not from hypericin as previously believed but rather from hyperforin. In rats, St. John's wort has been shown to increase the release of dopamine from the nucleus accumbens and striatum (Di Matteo et al., 2000). St. John's wort also interacts with GABA A and B receptors (Wong et al., 1998).

The half-life of hypericin is about one day (Wong et al., 1998), which allows for once-daily dosing and simplifies the overall administration of this drug. Its metabolic pathways are essentially unknown, although it appears to interact with a variety of other drugs as outlined below.

Drug-Drug Interactions

Because of its monoamine-oxidase-inhibiting activity, the possibility exists that St. John's wort could interact with anything that interacts with a monoamine-oxidase-inhibiting antidepressant (Wong et al., 1998). However, this monoamine-oxidase inhibition has not been demonstrated *in vivo*. Furthermore, to date, there have been no hypertensive reactions reported in association with St. John's wort (Cott, 2001) and dietary restrictions are not required to take St. John's wort, as they are for most if not all monoamine-oxidase inhibitors. Despite these reassurances, interactions between drugs that interact with monoamine-oxidase inhibitors and St. John's wort are possible (Wong et al., 1998). St. John's wort, when combined with specific-serotonin reuptake inhibitors, has the potential to cause a serotonin syndrome (Brenner et al., 2002), a concern supported by case reports suggesting that the combination of St. John's wort and selective serotonin reuptake inhibitors can induce a mild serotonin syndrome (Fugh-Berman, 2000).

St. John's wort can interact with several medications, however, via a different mechanism from monoamine-oxidase inhibition. Several cases, for instance, have been reported in which St. John's wort has appeared to lower concentrations of the immunosuppressant cyclosporine (Cott, 2001). St. John's wort has also been reported to interact with other drugs, including the cardiac drug digoxin, the protease inhibitor (used in HIV infection) indinavir, certain anticoagulants such as coumadin, and oral contraceptives (Cott, 2001). The combination of St. John's wort and some oral contraceptives can result in bleeding between menstrual periods (Izzo & Ernst, 2001). Finally, St. John's wort has been reported to lower blood concentrations of the tricyclic antidepressant amitriptyline, as well as concentrations of the antiasthmatic drug theophylline (Izzo & Ernst, 2001). In the short-term, St. John's wort appears to inhibit the cytochrome P450 enzyme 3A4 but induce it when given chronically (Cott, 2001), making drug-drug interactions possible with agents dependent upon cytochrome P450 for their metabolism.

Adverse Effects

In general, St. John's wort appears to be fairly well tolerated (Pies, 2000), although there is little data systematically evaluating its adverse-effect profile (Pies, 2000). Among the adverse effects reported for St. John's wort are skin sensitivity to sunlight, sedation, dry mouth, dizziness, and gastrointestional upset (Wong et al., 1998). Like most other antidepressants, St. John's wort may induce mania (Boniel & Dannon, 2001). In his review, Ernst (2002) concludes that when taken alone, St. John's wort's safety is better than conventional antidepressants.

Uses

Depression. Two separately conducted meta-analyses of the literature concerning the clinical efficacy of St. John's wort for depression concluded that, overall, St. John's wort appears to be superior to placebo and comparable to conventional antidepressants (Linde et al., 1996; Stevinson & Ernst, 1999). Many of the studies, however, included in these meta-analyses suffered from a variety of methodological problems, including short duration of the clinical trial, non-standardized diagnosis, and poor assessment tools. A review of the uses of St. John's wort in depression published in 2000 found that five of nine controlled- and standardized-clinical trials of St. John's wort showed that it was better than placebo, and four studies showed that it was as effective as standard antidepressants (Beaubrun & Gray, 2000). The first large-scale, randomized, placebo-controlled clinical trial in the United States in moderate to severe major depression found St. John's wort to be ineffective in the treatment of depression over eight weeks of treatment (Shelton et al., 2001). However, in this study, St. John's wort did appear to be safe and well tolerated.

Obsessive-Compulsive Disorder.   A small, uncontrolled study involving twelve patients with obsessive-compulsive disorder found improvement in obsessive-compulsive symptoms from St. John's wort (Taylor & Kobak, 2000). The limitations of small, non-placebo-controlled trials make it difficult to assess this information, and additional work is required prior to concluding that St. John's wort is effective in treating obsessive-compulsive disorder.

Anxiety.   While St. John's wort is used extensively for the treatment of anxiety, little evidence supports this practice, although St. John's wort was found effective based upon case reports in the treatment of a small number of people with generalized anxiety disorder (Davidson & Connor, 2001b).

GINKGO

A top-selling herbal medication in the United States as of 1998, accounting for $151 million in retail sales (Blumenthal, 1999), ginkgo is produced from the bi-lobed leaves of the ginkgo tree (*Ginkgo biloba*) (Wong et al., 1998). Native to Korea and China and introduced into Europe, Japan, and the United States (Zimmerman et al., 2002), ginkgo has been used in China and Europe as a medicinal herb (Wong et al., 1998). In addition to having been investigated for use in dementia in Europe and the United States (Sommer & Schatzberg, 2002), ginkgo has been used in a wide array of other diagnoses, including asthma, chilblains, glaucoma, and poor concentration (Ernst, 2002; Granger, 2001). However, much of the lack of research that hampers the clinical use of other herbal medications also hinders the widespread acceptance of ginkgo.

Mechanism of Action, Pharmacology, and Metabolism

While its mechanism of action is not completely known, ginkgo does appear to be a free-radical scavenger, diminishing, in theory, damage done to neurons and neuronal cell membranes by free radicals (Kade & Miller, 1993). Additive effects between some of the various chemical constituents of ginkgo, such as flavonoids, terpenoids, and organic acids, may account for ginkgo's free-radical scavenger properties (Le Bars, 1997). Components of ginkgo such as ginkgolide B also inhibit platelet-activating factor (Braquet et al., 1985), a process that presumably results in better blood perfusion into the brain. Ginkgo may also improve brain blood flow by altering blood vessel tone (Wong et al., 1998). Furthermore, evidence supports the idea that gingko may increase muscarinic acetylcholine receptors (De-Feudis, 1998). As Alzheimer's dementia appears to involve a reduction of the neurons that contain acetylcholine and drugs used to treat the cognitive problems of Alzheimer's disease increase the concentration of brain acetylcholine, the ginkgo-induced effects on acetylcholine physiology may be an integral part of ginkgo's mechanism of action (Sommer & Schatzberg, 2002). Alternatively, in a study of aged rats, ginkgo appeared to affect the norepinephrine system (Huguet & Tarrade, 1992). Finally, in general, little is known about the pharmacokinetics and metabolism of ginkgo, although in a study involving healthy volunteers, ginkgo reached maximum concentration in the blood about 2.3 hours after ingestion (Drago et al., 2002).

Drug-Drug Interactions

Several reports have suggested that ginkgo may have an anticoagulant effect and increase the chances of spontaneous bleeding, including hemorrhaging within the brain (Rowin & Lewis, 1996; Vale, 1998). This suggests that ginkgo should be used only with great caution with other anticoagulants, such as aspirin, nonsteroidal, anti-inflammatory drugs (such medications as ibuprofen and acetaminophen), and coumadin (Boniel & Dannon, 2001). Elevated blood pressure has also been reported from a combination of ginkgo and a thiazide diuretic (a blood-pressure lowering agent) (Izzo & Ernst, 2001). Finally, coma has been reported from ginkgo taken together with the antidepressant trazodone (Desyrel) (Izzo & Ernst, 2001).

Adverse Effects

In general, ginkgo is well tolerated with a low incidence of reported adverse effects (Wong et al., 1998), although adverse effects have occurred. Among the known adverse effects from ginkgo are headache, heartburn, low blood pressure (Itil, 2001), and gastrointestional upset (Wong et al., 1998). As might be expected from its reported propensity for some anticoagulation effects, excessive bleeding has occurred from the use of ginkgo (Rowin & Lewis, 1996). A case of hypomania in a woman with mild head injury and depression was reported after a combination of ginkgo and St. John's wort was added to her existing medication regimen of flu-oxetine and buspirone (Spinella & Eaton, 2002). After the ginkgo and St. John's wort were discontinued, the hypomania resolved. Of course, case reports such as this are often difficult to assess as any number of factors could have contributed to the woman's hypomania in addition to the ginkgo, such as the St. John's wort, the history of mild brain trauma, and the presence of the existing medications. However, the potential of herbal medications to have unexpected consequences cannot be overlooked.

The dangers of ginkgo, however, are not limited to adverse effects. Ginkgo seeds can be poisonous and, in addition to being associated with diarrhea and vomiting, can cause repeated seizures, which may lead to death (Kajiyama et al., 2002). Administration of pyridoxal phosphate may, however, prevent ginkgo-seed seizures (Kajiyama et al., 2002). Ginkgo extracts also contain allergens and can cause dermatitis. A case of diffuse morbilliform eruption was reported in a woman who had ingested ginkgo (Chiu et al., 2002). Finally, two epileptic patients who had been seizure free on anticonvulsant medications were reported to develop recurrent seizures after starting a course of ginkgo (Granger, 2001). The seizures, however, resolved after discontinuation of the ginkgo, suggesting that ginkgo may alter seizure thresholds in some people.

Uses

Dementia.   Beaubrun and Gray (2000) reviewed forty controlled studies of the use of ginkgo in dementia and found that in thirty-nine of these studies, ginkgo resulted in clinically significant improvement in memory, concentration, and affective symptoms. However, as is often the case, these studies were limited by poorly characterized study participants and small sample sizes. In a placebo-controlled trial from the United States, Le Bars et al. (1997) found that in demented patients with mild to moderately severe cognitive impairment, ginkgo improved cognition, daily living, and social behavior. While these changes were modest, caregivers of the subjects noticed improvement. More recently, Le Bars et al. (2002) observed improvement in cognition and social behavior in people with very mild to mild impairment and decreased deterioration or even stabilization in more severe cases. While these studies are promising, they require additional work to establish more clearly and fully ginkgo's place in the treatment of dementia (Sommer & Shatzberg, 2002).

Ginkgo may increase aspects of cognitive function in healthy people (Sommer & Schatzberg, 2002). In a sample of cognitively normal participants—participants who were free from dementia—a thirty-day trial of ginkgo resulted in significant improvement compared to placebo in working memory (Stough et al., 2001). In another study, healthy subjects who were given a combination of ginkgo and ginseng in a controlled, double-blind fashion demonstrated improvement at the higher doses in what the authors referred to as quality of memory. Conversely, the participants experienced a dose-dependent decrease in performance in the "speed of attention" domain (Kennedy et al., 2001), underscoring the importance of investigating different aspects of cognitive function when evaluating cognitive- and memory-enhancing drugs. Yet another study found that while well tolerated, ginkgo did not enhance memory in healthy male subjects (Moulton et al., 2001).

As is the case with ginkgo and dementia, these studies are intriguing but the place of ginkgo in memory enhancement (not to mention the ethical concerns) requires additional research. Keeping in mind the difficulties extrapolating findings from animal studies to humans, Topic and colleagues (2002) found preliminary evidence that zingicomb, which is composed of both *Zingiber officinale* and ginkgo, increased spatial learning ability in aged rats.

Early Use in Schizophrenia.   An early but nevertheless intriguing study found that ginkgo might enhance the effects of haloperidol (Haldol) in otherwise treatment-resistant schizophrenia. Basing the rationale for this study on indications that the etiology of schizophrenia could involve excessive free radicals and on suggestions that free-radical scavengers might improve the symptoms of schizophrenia, the researchers found that the use of ginkgo with haloperidol decreased the positive symptoms of schizophrenia more so than haloperidol alone and possibly reduced extrapyramidal side effects (Zhang et al., 2001), although it must be kept in mind that this work is preliminary.

Tinnitus.   Tinnitus is an annoying ringing and buzzing sound that may be associated with microvascular disease. As ginkgo appears to decrease the viscosity of blood and might increase the flow of blood through the microvasculature, ginkgo has been investigated for the treatment of tinnitus. Few randomized, controlled trials for the effects of ginkgo on tinnitus exist, but a review of the available studies found that ginkgo may be helpful in the treatment for tinnitus (Ernst & Stevinson, 1999).

Intermittent Claudication.   From the Latin *claudere* (to limp), intermittent claudication is a disease of the vascular system of the legs that results in painful limping upon walking due to insufficient blood supply to the lower extremities. Similar to the rationale for the use of ginkgo in tinnitus and ginkgo's ability to increase circulation (McKenna et al., 2002), several studies have investigated the use of ginkgo for intermittent claudication, finding that there is a moderate positive effect from ginkgo in this disease (Ernst, 2002).

KAVA

Kava is an extract of the kava-kava plant (*Piper methysticum*), which is found on islands in the South Pacific (Mischoulon, 2002), where indigenous peoples have used it for centuries. Polynesians reported that a kava drink had calming effects without disrupting consciousness (Singh, 1992). In Europe, where it has been known of for only a century, kava has been used for a diverse range of conditions such as asthma, gonorrhea, some skin disorders, and urinary tract infections (Connor et al., 2001). However, kava is no longer considered a main treatment for any of these diseases.

Mechanism of Action, Pharmacology, and Metabolism

Several biologically active compounds have been found in kava, but its mechanism of action remains unknown. Antioxidant activity has been identified in some of these compounds (Wu et al., 2002). In addition, the kavapyrones found in kava may have muscle-relaxing properties as well as anticonvulsant properties (Ernst, 2002). Kava also has been suggested to enhance the action of GABA in the amygdala but does not seem to be an agonist itself at these receptors (Jussofie et al., 1994). Such a mechanism could account for the putative anxiolytic effects from kava. In a study involving rats, certain kavapyrones were shown to inhibit the reuptake of norepinephrine in the cortex and hippocampus (Seitz et al., 1997). Kavapyrones have half-lives that vary from an hour and a half to several hours (Mischoulon, 2002).

Drug-Drug Interactions

In general, there have been relatively few drug-drug interactions reported for kava. The combination of kava and alcohol was reported to result in greater cognitive impairment than occurs from both agents when taken alone (Foo & Lemon, 1997). Furthermore, an isolated case report suggested an interaction associated with lethargy and disorientation between kava and the benzodiazepine alprazolam (Xanax) (Almeida & Grimsley, 1996), although, in general, kava does not seem to potentiate the cognitive effects of central nervous system depressants (Stevinson et al., 2002). Finally, kava, when used in conjunction with the anti-Parkinsonian drug levodopa, may shorten the time that levodopa is helpful (Izzo & Ernst, 2001).

Adverse Effects

In general, the reported adverse effects from kava have been rare and mild (Stevinson et al., 2002) and include gastrointestinal upset and headaches (Schultz et al., 2001). However, serious events have been reported, including dermatological reactions and liver damage (Stevinson et al., 2002). In fact, due to rare liver toxicity, kava has been banned in the United Kingdom (Walsh, 2003). Chronic use of high-dose kava has also been associated in the South Pacific with dry, yellowish skin and diminished auditory acuity (Norton & Ruze, 1994). Kava also has been noted to produce dizziness in some people (Wheatley, 2001). Finally, there is a case of kava inducing severe features of Parkinson's disease in a woman whose family history was notable for essential tremor (Meseguer et al., 2002). However, a double-blind, placebo-controlled trial of kava in generalized anxiety disorder found no significant differences in the incidence of reported adverse effects between kava and placebo (Connor et al., 2001). Despite the putative anxiolytic properties of kava, it is claimed that kava is free from dependence, a feature that so often complicates the use of other anxiolytics such as benzodiazepines and barbiturates (Wheatley, 2001).

Uses

Anxiety.   In part due to limitations of other, more conventional anxiolytic drugs, people have turned to alternative compounds including kava for anxiety treatment (Mischoulon, 2002). A review of the uses of kava reported that several double-blind, placebo-controlled clinical trials had found that kava does have anxiolytic properties, although the authors noted that these studies were limited in their generalizability by small sample sizes, clinical populations that were poorly characterized, and short durations of the actual clinical trials (Beaubrun & Gray, 2000).

Insomnia.   Kava has been found to diminish both stress and insomnia in a non-blinded study of stress-induced insomnia (Wheatley, 2001).

VALERIAN

Valerian is the common name for the approximately 170 species of the *Valeriana* genus, of which *Valeriana officinalis* is perhaps the most widely used in herbal medicine (Krystal & Ressler, 2001). The pink-flowered *Valeriana* species grow throughout North America, Europe, and Asia (Krystal & Ressler, 2001). Its sedative effects described for a thousand years (Krystal & Ressler, 2001), valerian was used in the time of Hippocrates to treat urinary tract disorders, gastrointestional disorders, and flatulence and is used widely now for a variety of ailments (Krystal & Ressler, 2001). Valerian also has been used in folk medicine as an anticonvulsant (Ortiz et al., 1999). Like many other herbal medications, the concentrations of valerian's constituents can vary widely from preparation to preparation, depending upon growing conditions and processing methods (Barrett et al., 1999).

Mechanism of Action, Pharmacology, and Metabolism

Valerian is composed of many potentially psychoactive compounds, including monoterpene bornyl acetate and sesquiterpene valerenic acid (Houghton, 1999), but it is unknown which, if any, of these substances accounts for the mental effects of valerian. It does appear, however, that valerian has GABA-like effects in that it interacts with the GABA receptor itself and not the benzodiazepine receptor, although one compound found in valerian, hydroxypinoresinol, does bind to benzodiazepine receptors (Houghton, 1999). Furthermore, valerian itself actually may contain GABA (Wong et al., 1998). In addition, valerenic acid, another component of valerian, may inhibit the metabolism of GABA (Houghton, 1999), increasing GABA concentrations in the brain. These factors may account for some of the putative anxiolytic and sedative effects associated with valerian. Valerian also appears to alter sleep architecture in the electroencephalogram (Balderer & Borbely, 1985). Furthermore, some evidence also indicates that valerian may displace melatonin, increasing free concentrations of this hormone, which is also related to sedation (Bodesheim & Holzl, 1997). Finally, a valerian-hops mixture was found to increase delta and decrease alpha and beta frequencies of the electroencephalogram (Vonderheid-Guth et al., 2000), suggesting a slowing of brain electrical activity, although the addition of hops to valerian complicates interpretation of this data study.

Adverse Effects

Valerian can cause several potentially serious adverse effects. Nephrotoxicity (a toxic reaction of the kidneys), headaches, and chest tightness have all been associated with valerian use. In addition, valerian use is related to abdominal pain and tremors of both the hands and the feet (Boniel & Dannon, 2001). Valerian use also has been associated with vivid dreams (Wheatley, 2001). Four cases of hepatitis have also been reported in people who were taking both valerian and another herbal medication, skullcap (Krystal & Ressler, 2001), making the contribution of valerian alone to hepatic toxicity difficult to assess. Impairment of reaction time and alertness is a concern with any drug that has sedative and anxiolytic effects, but a recent randomized, placebo-controlled, double-blind study found neither a single evening dose or repeated (over fourteen days) evening doses of valerian had a negative effect on reaction time, alertness, or concentration the morning after the drug was ingested (Kuhlmann et al., 1999), although use of valerian is associated with sedation (Wong et al., 1998). This finding suggests that, at the doses evaluated, valerian may be relatively free from the adverse cognitive effects that have so troubled treatment with barbiturates and benzodiazepines. A related issue is that valerian is supposedly free also from addictive and abuse potential (Wheatley, 2001). In a reported case of overdose on valerian, at approximately twenty times the suggested clinical dose, the patient had relatively mild symptoms consisting of abdominal cramping, lightheadedness, hand and foot tremors, and chest tightness, of which all resolved within twenty-four hours (Willey et al., 1995). Table 13.1 summarizes the adverse effects and proposed uses of St. John's wort, gingko, kava, and valerian.

Uses

Insomnia.   A literature review of nine randomized, placebo-controlled, double-blind clinical trials investigating the effects of valerian on insomnia found that the effects of valerian of insomnia were often contradictory and that there was extensive inconsistency between studies, with the authors concluding that the evidence supporting the use of valerian in insomnia is inconclusive (Stevinson & Ernst, 2000). However, in another, carefully designed sleep study, while no differences

TABLE 13.1   Herbal Medications: Their Adverse Effects and Uses

TYPE OF HERBAL MEDICATION	ADVERSE EFFECTS	PROPOSED USES
St. John's Wort	Dry mouth, sedation, dizziness, skin sensitivity to sunlight, confusion.	Depression, Obsessive-Compulsive Disorder, and Anxiety.
Ginkgo	Headache, heartburn, low blood pressure, excessive bruising and bleeding, hypomania, seeds can be poisonous, and extracts also contain allergens and can cause dermatitis and diffuse morbilliform eruption.	Dementia, Tinnitus, and Intermittent Claudication.
Kava	Gastrointestional upset, headaches, dermatological reactions, liver damage, dry, yellowish skin, diminished auditory acuity, and dizziness.	Anxiety and Insomnia.
Valerian	Nephrotoxicity, headaches, chest tightness, abdominal pain, tremors of both the hands and the feet, vivid dreams, possibly hepatitis, and, possibly impairment of reaction time and alertness.	Insomnia, Anxiety, and Depression.

between valerian and placebo were found in sleep structure (as assessed by polysomnography) and subjective reports of sleep quality, multiple doses of valerian resulted in a reduced latency time to slow-wave sleep and an increased percentage of time spent in slow-wave sleep, as well as a subjectively shorter latency to sleep onset (Donath et al., 2000). This finding suggests that valerian has positive effects on sleep architecture and subjective perception of improved sleep. Valerian also has been reported to decrease the number of nighttime awakenings (Beaubrun & Gray, 2000). In another study of stress-induced insomnia, valerian was found to both relieve stress and insomnia (Wheatley, 2001).

Anxiety.   Valerian has been reported to have anxiolytic properties (Boniel & Dannon, 2001). With little information available about its anxiolytic effects, the role of valerian in the treatment of anxiety disorders requires additional research.

Depression.   Reports have suggested a use for valerian as an antidepressant (Boniel & Dannon, 2001). The work done in major depression with valerian, however, has been done in combinations of valerian and some other herbal medication, such as St. John's wort, severely limiting the conclusions that can be drawn (Krystal & Ressler, 2001). Clearly, additional research is required to more carefully evaluate the antidepressant properties of valerian. In animal models used to predict antidepressant response in humans, valerian has shown effects similar to more traditional antidepressants, responses that suggest the possibility of antidepressant features (Sakamoto et al., 1992).

SUMMARY

Herbal medications that in some cases have been used for bodily ailments for millennia have seen sharp increases in sales in recent years. The four herbal medications reviewed here are remarkable for their novel proposed mechanisms of action such as antioxidant properties, as in the case of ginkgo, and for actions that are more familiar, as with St. John's wort and its possible inhibition of the reuptake of norepinephrine, serotonin, and dopamine.

Intriguing and in some instances promising research suggests that St. John's wort, ginkgo, kava, and valerian may have effects on mood, anxiety, and in the case of ginkgo, dementia and memory difficulties. The most clearly defined uses for St. John's wort appear to be for the treatment of mild to moderate depression. Kava and valerian seem to have their most well supported use in the treatment of mild to moderate anxiety, as well as insomnia. Ginkgo's role involves the treatment of mild to moderate dementia. Despite the existing evidence supporting these uses of these herbal medications, many of these studies are confounded by methodological flaws, urging caution in the use of these herbal medications. Additional research, simply put, is required before the roles and limitations of these medications can be clearly defined.

While St. John's wort, ginkgo, kava, and valerian are in general well tolerated, adverse effects, some of them quite serious, as with all medications, can occur. Drug-drug interactions, again some of them clinically significant, have been reported, a problem confounded by the tendency for patients to not inform their physicians that they are taking herbal medications.

STUDY QUESTIONS

1. Discuss the mechanism of action, adverse effects, potential for drug-drug interactions, and putative uses for St. John's wort.
2. Discuss the mechanism of action, adverse effects, potential for drug-drug interactions, and putative uses of ginkgo.
3. Discuss the mechanism of action, adverse effects, potential for drug-drug interactions, and putative uses of kava.
4. Discuss the mechanism of action, adverse effects, potential for drug-drug interactions, and putative uses of valerian.
5. What factors would you consider if a patient of yours expressed an interest in using herbal medications?

REFERENCES

Almeida JC, Grimsley EW (1996): Coma from the health food store: Interaction between kava and alprazolam. Annals of Internal Medicine 125:940.

Balderer G, Borbely AA (1985): Effect of valerian of human sleep. Psychopharmacology (Berlin) 87:406–409.

Barrett B, Kiefer D, Rabago D (1999): Assessing the risks and benefits of herbal medicine: An overview of scientific evidence. Alternative Therapies in Health and Medicine 5:40–49.

Beaubrun G, Gray GE (2000): A review of herbal medications for psychiatric disorders. Psychiatric Services 51:1130–1134.

Blumenthal M (1999): Herbal market levels after five years of boom. HerbalGram 47:64–65.

Bodesheim U, Holzl J (1997): Isolierung, strukturaufknlorung und radiorezeptorasays von alkaloiden und lignanen aus Valeriana officialis L. Pharmazie 52:387–391.

Boniel T, Dannon P (2001): [The safety of herbal medications in psychiatric practice]. Harefuah 140:780–783, 805.

Braquet PG, Spinnewyn B, Braquet M (1985): BN 52021 and related compounds: a new series of highly specific PAF-acether antagonists isolated from *Gingko biloba* L. Blood Vessels 16:558–572.

Brenner R, Bjerkenstedt L, Edman G (2002): *Hypericum perforatum* extract (St. John's wort) for depression. Psychiatric Annals 32:21–26.

Chiu AE, Lane AT, Kimball AB (2002): Diffuse morbilliform eruption after consumption of ginkgo biloba supplement. Journal of the American Academy of Dermatology 46:145–146.

Connor KM, Davidson JRT, Churchill LE (2001): Adverse-effect profile of Kava. CNS Spectrums 6:848–853.

Cott JM (2001): Herb-drug interactions: Focus on pharmacokinetics. CNS Spectrums 6:827–832.

Davidson JRT, Connor KM (2001a): Evaluating medicinal herbs. CNS Spectrums 6:826.

Davidson JRT, Connor KM (2001b): St. John's wort in generalized anxiety disorder: Three case reports. Journal of Clinical Psychopharmacology 21:635–636.

DeFeudis FV (1998): *Gingko biloba* extract (EGb 761): From chemistry to the clinic. Wiesbaden, Germany: Ullstein Medical Verlagsgessellschaft.

Di Matteo V, Di Mascio M, Di Giovanni G, Esposito E (2000): Effect of acute administration of *Hypericum perforatum*-CO_2 extract on dopamine and serotonin release in the rat central nervous system. Pharmacopsychiatry 33:14–18.

Donath F, Quispe S, Diefenbach K, Maurer A, Fietze I, Roots I (2000): Critical evaluation of the effect of valerian extract on sleep architecture and sleep quality. Pharmacopsychiatry 33:47–53.

Drago F, Floriddia ML, Cro M, Giuffrida S (2002): Pharmacokinetics and bioavailability of a Gingko biloba extract. The Journal of Ocular Pharmacology and Therapeutics 18:197–202.

Druss BG, Rosenheck RA (1999): Associations between use of unconventional therapies and conventional medical therapies. Journal of the American Medical Association 282:651–656.

Eisenberg DM, Davis RB, Ettner SL, Appel S, Wilkey S, Van Rompay M, Kessler RC (1998): Trends in alternative medicine use in the United States, 1990–1997: Results of a follow-up national survey. JAMA 28:1569–1575.

Ernst E (2002): The risk-benefit profile of commonly used herbal therapies: Ginkgo, St. John's wort, ginseng, echinacea, saw palmetto, and kava. Annals of Internal Medicine 136:42–53.

Ernst E, Stevinson C (1999): *Gingko biloba* for tinnitus: A review. Clinical Otolaryngology and Allied Sciences 24:164–167.

Fetrow CW, Avila JR (1999): *Professional's handbook of complementary and alternative medicines.* Springhouse, PA: Springhouse.

Foo H, Lemon J (1997): Acute effects of Kava, alone or in combination with alcohol, on subjective measures of impairment and intoxication and on cognitive performance. Drug and Alcohol Review 16:147–155.

Fugh-Berman A (2000): Herb-drug interactions. Lancet 355:134–138.

Gaster B, Holroyd J (2000): St. John's wort for depression: A systematic review. Archives of Internal Medicine 160:152–156.

Gorman JM (2001): Alternative, complementary, or not: Is mainstream medicine ready for herbal medicine? CNS Spectrums 6:825.

Granger AS (2001): Ginkgo biloba precipitating epileptic seizures. Age and Ageing 30:523–525.

Healy D (1997): *The antidepressant era*. Cambridge, MA: Harvard University Press.

Houghton PJ (1999): The scientific basis for the reputed activity of Valerian. The Journal of Pharmacy and Pharmacology 51:505–512.

Huguet F, Tarrade T (1992): K_2-Adrenoceptor changes during cerebral ageing: The effect of Gingko biloba extract. The Journal of Pharmacy and Pharmacology 44:24–27.

Itil TM (2001): Uses and contraindications of *Gingko biloba* in psychiatry. Psychiatric Times (November):47–49.

Izzo AA, Ernst E (2001): Interactions between herbal medicines and prescribed drugs: A systematic review. Drugs 61:2163–2175.

Jussofie A, Schmiz A, Hiemke C (1994): Kavapyrone enriched extract for *Piper methysticum* as modulator of the GABA binding site in different regions of rat brain. Psychopharmacology (Berlin) 116:469–474.

Kade F, Miller W (1993): Dose-dependent effects of Gingko biloba extract on cerebral, mental, and physical efficiency: A placebo-controlled double-blind study. British Journal of Clinical Research 4:97–103.

Kajiyama Y, Fujii K, Takeuchi H, Manabe Y (2002): Ginkgo seed poisoning. Pediatrics 109:325–327.

Kennedy DO, Scholey AB, Wesnes KA (2001): Differentia, dose-dependent changes in cognitive performance following acute administration of a Ginkgo biloba/Panax ginseng combination to healthy young volunteers. Nutritional Neuroscience 4:399–412.

Kessler RC, Soukup J, Davis RB, Foster DF, Wilkey SA, Van Rompay, Eisenberg DM (2001): The use of complementary and alternative therapies to treat anxiety and depression in the United States. American Journal of Psychiatry 158:289–294.

Krystal AD, Ressler I (2001): The use of valerian in neuropsychiatry. CNS Spectrums 6:841–847.

Kuhlmann J, Berger W, Podzuweit H, Schmidt U (1999): The influence of valerian treatment on "reaction time, alertness, and concentration" in normal volunteers. Pharmacopsychiatry 32:235–241.

Le Bars PL, Katz MM, Berman N, Itil TM, Freedman AM, Schatzberg AF (1997): A placebo-controlled, double-blind, randomized trial of an extract of Gingko biloba for dementia. Journal of the American Medical Association 278:1327–1332.

Le Bars PL, Velasco FM, Ferguson JM, Dessain EC, Kieser M, Hoerr I (2002): Influence of the severity of cognitive impairment on the effect of Ginkgo biloba extract EGb 761 in Alzheimer's desease. Neuropsychobiology 45:19–26.

Lee A, Minhas R, Matsuda N, Lam M, Ito S (2003): The safety of St. John's wort (*Hypericum perforatum*) during breastfeeding. Journal of Clinical Psychiatry 64:966–968.

Linde K, Ramirez G, Mulrow CD, Pauls A, Weidenhammer W, Melchert D (1996): St. John's wort for depression: An overview and meta-analysis of randomized clinical trials. British Medical Journal 313:253–258.

Lipman AG (2004): The federal ban of ephedrine dietary supplements: An important event for pain practitioners and patients. Journal of Pain & Palliative Care Pharmacotherapy 18:1–4.

McKenna DJ, Jones K, Hughes K (2002): Efficacy, safety, and use of ginkgo biloba in preclinical and clinical applications. Alternative Therapies in Health and Medicine 7:70–86.

Meltzer-Brody SE (2001): St. John's wort: Clinical status in psychiatry. CNS Spectrums 6:835–840.

Meseguer E, Toboada R, Sanchez V, Mena MA, Campos V, Garcia De Yebenes J (2002): Life-threatening parkinsonism induced by kava-kava. Movement Disorders 17:195–196.

Mischoulon D (2002): The herbal anxiolytics kava and valerian for anxiety and insomnia. Psychiatric Annals 32:55–60.

Moulton PL, Boyko LN, Fitzpatrick JL, Petros TV (2001): The effect of Ginkgo biloba in memory in health male volunteers. Physiology & Behavior 73:659–665.

Müller WE, Kasper S (1997): Clinically used antidepressant drugs. Pharmacopsychiatry 30 (supplement):S71.

Norton SA, Ruze P (1994): Kava dermopathy. Journal of the American Academy of Dermatology 31:89–97.

Ortiz JG, Nieves-Natal J, Chavez P (1999): Effects of Valeriana officinalis on [3H] flunitrazepam binding, synaptosomal [3H]GABA uptake, and hippocampal [3H]GABA release. Neurochemical Research 24:1373–1378.

Pies R (2000): Adverse neuropsychiatric reactions to herbal and over-the-counter "Antidepressants." Journal of Clinical Psychiatry 61:815–820.

Rowin J, Lewis SL (1996): Spontaneous bilateral subdural hematomas associated with chronic Gingko biloba ingestion. Neurology 46:1775–1776.

Sakamoto T, Mitani Y, Nakajima K (1992): Psychotropic effects of Japanese valerian root extract. Chemical & Pharmaceutical Bulletin 40:758–761.

Schultz V, Hansel R, Tyler VE (2001): *Rational phytotherapy: A physician's guide to herbal medicine* (4th ed.). Berlin: Springer.

Seitz U, Schule A, Gleitz J (1997): [3H]-monoamine uptake inhibition properties of kava pyrones. Planta Med 63:548–549.

Shelton RC, Keller MB, Gelenberg A, Dunner DL, Hirschfield R, Thase ME, Russel J, Lydiard RB, Crits-Cristoph P, Gallop R, Todd L, Hellerstein D, Goodnick P, Keitner G, Stahl SM, Halbreich U (2001): Effectiveness of St. John's wort in major depression: A randomized controlled trial. Journal of the American Medical Association 285:1978–1986.

Singh YN (1992): Kava: An overview. Journal of Ethnopharmacology 37:13–45.

Solecki RS, Shanidar IV (1975): Neanderthal flower burial in northern Iraq. Science 190:880.

Sommer BR, Shatzberg AF (2002): Ginkgo biloba and related compounds in Alzheimer's disease. Psychiatric Annals 32:13–18.

Spinella M (2002): The importance of pharmacological synergy in psychoactive herbal medicines. Alternative Medicine Review: A Journal of Clinical Therapeutic 7:130–137.

Spinella M, Eaton LA (2002): Hypomania induced by herbal and pharmaceutical psychotropic medicines following mild traumatic brain injury. Brain Injury 16:359–367.

Stevinson C, Ernst E (1999): Hypericum for depression: An update of the clinical evidence. European Neuropsychopharmacology 9:501–505.

Stevinson C, Ernst E (2000): Valerian for insomnia: A systematic review of randomized clinical trials. Sleep Medicine 1:91–99.

Stevinson C, Huntley A, Ernst E (2002): A systematic review of the safety of kava extract in the treatment of anxiety. Drug Safety 25:251–261.

Stough C, Clarke J, Lloyd J, Nathan PJ (2001): Neuropsychological changes after 30-day Ginkgo biloba administration in healthy participants. International Journal of Neuropsychopharmacology 4:131–134.

Taylor LVH, Kobak KA (2000): An open-label trial of St. John's wort (Hypericum perforatum) in obsessive-compulsive disorder. Journal of Clinical Psychiatry 61:575–578.

Topic B, Tani E, Tsiakitzis K, Kourounakis PN, Dere E, Hasenohrl RU, Hacker R, Mattern CM, Huston JP (2002): Enhanced maze performance and reduced oxidative stress by combined extracts of zingiber officinale and ginkgo biloba in the aged rat. Neurobiology of Aging 23:135–143.

Upton R (1999): St. John's wort (*Hypericum perforatum*). Herbalgram (American Herbal Pharmacopia, Santa Cruz, CA) 40:1–32.

Vale S (1998): Subarachnoid hemorrhage associated with gingko biloba. Lancet 352:36.

van Rijswijk E, van de Lisdonk EH, Zitman FG (2000): Who uses over-the-counter psychotropics? Characteristics, functioning, and (mental) health profile. General Hospital Psychiatry 22:236–241.

Vonderheid-Guth B, Todorova A, Brattstrom A, Dimpfel W (2000): Pharmacodynamic effects of valerian and hops extract combination (Ze 91019) on the quantitative-topographical EEG in healthy volunteers. European Journal of Medical Research 5:139–144.

Wagner H, Bladt S (1994): Pharmaceutical quality of Hypericum extracts. Journal of Geriatric Psychiatry and Neurology 7(supplement 1):65–68.

Wagner PJ, Jester D, LeClair B, Taylor AT, Woodward L, Lambert J (1999): Taking the edge off: Why patients choose St. John's wort. Journal of Family Practice 48:615–619.

Walsh N (2003): Kava formally banned in the U.K. due to hepatotoxicity. Clinical Psychiatry News 31:57.

Wheatley D (2001): Kava and valerian in the treatment of stress-induced insomnia. Phytotherapy Research 15:549–551.

Willey LB, Mady SP, Cobaugh DJ, Wax PM (1995): Valerian overdose: A case report. Veterinary and Human Toxicology 37:364–365.

Wong AH, Smith M, Boon HS (1998): Herbal remedies in psychiatric practice. Archives of General Psychiatry 55:1033–1044.

Wu D, Yu L, Nair MG, DeWitt DL, Ramsewak RS (2002): Cyclooxygenase enzyme inhibitory compounds with antioxidant activities from Piper methysticum (kava kava) roots. Phytomedicine 9:41–47.

Yager J, Siegfreid S, DiMatteo T (1999): Use of alternative remedies by psychiatric patients: Illustrative vignettes and a discussion of the issues. American Journal of Psychiatry 156:1432–1438.

Zhang XY, Zhou DF, Zhang PY, Wu GY, Su JM, Cao LY (2001): A double-blind, placebo-controlled trial of extract of Gingko biloba added to haloperidol in treatment-resistant patients with schizophrenia. Journal of Clinical Psychiatry 62:878–883.

Zimmerman M, Colciaghi F, Cattabeni F, Di Luca M (2002): Ginkgo biloba extract: From molecular mechanisms to the treatment of Alzheimer's disease. Cellular and Molecular Biology 48: 613–623.

ELECTROCONVULSIVE THERAPY, TRANSCRANIAL MAGNETIC STIMULATION, AND VAGAL NERVE STIMULATION

Although electroconvulsive therapy (ECT), transcranial magnetic stimulation (TMS), and vagal nerve stimulation (VNS) are not pharmacological agents per se, operating instead through electrical and magnetic fields, they are used for the treatment certain mental disorders. Additionally, these modalities cause a myriad of biochemical changes in brain tissue, in many cases similar to those induced by the more traditional drugs of psychopharmacology. ECT has long been approved for use in the United States and continues to be widely performed, particularly for psychotic and major depressions that have not responded to other approaches. TMS is approved in Canada for the treatment of depression and is widely used in research, for both its putative therapeutic properties as well as a neuropsychological probe secondary to its ability to cause so-called temporary virtual lesions. While it has been considered for a variety of disorders, TMS is used primarily for the experimental treatment of depression and has been considered as an alternative to ECT in certain cases. VNS is still in the experimental stages but offers a potentially unique approach to the treatment of mental and other disorders and thus merits inclusion in this chapter.

Despite significant controversy, even within psychiatry itself, ECT continues to be widely used. Given under general anesthesia and pharmacologically induced paralysis to minimize injury, ECT passes electricity through the brain to induce a seizure. The mechanism of action of ECT is unknown, although some biochemical changes follow ECT treatment that closely mimic those of various psychopharmacological drugs, including changes in certain neurotransmitters. Confusion and memory loss may worsen throughout the course of ECT but generally are believed to improve after the course of ECT is done. However, controversy about memory loss continues. The primary indications of ECT are depression, psychotic depression, mania, and catatonia.

TMS generates a magnetic field from magnets held near the scalp. This magnetic field passes unimpeded into the brain, where an electrical field is generated. This electrical field in turn is believed to cause neuronal hyperpolarization. While still a research tool in the United States without general approval from the Food and Drug Administration, early evidence indicates that TMS may possess antidepressant properties, particularly when TMS is applied over the prefrontal areas of the brain. Should TMS indeed prove effective for the treatment of depression, advantages over ECT could include fewer adverse memory and cognitive effects, less expense, and no requirement for general anesthesia.

An invasive treatment, VNS involves the implantation of an electrode under the skin of the lower neck that stimulates the vagus nerve. The tenth cranial nerve, the vagus nerve arises from the medulla, runs through the neck, and undergoes extensive branching, sending nerve fibers to the pharynx, larynx, lungs, aorta, and gastrointestional system. In the brain, it is connected to a variety of other brain regions, some of which may be involved in mood and emotion. Stimulation of this nerve presumably affects the medulla, which then can alter additional neural circuits in an as yet poorly described manner.

A highly controversial treatment (Gorman, 2003), electroconvulsive therapy (ECT) was introduced in 1938 (Bolwig, 2003). Although it is still widely used (American Psychiatric Association Committee on ECT, 2001), potential adverse effects (Bolwig, 2003) and controversy have led to other forms of treatment. A possible alternative to ECT for some cases of depression (Janicak et al., 2002), transcranial magnetic stimulation (TMS) was first developed in 1985 (Barker et al., 1985) and is approved for the treatment of depression in Canada. The seemingly least likely modality to have antidepressant effects, vagal nerve stimulation (VNS) was first used in the late 1880s by New York neurologist James Corning for the treatment of seizures (Lanska, 2002). However, at that time, VNS did not gain widespread acceptance and actually had fallen out of use by the end of the nineteenth century (Lanska 2002), only to be revived again in the late twentieth century.

While ECT, TMS, and VNS are clearly not drugs, they have been and are still used in psychiatry alongside drugs to alter brain physiology in the hopes of producing emotional and behavioral changes, especially in cases where drugs have proven ineffective or poorly tolerated. That methods of directly and indirectly electrically stimulating the brain can result in affective changes is illustrated by deep-brain stimulation. In this highly invasive technique (Goodnick et al., 2001), a lead is inserted surgically into different brain regions and electrical current applied from a generator placed in the chest (Bolwig, 2003). Although not used clinically in mental disorders, mood changes from the deep brain stimulation have been reported, including electrically induced feelings of sadness (George et al., 2000). Used for Parkinson's disease (Bolwig, 2003) and treatment-resistant epilepsy (Gorman, 2003), deep brain stimulation is not used in mental disorders (Goodnick et al., 2001) but provides a theoretical rationale for the use of similar, less invasive procedures.

ELECTROCONVULSIVE THERAPY (ECT)

Before ECT was introduced, Joseph Ladislas von Meduna used camphor and later metrazol to induce seizures in people with schizophrenia. Von Meduna based his work with drug-induced seizures on the mistaken notion that seizures were protective against schizophrenia (Valenstein, 1998). However, it was observed that people with depression responded better to the seizures than did people with schizophrenia (Valenstein, 1998). Ease of administration and improved safety, however, led to the demise of drug-induced seizures, and ECT became the preferred method of inducing seizures (Valenstein, 1998). Despite continuing controversy and the social stigma associated with ECT (Fink, 2003), ECT appears to be effective for a variety of mental disorders, including certain types of depression, mania, and the tremors associated with Parkinson's disease (Gorman, 2003), although, perhaps, no area of psychiatric treatment has generated as much contention as ECT (Gorman, 2003). Even the portrayal of ECT in the movies has become increasingly negative (McDonald & Walter, 2001). Heightening the disagreement over its use, ECT is one of the few medical treatments subjected to legal restraints (Scull, 1995).

In order for an antidepressant effect to occur, ECT appears to require the induction of a seizure lasting at least 20 seconds (Bolwig, 2003). Generally, a course of ECT requires six to twelve sessions (Bolwig, 2003). Although many of the issues regarding ECT remain unresolved (Scull, 1995), vast improvements in the method of administration of ECT have occurred. For example, ECT is now done under anesthesia. The most commonly used anesthetic for ECT is methohexital (Brevital) (Calarge et al., 2003), but other agents also are used. Ketamine, for example, may prolong seizure duration (Krystal et al., 2003), a possible advantage if seizures induced in the presence of methohexital are too brief. Alternatively, the anesthetic propofol can be used in cases complicated by prolonged ECT seizures (Bailine et al., 2003). To mitigate injury occurring during the procedure, bite blocks are used to prevent oral damage during ECT (Lippman et al., 1993).

ECT is administered through electrodes placed on the scalp. In general, bilateral electrode placement is associated with greater efficacy in depression (Bolwig, 2003) but more adverse cognitive effects (Lisanby et al., 2003). The muscle relaxant succinylcholine is used to inhibit the severe muscle contractions that otherwise occur during ECT administration (Cheam et al., 1999). In order to visually monitor the subsequent seizure activity, succinylcholine is prevented by means of a tourniquet restricting the blood supply from penetrating to a foot or hand, allowing the physicians to observe this isolated body part undergoing the muscle activity associated with the seizure (Lippman et al., 1993). Seizure activity also is monitored by electroencephalography, in addition to the muscle movements observed in a foot or hand (Lippman et al., 1993). The seizure threshold increases over the course of ECT (Bolwig, 2003), which can make it more difficult to induce subsequent seizures. To facilitate seizure induction, caffeine and other anesthetic agents, such as ketamine, may be used (Datto et al., 2002).

It may be that for optimal therapeutic efficacy to occur not only must the seizure threshold be exceeded, but it also must be exceeded by a certain degree. For example, some findings suggest that the efficacy rate in depression is 80 percent when the seizure threshold was exceeded by a factor of six, but only 17 percent when the seizure threshold was barely exceeded (Mann, 2001).

Mechanism of Action

Despite years of clinical use, the mechanism of action of ECT remains unknown. ECT does seem to require the induction of a generalized seizure to achieve efficacy (Lisanby et al., 2003). An intriguing finding about ECT is the aforementioned increase in seizure threshold (Bolwig, 2003). The mechanism of the increased seizure threshold may be related to increased GABA function (Bolwig, 2003). Not only of practical concern in inducing seizures during a course of ECT, neurochemical alterations particularly in the hippocampus that are associated with the ECT-induced increase in seizure threshold may be relevant to ECT's antidepressant properties (Bolwig, 2003). In addition to its effects on seizure threshold, ECT also may increase brain-derived neurotrophic factor (Bolwig, 2003), a biochemical that appears involved in the etiology of depression (Shimizu et al., 2003). The putative increase in brain-derived neurotrophic factor associated with ECT is consistent with the finding that several antidepressants may increase brain-derived neurotrophic factor in the hippocampus and cortex (Vaidya & Duman, 2001). Suggesting connections with the monoamine system, ECT down regulates beta adrenergic receptors (Bolwig, 2003). Similar to antidepressants, ECT in rats appears to desensitize hippocampal autoreceptors resulting in increased transmission of hippocampal serotonin (Dremencov et al., 2002). Finally, in animals, electroconvulsive shock increases the growth of new neurons in the hippocampus (Lisanby et al., 2003), and ECT may promote the growth of neurons in humans, although the meaning of this putative finding is unknown (Gorman, 2003).

Adverse Effects

Several adverse effects are associated with the use of ECT. People undergoing ECT, for example, often become increasingly confused and disoriented during the course of treatment (Leung et al., 2003), and delirium occurs in approximately 12 percent of people subsequent to an ECT-induced seizure (Fink, 1993). Agitation can complicate the course of ECT (Augoustides et al., 2002). Headaches are a frequent side effect also of ECT (Weiner et al., 1994) and can be treated with nonsteroidal anti-inflammatory drugs or narcotics (Leung et al., 2003). Pretreatment with ibuprofen appears beneficial in post-ECT headaches (Leung et al., 2003).

But it is the loss of memory that has so bedeviled ECT. Many people undergoing ECT experience a transient loss of memory that appears to return to baseline within a few months (Gorman, 2003). In fact, there is little evidence that ECT causes permanent deficits in memory or cognition (Gorman, 2003). There is no evidence that ECT produces observable brain damage (Lisanby et al., 2003). However, one review found that a significant number of patients who had undergone ECT reported persistent memory loss from the ECT (Rose, et al., 2003), suggesting a need for continued investigation into the effects of ECT on memory function.

Concerns exist about a possibly elevated death rate occurring from ECT. In a study that evaluated death occurring within fourteen days from ECT over the period from 1993 to 1998 in Texas, death rates from ECT were estimated at 2 to 10 deaths per 100,000 ECT treatments, compared to death rates of approximately 3.3 to 3.7 per 100,000 from general anesthesia, which of course is part of ECT. Causes of death in this study included cardiac causes, aspiration, and laryngospasm (Finn, 2001).

Uses

Major Depression. About 100,000 people undergo a course of ECT each year in the United States (American Psychiatric Association Committee on ECT, 2001). A review published in 2003 concluded that ECT is effective in the treatment of depression (UK ECT Review Group, 2003). Furthermore, there was evidence that ECT may be more effective for depression than antidepressant medication (UK ECT Review Group, 2003). A significant problem with use of ECT in depression, however, is the high rate of relapse after an initial successful response with up to 50 percent of patients who respond favorably to an initial course of ECT relapsing (Shapira et al., 1995). The percentage of relapse after ECT may be even higher for patients who have been treatment resistant to antidepressant medication (Devanand et al., 1991). To overcome the high rate of relapse after ECT, monthly maintenance ECT treatments can be used (Gorman, 2003). Antidepressant drugs are an important component of treatment after a course of ECT to minimize relapse (Lisanby et al., 2003).

ECT can be used in other cases of depression. For example, ECT is considered a particularly potent treatment for psychotic depression (Wheeler Vega, 2000). In fact, some evidence suggests that ECT may treat psychotic depression faster than it does depression without psychosis (Fink, 2001). ECT is used in psychotically depressed geriatric patients, as well (MacNeil, 2002). As an alternative to antidepressant medication, ECT has been used in pregnant women and is generally considered relatively safe in all trimesters during pregnancy (Rabheru, 2001). Likewise, careful medical and anesthesia management allows some medically ill, elderly depressed patients who may not tolerate psychotropic medications well to undergo safely a course of ECT (Rabheru, 2001). Although its use is controversial due to questions of safety, ECT is sometimes used as a treatment for depressed children (Findling et al., 2004).

Mania. While drug treatment is generally used in the treatment of mania (see Chapter 10), ECT can be an option, because mania can be treated effectively with ECT (Kahn & Chaplan, 2002). As an example, in acute mania, one review reported a positive response rate of approximately 80 percent for ECT, compared to a response rate of approximately 80 percent for lithium (Gelenberg & Hopkins, 1993).

Schizophrenia.   Induced seizures were originally performed in psychotic patients based on the erroneous observation that psychosis did not seem to occur in epilepsy patients (Valenstein, 1998). However, ECT may have efficacy in some cases of schizophrenia, particularly when used in combination with antipsychotic medication (Tharyan & Adams, 2002). For example, in select cases, ECT has been used concurrently with antipsychotic drugs, including clozapine (Clozaril) (Klapheke, 1993).

Catatonia.   Associated with mood disorders, psychosis, and a variety of medical conditions including metabolic diseases, catatonia presents with mutism, staring, and rigidity (Taylor & Fink, 2003). The response of catatonia to ECT can be remarkable, with patients often responding in a few days (Philbrick & Rummans, 1994). ECT also is used in children with catatonia (Takaoka & Takata, 2003).

Use in the Medically Ill.   ECT is used in the treatment of depression in the medically ill (Fink, 2001). Complications from ECT in this population can be minimized by appropriate precautions and medical monitoring during and after the ECT procedure (Rasmussen et al., 2002).

Parkinson's Disease.   ECT may be beneficial for the movement abnormalities of Parkinson's disease (Kennedy et al., 2003), although the data supporting the use of ECT in Parkinson's disease are poorly controlled and rely heavily on case reports and open studies, with only one randomized, controlled trial available (Kennedy et al., 2003). The mechanism by which ECT could result in motor improvement in Parkinson's disease is unknown, but may be due to increases in dopamine transmission that possibly are mediated by changes in dopamine receptor sensitivity (Kennedy et al., 2003).

TRANSCRANIAL MAGNETIC STIMULATION (TMS)

Introduced in 1985 (Barker et al., 1985), TMS has been used as both a tool to map aspects of brain function (Rafal, 2001) and as a therapeutic modality (Nadeau et al., 2002). Fairly noninvasive (Schlaepfer, 2003), TMS can be applied to a relatively small region of the brain (Gorman, 2003) and subsequent changes in cognition, emotion (Gorman, 2003), and motor function evaluated (Hoffman & Cavus, 2002). By temporarily and non-invasively altering a small region of brain activity, TMS can act as a virtual lesion (Rafal, 2001). For example, TMS has been used to evaluate the localization of cortical and motor function (Maeda & Pascual-Leone, 2003).

Mechanism of Action

An advantage of TMS compared to ECT is that TMS does not require the generation of a seizure (Koren et al., 2001) as does ECT (Bolwig, 2003). In TMS, an electrical current is passed through a metal coil held near the scalp (Janicak et al., 2002). The electrical current induces a magnetic field of approximately 2 tesla (Maeda & Pascual-Leone, 2003), which passes painlessly (George et al., 2003) [in contrast to direct electrical stimulation of the scalp, which is quite painful (George et al., 2003)] into the brain (Hoffman & Cavus, 2002), where it in turn generates a second electrical field within the brain itself (Maeda & Pascual-Leone, 2003). TMS is thus a method of generating a small electrical field in the brain (Hoffman & Cavus, 2002). This electrical field in the brain then presumably alters neuronal function temporarily (Dowd & Janicak, 2003) and can result in depolarization locally (Fitzpatrick & Rothman, 2000) and possibly in more distant brain regions as well (Bolwig, 2003). Whether neuronal excitation or inhibition occurs from TMS may depend in part on the frequency of the stimulus. In some situations, low frequency can result in neuronal inhibition and high frequency TMS causes in some instances neuronal excitation (George et al., 2003). Like ECT, TMS down regulates beta adrenergic receptors (Bolwig, 2003). In contrast to ECT, which appears to alter gene expression in the hippocampus, TMS seems to change gene expression primarily in the hypothalamus (Bolwig, 2003). Furthermore, TMS does not need to induce seizures for a therapeutic effect to occur (Bolwig, 2003).

Adverse Effects

Generally well tolerated (Maeda & Pascual-Leone, 2003), TMS appears to be safer than ECT, with fewer adverse effects. However, the long-term adverse effects of TMS, in part due to its relative novelty, are not known (Belmaker et al., 2003). Unlike ECT, TMS does not require the induction of a seizure for its clinical effect to occur (Bolwig, 2003). However, cases of seizure induction have been reported, although this adverse effect seems to be rare (Dowd & Janicak, 2003) and associated with high frequencies of stimulation (George et al., 2003). There have been concerns about TMS-induced cognitive dysfunction, although little evidence exists suggesting that TMS does cause cognitive difficulties (Dowd & Janicak, 2003), at least when given over short periods. For instance, a study of normal volunteers exposed to a single session of TMS found no evidence of neuropsychological dysfunction (Koren et al. 2001). In a clinical trial with TMS, side effects were relatively uncommon, although some patients complained of sleeplessness (Boughton, 2002). Pain over the application site has been reported, as have headaches (Fitzgerald, 2003) that may last for a few hours after TMS application (Klein et al., 1999). Some TMS researchers have considered the possibility of hearing loss as a consequence of TMS, not from the TMS *per se*, but rather from the loud clicking noises the TMS delivery machine makes. To avoid this potential complication, patients are often required to wear earplugs during the actual treatment (Dowd & Janicak, 2003). As TMS is a relatively novel treatment modality working through a presumably unique mechanism of action, safety issues, however, do persist.

Uses

Depression.   Numerous studies have suggested that TMS has an antidepressant effect in animal models of depression and in human trials (Dowd & Janicak, 2003). In particular, TMS applied over the prefrontal cortex appears associated with antidepressant effects (Klein et al., 1999). In a study of severely depressed patients, a two- to four-week course of TMS was found to be comparable to two to four weeks of ECT. Most of the subjects in this trial had failed several previous trials of antidepressants, suggesting that at least some of these subjects were treatment resistant (Boughton, 2002). The findings that TMS may have efficacy in treatment-resistant major depression (Fitzgerald et al., 2003) have been supported by additional work (Fitzgerald et al., 2003; Janicak et al., 2002). One randomized study comparing the efficacy of TMS to ECT in the treatment of severely depressed patients found no significant differences between the two treatments, suggesting that TMS may be an alternative in some cases to ECT (Janicak et al., 2002). There are cases reported in which TMS induced mania in depressed bipolar patients and in one patient with major depression and no history of mania (Ella et al., 2002). Based upon early data, TMS is approved for the treatment of depression in Canada (George et al., 2003), although not in the United States (George et al., 2003), except in clinical trials that have been approved by the United States Food and Drug Administration (Dowd & Janicak, 2003). An apparent advantage of TMS over ECT is that TMS does not appear to cause the cognitive and memory disturbances that are associated with ECT (Koren et al., 2001) and does not require anesthesia as does ECT (Janicak et al., 2002). Finally, TMS is less expensive than ECT to administer (Janicak et al., 2002). In cases of depression with psychotic features, however, ECT appears to be more beneficial than TMS (George et al., 2003).

Obsessive-Compulsive Disorder.   Preliminary evidence suggests that TMS may have some effects in obsessive-compulsive disorder. For example, one study found a reduction in features of obsessive-compulsive disorder in one-quarter of treatment-resistant subjects who had failed both drug treatment and in most cases psychotherapy (Sachdev, 2001). Not all studies of TMS in obsessive-compulsive disorder, however, have been positive (Hoffman & Cavus, 2002), underscoring the need for additional investigation into the effects of TMS on obsessive-compulsive disorder.

Schizophrenia.   The effects of TMS on schizophrenia are unclear; however, one pilot double-blind, placebo-controlled (sham treatments are given in which the subject is not exposed to electrical or magnetic fields) found no beneficial effects from TMS given of the right prefrontal cortex in actively psychotic subjects with schizophrenia (Klein et al. 1999). In another study, TMS given over the left temporoparietal cortex diminished auditory hallucinations in people with schizophrenia (Hoffman & Cavus, 2002). Overall, the effects of TMS on schizophrenia remain mixed, however (George et al., 2003).

VAGAL NERVE STIMULATION (VNS)

In addition to ECT and TMS, as well as other techniques, VNS has been developed as a potential alternative to traditional forms of treatment for mental disorders. Approved in the United States since 1997 for the adjunctive treatment of medication-resistant partial-onset seizures in people over the age of 12 (Kosel & Schlaepfer, 2003), VNS initially requires surgical placement of a pulse generator near the clavicle (Kosel & Schlaepfer, 2003). Electrodes are placed in contact with the left vagus nerve in the neck in a separate incision, with their leads traveling under the skin to connect to the VNS device in the neck (Kosel & Schlaepfer, 2003). The stimulus parameters (i.e., "dose") can be changed noninvasively by a telemetric device and computer (George et al., 2000), precluding the need to extract and reinsert the device each time the stimulus requires changing. Adverse effects such as discomfort from the stimulus can be disrupted temporarily by the patient by means of an external magnet should the VNS settings be too high (George et al., 2000). Because it is the vagus nerve that is directly stimulated by VNS (Kosel & Schlaepfer, 2003), VNS is not directly invasive in the brain and does not require repeated periods of general anesthesia, as does ECT. Although not a traditional pharmacological agent, VNS is clearly a biological therapy that appears to alter neurochemistry in a novel way without the use of drugs.

Mechanism of Action

The mechanism of action of VNS hinges in part upon the anatomy of the vagus nerve (George et al., 2000). The tenth cranial nerve, the vagus exits the central nervous system from the medulla in the brainstem (Brodal, 1992). Branching widely, it sends fibers to the larynx, aorta, heart, lungs, and gastrointestinal tract (Brodal, 1992). The vagus nerve also transmits sensory information from the periphery into the brain via a pathway known as the nucleus tractus solitarius, from whence it can project to many brain regions (Bailey & Bremer, 1938; Goodnick et al., 2001) including the amygdala (Goodnick et al., 2001), thalamus (Kosel & Schlaepfer, 2003), and indirectly to the locus coeruleus (Kosel & Schlaepfer, 2003). In fact, approximately 80 percent of the fibers of the vagus nerve are sensory, relaying information to the brain (George et al., 2000). During investigations into the effects of electrical stimulation of the vagus nerve, it was noted that vagal stimulation could block seizures (Goodnick et al., 2001), an observation that spurred the development of VNS as an anticonvulsant. Overall, stimulation of the vagus nerve appears to be an effective entrance into several brain regions (Bolwig, 2003; Goodnick et al., 2001; Kosel & Schlaepfer, 2003). While the electrochemical mechanism of action of VNS is unknown (Kosel & Schlaepfer, 2003), it has been postulated that VNS increases gamma aminobutyric acid (the major inhibitory neurotransmitter in the brain and an anticonvulsant itself) (Goodnick et al., 2001). Another potential mechanism of action of VNS is a possible reduction of glutamate (Goodnick et al., 2001). Even less well understood is the mechanism of action of VNS for depression, although it has been suggested that stimulation of the vagus nerves interacts via the nucleus tractus solitarius with the locus coeruleus to increase to release on norepinephrine (George et al., 2000; Goodnick et al., 2001). Animal studies have shown increases in norepinephrine in the locus coeruleus (Walker et al., 1999), which in turn projects to many brain regions, among which is the prefrontal cortex. VNS (in people with epilepsy) has resulted in increases in 5-hydroxyindoleacetic acid, the major metabolite of serotonin in cerebral spinal fluid (Ben-Menachem et al., 1995). In addition to these possible alterations in neurotransmitter function, positron emission tomography (PET) imaging (a technique of imaging brain function) has shown changes in brain activity, such as changes in blood flow to some brain regions, after treatment with VNS that are similar to effects observed from certain antidepressant drugs (Henry et al., 1998). Changes in brain blood-flow patterns after VNS administration have been found in the hypothalamus, medulla, thalamus, hippocampus, amygdala, and cingulate cortex (Goodnick et al., 2001), although it is not known which, if any, of these changes is related to the putative antidepressant effects from VNS.

Adverse Effects

Like ECT, TMS, and psychotropic drugs, VNS is associated with some adverse effects. As implantation is required for VNS, surgical complications can occur, including postoperative infection, hoarseness, and pain (Kosel & Schlaepfer, 2003). Adverse effects from VNS itself consist most commonly of a cough, hoarseness, headaches, and pain (Kosel & Schlaepfer, 2003). Paresthesias (pain from abnormally functioning nerves) can also occur, as can a feeling of shortness of breath (Kosel & Schlaepfer, 2003). Voice changes are a common adverse effect from VNS (Kosel & Schlaepfer, 2003). Notably, the cognitive side affects that have complicated treatment with traditional anticonvulsant drugs (which are now extensively used in the treatment of bipolar disorder other behavioral conditions; see Chapter 10) have not been reported with VNS (Ben-Menachem, 2001). In fact, motor speed, executive function, and language were reported to improve in proportion to improvement in depressive symptoms in depressed people treated with VNS (Sackeim et al., 2001a). VNS may also enhance recognition memory in humans (Clark et al., 1999).

Cardiac complications from VNS may occur. For example, transient asystole (lack of a heart beat) lasting 10 to 20 seconds have been reported during implantation of the VNS device (George et al., 2000). While sudden death has been reported in epilepsy patients treated with VNS, the rate of this does not appear any higher, and is possibly lower, than that associated with sudden, unexplained death from epilepsy (Annegers et al., 1998). As with all novel procedures and treatments, the effects of long-term use remain unknown, although the available data suggest that adverse effects from VNS tend to diminish with time (George et al., 2000).

Uses

Depression.   VNS was first used for treatment-resistant depression in 1998 (Kosel & Schlaepfer, 2003). Based in part on observations of mood improvement in patients with epilepsy (Goodnick et al., 2001) who underwent treatment with VNS and on biochemical changes associated with VNS (Goodnick et al., 2001; Kosel & Schlaepfer, 2003), VNS has been investigated as a potential antidepressant (Kosel & Schlaepfer, 2003). In one study, sixty patients with depression who had not adequately responded to two trials of antidepressant from two different classes were given VNS for ten weeks. The study authors concluded that VNS appeared most effective for patients with a history of low to moderate resistance to previous antidepressant trials (Sackeim et al., 2001b). VNS is approved for use in treatment-resistant depression and bipolar depression in Europe and Canada (Goodnick et al., 2001). At this stage, however, the evidence at best is preliminary regarding the place of VNS in treatment-resistant depression, and as one editorial had it, psychiatrists "must abide for now with some circumspection until efficacy is established" (Rosenbaum & Heninger, 2000). While touted as possibly efficacious for treatment-resistant depression, one study found that no response in depressive symptoms to a previous trial of ECT was a predictor of nonresponse to VNS (Rush et al., 2000), although this was a relatively small study, limiting the conclusions that can be drawn. Finally, similar to many other antidepressants, VNS appears to have some potential to induce at least hypomania in some people (Rush et al., 2000).

Epilepsy.   Initially found to prevent seizures in animals (Kosel & Schlaepfer, 2003), VNS has been approved by the United States Food and Drug Administration for otherwise refractory, partial-onset seizures in people 12 years of age and older (Kosel & Schlaepfer, 2003); it has become an accepted method for the treatment of certain types of epilepsy that are resistant to other anticonvulsant medication (Kirchner et al., 2001). For example, the Lennox-Gastaut is a severe type of childhood epilepsy (Karceski, 2001) that frequently does not respond to medications (Benbadis et al., 2000) and for which corpus colosotomy, a highly invasive intracranial surgery in which the corpus collosum is cut, is sometimes performed in cases of medication resistance. However, VNS now offers an alternative to corpus colosotomy in some cases (Schmidt & Bourgeois, 2000). For partial seizures, VNS appears to result in progressive improvement in seizure control over two to three years of treatment (Goodnick et al., 2001). As of 2001, VNS had been used in over 11,500 patients with epilepsy (Goodnick et al., 2000).

Chronic Pain.   Depending on the stimulus intensity, VNS can both elicit and inhibit the perception of pain. While of mechanism of this antinocioception is un-

TABLE A1.1   Nonpharmacological Agents

MODALITY	ADMINISTRATION	USES
Electroconvulsive Therapy (ECT)	Requires the induction of a generalized seizure to achieve efficacy.	Major Depression, Mania, Schizophrenia, and Catatonia.
Transcranial Magnetic Stimulation (TMS)	Induces an electrical field within a circumscribed region of brain tissue itself without the induction of a seizure, administered by placing a coil near the scalp.	Putative uses in Depression, Obsessive-Compulsive Disorder, and Schizophrenia.
Vagal Nerve Stimulation (VNS)	Initially requires surgical placement of an electrode near the vagus nerve in the lower neck. It is not directly invasive in the brain and does not require repeated periods of general anesthesia. The VNS device is placed surgically. The stimulus parameters (e.g., "dose") can be changed non-invasively by a telemetric device and computer.	Depression, Epilepsy, and Chronic Pain.

known, it has been postulated to involve alterations in neurobiochemistry (Kirchner, 2001).

Alzheimer's Disease.   Because VNS may enhance memory in rats (Clark et al., 1995) and verbal recall in humans (Clark et al., 1999), it may have a possible role in the treatment of Alzheimer's disease (Sjögren et al., 2002). Cognitive improvement was noted in a small group of subjects with Alzheimer's disease who were treated with VNS in an open-label fashion (i.e., no placebo, all subjects received treatment) (Sjögren, 2002).

Table A1.1 summarizes the administration and proposed uses of ECT, TMS, and VNS.

SUMMARY

ECT, TMS, and VNS are nonpharmacological techniques that appear to alter certain neurotransmitters, similar to antidepressant drugs. ECT is perhaps the most controversial of these therapies and has been used the most extensively. Given under general anesthesia, ECT requires the induction of a generalized seizure for efficacy. Usually, a course of ECT consists of six to twelve treatments given over several weeks. Despite some intriguing hints, the mechanism of action of ECT is unknown. The primary clinical use of ECT is for treatment-resistant depression, although it is used in other situations for depression, such as during pregnancy or in medically ill people. ECT also can be effective in a variety of other conditions under certain circumstances, including mania, catatonia, and schizophrenia.

Developed in 1985, TMS is used both as an investigational probe of neuropsychological function and as a therapeutic agent. Although TMS generates an electrical field within the brain that presumably alters neuronal function and results in changes in neurotransmitters, its mechanism of action remains essentially unknown. Unlike ECT, TMS does not require the induction of a seizure and does not require general anesthesia for administration. Generally well tolerated and with little evidence to suggest significant cognitive and memory adverse effects, TMS appears to possess antidepressant properties and has compared favorably with ECT. While TMS has been investigated in other conditions, such as schizophrenia and obsessive-compulsive disorder, its use in these situations is even less clearly defined than its role in the treatment of depression.

Although initially used in the latter part of the nineteenth century, VNS was no longer in use by the beginning of the twentieth and remained so until the 1990s, when it was revived first with investigations into epilepsy and then depression. VNS operates by electrically stimulating the vagal nerve in the neck via a pacemaker-like device implanted in the upper chest. The stimulation is transmitted in the brain via the tractus nucleus solitarius to multiple brain regions including the locus coeruleus. Like both ECT and TMS, VNS results in various changes in certain neurotransmitters, including norepinephrine, serotonin, GABA, and glutamate. Additionally, VNS may alter blood flow in different brain regions in a manner similar to some antidepressants. Used to treat some types of treatment-resistant epilepsy, VNS is used as an investigational antidepressant.

STUDY QUESTIONS

1. Describe the proposed mechanisms of action for ECT.
2. Why is the seizure potential important in discussions of ECT efficacy?
3. Describe the putative mechanism of action of TMS.
4. For what conditions is ECT used?
5. It appears almost counterintuitive that stimulation of a nerve in the neck could result in mood improvement. Describe how VNS could alter brain function even though it is administered peripherally.
6. Contrast the adverse effects from ECT, TMS, and VNS.
7. A 32-year-old, five-months' pregnant woman presents with a twelve-month course of worsening depression. While she is not on any antidepressant medication now, two previous trials of medications (one of an SSRI and one of venlafaxine) have proven unsuccessful. Discuss treatment options and their pros and cons.

REFERENCES

American Psychiatric Association Committee on ECT (2001): *The Practice of Electroconvulsive Therapy: Recommendations for Treatment, Training, and Privileging* (2nd ed.). Washington, DC: American Psychiatric Press.

Annegers JF, Coan SP, Hauser WA, Leetsma J, Duffell W, Tarver B (1998): Epilepsy, vagal nerve stimulation by the NCP system, mortality, and sudden, unexpected, unexplained death. Epilepsia 39:206–212.

Augoustides JG, Greenblatt E, Abbas MA, O'Reardon JP, Datto CJ (2002): Clinical approach to agitation after electroconvulsive therapy: A case report and literature review. Journal of ECT 18:213–217.

Bailey P, Bremer F (1938): A sensory cortical representation of the vagus nerve. Journal of Neurophysiology: 405–412.

Bailine SH, Petrides G, Doft M, Lui G (2003): Indications for the use of propofol in electroconvulsive therapy. Journal of ECT 19:129–132.

Barker AT, Jalinous R, Freeston IL (1985): Non-invasive stimulation of the human motor cortex. Lancet 1:1106–1107.

Belmaker B, Fitzgerald P, George MS, Lisanby SH, Pascual-Leone A, Schlaepfer TE, Wassermann E (2003): Managing the risks of transcranial magnetic stimulation. CNS Spectrums 8:489.

Benbadis S, Tatum W, Vale F (2000): When drugs don't work: An algorithmic approach to medically intractable epilepsy. Neurology 55:1780–1784.

Ben-Menachem E (2001): Vagus nerve stimulation, side effects, and long-term safety. Journal of Clinical Neurophysiology 18:415–418.

Ben-Menachem E, Hamberger A, Hedner T, Hammand EJ, Uthman BM, Slater J, Treig T, Stefan H, Ramsay RE, Wernicke JF, et al. (1995): Effects of vagus nerve stimulation on amino acids and other metabolites in the CSF of patients with partial seizures. Epilepsy Research 20:221–227.

Bolwig TG (2003): Putative common pathways in therapeutic brain stimulation for affective disorders. CNS Spectrums 8:490–495.

Boughton B (2002): Study finds rTMS comparable to ECT. Clinical Psychiatry News 30:4.

Brodal P (1992): *The Central Nervous System*. New York: Oxford University Press.

Calarge CA, Crowe RR, Gergis SD, Arndt S, From RP (2003): The comparative effects of sevoflurane and methohexital for electroconvulsive therapy. Journal of ECT 19:221–225.

Cheam EW, Critchley LA, Chui PT, Yap JC, Ha VW (1999): Low dose mivacurium is less effective than succinylcholine in electroconvulsive therapy. Canadian Journal of Anaesthesia 46:49–51.

Clark KB, Krahl SE, Smith DC, Jensen RA (1995): Post-training unilateral vagal stimulation enhances retention performance in the rat. Neurobiology of Learning and Memory 63:213–216.

Clark KB, Naritoku DK, Smith DC, Browning RA, Jensen RA (1999): Enhanced recognition memory following vagus nerve stimulation in human subjects. Nature Neuroscience 2:94–98.

Datto C, Rai AK, Ilivicky HJ, Caroff SN (2002): Augmentation of seizure induction in electroconvulsive therapy: A clinical reappraisal. Journal of ECT 18:118–125.

Devanand DP, Sackeim HA, Prudic J (1991): Electroconvulsive therapy in the treatment-resistant patient. Psychiatric Clinics of North America 14:905–923.

Dowd SM, Janicak PG (2003): The attraction of magnetism: How effective—and safe—is rTMS? Current Psychiatry 2:59–66.

Dremencov E, Gur E, Lerer B, Newman ME (2002): Effects of chronic antidepressants and electroconvulsive shock on serotonergic neurotransmission in the rat hypothalamus. Progress in Neuropsychopharmacology & Biological Psychiatry 26:1029–1034.

Ella R, Zwanzger P, Stampfer R, Preuss UW, Muller-Siecheneder F, Moller HJ, Padberg F (2002): Switch to mania after slow rTMS of the right prefrontal cortex [Letter]. Journal of Clinical Psychiatry 63:249.

Findling RL, Feeny NC, Stansbrey RJ, DelPorto-Bedoya D, Demeter C (2004): Somatic treatment for depressive illnesses in children and adolescents. Psychiatric Clinics of North America 27:113–137.

Fink M (1993): Post-ECT delirium. Convulsive Therapy 9:326–330.

Fink M (2001): The broad clinical activity of ECT should not be ignored. The Journal of ECT 17:233–235.

Fink M (2003): When to consider ECT: Algorithm seeks respect for neglected therapy. Current Psychiatry 2:49–56.

Finn R (2001): Rate of mortality related to ECT is extremely low. Clinical Psychiatry News 29:41.

Fitzgerald PB, Brown TL, Marston NAU, Daskalakis ZJ, de Castella A, Kulkarni J (2003): Transcranial magnetic stimulation in the treatment of depression. Archives of General Psychiatry 60:1002–1008.

Fitzpatrick SM, Rothman DL (2000): Meeting report: Transcranial magnetic stimulation and studies of human cognition. Journal of Cognitive Neuroscience 12:704–709.

Gelenberg AJ, Hopkins HS (1993): Report on the efficacy of treatments for bipolar disorder. Psychopharmacology Bulletin 29:447–456.

George MS, Nahas Z, Kozel A, Li X, Yamanaka K, Mishory A, Bohning DE (2003): Mechanisms and the current state of transcranial magnetic stimulation. CNS Spectrums 8:496–502.

George MS, Sackeim HA, Rush AJ, Marangell CB, Nahas Z, Husain MM, Lisanby S, Burt T, Goldman J, Ballenger JC (2000): Vagus nerve stimulation: A new tool for brain research and therapy. Biological Psychiatry 47:287–295.

Goodnick PJ, Rush AJ, George MS, Marangell LB, Sackeim HA (2001): Vagus nerve stimulation in depression. Expert Opinion in Pharmacotherapy 2:1061–1063.

Gorman JM (2003): New methods of brain stimulation: What they tell us about the old methods and about the brain. CNS Spectrums 8:475.

Henry TR, Bakay RAE, Votaw JR, Pennell PB, Epstein CM, Faber TC, Grafton ST, Hoffman JM (1998): Brain blood flow alterations induced by therapeutic vagus nerve stimulation in partial epilepsy: Acute effects at high and low levels of stimulation. Epilepsia 39:983–990.

Hoffman RE, Cavus I (2002): Slow transcranial magnetic stimulation, long-term depotentiation, and brain hyperexcitability disorders. American Journal of Psychiatry 159:1093–1102.

Janicak PG, Dowd SM, Martis B, Alam D, Beedle D, Krasuski J, Strong MJ, Sharma R, Rosen C, Viana M (2002): Repetitive transcranial magnetic stimulation versus electroconvulsive therapy for major depression: Preliminary results of a randomized trial. Biological Psychiatry 51:659–667.

Kahn D, Chaplan R (2002): The "good enough" mood stabilizer: A review of the clinical evidence. CNS Spectrums 7:227–237.

Karceski S (2001): Vagus nerve stimulation and Lennox-Gastaut sydrome: A review of the literature and data from the VNS patient registry. CNS Spectrums 6:766–770.

Kennedy R, Mittal D, O'Jile J (2003): Electroconvulsive therapy in movement disorders: An update. Journal of Neuropsychiatry and Clinical Neurosciences 15:407–421.

Kirchner A, Birklein F, Stefan H, Handwerker HO (2001): Vagusstimulation—eine Behandlungoption fur chronishe Schmerzen? [Vagus nerve stimulation—a new option for the treatment of chronic pain syndromes?] Schmerz 15:272–277.

Klapheke MM (1993): Combining ECT and antipsychotic agents: Benefits and risks. Convulsive Therapy 9:241–255.

Klein E, Kreinin I, Chistyakov A, Koren D, Mecz L, Marmur S, Ben-Shachar D, Feinsod M (1999): Therapeutic efficacy of right prefrontal slow repetitive transcranial magnetic stimulation in major depression: A double-blind controlled study. Archives of General Psychiatry 56:315–320.

Koren D, Shefer O, Chistyakov A, Kaplan B, Feinsod M, Klein E (2001): Neuropsychological effects of prefrontal slow rTMS in normal volunteers: A double-blind sham-controlled study. Journal of Clinical and Experimental Neuropsychology 23:424–430.

Kosel M, Schlaepfer TE (2003): Beyond the treatment of epilepsy: New applications of vagus nerve stimulation in psychiatry. CNS Spectrums 8:515–521.

Krystal AD, Weiner RD, Dean MD, Lindahl VH, Tramontozzi LA III, Falcone G, Coffey CE (2003): Comparison of seizure duration, ictal EEG, and cognitive effects of ketamine and methohexital anesthesia with ECT. Journal of Neuropsychiatry and Clinical Neurosciences 15:27–34.

Lanska DJ (2002): J. L. Corning and vagal nerve stimulation for seizures in the 1880s. Neurology 58:452–459.

Leung M, Hollander Y, Brown GR (2003): Pretreatment with ibuprofen to prevent electroconvulsive therapy-induced headache. Journal of Clinical Psychiatry 64:551–553.

Lippman S, Haas S, Quast G (1993): Procedural complications of electroconvulsive therapy: Assessment and recommendations. Southern Medical Journal 86:1110–1114.

Lisanby SH, Morales O, Payne N, Kwon E, Fitzsimons L, Luber B, Nobler MS, Sackeim HA (2003): New developments in electroconvulsive therapy and magnetic seizure therapy. CNS Spectrums 8:529–536.

MacNeil JS (2002): Electroconvulsive therapy effective for depressed elderly. Psychiatric Times 4:20.

Maeda F, Pascual-Leone A (2003): Transcranial magnetic stimulation: Studying motor neurophysiology of psychiatric disorders. Psychopharmacology 168:359–376.

Mann A (2001): Earlier of use of antidepressants, tapered doses reduce relapse rate post ECT. Clinical Psychiatry News 29:41.

McDonald A, Walter G (2001): The portrayal of ECT in American movies. Journal of ECT 17:264–274.

Nadeau SE, McCoy KJM, Crucian GP, Greer RA, Rossi F, Bowers D, Goodman WK, Heilman KM, Triggs WJ (2002): Cerebral blood flow changes in depressed patients after treatment with repetive transcranial magnetic stimulation. Neuropsychiatry, Neuropsychology, and Behavioral Neurology 15:159–175.

Philbrick KL, Rummans TA (1994): Malignant catatonia. Journal of Neuropsychiatry and Clinical Neuropsychiatry 6:1–13.

Rabheru K (2001): The use of electroconvulsive therapy in special patient populations. Canadian Journal of Psychiatry 46:710–719.

Rafal R (2001): Virtual neurology. Nature Neuroscience 4:862–864.

Rasmussen KG, Rummans TA, Richardson JW (2002): Electroconvulsive therapy in the medically ill. Psychiatric clinics of North America 25:177–193.

Rose D, Fleischmann P, Wykes T, Leese M, Bindman J (2003): Patients' perspectives on electroconvulsive therapy: Systematic review. BMJ 326:1363.

Rosenbaum JF, Heninger G (2000): Vagus nerve stimulation for treatment-resistant depression. Biological Psychiatry 47:273–275.

Rush AJ, George MS, Sackeim HA, Marangell LB, Husain MM, Giller C, Nahas Z, Haines S, Simpson RK, Goodman R (2000): Vagus nerve stimulation (VNS) for treatment-resistant depressions: A multicenter study. Biological Psychiatry 47:276–286.

Sachdev PS, McBride R, Loo CK, Mitchell PB, Malhi GS, Croker VM (2001): Right versus left prefrontal transcranial magnetic stimulation for obsessive-compulsive disorder: A preliminary investigation. Journal of Clinical Psychiatry 62:981–984.

Sackeim HA, Keilp JG, Rush AJ, et al. (2001a): The effect of vagus nerve stimulation on cognitive performance in patients with treatment-resistant depression. Neuropsychiatry, Neuropsychology, and Behavioral Neurology 14:53–62.

Sackeim HA, Rush AJ, George MS, Marangell LB, Husain MM, Nahas Z, Johnson CR, Seidman S, Giller C, Haines S, Simpson RK Jr., Goodman RR (2001b): Vagus nerve stimulation (VNS) for treatment-resistant depression: Efficacy, side effects, and predictors of outcome. Neuropsychopharmacology 25:713–728.

Schlaepfer TE (2003): Progress in therapeutic brain stimulation in neuropsychiatry. CNS Spectrums 8:488.

Schmidt D, Bourgeois B (2000): A risk-benefit for assessment of therapies for Lennox-Gastaut syndrome. Drug Safety 22:467–477.

Scull A (1995): Psychiatrists and historical "facts" Part One: The historiography of somatic treatments. History of Psychiatry 6:225–241.

Shapira B, Garfine M, Lerer B (1995): A prospective study of lithium continuation therapy in depressed patients who have responded to electroconvulsive therapy. Convulsive Therapy 11:80–85.

Shimizu E, Hashimoto K, Okamura N, Koike K, Komatsu N, Kumakiri C, Nakazato M, Watanabe H, Shinoda N, Okada S, Iyo M (2003): Alterations of serum levels of brain-derived neurotrophic factor (BDNF) in depressed patients with or without major depression. Biological Psychiatry 54:70–75.

Sjögren MJC, Hellström PTO, Jonsson MAG, Runnerstam M, Silander HC, Ben-Menachem E (2002): Cognition-enhancing effects of vagus nerve stimulation in patients with Alzheimer's disease: A pilot study. Journal of Clinical Psychiatry 63:972–980.

Takaoka K, Takata T (2003): Catatonia in childhood and adolescence. Psychiatry and Clinical Neurosciences 57:129–137.

Taylor MA, Fink M (2003): Catatonia in psychiatric classification: A home of its own. American Journal of Psychiatry 160:1233–1241.

Tharyan P, Adams CE (2002): Electroconvulsive therapy for schizophrenia. Cochrane Database of Systematic Reviews, CD000076.

Thuppal M, Fink M (1999): Electroconvulsive therapy and mental retardation. Journal of ECT 15:140–149.

UK ECT Review Group (2003): Efficacy and safety of electroconvulsive therapy in depressive disorders: A systematic review and meta-analysis. Lancet 361:799–808.

Vaidya VA, Duman RS (2001): Depression—emerging insights from neurobiology. British Medical Bulletin 57:61–79.

Valenstein ES (1998): *Blaming the Brain: The Truth about Drugs and Mental Health.* New York: Free Press.

Walker BR, Easton A, Gale K (1999): Regulation of limbic motor seizures by GABA and glutamate transmission in nucleus tractus solitarius. Epilepsia 40:1051–1057.

Weiner SJ, Warn TN, Ravaris CL (1994): Headaches and electroconvulsive therapy. Headache 34:155–159.

Wheeler Vega JA, Mortimer AM, Tyson PJ (2000): Somatic treatments of psychotic major depression: Review and recommendations for practice. Journal of Clinical Psychopharmacology 20:504–519.

LIST OF GENERIC DRUG NAMES, TRADE NAMES, AND MANUFACTURERS

Generic Name	Trade Name(s)	Manufacturer(s)
Acamprosate	Campral	Forest Laboratories
Alpha-Tocopherol	Vitamin E	Arco, A. L. Grace, Carlson, Montieff, Podirol
Alprazolam	Xanax	Pharmacia & Upjohn
Amantadine	Symmetrel	Endo Labs
Amisulpride	Solian	Sanofi-Synthelabo
Amitriptyline	Elavil	Merck Sharp & Dohme
Amobarbital	Amytal	Flynn
Amoxapine	Asendin	Wyeth
Aripiprazole	Abilify	Bristol-Myers Squibb
Atomoxetine	Strattera	Lilly
Benztropine	Cogentin	Merck
Biperidin	Akineton	Par
Buprenorphine	Subutex	Reckitt Benckiser
Bupropion	Wellbutrin, Wellbutrin SR, Wellbutrin XL, Zyban	GlaxoSmithKline
Buspirone	Buspar	Medochemie
Butabarbital	Butisol	Wallace
Carbamazepine	Tegretol	Novartis
Chloral hydrate	Noctec	Pharmaceutical Associates
Chlordiazepoxide	Librium	ICN
Chlorpromazine	Thorazine	GlaxoSmithKline

Generic Name	Trade Name(s)	Manufacturer(s)
Citalopram	Celexa	Forest
Clomipramine	Anafranil	Mallinckrodt
Clonazepam	Klonopin	Roche Laboratories
Clonidine	Catapres	Boehringer Ingelheim
Clozapine	Clozaril	Novartis
Cyproheptadine	Periactin	Merck
Desipramine	Norpramin	Aventis
Dextroamphetamine	Dexedrine	GlaxoSmithKline
Diazepam	Valium	Roche Laboratories
Disulfiram	Antabuse	Odyssey
Donepezil	Aricept	Pfizer
Doxepin	Sinequan	Pfizer
Dronabinol	Marinol	Unimed
Droperidol	Inapsine	Akorn
Duloxetine	Cymbalta	Eli Lilly
Escitalopram	Lexapro	Forest
Fenfluramine	Pondimin	Wyeth-Ayerst
Fentanyl	Duragesic	Janssen
Flunitrazepam	Rohypnol	Hoffman-La Roche
Fluoxetine	Prozac	Lilly
Fluphenazine	Prolixin	SmithKline Beecham
Flurazepam	Dalmane	ICN
Fluvoxamine	Luvox	Solvay Pharma
Gabapentin	Neurontin	Parke-Davis
Galantamine	Reminyl	Janssen
Gamma-hydroxybutyrate	Xyrem	Orphan
Halazepam	Paxipam	Schering
Haloperidol	Haldol	Ortho-McNeil
Hydromorphone	Dilaudid	Abbott
Imipramine	Tofranil	Mallinckrodt
Isocarboxazide	Marplan	Oxford Pharmaceuticals
Lamotrigine	Lamictal	GlaxoSmithKline
Levomethadyl acetate hydro- chloride oral solution	LAAM	Roxane
Lithium	Lithobid, Solvay, Eskalith	GlaxoSmithKline
Lorazepam	Ativan	Wyeth
Loxapine	Loxitane	Watson
Maprotoline	Ludiomil	Mylan
Memantine	Namenda	Forest
Meperidine	Demerol	Sanofi-Synthelabo
Meprobamate	Miltown	Wallace
Methadone	Dolophine	Roxane
Methohexital	Brevital	Jones

Generic Name	Trade Name(s)	Manufacturer(s)
Methylphenidate	Ritalin	Novartis
	Concerta	McNeil Consumer
	Metadate CD	Celltech
Midazolam	Versed	Roxane
Mirtazapine	Remeron	Organon USA
Moclobemide	Aurorix	Roche
Modafinil	ProVigil	Cephalon
Molindone	Moban	Endo Labs
Nalmefene	Revex	Baxter Anesthesia
Naltrexone	ReVia, Trexan	Dupont
Nefazodone	Serzone	Bristol-Myers Squibb
Nortriptyline	Pamelor	Mallinckrodt
Olanzapine	Zyprexa	Lilly
Oxazepam	Serax	Wyeth
Paroxetine	Paxil	GlaxoSmithKline
Pemoline	Cylert	Abbott
Phenelzine	Nardil	Parke-Davis
Phenobarbital	Luminal	
Phentermine	Adipex-P, Fastin, and others	Gate
Phenytoin	Dilantin	Parke-Davis
Pimozide	Orap	Gate
Pregabalin	Lyrica	Pfizer
Procyclidine	Kemadrine	GlaxoWellcome
Propranolol	Inderal	Wyeth
Protriptyline	Vivactyl	Odyssey
Quetiapine	Seroquel	Astra Zenec
Reboxetine	Edronax	Pfizer
Risperidone	Risperdal	Janssen
Rivastigmine	Exelon	Novartis
Secobarbital	Seconal	Eli Lilly
Selegiline	Eldepryl	Somerset
Sertraline	Zoloft	Pfizer
Sildenafil	Viagra	Pfizer
Tacrine	Cognex	Parke-Davis
Temazepam	Restoril	Mallinckrodt
Tetrahydroaminoacridine	Cognex	
Thioridazine	Mellaril	Novartis
Thiothixene	Navane	Pfizer
Tiagabine	Gabitril	Cephalon
Topiramate	Topamax	Ortho-McNeil
Tranylcypromine	Parnate	GlaxoSmithKline
Trazodone	Desyrel	Geneva
Triazolam	Halcion	Pharmacia & Upjohn

Generic Name	Trade Name(s)	Manufacturer(s)
Trifluoperazine	Stelazine	GlaxoSmithKline
Trihexiphenidyl	Artane	Lederle
Trimipramine	Surmontil	Odyssey
Valproic acid	Depakote, Depakene	Abbott
Venlafaxine	Effexor, Effexor XR	Wyeth
Zaleplon	Sonata	Monarch
Ziprasidone	Geodon	Pfizer
Zolpidem	Ambien	Sanofi-Synthelabo

LIST OF TRADE DRUG NAMES (WITH GENERIC NAMES IN PARENTHESES)

Abilify (aripiprazole)
Adipex-P (phentermine)
Akineton (biperidin)
Ambien (zolpidem)
Amytal (amobarbital)
Anafranil (clomipramine)
Antabuse (disulfiram)
Aricept (donepezil)
Artane (trihexiphenidyl)
Asendin (amoxapine)
Ativan (lorazepam)
Aurorix (moclobemide)
Brevital (methohexital)
Buspar (buspirone)
Butisol (butabarbital)
Campral (acamprosate)
Catapres (clonidine)
Celexa (citalopram)
Clozaril (clozapine)
Cogentin (benztropine)
Cognex (tacrine, tetrahydroaminoacri-
   dine)
Concerta (Ritalin)
Cylert (pemoline)
Cymbalta (duloxetine)
Dalmane (flurazepam)
Demerol (meperidine)
Depakene (valproic acid)
Depakote (valproic acid)
Desyrel (trazodone)

Dexedrine (dextroamphetamine)
Dilantin (phenytoin)
Dilaudid (hydromorphone)
Dolophine (methadone)
Duragesic (Fentanyl)
Edronax (reboxetine)
Effexor (venlafaxine)
Effexor XR (venlafaxine)
Elavil (amitriptyline)
Eldepryl (selegiline)
Eskalith (lithium)
Exelon (rivastigamine)
Fastin (phentermine)
Gabitril (tiagabine)
Geodon (ziprasidone)
Halcion (triazolam)
Haldol (haloperidol)
Inapsine (droperidol)
Inderal (propranolol)
Kemadrine (procyclidine)
Klonopin (clonazepam)
LAAM (levomethadyl acetate
   hydrochloride oral solution)
Lamictal (lamotrigine)
Lexapro (escitalopram)
Librium (chlordiazepoxide)
Lithobid (lithium)
Loxitane (loxapine)
Ludiomil (maprotoline)
Luminal (phenobarbital)

Luvox (fluvoxamine)
Lyrica (pregabalin)
Marinol (dronabinol)
Marplan (isocarboxazide)
Mellaril (thioridazine)
Metadate CD (methylphenidate)
Miltown (meprobamate)
Moban (molindone)
Namenda (memantine)
Nardil (phenelzine)
Navane (thiothixene)
Neurontin (gabapentin)
Norpramin (desipramine)
Noctec (chloral hydrate)
Orap (pimozide)
Pamelor (nortriptyline)
Parnate (tranylcypromine)
Paxil (paroxetine)
Paxipam (halazepam)
Periactin (cyproheptadine)
Pondimin (fenfluramine)
Prolixin (fluphenazine)
ProVigil (modafinil)
Prozac (fluoxetine)
Remeron (mirtazapine)
Reminyl (galantamine)
Restoril (temazepam)
Revex (nalmefene)
ReVia (naltrexone)
Risperdal (risperidone)
Ritalin (methylphenidate)

Rohypnol (flunitrazepam)
Seconal (secobarbital)
Serax (oxazepam)
Seroquel (quetiapine)
Serzone (nefazodone)
Sinequan (doxepin)
Solian (amisulpride)
Sonata (zaleplon)
Stelazine (trifluoperazine)
Strattera (atomoxetine)
Subutex (buprenorphine)
Surmontil (trimipramine)
Symmetrel (amantadine)
Tegretol (carbamazepine)
Thorazine (chlorpromazine)
Tofranil (imipramine)
Topamax (topiramate)
Trexan (naltrexone)
Valium (diazepam)
Versed (midazolam)
Viagra (sildenafil)
Vitamin E (alpha-tocopherol)
Vivactyl (protriptyline)
Wellbutrin (bupropion)
Wellbutrin SR (bupropion)
Wellbutrin XL (bupropion)
Xanax (alprazolam)
Xyrem (gamma-hydroxybutyrate)
Zoloft (sertraline)
Zyban (bupropion)
Zyprexa (olanzapine)

GLOSSARY

Acetylcholine. A neurotransmitter produced by neurons whose cell bodies are in the nucleus basalis of Meynert. Acetylcholine binds to nicotinic and muscarinic receptors and is involved with learning and memory.

Action potential. The wave of depolarization mediated by voltage-dependent ion channels that transmits the intraneuronal flow of information.

Adverse effect. Unwanted results from a drug.

Affective disorder. A mood disorder, such as depression, dysthymia, or bipolar (manic-depressive) disorder.

Agonist. A drug that interacts with a receptor such that the receptor responds in the same manner that it would when interacting with its own naturally occurring neurotransmitter.

Agranulocytosis. The loss of granulocytes, which are important white blood cells involved in protection from infection. Certain drugs, such as the atypical antipsychotic drug clozapine, can sometimes cause agranulocytosis.

Aldehyde dehydrogenase. An enzyme involved in the metabolic breakdown of alcohol. Disulfiram inhibits the action of aldehyde dehydrogenase, leading to a noxious reaction in the presence of alcohol.

Alzheimer's disease. The most common type of dementia, characterized by cognitive deterioration, amyloid plaques, and neurofibrillary tangles.

Akathisia. An extrapyramidal effect from dopamine 2 antagonism in the nigrostriatal pathway characterized by feelings of inner restlessness that can lead to difficulty with sitting and standing still.

Antagonist. A drug that prevents a receptor from performing its normal function.

Anticonvulsant drug. A drug used to treat seizures. Certain anticonvulsants also function as mood stabilizers and are used in the treatment of bipolar disorder.

Antidepressant drug. A drug used to treat depression. Many antidepressants also are used in the treatment of other disorders, such as anxiety.

Antipsychotic drug. A drug used in the treatment of psychotic disorders, such as schizophrenia.

Anxiolytic drug. A drug that is used for the treatment of anxiety disorders.

Attention-deficit, hyperactivity disorder. A mental disorder occurring in adults and children and characterized by attention deficits, hyperactivity, and impulsivity.

Atypical antipsychotic drug. An antipsychotic drug that generally has fewer extrapyramidal effects and less prolactin elevation than a typical antipsychotic drug.

Atypical depression. A depressive illness characterized by an increase in appetite and sleep, in addition to depression.

Barbiturates. Little used sedative-hypnotics with a low therapeutic index that affect the $GABA_1$ receptor.

Benzodiazepines. Sedative-hypnotics used for the treatment of some anxiety disorders and alcohol withdrawal.

Bipolar affective disorder. A mood or affective disorder characterized by periods of depressive mania or hypomania, or both.

Brand name. The commercial name of a drug. For example, the brand name of the antidepressant fluoxetine in Prozac.

Cannabis sativa. The scientific name of the marijuana or hemp plant.

Central nervous system. The portion of the nervous system comprising the brain and spinal cord.

Cognitive enhancer. A drug used to improve or maintain cognition, particularly in the context of dementia.

Cytochrome P450 system. A system of enzymes located primarily in the liver but also the small intestine that is involved in the metabolism of numerous drugs. Many drugs also can inhibit cytochrome P450 enzymes, potentially creating drug-drug interactions.

Delirium tremens. An extreme form of alcohol withdrawal characterized by severe agitation, hallucinations, and even seizures.

Delta 9-tetrahydrocannabinol. The active constituent of marijuana.

Dementia with Lewy bodies. A type of dementia accounting for approximately 20 percent of cases of dementia and characterized by cognitive deterioration, a fluctuating mental status, hallucinations, and motor abnormalities.

Dependence. The physical or psychological need to continue to take a drug. Physical dependence can result in a withdrawal syndrome when the drug is reduced or discontinued abruptly, whereas psychological dependence results in a craving for the drug.

Dopamine. A neurotransmitter found in the tuberoinfundibular, nigrostriatal, and mesocorticolimbic brain pathways and involved in addition, brain-reward systems, psychosis, and movement.

Dose-response curve. The concentration of a drug on the x-axis plotted against the drug's effect on the y-axis. The resulting curve may be concave, linear, or sigmoid in shape and can provide important information about the dose of a drug and its clinical response.

Drug. A chemical that alters physiological function.

Drug toxicity. The development of unwanted effects from a drug.

Dystonia. Muscle spasm that often occurs from dopamine 2 antagonism in the nigrostriatal pathway.

Electroconvulsive therapy. The electrical induction of a seizure to treat depression and catatonia.

Endorphin. An endogenous opiate.

Enkephalin. An endogenous opiate.

Extrapyramidal effect. An adverse effect caused by drug antagonism of dopamine 2 receptors in the nigrostriatal pathway manifested by dystonia, akathisia, muscle rigidity, and slowed movements.

First-generation antipsychotic. A typical antipsychotic, whose mechanism of action appears to involve dopamine 2 antagonism.

Frontotemporal dementia. A type of dementia with neuronal loss typically beginning in the frontal and temporal lobes. Pick's disease is a type of frontotemporal dementia.

Gamma aminobutyric acid. The brain's major inhibitory neurotransmitter.

Generalized anxiety disorder. A mental disorder characterized by excessive worry and anxiety that is often accompanied by somatic manifestations of anxiety including muscle tension and gastrointestinal upset.

Generic name. The noncommercial name of a drug. For example, fluoxetine is the generic name of the antidepressant Prozac.

Glial cell.   A non-neuron class of brain cell outnumbering neurons approximately ten to one involved in numerous functions including, depending upon the type of glial cell, myelin production, formation of part of the blood-brain barrier, and immune response.

Glutamate.   The brain's major excitatory neurotransmitter.

Half-life.   The amount of time required for 50 percent of a drug to be eliminated from the body. As a general rule, four or five half-lives of a drug are needed before the drug can be considered cleared from the body.

Hallucinogen.   A class of drugs including lysergic acid diethylamide (LSD) that can produce hallucinations and alterations in consciousness at doses not otherwise toxic.

Ion.   An atom with either a positive or negative charge.

Lewy body.   An intraneuronal inclusion body formed from proteins and found in Parkinson's disease and Lewy-body dementia.

Major depression.   An affective disorder characterized by depressed mood, anhedonia, disturbances in appetite and sleep, diminished energy, and deficits in cognition.

Mania.   A mood disturbance characterized by an elevated mood, euphoria, diminished need for sleep, irritability, grandiosity, and pressured speech.

Monoamine oxidase.   An enzyme involved in the breakdown of the monoamines, such as dopamine, serotonin, and norepinephrine.

Mood stabilizer.   A drug used to treat mania or depression but which does not induce mania.

Neurogenesis.   The production of new neurons.

Neuroleptic.   Usually a first-generation, or typical, antipsychotic drug.

Neuroleptic malignant syndrome.   A constellation of findings sometimes resulting from first- or second-generation antipsychotics. Neuroleptic malignant syndrome is characterized by fever, muscle rigidity, confusion, unstable vital signs, and death in up to 25 percent of untreated cases.

Neuron.   A specialized cell that processes and transmits information.

Norepinephrine.   A neurotransmitter produced in neurons whose cell bodies are in the locus coeruleus. Norepinephrine is involved in attention and mood regulation.

Obsessive-compulsive disorder.   An anxiety disorder characterized by obsessions and compulsions.

Partial agonist.   A drug with relatively weak affinity for a receptor that under conditions of high concentrations of the receptor's naturally occurring neurotransmitter acts as an antagonist by preventing full access of the neurotransmitter to the receptor, while under conditions of low concentrations of the naturally occurring neurotransmitter acts as an agonist due to its weak affinity for the receptor and relative absence of the naturally occurring neurotransmitter.

Peripheral nervous system.   The part of the nervous system that is located outside of the brain and spinal cord.

Pick bodies.   An intraneuronal protein body found in Pick's disease.

Pick's disease.   A frontotemporal dementia characterized pathologically by Pick's bodies.

Posttraumatic stress disorder.   A mental disorder occurring after exposure to a significant stress characterized by the re-experiencing of the trauma (often in the form of nightmares and flashbacks), avoidance of places or events that are reminiscent of the trauma, and hypervigilance.

Proband.   A term used in genetic research to identify a member of a family or pedigree who has the disease in question.

Prolactin. A hormone produced by the pituitary gland involved in lactation and regulated in part by dopamine in the tuberoinfundibular pathway.

Psychopharmacology. The science and clinical discipline of the effects of drugs on brain function and behavior.

Psychotropic drug. A chemical affecting brain structure or function, as well as behavior.

Receptor. A three-dimensional structure found in the cell membrane or in some cases intracellularly that can bind to drugs, neurotransmitters, peptides, or hormones. Receptors are often named after the neurotransmitters with which they bind.

Reuptake. The process by which a neurotransmitter is taken back into the presynaptic neuron from which it came.

Schizophrenia. A psychotic disorder characterized by disturbances in perception, thought, language, reality testing, and cognition.

Second-generation antipsychotic. An atypical antipsychotic that tends to cause fewer extrapyramidal effects and less prolactin elevation than first-generation, or typical, antipsychotics.

Serotonin. A neurotransmitter produced by neurons whose cell bodies are in the raphe nuclei in the brainstem. Serotonin is implicated in a variety of functions and conditions, including mood regulation, psychosis, and obsessive-compulsive behavior.

Serotonin syndrome. A condition presumably resulting from the excessive transmission of serotonin (sometimes due to the concurrent use of two or more drugs that increase the transmission of serotonin) and characterized by an elevated heart rate, excessive sweating, increased reflexes, and confusion.

Side effect. An unwanted effect from a drug.

Social anxiety disorder. A mental disorder characterized by excessive anxiety in social situations, particularly those in which a person may become the center of attention or target of scrutiny.

Steady state. The condition of relatively constant drug concentrations in the body obtained when the amount of drug coming into the body equals the amount cleared from the body.

Tardive dyskinesia. Abnormal movements of the tongue, mouth, neck, arms, legs, and trunk that can occur from antipsychotic drugs.

Tau proteins. Proteins found in normal neurons where they function in intracellular transport. Tau proteins also form neurofibrillary tangles in neurons of people suffering from Alzheimer's disease.

Tolerance. The need for higher doses of a drug to maintain the same effect or the loss of an effect previously obtained from the same dose of drug.

Transcranial magnetic stimulation. A technique by which a magnetic field is passed into the brain where it generates an electrical field that can alter neuronal function.

Typical antipsychotic drug. A first-generation antipsychotic drug, one whose primary mechanism of action appears to be antagonism of dopamine 2 receptors.

Vagal nerve stimulation. Electrical stimulation of the vagus nerve to alter brain function.

Vascular dementia. A type of dementia occurring from disease related to disease in the brain's vascular system.

Withdrawal syndrome. The symptoms produced when a drug to which physical dependence has occurred is abruptly stopped or lowered.

INDEX